# CRUSTS

*The Ultimate Baker's Book*

# Crusts

13-Digit ISBN: 978-1604337365
10-Digit ISBN: 1604337362

This book may be ordered by mail from the publisher. Please include $5.99 for postage and handling.
Please support your local bookseller first!

Books published by Cider Mill Press Book Publishers are available at special discounts for bulk purchases in the United States by corporations, institutions, and other organizations. For more information, please contact the publisher.

Cider Mill Press Book Publishers
"Where good books are ready for press"
PO Box 454
12 Spring Street
Kennebunkport, Maine 04046

Visit us online!
cidermillpress.com

Cover design by Cindy Butler
Interior design by Jaime Christopher
Typography: Adobe Garamond, Brandon Grotesque, Lastra, Sackers English Script
Illustrations by Annalisa Sheldahl
Image credits: see pages 816-817

Printed in China

1 2 3 4 5 6 7 8 9 0

First Edition

# CRUSTS

## The Ultimate Baker's Book

---

### BARBARA ELISI CARACCIOLO

WITH MORE THAN 300 RECIPES
FROM EXPERT AND ARTISAN BAKERS, COVERING BREADS,
CROISSANTS, FLATBREADS, PIZZA, PIES—

**ALL FOODS THAT DEMAND THE PERFECT CRUNCH**

CIDER MILL
PRESS

BOOK
PUBLISHERS
KENNEBUNKPORT, MAINE

# CONTENTS

# FOREWORD

It all started with a toy oven I received as a present when I was seven years old. In no time, my toy oven and I became very good friends, in spite of the fact that the only cake it could bake was a chocolate sponge that looked and tasted between a failed lava cake and an over-baked bread.

I kept making that same little cake every afternoon and I am still grateful to my father for having pretended, day after day, that the cake was, indeed, wonderful. Soon I became confident enough to use our kitchen oven, and I spent many afternoons during my early teens in Rome unraveling the mysteries and wonders of baking.

Growing up, I found other passions, among which were neuroscience and epidemiology. Then one day I felt the itch to bake again. Since relocating to Sweden for my PhD work, I had been longing for some authentic Roman country sourdough, like the one I used to eat with my family during our Sundays by the lake.

The wish to recreate those long lost flavors made me put aside my scientific papers to bake again, and I have never stopped since.

I started to write *Bread & Companatico* to share my enthusiasm for bread and baking, and it has been amazing to be able to help many to take their first steps into bread baking. More recently, I opened Spigamadre, where I can dig in to my ever-growing passion for bread and grains, and share it with a very supportive community. Writing *Crusts* has enabled me to stop and think, and remember once more why I love baking so much.

Baking, especially when made using yeast or sourdough fermentation, is a continuous transformation that speaks of life and regeneration. There is so much happening in a bread dough, and most of it is not done by us. In bread baking, I feel just the initiator and the sentinel of a multiplicity of processes that start when I combine my ingredients—but actually continues to happen in my starters. I am, in fact, never tired of spying on the activity of my many ferments, always growing and thriving in my home and bakery kitchens. To me, it feels like they are their own thing and I am just the zookeeper, and they never stop filling me with a sense of awe and gratitude.

Bread—and anything baked, really—is also our memory. Something so deeply rooted in us that often one single bite can bring up episodes that were long lost in the recesses of our minds. That bite may remind you of some special bread or baked good you ate before, maybe delivered to you by the hands of a loving parent, grandparent or an aunt. Or maybe it was a bread coming from a bakery that has been long closed since. Baking at home gives you the power of recreating your all-time favorite baked goodies and make them known to your loved ones.

By learning the craft of baking and remaking old baking classics, you are also keeping alive a knowledge that has been at the core of countless cultures, since the time when culture began, really. Baking, and bread baking in particular, is our heritage. While doing the research for this book, I have been humbled thinking of all the work, love, and care that brought to us all the traditional techniques and recipes available today. It is truly touching to think to all the history and lives that have revolved around these breads, and realizing once more how central baking has been to humankind since we became human in the full meaning of the term.

My hope is that in this book you will find some of your heritage, too, together with the means and tools to bake whatever your heart feels inspired to bake, at each moment and for every occasion, although one does not need a special occasion to bake. If you really need an occasion, make it a celebration of your quality time with yourself. Even feeding your sourdough starter can become part of this precious time, rather than a chore.

When you feel like the whole world is spinning too fast around you, just put on your apron, take a deep breath, and bake. Be assured that you will bring to life something always new and always good, no matter what.

Happy baking!

*Barbara*

# INTRODUCTION

When flour is combined with water, something really special happens. Technically, the molecules in flour become "hydrated." Practically, we are now in the presence of a substance that was not there before. Flour and water combined have, in fact, become a dough, which can be kneaded, folded, stretched, rolled, shaped, filled, or left alone to ferment. Subsequently, the dough can be cooked, boiled, fried, or baked, and the resulting flour-based product will be called simply bread, bagel, pizza, pie, or any of the millions of terms that we have used over time to call the many different types of "crusts." The inclusive term *baking* generally refers to the action of transforming a dough into an edible food, even when the dough is actually not baked but cooked outside of an oven.

A big fan of dough and baking since childhood, I used to have the habit of jumping to the end of comprehensive cookbooks to read the eventual baking section. I was never satisfied even if there was one, because there were always too few recipes and way too little information to satisfy my endless curiosity about any preparation that had a dough as its starting point. When, later on, I started to buy specialized books on bread and baking, I still could not seem to find answers to all of my questions. This is how I ended up owning dozens of books, without quite finding "the book," the one to use as a reference for my everyday baking and which could finally answer most of my questions—questions that were not only about *how* to achieve a specific baking outcome, but also *what* the historical and regional context is that created a recipe. Such a book I would keep on my kitchen countertop rather than in a forgotten bookshelf, and consult each time

I need to venture into uncharted baking territory. *Crusts* is such a book.

*Crusts* intends on becoming your one book to always have at hand—a comprehensive collection of facts, tips, and recipes about the most disparate types of breads and "crusts," a book to keep us company in countless baking adventures, with our favorite pages and recipes bookmarked by dried dollops of dough.

Before starting with the methods and the recipes, I recommend an in-depth incursion into the history of bread (see page 31), which will make you better appreciate the incredible heritage that comes with every single bread you bake. It will also help you not take for granted all the amazing technological advantages we have achieved, starting from dense unleavened breads cooked on a griddle to the well-risen and light loaves baked in sophisticated, modern ovens like the ones we have in our kitchens.

We would surely not have managed to get those light and well-risen loaves without learning to master fermentation. In Part II, you will be introduced to dough fermentation and have the chance to become accustomed to the different families of the friendly microorganisms that make our bread rise.

If you never baked a loaf, *Crusts* will teach you bread baking basics and beyond, enough for you to make authentic artisan bread at home. If sourdough baking is something you are curious about, in Part II, you will be guided though all the steps to make and keep a foolproof sourdough starter.

Loaves are ambitious bakes, but flatbreads have their charm, too (Part V). From pita bread to injera, passing through roti and tortilla, there is no limit to all the regional contexts and

baking traditions you will be able to explore, now that you have found *the* book.

Pizza is a very special flatbread that started as a food for the poor and is now known and loved in every corner of the world, often dignified by luxury toppings. In Part VII, you will learn about what makes an authentic Neapolitan pizza, as well as the many scrumptious non-authentic variations. You will be given the tools to become a skilled *pizzaiolo* in no time.

If you wonder about grains and what use you can have of each of them, in Part III, we have devised a grains encyclopedia, which we hope will clear every doubt you may have on the main ingredient of any dough—flour. In Part II, you will also have a foolproof guide to all the different types of flours, and an easy tutorial on how to make and keep fresh flour at home.

There is always a good occasion to bake a sultry sweet bread. In Part IX, a rich collection of sweet breads will make you travel to differ-ent times and cultural contexts, and challenge you with some of the most ambitious leavened breads you can bake. Finally, *Crusts* would not be complete without an incursion into pie baking, with its long history and unwritten rules, and an in-depth mention of other celebrated baked glories such as croissants, bagels, and scones (Part VI).

In approaching your first bakes, or in upgrading to more challenging ones, be aware that you do not need plenty of special powers or tools to become a skilled baker. Most of the necessary tools are probably already in your kitchen and, if not, they are quite cheap and easy to get. Speaking of special powers, maybe you need just two: to learn to feel the dough and to trust your instinct. Differently from what is commonly believed, there is indeed nothing overly scientific in baking. Although it is true that every minimal aspect of the art of baking has been analyzed and made into a seemingly exact science, it does not have to be so.

Too many numbers, one may think. Too many rules. Numbers, like those used to weight ingredients and measure dough temperature, are surely useful tools. However, numbers are not necessary, and not even sufficient, to turn you into a good baker. Many skilled professional bakers would agree that the best bakers ever were probably the moms and grandmas traditionally in charge of baking bread for their community. They had no knowledge of numbers and owned no sophisticated tools to help them master their doughs. Nonetheless, those women surely knew what counts most. They knew that you need to look at, and really feel, the dough in order to learn how to tame it. The recipe is, in fact, nothing more than a *canovaccio*, or a roughly written script, which can get you started until you develop your own version of each single recipe. Only you will know how to complete your canovaccio, your script, in every specific baking occasion.

With this in mind, feel confident in using *Crusts'* palette of different methods and baking techniques, which will be the perfect base and complement to your own creativity. Know that you are building on more than 10,000 years of baking tradition and that, through your skilled hands, every recipe has the chance to come back to life and become actual again.

Baking is indeed a very important piece of our heritage as human beings, and it surely represents a wonderful responsibility to carry forward. Feel free to be humbled by this rich tradition but do not be scared: working with dough is so ingrained in us that you just need to listen to your inner baking mojo.

As you listen, you will see that your dough will listen back, and that synergy will create magic. This magic will nourish your soul in ways that you may not have expected. The best part of it is that after the very personal interaction with dough, you are left with an edible piece of craft that can be shared with the people we love and care for. What can be better than this?

# THE FUNDAMENTALS OF BREAD

There is something magical about making your own bread, in your own kitchen, with your own hands. It makes one feel like some sort of master of all things when from simple and apparently inert ingredients like flour, water, and salt, one manages to create a food as complete, delectable, nourishing, beautiful, and alive as bread.

To make the simplest bread, one does not even need a rising agent. It is enough to combine flour with water to create something completely new, which we call *dough*. If you then add some salt, shape the dough into small rounds, and bake it in a hot oven, you have bread. While simplistic in its approach, it may surprise you.

If you repeat the same procedure, adding baker's yeast or sourdough starter to your dough, give it the time to rise, and then you will bake a bread that will more closely resemble your idea of the classic loaf.

When you feel confident enough to experiment with variations of the type or percentages of the basic ingredients (flour, water, salt, yeast and time), you will realize that the shapes and flavors of bread are virtually infinite. Later on, when you venture into adding other ingredients to your basic yeasted doughs, you will feel like a full-blown magician. However, between your first simple creation and the many variations and improvements to follow, there is less difference in the process than you may think.

It is all bread, a thing of absolute magic, even in its simplest form.

## BASIC INGREDIENT LIST & DESCRIPTIONS

### Flour

For most people flour is just a powdery substance sold in a paper package. Like sugar, cornstarch, or baking soda.

For professional and home bakers alike, flour is like the colors of a painter's palette. In that paper package lies a whole world to discover. As an apprentice home baker, you will soon realize that a big part of your baking successes and failures are largely explained by the type of flour you use. You will find out how each flour characterizes the bread you make in peculiar ways. Soon, hunting for flours will become just as natural as hunting for the freshest and plumpest fruits at the grocery store.

Technically, flour derives from the grinding of seeds, nuts or roots. The most commonly used flour in bread making comes from wheat, but flours from other grains, or cereals, are also very common (see Part III).

Wheat is the world's most widely grown cereal. As of 2017, wheat alone accounted for nearly one-third of the global cereal harvest (FAO data). One good reason for the supremacy of wheat over other cereals is its superior baking properties. Another name for common modern wheat

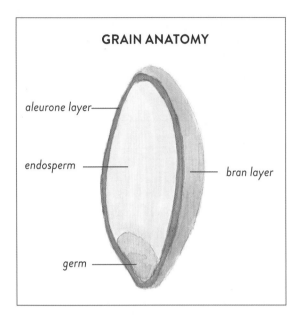

**GRAIN ANATOMY**

aleurone layer

endosperm

bran layer

germ

proteins to be more available in the finest fractions of milled flour. A dough made with finer flour is also more extensible, allowing for easier shaping. The result is a beautiful looking bread with higher volume, lighter texture, and better color as compared with bread made with coarser flours.

Although high fineness is desirable in breads that are meant to develop much in volume and have a very light crumb, there is a huge variety of breads with different characteristics, which do not call for a fine or superfine flour. For example, there are many breads made with the coarse, but delicious, semolina flour and whole-rye breads, which are not supposed to be light or high in volume. A coarser type of flour is also the preferred option in several traditional flatbreads and in a wide variety of crackers.

Flour whiteness is a quality that has been associated with wheat for a very long time. The origin of the term *wheat* is related to the color white. The word comes from the old German name *weizzi*, also reportedly *wēte*, which derives from the word *hwīta*, meaning white. The association of wheat and white may be due to the comparison of wheat flour to flour made with other cereals, such as barley, rye, and oats.

The superior baking properties of wheat also confer to whiter bread made with wheat, as compared to breads made with other grains. In order to obtain an even lighter and airier consistency in wheat bread, the bran is partially or totally eliminated or sifted out. Bran removal has been done since antiquity, using increasingly sophisticated milling and sifting techniques.

Based on the level of whiteness in wheat flour, i.e. the relative amount of bran present in the milled flour, different labels are applied, such as: whole wheat or wholemeal, sifted, unbleached white, and white (i.e. bleached white).

is, in fact, bread wheat. Read more on this in Part III.

Wheat seeds possess an inner body mostly composed of the large starchy endosperm and the oily germ, all enclosed in an outer layer of bran. Fibers are mostly concentrated in the bran, while the endosperm is where the starches and most of the proteins are stored. Fats are stocked in the germ of the wheat kernel.

Wheat and other cereals can be ground into flours with different degrees of fineness. The level of fineness of the grinding will give us flours that can be coarse, like semolina flour, best suited for pasta making, or fine, like the widely used all-purpose flour.

Flour fineness is an important quality for bread baking. If you want to make a bread or pastry with a feathery light texture, you will need to look for "superfine flour." Superfine flour has a silky sensation to the touch and confers special powers to your rising dough.

Laboratory research comparing flours of different fineness shows that the water absorption of wheat flour increases with reduction in particle size. Both dough development time and dough stability increase with increased fineness of the flour. This is due to the tendency of flour

Whole wheat flour is obtained when all the bran contained in the wheat kernel is included in the milled flour. Not all whole wheat flours are the same though. Most store-bought whole wheat flours are not made by grinding the whole seed at once, but rather by adding the bran, which was previously removed, back in to the refined flour. The resulting flour, even if it's called whole wheat or wholemeal, will not truly include the whole ground wheat kernel, but only the endosperm and bran fractions. In fact, the vitamins and essential fat-rich wheat germ is not included in most industrial whole wheat flours.

Sifted flour is obtained by sifting flour derived by milling the whole kernel at once. In general, the sifting process is aimed at removing the bran, leaving the endosperm and wheat germ in the flour. Both milling and sifting can be achieved with different methods. Different degrees of sifting can give flours with different percentages of bran, or ashes. Depending on

the ashes or bran content, the resulting flour will have a different degree of whiteness. The wheat germ, however, will always remain in the flour, if the kernel is truly milled whole.

Unbleached white flour is obtained with roller mill technology. This sophisticated method involves mechanically isolating the endosperm from the bran and the wheat germ, in order to mill the endosperm alone. This process gives a lighter and whiter flour compared to sifted flour. Such flour is extremely versatile and has a long shelf life. The term *unbleached* means that no bleaching agent is added to the flour to increase its whiteness. Unbleached, however, does not mean that the flour is necessarily free from chemical additives. A very common additive that can be found in unbleached flour is sodium bromate, which improves the baking performance of the flour. However, this additive has been linked to unfavorable health

outcomes, and is banned in several countries outside the United States. Therefore, you may want to check that your unbleached white flour is also unbromated.

White flour may mean that the flour has been bleached. Bleaching is done to increase whiteness but also to improve baking properties. Through bleaching, the flour is oxidized, which can mimic the natural aging of flour (see page 42).

### Other commonly used labels

Pastry flour refers to superfine white wheat flour with a protein content that is ideal for pastries. This means that the protein content is relatively low. Soft wheat is the main grain used here.

Graham flour refers to a coarse, 100% whole wheat flour.

Bread flour refers to white flour with a high protein content, which is ideal for bread baking. It is generally obtained from hard wheat grains.

All-purpose flour refers to white flour that can be used for all sorts of baking purposes. It is generally a combination of hard and soft wheat.

Stone-milled flour refers to flour that has been milled with the traditional milling technique of grinding the whole kernel between stones. Authentic stone-milled flour can be sifted or unsifted (stone-milled whole wheat), but can never be white or superfine. It is very common, however, to find stone-milled flours in which stone milling is only one part of the milling process, with the remaining milling carried out with more sophisticated techniques. These flours resemble roller-milled flours.

## Local Mills or Store-Bought?

Not so long ago, there were thousands of local mills in the United States. With the advent of modern milling techniques in the second half of the 19th century, large milling plants gradually substituted the small and less technologically advanced gristmills. By the turn of the last century, industrial mass-produced flour had already become the norm in both the new and the old continents, with the new leading the way and becoming a worldwide wheat flour leader.

Today, we are witnessing a revival of local artisan milling, and the availability of flour milled without the use of advanced technology is increasing. However, local mills are still too few and too scattered to provide a significant proportion of our wheat. Access to a large distribution channel is limited for local mills. The best way to buy flour from a local mill is online.

Most contemporary artisan mills use the ancient technique of stone milling. This technology is as old as agriculture, although important developments have occurred. In particular, the source of power that makes the stones rotate against each other to grind the grains' kernels has considerably changed over time: from the first hand-operated mills, ancient Rome's watermills, and medieval windmills, to today's modern electricity-powered stone mills.

Even with these notable differences, the basic mechanisms that make stone mills run have changed little, particularly when compared to their 18th century relatives. Consequently, genuine stone-milled flours are in all likelihood similar to pre-industrial flours, just like the bread made with such flours. With local stone mills today, we can experience a bread that holds the charm of something lost in time, evoking ancestral memories.

Flours commonly found in grocery stores are instead processed in highly automated roller mill plants. Roller mills break open the kernel and scrape the endosperm from bran and germ through break rolls. Through a repeated action of sifters and purifiers, we are left with a completely refined wheat, which contains only the finely ground endosperm.

Sifters and purifiers are used in most local mills, too, but if the kernel is ground whole—like in stone milling—it is not possible to later filter out all the bran from the flour. Similarly, the fats contained in the wheat kernel's germ are released into the flour during milling when the kernel is broken. These fats end up coating flour particles, making them stick together more and interfere with water absorption during dough development.

This is why, when using flours produced in an authentic stone mill, we should not expect the superfine, powdery, white substance many of us grew up calling flour. Similarly, the breads made with the darker, coarser stone-milled flours will never equate the characteristics of the breads made with standard white flours. Bread volume will most likely be affected, as well as crumb density and crust color.

Still, there are small artisan mills that use more advanced technology and can offer whole flours with better baking performance compared to traditional stone mills. The main point of artisan mills is not to revive old technology, but rather to offer us a more wholesome flour from the whole grain.

So, when deciding if it is better to use flour from local artisan mills or store-bought flour, one should first answer this question: *what is most important to me?* If your aim is to learn to bake an awe-inducing and feathery light baked good to compete with bakery or magazine perfect bread and pastry, industrial flours are the way to go. If you instead value taste and nutritional properties, over the appearance and consistency, local mills have much more to offer.

Finally, if you find yourself wanting it all, then you must have a variety of different flours at hand and learn to combine them in a way that can give you an uncompromised beautiful looking bread. This is also the best type of bread you could possibly eat, both in taste and nutrition.

## It's in the Water

Water is a key ingredient in making bread dough. Adding water to flour hydrates the molecules, which have a strong affinity for this solvent. In addition to hydrating the macromolecular components, water allows the formation of gluten regulates enzymatic activity, gives life to yeast (page 54), hydrates starch granules during baking, allows gelatinization, and exerts an important solvent effect on other dough ingredients, such as glucose, sucrose, and salt.

The first condition for the water you use for your dough is that it is suitable for human consumption. In other words, the water you use in your bread needs to be reasonably clean and therefore drinkable.

You may have heard claims that a certain bread or food cannot be made in any place other than its original geographical area, because the real secret for the recipes success is "in the water." Neapolitan pizza is a good example. It is often claimed that an authentic Neapolitan pizza can only be made in Naples, because of the water. This may actually be an exaggeration, as it was noticed that New York's tap water is not so dissimilar from the mystical water of Naples, and so are other waters. Nonetheless, local differences are sometimes truly relevant and can explain the failure in replicating a bread recipe.

There are three main water characteristics that should be considered in bread baking.

### Water hardness

In the baking industry, water is classified according to its hardness, measured in French grades. The hardness of water depends on its concentration of mineral salts, especially calcium and magnesium. These minerals interact with proteins, affecting the dough development in different ways. Specifically, a very soft water (up to 5°F) can collapse a dough, while too hard of a water (over 20°F) results in poor production of gasses, reduces the activity of the yeasts, and creates a tighter gluten net, which results in a forced prolongation of leavening times. Information on water hardness is often made available by municipalities. If you plan to use your tap water, you may want to check this information and evaluate if you need to dilute your water with bottled water to reach the right balance of minerals. Water filters may also come in handy if your water is too hard.

## Water pH

A neutral solution has a pH of seven, a basic pH is greater than seven, and an acidic solution has a pH less than seven. For bread dough, it is generally preferable to use a slightly acidic water, with a pH around five to six, but Neapolitan pizza likes a higher pH of seven. If your tap water is highly basic, you may consider diluting it with bottled water with a lower pH. Testing for pH is very easy nowadays thanks to the availability of home kits.

## Water temperature

Professional bakers consider it fundamental to have control over the internal temperature of their doughs. Water is a very smart way to easily achieve desired dough temperature, as it is easy to warm up or cool down water before combining it with flour. There are more or less complicated formulas to calculate the ideal water temperature based on desired dough temperature. They all consider 1) room and/ or flour temperature and/or preferment temperature; 2) desired dough temperature; and 3) estimated added temperature generated by dough mixing (including hand mixing). These formulas can be useful, but they are always an approximation. A good way to easily get by with water temperature is to consider that if your kitchen temperature is high, you can still obtain a lower dough temperature by adding cold water, but not below 40°F. If your room temperature is cold, you can achieve a higher desired dough temperature by adding warmer water, but not warmer than 77°F. Finally, if you are using a mixer and know that it tends to overheat the dough, cooling your water before adding it to the dough is a good idea, especially if your room temperature is higher.

## Salt

Contrary to common thought (by non-bakers), the primary reason for adding salt to a dough is not for taste. Although salt does improve the taste of bread considerably, its other functions are far more important.

Have you ever tried baking bread without adding salt? The result will be a flat and pale loaf, so far away from the rustic beauty you may have aimed for. Middle Age Pisans knew this very well and, consequently, used a salt embargo in their rivalry with Florence. Florentines were thus forced to make bread without salt, which has since become typical of that region. Tuscan bread (*pane sciocco*) is, however, quite an acquired taste, and non-Tuscans can have a hard time appreciating this flat and pale type of bread.

The presence of salt in dough slows down the activity of the yeasts and bacteria as well as the activity of the enzymes, so that there will still be spare activity and sugars for when the loaf is baked, allowing for good oven spring and browning of the crust. This is particularly important for rye bread, which has a very high enzymatic activity.

Thanks to its slowing action on bacterial activity, salt also works like a natural disinfectant, inhibiting the action of potentially harmful bacteria, both during fermentation and after baking, working as an effective anti-molding agent. Even good bacteria are partially inhibited, with a consequent reduction of acidity in the final loaf.

Salt helps creating good structure in bread, acting positively on gluten, by making the gluten net more resistant and more effective in keeping the gasses in, and the resulting loaf higher in volume and with a more open crumb.

Salt absorbs water, thus, a dough containing salt will be more dry and elastic, and will be less sticky during handling and shaping. On the contrary, a dough without salt is sticky and difficult to be worked.

Salt stiffens the dough and this is why it is generally added during the last phases of mixing/kneading rather than at the beginning, so not to toughen the dough too early.

Too much salt can, however, negatively affect dough development and baking. The ideal amount of salt is a mere 2% on the total amount of flour, which means 0.7 ounce per 35 ounces of flour.

Although the amount of salt needed for optimal dough development is rather small, several countries are addressing salt in bread, trying to reduce it for supposed health reasons. If you love bread, I would suggest reducing the amount of processed food, which contains unnecessary high amounts of salt, and leaving salt in your homemade loaf. The choice is of course up to the baker!

## Enzymes in Flour

Enzymes are molecules, generally proteins, which bring about biochemical reactions. In bread baking science, amylases are the class of enzymes we most care about. The amylases present in wheat flour help reduce starch and fructose to simpler sugars. In particular, amylose and amylopectin bonds in wheat starch need to be broken, producing dextrin and maltose, which are easily fermentable sugars. These sugars can then be "eaten" by yeast cells, and the resulting fermentation process will produce carbon dioxide, which is what makes the dough rise. Proper enzymatic balance in flour is also essential for the color and flavor of the final loaf.

Amylase naturally occurs in sprouted grains. During sprouting, however, starches are damaged, which affects the baking properties negatively. This is why sprouting is generally avoided, and grains are harvested and dried before this happens.

A natural way to balance enzymes in ground flour is to use small amounts of malted barley. Malted barley is simply sprouted barley. After sprouting, grains are milled and sold as malt flour (or malted grain flour), or processed into malt extract through further processing. Malt extract is produced by mixing the malt flour with water, then reactivating the enzymatic activity to further transform the starch into simple dextrose sugars. The result is a sticky, semi-sweet, and dark-colored malt extract.

The malt produced in this way is very useful in baking as it contains an enzyme called diastase: this term refers to either $\alpha$-, $\beta$-, or $\gamma$-amylase (all of them are called hydrolases) that are all capable of transforming a very complex sugar, such as starch, into simple sugars that are easily metabolized by yeasts.

Adding small amounts of malt (usually about 1% of the amount of flour used) increases the availability of yeast nourishment. Thanks to the Maillard reaction, the crust of the cooked product acquires a nice, uniform brown color.

### Know your grains

One important advantage of milling at home is the reappropriation of our long-lost relationship with grains. Having the ability to access whole grains, learn about their different shapes, colors, smells, and hardness, brings a different approach to the whole baking process. The milled grains become the real stars, giving a distinctive character to each and every bake. You will also become aware of the value and importance of quality grains, surely much more than when buying industrially milled flours at the grocery store.

### Bake fast

One main argument for home milling is the freshness of milled flour. With the easy-to-use home mills available nowadays, one can grind just enough flour for a bake and use it immediately after milling. The advantage of this routine is to preserve the nutrients contained in the grain. The quality and concentration of both vitamins and essential fats start to decrease soon after milling. Thus, being able to make your own flour will give you the most nutrient-packed bread you could possibly eat. It is important to note, though, that home mills can have drawbacks. The main defect is that some of them overheat flour in a way that commercial mills may not. Heat, like time, is another born enemy to nutrient-rich flour. Therefore, a local mill could be the best option if your main concern is using a nutrient-packed flour. Just ask your local miller for their freshly milled flour.

### Know you miller/farmer

Milling your grains could help you establish relationships with local millers. Unless you grow your own grains or live close to a wheat farm, your nearest artisan mill is your best chance to get quality grains to mill at home. Having to directly interact with millers and farmers will make you feel like you more closely know the chain that leads from the cultivated grains to your baked loaf. Dealing with millers and farmers will also shorten the distribution chain, by-passing intermediaries and giving you a safest grip on the bread you will be eating. It can benefit you, as you benefit your local grain community by supporting the cultivation of quality seeds for your flour.

## General Notes About the Recipes

Flour: For simplicity, most recipes refer to all-purpose or bread flour. Feel always free to substitute the flour with different types of flours, like spelt, emmer, einkorn, rye, heritage wheat, as well as whole wheat flour and home-milled, too. A recipe will be negatively affected only if the change is over 40% of the total flour amount, and only for flours that have worse baking properties compared to regular white flour.

Sourdough starter: Unless otherwise specified, when "sourdough starter" is listed as an ingredient, we refer to a 100% hydration white wheat flour starter (see page 56). Feel always free to change the type of flour used to feed the starter, but if changing the hydration (the water/flour ratio) of the starter, the amount of water in the recipe will need to be changed accordingly.

Preferments: Whenever a recipe calls for a sourdough starter, know that this can be substituted by an equal amount of any other type of preferment. See page 56 for suggestions on the alternatives.

Kneading: There is almost never only one right way of kneading/working a dough. For each recipe, feel free to use your favorite way, just making sure that the end-result achieves the recipe's needs in terms of dough development and gluten strength.

Fermentation: Times for the first and second fermentation are always just an indication; they can never be precise, because fermentation time depends on several variables that only you know, such as your room temperature, initial ingredients' temperature, force of your leavening agent, and so on. Learn to understand the dough and always have an eye on it rather than on the timer.

# A BRIEF HISTORY OF BREADMAKING

## THE FERTILE CRESCENT: WHERE WHEAT GREW WILD

The origins of bread are inseparable from the origins of wheat cultivation. Wheat cultivation started in the Middle East, in an area called the Fertile Crescent, which today includes Syria, parts of Turkey, Iraq, and Iran.

Long before the actual cultivation of common wheat, grains that are closely related to it used to grow wild and abundant in the Fertile Crescent. Barley and emmer, as well as einkorn and rye, were all present in different areas of this large region. There was something special about the seeds from these grasses: they were big and full of starches, easy to reach, and easy to store. The oldest seeds that have been preserved in our time date back 33,000 years. These seeds, found in Mount Caramel in northern Israel, were identified as emmer, a close relative of modern wheat. So, the hunter-gatherers of the Fertile Crescent were progressively incorporating more plant-based foods in their diet by gathering plenty of wild grains in the summer, and using them until the next harvest of spontaneously growing grasses.

In the beginning, wild relatives of wheat were presumably crossed or ground, combined with water, and then cooked. The resulting food preparation resembled porridge or polenta.

Between 10,000 and 12,000 years ago, humans began domesticating wild cereals, and agriculture was born. The wild grains were progressively selected to give richer and easier harvests, and soon they mutated in a way that made them incapable of surviving without the human hand, as well as making humans heavily dependent on the grains themselves. The advent of agriculture and the increased availability of stored grains also brought new ways of eating cereals, and so, bread was born.

First came unleavened flatbreads. The mixture of ground grains and water was now baked in rudimental ovens, rather than being boiled. An example of an ancient oven is the tannour (also called tannur, tabun or tanur), a cylinder deeply placed in the ground, with fire coming from the bottom. The flatbread was cooked by adhering the dough to the hot sides of the oven. These ovens are still built and used in rural areas in the Middle East.

## EGYPT: BREAD THAT BUILT PYRAMIDS

The first historical documents reporting the existence of leavened bread date back to the second millennium BC. At that time, Egyptians had possibly the most advanced culture in the world, thanks to their highly developed agriculture.

# PANIS FARREUS

YIELD: 1 LOAF / **ACTIVE TIME:** 50 MINUTES / **TOTAL TIME:** 6 HOURS

This bread is inspired to the ancient Roman bread *panis farreus,* which was made of emmer (farro), but possibly also with einkorn in early times. It was linked to a very special occasion, the *Confarreatio* (meaning "with farro"), the traditional Roman wedding ceremony.

**INGREDIENTS:**

- 14 ounces (400 g) 100% hydration sourdough starter

- 1⅘ pounds (800 g) einkorn flour

- 14 ounces water

- 2 teaspoons sea salt

1 Combine all ingredients but the salt, and knead for about 10 minutes. Dissolve the salt in 2 tablespoons of water and add to the dough. Knead for another 5 minutes.

2 Let rest, covered, for 2½ hours in a warm spot. Try using the oven with the light on and a crack open.

3 Transfer the dough onto a floured surface and gently shape into a round.

4 Cover a large round basket—or a medium-sized round tray—with kitchen towels and heavily coat with flour. With the floured linen, create a little hill in the middle of the basket.

5 Make a hole in the middle of your round and delicately enlarge the hole, flattening the round a bit to look like a big doughnut.

6 Place the "doughnut" in the basket, making sure that the central part of the linen sticks out of the hole. This will help keep the shape. There are also special bread baskets that can help to shape loaves this way. Let rest, covered, for 2 to 3 hours at room temperature.

7 Preheat your oven to 480°F. Bake for 10 minutes with steam (see pages 48-49 for tips), then open to let the steam out and lower the temperature to 390°F. Bake for 1 more hour and let cool.

The fall of the Roman Empire coincided with a time of technological recession in bread baking and wheat availability. Imports stopped and wheat circulation across Europe became more difficult. Agricultural techniques also went backwards, making local harvests poorer and more unpredictable. In this time, a large proportion of farmland was completely abandoned and turned into wilderness again. Famines and plagues became frequent, and the sultry white bread of the late Romans became a memory of a long lost golden age. However, in monasteries, the monks continued to cultivate grain.

Later on, when feudalism was instituted, the peasants worked in the land of the feudal lord, receiving a part of the harvest and the right to bake bread in the lord's oven in return. The lords were served white bread made with the sifted flour, and peasants ate black bread made with the bran discarded from the sifting and a small amount of flour.

Where wheat did not grow, common people ate bread made with grains other than wheat, such as barley and oats in Nordic countries or rye in Eastern Europe, France, and Northern Italy. Millet was also used to make bread, and in Mediterranean areas they used durum wheat. All of these grains were considered of poorer quality and lower nutritional value compared to bread made with common wheat. This is probably because they produced a bread with inferior baking properties, which was denser and took a long time to bake. Nobility and royalty, however, could afford to buy wheat from merchants, even in areas where wheat did not grow, so aristocracy continued to have white bread on the table.

Often, common people did not have enough of any type of grain to make bread, and needed to make flour from the most diverse sources—anything to satisfy the hunger and bake a loaf. Examples include tree bark in Nordic countries, chestnuts in Southern Europe, and even acorns in times of famine. Legumes were also used, and later on potatoes—and the list is much longer. All of these alternative ingredients, as well as grains other than wheat, were used for necessity rather than by choice, but ended up characterizing European local breads in peculiar and fascinating ways. It is thanks to these local restrictions that a very important part of Europe's culinary and bread heritage was born.

Therefore, the middle age was prolific in giving birth to countless different local breads, but it did not produce any substantial technological progress in bread baking, with the exception of the invention of the windmill in seventh century AD. Windmills have Persian origins and were used to grind grains and operate field irrigation pumps. However, written evidence proves that the use of windmills did not reach Europe until at least the 12th century.

During the Renaissance, and starting in Italy, commerce flourished again, and wheat's exchange and transportation became easier. White bread was no longer associated with the noble rank, but was still a sign of wealth. Cities' middle classes could buy it from the many bakeries, and well-off peasants could bake it in their ovens.

Around this time, beer-derived yeast was reintroduced. This was a relative of modern baker's yeast and had been long lost since the Roman Empire, where it was often used as an alternative to sourdough. Once reintroduced, yeast quickly became favored over sourdough, because it could make lighter bread. It is said that Maria De Medici made baker's yeast popular again. The Tuscan noblewoman, who became queen of France, apparently brought her crew of Italian bakers to Paris, and it is said that the superiority of French luxury bread and pastries started from there.

After the French revolution, and with the success of Napoleon, wheat-based breads and pastries became more popular in Northern and Eastern Europe, and in the United States. It was the type of bread eaten by the French—or, at least, by the Emperor's court and by the citizens of Paris, the Empire's capital.

## NORTH AMERICA: INDUSTRIAL WHEAT AND FLOURS

Wheat was introduced to North America by the colonists, but it took a couple of centuries for it to become the main grain. Initially rye, oats, and corn were much more popular than wheat, but the French influence was felt in the young United States and the cultivation of wheat was driven forward. However, it was not until the mid-19th century that substantial progress occurred in American wheat breeding and milling techniques.

There were two major events that determined the future of wheat farming and trading in North America. The first event occurred in Canada. A Canadian farmer, David Fife, was not pleased with the performance of his wheat. So, he asked one of his workers, a native of Scotland, to find him another variety of wheat in his home country. The worker went to the harbor and found a ship full of wheat. He bought a small amount of it and sent it to Mr. Fife in Canada. Unfortunately, the wheat was mistakenly sown right away. It was a winter wheat, and needed instead to be sown in the fall. The story goes that the first disastrous harvest was just one spike of wheat, from which a few seeds were saved, and then sown at the right time. In a few years, the seeds of this mysterious wheat, Red Fife, had multiplied and given fantastic harvests. This wheat was a hard wheat and made a flour that allowed bread to rise higher, which made it immediately popular among bakers. Soon this wheat was grown in most of the United States, and other high performing hard wheats followed, like Turkey Red and Marquis. This growing wheat empire had its center in Minneapolis, Minnesota.

The second major innovation was aimed at solving the problems that arose with the milling of Red Fife. This wheat had superior baking properties, so bakers wanted it as refined as possible. However, stone mills had problems dealing with its hardness, and as a result the flour could not be properly sifted. To make matters worse, the stones of the mills wore up faster when milling hard wheats like Red Fife and Turkey Red. This is the main reason that the milling industry began to seek different techniques of milling, and in a few decades roller mills were born.

Roller mills were made with metal, rather than stone, and could separate the endosperm from the bran through purifiers. Later, extractors were able to isolate the wheat germ from the endosperm. The levels of fineness and

# VIKING UNLEAVENED BARLEY BREAD

YIELD: 16 FLATBREADS / ACTIVE TIME: 1 HOUR / TOTAL TIME: 2 DAYS

This recipe is inspired by the authentic remain of a Viking bread found in a grave in Birka, Sweden, dated ninth to tenth century AD. Interestingly, at the time flaxseeds were quite popular in Northern Europe.

**INGREDIENTS:**

10½ ounces (300 grams) barley flour

3½ ounces (100 grams) graham flour

2 tablespoons (30 grams) crushed flaxseed

1¼ cups water

1 tablespoon lard

1 teaspoon salt

1 Combine both flours and the flaxseed with ¾ cup of the water. Check the consistency of the dough. It should be sticky, but not too wet. If the dough absorbs the first half of the water, add the remaining water.

2 Add the lard and salt, and knead just enough to combine all of the ingredients.

3 Place in a bowl sealed with plastic wrap or in an airtight container, and place in the fridge for two days.

4 Preheat the oven to 375°F.

5 Transfer the dough onto a heavily floured surface, divide in four pieces and then divide each piece in four smaller pieces (you need 16 pieces overall).

6 Shape the dough pieces into balls. Then, flatten the balls into rounds.

7 Make four big incisions in the dough so it will look like a clover, and then make a few small incisions with a fork.

8 Bake for 10–20 minutes, or until golden brown.

whiteness obtained by these mills were unprecedented, and soon the United States began to export large amounts of white flour to Europe. Later on, when Europe imported roller mill technology, the United States became the largest exporter of wheat to the old continent.

Having wheat become so important in the United States, sizable investments were made in research. Wheat was studied in increasingly sophisticated laboratories and was bred, cross-bread, or directly modified. This was, and continues to be, with the aim of selecting plants with improved baking properties, as well as improved resilience to pests, drought, and weather. The result was wheat varieties, which gave immensely productive harvests that are apt to be extensively grown without need of much care from the farmer.

# WORLD: THE REDISCOVERY OF ARTISAN BREAD AND LOCAL WHEAT VARIETIES

In the 20th century, the availability of high performing and cheap white flour resulted in its massive use for baking and cooking, alike to what had happened for refined sugar.

The spread of industrial flour was followed by that of *industrial bread*. Progress in food appliances as well as advances in food chemistry resulted in a new type of bread. Thanks to the use of high-speed mixers, and chemical dough conditioners and improvers, the rising process could be sped up like never before. At the same time, machines were capable of substituting bakers in every stage of the baking process, so that thousands of loaves of bread could be made and baked at once. The advantages in terms of productivity and cost are clear.

As a delayed reaction to an overflow of cheap bread, a long wave of artisan bread nostalgia started to spread in the '70s, fully bloomed in the '90s, and hasn't faded since. The term *artisan bread* generally refers to a bread made either at home or in a non-industrial bakery. In an authentic artisan bakery, the baker has full control over the baked product; in other words, the process of making bread is not fully automated. As opposed to quick risen packaged bread, artisan bread is expected to have undergone a proper, longer fermentation and to be free from additives.

The interest in breads recreating local traditions has grown, all in a search for authenticity in bread that was perceived by some to be forever lost. Small artisan bakeries inspired by the European bread tradition are successfully opening in every corner of the world including, curiously, the Far East, where there was never such a tradition. At the same time, more and more households are learning to make their own bread and regaining control over the quality of their bread.

Paralleling the revival of artisan bread, scientists, farmers, and wheat lovers started to hunt for old wheat varieties. Sources were mostly seed banks, where original seeds from different regions of the world were stored. Other important sources were isolated pockets of farmland where growers have kept using local wheat varieties, rather than converting to the dominant, modern ones. Sometimes old seeds were recuperated out of pure luck, in the attic of an elderly relative, or a disused barn.

In every corner of the world, with a longstanding tradition of wheat and cultivation, the hunt and study of autochthon grain varieties is ever growing. There is much to research and try, since hundreds and hundreds of old varieties of wheat are still around, notwithstanding our continued attempts to push only a few highly efficient cultivars.

This is good in many ways. First of all, there is the big advantage of preserving biodiversity. As agronomists tell us, we cannot foresee all of the climatic changes to come, and biodiversity in our wheat is a guarantee that we will have

bread on our table for time to come. Foodies will also appreciate having a wide array of different grains and wheat varieties, adapted to particular soils and weather conditions. As with cheese and wine, different local varieties present a rich array of different flavors for consumers. Each local variety will, therefore, give our bread different characteristics in terms of taste, consistency, and the overall look of the baked bread.

Finally, there are also health-related benefits in reintroducing old wheat varieties in our diet. It has been argued that modern wheat has undergone excessive changes, or that those changes occurred too fast for our biology to adapt to them. It is indeed true that older varieties of wheat have been consumed for a longer amount of time, and they have already passed the test as reliable food staples. Studies tend to confirm that older wheat varieties are superior to newer ones

in terms of digestibility, and often in their nutritional profile, too.

Thanks to all these considerations and to the contagious enthusiasm of wheat "archeologists," old varieties are becoming one of the next big things in bread baking. As an example, in California the cultivation of wheat almost became a memory from the past, but interest in heritage wheat varieties has revived the local grain economy, and now more and more land is being converted to wheat agriculture. Similar phenomena can be observed in Sicily, which was once the cradle of wheat, and has now been reborn as a heritage wheat paradise. France is also rediscovering its many precious local wheat varieties, and so on.

These are still just pockets compared to the vastly dominant conventional wheat farming that rules global imports and exports. However, the number of these pockets are growing exponentially.

## MILLING YOUR OWN FLOUR

### The Grains

If you were to grow wheat in your garden, you would have to find a way to do the hardest part of all: threshing the grains. This means removing the wheat kernel from the inedible chaff that surrounds it, something that is not easily done by hand.

In the most likely case that you are instead buying grains, you may purchase them already cleaned and ready to be milled. Make sure not to buy grains destined to be cooked rather than milled, like those sometimes found in a grocery store. If those grains are not meant for home milling, they have possibly been heated. When grains are heated, starches get damaged and can no longer give you good bread.

The best way to buy grains for milling is either from a farmer or from a small mill. There are also specialty stores that sell quality grains for milling.

### Storage

Storage is a fundamental aspect of your new endeavor as a home-miller. Grains can maintain most of their properties for a very long time, if properly stored. Therefore, unless your grains come to you in a vacuum package, there are several actions you should take.

First, freeze your grains. This will kill any larvae present in the grains and will save you from unpleasant pantry bugs. If you have space in your freezer, you could keep the grains there until you decide to use them. Otherwise, store them in a fresh and dry part of your home. If you have a storage room with such properties somewhere outside of your kitchen, that would be best, because kitchens tend to undergo steep variations in temperature, which is not optimal for grains. Ideally, grains should not be stored in thick plastic boxes, because they are alive and tend to generate heat. Plastic is a good insulator, which means that it retains heat. The best grain container is one made of glass or stainless steel.

## Tempering

Commercial mills temper (soak) wheat kernels with water before processing them. This is done by adding water to the kernels in special machines that distribute the humidity evenly. Tempering allows you to easily separate the bran from the endosperm. Similarly, the home-miller can temper their grains at home and obtain a flour where the bran more easily "peels off" during milling, and therefore, can be more easily separated by the rest of the flour while sifting. To temper your grains, add minimal amounts of water (5% of the amount of grains is a good start) to your grains, shake them vigorously, let rest, and shake again. Let the process last between 24 to 48 hours. One limit of tempering your grains is that the resulting flour will contain more water and so the flour will spoil fast if not used rather quickly.

## Milling

Unless you have a hand-operated mill, the actual milling operation is quite simple and effortless. For most home-mills, you will simply need to place your grains into the hopper, press a button, and wait for the flour to come out. It could not be simpler than this.

In most mills, you have the possibility of regulating the fineness of the output. This will depend on the type of flour you are after, which in turn will depend on the kind of bread you want to make. If your aim is an earthy rye bread, you will want your mill to be set on a coarse grinding. If you wish to make a baguette or a fluffy cinnamon bun, you most definitely will want the mill's finest grinding setting. In the latter case, make sure that the mill does not overheat the flour, because this could affect the success of your loaf. At temperatures over 105°F, the enzymes contained in the grains, which are important for the leavening process, start to deteriorate (see page 25). Be aware that heat is produced on the finest settings of the mill. One solution is to first choose a coarse grinding, then cool the flour and mill it again, this time using the finest setting. Re-milling is, however, not recommended for all types of mills, so please read the instructions first.

## Sifting

Hand sifting is not the most time efficient method, but it can be useful if one wants to use home-milled flour even for the most ambitious breads. The methods available to the home-miller are generally quite similar to the ones that were used in our past when hand sifting. It is based on the use of hand-operated sieves that come with meshes of different fineness. The flour is first passed through a sieve with a wider mesh and is then sifted again through another sieve with a finer mesh, and so on. Many skip the sifting and the tempering altogether and prefer to use their whole wheat flour as it is, often in combination with sifted and white flours from local and industrial mills.

## Fresh or Aged?

There has been much debate regarding the issue of using freshly milled flour vs. aged flour. Aged flour is a flour that has been left to age in a vessel that allows the flour to breathe (such as a paper sack) for a few weeks. Flour that has not been aged is called "green." Mills and professional bakers generally agree that aged flour is better for bread baking. Home-millers, however, believe that their flour should be consumed as fresh as possible. The rationale behind the average home-miller's position is in the superior nutritional value of freshly milled flour. The preference of skilled bakers for aged flour derives instead from their knowledge of basic baking chemistry. An oxidized flour helps the gluten strands of the dough to fully develop. Without some level of oxidation created by exposing the flour to air, the baked bread may have lower volume and poorer structure.

## Learn About your Flour

Once you have your home-milled flour, you will need to learn how to use it in a dough. Your flour could be coarse or fine, sifted or whole-wheat, fresh or aged. Depending on the quality of the grains, it could have high, low, or medium enzymatic activity. It could be strong or weak, and so on. These considerations are important to have in mind with every new flour, even a store-bought one. The best way to learn about your flour is to test it. Try the flour in a bread recipe you know well, and that is as simple as possible. Always remember to have an eye on the dough and to adjust all the other ingredients around the flour.

# EQUIPMENT & TOOLS
# FOR BREAD BAKING

To start making bread, you do not need any special tools. You can manage to bake your first bread using only what is commonly found in an average kitchen. However, if you want to become a skilled bread baker, you can have fun setting up your own little home bakery. Having the right tools at hand will make bread baking more enjoyable and may greatly improve the quality of your loaves.

## ESSENTIALS

### Scale

A scale will be your best friend through your bread baking endeavors. Your scale, along with your oven, is one appliance you should learn to know and love. The international bread baking language runs on weights, rather than volumes, and this is how all the best recipes, also called formulas, are written.

There are several good reasons why measurement expressed in weights are preferable to volumetric ones. Flour can vary in volume depending on its fineness. A coarser flour has a smaller volume compared to a more finely ground one, therefore, the weight of a cup of flour varies according to the type of flour. Other ingredients, like water, need to be scaled based on the total amount of flour, something that is easily done using weights. If you are unfamiliar with your kitchen scale, start by weighting volumes you are used to (like a cup, a spoon, etc.) so that you start getting the grip of the new system. In no time, you will become very fond of your scale. Just rely on the fact that it will make bread baking infinitely easier.

You absolutely do not need a highly technological scale. Choose based on your budget, and know that almost any scale will serve the purpose. There are bakeries that still use decades old analogical scales and have no intention to change them for the newest one. Just make sure of two things:

**1.** *Weight range.* You will need to measure everything from a pinch of salt to a few pounds of flour, so make sure that your scale can reliably handle weights in this range. In case your scale is not reliable for the lower end, you can always buy an extra scale dedicated to weigh small amounts.

**2.** *Dimension.* This aspect regards both the actual dimensions of the scale and the scale's weighing surface. The actual dimension needs to properly fit your kitchen space requirements. It also depends on where you plan to store the scale—in a drawer or always on the counter? Even more important is the size of the scale's weighing surface. In order to be able to comfortably weigh a big piece of dough, you need a large enough weighing surface.

### Assorted Containers

You will need several containers of different sizes to mix ingredients and allow your dough and preferments to rest and rise.

*Container Size.* The size of your containers depends on the amount of dough you preferably work with. Always consider that both your preferments (yeasted or sourdough-based) and your dough need to have enough space in order to triple in volume. Dough and preferments generally double in volume, but you do not want to be unprepared for the days when your yeasts are unusually active.

*Container Type.* Containers with straight walls are preferred, as they are easy to keep clean with sticky dough. A lid that can effectively seal the container is also preferable to a looser one. Alternatively, you can always use multi-purpose bowls that you surely already have in your kitchen, and cover them with plastic wrap or with a pan lid that fits the bowl.

## Spatula

You will not be able to keep the walls of your containers tidy and remove sticky dough without a spatula. A clean container means an unfavorable ground for the proliferation of unwanted microorganisms, so make sure you always have a few spatulas at hand.

## Proofing Baskets

It is possible to make bread without using proofing baskets, but once you start using them, you will realize that they make the process much easier. With your shaped loaf in the basket, you can easily move the dough around your kitchen without disturbing the dough. This comes in handy when baking at home, where kitchen space is not exclusively dedicated to bread. Bread proofing baskets come in different shapes and materials, and nowadays are very reasonably priced and easy to get. You may start with a couple of round baskets, and a couple oval-shaped ones. There is always time to expand the collection.

## Kitchen Towels

It is always good to have clean kitchen towels at hand. You can use any clean piece of cloth made of cotton or linen. The lighter the better. They can be very useful when dealing with wet doughs or to line the bread baskets. If properly floured, they will ensure that the dough won't stick to the basket—or to the kitchen towel.

## Dough Scrapers

These come in different materials and shapes. You will want to have at least two of them. One should have round edges and be used to detach your dough from the container where you mix it or proof it. The other essential type of scraper has a blade with a straight edge, and the best ones are made of stainless steel. The metal scraper will enable you to easily cut your dough, as well as help you to scrape dough off of your working table, keeping it clean. In fact, it could become one of your most important tools. A good metal scraper will enable you to cut the risen dough without deflating it. It can also help you shape very wet doughs—many bakers use it as a "second hand" in shaping. So, choose a quality scraper, and make sure it is not too small, so that it can handle bigger doughs.

## Working Surface

This is another fundamental aspect of your little home bakery. Check your kitchen for a working surface that has a good height for you. It could be a corner of your countertop, your kitchen table, or a kitchen island. Make sure that, whatever the surface, it gives stable support. In the bread baking process, you may need to punch your dough (literally) or slap it around, and in order to do so you need stability.

If you have the chance of choosing the material of your working table/surface, there are different possibilities. Both marble and wood are good. Stainless steel is not considered optimal by many—yet that is what most professional bakers have to use, because of hygienic regulations. The reason why both stone and wood are preferred is that they are not as "cold" as stainless steel. In other words, they will not affect dough temperature. Stainless steel instead will cool down the dough slightly, becoming an extra variable to take into account. Wooden surfaces are also gener-

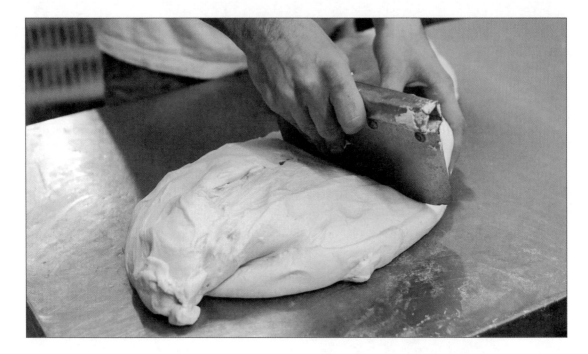

ally good to work with because of the uneven texture of wood, an advantage when shaping medium-hard doughs. Marble, on the other hand, is easier to keep clean, and its smoothness may be the best surface for very wet and sticky dough. Yet, ultimately, it all depends on what feels best when you work a dough on it.

## Dough Thermometer

Like with your scale, you will become very fond of your baking thermometer. It will be an invaluable tool to help you control one of the most important variables in bread baking: temperature. You do not need to get the most technological device on the market and you do not need all of the extra functions some thermometers offer—unless you really like them. All you need is a sensor that can easily penetrate in the dough and liquids (like water or milk) with a display to inform you about their temperature. Simple multi-purpose kitchen thermometers are nowadays easy to find and quite inexpensive. Do not hesitate to get one at the first occasion.

## Assorted Loaf Pans

It is essential to have a few loaf pans of different sizes at hand. You will need them for quick breads and breads with a high percentage of whole-grains and seeds, which require the dough to be very wet and do not have a strong gluten structure to keep their shape without the loaf pan.

## Parchment Paper

Good parchment paper always comes in handy. It can make loading the loaves in the oven a much easier job, especially in the beginning. Just make sure that your baking paper can tolerate temperatures up to 500°F or higher.

## Oven

This is one appliance you surely cannot do without in bread baking. However, keep in mind that in case of necessity, there is also the possibility of making bread on a stove (see the Flatbreads section). Like any other tool, your oven does not need to be high-tech. Old kitchen ovens can sometimes bake the best bread. So, do not think that you will have to trade an old oven for a new one to become a bread master. Your old oven may hold some good surprises— just as your brand new one could. The most important thing is to know your oven, and use it at its full potential.

If you need to buy an oven for your kitchen, one important aspect to check for is maximum temperature. Both breads and pizzas love a very hot oven, so make sure to invest in an oven that can reach at least 500°F. The hotter, the better. If you can also find a kitchen oven that is good at retaining steam, that is a bonus. There are some rather new kitchen ovens designed for the most ambitious home chefs that can generate steam. Buying one of these could be the best option, but the steam control must be effective. In other words, you need to make sure that your technological oven with steam function can be used for bread baking. In order for this to be possible, it is necessary to have full control of when to release steam, and for how long.

In the most common scenario of having to adapt your kitchen oven to your new passion, here are some tips.

*Heat.* To generate and retain heat is the main characteristic of any oven. Unfortunately for home bakers, common kitchen ovens are not made to reach and retain the high temperatures loved by bread. Luckily, there are a few tricks that can help make your oven more efficient, both in generating and retaining heat. For instance, you can use baking stones and place them on the middle and bottom racks of the oven. Remember, however, that baking stones absorb and release heat slowly and this is why (to benefit from this system) the oven should undergo a long preheat: 1½ to 2 hours before loading a loaf is a good interval. If you have cast-iron pans, they can also be used to absorb heat. Just place the pans on the bottom of the oven when you start preheating.

*Steam.* Steam is naturally released from the loaf when the heat of the oven makes water contained in the dough evaporate. In a traditional wood-fired oven, the steam generated by the baking process is not efficiently dispersed outside of the oven, which is good for bread. In the absence of ambient steam, the loaf quickly forms a crust and the loaf's inner gasses are no longer able to make the bread expand further. The resulting bread will have a smaller volume, be denser, and take longer to bake. It is then clear why in modern ovens, with more efficient ways to disperse fumes and steam, we need to add steam during baking in order to compensate for the loss of it. This is most important in the initial stages of baking. Later on, when the crust has already formed, it is good to allow all of the steam out and let the loaf dry in the oven.

There are several ways to create steam in your home oven:

Ice cubes. It may sound strange, but ice cubes are a very effective way to create steam, because they vaporize slower than water. Make sure you place a baking dish or a cast-iron pan on the bottom of your oven when you start preheating. Then you will just need to throw a few ice cubes on your baking dish or pan when you insert the loaves on the upper oven rack.

Lava stones. A very effective way to increase the oven's temperature and create steam is using lava stones. Lava stones are easily found in shops that sell grilling supplies. The process is simple: Place the lava stones on a baking tray or cast-iron pan and set on the bottom of the oven when preheating. To generate steam, pour a glass of water over the hot stones when you load your loaves into the oven.

*Water.* The old-fashioned way to generate steam in a home oven is to place a small pot with water in the bottom of the oven. However, this system is not preferred, because the resulting steam tends to be concentrated in only one part of the oven, and risks creating asymmetry in the baked loaves. It is better to pour a hot cup of water directly on a hot baking dish or a cast-iron pan placed in the bottom of the oven. Another way to add water to the oven and generate steam is to use a spray bottle and spray the walls of the oven soon after loading the loaves, repeating a few minutes later.

## Stone

Adding one or more baking stones to your oven will drastically improve the quality of your bread. With the use of baking stones, you will obtain crusts that resemble those baked in a wood-fired oven. There are several types of baking stones available, made of different materials, and overall, they will all be efficient. However, some aspects make a baking stone superior to others. One aspect to consider is the thickness of the stone. A good bread baking stone should be at least half an inch thick. Also, be aware that rectangular stones are more useful than round ones, as they cover more oven surface. Ideally, your stone should cover all of your baking rack, leaving just a margin on all sides to allow air circulation.

## Dutch Oven

This is not as essential as a baking stone, but can help you make bakery-perfect loaves, especially when combined with one or more baking stones. A Dutch oven is any ovenproof pot or pan with a lid. You may already have one at home; look through your collection of pots and pans and you may be surprised. If you buy one, a deep cast-iron skillet with a lid is the best choice for bread. The advantage of using a Dutch oven is that the lid helps retain steam in the bread, therefore, using the natural steam generated by the baking loaf to the maximum. It is common to remove the lid halfway through the baking time, so that the steam can be released and the crust can get some color.

The small dimensions of the Dutch oven also maximize oven temperature by creating an oven

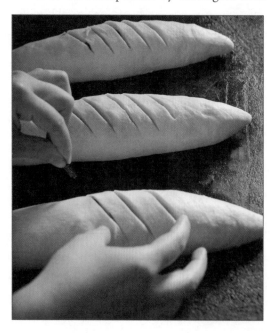

within the oven. Remember that if using this method, the pan should be placed in the oven upon starting the preheat. The limits of this method are that the shape and dimension of the breads you bake are conditional to the shape of the pot or pan used. This method can thus be used when baking specific types of breads, but surely not all of them.

## Peel

A baker peel is essential to load a delicate, fully risen dough in the oven without deflating it. It is also helpful in unloading baked breads without burning oneself. Peels can be made out of wood or metal. Both materials do the job, and the choice is up to the baker. As to the dimension, it depends, again, on the baker. If you prefer to load one loaf at a time, then a narrow peel will be the best. If you like to load multiple loaves at once, then the peel should be almost as wide as the inside of your oven. Always remember to sprinkle some coarse semolina or cornmeal on the peel—it will help unload the breads.

## Oven Gloves

Considering that in bread baking you need to work with a very hot oven, good protective gloves are mandatory. Having good oven gloves becomes truly imperative if working with the Dutch oven method. When choosing, I prefer gloves that allow for fine hands movements, as ordinary kitchen mittens may not. You will need to be able to move your hands quickly to get the best out of your oven. It is also important to choose long gloves, because it is common to get burns on the forearms when wearing normal length gloves.

## Scoring Lames/Blades

It is common, but not always necessary, to score your loaves before baking them. Scoring a loaf of bread allows the crumb to have space to fully expand during baking without being stopped by the external layer of the loaf, which will become the crust. The external layer generally hardens and dries slightly during the last stages of dough rising (proofing) and will continue to harden during baking. If the growth in volume, also called oven spring, is accentuated, the external layer could also spontaneously break, altering the look of the bread in undesirable ways. This is why scoring needs to be precise in order to make the bread expand harmoniously. An exception is very wet dough, where the external layer does not generally dry enough to be a problem. There are different types of scoring tools. Some use a lame, like that of a serrated knife. Most prefer razor blades, either held in the hand or mounted on a blade holder. Those bakers who are perfectionists change their blades very often to ensure a clean cut.

## EXTRA TOOLS

### Mixer

There is a wide array of machines used to mix and work dough. Although commercial bakeries would have a hard time without such machines, they are not essential to the home baker. When amounts of dough are as small as the ones made at home, hand mixing and kneading are perfectly viable options. It is, however, useful to have a mixer, especially when handling sweet doughs that can be very sticky and require intense kneading.

The type of mixer generally available to the home baker is the stand-mixer, also called planetary mixer. There are several reasonably priced models on the market. For bread baking, you want to select a machine with a good dough hook, a powerful motor, and a large bowl. Having several speeds is another important characteristic. Bread dough likes a gentle low speed mixing in the first stages, but can benefit from shorter medium-high speed mixing in later stages of the process. Sweet bread doughs often require more vigorous mixing.

### Mill

As with the mixer, owning a mill is not a necessity in bread making, but it can become an added pleasure. The aroma of freshly milled grains is indeed quite addictive, and you may quickly become fond of your home mill. Nowadays, there are plenty of different types and brands to choose from.

*Countertop electric stone mills.* This type of mill is a miniature version of the modern stone mills used by commercial artisan mills. They can look very appealing on the kitchen countertop, and can produce coarse to relatively fine flour, although not as fine as the flour produced with larger stones in commercial facilities. Small stone mills also tend to overheat flour, unlike commercial models.

*Countertop electric mills.* This type of mill uses metal plates instead of stone to grind the grains. They are less attractive, but just as effective as stone mills. Some models can give finer flour than others and can also overheat the flour, so check these aspects before buying.

*Countertop manual mills.* These mills can use either stone or metal plates and are run on manual, rather than electric, power. They require a full workout from your side, but it may be worth it. The big advantage of manual over electric mills is increased control over grains grinding. Manual mills offer the possibility to vary intensity of the grinding based on the feedback from the grains. In other words, with practice, the home miller develops a "feel" for milling and understands when the grains need a gentler action. This will benefit the flour by damaging the grains as little as possible during the milling process.

*Mill mixer attachments.* Mixer attachments generally run on metal disks. If you already have a mixer, this option could come in handy, because most mixers have a mill attachment. Before choosing an attachment instead of a countertop mill, look into the quality of your mill mixer attachment. Check for the flour maximum fineness and level of overheating when the mill is set on its finest gear.

# FERMENTATION IN BREAD BAKING

The term *fermentation* derives from the Latin *fervere*, which means to burst, like the bubbles on grapes during the wine-making process. Similar fermentative processes are involved in bread baking.

Fermentation is a metabolic process performed by microorganisms that extract energy from carbohydrates releasing a series of by-products, among which is carbon dioxide ($CO_2$). $CO_2$ is the main agent responsible for the increase in volume in bread dough. This gas stays in the dough only if entrapped by a tight gluten net. In the absence of this characteristic, the $CO_2$ is released into the environment.

In bread baking, we have two main types of fermentation: alcoholic fermentation and lactic fermentation.

## ALCOHOLIC FERMENTATION

Yeasts are single-celled microorganisms classified as fungi. They are special, because they're capable of obtaining energy both under anaerobic and aerobic conditions. Anaerobic processes evolved first in the very beginning of life on Earth when oxygen was not yet available. Later on, yeast cells developed mechanisms to obtain energy also in the presence of oxygen.

In bread baking, the dominant type of yeast fermentation is anaerobic. In such conditions, yeasts obtain energy through alcoholic fermentation. In short, during dough fermentation yeast cells multiply in number, and break down starches and sugars that naturally occur in flour, to produce energy for their survival. This process is called glycolysis, which is aimed to provide energy to the yeast cells, and, in alcoholic fermentation, generates as by-products alcohol and carbon dioxide. The carbon dioxide makes the dough rise, while the alcohol tends to slowly evaporate from the dough.

## LACTIC FERMENTATION

This type of fermentation is not performed by yeast cells but is instead the result of the proliferation and life maintenance functions of another type of microorganism, lactic acid bacteria (LAB). The basic mechanism is the same as in alcoholic fermentation. LAB, just like yeasts, are capable of carrying out glycolysis. This complex series of biochemical reactions are performed in the absence of oxygen, and aimed at extracting energy from starches and sugars. The difference is in the by-product. In lactic fermentation, the main by-product of LAB activity is lactic acid, followed by $CO_2$, alcohol, and acetic acid. The latter molecules can, however, only be produced by specific types of LAB.

*Homofermentative.* LAB only generate lactic acid as a by-product of glycolysis. In bread baking, lactic acid serves several functions, but does not contribute to any rise in volume in the dough.

*Heterofermentative.* LAB instead can do much more for your dough. Besides producing lactic acid, they also release $CO_2$, which can help the dough rise.

## BAKER'S YEAST

The discard of beer production, a yeasty froth evolved during brewing commonly called barm, has been used since antiquity to leaven bread (see page 32).

Nowadays, yeast for baking is produced through industrial multiplication and processing of isolated cultures of one single type of yeast cell, *Saccharomyces cerevisiae*, which is the anaerobic yeast most commonly found in traditional beer brewing.

There are different types of packaged yeast, all containing live cultures of *Saccharomyces cerevisiae*.

**Active dry yeast** is the most easily found baker's yeast, and it consists of almost completely dried yeast cells. It needs to be activated before use by combining it with warm water and letting it sit for a few minutes. It does not like the cold, so you should never combine it with cold water.

**Instant yeast** is a little more difficult to find,

and it is made of partly dried yeast cells. It is more "alive" than active dry yeast, and lasts for a much shorter time after it has been exposed to air. You can easily distinguish the two by looking at the granules that compose these commercial yeasts. Instant yeast granules are bigger. Instant yeast does not require activation in water, so it can be sprinkled on the dough at any time of the mixing process.

**Fresh yeast** is also known as cake yeast, and is not easy to find in the United States nowadays. It needs refrigeration, and lasts for only two weeks. Like instant yeast, it does not need to be activated, and can be simply crumbled and added to the dough during mixing. It is less concentrated than the other two types of commercially sold yeasts, and, therefore, you will need about three times more yeast to achieve the same leavening effect. This could affect the taste of the baked bread, giving it a stronger yeast flavor.

## FERMENTATION WITH BAKER'S YEAST

This type of fermentation is carried out by one single type of microorganism, *S. cerevisiae*, and relies only on the alcoholic fermentation processes. As a by-product, the yeast cells will give us plenty of $CO_2$, but no lactic acid.

There are two main methods that can be followed when fermenting dough with baker's yeast: the direct and the indirect method.

### Direct method

This simply means that yeast is added to the mixture of flour and water directly, i.e., while

all the ingredients are combined. Recipes using the direct method are faster, but this also means that the fermentation process goes faster. Consequently, some of the biochemical reactions that normally take place in a long-fermented dough simply do not happen, or are reduced. Industrial bread is based on the direct method, because of obvious advantages in production rate.

## Indirect method

With this term, bakers refer to bread recipes that require the preparation of a preferment before the actual mixing of the final dough. There are several types of yeast-based preferments. What is common to all of them is that they require fermenting part of the flour and water called by the recipe ahead of time.

Poolish, a liquid preferment, was first developed in Poland, as suggested by the name. It is made with equal amounts of water and flour, and can also be referred to as a 100% hydration preferment. The amount of yeast added to a poolish varies according to the desired leavening time of the preferment. Less yeast is added to the preferment for longer leavening times, while more yeast is added to speed up the process.

For example: ⅓ lb (150 g) flour and ⅓ lb (150 g) water is fermented with 1.5 teaspoons (4 g) of active dry yeast for a fast rise of 3 hours at room temperature, versus ⅓ teaspoon (1 g) of active dry yeast is used for a longer rise of 12 hours at room temperature.

Biga is another preferment that was first developed in Italy. Its name evokes an ancient Roman's carriage, perhaps to signify the role that the preferment has in carrying forward the fermentation. Unlike poolish, biga is a stiff preferment and is generally made with half of the amount of water as compared with flour. Like poolish, the relative amount of added yeast determines the length of the fermentation needed for a biga.

For example: ⅓ lb (150 g) flour and 2.6 oz (75 g) water fermented with ½ teaspoon (5 g) of active dry yeast for a faster rise of 3 hours at room temperature, versus ⅓ lb (150 g) flour and 2.6 oz (75 g) water fermented with ⅕ teaspoon (⅕ g) of active dry yeast for a longer rise of 22 to 24 hours at room temperature.

# SOURDOUGH FERMENTATION

This type of fermentation is accomplished by a culture containing several populations of microorganisms that thrive in a regularly fed mixture of water and flour. Both yeasts and LAB are commonly found in sourdough cultures. There can be substantial variations between one culture and another, especially if the cultures originated in different geographical areas, due to the various nature of wild yeasts and LAB that can populate a sourdough culture.

Thanks to the rich microcosmos of living fungi and bacteria, making sourdough bread includes both alcoholic and lactic fermentation processes. The baked breads will differ considerably in terms of volume, texture, and flavor depending on the specific type of sourdough culture used and the way the culture is kept. When a sourdough culture is stable and capable of rising a dough, it is called sourdough starter. When a sourdough starter is heavily neglected, yeast populations become very small and the type of homofermentative LAB that produces acetic acid will become prevalent, giving us a very sour bread with poor volume development. On the other hand, a sourdough culture that pullulates yeast and has a predominance of heterofermentative LAB will reward our careful attention by producing a well-developed loaf, with ideal volume and texture, in which flavor is complex but not acidic.

Types of starters. Different types of bread recipes call for different types of starters. They can vary based on the kind of grain used (wheat or rye-based), or on the degree of whiteness (white, sifted, or whole wheat). Starters are also classified based on the relative proportion of water to flour contained in the mixture. Here some examples:

*100% hydration*, also called a liquid starter, refers to a sourdough starter in which the proportion of water to flour is 1:1. In other words, there is as much water as flour, in terms of

weight. Hydration means just this: how much water there is as compared with flour. This level of hydration is most commonly used by American, German, and Nordic bakers.

*80% hydration* refers to a soft sourdough starter in which the proportion of water to flour is 0.8 to 1, or 8 to 10. In other words, there is 80% as much water compared to flour. The same math applies to a 70% or 60% hydration starter, and so on. Medium stiff preferments were traditionally preferred by French bakers.

*50% hydration* refers to a stiff starter in which the amount of water is half as much as the flour. This is the type of starter commonly found in Italian sourdough bread recipes, called pasta madre.

All doughs made with sourdough as the rising agent are based on the indirect method. To use sourdough in a dough, one needs an active sourdough starter that has been recently fed water and flour. As with yeast-based preferments, fermentation time in sourdough-based baking is determined by the relative amount of sourdough added to the mixture of flour and water ahead of adding it to the final dough.

For example: 7 ounces (200 g) flour and 7 ounces (200 g) water fermented with 2 teaspoons (35 g) of 100% hydration sourdough starter allows for a slow rise of 12 to 16 hours at room temperature, while a much larger amount of starter (1 cup minus 2 tablespoons [200 g]) can be ready to be added to the dough in only 3 to 4 hours.

Increased digestibility. Scientific evidence shows bread made with sourdough is more digestible as compared to bread made with baker's yeast. This is due to two main reasons: time and lactic fermentation. Regarding time, fermentation with sourdough is generally longer than a yeast-based one, because in sourdough baking it is neither possible to use the direct method, nor to shorten final fermentation time below a minimum of 3 to 4 hours. It must be said that yeasted breads using preferments have some of the good characteristics of sourdough.

The second "superpower" of sourdough is lactic fermentation. While it does not help to rise the dough, it does plenty to make it more gut-friendly. The processes involved are complex, but the main point is simple: lactic fermentation is superior to alcoholic fermentation in catabolizing proteins, such as gluten, which are potentially problematic for our digestive system.

## FERMENTATION WITH OLD DOUGH

Finally, there is what the French call *pate' fermentee* and the Italians call *pasta di riporto*, which is simply a piece of old dough from a previous batch made with yeast or sourdough that can be used to ferment a new dough.

This system in the United States is also called "gold rush starter" or "cowboy starter," because the Californian gold hunters used it in the 19th century.

Using old dough is the simplest way to keep a starter and, in fact, it was the preferred method used by old-time homemakers. Nowadays, the method is widely used by professional bakers, but is often ignored by home bakers.

This is probably due to the fact that old dough needs to be used within a week, and most contemporary home bakers do not bake that often, but perhaps this simple method can help inspire home bakers to use this technique again.

If you want to revive the tradition of the gold rush starter, save a piece of dough when you make your next bread. It can be cut out before or after adding salt, but know that when it contains salt it will rise slower, giving you more days to use it.

The dough is kept in a container with lid placed in the refrigerator, making sure to leave the lid slightly open, to allow the dough to

exchange humidity and air with the environment. To make new bread, simply add the old dough to the new one. This type of starter can be used up to a week, and, as mentioned earlier, longer if containing salt. If you notice that the old dough looks over-ripe, i.e., the fermentation has gone too far and the dough has a very soft consistency, just feed it like you would do with a stiff starter and wait for it to double before adding it to your final dough. Then simply remember to reserve a piece of dough for the next bake. See page 65 for the recipe.

## HOW TO MAKE A SOURDOUGH STARTER

It is possible to get a starter from a friend or to buy it online from trusted sellers. However, making your own starter is a highly rewarding endeavor that you do not want to miss. Once a stable starter has been created, it can be maintained indefinitely, given the right care. There are several ways to create a starter. The most straightforward method is to make use of the many wild yeasts and good bacteria naturally occurring in flour and in the air, and allow time to do the rest. Here, find the recipe for a 100% hydration wheat-rye starter.

*Day 1, Morning*
¼ cup (60 g) lukewarm water (around 85°)
⅛ cup (30 g) white flour
⅛ cup (30 g) whole-grain rye flour

Mix the ingredients together, and put the mixture in a washed and rinsed container, making sure that the mixture takes up no more than one-third of the container. Put the lid on (if you are using a glass jar, do not screw the lid). Place the container in a warm (but not hot) spot. Ideally, the temperature should be around 80°F.

You may want to use bottled water to create a starter, because chemicals in tap water could inhibit its development in the early stages.

### Day 2, Morning

⅓ cup (80 grams) of your starter from the day before

⅓ cup (80 grams) lukewarm water

7½ tablespoons (60 grams) white flour

2½ tablespoons (20 grams) whole-grain rye flour

Discard the rest of your starter. Add the water and mix. Then add the flours, mix and scrape the walls of the container well to keep it clean. Place the container back in its warm spot.

### Day 2, Evening

⅓ cup (80 grams) of your starter from the day before

⅓ cup (80 grams) lukewarm water

7½ tablespoons (60 grams) white flour

2½ tablespoons (20 grams) whole-grain rye flour

Discard the rest of your starter. Add the water and mix. Then add the flours, mix and scrape the walls of the container well to keep it clean.

Place the container back in its warm spot.

At this point, you should be seeing some sign of life, some activity, which will manifest itself as bubbles.

### Day 3, 4, 5 and so on

Continue to do what was described for Day 2, until your starter can double itself within 12 hours, is all bubbly, and smells good (not too acidic). Make sure that the color stays within the yellow-brown shades, and does not take any orange or blueish tone.

### Day 6 or 7

You may have successfully created a starter. Does it double in 12 hours? Does it smell sweet and is it full of bubbles? If the answer is no, then continue as in the previous days. Hopefully, your sourdough culture will soon come to life, but if it does not, discard and start over. If instead you have given birth to a stable sourdough culture, jump to "How to Maintain a Sourdough Starter."

## HOW TO MAINTAIN A SOURDOUGH STARTER

Learning how to keep your starter healthy is the secret to good sourdough bread. Unless you want to make a new starter for each bake, you will need to learn how to keep it in good shape.

You have two main options for how to maintain your sourdough starter: either refrigerating the starter, or keeping it at room temperature.

Important: If you just started a sourdough culture, it is not recommended to shift to refrigerated maintenance for a few weeks. During those first few weeks at room temperature, strains of yeast and bacteria that are optimal for bread baking will be selected. Once the culture is stable, periods of refrigeration will not disrupt its main composition. Of course, this all depends on how good you are at feeding the starter at the right time.

Feeding schedule, room temperature: When keeping the starter at room temperature, it is ideal to feed it once every 12 hours: two times a day. In the beginning, use the same amount of starter, water, and flour, in a 1:1:1 ratio for each feeding. This means that every 12 hours you will take some of your starter and combine it with equal amounts of water and flour (in terms of weight, not volume). The remaining starter can be discarded or used for baking.

After several days at room temperature, your starter should become very active and you will need to change the ratio. The relative amounts for your feedings could then become, for instance, 0.5:1:1. This means that you will use half the amount of starter, keeping the same amounts of water and flour. What matters is that the hydration (the proportion of water to flour) remains constant. The amount of starter from the previous feeding can instead change depending on how active the starter is from day to day, how warm your room temperature is, and how capable you are to do two feedings in a day. If you want to feed your starter only once a day, you can inoculate a small amount of starter in your mixture of water and flour.

Feeding schedule, refrigerated: When your sourdough culture has stabilized, you can make life easier by alternating between leaving the starter unfed in the fridge, and bringing it to room temperature, feeding as described previously.

Ideally, you want to leave the starter unfed in the fridge for no more than five days, and then feed it at room temperature at least three times before putting the starter, just fed, back into the fridge.

Always choose the least cold spot of your fridge to keep your starter, and make sure the overall temperature of the fridge does not go below 40°F.

Although not optimal, if it does happen that you leave your starter unfed in the fridge for a prolonged amount of time, do not worry. It takes a very long time to kill a stable sourdough culture. If this occurs, let your sourdough starter stay at room temperature longer, with repeated feedings, to regenerate all the yeast cells and the good bacteria.

## HOW TO MAKE A DOUGH

### Mise En Place

Before you start mixing a dough, it is important to make sure that you have all the ingredients at hand and ready.

Ready means two main things: 1) weighted/measured and 2) at the right temperature. Additionally, there could be ingredients that need to be prepared ahead, like cooked and drained vegetables or grains, crashed spices and so on. All of this, including the weighting/measuring and the bringing the ingredients to the right temperature, requires extra time.

You do not want that extra time to impact on your fermentation schedule. When the leavening agent is added to flour and water, you want to devote your full attention to dough development. So do make sure to have everything ready before the fermentation starts, and your chances of success will increase considerably.

### Mixing

The way you combine ingredients together does impact on dough development. Many professional bakers could confirm you that the mixing stage determines a big proportion of the outcome of a batch of dough.

You can combine the ingredients by hand or using a mixer, which in a home kitchen will most likely be a planetary mixer, also called *stand-mixer* (see page 51 about mixers).

The traditional way is to combine all on a wooden board, making a dwell in the center of the flour and adding the wet ingredients gradually. Nothing wrong with using this method. It is, however, even simpler to start by combining the ingredients in a large bowl and then transfer the dough on a clean surface for working it further.

When mixing in a bowl, by hand or machine, it is easier to start with the main wet ingredients and then add the flours. This will ensure that no dry flour remains on the bottom of the bowl. On the other hand, when using this method, it is advisable to never add all the main wet ingredients at once, but always reserving a proportion to be added after the main dry ingredients have been incorporated in the mix. This is done because it is better not to change the amount of flour in a bread recipe, because that would alter the proportions with the other ingredients, including salt and starter/yeast. What instead is easily done and will not alter all the other proportions, is adding more liquids, i.e., changing the hydration of the dough.

After the full amount of flour is added to the forming dough, it is easy to see how the dough is coming up together and decide if adding more liquids, and how much of them. This is needed because no recipe will ever be able to tell you how many liquids your specific flour will be able to absorb in the specific conditions your kitchen will be at each specific moment.

This is the art of mixing: understanding the optimal hydration for each specific recipe. As every skill, it will develop with time. Use the recipe as your basic script, remember to reserve some of the liquids indicated for later, and be ready to add less or more liquids than indicated by the recipe depending on how your dough will feel and look.

## Kneading

Although it is possible to make good bread in a no-knead manner, a dough benefits from being worked in some way or another. The mechanical action of working a dough helps the gluten net to develop, helps distributing the gasses, and oxygenates the mixture. Below a brief description of some of the options.

### Mixer basics

When using a mixer, start combining ingredients at the lowest speed available. This will give time to the dough to come together without stressing or overheating it. It is also advisable to take breaks, to allow the gluten net to form

spontaneously (autolysis). In later stages of the mixing process, when the gluten net is close to be well developed, the speed can be increased. This will be mostly necessary for sweet doughs and high hydration doughs.

### Traditional hand kneading

The old fashioned but always valid way of working a dough consists in transferring the already combined ingredients on a clean and flat surface and then press the dough in a rhythmic way, using mostly the heels of your hands. The dough should be worked in an even way. Therefore, it does help to rotate the dough and repeat the kneading from different points of pressure, and repeat. Like with mixer-based kneading, it saves you effort to take breaks, allowing the dough to benefit from the spontaneous processes involved in autolysis.

### Slap-and-fold

This is a modern technique of French origin, made popular outside of France mostly by Richard Bertinet. This technique highly simplifies the hand kneading work, and is particularly good for sticky doughs with high hydration.

It consists of performing series of slap-and-folds on the dough. The dough needs to be pulled up toward you, stretched sideways while is being stretched vertically, and then folded back on itself and away from you (do look at the many available online tutorials to better understand this method). Then the dough is rotated and the process is repeated again. Series of slap and fold are alternated to periods of rest of the dough (autolysis), until the right dough development is achieved and the dough feels smooth and elastic when pulled and stretched.

### Stretch-and-fold

This technique is commonly used in contemporary baking. Stretch-and-fold consists is pulling the dough from one side and stretching it vertically, then folding the stretched strand over the rest of the dough. The routine is repeated from each side of the dough, in a circular fashion.

One can do this without taking the dough out of its resting bowl/container or alternatively by transferring the dough on a clean surface first. Some also flip the dough upside-down after the first set of stretch and folds and the repeat the series from all sides, then flip the dough again and let it rest in its bowl/container.

This method can be used alone, in which case several series of stretch and folds needs to be performed in the first stages of the fermentation, or it can be used to complement hand or mixer-based kneading. In this case, a few series of stretch and folds are given at regular intervals while the dough is undergoing its first fermentation.

## Bulk Proofing/First Fermentation

After the mixing stage, which can be followed by traditional hand kneading, mix-based kneading, or modern slap-and-fold or stretch and fold techniques, the dough needs to be left alone to rise. It is always important to cover the dough at this stage, to ensure that humidity is preserved. Bulk proofing, or first fermentation, really starts from the moment the starter or yeast is added to the dough, so do count your overall fermentation time accordingly and know that the longer you will be kneading/working the dough, the shorter your bulk proof will be.

Understanding when to stop the first fermentation and proceed to shaping is a true art, and it will develop with time, as you try specific loaves over and over again. Remember that practice do makes perfect. However, be also aware that perfection in bread baking is never fully achieved, because the dough will surprise you, from time to time. This is the true beauty of bread baking, though, so do keep an eye on fermentation but try not to be overly pedantic about it.

## Shaping

When the dough has undergone bulk proofing, it is time to shape it and let it rest some more. Always make sure to do a *mise en place* before you actually start shaping. Prepare the shaping surface, the proofing baskets, the scale, the cutters, the eventual baking dishes, and so on. This because shaping needs to be done fast in order not to dry the dough, so you better do your preparation ahead, while your dough is still resting in its bowl/container.

Some recipes require a special shaping, but most breads are generally shaped either like a round (*boule* in French) or like a short log (*batard* in French, *filone* in Italian).

### Shaping a batard/filone

1. Roughly pre-shape your dough into a ball. Let it rest 10–15 minutes, covered.

2. Flatten the round with the palm of your hand.

3. Flip the far end of the dough on two-thirds of remaining dough and seal.

4. Fold on themselves the corners at far top of the dough, sealing.

5. Roll the far end of the dough over itself.

6. Continue rolling until you end with a short log.

7. Seal the ends of the log and eventually roll the log to elongate it to fit your desired length.

### Shaping a round/boule

1. Do all the steps necessary to shape a batard/filone as described previously.

2. Once you have obtained a batard, flip it so that the seam is now facing up.

3. Roll the batard on itself starting from the end closest to you.

4. Turn the rolled batard 90° so that one of the ends is now facing you.

5. Place your hands at the far end of the rolled batard and drag it toward you, creating tension.

6. Turn the round 90° and repeat the movement as at step 5.

7. Repeat step 5 one last time and you now should have an even round.

## Final Proofing/Second Fermentation

Once your loaves are shaped, all you have to do is place them in the appropriate basket/tray and let them rest some more.

It is important to make sure that the loaves will not dry at this point. So do cover the proofing baskets or trays with a light and slightly floured kitchen towel, oiled plastic wrap or place the whole proofing basket/tray into a clean and food approved plastic bag. The recipe you are following will give you indications on the length of time needed to final prove your loaves, but your eye will come in handy, too.

As a rule of thumb, do not wait for the loaves to double their size as sometimes suggested by recipes. If you see a visible rise, about one and a half from the initial volume, that can suffice. You can also try to gently push the dough with your finger. If it leaves an indent that springs back relatively fast, the loaf is proofed.

## Scoring

It is common to make a variable number of cuts, of a variable depth, on the top of bread loaves before baking them (see page 50). This is done for two main reasons.

The phenomenon commonly called "oven spring" causes the loaves to rise and their skin to tear and progressively open up. This happens more if there is steam introduced in the oven. A scored loaf will, hopefully, open up along the cuts rather than spontaneously tearing in undesirable spots. This will make a properly scored loaf look more regular compared with a loaf that is tore apart in unpredictable ways.

The cuts, if deep enough, also help the loaf to fully rise in height, rather than in width, giving the impression of better risen loaves, which may otherwise look more flat. This also ben-efits the steam flow and its distribution in the crumb.

Scoring is an art, and mastery comes with repetition and multiple tries, as for any other skill. It helps to see how other bakers score their loaves, so it is OK to initially imitate others people's scorings and then later on develop your own signature style.

Be, however, aware that scoring is not always necessary. In most traditional Italian country loaves, for instance, bread is unscored and the irregular way in which every loaf breaks open (or doesn't open at all) during baking is part of its charm.

## Baking

There are several different techniques for obtaining a perfect oven temperature, see pages 48-49 for suggestions.

Regarding knowing when your bread is ready, color will help in giving you an indication of how cooked a loaf is, but there are also other cues that can help. A traditional way of knowing if a loaf of bread is ready is lifting it and knocking on its bottom. If it makes a hollow sound, the loaf is ready. This method is however useless with sweet breads, that are not supposed to develop a crust. In such cases, providing yourself of an dough thermometer will do wonders, as you can check when your bread reaches the temperature that indicates that the bread is properly cooked, not only on the outside but also inside. Most breads are ready when the internal temperature reaches 200°F.

Finally, allowing the bread to cool down before cutting into it ensure that the cooking is complete, because cooking continues until the loaf is hot.

# BREAD FROM OLD DOUGH

**YIELD:** 1 BIG OR TWO SMALL LOAVES / **ACTIVE TIME:** 50 MINUTES / **TOTAL TIME:** 6.5–7.5 HOURS

It often happens to have some leftover dough from a previous batch. Instead of throwing it, it can be used to make a new batch of bread, which will be particularly tasty and rich of flavor.

**INGREDIENTS:**

- 12.3 oz (350 g) water, warmed to 82° F
- 17.6 oz (500 g) bread flour
- 6.2 oz (175 g) old dough***
- 1½ tsp (8.5 g) salt

***leftover dough from a previous batch of bread, kept in the fridge up to 1 week. See pages 58-59.

1 In a large bowl, combine the water with the flour.

2 Start working the dough, either with a stand-mixer or by hand (see the next page for tips on kneading).

3 Add the old dough in pieces, continuing to work the dough for about 10 minutes from the start of the mixing.

4 Let rest, covered, for 20 minutes.

5 Add the salt and knead for further 5 minutes, at higher speed if using a stand-mixer or with slap-and-fold by hand.

6 Let the dough rest, covered, in a warm spot for 3 to 3½ hours, or until the dough has increased its volume one and a half times. Using a cold and unfed starter like old dough will slow down the process, so this phase could take long.

7 Transfer the dough on a clean and floured surface and shape into a large round or in two filoni or batards (see page 63 about shaping).

8 Preheat oven to maximum temperature, with the stone in if you own one.

9 Let rest, covered (for instance by placing the loaf into a clean plastic bag) for 3 to 3½ hours or until visibly risen.

10 Invert the loaf/loaves on a baker's peel or flat tray dusted with coarse semolina or corn flour.

11 Transfer to the hot oven producing steam (for instance, by throwing some ice cubes on the bottom part of the oven).

12 Reduce immediately heat to 480°F and bake for 25 minutes.

13 Let the steam out, reduce heat to 220°F and bake for 20–25 minutes or until deep golden brown.

# ENCYCLOPEDIA *of* GRAINS *and* PULSES

What we commonly know as grains are more precisely defined *cereals*. Cereal designates a variety of herbaceous plants that produce the seeds or "berries," from which we mill flour. The term *cereal* derives from Latin, meaning, "what belongs to the goddess Ceres," the Roman goddess of the harvest.

Most grains are varieties of common grass, also known as *poaceae*. Given that poaceae grasses are the most widely found plant on earth, it is not surprising that humans and animals alike have grown to thrive on them. Cereals such as wheat, emmer, einkorn, barley, rye, oats, rice, maize, millet, sorghum, and teff are all types of poaceae grass, whereas buckwheat, amaranth, and quinoa are entirely different plants, called *pseudocereals*. In addition to cereals and pseudocereals, flour can also be milled from a number of other plants. For instance, most pulses can be dried and ground into flour, as can root vegetables, nuts, seeds, and even coffee plants.

These days, heritage grains varieties are gaining increasing popularity. Here you will find listed the most commonly known old varieties—be aware, though, that these are just *some* of the countless varieties of grains that are cultivated or stored in seed banks across the globe. In our encyclopedia we have included all the main sources of flour used to make different breads, crusts, and other grain-based products. This knowledge will help you to move around with confidence in the vast world of grains and flours.

# WHEAT

People have grown wheat for thousands of years, dating back to the very dawn of farming. Through intensive, continuous cultivation, many different varieties of wheat have developed, due to adaptation, evolution, and the work of farmers and agronomists. Starting in the 1700s, farming methods began to advance rapidly, and there are now thousands of wheat varieties worldwide, with new ones every year. The 20th century ushered in the Green Revolution, a set of studies and initiatives led by Norman Borlaug, which gave rise to a radical increase in agricultural productivity around the world, aided by mechanization, irrigation, chemical fertilizers, genetic modification, and pesticides. The Green Revolution is believed to have saved over a billion people from starvation, a feat for which Borlaug deservedly received the Nobel Peace Prize. However, it also resulted it many ancient varieties of wheat and heritage landraces falling out of use. Fortunately, these have recently seen a resurgence alongside the growing market for organic food.

### Einkorn Wheat (*Triticum monococcum*)

Einkorn wheat was one of the earliest types of wheat to be domesticated. It initially grew only in the northern part of the Fertile Crescent and later spread to the Caucasus and Central Europe. This type of wheat prefers colder climates and, while largely replaced by common wheat, has continued to grow sporadically in Northern France and elsewhere. Although einkorn produces low yields and can be a challenge to farm, it has become increasingly popular due to its digestibility compared to common wheat and other cereals.

### Emmer (*Triticum turgidum dicoccum*)

Like einkorn, emmer was among the first wheat to be domesticated. Though more widely farmed than einkorn, it was likewise supplanted by common wheat. Nevertheless, its cultivation is growing once more, particularly in Italy. Much like einkorn wheat, the renewed popularity of emmer is largely due to its digestibility. Emmer is also prized for the unique flavor it lends to both bread and pasta. In Tuscany, whole grains of emmer are often used in soups.

### Black Winter Emmer

An old variety of emmer that dates back to 5000 years ago, this wheat is prized for its dark purple and black husks. It can grow in quite extreme weather, tolerating both heavy rain and drought. There is currently a scarcity of this variety of emmer, though limited amounts of seed are available. It is difficult to thresh and mostly used for ornamental purposes.

### Ethiopian Blue Tinge

This dark purple Ethiopian variety of emmer is easy to thresh and gives a high yield, making it much more popular than the similar-looking Black Winter Emmer. Ethiopian Blue Tinge is widely believed to have additional health benefits because of the high concentration of polyphenol antioxidants it contains. Interestingly, this wheat is said to taste like tea.

### Durum Wheat (*Triticum turgidum durum*)

Durum wheat is a modified type of emmer, developed through hybridization about 9000 years ago. "Durum" means hard—it is in fact the hardest of all wheat species. However, it is not to be confused with hard wheat, a variety of common wheat that is genetically very different from durum. The hardness of this wheat makes it difficult to mill it into very fine flour, and its gluten is also different than that found in common wheat. This is why durum is mostly used for pasta, semolina, and couscous as opposed to bread baking. After common wheat, durum wheat is the most cultivated, growing much better in hot and arid climates. Like common wheat, durum has been cultivated intensively for thousands of years and undergone extensive genetic manipulation. However, old varieties are once more enjoying a renewal in popularity.

### Bulgur

A durum wheat product used the same way as rice. To become bulgur, wheat is boiled, then dried, and subsequently cracked into pieces. The pieces are then sieved to divide pieces by size. This method was a common way to preserve wheat already in ancient Babylon, which then spread to the Middle East, where it is still a staple in local cuisine.

### Freekeh

Freekeh is made of "green" durum wheat, which is harvested before the ripening process is complete. The wheat is then immediately toasted and cracked. In Lebanon, where freekeh is particularly common, wheat is piled and left to dry in the sun for 24 hours before being set alight. Though the straw and chaff burn away, the seeds remain intact because of their moisture content. Served much like rice, it is part of many traditional North African and Mediterranean dishes.

## OLD VARIETIES OF DURUM WHEAT

### Hourani

This variety of durum wheat was cultivated for millennia in the Houran plateau of Northern Jordan and Southern Syria. According to food anthropologist Eli Rogosa, this ancient variety of wheat was discovered in the 1960s during the excavation of the Masada Fortress, where it had been stored 2000 years. Almost extinct today, it was eaten by the ancient people of what is now Israel.

### Senatore Cappelli

Named after Italian nobleman Raffaele Cappelli, it was developed from a Tunisian hard wheat (Jenah Rhetifah) 100 years ago by wheat genetist Nazareno Strampelli. This variety produces very tall plants, with ears of wheat characterized by beautiful dark awns. It has a high protein content and makes superior quality bread and pasta. This variety was abandoned after the 1960s in favor of lower quality varieties, but it is now widely grown again in Southern Italy.

### Sicilian Durum Wheat

In Sicily several old varieties of local wheat are being cultivated once more, thanks to the ongoing efforts of Stazione Consorziale Sperimentale di Granicoltura per la Sicilia. This local center for the preservation of regional cereals has studied and stored wheat seeds since the 1930s. The most common types of old Sicilian durum wheat are Timilia, Perciasacchi and Russello. These varieties have been used for centuries (some say millennia) to make both pasta and bread.

### Khorasan Wheat (*Triticum turgidum turanicum*)

This is an ancient variety of durum wheat. It is named after the historical Khorasan region of Central Asia, where it is still grown today. Khorasan wheat is now grown in numerous countries for its digestibility and nutritional value. Like other durum wheat, it tolerates drought well.

### Saragolla

An Italian variety of Khorasan, introduced to the Abruzzi region in the fifth century AD. Its longtime cultivation is evidenced by several historical docu-

ments praising its qualities. Saragolla wheat was eventually succeeded by Senatore Cappelli, and later still by dwarf varieties of durum wheat. Its cultivation, however, continued in parts of central Italy and it is now expanding once more.

### Kamut

Kamut is a patented variety of Khorasan created by two farmers from Montana, Mack and Bob Quinn, who started to cultivate it in the '70s and registered it in 1990. Khorasan wheat actually owes much of its popularity to the Kamut brand, which has also financed scientific studies to prove the health claims of this grain.

## COMMON WHEAT

### Common Wheat (*Triticum aestivum*)

Common wheat was developed between 2000–3000 years ago through the selection and hybridization of ancient wheat varieties. Dating is uncertain, as precursors of our common bread wheat were surely available at an earlier time, but we know that this type of wheat became widely available in the Western World right around the first century A.D. The intent of ancient wheat breeders was likely to increase their yields and create better bread—in fact, common wheat is often referred to as bread wheat. The gluten in common wheat is indeed ideal for baking, which is why it has been favored for so long. Of course, there are many other varieties of wheat, both old and new.

### Hard Red Winter

This is a group of modern North American wheat grasses modified from locally adapted Eurasian varieties. It has a high yield and is resistant to pests and disease. Grown extensively across the Great Plains between Texas and Montana, Kansas

is the biggest cultivator of Hard Red Winter wheat. "Winter" refers to the fact that the seeds are planted in the fall. It has a strong gluten that makes it ideal for breads and Asian-style noodles.

### Hard Red Spring

Called "the aristocrat of wheat for baking bread," this group of modern North American wheat grasses thrive better when planted in spring and harvested in early fall. It is grown mostly in North Dakota, Montana, South Dakota, and Minnesota. Like Hard Red Winter, this family of wheat also produces a high yield and is resistant to diseases and pests. It is planted in spring and harvested at the end of the summer.

### Soft White Wheat

Soft white wheat is a group of modern North American varieties grown Ohio, Kentucky, Indiana, Washington, Oregon, Idaho, Michigan, and New York states. It has a much lower protein content and gluten quality than Hard Red Spring and is therefore mostly used for pastries, cookies, cakes, pancakes, waffles and crackers. Soft white wheat is the base for pastry flour, and is combined with hardier wheats to make all-purpose flour.

### Hard White Wheat

Originally derived from hard Red Wheat, Hard White Wheat is a commonly grown wheat variety in Australia. However, it is relatively new to North American agriculture, and has only become widely grown over the last 20 years. Like Hard Red Wheat, it has a high protein and gluten content, but its bran is lighter in color and it is less bitter in taste.

### Ivory Wheat Flour

Ivory Wheat Flour is derived from North American Hard White Wheat. It is a whole wheat flour, containing every part of the ground wheat berry. Its name comes from the bran of Hard White wheat, which is genetically selected to be free of color pigments, which means that whole wheat flour milled from it actually looks white. The taste is mild with good protein content, and it is good for making both breads and pastries.

## OLD VARIETIES OF COMMON WHEAT

### Banatka Winter Wheat

This wheat variety was recently created by food anthropologist Eli Rogosa by cross-breeding two Eastern European heritage wheat landraces: Bankuti, loved for its intense flavor, and Ukrainka, a wheat variety valued for its high productivity, adaptability, and excellent baking qualities. Banatka can tolerate rain and humidity, and has thus far shown high productivity and a good disease resistance. It performs best when planted in early fall.

### Sonora Wheat

This variety of soft wheat was introduced to North America by Spanish missionaries in the early 1700s. It has been used for centuries to make flour tortillas and was a staple crop in the West up until the Civil War. It performs best in milder climates, and should be planted in the spring.

### Turkey Red

Introduced to the United States by German Russian Mennonites in 1874, Turkey Red is the ancestor of all modern varieties of Hard Red Winter Wheat. Although its cultivation languished for many years, it popularity is on the rise, as it is easy to digest, and its good baking properties makes it perfect for bread making.

### Red Fife

The story tells that back in the 1800s, Scottish-born farmer David Fife was looking for a wheat variety that could grow well in Canada. A friend from his homeland sent him some hard wheat seeds thought to have come from what is now the Ukraine, and from these first seeds David Fife eventually developed his sturdy Red Fife wheat. It grew which grew so well across Canada and the United States that for a time it was one of the most popular varieties. Largely abandoned after 1900, it is now gaining new interest.

### Carosella

This old variety of "soft" common wheat is traditionally cultivated in the region of Cilento, Southern Italy, and known to have been cultivated in ancient Rome. Although it does not have a very high protein content, Carosella wheat is used to make traditional pasta, and has been appreciated for millennia for its good baking properties. Its production is still limited but interest in this ancient grain is on the rise.

### Gentil Rosso

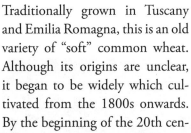

Traditionally grown in Tuscany and Emilia Romagna, this is an old variety of "soft" common wheat. Although its origins are unclear, it began to be widely which cultivated from the 1800s onwards. By the beginning of the 20th century it was the most grown variety of common wheat in Italy, but quickly fell out of favor due to the introduction of modern wheat varieties. Happily, after nearly a century of neglect, it is now grown again. It has good baking properties and works well in both pastries and bread.

### Rouge de Bordeaux

Like Gentil Rosso, this is an older variety of "soft" common wheat, developed created in the 1800s and grown in Bourdeaux, France. The ears of the wheat are a little reddish at maturity and a little bit bearded like barley. It is renowned for its baking properties. It is one of several wheat varieties of French wheat becoming popular outside France.

### Marquis

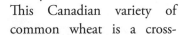

This Canadian variety of common wheat is a crossbreed of Hard Red Calcutta and Red Fife. Dr. Charles Saunders developed it in 1904, and it soon became incredibly popular, replacing all other hard wheat being cultivated in Canada at that time. Marquis is shorter than Red Fife and matures 7–10 days earlier. It has a very high yield, as well as a high protein and gluten content.

### Spelt (*Triticum aestivum subspecies spelta*, or, *Triticulm spelta*)

Closely related to common wheat and considered a subspecies by some, spelt has been continuously cultivated since around 5000 BC. It is particularly suited to Northern climates, and while its cultivation in North America peaked in 1900, it has continued to be farmed in Germany, Switzerland, and across Scandinavia. Although it gives inconsistent yields, it has become popular in recent years as a supposedly healthier alternative to modern varieties of common wheat. Acreage devoted to spelt is increasing also in North America as in many other regions of the world. The baking properties of spelt flour are similar to that of flour milled from common wheat.

### Triticale (*Triticosecale*)

Triticale is a hybrid of Rye and Wheat. Created at the end of the 19th century, it has only recently been cultivated on a large scale. It has the advantages of rye, is resistant to cold, and has the all the baking properties of wheat. It is a good alternative in soils and climates suitable to rye. Though largely used as grass feed, it is increasingly being used in baking.

# JAMES A. BROWN

*Barton Springs Mill, Texas, USA*

Barton Spring Mills is the fulfillment of James A. Brown's dream to make quality grains and flours accessible to his community. James has managed in no time to tie up relationships with a rich network of local farmers, inspiring them to grow heirloom grains. Local grains are freshly milled with an authentic stone mill, and then distributed to private companies, but also chefs and bakers, who are encouraged to use heirloom whole grains in their baking and cooking.

"Initially my inspiration was to make a tasty loaf of bread. It seems like an extreme to go to just to get that!"

*1. What is your story? How did you end up cultivating and milling grains?*

As a former chef and hobbyist baker, I wanted to get into baking bread from locally and regionally grown and milled grains. After doing some research, I discovered there was no place in Texas to get those items, and it occurred to me that milling might be a great fit for me as a second career. I started my research in January 2015, and on January 2, 2016, we turned on our mill for the first time.

*2. What inspired you?*

Initially my inspiration was to make a tasty loaf of bread. It seems like an extreme to go to, just to get that! The more I talked to farmers, millers, and experts in heirloom and landrace grains, the more inspired I became. It became very clear to me that I was going to have to get involved in the entire process from sourcing the seed, to finding farmers with the requisite talent to grow these rare grains, to cleaning, processing and storing them in a safe way, as well as milling. Glenn Roberts of Anson Mills was a particular inspiration. Every conversation with him was information-packed! It often took me a couple of months to unpack everything he would tell me in just a 10-minute conversation.

*3. What made you decide on stone milling? What are the advantages?*

I'm interested in using the entire grain, and I feel the best way to do that is through stone milling. This process creates finer bran, and thoroughly expresses the germ oil throughout the endosperm. It makes for a flour that is very easy to use in a one-for-one, substitution with modern white flours. We do some sifting in our facility, but I'm always trying to move bakers, chefs, and end-users toward using more whole grains. Total utilization in any food system is key, and it seems a shame not to use whole-grain. Even when we do sifting, we find a home for all of the other parts that become byproducts in our process. Some goes to organic farmers for the feeding of livestock. Other parts go on to be used in making other food items, such as soy sauce, or compost for mushrooms.

*4. What are the challenges of running a stone milling facility?*

I think perhaps the easiest part is the milling activity. Some of the most important work starts before the grain ever falls into the mill: expectations set with farmers about planting rates, cover crops, crop rotation, methods of harvest. Grain cleaning and storage. Maintaining the strength and purity of these rare seeds. All these things lead to quality of grain that shines through once milled into flour. I would say that three-quarters of the effort goes into these processes before we even begin to mill.

*5. Are your grains organic? Do you believe in organic farming or do you trust conventional farming?*

All of our grains are certified organic by the Texas Department of Agriculture. Currently our facility is not certified organic. I'm a firm believer in organic and sustainable farming practices, although I'm not always a staunch supporter of the policies that are in place to enforce the standards.

*6. What type of grains and wheat do you grow and mill?*

For 2017, we grew Marquis, Red Fife, Sonora, Turkey Red, and TAM 105 hard red winter wheats. We also grew northern European and Danko Ryes. As I write this, we are preparing to go in with Rouge de Bordeaux, Yecora Rojo, and Warthog hard red winter wheats, and Wren's Abruzzi rye. We also mill Bloody Butcher Red, Oaxacan Green, and Hopi Blue corn, as well as Mancan buckwheat.

*7. Do you make your own seeds or do you buy them from big companies?*

We purchased all of our initial seed stock from small farms and producers, as these varieties open-pollinated. Starting in 2017, we now save our own seed and work constantly to keep the purity and strength of these varieties. Prior to the planting of our 2017 Bloody Butcher Red corn crop, we held "sorting parties" to sort 350 pounds of corn seed, one seed at a time. Not only did this spread the workload among many, it afforded us the opportunity to share with chefs and consumers what it takes to preserve these rare varieties. It's a great responsibility and one that requires a fair amount of diligence and energy. Even after planting, we will walk the fields near harvest-time and rogue our crops in order to eliminate anything that is not true to variety.

*8. What keeps you motivated?*

I'm motivated and inspired by the changes I've seen in our local food scene with the addition of freshly milled heritage and landrace grains. I still make all of my own local deliveries, and I'm in the kitchens of every one of my restaurants, speaking with chefs and bakers. That constant back-and-forth not only fuels my drive, but provides constant feedback about how we can improve what we're doing, and gives me inspiration for what we should be doing in the future, whether it be new varieties of grain or new processes that will expand the utilization of these grains.

*9. What do you do differently from other millers or farmers?*

We are utilizing a relatively new technology from the Netherlands that allows for MAPing (modified atmosphere packaging) of our grain totes. This is a process where we seal 1-ton sacks inside a vacuum bag, remove all of the oxygen, and replace it with $CO_2$. This protects against insect invasion, allowing us to keep all of our grains at room temperature, rather than in cold storage. This radically reduces the cost of storage so we can keep more grain on hand and buy more grain from our farmers without risk of damage. This has allowed us to work at a scale that is sustainable for our farmers, and is helped to keep the price of grain and flour low, thereby making it accessible and affordable to a broader section of the population.

*10. What are the challenges of growing wheat and grains in this changing climate? Will we still have bread on our tables 500 years from now?*

Here in Texas, I see our greatest challenge to be precipitation during the time that we need to harvest. It is always been a problem here in central Texas, but it seems to be an increasing challenge now even in more arid parts of the Panhandle. Historically, there were varieties of wheat in the 19th and early 20th century that were bred specifically to mature early and avoid these harvest-time rains. We are trying to reintroduce those varieties, like Quanah and Westar, and gauge their suitability in today's climate. But, we're starting with a few ounces, so it will take time. I firmly believe we will have bread on our tables 500 years from now. There are now a few wheat breeders who are working with the right set of priorities who I believe can create safe, suitable, nutritious, and delicious wheat varieties that will thrive in our future climate.

*11. What do you think of household mills? Are you concerned that they could replace commercial mills?*

I am a proponent of household mills, and even mills for small restaurants and bakeries—anything that gets more of these grains on peoples' plates. I'm happy to sell whole berries to anyone who wants them. I don't think that they always make as fine a flour as my mill makes, but that's not always necessary either. I think there will always be a place for both. I especially like small-scale mills for milling amendments to a recipe at the last minute. But I *am* biased about the quality of the flour that comes from our mill. It's pretty hard to replicate our flour on a stone mill that is 2 to 3 inches in diameter, when ours is 48 inches in diameter.

*12. What can people do to support small-scale millers and farmers?*

Eat more whole grains. Foster a curiosity about the lesser-known ones. Learn more about the wide diversity in the flavors of ryes, for example. Ask your local bakery or local grocery store where they get their flour. Support farmers at local farmers markets. If you have a local or regional mill that sells retail, buy directly from them. Expect to pay more for these grains, and do it cheerfully. Regard your grains the same way you regard an heirloom tomato, and the world will be a better place for it.

# OATS

## (*Avena sativa*)

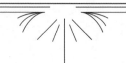

Oats are a widely cultivated cereal, and are used in a great variety of foods. Only domesticated roughly 3000 years ago, they are believed to be the product of the spontaneous cross-breeding of cultivated wheat and barley with nearby weeds. Oat is more tolerant of rain than any other cereal, making it extraordinarily popular in places like the United Kingdom, Scotland, Scandinavia, and Russia. Although oat flour is often used in baked goods, it cannot leaven bread. When rolled or flaked oats, oats can be used in porridge or granola. It is a very nutritious cereal, and can even be consumed by some people with celiac disease. However, it should be noted that oats *do* contain a protein similar to gluten that *can* be toxic for the gluten sensitive, so even so-called gluten-free oats grown in isolation should be eaten with caution by people who react to gluten.

### Naked Oats (*Avena nuda*)

This variety of oat is originally from China, where it was grown for thousands of years. Its kernels are loose and easy to free from the chaff during threshing. Naked oats are more nutritious than common oats, and are easy to flake or process into flour.

### Groats

Groats are simply hulled oats. They retain both the germ and bran of the grain and cannot be eaten raw. They can be used whole (in which case they are typically soaked in water), sprouted, or sliced into Steel Cut Oats.

### Steel Cut Oats (*Irish Oats, Pinhead Oats*)

These are oat groats that have been chopped by large steel blades into pieces.

They can be used to make porridge, though the process is of course longer than that required when using instant, rolled, or Scottish oats. They have a nuttier flavor and are chewier than other types of oat.

### Scottish Oats

These are oats that have been coarsely ground with a stone mill into a meal, they are the typical base for oatmeal porridge. They cook quickly, and continue to be a staple in Scotland, the United Kingdom, and North America.

### Rolled Oats

Rolled oats are groats that have been dehusked and either steamed or lightly baked and then rolled or pressed into flakes. They are widely used in porridge, muesli and granola. They can also be ground and made into flour.

# RYE

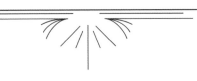

*(Secale cereale)*

One of the younger domesticated cereals, the origins of rye are unclear. Like oat, it came from the spontaneous cross-breed of weeds with cultivated wheat and barley. Since Roman times, rye has been grown extensively, and became increasingly popular in Northern and Central Europe after the Middle Ages because of its ability to adapt to poor soils, where other grains would not easily grow. Rye is also extremely tolerant of cold and can keep alive under a carpet of snow. It is, however, susceptible to ergot, a fungus that can be poisonous to both humans and animals. Fortunately, modern farming has given rise to efficient methods to prevent and control the growth of ergot. The gluten found in Rye is different from that found in wheat, and *can* be used to make bread rise. Rye bread is popular in many countries, including the United States, Germany, and Russia.

### Winter Rye

This is a rye that is planted in the fall and harvested during summer. Most rye is used as a winter crop because is an excellent winter cover. Due to its deep roots, rye prevents soil erosion, protecting cultivated land during even the harshest winters.

### Abruzzi Rye

Abruzzi is an old variety of rye that was cultivated by early North American colonists. This variety of rye produces plants capable of growing two feet taller than a standard rye. Abruzzi rye flour was traditionally used in thirded bread, a dense loaf made by the colonists before white wheat became widely available.

### Rye Berries

Rye berries are the whole-wheat kernels of threshed and harvested rye, with all the germ and bran included. They are often used in baking (though only after a proper soaking). Traditional Nordic breads, like Danish rye bread, include whole rye berries, which are sometimes boiled before being added to the dough.

### Rye Chops

Similar to steel-cut oats and cracked wheat, rye chops are just that—roughly chopped rye berries. Rye chops are quicker to cook and can be used in porridges as well as baking.

### Rye Flakes

Rye flakes are processed similarly to rolled oats. They are first steamed, before being flaked through a rolling system, and then dried. They are a useful addition to several different types of bakes and can also be used in porridge and granola.

# BARLEY

## *(Hordeum vulgare l.)*

Barley cultivation predates all but that of the most ancient varieties of wheat. This cereal adapts well to different climates, and tolerates both cold and drought. It was the most commonly cultivated grain in ancient India and Greece and, along with emmer, was also a staple in Egypt. Even after wheat became the preferred grain for breadmaking, barley continued to be grown for the brewing of beer and distillation of whiskey. Since its farming required less care than that of other cereals, barley was historically more affordable to those of lesser means. As such, it developed a longstanding reputation as a "*humble*" grain. Because the particular type of gluten of found in barley does not retain the gases needed for fermentation, it is rarely used in leavened bread. Instead, it has historically been used to make flatbreads, porridge and soups. While barley is currently the fourth most cultivated cereal in the world, it is mostly used for its malt and as animal feed. This cereal is, however, extremely rich in nutrients, and can be a healthy addition to one's diet. The biggest producer of barley is Russia.

### Flaked Barley
This is barley that has been dehulled, pearled, cooked, dried and rolled into flakes. It can then be used in granola or porridge, as well as in baking, cooking, and brewing, where it is said to impart beer with a rich and grainy flavor.

### Hulled Barley
Hulled barley is as closest thing to "whole-grain" barley sold commercially. It has only the outer part of the hull moved, through a process aimed to leave part of the bran attached to the grain. It has a lengthy cooking time and needs to be soaked or boiled before it can be used in baking.

### Pearl Barley
Pearl barley are grains that have had both their tough bran and inedible hull removed, and are then carefully polished. Unfortunately, this polishing process also removed many of the grain's

nutrients. Fine barley flour is milled from pearl barley.

### Pot Barley
Pot Barley is a processed form of barley that is milled three times, after which the husk is partly removed and only some of the bran is left. Cooking pot barley takes about an hour. It is typically used in soups, as suggested by the name.

### Quick-Cooking Barley
Quick cooking barley is the most processed barley available. It has been dehulled, polished, and then steamed, so it is pre-cooked, making it much faster to prepare. Generally, it takes roughly ten minutes to cook.

### Bere Barley
This ancient variety of six-row barley looks very different from its relatives. It was once a staple in Scotland where it was

used in a number of local foods, like the traditional bere bannock loaf. Today, its cultivation is largely confined to the Orkney islands.

### Arizona Barley (*Hordeum arizonicum*)

A wild variety of barley, it originates from a region spanning northern Mexico and the southwestern United States. It is an annual grass and grows in salt-rich habitats, like irrigations ditches, canals, and ponds. Although it is considered to be at risk of extinction in the wild, farmers have been known to use it to enhance cultivated barley.

### Meadow Barley (*Hordeum brachyantherum*)

This cool season perennial grass is native to the western United States and can be found from California to Alaska. It is often used as a quick cover for soil stabilization on wet, dry, and salt-rich land. Although its seeds are edible, it is not typically grown for sustenance, and is usually only consumed by wild animals.

### Low Barley or Dwarf Barley (*Hordeum depressum*)

This wild variety of barley is also found in the western United States,

growing from Idaho to California. An annual grass, dwarf barley prefers moist habitats. Like other kinds of wild barley, it is used to enhance cultivated varieties through crossing.

### Purple Barley

This heirloom variety of domesticated barley is notable for both its striking purple hue and for being "hulless". This means that though the seed does indeed have a hull, it is loosely attached and easy to remove without the need to "pearlize" the barley. First brought to North America in the early 1920s, its origins go back to Tibet and the Middle East. For many years, purple barley was stored in the USDA Seed Repository, and it has only recently started to be grown in North America as a gourmet variety.

### Black Nile Barley

This variety was derives from a domesticated North African Barley, and was introduced to North America fairly recently. Like Purple Barley, Black Nile Barley is a hulless barley, and does not require pearlizing.

# GLUTEN-FREE

## RICE

Almost as old as wheat, rice was domesticated in China between 10,0000 and 12,000 years ago. Consumed by more people than any other cereal, rice is the third highest-produced agricultural commodity on the planet. It is mostly eaten in grain form, but can also be ground into flour or pressed into milk. Since rice does not contain gluten, it cannot serve to leaven bread but can be used in combination with wheat, or combined with ingredients that mimic natural leavening to make gluten-free breads. Rice is very nutritious and highly digestible but, unfortunately, easily absorbs chemicals from the soil in which it grown, including arsenic. While arsenic can occur naturally in soil, widespread use of chemical fertilizers has increased its concentration significantly. It is therefore important to know where your rice comes from. Rice is grown extensively around the globe, and China is its biggest producer.

### White Rice

White rice are grains which have had their husk, bran, and germ removed. The practice of polishing rice dates back to ancient China, as the process prolonged its shelf-life, enhanced its flavor, and made it easier to digest. Like other processed grains, white rice has had part of its nutrients stripped, but it can be part of a healthy diet.

### Brown Rice

Like white rice, brown rice grains have had their husks removed. However, their bran is left intact. Brown rice flour makes an ideal coating for artisanal loaves, as it has a more subtle color than that of white rice flour. As a whole grain, brown rice has long been considered a healthier alternative to white rice. However, recent studies have shown that it is actually the bran and the husk of the rice that retain the most chemicals and minerals from the soil, including trace amounts of arsenic. We recommend checking the area of origin (rice from California, India,

and Pakistan are good options) and taking the time to rinse rice before cooking it, cook it with plenty of water, and then drain it afterward.

### Arborio

Selected by the Italian agronomist Domenico Marchetti in 1946, this variety of northern Italian rice is derived from the older *Vialone Nano*. It has large grains that absorb lots of water during cooking and can increase in weight up to five times, making it the ideal rice for risotto.

### Parboiled

Parboiled rice is rice that has been partly pre-cooked. This process originated in India and West Africa as way of de-husking rice by steaming it, and it was later adapted commercially to reduce cooking time.

### Basmati

A long and slender variety of rice native to India, which was later introduced to the Middle East by merchants. Although Basmati plants and grains have been cultivated in the United States, the Indian government has argued that these strains are but imitations of true Basmati, which only grows in certain parts of India and Pakistan. Basmati rice has a lower glycemic index score than most other rice varieties.

### Black

Different varieties of black rice, characterized by their dark color, can be found across Asia. Some of these are glutinous varieties, have a similar texture to sticky rice, and are commonly used in sweet desserts.

### Jasmine

Mostly grown in Southeast Asia, this popular long grain rice is named for its floral scent. It has the ideal consistency for woks, and is often used in stir-fried dishes. It has a higher glycemic index score than Basmati.

### Rosematta (*Matta*)

This Indian rice originates from the Palakkad region of Kerala. It has a rich and unique flavor and is considered an excellent accompaniment to meat dishes. The rice is parboiled in its red husks, giving grains a yellow-pink color.

### Red Cargo

A long whole grain rice with a red colored bran, its name comes from the fact that it used to arrive to the United States in bulk, transported via ships (unlike white rice, which was imported pre-packaged).

### Valencia (*Bomba*)

Named for its native Valencia, Spain, this variety of rice has short, rounded grains that expand considerably when cooked without becoming sticky. It is used in numerous traditional Spanish dishes, most notably *paella.* Valencia rice is in fact so highly valued that its cultivation and native wetlands are protected by the Spanish Department of Agriculture.

### Bhutanese Red Rice (Himalayan)

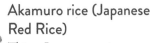
Grown in the eastern Himalayas at an elevation 8,000 feet, Bhutanese rice comes in both short and long grain varieties. The short type cooks relatively quickly, at a similar speed to white rice. When processed, the red colored bran is left intact, making this rice a whole grain. It is slightly sticky and very flavorful.

### Akamuro rice (Japanese Red Rice)

This Japanese rice variety comes from Hokkaido and is a translucent reddish brown color. Akamuro matures fast and grows well on lowland. Unlike most rice, it can tolerate a cold climate. It has a delicate flavor and as recently been cultivated in North America on a small scale.

### Duborskian Rice

A Russian rice variety that grows well on upland and does not require the soil to be flooded to grow. Like Akamuro rice, it does well in cold climates and has also started to be farmed in North America on a small scale.

## WILD RICE

There are four species of Wild Rice, most of which are native to North America. These grasses are from the *Zizania* plant family, which is only indirectly related to most rice of Asian origin. There are four species of this aquatic cereal, all of which prefer shallow waters, ponds, and slow flowing rivers.

It often serves as sustenance for nearby wildlife (ducks, for instance), and in recent times has been planted with the intention of helping local fauna. It was a staple cereal for both the Native American and ancient Chinese peoples. It is now mostly cultivated in Minnesota, California, Canada, Hungary and Australia. Since the 1970s wild rice has become increasingly popular as a gourmet food. Although wild rice flour is not particularly common, it is sometimes used in bread and baked goods, giving them a nutty flavor.

### Northern and Southern Wild Rice (*Zizania palustris* and *Zizania aquatica*)

These two closely related types of wild rice were the staple cereals of Native Americans, who considered wild rice sacred. Native Americans threshed the mature seeds directly from canoes, making sure to allow some seeds to fall into the water, so that they would generate the next harvest. Both varieties still grow wild in different regions of North America, as their names suggest, and continue to be cultivated today.

### Manchurian Wild Rice (*Zizania latifolia*)

This plant is a close relative of North American wild rice and was used as a staple grain in ancient China. Nowadays it has almost entirely disappeared in the wild and is usually grown for its stems, which are eaten as vegetables.

### Texas Wild Rice (*Zizania texana*)

This variety of rice grows wild in Texas and is considered an endangered grass species. Farmers do not cultivate Texas wild rice as a crop.

## CORN (MAIZE, ZEA MAYS)

Corn is the second most cultivated cereal in the world, and is used for a massive range of products, from cattle feed and ethanol, to cornstarch and syrup. It was domesticated in Mexico around 8000 BC. Like rice, corn does not contain gluten and cannot leaven bread. However, many varieties of flatbread are made with maize flour. Stoneground cornmeal or hominy can also be used to make thick savory porridges like grits, polenta, or the Brazilian dish *angu*. Sweet corn is often eaten whole, boiled or roasted, and the boiled grains are a popular addition to stews and salads. Corn is a good source of carbohydrates but is nutritionally less valuable than other grains. It lacks Vitamin B3, which is why Europeans who once used it as a staple cereal ended up with a sickness called *pellagra*. In a rich and varied diet, maize certainly has its place, but there is some concern regarding the massive industrialization of much of its cultivation. The United States is the world's largest producer of corn.

### Dent Corn (*Zea mays var. indentata*)

The great majority of farmed corn is dent corn, also called *field corn* and *yellow corn*. Harvested when the kernels are tough, it must be processed into flour and then cooked to become edible. Most crops have been genetically modified to increase their yield. Commonly grown for cattle feed and practically ubiquitous in processed foods, it is found in corn flakes, corn starch, gluten-free pasta and bread, corn meal, tortillas, high fructose corn syrup, and much more.

### Sweet Corn (*Zea mays convar. saccharata var. rugosa*)

Sweet corn is typically consumed as a vegetable, often served as "corn on the cob" or as whole kernels rather than being processed like a grain. It is harvested when the kernels are still soft and is either eaten when fresh or preserved through canning or freezing. While hugely popular, it actually only accounts for a minimal part of North American corn cultivation. GMO varieties are widely sold although heritage varieties are still grown.

### Flint Corn (*Zea mays var. indurata*)

Historically cultivated by Native Americans, flint corn has a hard outer layer and is similar to dent corn, but is often used for ornamental purposes because of its multicolored kernels. It was used to make *hominy*, a food made of corn that has been treated with lye or slaked lime to soften it. It can then be added to stews and beverages, or used to make grits or masa.

### Blue Corn (*Hopi Maize*)

Blue corn is grown in Mexico and southwestern United States. The varieties of blue corn found in the United States were originally developed by the people of the Hopi tribe, who used it to make *piki*, a traditional Hopi bread. In Mexican cuisine it is used to make *tlacoyo* and tortillas. It has a higher antioxidant and protein content compared to yellow corn.

### Waxy Corn

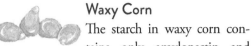

The starch in waxy corn contains only amylopectin and no amylose, a mutation that makes it far more digestible than dent corn. When used as feed, it also encourages more efficient weight gain and growth in animals than dent. This rare variety has unclear origins and has been subject much research; in the early 20th century it was found growing in China, Burma, and the Philippines. It is now widely thought it travelled to China from the Americas in or around the 1500s, and that the mutation occurred sometime afterward.

### Iroquois White Corn

This is a true heritage variety of corn similar to common sweet corn. The Iroquois tribe cultivated this white corn before their farmlands were destroyed by European settlers. Fortunately, some seeds survived and continued to be cultivated, and Iroquois White Corn is now commercially available in the form of dried seeds and flour. The flour is a good gluten-free alternative in breads and cookies, and is also used in tortillas and other maize breads.

## BUCKWHEAT

The most common type of buckwheat, *fagopyrum esculentum*, is not a grass, but actually more closely related to the rhubarb plant. It originated in East Asia about 10,000 years ago and from there it spread to the rest of the continent, and on the Europe. Historically, buckwheat was a popular cereal and key component in many regional cuisines, where it was the base for pancakes, bread, pasta, and noodles. Buckwheat is also used to make beer. With the advent of modern agriculture, buckwheat production declined, as it responds poorly to fertilizer. However demand is on the rise once more, due to the fact that buckwheat is nutrient-rich as well as gluten-free. The biggest producer of buckwheat is Russia.

### Buckwheat Groats

Buckwheat groats are crushed buckwheat seeds that have had their hull removed. They can be cooked like rice, made into porridge or ground into flour. Sometimes buckwheat is

# PHILIPPE GUICHARD

*Paysanbio Semences Paysannes,
Aquitaine, France*

Farmer by birth but heritage wheat champ by choice, Philippe is a force for the whole heritage grains' movement in France. He has developed his own collection of old landraces of wheat and grows them together, following an evolutionary approach. Such an approach allows the plants to select themselves, rather than being selected by agronomists or a laboratory. Paysanbio Semences Paysannes farm provides high-quality heritage wheat flours to several French bakeries and restaurants.

"...they are the seeds that have been cultivated by my ancestors, who were also farmers like me."

*1. What is your story? How did you become a wheat farmer and miller?*

My father was a farmer, and always cultivated wheat. My maternal grandfather was a farmer and a miller, and my paternal grandmother made bread for the entire family. So the sowing and harvesting of wheat at the family farm was the backdrop to my childhood. After I learned more and more about it, I listened to the call of the earth and decided to become a farmer.

I did not want to take over my father's family farm because at the time he had a negative opinion about organic farming, so I went out on my own a couple of decades ago. I became an organic farmer and began to work with old wheat varieties in 1991–1992. Very few people were interested in organic farming at that time, and even less were interested in heritage seeds or old varieties of wheat.

However, I soon became convinced that these old varieties of wheat were among the tools that I needed to succeed as a farmer. I have been cultivating a mix of about a hundred different heritage varieties of wheat for a long time, and I have been selling the milled flour of my unique heritage wheats mix across France.

*2. Is wheat the only thing you farm?*

No, on an organic farm, cultivating exclusively wheat does not make sense and is not sustainable. A coherent organic farm that is in accordance with the main principles of agronomy and ecology must include the cultivation of several species and varieties. For my farm, which does not have animals, I have chosen a variety of legumes, which work well in rotation and add a lot of nitrogen to the soil. This in turn makes the soil more fertile and guarantees a good wheat harvest. Depending on the year and on the condition of the crops, I grow alfalfa, fava beans, protein peas, lentils, chickpeas, and soybeans.

*3. What keeps you motivated?*

I am passionate about my work, and constantly have new things to learn, observe, and experiment with. The recognition from my customers, who rave about the products I make and transform, also keeps me motivated.

*4. What do you think you do different from other farmers?*

I think I am much more concerned than some other [farmers or millers] about the final quality of my product. I have always been very demanding with myself as well as those who work with me, so that the product is as close to perfect as possible. This high standard has contributed to the recognition of the quality of my products, both in the world of agriculture and in that of gastronomy and baking.

*5. Do you make your own seeds or do you buy them from another company?*

I produce 90% of the seeds I grow. Once in a great while I buy seeds for the green manure I grow, but that's it.

*6. Why are heritage wheat varieties so important?*

To me the main reason to grow heritage wheat is the soil! In fact, these varieties of wheat, with their high stems, allow for a replenishment of the soil through their straws, and guarantee that enough nitrogen is present. This ensures that the soil maintains its fertility without the need of organic fertilizers. My second reason is sentimental: they are the seeds that have been cultivated by my ancestors, who were also farmers like me. The third reason there is the current demand for these old varieties.

*7. Are your methods 100% organic?*

Yes, the farm has been 100% organic for over 25 years.

mix and then say that they are selling heritage wheat flour. They often deceive bakers and consumers without the knowledge to recognize flour made from older wheat varieties. There are also farmers who might claim to cultivate ancient wheat but deceive their buyers.

Over time, by educating consumers and showing pictures of our cultivated fields and wheat, we can help distinguish the truth from the false. But one has to spend a lot of time explaining everything.

Another challenge to the industry are businesses with lots of money that contract farmers to cultivate old wheat varieties and then resell them at a very high price, profiting from the work of others.

*10. How do you envision the future of wheat farming in the face of climate change? Will we still have bread on our tables in 500 years from now?*

Yes, as long as there is still wheat and people to cultivate it! Old varieties will always be present because they possess great capabilities to adapt to changes in climate. They are much more adaptable than humans, for sure!

*11. What can people do to support small-scale millers and farmers?*

Sharing our work and its importance. We do not necessarily need to sell massive amounts of produce; we just need to sell it regularly. It is my farm (rather than my income) that suffers most because of inconsistent sales. Some months, I sell a lot of flour, to such a point that the mill runs incessantly. Other months, it barely runs. The production rhythms are often not regular enough to allow for the development of long term projects or investments at the farm.

*8. Do you think organic farming is more sustainable than conventional farming?*

Of course! Without any doubt this is obvious. The best indicator of the sustainability of an agricultural system is its dependence on external input. On my farm, with a turnover of about €65,000 per year, the expenses for materials/supplies external to the farm represent less than €10,000 per year, energy expenses for electricity and fuel included.

*9. Do you have much competition? What are the greatest challenges for independent wheat farmers?*

Yes, there is competition, but it is not a real competition. As no legislation regulates the pproduction of old varieties of wheat, many millers can claim to produce flours from heritage wheat varieties. Often they even have a farmer who cultivates an old wheat variety for them. They put this one single grain in their

milled without removing the hulls to make wholemeal buckwheat flour. The buckwheat hulls can also be used as a natural filling for pillows. Buckwheat flour can be used for many delicious foods, from the Breton *galette* to Russian *blini*.

### Kasha

This is a Slavic term that in English use is often applied to toasted buckwheat groats, but traditionally refers to buckwheat porridge, or porridge in general. Kasha is one of the oldest and most loved staples of Russian cuisine, and an important dish in Ashkenazi-Jewish cuisine. There are a number of sweet and savory variations, nearly all of which include plenty of butter.

### Old Varieties of Common Buckwheat

Common buckwheat has been a staple in many European regions. It tolerates cooler climates well, and thrives in acidic and low-fertility soils. It was once widely grown in Bretagne, Russia, and on the Alps. Farmers and researchers in Valtellina, Italy, have preserved two heritage Alpine varieties, and in doing so saved them from extinction: *Curunìn* from Baruffini and *Nustràn* from Teglio. Both varieties are milled into flour and used locally to make fresh pasta and bread.

### Tartary Buckwheat

A close relative of common buckwheat, tartary buckwheat grows mostly in Asia, and is particularly abundant in the Himalayas. However, it is not uncommon in Europe. This bitter variety can be used to make flour as well as porridge. Recently, researchers observed that Tartary buckwheat had a higher concentration of *rutin* (a bioflavonoid with several health benefits) than common buckwheat.

## QUINOA (CHENOPODIUM QUINOA)

This is a leafy cereal from the same plant family as amaranth (see page 92) and kaniwa (page 91). It was one of the staple foods of the Peruvian Incas and has become an increasingly popular alternative to rice and pasta. It originated in the Andes mountains around 3000 BC, in an area spanning what is now Peru and Bolivia. South America remains the world's biggest producer of quinoa but cultivation has also expanded to other areas, including China and the United States. Quinoa is often used as a substitute for rice, but can also be ground into flour and used to make bread. In terms of nutrition, quinoa is rich in proteins and several minerals and vitamins. Unfortunately, it is also rich in *saponins*, which can trigger symptoms for those with IBS (Irritable Bowel Syndrome). Consequently, while quinoa can be a great gluten-free alternative to many grains it may not be the best choice for people affected by digestive issues.

### Red, White, and Black Quinoa

These varieties of quinoa are all similar in terms of cultivation as well as their nutritional properties. Aside from color, their difference lies in cooking time and texture: red and black quinoa take longer to cook than white quinoa, which has a softer, fluffier texture. In contrast, red and black quinoa are chewier and lend themselves well to salads.

# MILLET

Millet is a family of grasses that produce small grains. Some varieties of millet have been grown in East Asia since at least 6000 BC. Millet went on to spread to from Asia to Europe, where it was popular throughout the Middle Age. It remains one of the most common cereals in hot, arid parts of the globe, including Africa and India, which is the world's leading producer. Millet is a valuable animal feed and makes good grazing grass. This cereal has is a key component in many traditional cuisines and is used in flatbreads, soups, and porridges as well as several alcoholic beverages. Millet contains no gluten and cannot be used to leaven bread, but it is safe for gluten sensitive people. Its nutritional profile is similar to that of wheat and rice, which makes millet a good staple cereal.

### Pearl (*Pennisetum glaucum*)

This is the most common type of millet and the most widely cultivated. It originated in West Africa around 4500 years ago and from there it spread to India. It is still a staple cereal in some parts of Africa, like Nigeria and Namibia, because of its high tolerance to both drought and flood.

### Foxtail (*Sataria italica*)

The oldest domesticated millet, Foxtail millet has been farmed in China for over 8000 years. It is still widely cultivated in the more arid regions of India and China. In warm climates, foxtail millet has proven to be extremely versatile, and can be grown in any season of the year.

### Little (*Panicum sumatrense*)

Found in Central India, where it has been cultivated since 2500 BC and continues to be common today. It is generally used like rice but can also be ground into flour, and used to make bread and other foods. It is often sold unpolished, with the bran intact.

### Kodo (*Paspalum scrobiculatum L.)*

Originally from West Africa and grown in India and East Asia. It grows well in tropical regions, with high temperatures and plenty of rain. It can be an asset in waterlogged and coastal areas where other cereals cannot grow, but spreads like an invasive weed when introduced to cultivated land.

### Finger (*Eleusine coracana*)

This variety originates from the highlands of Uganda and Ethiopia. It thrives in semi-arid climates and can grow at very high altitudes. It is also grown in the Himalayas as well as other regions of India. Finger millet has very small seeds, which makes difficult to separate the bran from the endosperm and therefore it is mostly used as whole-grain flour. Its flour is widely used in regional cuisine, including cakes, breads, puddings, porridge, and beverages.

### Proso (*Panicum miliaceum*)

Proso millet may have first been domesticated independently in both China and the Caucasus in 5000 BC. It became the dominant millet variety in the Near East and Europe, but never reached Africa. In North and South America it is grown for animal feed, though it has recently been considered as source for biofuel production. It thrives in arid regions and has been promoted as a gluten-free alternative, both as a grain and flour.

### Kaniwa (*Cañihua, Cañahua, Chenopodium pallidicaule*)

This crop is part of the same plant family as amaranth (see page 92) and quinoa (see page 90). Kaniwa is grown for it seeds, which can be boiled or milled into flour. It has been cultivated on the highlands of Bolivia and Peru for thousands of years. There are 200 varieties of kaniwa, but only 20 are still cultivated. Kaniwa is similar to quinoa but has a better nutritional profile. In particular, kaniwa has much lower concentrations of toxic saponins compared with quinoa.

### Teff (*Eragrostis tef*)

 Teff is a grass indigenous to Ethiopia and Eritrea, where it was domesticated sometime between 4000 BC and 1000 BC. Unlike wheat and many other grasses, it does not contain gluten. It is used in soups, stews and porridges, and is also a key ingredient in *injera*, a fermented traditional bread. This fermentation process is not intended to leaven the bread, but to release the grain's rich proteins and minerals. Teff grows best in warm, sunny climates at a high altitude. Its cultivation is still limited to a few regions of the globe, but demand is rising because of its nutritional profile and lack of gluten. There are dark and light varieties of teff, both of which are used in similar ways. Due to the small size of the seeds, teff is always ground whole, as it is impossible to isolate the bran from the starchy section.

### Sorghum (*Sorghum bicolor*)

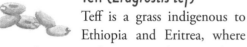 Like wheat, sorghum is part of the poaceae grass family. While there are many species of this grass, *sorghum bicolor* is by far the most widely cultivated. This variety is native to Africa and has been farmed for thousands of years, though it is unclear when it first became domesticated. Grown worldwide, Africa remains this nutritious gluten-free cereal's biggest producer. Sorghum is a resilient plant, and can tolerate poor soil, as well as extreme heat and drought. It is used in a number of traditional flatbreads throughout Asia and Africa, as well as a wide variety of other foods. These include sweet sorghum syrup, spirits, beer, and baked goods. It is also used as a source of biofuel and feed for livestock, although it can be difficult for animals to digest.

### Amaranth (*Amaranthus*)

 Unlike wheat, amaranth is not a grass but a leafy summer vegetable closely related to spinach, chard, and beet. It is part of the same plant family as quinoa (see page 90) and kaniwa (see page 91). Like these, it is primarily cultivated for its seeds, which are consumed as pseudocereals. Its domestication dates back to the Mayans, and it has been cultivated for over 8000 years. The diet of the Aztec people was overwhelmingly amaranth-based, and it was a key component in many religious rituals and festivities. Tragically, after the arrival of Spanish conquistadores in the 1500s, the farming of amaranth was forbidden and nearly all cultivated fields were burned. Luckily, the plant was not completely destroyed and cultivation began to spread once more in the 1970s. Much of the renewed interest in amaranth is due to its nutrient-rich profile and the fact that it does not contain gluten. Amaranth can be used to make flour and baked goods, and can also to be eaten whole in soups, stews, and other dishes. The Aztec people also "popped" it, much like popcorn. Introduction of amaranth to cultivated land can be difficult, since this plant does not like competition and will spread like an invasive weed. Consequently, most commercially produced amaranth has undergone genetic manipulation allowing it to tolerate chemical treatment to contain is growth. As such, it may be advisable to buy organic whenever possible. The current leading producer is China.

### Coconut (*Cocos nucifera*)

 The fruit of the coconut tree, the exact origin of the coconut has been subject to extensive debate. It is generally thought to be native to the Indian-Indonesia region, from where it gradually self-distributed. Protected by their sturdy shell, fruit from coastal coconut trees floated across the seas, spreading to the rest of the world. The flesh of the coconut can be used to make coconut milk and oil, from which the leftover pulp is often dried and ground into flour.

### Coixseed "Job's Tears" (Adlay Millet, *Coix lacryma-jobi*)

This grass is native to Southeast Asia, and has been domesticated in the southern United States as well as Central and Southern America. The gluten-free seeds of the plant can be dried and milled into flour for bread and other baked goods. This cereal has long been used in traditional Chinese medicine, and is believed to have many beneficial properties. Recent research has suggested that Job's Tears could help manage cholesterol levels, menstrual symptoms, and even be used in the treatment and prevention of cancer.

### Banana (Musa genus)

This genus of large fruit-bearing plants has been cultivated since 5000 BC, and is native to Southeast Asia. It has since spread to both Africa and the Caribbean. Banana flour is typically made from green bananas or plantains, but researchers in Chile have recently developed a way to make flour from overripe bananas and their peels.

### Plantain (Cooking Banana, *Musa x paradisiaca*)

In Europe and the Americas, "plantain" refers to sturdier, starchier, less sweet varieties of banana that are generally cooked as part of a meal rather than eaten as a fruit, and are used and sold at varying stages of ripeness. They can be dried and milled into flour, which is rich in resistant starches and therefore low in calories. It is worth noting that in other regions of the world, especially Asia and the islands of the Pacific, there is no distinction made between plantains and bananas.

## SEEDS

### Chia (*Salvia hispanica*)

A flowering herb once farmed by the Aztecs, chia is now widely cultivated for its seeds in Mexico, the southwestern United States, and parts of South America. Chia seeds can be added to a number of different foods or ground into a gel for use in desserts and as a vegan egg substitute. They can be ground into flour and used in bread and other baked goods. Although chia seeds are often promoted as a health food and are rich in omega-3 fatty acid, claims of their purported health benefits have yet to be fully proven.

### Grape seed

Grape seed flour is made from the seed and skin residue left over from winemaking. It is rich in antioxidants, and much research has gone into its nutritional properties. Many bakers and chefs have experimented with using it in bread and baked goods, and it can be an excellent way to add flavor, color, and nutritional value. However, it is widely agreed that adding more than a small amount can negatively impact the bread's flavor and texture.

### Pumpkin Seed

Native to North America, pumpkins produce seeds that are ideal for making gluten-free flour. Pumpkin seed flour, milled from whole seeds, is suitable to people with nuts allergies and can work as a substitute for almond meal. Pumpkin seed flour is rich in proteins, fats, and essential minerals.

### Sunflower Seed (*Helianthus*)

Sunflowers, a plant indigenous to the Americas, produce hearty seeds that are rich in omega and unsaturated fatty acids and minerals. Once they have been soaked and dehydrated, these seeds can be milled into flour. Like pumpkin seed flour, this is a good nut-free substitute to almond meal.

### Hemp

One of the first plants to be domesticated, hemp is a variety of *cannabis sativa* once used as a fiber crop. Today its uses span from the production of oil and paper and to plastics and biofuel. Hemp flour is milled from the "cake" left over after hemp seeds are pressed for oil. This gluten-free flour works best when blended with other flours, especially when making bread, as it will otherwise result in a very flat, dense loaf.

### Flax (Linseed, *Linum usitatissimum*)

Flax has been farmed since antiquity for its oil, fibers, and seeds. Flaxseed meal is made from milled whole flax seeds. It is very high in fats and therefore it cannot be used as a substitute for flour, but it can be an interesting addition to bread and baked goods.

## NUTS

### Almond

Almonds are the seeds of the widely cultivated tree of the same name, which is native to the Middle East. Ground and whole almonds are widely used in both baking and pastry making, and are also the main ingredient of marzipan paste. Very fine almond flour, or meal, has become popular as a gluten-free substitute for wheat flour. The flour keeps all the rich nutrients of the whole almonds.

### Acorn

Acorns are the nuts of the Oak tree. Throughout much of the world, acorns were considered inedible and only eaten in times of great need. However, one notable exception is that of the indigenous people of North America, particularly Californian Native Americans. A staple food for many, acorns were harvested and sun-dried to prevent mold and germination, and could be stored for long periods of time. They were often later crushed and ground into flour, and then leached in water to remove the flour of tannic acid. This processing method has been "rediscovered" in recent years, and acorn flour is increasingly available. It is extremely rich in antioxidants and gluten-free.

### Chestnut

Chestnuts are the nuts of the chestnut tree, found in temperate climates. Different varieties of chestnut can be found in Europe, East Asia and North America. Chestnuts, and flour milled from them, have been a source of food for millenia, and chestnut cultivation is thought to date back to 2000 BC. Chestnut flour is made from dried, ground chestnuts, and can be used alone or in combination with regular flour to make cakes, cookies, and bread. Chestnut flour is rich in minerals and vitamins, and low in fats.

### Peanut

Peanuts are in fact not nuts, but the seeds of the peanut legume. Although peanuts are native to Central and South America, Asia has become the world's largest producer. Crushed peanuts left over from the manufacture of peanut oil can be milled into peanut flour. This flour, unlike almond flour, is low in fat but still high in protein. It is generally used as a thickening agent in food, but can also be used in baking.

### Cashew

Cashews are the edible seeds of the tropical cashew tree, native to Brazil. Africa and Asia are the world's biggest producers of cashews. Much like almond flour, cashews are dried and milled to make flour. As a result, cashew flour is very high in fat, but also retains all of its nutrients.

### Pecan

Pecans are the nuts of the tree of the same name, which is native to both Mexico and North America, both of which remain the world's biggest producers of pecans. Used in a variety of foods, pecans can also be dried and ground into flour. Pecan flour is rich in fats, proteins, minerals, and vitamins and can be used as a substitute for almond.

### Hazelnut

Hazelnuts are the nuts of the hazel tree, also called Corylus. Native to the Eurasian continent, early traces of their processing were discovered in Scotland and dated to 6000 BC. Nowadays, the largest producer is Turkey. Hazelnuts have been used since antiquity in numerous foods, including baked goods. Hazelnut flour is similar most other nuts flours, and is made from ground, dried hazelnuts, retaining their fat and nutrients.

### Pistachio

Pistachios are the nuts of the pistachio tree. Native to Asia and the Middle East, they have become naturalized throughout the Mediterranean. Widely eaten since antiquity, pistachios are used in a variety of foods. However, finely milled pistachio flour is a relatively recent development. This flour has a distinctive flavor and is full of the same rich nutrients found in whole pistachios.

### Macadamia

Macadamia are a group of tree species native to Australia, all of which bear the macadamia nut. South Africa is currently the largest producer, followed by Australia and the United States. Macadamia nuts, like other nuts, can be dried (and sometimes roasted) and then ground into flour. The flour contains all the fats and nutrients of the macadamia nuts and can be used as one would almond flour.

## TUBERS

### Potato (*Solanum tuberosum*)

The fourth most cultivated crop in the world, potatoes are the tubers of herbaceous plants native to the Andes. Potatoes can be peeled, dried, and milled into potato flour, which can be used in baking in combination with regular flour or as a flour substitute in gluten-free baking. Potato *starch* is also widely used in both cooking and baking. This is extracted from pulverized potatoes and then dried into powder.

### Sweet Potato (*Ipomoea batatas*)

Sweet potatoes are the tuber of a flowering plant native to either Central or South America, and date back to at least 8000 BC and spread to the Pacific Islands as early as 1000 AD. A popular food in many cultures, this healthy and nutritious tuber can be dried and milled into flour. Sweet potato flour is low in fat and rich in nutrients.

### Tapioca

This starch is derived from the cassava root, which is indigenous to Brazil. As an extracted starch, it essentially contains only carbohydrates, with no proteins and nearly no fats, significant minerals, or vitamins. It is added to various food products as a thickener or jellifying agent, and is also used in baked goods, puddings, snacks, and drinks.

### Tigernut (*Cyperus esculentus*)

This is common tuber grows wild throughout much of the world, its cultivation dating back to 4000 BC in Egypt and 7000 BC in North America. Cultivation is currently concentrated in Spain and Egypt. Tubers can be eaten raw and are used in a number of dishes and beverages. They can also be toasted and then milled into flour. This flour is rich in starch as well as several nutrients, including proteins, fats, minerals and vitamins, making it a healthy gluten-free alternative.

### Yam (family *Dioscoreaceae*)

Although the terms *yam* and *sweet potato* are used interchangeably in parts of North America and Polynesia, true yams are the tubers of vine plants native to Africa and Asia. They are widely cultivated in Africa, which is the major producer. Rich in starch but low in other nutrients (particularly in protein), yams are traditionally sundried and milled into flour, which can be used in cooking and baking.

### Cassava (Yuca, Manioc, *Manihot esculenta*)

Cassava is the root of a shrub native to South America but now more widely cultivated in Africa and Asia. Cassava is a staple in sub-Saharan African countries, as it thrives arid climates and can do well in poor soils. However, raw cassava is in fact toxic and can cause cyanide poisoning. It must be boiled or otherwise processed to remove these toxins, after which it can be consumed or dried and milled into flour. Nutritionally speaking, processed cassava contains little more than carbohydrates.

### Water Chestnut (Chine Water Chestnut, *Eleocharis dulcis*)

The tuber of a grass native to East Asia, water chestnuts can also be also found in Australia, the Pacific Islands, and parts of Africa. It is particularly common in Chinese cuisine. Water chestnuts can be ground into a starch-rich flour that can be used in baking, frying, and as a thickener.

## BEANS AND LEGUMES

### Soybean (*Glycine max*)

Soybean is a legume native to East Asia. It is extremely rich in proteins and suitable for extensive farming, which is why it is widely cultivated in both North and South America. The United States, Argentina, and Brazil are the world's leading producers. In the United States, soybeans are harvested and processed for their oil and flour on an industrial scale. Soy flour is usually milled from the dry bean residue leftover after the soybeans have had their oil extracted, but can also be made from whole heat-processed soybeans.

### White Bean (Navy Bean, Haricot Bean, *Phaseolus vulgaris* family)

This variety of common bean is native to North America, and went on to become a widespread crop throughout the rest of the world. White bean flour is made from pulverized white beans and is packed with proteins and other important nutrients.

### Black Bean (Black Turtle Bean, *Phaseolus vulgaris* family)

Like white beans, black beans are a variety of common beans. Native to the Americas, they are staples of Mexican, Latin American, and

Dominican cuisine. Black bean flour is made from pulverized dried beans and contains the same nutrients found in whole black beans.

### Black Gram or Urad Bean (*Vigna mungo*)

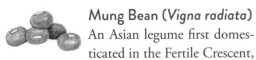 This Indian legume has been grown since ancient times and is a major part of Indian cuisine. Extremely nutritious, it is rich in high quality proteins, essential minerals, and vitamins. The dried beans can be ground into flour used in traditional foods such as chapatti and dosa.

### Mung Bean (*Vigna radiata*)

An Asian legume first domesticated in the Fertile Crescent, it has been farmed in India and nearby regions for millennia. The dry beans are often ground into a dry paste used in several traditional Indian dishes. Starch can also be extracted from the flour and used to make noodles.

### Green Pea (*Pisum sativum*)

A legume of Mediterranean origin, peas are have been widely cultivated for thousands of years, dating back to at least 4400 BC in Egypts and 3600 BC in India. Nowadays, green peas are usually eaten fresh, but in antiquity they were grown for their dry seeds. These seeds can be milled to make a pale green flour. It has a very mild flavor, and is easy to use in many baking recipes. Green pea flour is a good way to boost the nutritional value of bread and other baked goods.

### Fava Bean (Broad Bean, *Vicia faba*)

This legume is native to North Africa as well as South and Southwest Asia. Often eaten fresh, fava beans were also popular dried.

Dried fava beans can be milled into an earthy flour that lends itself well to savory baked goods, but may not work as well in more sweet or more delicately flavored bakes. Like other legumes, fava beans and their flour are low in fat but rich in proteins, minerals, and vitamins.

### Chickpea (Garbanzo Bean, *Cicer arietinum*)

Chickpeas are one of the earliest cultivated legumes, and were first domesticated in the Fertile Crescent in 5000 BC. They are grown for they dry seeds, which have become a staple in Medditerranean, Indian, Middle Eastern, and other regional cuisines. Chickpea flour, ground from the dry seeds, is the main ingredient of numerous flatbreads and other foods. Chickpeas are some of the most nutrients-rich legumes and are particularly high in vegetable proteins.

### Lentils (*Lens culnaris*)

Like chickpeas, lentils were one of the earliest legumes to be domesticated, in the ancient Near East. Cultivated for their dried seeds, which are generally boiled and used in several regional foods. Dry lentils can be milled into a versatile flour, which has a mild flavor and rich nutritional profile.

### Coffee

Remarkably, a process has recently been developed to extract flour from the very same plant from which we harvest coffee beans. This patented process repurposes the waste from coffee production, making a flour that can be used in baking. However, it should be noted that it may affect the dough's flavor and texture if added in large quantities.

# GIUSEPPE NINIVAGGI

### *Azienda Agricola Ninivaggi a Ferrandina*
### *Basilicata, Italy*

Giuseppe is the continuator of a family-owned farm located in the beautiful countryside outside Matera (Basilicata, Italy). Matera is world-known for its semolina bread, and the whole area is ideal for durum wheat cultivation, like the neighbor Apulia, with its famous Altamura bread (see Pugliese bread). Agricola Ninivaggi in Ferrandina farm is driven according to strict organic standards but, above all, is carried forward by the deep bond that Giuseppe Ninivaggi has with his land.

*1. What is your story? How did you become a farmer?*

I did not become a farmer so much as I was born into it. I belong to a family of farmers, who have cultivated our beautiful and sometimes harsh land for generations. As a child my father would bring me with him to the farm and it is from these early experiences that I learned to love nature and to cherish the work in the fields. As a farmer in Southern Italy, I became a wheat farmer by default, because this land is ideal for wheat cultivation, which has been grown here since antiquity.

*2. Is wheat the only thing you farm?*

I grow several other cereals on my farm, including emmer, barley, oats, as well as legumes like lentils, beans, chickpeas, and more. We also grow strawberries, flax, and fodder. In organic farming it is mandatory to follow a strict routine of crop rotation.

*3. What keeps you motivated?*

I come from ten generations of farmers, which is a great motivation. I am also excited by our ongoing projects, which include our plans to construct our very own flourmill as well as an artisan pasta-making facility, so we can sell our products directly to consumers.

*4. What do you think you do different from other farms, especially large conventional ones?*

Conventional farming and what I do are two completely different ways to approach nature and agriculture. What I do is organic farming, which does not involve the use of fertilizers and pesticides and which, above all, is done with great respect of the environment and the soil. If you look at climate change and global warming, well, conventional and intensive agriculture is one of the major contributors to this destructive change. On the contrary, organic farming is associated with the least amount of alteration of the soil and of the seeds. I see organic farming as the only way to give back to the environment, to nature, to the soil and, above all, to our atmosphere what we have been taking away for decades. Since the so-called Green Revolution, which brought enormous profit to many farmers, our climate has changed rapidly and has reached the level of environmental catastrophe. We are paying for it today with massive environmental pollution and loss of soil fertility. If we continue at this pace, we will continue to lose soil fertility and humus, and will be forced to increase the use of fertilizers and pesticides that pollute the environment.

*5. Do you make your own seeds or do you buy them from a big company?*

This is a very important aspect of our work. Every year we select seeds and land plots devoted to grow the seeds for the next season. Unfortunately, or fortunately, big seeds companies focus on patents and intensive farming, and their aims

are completely incompatible with my agricultural philosophy.

### 6. Why are heritage wheat varieties are so important?

For a long time, I have exclusively grown ancient varieties of wheat. The benefits to me are innumerable, both for our health and that of the soil, as well as for preserving biodiversity. With regards to our health, it took thousands of years for the human digestive system to adapt to the assimilation and digestion of wheat. Changing the type of wheat we consume so abruptly is the reason why, in recent years, the number of people with sensitivity to gluten and celiac disease has skyrocketed. Ancient grains have a much weaker type of gluten that is easier to digest. The big wheat farming companies, driven by the food industry, have selected super-high protein wheat with super strong gluten. It is extremely difficult to digest, hence gluten sensitivity and celiac disease.

As far as soil is concerned, organic farming does not make absolutely any use of herbicides, and here the ancient grains have another great value. The plants are very tall, so they naturally suffocate weeds, unlike genetically engineered dwarf wheat.

### 7. What are the greatest challenges you have faced so far as an organic wheat farmer?

I was born at the height of the Green Revolution, so I had to completely change my approach to the land. I had to study why our soil's humus was becoming more and more poor. Over the years I had to revolutionize my way of farming. It is still a challenge today, but it is the challenge I want to keep taking up in order to leave a better world for future generations.

### 8. What are the worst "enemies" to quality wheat farmers?

International agreements and laws can have a negative impact on good farming practices.

### 9. How do you envision future of wheat farming in the face of climate change? Will we still have bread on our tables in 500 years from now?

Cereals have been grown for more than 10,000 years and I cannot see why there shouldn't be wheat farmers in 500 years. Maybe climate change will change the areas that are best suited to wheat farming, but I think the cultivation of wheat will continue.

### 10. What can people do to support small-scale farmers?

We have to remember that "la salute vien mangiando"; health comes with eating. The most powerful medicine is nourishing ourselves with the highest quality products. These are often not produced by big food companies, because of practical reasons, since their primary focus is profit. To get the best quality food, it is necessary to buy directly from organic farmers. Learn their stories and get an idea of how that food was produced. I know it can be challenging but if one really wants to, it is possible.

# LOAVES

Bread is, by all means, the most universal food we have. From North to South, East to West, it is hard to find a local cuisine and culture without its own version of "the stuff of life." Bread is the best way to eat your grains, because it involves soaking, fermenting, and cooking them. All of these processes are aimed at transforming the seeds of different types of grasses, which can be eaten raw by other animals (but not by us), into one of the most nutrient-rich foods available to humans. From a traditionally made loaf of bread, one can get what our bodies and brains need most: complex sugars. In addition to this, and unlike other starchy foods like tubers, cereals are packed with vegetable proteins and essential fatty acids. They also contain vitamins that are fundamental for our body and difficult to find elsewhere. It is thus not excessive to state that, with minimal integration from other food groups, your loaf of bread could sustain you.

Bread is also portable and can last several days, even months in its dried versions. It is extremely versatile and can accompany any other food. It is, therefore, not surprising that bread was—and is—central to so many different cultures. Of course, different climates favor different cuisines, and determine the cereal used as the primary staple. We have wheat in Western and Southern Europe, rye in Eastern Europe, barley and millet in India, corn in Latin America, and teff in Africa. What we are left with is an incredibly deep cornucopia full of breads of any possible shape and flavor.

## French Bread

When we think of French bread, what comes instinctively to mind is a fragrant baguette. This bread is not just French, but is rather an accomplishment of the Parisian bread-baking tradition. The baguette is a light, white wheat bread with a thin and crunchy crust, and a fine and regular alveolation. It is fermented with yeast in a rather standardized way. This type of bread was part of an extremely rich variety of white breads and pastries that were reserved for the privileged, and that became the daily bread throughout Paris following Napoleon's time.

Outside of Paris and cities in general, the old tradition of Pain de Campagne survived up to relatively recent times. Pain de Champagne (see page 293) is generally made with sourdough and a mixture of sifted and whole wheat flours, with a variable percentage of rye. It is shaped as a round (*miche*), which was generally quite wide and heavy in order to feed entire families for several days. The miches were made at home and baked in communal ovens. This tradition survived up to WWII in small rural centers. However, with the artisan bread revival, Pain de Campagne has gained a renewed importance, reaching Paris where it is now baked in the best bakeries.

There are, of course, many other non-Parisian types of breads, and every French region has its own traditions. Just to mention a couple of examples, in southern Provence, it is typical to aromatize bread with the many local herbs, while in northern Normandy, we find Pain Brie, which has a very special scoring, and was traditionally kneaded for a very long time.

## Italian Bread

Italian bread is characterized by regional differences. Each and every Italian region, and often every little center within the region, has its own peculiar baking tradition, and takes pride in its breads.

During the 20th century, local traditions were increasingly replaced by standardized white bread. Only in recent times have efforts been made to recognize and preserve the invaluable heritage of traditional regional breads.

Traditional Italian bread comes in many different shapes and sizes, and the recipes are based on a variety of grains. Bread wheat is used in northern and southwestern Italy, while durum wheat is still the favored grain in southeastern Italy and the islands, Sicily and Sardinia. Moreover, in the north, wheat bread tends to be made with stiffer doughs and, therefore, has a denser crumb. On the other hand, in central and southwest Italy, wheat bread tends to be made with softer doughs and has a lighter crumb, with a more open alveolation. Durum wheat bread is instead always quite compact, and is characterized by a beautiful golden color.

In Italy, as in France, bread made in cities was typically based on yeast, whereas in rural areas, traditional sourdough baking has been kept alive.

Curiously, the best-known Italian bread outside of Italy is the ciabatta (pages 160-173), which is a modern creation attributed to a specific baker, Francesco Favaron, who developed it in the 80s as an Italian response to the French baguette. Ciabatta, like a baguette, is based on white wheat but is supposed to have a rather soft crust.

## English and Irish Bread

Wheat was brought to England by the Romans, and then to Ireland by the British. The type of wheat that was traditionally grown in these two islands was not like that grown in France or Italy. It was a soft wheat with very low protein content, and could not make a crusty bread. This is the reason why both British and Irish baking traditions are rich in cookies and biscuits, as well as cakes and soft, spongy breads.

In Britain, yeast and malt from beer making and other alcoholic beverages have been used to make bread rise since Roman times. Bread was generally made with wheat, but rye, oats, and barley were also used. As with the rest of Europe and up to the 19th century,

Pain de campagne

2,10€

only the privileged classes could afford white wheat bread, while commoners were eating a darker and heavier whole wheat bread mixed with flours from other cereals.

Since the wheat available in Ireland and England did not rise as much with yeast, it was easy to pass to chemical leavening when baking soda became available. Soda bread (pages 239-248) was first developed in England but became particularly popular in Ireland during the potato famine, and has become one of the symbols of Ireland since.

## Northern and Eastern European Bread

While wheat bread was predominant in southern and western Europe, the Nordic countries and eastern Europe used rye, barley, and oats.

Oats do not contain gluten proteins, and, therefore, cannot be the main grain of leavened bread. Rye and barley contain proteins that form a type of gluten that is different from the one formed in wheat. This type of gluten is not as good at keeping the gasses of fermentation in the dough as wheat gluten. Therefore, barley is more suited for flatbreads.

Rye, if properly fermented, can make leavened bread that is denser than wheat bread, but can be more flavorful. Every Eastern European and Nordic country highly prizes its own rye bread. We have pumpernickel (page 123) in Germany, borodinsky bread (page 292) in Russia, limppu (page 213) in Finland, rugbrød (page 214) in Denmark, and so on. All of these breads were traditionally made with rye sourdough, and tend to be sourer compared to Italian, French, Irish, and English breads. Although dark rye breads are quite popular in Poland and Sweden, rye flour is often sifted and combined with wheat to

Fougasse
au fromage
2,40€
200g

make soft and light rye breads.

## North American Bread

The colonists and later waves of immigrants brought their own diverse bread-baking traditions to North America.

The British preference for soft white bread ultimately led to contemporary packaged industrial bread. The British also influenced the American love for biscuits and fast-baked breads based on baking powder.

The Irish made soda bread popular; Eastern Europeans imposed an appreciation for rye; European Jewish people made their challahs known (pages 230-238); Latin Americans taught their corn-based breads; and Italians spread the love for the pizzas and focaccias. There are also countless small cultural pockets where descendants of immigrants still bake their traditional breads. For example, Finnish

limppu is still baked in Upper Michigan.

When it comes to commercially sold bread, the French baking school has been the main model for North American bakers and it keeps inspiring.

## Latin American Bread

In Latin America, corn was the staple cereal used to make bread for the native cultures, and remains a popular choice. For example, in modern Peru (once the center of the Inca civilization), pan de maiz is still made today. In Mexico, corn tortillas remain a staple, and are likely similar to what the Aztecs and Mayans called bread.

Corn has no gluten and cannot trap molecules of carbon dioxide; therefore, breads made with this cereal are, by definition, flat. They do not need an oven, and are simply cooked on a hot pan. Besides tortillas, traditional Latin

American corn bread also comes in the form of arepas, which are bread cakes that possess more volume than tortillas, and can be filled.

It is also very common to make light bread rolls with cheese. There are infinite variations of these rolls, but the typical recipe is based on flour made from the local root vegetable cassava. In Ecuador, this bread is called pan de yucca; in Paraguay its name is chipas; in Argentina and Brazil, pão de queijo; in Columbia, pan de queso; and in Bolivia, it is called cuñape. European-style soft white wheat bread is also very popular in Latin America, and is widely consumed.

## Asian Bread
South Asia. Wheat and barley have been staple grains in both India and Pakistan. Bread is a fundamental part of South Asian cuisine, and it is generally unleavened.

There is a very rich tradition of flatbreads in South Asia, which often combines different cereals. These flatbreads are typically unleavened and cooked on a hot iron griddle, like chapati or roti. Leavened variations are also popular, like naan bread (page 318), which is baked in a tandoor or clay oven.

Far East. Wheat has been grown in China even before rice was discovered. It grew particularly well in northern China, where leavened wheat bread became a staple, together with wheat noodles.

Bread generally came in the form of soft buns, called mantou (page 324), which are steamed instead of baked. Steaming was originally preferred, because ovens were not common in China. Mantou, in their plain form, are quite neutral tasting, as they contain no salt. There are flavored versions though, with fried meat, vegetables, or a bean paste used as a filing before steaming. Filled steamed buns are called baozi. There are also versions of mantou and baozi in southern China, but they are often smaller and sweet rather than savory.

Steamed leavened buns are also common in Japan and in the Philippines. Japan has developed a taste for sweet baked bread, which flourished after the 19th century. One example is Hokkaido Milk Bread, made with the Japanese Tangzhong method. Before the diffusion of baker's yeast, natural ferments were used to leaven bread in both south and east Asia.

## Middle Eastern and North African Bread
Many of today's traditional breads still eaten in Middle Eastern and North African countries have a very long history behind them. These are the regions where wheat cultivation was originally developed, and it is here that the first wheat breads were born.

It is also here that the first ovens were developed. In several rural areas, it is still possible to eat bread made in tannour ovens, which are cylinders made out of clay. Flat leavened breads are baked on the oven's hot sides. Tannours are very similar to the Indian tandoor ovens, and the breads made in these ovens possess similar characteristics.

It is even more common to find brick ovens derived from those used by ancient Egyptians. Egyptian sun bread or al-shamsi is still baked in the traditional way.

There is an extremely rich heritage of traditional leavened and unleavened flat breads in both the Middle East and North Africa, but the most common one is undoubtedly the pita. Pita is the European name given to this type of leavened flat bread, which is a real staple. In Arabic, pita is called khubz arabee.

## Ethiopian Bread
Stemming from the traditional Middle Eastern and North African flat breads, we find injera a little farther down the map. There are two qualities of injera that makes it deserve a special mention. The first one regards the grain used to make it, teff, which was very typical of Ethiopia and which gives the bread a very distinctive taste, consistency, and color. The other notable aspect of this bread is in the baking method. Traditionally, injera was fer-

mented without the addition of a preferment or a rising agent. In other words, no sourdough was added to the dough, nor any foam from beer or other fruit and vegetable ferments. The dough was simply left standing for several days, allowing it to ferment on its own, becoming a sourdough starter, and then it was cooked on a griddle. Nowadays, injera is sometimes made with baker's yeast, but most believe that the sour flavor of the authentic injera is unbeatable.

## Seven Stars Bakery

(401) 521-2200
www.sevenstarsbakery.com

820 Hope Street
Providence, RI 02906

342 Broadway
Providence, RI 02909

Rumford Center,
20 Newman Avenue
East Providence, RI 02916

When Lynn and Jim Williams met in California in the late 90's, baking was already an established part of their lives. Lynn longed to return to the Northeast and open her own bakery; Jim had already worked in the now-closed Bread Garden of Berkeley, and remained an avid follower of baking and fermentation processes. Eventually, they found a space they liked on Hope Street in Providence—and their customers are glad they did.

Their enterprise grew quickly. It wasn't long before two new locations had opened, and after a visit to Dave Miller's Miller's Bake House, Jim and Lynn purchased their first flour mill. For Jim, it was a long road from making Sunday morning waffles as a child. "I have no formal cooking or baking education, but I worked in lots of bakeries learning the craft. Baking is all about repetition. You have to put in the time and do the work."

Known for its flavorful breads and friendly service, Seven Stars does not skip steps. Their fermentation process is rigid, but worthwhile; the bakery uses four different types of preferments, and each loaf they bake requires at least one of them. These recipes are time-tested and made entirely in-house—and it shows in the bread.

The bread alone is enough to justify Seven Stars' popularity, but the bakery is active in the community as well. Aside from participating in local charity raffles and auctions year-round, they donate 100% of their profits to a local charity every year on their anniversary, January 2. And their commitment to locally sourced grains helps area farmers as well: "When we first started buying northeast-sourced flour, it was rough at best, but it's getting better and better. We are part of this revolution that is happening, and it's really great to be part of it. In the end, we need good-performing, great-tasting wheat, and the Northeast source has those two all-important elements in addition to supporting our emerging grain economy."

Seven Stars has entrenched itself firmly in the Providence community. And though its bread is so tasty that patrons would visit regardless, one can't help but smile at the way this local business has spread its roots.

# IN HIS OWN WORDS:
## JIM WILLIAMS, OF SEVEN STARS

*Who inspired you to bake? Who inspires you now?*

Jim: I had always been interested in cooking and baking growing up. I had a tremendous interest in bread and brewing beer. In 1993, two very inspirational books, *Bread Alone* by Daniel Leader and *The Village Baker* by Joe Ortiz, were published on European style, long fermented breads. I dove in head first, and realized that this is what I wanted to do with my life.

Lynn: I'm inspired by bakers that have been around for a while, and continue to push the limits with whole grain breads. Dave Miller and Mike Zakowski, both based in Northern California, come to mind.

*What is your golden rule(s) for baking?*

Time and temperature are everything. Control those two variables, and you control the final product.

*What does Seven Stars Bakery represent to you?*

We take pride in offering an outstanding product, while giving our employees an excellent place of employment all the while, providing excellent customer service. The three add up to what makes Seven Stars the special place that it is.

*What is your favorite thing to bake? Why? Least favorite thing to bake?*

My favorite thing would be freshly milled, long-fermented whole grain breads from one single variety of wheat. Wheat is no different than grapes, hops, or even cows! There are thousands of different varieties of wheat to explore—all with different flavors and fermentation profiles. I have a lot of respect for the sweet bakers of the world, but I'm not one of them!

*Where do you get your tools/materials? What non-essential items should every baker have?*

Large equipment, like ovens and mixers come from equipment companies. Any smaller items like scrapers, scoops, and buckets, can be found at any restaurant supply store.

The important non-essential item—though I would argue it *is* essential—would be a good plastic scraper! I like them made of hard, rigid plastic. Curved for some bowls and straight-sided for others. Flexible scrapers just don't work as well.

*What book(s) go on your required reading list for bakers?*

For the home and professional baker, *Bread* by Jeffrey Hamelman. *Advanced Bread and Pastry,* by Michel Suas, for the professional baker.

*What outlets/periodicals/newspapers do you read or consult regularly, if any?*

Instagram has a very good bread community. Also, the Bread Bakers Guild of America is an excellent organization for both home and professional bakers. They offer events throughout the year, and a quarterly newsletter that is worth the membership alone.

*Tell me about your most memorable collaboration with another chef.*

It's not exactly a collaboration, but my first visit to Dave Miller's bakery, Miller's Bake House, changed the way I think about bread, grains, and milling. That visit led to a new mentor, friendship, and direction, both for myself as a baker and for Seven Stars Bakery. Shortly after that visit, we purchased our first flour mill to start milling the northeast-sourced local grains we had previously been purchasing as flour. It led to Seven Stars becoming one of

the leaders in the country in sourcing regional grains, and milling them into whole grain flour. Very soon, we will take the next step with a new farmer. We'll be able to stand in a field of wheat, and say, "all of what I see is ours."

*Do you follow any cooking shows or chefs? If so, which is your favorite?*

Lately, our family has been watching "The Great British Baking Show." Quite entertaining, especially when they make bread!

*Brag about yourself a bit. What are your highest achievements and/or proudest moments as a chef?*

Bakers tend to be quiet types with not much to say about themselves. I'm proud of the work we do daily at Seven Stars and the work I've done with single-variety wheats. I believe that Seven Stars is a great place to work. I wish I worked in a place like ours when I was starting out!

*You mill in-house. What inspired you to make that choice, and how has it benefitted the bakery?*

After that first visit to Dave's I just knew milling was the next logical step. We jumped right in headfirst, and I couldn't see us going back to dead flour in a bag. Fresh milled flour has an aroma that you want to do everything you can to capture. We do our best to do that in our breads every day. One of the nicest side effects to milling in house is the interest generated by our staff. Of course, some people couldn't care less, but there are those that might have thought I was crazy at first. Not anymore. I can guarantee that there are a handful of bakers on our team that wouldn't think twice about adding a mill to their own bakery if they were to ever venture out on their own. Once you do it, it becomes what you do. There are no other options.

# MULTIGRAIN LOAF

YIELD: 3 LOAVES, OR 2 LARGE LOAVES / ACTIVE TIME: 1 HOUR / TOTAL TIME: 24 HOURS

Our multigrain bread has fresh stone-milled whole rye and wheat. The combination of whole grains with cracked grains and seeds has made it a customer favorite for 17 years!
—*Jim Williams, Seven Stars Bakery*

## DAY 1

1 Begin by making both of your sourdough cultures (levain and rye starter). In separate bowls, mix their respective ingredients until incorporated, then leave to ferment for 12–16 hours at room temperature (ideally 70°F). They can be doubled or tripled for ease of use—just discard whatever you don't need.

2 For your soaker, add water to grains and seeds, mix well and leave overnight.

## DAY 2

3 It's time to make your dough. Mix all ingredients except rye starter, levain, and salt in a bowl to incorporation, either by hand or using a mixer. Let rest for 30 minutes.

4 Add rye starter, levain and salt and mix the dough to a point of light development.

5 Bulk fermentation should take 3 hours at 77–80°F. During this time, give the dough 3 folds. Simply take the dough and fold it upon itself several times. Each time, the dough will feel stronger and more resilient.

6 After bulk fermentation, divide the dough into loaves. Give the dough a light pre-shape and rest 30 minutes.

7 Shape into final shapes and proof. The proof should last 3–5 hours, depending on the temperature and humidity in your home kitchen.

8 Preheat a cast iron Dutch oven, with the lid, in your oven. Turn heat up as hot as it will go.

9 Once proofed, lightly insert your proofed dough into the Dutch oven, score it, put the lid on, and place it into the oven. After 30 minutes of baking, remove the lid and finish to desired color. Let cool and enjoy.

## INGREDIENTS:

### RYE STARTER

| | |
|---|---|
| 2¾ | ounces whole rye |
| ¼ | cup or 2½ ounces water |
| ¼ | ounce sourdough culture |

### LEVAIN

| | |
|---|---|
| ¼ | cup stone-ground, fresh-milled wheat flour |
| ¼ | cup white all-purpose flour |
| ⅛ | cup water |
| ¼ | ounce sourdough culture |

### SOAKER

| | |
|---|---|
| 2 | ounces cracked wheat |
| 2 | ounces cracked rye |
| 2 | ounces cracked oats |
| 2 | ounces flax seeds |
| ¼ | cup millet |
| ¼ | cup sunflower seeds |
| ⅛ | cup pumpkin seeds |
| 1¾ | cups water |

### DOUGH

| | |
|---|---|
| 3 | cups white all-purpose flour |
| 2⅛ | cups fresh-milled, whole wheat flour |
| 1¼ | cups water |
| 5⅓ | ounces rye starter |
| 5 | ounces levain |
| 1½ | tablespoons honey |
| 1 | tablespoon salt |
| 26⅛ | ounces soaker |

# Amy's Bread

| Hell's Kitchen | The Village | The New York Public Library |
|---|---|---|
| 672 Ninth Avenue | 250 Bleecker Street | 476 5th Avenue (at 42 St) |
| (Between 46th & 47th Streets) | at Leroy Street | New York, NY 10018 |
| New York, NY 10036 | New York, NY 10014 | |
| (212) 977-2670 | (212) 675-7802 | The New York Library for the Performing Arts |
| Chelsea Market | The Pantry by Amy's Bread | 40 Lincoln Center Plaza |
| 75 Ninth Avenue | 672 Ninth Avenue | New York, NY 10023 |
| (Between 15th & 16th Streets) | (Between 46th & 47th Streets) | www.amysbread.com |
| New York, NY 10011 | New York, NY 10036 | |
| (212) 462-4338 | | |

It's hard to open a small business in New York City. It's even harder when that business is a bakery. Long hours, high rent, stiff competition—the life of a New York baker requires constant diligence. But Amy's Bread has persisted, even thrived, for over 25 years. And after a slice of owner Amy Scherber's rye bread, it isn't hard to see why: Amy's is as safe a bet as there is in the city for a beautiful slice or loaf. Her secret? Passion and resolve.

"[In 1992] I wanted to have a small, local bread bakery that served retail customers and wholesale customers such as local restaurants. I found a small space on Ninth Avenue in Hell's Kitchen, got loans from friends and family to start, and opened the business on a low budget without a business partner," Scherber explains. Not the easiest beginning, to say the least. But quality won out in the end. "We have seen so many ups and downs with the economy, snowstorms, power outages, hurricanes, low-carb trends, and gluten-free diets, but we have found our place within our city to survive through all of it."

In this way, Amy's is a distinctly New York bakery—there for the local who is rushing to work, or the tourist who has a few hours to kill before their next event. And as it's spread it roots across the city, its name has become synonymous with chewy, crunchy bread you can always count on. "Local bakeries in NY provide a friendly place for people to get a treat and take a moment to relax during the crazy, busy days we have. Walking down the street, riding the subway, dealing with the noise and the bustle, all become tiring after a while, but going to a bakery for an excellent coffee and delicious treat provide that respite from the stresses of daily life."

And while every bakery must be reliable, in New York, it's a zero-sum game. There is perhaps no greater compliment, then, than to simply say that Amy's has existed for 25 years for a reason. Whether looking for a sandwich, pastry, or a fresh loaf for your next dinner party, you can always count on Amy's to deliver.

# IN HER OWN WORDS:
## AMY SCHERBER

*How and when did you get your start baking?*

I found my passion for baking when I was in culinary school. On weekends I helped one of my chef instructors with freelance catering, and when it came to making pies and desserts for his events, I fell in love. I tried to get an externship in pastry at Bouley (in NYC) right after culinary school, but I landed on the savory side of the line. It took nearly two years to make my way back to the pastry kitchen, and I have been baking ever since.

*Who inspired you to bake? Who inspires you now?*

Both of my grandmothers and my mom were good bakers, and my dad worked for Pillsbury for 35 years. Pillsbury Bake-off recipes and new products were always the topic of conversation at our house! After working in pastry at Bouley, I realized that I wanted to be a bread baker. The most inspiring bread lessons I ever had were at the boulangerie school in Aurillac, France. The classes were taught by MOFs and geared to professional bakers from the Bread Bakers Guild of America. The instructors were incredible, so skilled in all aspects of bread making. It was a joy to watch them shape loaves and work with bread dough. And their bread smelled and tasted delicious. Today I get inspired by visiting bakeries in my travels in the United States and Europe. There is always something new to try.

*Amy's is a proper New York bakery. How have you tried to maintain your relationship with the local neighborhoods?*

For us, being a local neighborhood bakery has always been a top priority. I have lived near my bakery in Hell's Kitchen since we opened in 1992, and I know our café is a comfortable place for many people from the neighborhood to meet with friends or work associates. In all our locations we try to take special care of our local "regulars," we make donations to our neighborhood schools and local organizations, and we take pride in being members of our communities. We also think of the Broadway community as our neighbors and are lucky to bake cakes for many casts of Broadway shows! In Chelsea Market all the businesses are a community under one roof, and that is also a unique kind of neighborhood in a busy part of the city.

*What is your golden rule(s) of baking?*

Make the best bread you can by taking care of the details, never cutting corners on ingredients or time. It takes time to make excellent bread and good bread cannot be rushed.

*What does Amy's represent to you?*

Amy's Bread is a local business that takes care of its customers and its employees, while making the best breads, pastries, and savory foods we can make. For 25 years we have cared about people and products, and that commitment to caring is what it's all about for me.

*What is your favorite thing to bake? Why? Least favorite thing to bake? Why?*

I love to bake crusty, grainy, freeform whole wheat loaves. The aroma and taste are so satisfying, and getting the fermentation right is a good challenge. My least favorite thing to bake is soft white bread. It reminds me of industrial bakeries that make bread without any health benefits, and what's the point of eating it?

*How hard was it to get Amy's off the ground?*

I started Amy's Bread in June of 1992, 25 years ago. I wanted to have a small, local bread bakery that served retail customers and wholesale customers such as local restaurants. I found a small space on Ninth Avenue in Hell's Kitchen, got loans from friends and family to start, and opened the business on a low budget without a business partner. It took hard work and time to get it off the ground, but today my husband, Troy Rohne, runs the bakery with me. He is the VP and Director of Sales. It's great to work together to make it a success. We still have many employees that have been with us anywhere from 15 to 25 years, and our long-term staff help to keep our products consistent. They also take pride in being a part of the company for such a long time.

*What are your most popular items?*

Some of our most popular products are crusty white breads such as French Baguettes and Organic Rustic Italian loaves, Chocolate Sourdough bread twists, Semolina Raisin and Fennel Bread, Oat Scones and Cherry Cream Scones, Black and White Cake, Pecan Sticky Buns.

*Where do you get your tools/materials? What non-essential items should every baker have?*

We buy our ingredients from local vendors and some of our flour is grown and milled in upstate NY. We buy our tools on restaurant equipment websites and Amazon. All bakers need a good scale to measure ingredients in grams. I think a nice sturdy lame handle that can be used with a double-edge razor blade is the best way to score bread. And one must always have a good serrated knife to cut the bread after all the work is done!

*What book(s) go on your required reading list for bakers?*

A book I really like is *Bread: A Baker's Book of Techniques* and Recipes by Jeffrey Hamelman. You can pick it up and use any recipe without worrying about whether it will work. All the recipes and techniques are well tested and work great. For an entry-level baker I recommend *One Dough, Ten Breads: Making Great Bread by Hand,* by Sarah Black. It's a step-by-step guide to making all kinds of bread, building on one technique after another. It's a great way to learn! And of course Amy's Bread is an excellent resource for any bread baker. It demystifies how to use starters to make your bread, and it is clear and easy to use.

*What outlets/periodicals/newspapers do you read or consult regularly, if any?*

King Arthur Flour has a cool magazine called *Sift* that comes out two times per year. I love the recipes and photos. I look at *Bon Appetit, Food & Wine, Martha Stewart Living*

and *Edible Manhattan* to see what they are writing about, and I like *Bake* magazine which is a professional trade magazine. I always enjoy reading the Wednesday food section of *The New York Times. Eater* is another good source for news about the food world.

*Tell me about your most memorable collaboration(s) with another chef.*

Several years ago, I worked together with Chef Ed Brown who, at that time, was the chef at Sea Grill at Rockefeller Center. He always wanted new and different breads for his bread service and over the course of a couple of years, he suggested several new breads that he would like to try. He would give me a general request such as "green olive bread" and I would work on it until I had samples for him, then he would make further suggestions until it was just right. Through that process we came up with four really good breads that have been part of our repertoire for years.

*Brag about yourself a bit. What are your highest achievements and/or proudest moments as a chef?*

Starting a business in NYC and staying in business for 25 years is something I am very proud of! We have seen so many ups and downs with the economy, snowstorms, power outages, hurricanes, low-carb trends, gluten-free diets, but we have found our place within our city to survive and thrive through all of these times. The people that have worked with me over the years have all contributed to our success, and the collective energy and satisfaction from working together is also very gratifying.

*Where did you learn to bake?*

I spent a few months in France working in three bakeries. After watching the bakers there, I came back to New York and taught myself to bake using the bread books I had. I tested my breads on customers while I worked at Mondrian restaurant. I made all the bread and worked pastry service at night. Then I started Amy's Bread and learned even more on the fly. I continue to take courses taught by amazing bakers who are part of the Bread Bakers Guild of America. In my opinion, that is the best place to learn how to bake bread.

# BIGA (SPONGE) STARTER

YIELD: 1¼ CUPS

**INGREDIENTS:**

- ¾ cup + 2 tablespoons very warm water (105–115°F)
- ⅛ teaspoon active dry yeast
- 1½ cups + 2 tablespoons unbleached all-purpose flour

1 Mix all the ingredients together in a medium bowl and stir vigorously with a wooden spoon for 2 to 3 minutes, until a smooth, somewhat elastic batter has formed. The batter will be very stiff; it gets softer and more elastic after it has proofed. You may find it easier to mix the sponge using an electric mixer, with a paddle or a dough hook, on medium speed for 1 to 2 minutes. Scrape the sponge into a 2-quart clear plastic container and cover with plastic wrap.

2 At this point you have two options:

1) If you plan to make your dough later that same day, let the sponge rest at room temperature until it has risen to the point where it just begins to collapse. This will take 6 to 8 hours, depending on the temperature of the sponge, the temperature of the room, and the strength of the yeast. The sponge will triple in volume and small dents and folds will begin to appear in the top as it reaches its peak and then begins to deflate. The sponge is now in perfect condition to be used in dough. It's best if you have already weighed or measured out all of your other recipe ingredients before the sponge reaches this point so you can use it before it collapses too much.

2) If you're not planning to make your dough until the next day or the day after, put the covered sponge in the refrigerator and let it rise there for at least 14 hours before taking it out to use in a recipe. Be sure to compensate for the cold temperature of the starter by using warm water (85–90°F) in the dough instead of the cool water specified in the recipe. Or let the starter sit out, covered, until it reaches room temperature. This may take several hours, but be careful not to let it collapse too much before use.

# COARSE-GRAINED WHOLE WHEAT
## *with* TOASTED WALNUTS

YIELD: 2 1-POUND LOAVES / ACTIVE TIME: 3 HOURS / TOTAL TIME: 16–20 HOURS

*Made with a Biga starter (see page 118)*

I developed this recipe years ago with a goal of creating a crunchy, earthy bread with a deep walnut taste to complement rich cheese and charcuterie. The bread is great served lightly toasted to enhance its nuttiness. Refrigerate this dough overnight to intensify its walnut flavor and allow the walnut skins to impart a slightly purple color upon the dough.

—*Amy's Bread*

## INGREDIENTS:

¼ cup very warm water (105–115°F)

¾ teaspoon active dry yeast

1¾ cups whole wheat flour

⅞ cup unbleached bread flour

3 tablespoons medium yellow cornmeal, plus extra for sprinkling

1 tablespoon kosher salt

1 cup water (75°F)

1 cup biga starter (see page 118)

1 tablespoon honey

1 tablespoon walnut oil

1½ cups walnut pieces, toasted

½ cup cooked wheat berries

## DAY 1

1 Place the yeast and warm water in a medium bowl and stir with a fork to dissolve the yeast. Allow to stand for about 3 minutes.

2 Whisk the whole wheat flour, unbleached flour, cornmeal, and salt together in a medium bowl. Set aside.

3 Add the biga starter, cooler water, honey, and oil to the yeast mixture. Mix the ingredients with your fingers for 1 to 2 minutes, just to break up the sponge. The mixture should look milky and be slightly foamy. Add the flour mixture and stir with your fingers to incorporate the flour, scraping the sides of the bowl and folding the dough over itself until it gathers into a shaggy mass.

4 Move the dough to a lightly floured surface and knead for 5 to 7 minutes, until it becomes supple and elastic. If the dough seems too stiff and hard to knead, add additional cool water 1 tablespoon at a time until you get a malleable dough. Shape the dough into a loose ball and let it rest, covered with plastic wrap, on your work surface for 20 minutes.

5 Combine the walnuts and wheat berries in a small bowl. Set aside.

6 Flatten the dough and stretch it gently with your fingers to form a rectangle about 1 inch thick. Spread the walnuts and wheat berries evenly over the dough. Fold the whole mass into an envelope and knead it gently until the nuts and berries are well distributed, about 2 to 3 minutes. If the dough resists, let it rest for 5 minutes and then continue kneading it.

7 Shape the dough into a loose ball and place it in a lightly oiled bowl, along with any loose nuts and berries. Turn the dough to coat with oil and cover the bowl tightly with oiled plastic wrap. Let the dough rise at room temperature for 1 hour, or until it looks slightly puffy but has not doubled in size.

8 Push the dough down to de-gas it. Refrigerate the dough overnight to intensify the walnut flavor.

## DAY 2

9 Remove the dough from the refrigerator and allow it to rise at room temperature for 2 hours.

10 Gently remove the dough from the bowl and place it on a lightly floured work surface, pressing in any loose nuts and wheat berries. Divide it into 2 equal pieces and shape each piece tightly into a boule. Dust a baking peel or the back of a baking sheet generously with coarse cornmeal or a sheet of parchment paper. Place the loaves on the cornmeal or parchment, seam side–down, leaving several inches between them so they won't grow into each other as they rise. Cover with oiled plastic wrap and allow to rise for 2 to 3 hours, or until they have doubled in size (to test, press a finger lightly into the dough will leave an indentation).

11 30 minutes before baking, preheat the oven to 450°F. Place a baking stone in the oven to preheat and place an empty water pan directly below the stone.

12 When the loaves have doubled, dust with flour and cut a shallow X on top of each one with a very sharp knife. Gently slide the loaves onto the stone. Quickly pour 1 cup of very hot water into the water pan and immediately shut the oven door. After 1 minute, using a plant sprayer, mist the loaves quickly 6 to 8 times, then shut the oven door. Repeat the misting procedure 1 minute later.

13 Bake for 20 minutes, then reduce the oven temperature to 400°F and bake for 15 to 20 minutes longer, until the loaves sound hollow when tapped on the bottom. Transfer the loaves to a rack and allow to cool before serving. This bread freezes well, wrapped tightly in aluminum foil and a heavy-duty plastic freezer bag.

### COOKING WHEAT BERRIES

To save time, you can cook the wheat berries a day ahead. Place the berries in a saucepan with water to cover them by at least 1 inch, cover, and bring to a boil. Reduce the heat to low and cook until they're plump, 30 to 40 minutes. Let the berries cool, then drain, saving the cooking liquid to use as part of the water called for in the recipe. Refrigerate in an airtight container if you don't plan to use them immediately.

Wheat berries (and rye berries) triple in volume when they are cooked. To determine how many dry berries you need to cook, simply divide the measured amount in the recipe by 3 (e.g., if the recipe calls for ¾ cup of cooked berries, you need to cook about ¼ cup of dry ones).

# PUMPERNICKEL

YIELDS: 1 BIG LOAF / ACTIVE TIME: 30 MINUTES / TOTAL TIME: 4 HOURS PLUS GRAINS SOAKING AND STARTER BUILD

A traditional dark rye bread from the North Western German region Westphalia. It is based on rye sourdough starter and includes whole rye berries, so the process needs to be started the evening before the baking day.

1 Combine all ingredients with a spoon, adding the salt last.

2 Grease a ½-gallon loaf pan (best if with a lid) and pour the dough in the pan.

3 Let rest, covered, for 3½ hours.

4 Towards the end of the proofing, preheat the oven to 320°F.

5 Bake for 2½ hours.

6 Let cool for several hours before slicing.

### INGREDIENTS:

14 oz (400 g) dark rye flour

11.8 oz (350 g) rye sourdough starter (see page 59)

5.3 oz (150 g) rye berries, soaked in water overnight, boiled for ½ hour and drained

⅗ cup (150 g) water

⅕ cup (50 g) molasses

2 tsp (about 11½ g) salt

# Polestar Hearth

535 Woolwich Street
Guelph, Ontario N1H 3X9
Canada
(519) 265-4300
www.polestarhearth.com

Like many bakers, Polestar Hearth's Jesse Merrill didn't find his calling until later in life. "My education and background was in stringed instrument construction and repair, and I had a wonderful career in one of North America's premier vintage guitar shops. Eventually, I had a revelation that what I really wanted to do with my hands was work that maintained that same caliber of craftsmanship, but served my community directly, producing something so vital that it would affect the lives of folks of all demographics." At the time, Merrill had a home and family of his own, including a small brick oven he'd built himself in the backyard. So, he took a risk. He quit his job. "Soon after that teensy beginning, we bought a house with a small garage, which I was able to convert into a prep kitchen. I built a big brick oven in the backyard, and Polestar Hearth was born in earnest."

Things have changed significantly since then. While the team is still small, the output has increased exponentially. In addition to keeping his own retail hours, Merrill delivers bread to local retailers all week long. This process has helped Polestar gain some notoriety, widening its clientele to include people from all over the world. Merrill recounts a particular example in discussing his proudest moment: "Early on, an elderly European gentleman, dressed in a fine tweed suit, stopped me on delivery to tell me his story. With a hand holding my arm firmly, his eyes moist, he wanted me to know that he had spent 17 years in Canada, homesick the whole time until his wife had brought home a loaf of my bread the week before. 'Now it is ok; I can live here happily the rest of my life,

thanks to you!' What more resounding accolade could I get?"

Though it is not a Polish bakery ("Polestar" refers to the North Star, not Polish culture as often assumed), the bakery has made an impression on much of Ontario's European community—a testament to its authenticity and attention to detail. Another key factor in Polestar Hearth's popularity? The BreadShare. "This was a concept I dreamed up early on, based of course on Community Supported Agriculture. The first stumbling block in my professional baking career was learning that the local Farmer's Market didn't have room for me. So, I called up all my friends and asked them to buy a dozen loaves of bread before I made them. I was practically giving the stuff away, trying to buy myself a business. Before I knew it, I had 13 customers, and I had to figure out how to make 13 loaves! Word got out, and in its prime the Polestar BreadShare had hundreds of subscribers. It went through different phases as we grew. First delivered door to door by kids with wagons–eventually we had to switch it around and have the customers come to us." The idea reinforced what Merrill had set out to do in the first place: use his hands to better the community.

Despite its changing sales policies, the constant at Polestar is its bread. Crunchy and golden brown, it is always meticulously crafted with starters that have fermented for multiple days. The result is a bread bakery that withstands any critical eye—from a first-timer to someone whose baking legacy dates back to the old country.

## IN HIS OWN WORDS: JESSE MERRILL

*Who inspired you to bake? Who inspires you now?*

That was the early days of the internet, before there were rock star bakers in North America. I pored over every word in Daniel Wing's *Bread Builders*, eked out any little shred of information hidden between the lines of his chapter on Chad Robertson long before *Tartine Bread* was ever published. Left no stone unturned! These days some of my best inspiration comes from my bread brother Don Guerra of Barrio Bread, a giant among men, to be sure! And I have so many dear friends pushing me forward with new artistic ideas daily via social media. I'd love to name them all, but it would be hard to do. We are living in the golden age of bread, for sure!

*What is your golden rule for bakers?*

I'm in this to learn something from the bread, from the dough or the flour, every day. Don't ever plateau; don't get complacent. The bread can challenge you to greatness if you listen to what it has to teach you every day.

*What does Polestar Hearth represent to you?*

Polestar Hearth is always evolving. It's grown and changed for ten years in many unforeseen ways. What is important to me is that it is the answer to the biggest part of my creative energies—the part of me that would otherwise be drawing or sculpting or making music.

*What is your favorite thing to bake? Why?*

Bread! Long fermentation sourdough bread, to be specific. I get a real kick out of using heritage grains, especially when they have a cool backstory. We get a lot of our flour from an Amish mill, and I just love knowing that that grain was grown in clean fields using only horsepower and the sweat of hard-working folks who hold some of the last living knowledge of how our civilization was born.

*What is your most popular item?*

Our spelt bread is a total revelation to many folks. It's completely unlike the dry, sawdust-y, pallid loaves well-intentioned folks have been choking down since the anti-gluten war began. Our biggest seller is a light wheat bread packed with toasted seeds that we call SuperSeed.

*What non-essential items should every baker have?*

A French rolling pin, slightly fatter in the middle. This is one of the secrets to making our beautiful Couronne loaves (check 'em out on Instagram). And a simple homemade lame for scoring. Mine is whittled from a disposable chopstick from a Thai restaurant. Change your blades often. If you care about beautiful scoring (and I really do), don't be afraid to throw out the razor blade whenever you start to feel the slightest resistance to your cut. It should be like painting with an artist's brush, not hacking at a tomato with a crummy kitchen knife!

*Where did you learn to bake?*

Right in my own back yard!

*Can you talk a bit about the local grains you use? Where do you primarily get your ingredients, and why is it so important you keep things local?*

We live in the heart of Ontario, in a city surrounded by farmland, some of which has grown grain for more than 200 years. Waves of immigrants came to this area starting in the late 1700's looking for freedom and a self-sustaining livelihood. So, in one very direct way, we owe it to our ancestors to carry this self-reliance forward. To be quite honest, I don't get too hung up in historical varieties and the hype that surrounds them. We use a bit of Red Fife, but we use other wheats too, leaving varietal choices up to our Amish friends who horse farm and stone mill a good portion of the wheat and spelt we use. It's an incredibly grounding feeling to stand in a field of spelt taller than a man, and look out between the weaving stalks to watch the harnessed horses work the land, especially if you know you can take that same grain home and make a truly exceptional bread from it.

It isn't easy using local grains; some fields just don't produce well; some years are bad across the board. Yes, we do use a lot of organic wheat imported from the Canadian Prairies. It helps us keep things consistent. But to feed our belief in local economy, small farms, small business and truly great food, we use many tonnes of local flour milled for us by three local millers. We use a custom cracked rye and purple and yellow corn, and we use hard and soft wheat flours, kamut flour, spelt flours, and malted barley and rye from our local mills. And all those grains are grown right around here, within an hour and a half drive of the bakery.

# WALNUT SPELT BREAD

YIELD: 2 BIG PAN LOAVES / ACTIVE TIME: 30 MINUTES / TOTAL TIME: 16–24 HOURS

It took many years to develop this bread, and we consider it to be one of our most remarkable achievements at Polestar Hearth. Moist, chewy, and with a delectably earthy sense of terroir, this bread can be served to discerning guests with fine cheese or dressed down for your morning toast. You can also substitute soaked Thompson raisins or apricots for the walnuts, or leave out the additions altogether. We bake the plain loaves ten at a time in a pinewood frame—an ancient Scottish technique—with our signature star stenciled on the boldly baked crust. It's a head-turner!
—*Jesse Merrill of Polestar Hearth Bread*

1 Lightly stir soaker ingredients together. These grains are best soaked for at least 2 and not more than 5 hours ahead of mixing the dough. If you are pressed for time, use hot tap water and cool the mixture in the fridge for 15 minutes.

2 Mix soaker, water, and levain together until even.

3 Add flour and combine. The dough will be very wet, just a touch drier than a nice cornbread batter. Let sit (autolyse) for ½ hour.

4 Add salt and 2 tablespoons water and mix thoroughly. Add walnuts or soaked, drained fruit. You may divide the dough in half at this point and make two variations, adjusting the additions to your taste.

5 Leave dough in a covered container for 4 to 6 hours, folding gently at 1-hour intervals. Dough should expand to 1 ½ times its original volume. Don't let it go too far! Slow it down in the fridge if necessary—spelt generally ferments much faster than wheat doughs.

6 Turn the dough out onto a well rice- or wheat-floured table, divide in half and shape loosely into a log. Roll log in flour and quickly turn into oiled pan, seam side–down.

7 Refrigerate overnight, covered with plastic. The middle of the loaf should rise just about as high as the pan sides.

8 Optional: Using rice flour, stencil the top of the loaf with a special design you've cut into cereal box cardboard or a yogurt container lid. Objects such as scissors, leaves, flowers, and lace also make interesting stencils.

## INGREDIENTS:

### SOAKER:

- ½ cup cracked rye
- ¼ cup brown flaxseed
- 1 cup water, room temperature

### DOUGH:

- Grain soaker
- ⅔ cup sourdough starter, ripe but still sweet (a wheat-based levain is our go-to)
- 2 cups filtered water, room temperature
- 4⅓ cups light spelt flour
- ½ cup whole spelt flour
- ½ cup kamut flour
- 1 tablespoon sea salt
- 1⅓ cups walnuts

Like most artisan bakeries, our focus is on hearth-style loaves. However, in working with spelt, we've found that the most consistently great results are easier to obtain in a pan loaf. There's no shame in making pan bread if it's beautiful and delicious! If you have good wet dough–shaping abilities, by all means make a boule and bake it in a cloche. Our two best tips from working with spelt are to avoid overproofing the dough (it moves much faster than wheat!) and to bake it very hot. In our stone deck oven, we bake spelt at 550°F!

9  Preheat your oven to 500°F. Yup, stinking hot! Steam is not absolutely necessary for a pan loaf, but if you have a favorite steaming technique (such as a pan of boiling water in the bottom of the oven), it can help the crust color and oven spring. Bake for 35 minutes, remove from heat, and let cool for 10 minutes in pan before turning out.

# *Boulangerie, a Proper Bakery*

5 Nasons Court #12
Kennebunk, ME 04043
(207) 502-7112
www.aproperbakery.com

One could be forgiven for not guessing that one of the world's tastiest croissants can be found in Kennebunk, Maine. One could even be forgiven for treating this news with a fair dose of skepticism—after all, shouldn't the finest French pastries be in France? With respect to the many wonderful patisseries across the pond, the croissant at Boulangerie, a Proper Bakery can stand up to the best of them. And the credit goes to owners Amy and Zachary Tyson, and head baker Bre Jaworowski.

The Tysons have operated Boulangerie for over ten years—ever since they purchased the big red barn they currently operate from. Amy says, "Zachary and I worked on private motor yachts. We came to Maine for work, fell in love with Kennebunk, and purchased a home. We continued to work on yachts for a number of years, but we were always looking for our next step—off boats. There was a 'bakery café' in town; when it closed, it made me realize that I really wanted a bakery in town. And, my father always said, 'If you want something done, you have to do it yourself.' So, we started planning and saving and, five years later, we opened Boulangerie." Zachary adds, "Anywhere you go, the bakery is the happiest place in town." At Boulangerie, that's certainly true.

Theirs is a tried and true method: Amy is the "purist," Zachary the "engineer." She handles the spirit of the bread as he tinkers with the formulas. And Jaworowski makes everything go. Many of the recipes have come from Bre herself, tested over a period of months before she deems them acceptable to sell. "The ciabatta recipe we use today took me months to develop," says Jaworowski. "We knew we wanted a high-hydration dough but struggled to find the balance between hydration and strength." No matter where each recipe comes from, all the recipes Boulangerie uses have been tinkered with by the trio in charge to work with their bake schedule.

For many Boulangerie patrons, though, it all comes back to the croissant. Their most popular item by far, they often sell out early, to everyone's dismay. As Amy says, "Making our croissants is a four-day process, so it is difficult to whip up another batch as customers often ask us to do!" Still, baking at Boulangerie is a labor of love, even when things get a little intense. "I'm proud to give other bakers a chance to do their thing and produce beautiful, cared-for products. To be able to support some good people and give them a livelihood feels pretty amazing," says Zachary. Their proudest achievement? Amy puts it simply: "returning customers and a line out the door!"

## IN THEIR OWN WORDS:

## AMY AND ZACHARY TYSON
## AND BRE JAWOROWSKI

*How and when did you get your start baking?*

Amy: As a child, I watched cooking shows on PBS. Julia, Jacques, and *Great Chefs of the World*.

Zachary: "You see, there's this girl"—to impress a lady.

Bre: My love for baking actually started from television. During high school, I watched a lot of Food Network and at that time shows like *Ace of Cakes* and *Cake Wars* were the popular shows. I remember watching those shows and thinking how amazing those works of art were and how much patience those bakers must have had. Cakes were what first got me interested in baking.

*Who inspired you to bake? Who inspires you now?*

Amy: I suppose the celebrity chefs of PBS inspired me to bake. I jotted down a recipe for a French loaf while watching TV, baked it (and forgot the salt) and recognized the taste 15 years later in Florence while eating Pane Toscana—which is bread made without salt. It tastes quite good with fresh olive oil drizzled on it and sea salt sprinkled over it. My loaf many years prior was quite a disappointment.

Zachary: My most beautiful wife and loving partner, Amy.

Bre: My Aunt Joy is the person who ignited the fire first for my passion of baking. No one in my family baked besides her, and she seemed to have her own art form to it. She would make cookies, pies and my ultimate favorite, Chrusciki, which is a very thin and crispy Polish fried dough. My family inspires me now to continue baking.

*What is your golden rule(s) of baking?*

Amy: Trust your senses. Feel, smell, touch, sound, and experience serve you better than thermometers and timers.

Zachary: Don't F it up. Everything you do matters!

Bre: Patience. Every step in bread-baking requires patience and an understanding. You must not try to rush the process and you must go by feel, not time. You must respect what the dough requires.

*What does Boulangerie represent to you?*

Amy: My child—beautiful, difficult, expensive, and full of love.

Zachary: A culmination of a vision that functions well from the studs out. I saw it built; I trained the people in it. I know it is a place where I would be happy to spend my money with confidence that I'll be getting a quality product.

*What is your favorite thing to bake? Why? Least favorite thing to bake? Why?*

Amy: My favorite thing to bake is sourdough—I love the blisters and the rise. My least favorite is the Boulangerie Brownie, which is essentially a flourless chocolate cake. They smell amazing, but they are so moist that it is hard to tell when they are finished.

Zachary: My favorite is challah—the braid is challenging, and when done successfully it is quite satisfying. Least favorite: Ciabatta. Sticky.

Bre: French Baguettes are what truly drive my passion to bake. I believe a truly great baguette is hard to come by and even harder to create. There are so many aspects to a good baguette, such as crust, crumb, and scoring marks (also called "ears"), that it is easily the most judged item on a bakery's list. It has become a personal goal of mine to create one perfect French baguette in my career.

I honestly do not have a least favorite thing to bake. I do however have a least favorite item to finish and that would be cakes. The patience required to beautifully decorate a cake and beautifully hand craft a loaf of bread could not be any more different from one another. I do not have the patience and skill to finish cakes that they deserve.

*What are your most popular items?*

Amy: Croissants. Making our croissants is a four-day process, so it is difficult to whip up another batch as customers often ask us to do.

*Where do you get your tools/materials?*

Amy: San Francisco Baking Institute (SFBI), King Arthur Flour (KAF), and Maine Grains.

*What non-essential items should every baker have?*

Good shoes and/or good floor mats (sky mat, anti-fatigue mat).

*What book(s) go on your required reading list for bakers?*

Amy: *Bread* by Hamelman. *Professional Baking* by Gisslen. *Tartine* by Chad Robertson (he makes sourdough approachable).

Zachary: *Bread Science* by Emily Buehler.

Bre: *Tartine*, Book 3. This is a beautifully photographed and well-composed book of ancient grains and unique ingredients that expose you to a whole new world of flours that go way beyond white and wheat.

*What outlets/periodicals/newspapers do you read or consult regularly, if any?*

Bre: For answers to questions, recipes or advice, I turn to the Bread Bakers Guild of America. They have a wonderful database of recipes available for members and their member list contains bakers from all walks of life from all over the world. It is a wonderful community of like-minded people coming together to help one another.

Amy: If there are any good articles in the newspapers, our customers bring them to us!

*Tell me about your most memorable collaboration(s) with another chef.*

Amy: We created a bread for a restaurant that no one on my team had ever tried: Cristal bread. It is a Spanish version of ciabatta, but lighter, crisper, and made with plenty of olive oil. We had to incorporate different flours to balance a high hydration, and also give it enough folds and various stages to develop the gluten. The chef was very pleased and said it was like the real thing.

Zachary: Pulled Pork Focaccia using a local food truck's (Texas Grace) pulled pork.

*Do you follow any cooking shows or chefs? If so, which is your favorite?*

Amy: *Iron Chef* is fun. I don't watch much TV, but *The Great British Baking Show* is a good laugh!

Zachary: Anthony Bourdain.

*Where did you learn to cook? Please tell me about your education and/or apprenticeships.*

Amy: I worked at Eatery in NYC in pastry, then Spago in Las Vegas where I became the head of the Bread Department. We produced the bread for all of Wolfgang Puck's properties in Vegas—Spago, Postrio, and Chinois.

After working at Spago, I attended the Cordon Bleu in London. Zachary and I both attended specialized courses in hearth breads, sourdoughs, and croissants at both the International Culinary Center in NYC and King Arthur Flour Baking Education Center in Vermont.

Zachary: International Culinary Center, and King Arthur Flour. Trial and Error. Not my mother!

Bre: I received a Bachelor's Degree in Bak-

ing and Pastry Arts from Johnson and Wales University in Providence, RI. Through my schooling I interned at a high-end resort in Idaho and a small family-owned resort on St. Kitts in the Caribbean. The program at Johnson and Wales is truly wonderful, and exposes you to all aspects of baking, from bread to cakes to showpieces to plated desserts. It is thanks to Johnson and Wales and a few of my chef instructors that I got exposed to bread and discovered my life's passion.

# SPROUTED SPELT LOAF

YIELD: 1 LOAF / ACTIVE TIME: 2 HOURS / TOTAL TIME: 96 HOURS

This technique was developed and refined by Raymond Calvel, author of the seminal *Le Gout du Pain* (*The Taste of Bread*), and bread guru to Julia Child. These steps require strict timing—though the specific times can change, try to keep the time intervals as close to the suggested times as possible!
—*Amy and Zachary Tyson, Boulangerie*

## DAY 1

At 10 a.m., soak the spelt berries in cold water. Keep completely covered.

At 3 p.m., drain the berries. Rinse, toss, and aerate. Place in a large sieve and cover with cloth.

## DAY 2

At 4 a.m., rinse, toss, and aerate the berries. Cover.
At 3 p.m., rinse, toss, and aerate the berries. Cover.

## DAY 3

At 4 a.m., rinse, toss, and aerate the berries. Cover.
At 3 p.m., rinse, toss, and aerate the berries. Cover.
Make your spelt culture with an existing sourdough culture. Mix ingredients by hand, cover, and set aside overnight.

### INGREDIENTS:

**SPELT BERRIES**

| | |
|---|---|
| 1 | cup spelt berries |
| | Water for rinsing, as needed |

**SPELT CULTURE**

| | |
|---|---|
| ½ | cup wheat flour |
| ½ | cup spelt flour |
| ¼ | cup water |
| 2 | tablespoons sourdough culture |

**FINAL DOUGH**

| | |
|---|---|
| 3 | cups water, scantly poured |
| 1 | cup spelt culture |
| 3¾ | cups "HE" spelt flour |
| 2¼ | cups "HE" wheat flour |
| 1 | cup sprouted spelt berries |
| 1 | tablespoon + ½ teaspoon salt |

## WHAT IS AUTOLYSE?

The Greek word "autolysis," which translates literally to "self-splitting," is used in biology to describe the process of a cell digesting its own enzymes. The French cognate "autolyse" carries the same meaning, used primarily in baking to refer to the process wherein enzymes in flour (amylase and protease) begin to break down the starch and protein in the flour. The starch gets converted to sugar, and the protein gets reformed as gluten.

When you knead dough, you also oxidize it (expose it to oxygen). Over-oxidized (or, over-kneaded) dough usually causes your finished bread to lose color and flavor. By giving the mixed flour and water time to go through autolysis on their own, you achieve the same result, but without any of the unpleasant effects of oxidation!

## DAY 4: MAKING YOUR DOUGH

By now, your berries should have sprouted, so it's time to make your dough! Mix water, culture and flours in a mixer for 2 minutes on low speed—just until combined. Autolyse for 30 minutes, then add salt.

Mix for 3 minutes on low speed, then 2 minutes on medium speed.

Drop to low speed and add sprouted berries. Mix until incorporated.

Rest in a lightly oiled bowl for 1 hour, then fold. Rest an additional hour and fold again. After one last hour of rest, cut and pre-shape the dough into a bowl. Cover with a cloth and let rest for 20 minutes.

Shape into a bowl and place seam side–up in a floured basket or bowl lined with a floured linen/towel. Let proof in a warm area for 1 hour.

Preheat your oven to 475°F. Turn out dough onto a peel or tray and score as desired.

Bake at 475°F for 35 minutes, ideally on a stone. Steam the oven at the beginning of the bake using ice cubes on a tray in the oven or spraying a water bottle in the oven.

# Metropolitan Bakery

www.metropolitanbakery.com

Rittenhouse Square
262 South 19th Street
Philadelphia, PA 19103
215.545.6655

Reading Terminal
12th Street and Arch Street
Philadelphia, PA 19107
215.829.9020

Chestnut Hill
8607 Germantown Avenue
Philadelphia, PA 19118
267.766.3989

Metropolitan Café
264 S. 19th Street
Philadelphia, PA 19103
215.545.6655

University City
4013 Walnut Street
Philadelphia, PA 19104
215.222.1492

For Wendy Smith Born and James Barrett, the partnership came easily. While working together at the original White Dog Café in Philadelphia—Wendy as the managing partner and James as the pastry chef—the pair bonded over their shared love of the beautiful breads they'd enjoyed in Europe during their formative. In 1993, though, those loaves were not so easily found in Philadelphia. So, they decided to do something about it, opening their flagship bakery at Rittenhouse Square that same November.

Things have changed considerably in the 25 years since. Born and Barrett's labor of love has become a massive commercial success, found at locations all over Philadelphia and enjoying features in *Gourmet, Bon Appetit, The Oprah Magazine, Zagat*, and the *Today Show*. They've also developed a substantial online store, where they sell cakes, pies, to-go meals, and even their own ice cream to customers nationwide. But in spite of all that, Metropolitan remains a Philly staple first and foremost. "For us, Metropolitan Bakery is about community," says Born. "In addition to all-natural high-quality products (locally sourced whenever possible), we're proud to be part of our customers' daily lives and proud that we've provided job training and skills to thousands of Philadelphians."

It may sound like a platitude, but Born and Barrett practice what they preach. Metropolitan partners with many organizations to help give back to Philadelphia, including schools, environmental sustainability groups, coalitions addressing homelessness and poverty, and local farmers. For this alone, Metropolitan is a bakery worth supporting. But there's a much simpler reason, too: its baked goods. Baguettes, sourdough and multigrain loaves, millet muffins, and sour cherry chocolate chip cookies, all highlight their bestsellers, not to mention their granola, which was voted best in America by Epicurious.com. Even better, they make their own starter, usually referred to as "the chef" in-house. As Barrett says, "At Metro, it's all about the natural starter." This process (which Barrett explains in more detail below) helps create "loaves with rich, crackling, mahogany crusts and nutty, intensely fragrant interiors—the hallmarks of old world bread."

Metropolitan Bakery walks the tightrope of success as well as any bakery in the country, maintaining a local presence in its community while delivering good food to as many people as possible. Whether you're close to Philly or not, this is a bakery you'll want to order from.

~ metro bake
lemon bar
$2.50

# IN THEIR OWN WORDS:

## WENDY SMITH BORN AND JAMES BARRETT

*How and when did you get your start baking?*

James: I first learned about baking from my Grandmother Tucci, who would gather my brothers, sisters, and I in her kitchen. It was from her that I learned the ritual of baking, and how certain recipes evoke a feeling or a memory.

*Who inspired you to bake? Who inspires you now?*

James: I get my inspiration from other chefs, customers, employees, and sometimes the ingredients themselves. Other times, I'll have a craving and the only way to satisfy it is to make something. That's how many Metro favorites, like our award-winning granola,

came to be.

*What is your golden rule of baking?*

James: Always use the best ingredients, locally sourced if possible, and stay true to time-honored techniques. If you take the easy way out, you can taste it.

*What is your favorite thing to bake? Why?*

James: My favorite thing to bake is our *miche*. It takes almost *60* hours to produce from start to finish. It is awesome watching the loaves have their final oven spring and slowly bake to a rich dark caramel color. The smell is incredible and complex.

*What are your most popular items?*

Wendy: Our most popular breads are the levain, multigrain, sourdough, French baguette, and, when available, our chocolate cherry bread. We also sell a lot of millet muffins, sour cherry chocolate chip cookies, chocolate layer cake, French berry rolls, and handmade granola. Many of these products are available nationwide via our website.

*Where do you get your tools/materials? What non-essential items should every baker have?*

James: I get my tools from Fante's Kitchen Shop and various professional equipment companies.

*What book(s) go on your required reading list for bakers?*

James: Two great resources are *Advanced Bread and Pastry* by Michel Suas *and How to Bake Bread* by Michel Kalanty.

*What outlets/periodicals/newspapers do you read or consult regularly, if any?*

James: I like Instagram, *The New York Times* Food Section, and the Bread Bakers Guild newsletter.

Wendy: I also read *The New York Times*, plus the *Washington Post* and *Food52*.

*Tell me about your most memorable collaboration(s) with another chef.*

James: I have enjoyed working with Alice Waters, Nancy Silverton, Mark Peel, and Paul Bertolli, to name a few.

*Do you follow any cooking shows or chefs? If so, which is your favorite?*

James: I love PBS and Netflix cooking shows and series.

*Where did you learn to cook? Please tell me about your education and/or apprenticeships.*

James is a trained chef as well as a master baker. He graduated from the Culinary Institute of America, and has studied in Europe at the Ecole Française de Boulangerie d'Aurillac.

*How do you make your starter, "the chef?" How long does this process usually take?*

James: Wild yeasts in the air are allowed to feed on a mixture of flour, water and catalysts such as mashed bananas, raisins or Concord grapes. For two weeks, the mixture is fed a steady diet of breakfast, lunch, and dinner, allowing it to ferment and multiply. Eventually, it becomes the bubbly, pleasantly sour-smelling natural starter called the "chef." Then, over two days, the dough will be mixed, hand-shaped, and signed, before it's left to rise in rye-dusted wicker baskets in cool, dark rooms. Only after this "long-slow-cool" rise are the loaves ready to be baked in steam-injected, stone-deck Bongard ovens.

*Where can people find more recipes, or buy products?*

James: Metropolitan Bakery products are available at our three retail shops in the Philadelphia area, and throughout the United States via www.metropolitanbakery.com. Our site also features additional recipes, videos, and information for other retailers.

Baking enthusiasts can also follow us on Twitter at @metrobakes or on Instagram at metrobakesPHL.

# WHOLE WHEAT LEVAIN

A levain is a 3-step refreshment process that begins with a ripe starter. During each refreshment, fresh water and enough bread flour are added to develop a soft dough.
—*Metropolitan Bakery*

## DAY 1 (FIRST REFRESHMENT)

⅓ cup active Whole Wheat Starter (see page 56)

3 tablespoons water (70°F)

½ cup bread flour

1 tablespoon + 1 teaspoon whole wheat flour

1  In a large bowl with a wooden spoon, stir together the starter and water. Add the bread flour and whole wheat flour and stir until a soft dough is formed.

2  Cover the bowl tightly with plastic wrap and let the mixture ferment at room temperature for 12 hours, until doubled in size.

## DAY 2 (SECOND REFRESHMENT)

¾ cup water (70°F)

1 cup + 2 tablespoons bread flour

½ cup whole wheat flour

1  Check to see that the levain has doubled in size then collapsed slightly. In the bowl of a heavy-duty mixer with a dough hook attachment, dissolve the First Refreshment in the water at low speed. Add the bread flour and whole wheat flour and mix until a soft dough is formed—about 2 minutes.

2  Transfer the dough to a lightly oiled bowl; cover the bowl tightly with plastic wrap. Let the dough stand at room temperature for 4 hours, until active but not doubled in size. Refrigerate the dough overnight.

## DAY 3 (THIRD REFRESHMENT)

1 ½ cups water (70°F)

2 ⅓ cups bread flour

1 cup + 1 tablespoon whole wheat flour

1  Check to see that the Second Refreshment has doubled in size then collapsed slightly, then transfer to the bowl of a heavy-duty mixer. With a dough hook attachment at low speed, dissolve the Second Refreshment in the water. Add the bread flour and whole wheat flour. Mix until a soft dough is formed—about 3 minutes, when it is smooth and slightly elastic.

2  Return the dough to the oiled bowl and cover the bowl tightly with plastic wrap. Let the dough stand at room temperature for 4 hours until it begins to rise. Then refrigerate the dough overnight.

## DAY 4

The levain is now ready to use. It should have doubled in size. Before using, let the levain come to room temperature, 1 to 2 hours. After measuring the amount of levain you'll need for a recipe, set aside ⅓ cup, discarding any of the remaining levain. Refrigerate the reserved levain for up to 2 weeks or freeze up to 3 months. Before you use the reserved levain in a recipe, return it to room temperature (thawing it in the refrigerator overnight, if frozen). Repeat the 3-step refreshment process, starting with Day 1 (the ⅓ cup of reserved levain will now replace the whole wheat starter).

# BAKING TIPS

These helpful tips come courtesy of Wendy Smith Born and James Barrett of Metropolitan Bakery (page 138). You may want to save yourself the time and just dog-ear this page now!

## TESTING GLUTEN DEVELOPMENT
Here's how to test for gluten development (or the dough's extendability).

1. Tear off a small piece of kneaded dough. With lightly floured hands, very gently stretch and turn the dough (as if you were shaping a pizza crust) until it becomes sheer enough to see through. The dough should stretch evenly without tearing. If it tears before it is sheer, continue kneading for 2 to 3 minutes to develop the gluten and then test again.

2. Insert an instant-read thermometer into the dough. Wait a few seconds to register the temperature. If the dough does not register 78 to 80°F, return the dough to the mixer and knead 1 minute more.

## CREATING STEAM IN YOUR OVEN
Utilizing steam during the first part of bread-baking helps to soften the exterior crust. This allows for optimum loaf expansion during the final activity of the yeast before it expires. It also gelatinizes the surface of the loaf, creating a shiny finish.

If you don't have a spray bottle to create steam, place a baking pan at least 2 inches deep on the floor of your oven. Preheat the pan along with the baking stone at least 20 minutes before baking. Just before placing the loaf in the oven, very carefully pour lukewarm water into the pan.

## SCORING YOUR LOAVES
Scoring a loaf is the baker's signature. The scoring allows the loaf to expand without bursting wildly in the oven and lends a decorative appearance to the load. Scoring works best using a 3-inch lame to which you attach a double-edge razor blade. Alternatively, a sharp serrated knife may be used.

# WHOLE GRAIN SANDWICH BREAD

YIELD: 2 LOAVES / ACTIVE TIME: 1 HOUR 15 MINUTES / TOTAL TIME: 6 - 15 HOURS

The grains in this bread are toasted so their natural flavor is highly pronounced. The addition of yeast to this whole wheat levain bread helps to lighten the texture, making it adaptable to both sandwiches and toast.

—*Wendy Smith Born and James Barrett of Metropolitan Bakery*

**INGREDIENTS:**

- 1 ¾ cups active **Whole Wheat Levain** (see page 141)
- 1 ¾ cups water (72°F)
- 1 teaspoon active dry yeast
- 2½ cups bread flour, plus extra flour for preparation
- 1¼ cups whole wheat flour
- 1¼ cups (8 ounces) **Toasted Grain Mix** (see page 144)
- 2 tablespoons molasses
- 2 tablespoons honey
- 2 tablespoons grits
- 2 tablespoons cracked wheat
- 2½ teaspoons fine sea salt

1 In the bowl of a heavy-duty mixer, combine the levain, water, and yeast. With a dough hook attachment at low speed, mix to dissolve the levain and the yeast. Add the bread flour, whole wheat flour, grain mix, molasses, honey, grits, and cracked wheat. Mix until the dough forms a shaggy mass, about 3 minutes. Sprinkle the salt over the dough and let rest for 20 minutes.

2 At low speed, mix the salt into the dough for 2 minutes. Increase the speed to medium and knead the dough for 8 to 10 minutes. Test for proper gluten development (see page 142 The dough should be smooth and elastic, but wet to the touch. The temperature should be 78 to 80°F when tested with an instead-read thermometer. Transfer the dough to a lightly oiled bowl or container at least twice its size and cover tightly with plastic wrap. Let rise in a cool, draft-free place until doubled in size, about 2 hours.

3 Lightly brush the bottoms and sides of two 8 ½ by 4 ½-inch pans with safflower oil (or use 2 nonstick loaf pans). Set aside.

4 Turn the dough out onto a lightly floured surface and divide into 2 equal pieces. Flatten 1 piece of dough into a 5 by 7-inch rectangle, with 1 short side facing you. Starting from a short side, roll up the length of the dough, pinching the crease with each rotation. Starting from the left, use the palm of your hand to seal the seam closed. Gently roll the cylinder back and forth until it is even; do not taper the ends. Place the loaf, seam side–down, in a prepared pan (the ends of the loaf should reach the ends of the pan). Repeat the process with the remaining dough.

5 Place the loaf pans on a large baking tray. Cover the pans loosely with plastic wrap. Let rise at room temperature until doubled in size, about 2 hours. (Or refrigerate the loaves to rise slowly overnight or up to 10 hours. The next day, let the loaves come to room temperature to finish rising, approximately 1 hour.

6 Preheat the oven to 400°F. Working quickly, open the oven door and generously spray the entire oven cavity with water

(taking care not to spray the oven lightbulb) to create steam. (See "Creating Steam in Your Oven," page 142.) Uncover the loaves and arrange the baking tray on the center oven rack. Close the oven door. Bake 3 minutes. Open the oven door and spray all around the loaves. Close the oven door. Bake 3 minutes. Repeat spraying the oven walls. Close the oven door. Bake 35–40 minutes, until loaves are dark golden brown. (To test for doneness, remove 1 loaf from a pan. It should sound hollow when tapped on the bottom.) Cool the loaves in the pans on a wire rack for 5 minutes. Remove the loaves from the pans and cool completely on the wire rack. If the loaves are left in the pans to cool, they will become soggy.

# TOASTED GRAIN MIX

**YIELD:** 1 ½ CUPS / **ACTIVE TIME:** 15 MINUTES / **TOTAL TIME:** 15 MINUTES

Preheat the oven to 350°F. In a bowl, combine the grains and seeds. Spread the mixture in an even layer on a baking tray. Bake on the center rack for 12 to 15 minutes, until toasted and golden brown.

**INGREDIENTS:**

¼ cup sesame seeds

¼ cup millet

¼ cup flax seeds

¼ cup sunflower seeds, shelled

¼ cup pumpkin seeds, shelled

¼ cup old-fashioned oats

# SESAME LOAF

**YIELD:** 1 SMALL ROUND / **ACTIVE TIME:** 25 MINUTES / **TOTAL TIME:** 3 HOURS

As you master bread making in the cast-iron Dutch oven, you can experiment in all kinds of ways. If you like toasted sesame seeds, this is a real treat.

—*Dominique DeVito*

**INGREDIENTS:**

| | |
|---|---|
| ¼ | teaspoon instant yeast |
| ¼ | teaspoon sugar |
| 1½ | cups water (110 to 115°F) |
| 1 | teaspoon kosher salt |
| 3 | cups all-purpose flour plus more for kneading and dusting |
| 1 | egg yolk beaten with 1 tablespoon water |
| ½ | cup sesame seeds |

1 Put the yeast and sugar in a measuring cup and add about ½ cup warm water in a drizzle. Hot water will kill the yeast, so it's important that the water be warm without being hot. Cover the measuring cup with plastic wrap and set it aside for about 15 minutes. If the yeast doesn't foam, it is not alive and you'll need to start over.

2 When the yeast is proofed, pour it into a large bowl and add the additional cup of warm water. Stir gently to combine. Add the salt to the flour, and add the flour to the yeast mixture. Stir with a wooden spoon until combined. The dough will be wet and sticky.

3 Put a dusting of flour on a flat surface and lift out the dough. With flour on your hands and more at the ready, begin kneading the dough so that it loses its stickiness. Don't overdo it, and don't use too much flour; just enough that it is more cohesive.

4 Place the dough in a large bowl, cover the bowl with plastic wrap, and allow to rise untouched for at least 1 hour, and up to several hours. On a gently floured surface, turn out the dough and gently punch it down. Put a large piece of parchment paper in the bowl in which the bread was rising before. Return the dough to the bowl on the parchment paper, cover with plastic wrap, and allow to rise again for another 30 minutes or so.

5 While the dough is on its final rise, preheat the oven to 450°F. Put a piece of parchment paper on the bottom of the Dutch oven and put it in with the lid on so it gets hot. When the oven is ready and dough has risen, carefully remove the lid and gently scoop the dough from the bowl into the pot, brush with the egg wash, and sprinkle generously with the sesame seeds. Cover and bake for 15 minutes. Remove the lid and continue to bake for another 15 to 20 minutes until the top is golden and it sounds hollow when tapped.

6 Remove the pot from the oven and use tea towels to carefully remove the bread. Allow to cool before slicing.

BOULTED BREAD

## Boulted Bread

614 W. South Street,
Raleigh, NC 27603
(919) 999-3984
www.boultedbread.com

"Initially, Boulted Bread was a pretty selfish endeavor; a means to explore our own ideas of bread and pastry while indulging our own creativity, but that self-indulgence vanished pretty quickly once we opened our doors." The speaker is Joshua Bellamy. Alongside Fulton Forde and Sam Kirkpatrick, he owns and operates Boulted Bread in Raleigh, where the three men bake beautiful loaves and pastries for the local community.

Their original focus may have been bread experimentation, but Boulted has a new priority these days: "doing right by the people who sustain it: our customers and our employees." This is the fundamental obligation of any bakery, says Josh, and it ties in nicely with their original goal. "Our products aren't pigeonholed by rigid morality, other than this quest for taste. We want our customers to be shocked at and to revel in the fertility of flavor in everything we make. This ambition toward a nebulous ideal keeps us honest and driven." In other words: creativity is still encouraged.

Boulted got its start in 2014, when Fulton and Josh met at the Asheville Bread Festival. They immediately recognized one another as "like-minded idiots," and it wasn't long before Fulton and his longtime friend Sam reached out to Josh with their plans to open a bakery; all three men are Raleigh natives themselves, and felt it was important to bake for the community they knew and loved. Boulted was soon up and running, establishing itself as a part of the community just as quickly. With its loaves, both chewy and crunchy, and its buttery pastries, it's not hard to see why.

With the Boulted's success came a natural push away from the day-to-day baking duties, but Josh has held firm on that score. "I love to bake bread, and so far, thank goodness, the success and growth of Boulted Bread has not come at the expense of what I love." Members of the Raleigh community certainly agree—their products can be found at over 15 restaurants and cafés in the city!

# IN HIS OWN WORDS:

## JOSHUA BELLAMY

*How and when did you get your start baking?*

I've worked at bakeries and coffee shops since high school, but my first real urge to bake came later in life, after college. At the time, I was running an afterschool program for at-risk middle school students, and it was a lot. I started baking bread at home to relieve the stress of it, and things snowballed pretty rapidly from there.

*Who inspired you to bake? Who inspires you now?*

Initially, my curiosity was piqued by Peter Reinhart's books. They gave me a window into a world of which I had such limited understanding, and I knew pretty quickly that I wanted to explore more.

Currently, no baker inspires me more than Jim Lahey of Sullivan Street Bakery. His con-

tinued evolution as a baker proves his persistent curiosity, which I find deeply impressive.

*What is your golden rule(s) for baking?*

My only "golden rule" for baking is that I only bake things I'd like to eat. Does it taste good? Despite other moral and ethical proclamations, I believe that's really the essential goal of baking.

*What is your favorite thing to bake, and why? Least favorite?*

Baguettes are the ultimate challenge for me: the purest expression of a baker's proficiency, focus, and ethos. A perfect baguette requires so many distinct skills and such precise execution. If you're even fractionally off your game, the whole thing can fall apart. For the same reason, baguettes are also my least favorite thing to bake. Nothing has caused me more stress, grief, and sleepless nights.

*Where do you get your baking tools? What non-essential items should every baker have?*

We purchased almost all of our equipment secondhand. We also did most of the build-out ourselves, asking friends and family to pitch in when our construction skills were found lacking.

And, bountiful, high-quality bench scrapers are an absolute must for us! We use these orange, hard plastic scrapers from King Arthur Flour exclusively. They're amazing.

*What book(s) go on your required reading list for bakers?*

*Bread Builders* by Daniel Wing and Alan Scott and all of the *Tartine* books played a role in informing our overall ethos toward baking. For technical knowledge, nothing beats *Advanced Bread and Pastry* by Michel Suas and *Bread* by Jeffrey Hamelman. *Practical Milling* by B.W. Dedrick is also great for an informative trip into the history and mechanics of milling.

*What outlets/periodicals/newspapers do you read or consult regularly, if any?*

The online forum for the Bread Baker's Guild of America offers an amazing, ongoing conversation on all things bread and pastry–related.

*Tell me about your most memorable collaboration with another chef.*

It's always really exciting to see how Drew Maykuth of Stanbury (in downtown Raleigh) uses our bread. We've created some custom loaves for chefs in the past, and it's interesting to see how our vision of bread pairs with what chefs are accomplishing in their restaurants. Drew always finds a way to enhance and highlight the best qualities of our loaves. He's a real hero.

*Where did you learn to cook? Please tell me about your education and apprenticeships.*

After struggling to unlock some bread-baking mysticism at home, I moved to Vermont and got a Certificate of Professional Baking from the New England Culinary Institute. It was a short and wonderful experience. I worked with some really talented instructors, learned all the important fundamentals, and got a great taste of what it would be like to work in a production setting.

I completed my apprenticeship at Elmore Mountain Bread in Wolcott, Vermont with Blair Marvin and Andrew Heyn. They were gracious enough to let me stick around after the internship and gave me an immense wealth of knowledge, ethics, and skills with which to grow my career. I am forever in their debt, and I'm lucky to count them as my friends.

*Tell me about your milling process. How long have you been using a stone mill in-house? Why do you prefer it?*

Our stone mill has been the focal point of our bakery, both physically and ethically, since our inception. It was designed and built by our very own Fulton Forde, as part of New American Stone Mills. We now fresh-mill over 60% of our flour and plan to increase that number in the next few years.

We try to stay loose with our milling dogma and avoid sacrificing product integrity, identity, and flavor for the sake of fresh milling. That being said, milling most of our flour in-house gives us a number of distinct benefits. We have access to a wide variety of grain, directly from the farm, and the fresh flour has a sweeter aroma and fattier flavor than conventionally milled grains. We use our mill, in conjunction with several other techniques, as a tool to elevate and deepen the flavors in our products.

# GRITS BREAD

YIELD: 1 LOAF / ACTIVE TIME: 4 HOURS / TOTAL TIME: 20 HOURS

How do the guys at Boulted Bread do such justice to this corn-bread cousin? Extra butter. Beloved in the South (if a bit harder to find), this moist yet crumbly loaf agrees quite well with a little extra spread on top.

*—recipe courtesy of Joshua Bellamy, Fulton Forde, and Sam Kirkpatrick of Boulted Bread*

1 At least 12 hours prior to cooking, soak 150 grams of corn grits with 2⅛ cups of water.

2 Eight hours prior to mixing, mix cornmeal and the soaker buttermilk. Cover and let sit at room temperature in a cool kitchen.

3 At the same time (8 hours prior), mix levain flour with cold levain water in a separate bowl. Let sit at room temperature in a cool kitchen.

4 At least two hours prior to mixing, heat the grits and water to a boil and then drop to a simmer. Cook your grits until tender, then add butter, cream, and salt to taste. You will probably have some excess grits...lucky you!

5 Mix cooked grits, soaked cornmeal, levain, the remaining buttermilk, flour, and salt on low speed until all ingredients are thoroughly incorporated. This can be done in a mixer with a dough hook attachment or by hand. The resulting dough will be a shaggy mess.

6 Cover the mixing bowl with plastic wrap and place dough in a warm location. Allow to bulk ferment for 4 hours. During bulk fermentation, wet your hand and fold all of the sides into the center of the bowl every 45 minutes.

7 This dough is a mess and very difficult into shape. Luckily, it doesn't really matter! Dump the dough to a greased, buttered, or oiled loaf pan until the dough is about 2 inches from the top lip of the pan.

8 Let proof in a warm location for 2 hours or until the dough is about ½ inch from the top lip of the pan.

9 Preheat your oven to 450°F. Place a small baking sheet on the bottom rack of your oven and fill with water immediately before adding your proofed pan loaf to the oven on the rack above. This will help to steam the top of the loaf.

10 Bake for approximately 1 hour or until the top is a deep golden brown. Remove from heat and let cool completely before slicing.

INGREDIENTS:

FOR LEVAIN:

½ cup cold water

½ cup whole wheat flour

FOR SOAKER:

2¾ cups organic cornmeal

447 grams organic buttermilk

FOR DOUGH:

447 grams cooked organic grits

596 grams organic buttermilk

1½ tablespoons salt

3⅔ cups bread flour

Just under ½ cup water

Just over ¾ cup whole wheat flour

Soaker

Levain

# BASIC WHITE BREAD

I was skeptical of the recipes I found for baking bread in a cast-iron Dutch oven. They called for heating the cookware in the oven while the oven preheated (to a very high 450°F) and leaving the lid on for part of the baking time. But the photos looked good, so I dove in. This was the first recipe I made, and it was a great success and huge hit. I'm definitely a convert. Hope you will be, too.
—Dominique DeVito

**INGREDIENTS:**

¼   teaspoon active dry yeast

¼   teaspoon sugar

1½  cups water (110 to 115°F)

1   teaspoon kosher salt

3   cups all-purpose flour plus more for kneading and dusting

1 Put the yeast and sugar in a measuring cup and add about ½ cup warm water in a drizzle. Hot water will kill the yeast, so it's important that the water be warm without being hot. Cover the measuring cup with plastic wrap and set it aside for about 15 minutes. If the yeast doesn't foam, it is not alive and you'll need to start over.

2 When the yeast is proofed, pour it into a large bowl and add the additional cup of warm water. Stir gently to combine. Add the salt to the flour, and add the flour to the yeast mixture. Stir with a wooden spoon until combined. The dough will be wet and sticky.

3 Put a dusting of flour on a flat surface and lift out the dough. With flour on your hands and more at the ready, begin kneading the dough so that it loses its stickiness. Don't overdo it, and don't use too much flour; just enough that it is more cohesive.

4 Place the dough in a large bowl, cover the bowl with plastic wrap, and allow to rise untouched for at least 1 hour, and up to several hours. Gently punch it down, recover with the plastic, and allow to rise again for another 30 minutes or so.

5 While the dough is on its final rise, preheat the oven to 450°F. Put a piece of parchment paper on the bottom of the Dutch oven and put it in with the lid on so it gets hot. When the oven is ready and dough has risen, carefully remove the lid and gently scoop the dough from the bowl into the pot. Cover and bake for 15 minutes. Remove the lid and continue to bake for another 15 to 20 minutes until the top is golden and it sounds hollow when tapped.

6 Remove the pot from the oven and use tea towels to carefully remove the bread. Allow to cool before slicing.

# PORTUGUESE SWEET BREAD (PÃO DOCE)

YIELDS: 2 LOAVES / ACTIVE TIME: 40 MINUTES / TOTAL TIME: 3½ HOURS

Also known as Hawaiian Bread, páo doce is a traditional Portuguese sweet bread eaten during holidays, but it is also available all-year-round. It is common in areas with Portuguese American influences, such as Hawaii, New Jersey, southern Florida, California, and Toronto.

1 Heat the water to 100–110°F. Dissolve the yeast in the water and let rest for 5 minutes. In a large bowl, combine the water-yeast mixture with the milk (warmed to 100°F) Add the flour and the sugar and start working the dough, either with a stand mixer or by hand (see page 63 for tips on kneading). Continue working the dough and add 1 egg at a time.

2 Add the butter in pieces, continuing to work the dough, and incorporate the salt towards the end of kneading the dough until it feels smooth. The mixing process takes about 20 minutes from start to finish. Let the dough rest, covered, in a warm spot until it looks fully risen. This should take about 1 to 1½ hours. Transfer the dough to a clean and floured surface, divide in two pieces, and shape into two rounds.

3 Prepare a baking dish lined with parchment paper and dusted with flour. Place the dough rounds on the parchment paper and slightly flatten them. As an alternative, you can also place the rounds in 2 greased, round baking pans. Preheat oven to 350°F. Let the rounds rest, covered, for about 1 to 1½ hours, or until fully risen. Brush the rounds with the egg whisked with 1 tablespoon of water, and sprinkle with sugar. Bake for 35 to 40 minutes, covering with aluminum foil if the rounds are browning too fast.

## INGREDIENTS:

- 2 tsp (8½ g) active dry yeast
- 1.4 oz (40 g) water
- 5.6 oz (160 g) milk
- 17.6 oz (500 g) all-purpose flour
- 3½ oz (100 g) sugar
- 2 eggs
- 2.2 oz (60 g) butter
- ¾ tsp (4 g) salt

## FINISH

- 1 egg
- 1 tbsp water
- Sugar

## Bellegarde Bakery

www.bellegardebakery.com

One of the most respected bakers in New Orleans, Graison Gill has been featured on platforms such as *Saveur, Edible New Orleans* and *The Wall Street Journal*. But his proudest moment took place on a different sort of stage: the Louisiana House of Representatives. A resolution he co-wrote, aimed to protect and promote organic and local agriculture, passed with a whopping 92-0 vote. "My initial smug pride quickly buckled under a very humbling and empowering feeling that, really, it is possible to help change the laws in America," says Graison.

This larger awareness is not merely tangential to what Bellegarde does, but woven into the bakery's identity. Everything stems from Graison's own ethos, which he summarizes thusly: "I gradually had the epiphany that everything is inherently imperfect, but bread always proved to be a potential rubric of perfection. It *is* possible to make a perfect loaf of bread; realizing that you have inspiration that, however ephemeral, achievement and fulfilment are possible.

It proves that there can be a map between head and heart, between intention and experience. I found purchase in this belief. And to me the perfect loaf of bread became a medallion to be spent against everything else, to be spent against the things that didn't come out right."

If things didn't come out right in the beginning, they certainly do now. Producing only four loaves on regular rotation—ciabatta, country, baguette, and rye—has allowed Bellegarde to fine-tune their recipes to near perfection. To enhance their refinement process, the team at Bellegarde makes everything by hand for a more deliberate approach. And though plenty of world-class bakeries don't follow this method, one can certainly appreciate the personal touch at Bellegarde.

Graison Gill is a baker, first and last, but his poetic style is more than just a way of speaking. It shines through in his bread as well—each result a labor of love, representing his hope to, one day, create the sublime loaf.

# IN HIS OWN WORDS:

## GRAISON GILL

*How and when did you get your start baking?*

I began baking in my first New Orleans apartment, on Royal Street, in 2009. I arrived in New Orleans on a Greyhound bus on August 15, 2009 and that summer I began sharing a commercial kitchen in the Bywater with local chefs and caterers. From there, I began selling bread to neighbors and at a farmers' market. I was attracted to baking because of its nature: I was working with my hands. Bread-baking is the manifestation of many metaphors: failure, exile and solitude, intimacy, nurturing, consistency, moderation. I was mesmerized by the ingredients, the history, the process. More than anything, I found the experience of a bad loaf—its hubris—humbling and necessary, especially as a young man. Loaves competed between my expectation and their reality.

*How and when did the bakery get its start?*

I began the bakery with a SBA loan. My best friends and I did some painting and assembling of used equipment in the rented warehouse. For about six months, I worked alone: baking, mixing, delivering, bookkeeping, cleaning. For about one-and-a-half years I worked seven days a week; on Mondays, I woke up at 7 a.m., the rest of the week at 4 a.m.

*Who inspired you to bake? Who inspires you now?*

Sebastien Boudet (Petite France), Christophe Vasseur (Du Pain et Des Idées), Chris Bianco (Pizzeria Bianco), Nan Kohler (Grist & Toll), Mike Zakowski (The Bejkr), Scott Peacock (formerly of The Watershed), Glenn Roberts (Anson Mills)—these individuals and my family have been the strongest compasses and brightest stars in my life. When the bakery began, there was nothing but personal inspiration. I merely had the desire to create a place where I could do right.

*What is your golden rule(s) of baking?*

Chris Bianco once said, "Whether it's a tomato or a rumor, you must always consider the source." For me, baking is about terroir. Not only the terroir of the grain, but also of the salt, the water, the baker, the process, the style. Ninety-nine percent of American wheat products are made with white flour. White flour is a dead, inert product. It has little flavor, minimal nutritional value, and is entirely uninspiring. American bakers are groomed to work with this product for their entire careers; I certainly was. It really had no bearing upon who I was or what I was seeking. It's as if you were a musician and were asked only to play cover songs.

There is not much inspiration or imagination in constantly performing the work of others. And so, my golden rule is that chefs and bakers need to be like midwives. We don't create, we don't parent, in the way a farmer or winemaker does. Instead, we merely facilitate a process, and we allow ingredients to speak for themselves.

*What does Bellegarde represent to you?*

At its best, Bellegarde is a manifestation of my life. Everything I've experienced, everywhere I've traveled, everything I've done, and most importantly, all the things I haven't done.

*Where do you get your tools/materials? What non-essential items should every baker have?*

We do everything by hand; we don't use tools at Bellegarde. The only machines we have are our mixer, our walk-in fridge, our oven, and our mill.

*What book(s) go on your required reading list for bakers?*

Jeffrey Hammelman's *Bread* is the most essential and critical text for every baker. It is exceptional, flawless, and graceful. No other book was more important to me. Chad Robertson's *Tartine* is also beautiful for its iconoclasm. I'd relate both of them, respectively, to The Beatles and to The Rolling Stones: in order to break the rules, one must learn them first.

*Tell me about your most memorable collaboration(s) with another chef.*

I am working with Professor David Shields of USC and Glenn Roberts of Anson Mills to perform a tactile and historical review of heirloom southern grains. The plan is for David to present on the narratives of certain grains and then for Glenn to discuss their horticultural experience. That discussion will include who grew them, why, where—all the interrogatives. And, if pertinent, how Glenn found those seeds.

The Judgment of Paris in 1976—when California wines usurped French wines—inspired this event. We have so many programmed expectations and qualifiers for breads; yet, as a culture, we have no emotional or literal vocabulary to speak about bread. Before 1976, the world thought only France could make great wine; those blind tastings disproved our cognitive bias. You don't have to be in Rome to be a priest.

*Where did you learn to bake?*

I trained at the San Francisco Baking Institute. My teachers—particularly Mac McConnell and Frank Sally—were incredibly influential to the character, ethics, and discipline of my career. What Michel Suas has done at SFBI is incredible. If it weren't for that foundation, I would not be who I am today.

*Bellegarde uses its own stone mill. Why is this process so important to you, and what grains do you prefer to use? Do you ever experiment with more uncommon grains?*

Milling our own flour has become the defining aspect of Bellegarde. I wasn't born into a baking family, nor was I raised with strong food rituals. My craft chose me and I practiced it constantly, often at the cost of other aspects and relationships in my life. Like athletes, a baker only gets out what they put in. Everything that goes around comes back again, like the tide; nothing is ever created, it is merely transferred. It is for this reason that we mill most of our own flour. Our baking process and its methods are incredibly intimate: on busy weeks, we make 5,000 loaves of bread. Every single aspect of the ceremony is performed by hand; I felt that it would be an awkward hypocrisy if we were doing all this work by hand while using store-bought white flour. Machines and technology went into creating that white flour; granite and soil went into stone milling our wheat flour. It is because of this desire for continuity and connection that we stone mill flour in-house. And of course, fresh flour tastes better.

# BELLEGARDE BAKERY'S CIABATTA BREAD

YIELD: 2 2-POUND LOAVES / ACTIVE TIME: 2½ HOURS / TOTAL TIME: 16 HOURS

It wouldn't be a stretch to say that the United States has had a love affair with ciabatta over the last few years, so much so that one couldn't be blamed for getting a little sick of the stuff. Consider this recipe the antidote to your ciabatta exhaustion. Spongy yet sturdy, it will have you falling in love all over again.

— *recipe courtesy of Graison Gill, Bellegarde Bakery*

**INGREDIENTS:**

| | |
|---|---|
| 950 | millilitres water, 78°F (hold back some water) |
| 28 | grams salt |
| 2 | grams instant dried yeast |
| 24 | grams extra virgin olive oil |
| 35 | grams levain |
| 1096 | grams freshly milled whole wheat flour, 78°F |
| 20 | grams toasted wheat germ |

1   Add flour, levain, and 90% of total water into a shaggy mass. Sprinkle the salt, yeast, EVOO, wheat germ, and remaining on top. Mix by hand in a bus tub or large bowl. Once combined, the ingredients should have a mutual temperature of 78°F. If this temperature is not achieved, place the covered dough in a drafty or warmer area of the kitchen in order to reduce or increase its overall temperature. Then cover with a lid or towel and let rest for 90 minutes. This is your autolyse period.

2   After 90 minutes, fold the dough 5 to 7 times, depending on its strength and elasticity (see pages 62-63 for instruction on folding). Do this every 12 minutes.

3   Lightly oil a container. Transfer the dough to the oiled container and store in fridge overnight.

4   Remove dough from fridge and portion equally into 2 pieces; let the dough rest in couche. Allow dough to proof about 30 minutes before baking.

5   Preheat a baking stone in your oven to 500°F. When the oven is ready, place dough on top of baking stone and immediately drop the temperature to 450°F. Bake to desired doneness, about 25 minutes.

## LEVAIN MEANS SOURDOUGH:

Our sourdough is composed of 100% flour, 80% water, and 40% seed (fermented sourdough). We mix it to 80°F and let it sit for 4 hours before use.

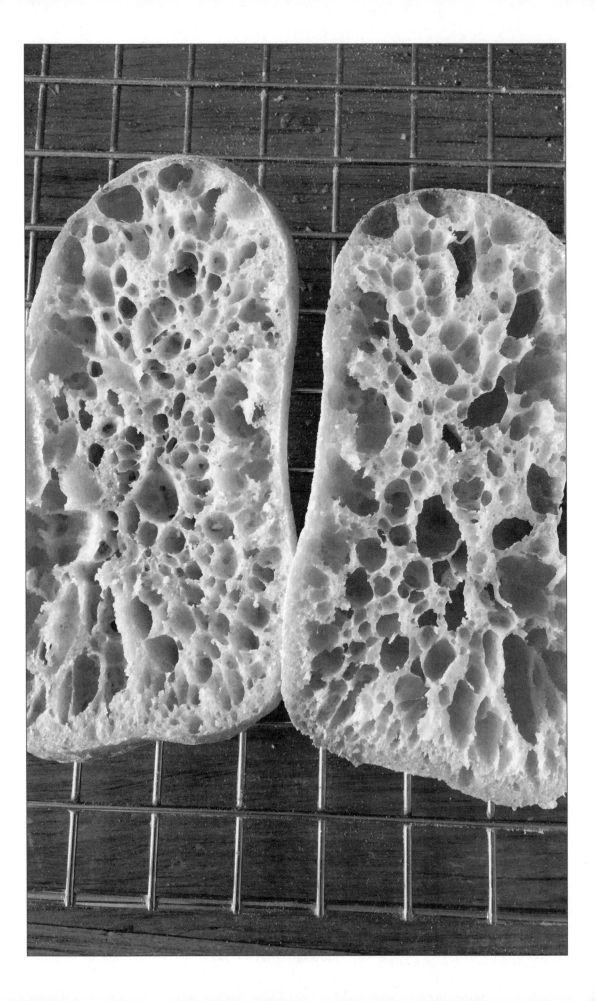

# POOLISH CIABATTA

**YIELDS:** 8–10 CIABATTAS / **ACTIVE TIME:** 50 MINUTES / **TOTAL TIME:** ABOUT 4½ HOURS + POOLISH BUILD

Ciabatta is a bread roll with a high ratio of water to flour that is meant to be filled. Arnaldo Cavallari and Francesco Favaron are the Italian bakers who created ciabatta in 1982. This is a rather easy approximation of the typical recipe and requires an overnight fermentation of part of the flour with commercial yeast.

1 The night before the baking day, prepare the poolish by combining all poolish ingredients with a spoon and leaving the mixture to ferment overnight in a container with a lid.

2 The morning after, combine all the poolish with the final dough ingredients, leaving aside the extra 1.8 oz water and the salt.

3 Let the dough rest for ½ hour, covered.

4 Add the salt and the remaining water, and work the dough through a series of stretch and folds every 20 minutes for the first hour (check page 63 for tips about kneading and folding).

5 Let rest for ½ hour, covered.

6 Transfer to a clean and floured surface, divide in two, and fold into two logs without deflating the dough. Cut each log into 5 pieces of equal weight. If you like bigger ciabattas, divide in fewer pieces, 4 or even 3.

7 Transfer the pieces to a heavily floured tray and sprinkle with abundant flour.

8 Preheat the oven to 480°F. If you have a baking stone, place it in the oven to preheat.

9 After about 1½ hours, prepare a baking peel or flat tray covered with parchment paper and place the pieces of dough on the parchment paper after stretching each piece lengthwise. This gives the baked breads the look of ciabattas (slippers).

10 Bake with steam (see page 142) for 10 minutes, let the steam out by opening the oven door, reduce the temperature to 410°F, and bake another 10 to 20 minutes, depending on how pale or brown you like your ciabattas and on how big you cut the pieces.

## INGREDIENTS:

**POOLISH**

¾   tsp (4.3 g) active dry yeast

2.8   oz (80 g) water

3½   oz (100 g) all-purpose flour

**DOUGH**

Poolish

17½   oz (500 g) all-purpose flour

12½   oz (350 g) water + 1.8 oz water

1¾   tsp salt

# BOULANGERIE'S CIABATTA

YIELD: 2 LOAVES / ACTIVE TIME: 40 MINUTES / TOTAL TIME: 24 HOURS

The Italian answer to the French baguette, ciabatta bread has staked its claim as one of the most popular breads in the world. As this recipe uses a high-hydration dough, we use the double-hydration method—adding the water in two parts so the dough gets a chance to build some gluten and form a structure before it receives the additional water.

—*Amy and Zachary Tyson, Boulangerie*

## DAY 1

1 The day before the mix, make the biga: Combine all ingredients in a bowl, mix by hand until incorporated, then cover and set aside for 16–18 hours.

## DAY 2

2 The next day, begin your dough. Combine all dough ingredients except the ½ cup of water, mixing for 5 minutes on low speed. Mix for 5 more minutes on medium speed.

3 After the 10 minutes of mixing, lower the speed and gradually add the second amount of water. Mix for 5 more minutes, adding up to 15 total minutes of mixing.

4 Place dough in an oiled bin, preferably square in shape, and let proof for 45 minutes. Fold dough and let proof an additional 45 minutes. Repeat this process 3 more times for a total of 4 folds, each followed by a 45-minute rest time.

5 Turn dough out onto a generously floured surface. Work with precision so as to not deflate the dough!

6 Sprinkle flour on top of the dough. Divide the dough in half, using 2 floured bench knives or scrapers. Pick up the dough and place it on a parchment-lined tray. If you're baking on a stone, place dough onto a generously floured tray.

7 Preheat the oven to 470°F. Let dough proof for 30 minutes in a warm area. Place tray in the oven, or transfer the dough from a floured sheet onto the stone with a peel.

8 Bake at 470°F for 25 minutes, until the bread is golden brown.

## INGREDIENTS:

### BIGA (MAKES 4 ½ CUPS)

- 1 cups + 2 tablespoons water
- ⅛ teaspoon fresh red yeast
- 3⅓ cups King Arthur Special Patent Flour

### DOUGH

- 2⅔ cups + ½ cup water, kept separately
- 2½ teaspoons red yeast
- 6½ cups King Arthur Special Patent Flour
- 3 cups biga
- 1 tablespoon salt

# King Arthur Flour Baking School

135 US-5
Norwich, VT 05055
(802) 649-3361

11768 Westar Lane
Burlington, WA 98233
(800) 652-3334
www.kingarthurflour.com/baking-school

The Baking School at King Arthur Flour is a living, hands-on lab for bakers of all abilities and ages—from the seasoned professional looking to fine-tune her sourdough skills to the 9-year-old just baking his first cupcake. For those who love to bake, it's a dream destination.

"We believe we're the largest educator of home bakers in the world, and certainly in this country," says Baking School director Susan Miller. "We teach baking to thousands of people every year, both here in Norwich, VT and at our new campus at the Bread Lab in Washington State."

A longtime dream of former owners Frank and Brinna Sands, the school was founded in 2000. Since then, it's moved from one small room to three large, fully-equipped classrooms where students work at shared stations measuring flour, beating up batter, and kneading dough. Their handcrafted creations are baked in anything from a home-style oven to steam-injected deck ovens to a massive brick-and-stone, wood-fired hearth oven.

The professionally trained, full-time staff is augmented by a wide variety of guest instructors, including experts internationally noted in their field. But the best part about the Baking School? The stress-free, welcoming atmosphere. Students work cooperatively side-by-side, helping one another determine when the butter and sugar are fully creamed, the sourdough starter is at its peak, and the pizza has reached its ultimate balance of crispy crust and melted cheese.

"Baking is a wonderful, creative pursuit. And it's an incredible opportunity to share, as well," notes Miller. "Not just knowledge—but the bread or layer cake or tarts you go home with. What could be better than enjoying a relaxing afternoon doing something creative, then walking out with something delicious to share?"

The Baking School's multitude of happy students couldn't agree more.

# CIABATTA *with* OLIVE OIL

YIELD: 2 LOAVES / ACTIVE TIME: 30 MINUTES / TOTAL TIME: 4½ HOURS

Ciabatta, with its large holes, delightfully chewy texture, and crisp crust, is Italian country bread at its finest.
—*courtesy of King Arthur Flour*

**INGREDIENTS:**

- 4¼ cups (18 ounces) King Arthur Unbleached All-Purpose Flour
- 1¾ teaspoons salt
- 1 teaspoon instant yeast
- 1½ cups (12 ounces) water, room temperature
- 2 tablespoons (1 ounce) olive oil

**1** Place all of the ingredients in a large mixing bowl. Stir everything together to make a soft, tacky dough.

**2** Cover the dough and let it rest at room temperature (65°F to 75°F) for 3 hours. Every 30 minutes, use a spatula or bowl scraper to fold the edges of the dough into the center. This strengthens and aerates the dough.

**3** After 3 hours, turn the dough out onto a well-floured work surface. Cut in half and gently stretch to a rough rectangle, about 4 by 10 inches. These are your loaves. Place the loaves on a piece of parchment paper, sifting a bit of flour over the top. Cover loosely with plastic wrap.

**4** While the dough is rising, preheat your oven to 500°F with a baking stone inside. Place a medium-sized cast iron pan on the lowest oven rack. Allow the oven to heat for at least 30 minutes.

**5** Let the ciabatta rise until it's light and airy. This will take about 1 hour if your room temperature is around 70°F.

**6** Use a peel to transfer the loaves onto the hot stone. If you're baking the loaves without a stone, transfer them to a baking sheet and place the pan on the oven's middle rack. Pour about ½ cup boiling water into the preheated cast iron frying pan on the shelf below, and immediately shut the oven door. The steam created will both help the ciabatta rise and enhance its crust.

**7** After 5 minutes, lower the oven temperature to 450°F. Continue baking the ciabatta until they're a deep golden brown and feel firm when you prod their sides, about 26 minutes. They'll feel very light for their size when they're fully baked.

**8** Remove the ciabatta from the oven and cool them on a rack. Ciabatta are best enjoyed the same day they're made. Store leftovers for a day or so at room temperature, loosely wrapped in plastic. Freeze for longer storage.

# SOURDOUGH CIABATTA

YIELD: 8 SMALL CIABATTAS / ACTIVE TIME: 30 MINUTES / TOTAL TIME: 4½ HOURS

Ciabatta is not a traditional Italian bread and is not originally based on sourdough. When made with sourdough, though, ciabattas take on a lovely rustic look that will not disappoint you.

1 Combine the sourdough starter with 1⅓ cups water, leaving ⅛ cup for later.

2 Add the flours and mix well. Knead for a few minutes by hand or with a stand-mixer.

3 Let the dough rest, covered, for 30 minutes.

4 Incorporate the salt and the malt (optional). Add the extra water if the dough can absorb it. This dough is supposed to be well hydrated, but not liquid.

5 Knead more, by hand or with a stand-mixer, until the dough appears elastic when pulled (10 minutes). Alternatively, you can skip the kneading and do a series of folds. See pages 62-63 for tips about kneading and folding.

6 Let the dough rest, covered, for 2 hours.

7 Transfer the dough on a floured surface, divide in 2 and fold into 2 logs without deflating the dough. Cut each log into 4 pieces of equal weight. If you like bigger ciabattas, divide in fewer pieces, 3 or even 2.

8 Transfer the pieces on a heavily floured tray and sprinkle with abundant flour.

9 Preheat the oven to 440°F, with the baking stone in, if you have one.

10 After about 1½ hours have passed, prepare a baking peel or flat tray covered with parchment paper and place the pieces of dough on the parchment paper after stretching each piece lengthwise. This gives to the baked breads the look of ciabattas (slippers).

11 Bake with steam (see page 49) for 10 minutes. Let the steam out by opening the oven door and bake for further 10-20 minutes, depending on how pale or brown you like your ciabattas.

INGREDIENTS:

½ cup (125 g) 100% hydration sourdough starter (see page 59)

10.5 oz (300 g) bread flour

3.5 oz (100 g) all-purpose flour

1⅓ (335 g) cups plus ⅛ (30 g) cup water

1 tsp diastatic malt powder (optional)

½ tsp salt

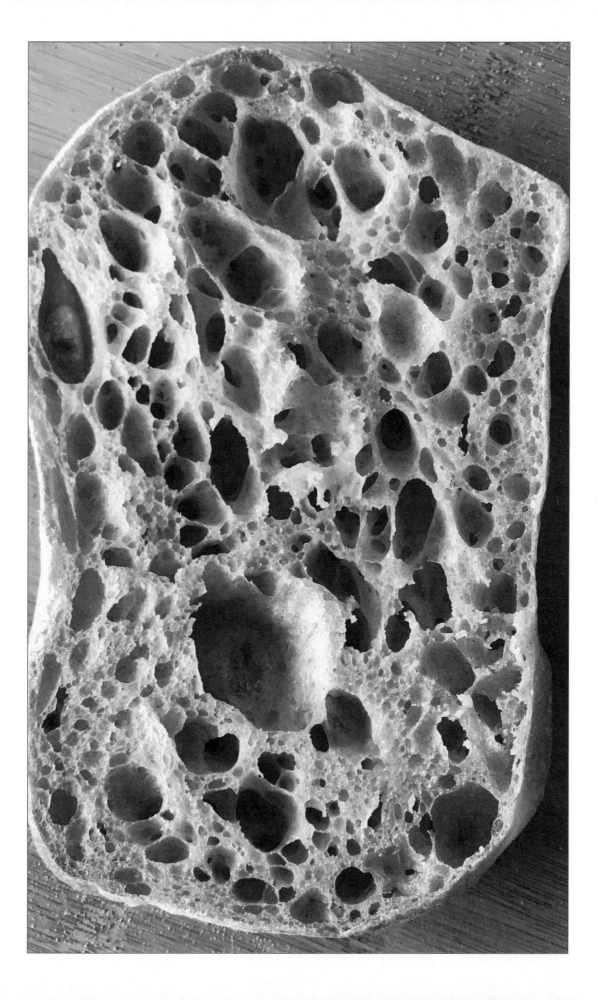

# ASSORTED SOURDOUGH CIABATTAS

**YIELD:** 15 CIABATTAS / **ACTIVE TIME:** 50 MINUTES / **TOTAL TIME:** 5 HOURS

The main idea behind these ciabattas is allow for a long first fermentation (bulk proof) and then just play with the dough as you wish, creating a variety of different types of ciabatta-like rolls. Some simple and some filled as you prefer (below some suggestions).

1 Combine the sourdough starter with 1⅓ cups water, leaving ⅛ cup for later.

2 Add the flours and mix well. Knead for a few minutes by hand or with a stand-mixer. Let the dough rest, covered, for 30 minutes.

3 Incorporate the salt and the malt (the malt is optional). Add the extra water if the dough can absorb it. This dough is supposed to be well hydrated, but not liquid.

4 Knead more, by hand or with a stand-mixer, until the dough appears elastic when pulled (about 10 minutes). Alternatively, you can skip the kneading and do a series of folds. See pages 62-63 for tips about kneading and folding.

5 Let the dough rest, covered, for 4 hours.

6 Preheat the oven to 480°F with the stone in if you own one.

7 When the oven is ready, transfer the dough on a floured surface and fold it on itself, delicately.

8 After 15 minutes, start shaping your ciabattas as you prefer. For the straight ciabattas, just cut rectangular pieces of dough and bake them as they are. You can even twist some ciabattas on themselves, making interesting looking twisted ciabattas.

9 For the filled ciabattas, a good option is chopped olives and chopped taleggio cheese (or other medium-hard cheese), or a baby pepper filled with the cheese.

10 To trap the filling in, wrap the dough over the cheese/olives/peppers and seal the dough pocket with a gruyere stick, eventually making small holes where to insert the gruyere, if the dough is stronger than the cheese.

11 Bake right away for 20–30 minutes depending on the size of your ciabattas, creating steam in the beginning by throwing a few ice cubes on a hot baking dish placed on the bottom of the oven.

**INGREDIENTS:**

- 1 cup (226 g) sourdough starter (see page 59)
- 21 oz (600 g) bread flour
- 7 oz (200 g) all-purpose flour
- 2⅔ (670 g) cups plus ¼ (60 g) cup water
- 2 tsp diastatic malt powder (optional)
- 3 tsp salt

For the filling: taleggio, cut in small squares; gruyere, cut in rectangular sticks; green olives; baby sweet peppers

# SOURDOUGH

In our time, we are witnessing an almost unprecedented bread renaissance, and sourdough bread is the absolute star of it. This is quite surprising considering that sourdough baking had long been forgotten in favor of baker's yeast or chemical rising agents like baking soda and baking powder.

There have always been places, both in Europe and North America, where sourdough baking has been kept alive. In the United States, San Francisco is the place where ferments have grown wild since the 19th century. It is unquestionable that today's artisan bread and sourdough revival is largely due to the influence of San Francisco's bakers over the whole of North America, and to Northern American influence over the rest of the world.

The story goes that during the California Gold Rush in 1849, some unknown gold miners brought a sourdough mother dough to San Francisco, which became the center of this massive migration. Using this mother dough to make bread became very popular among the miners. Isolated for long periods, they could still make their own bread using a piece of dough saved from their previous bake (see page 65).

The gold miners also passed on their mother dough to a French immigrant who belonged to a family of boulangers (French for baker). In 1849, Isidore Boudin opened the first sourdough bakery in San Francisco. His original starter has been kept alive ever since.

The influence of Boudin's bakery strongly characterized San Francisco baking, giving it a strong French, or rather Parisian, attitude. This, combined with a devotion to sourdough, has survived even in Paris, where no one was using natural fermentation anymore. The advent of industrial baker's yeast, originally commercialized as Fleischman's cake yeast, converted most European and American bakers to yeast. Skilled bakers already used yeast, but industrial yeast made it so available that sourdough could no longer compete.

Even when the gold miners disappeared, sourdough baking remained, and ended up characterizing the bread of San Francisco. It is even probable that the artisan bread renaissance as we know it may not have happened without the contribution of the gold miners, who somehow managed to time travel sourdough baking into a 21st century hungry for authentic bread.

The fame of San Francisco sourdough also reached bread science laboratories, where a special type of sourdough bacteria (LAB) was identified and called *Lactobacillus sanfranciscensis*. This type of LAB (see page 54) is of the heterofermentative type; therefore, it makes the sourdough starter type that makes bread rise in volume, and does not produce much acetic acid. A bread with this type of starter can be perfectly risen without a strong tang. *Lactobacillus sanfranciscensis* is not unique to San Francisco, but it is one of the good bacteria that a baker wishes to have in a sourdough starter.

San Francisco's history, combined with the biochemistry of San Francisco's starter, makes for great sourdough bread, and the city has a long tradition of top quality bakeries. To mention just a few, Boudin Bakery is still up and running, while maintaining high standards. Their variety of sourdough loaves is very popular, and tourists in particular like the selection of breads shaped like animals (turtles, alligators, and teddy bears to name a few). Tartine Bakery, founded by Chad Robertson, has become a cult favorite for the international artisan bread community. Tartine's homonymous and hugely successful bread book teaches in detail how to achieve a perfect San Francisco sourdough loaf, or rather Robertson's version of it. Another major success, Arizmendi Bakery, named after a labor organizer of Basque origins, is known for its fragrant baguettes, flavored sourdoughs, and sourdough croissants. The French inspiration never dies in the United States, as clearly seen through the names of other top bakeries, such as Le Marais Bakery and La Boulangerie de San Francisco.

# SOURDOUGH LOAF

YIELD: 3 LOAVES, OR 2 LARGE LOAVES / ACTIVE TIME: 1 HOUR / TOTAL TIME: 24 HOURS

A mild sourdough that uses fresh stone-ground whole wheat flour.
—*Jim Williams, Seven Stars Bakery*

## DAY 1

1 Mix your sourdough culture until incorporated and leave to ferment for 12–16 hours at room temperature (ideally 70°F). They can be doubled or tripled for ease of use—just discard whatever you don't need.

## DAY 2

1 Mix all ingredients except levain and salt in a bowl to incorporation, either by hand or using a mixer. Let rest for 30 minutes.

2 Add rye starter, levain, and salt and mix the dough to a point of light development.

3 Bulk fermentation should take 3 hours at 77–80°F. During this time, give the dough 3 folds. Simply take the dough and fold it upon itself several times. Each time, the dough will feel stronger and more resilient.

4 After bulk fermentation, divide the dough into loaves. Give the dough a light pre-shape and rest for 30 minutes.

5 Shape into final shapes and proof. The proof should last 3–5 hours depending on the temperature and humidity in your home kitchen.

6 Preheat a cast iron Dutch oven, with the lid, in your oven. Turn heat up as hot as it will go.

7 When proofed, lightly insert the proofed dough into the Dutch oven, score it, put the lid on and into the oven.

8 After 30 minutes of baking, remove the lid and finish to desired color. Let cool and enjoy!

**INGREDIENTS:**

**LEVAIN**

½ cup stone ground, fresh-milled whole wheat flour

⅓ cup white all-purpose flour

¼ cup water

⅓ ounce sourdough culture

**DOUGH**

7⅛ cups white all-purpose flour

¾ cups fresh-milled, stone-ground whole wheat flour

3¼ cups water

7¾ ounces levain

1⅓ tablespoons salt

Olive Bread: As a variation, you can add olives to the dough and make olive bread. Add 1⅔ cups of Kalamata olives and ⅔ cup of oil-cured olives, or any type you prefer, during your first fold. Just spread the olives on the dough and give it a light fold. Don't worry about fully incorporating the olives at this point—every time the dough is folded, the olives will incorporate further.

# OLIVE LOAF

YIELDS 1 SMALL ROUND / **ACTIVE TIME:** 25 MINUTES / **TOTAL TIME:** 3 HOURS

I love the earthy-salty flavor of dark olives like Kalamatas. They are delicious in bread, too. Rather than taking the time to slice a lot of Kalamata olives, I like to use a top-shelf tapenade (olive) spread, which is easy to spread and distribute in the dough, too.
—*Dominique DeVito*

**INGREDIENTS:**

- ¼ teaspoon instant yeast
- ¼ teaspoon sugar
- 1½ cups water (110 to 115°F)
- 1 teaspoon kosher salt
- 3 cups all-purpose flour plus more for kneading and dusting
- ½ cup tapenade (olive spread) or ½ cup Kalamata olives
- 1 tablespoon olive oil

1 Put the yeast and sugar in a measuring cup and add about ½ cup warm water in a drizzle. Hot water will kill the yeast, so it's important that the water be warm without being hot. Cover the measuring cup with plastic wrap and set it aside for about 15 minutes. If the yeast doesn't foam, it is not alive and you'll need to start over.

2 When the yeast is proofed, pour it into a large bowl and add the additional cup of warm water. Stir gently to combine. Add the salt to the flour, and add the flour to the yeast mixture. Stir with a wooden spoon until combined. The dough will be wet and sticky.

3 Put a dusting of flour on a flat surface and lift out the dough. With flour on your hands and more at the ready, begin kneading the dough so that it loses its stickiness. Don't overdo it, and don't use too much flour; just enough that it is more cohesive. Incorporate the tapenade or olive pieces while you're kneading.

4 Place the dough in a large bowl, cover the bowl with plastic wrap, and allow to rise untouched for at least 1 hour, and up to several hours. Gently punch it down, recover with the plastic, and allow to rise again for another 30 minutes or so. Brush with the olive oil.

5 While the dough is on its final rise, preheat the oven to 450°F. Put a piece of parchment paper on the bottom of the Dutch oven and put it in with the lid on so it gets hot. When the oven is ready and dough has risen, carefully remove the lid and gently scoop the dough from the bowl into the pot. Cover and bake for 15 minutes. Remove the lid and continue to bake for another 15 to 20 minutes until the top is golden and it sounds hollow when tapped.

6 Remove the pot from the oven and use tea towels to carefully remove the bread. Allow to cool before slicing.

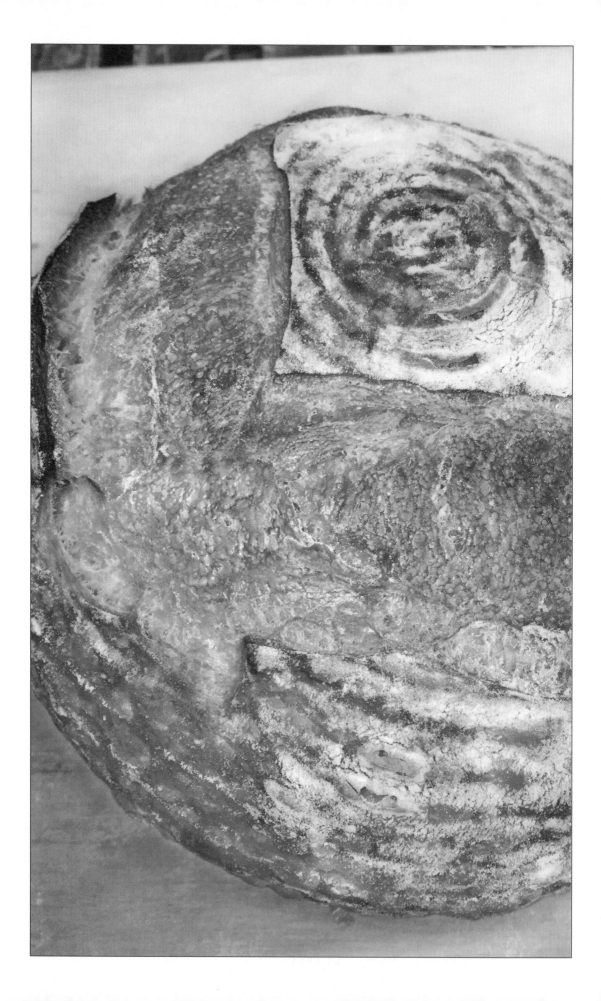

# BOULANGERIE'S SOURDOUGH

YIELD: 2 LARGE BOULES, PRE-SLICED / ACTIVE TIME: 1 ½ HOURS / TOTAL TIME: 6½-15½ HOURS

Whipping up some homemade croutons is fairly simply no matter how you do it, but if you're going to make some from scratch, it's worth using the Boulangerie croutons recipe. They use their old loaves to make delicious croutons in-house!

—*courtesy of Amy and Zachary Tyson, Boulangerie*

### INGREDIENTS:

- 5⅙ cups water
- 1½ cups culture
- 5⅙ cups Sir Galahad all-purpose flour
- 1¾ cups King Arthur Special Patent Flour
- 1½ tablespoons salt

1 Mix water, culture, and flours in a large bowl. Let sit for 30 minutes. This is your autolyse period.

2 In a mixer with a dough hook attachment, mix in the salt on 1st speed for 5 minutes. Then mix on 2nd speed for 3 minutes.

3 Allow to bulk ferment for 3 hours, or overnight if possible. If baking the same day, fold the dough every hour as you wait.

4 Divide the dough in half and preshape into a rough ball. Let rest for 30 minutes.

5 Do your final shaping and place dough bottom side–up in a basket or bowl lined with a floured cloth.

6 Proof for 45 minutes and preheat the oven to 450°F.

7 Invert dough onto a peel dusted with semolina or flour. Score the dough.

8 Spray oven with water bottle and bake for 30–45 minutes, until the bread sounds hollow.

## FEEDING YOUR CULTURE:

Begin with 1¾ ounces of sourdough culture, ¾ cup of water, and 2 cups of all-purpose flour. Refrigerate and feed once a week until you're ready to bake. Three days before mixing your dough, begin feeding your culture daily and leaving covered at room temperature. Use the same portions for every feeding.

# EASY WHITE SOURDOUGH

**YIELD:** 1 BIG LOAF / **ACTIVE TIME:** 50 MINUTES / **TOTAL TIME:** 5 HOURS PLUS STARTER FEEDING

This recipe can give you a wonderful basic sourdough bread that can accompany any meal and it is great to make rustic sandwiches. The one and only secret for its success is having a lively sourdough starter, the rest will pretty much take care of itself.

**INGREDIENTS:**

- 5 oz (150 g) wheat sourdough starter (see page 59)
- 12 oz (350 g) water
- 17½ oz (500 g) bread flour
- 1¾ tsp salt

1 Combine the water (at room temperature) with the sourdough starter.

2 Add the flour, combine well, and let rest for 20 minutes, covered.

3 Add the salt and knead by hand for a couple of minutes.

4 Make a series of folds with intervals for the first 1½ hours (see page 62 for tips about folding techniques).

5 Let the dough rest, covered, for 1-1½ hours, or until it is nearly doubled.

6 Preheat oven to maximum temperature, with the stone in if you own one.

7 Transfer the dough on a clean and floured surface and shape into a large round, without deflating the dough.

8 Place the round into a proofing basket lined with a kitchen towel and dusted with flour.

9 Invert the loaf on a baker's peel or flat tray dusted with coarse semolina or corn flour and transfer into the oven, creating steam (see page 49) and lowering the temperature to 460°F.

10 Bake for 20 minutes, then open the oven and release the steam, lowering the temperature to 410°F and baking for further 25–30 minutes or until pleasantly browned.

# 24-HOUR SOURDOUGH

YIELD: 1 BIG LOAF / ACTIVE TIME: 30 MINUTES / TOTAL TIME: 24 HOURS

When time at home is rare, even baking a basic sourdough loaf can become impossible. No worries. You can let the wild yeasts and lactobacilli work for you while you attend your daily routine. It is easy to adapt the suggested time schedule to any bread recipe.

## DAY 1, MORNING (AROUND 7 A.M.)

Prepare the young sourdough starter and let rest covered.

## DAY 1, EVENING (AROUND 6 P.M.)

1 Combine the starter and the water, then add the flours and salt (already combined).

2 Mix for 5 to 6 minutes by machine on low speed, or 7 to 8 minutes by hand.

3 Transfer to a plastic, ceramic, or glass container and let rest, covered, for about 3 hours, folding twice at the 30 and 60–minute marks.

4 Shape 1 large round (2¼ pounds) and a medium-sized torpedo (1⅓ pounds) and place in heavily floured rising baskets that have been sealed into plastic bags.

5 Place in the fridge and let ferment for 18 hours.

## DAY 2, EVENING (ABOUT 6 P.M.)

1 Take the loaves out of the fridge and let rest at room temperature for 3 hours, still sealed in the plastic bags. Meanwhile, preheat your oven to maximum heat.

2 Invert the dough on a heavily floured baker's peel covered with parchment paper, score as you like, and then transfer to an already-hot baking dish or onto a baking stone in your oven. Make sure to create some steam by throwing a few ice cubes in a hot baking dish placed on the bottom of the oven.

3 Reduce the temperature to 445°F and bake for 25 to 30 minutes, depending on the size of the loaf.

4 Reduce the temperature to 410°F and bake for 25 to 30 additional minutes.

**INGREDIENTS:**

5 oz (150 g) wheat sourdough starter (see page 59)

11⅕ oz (350 g) water

17½ oz (500 g) bread flour

1¾ tsp salt

# 48-HOUR RUSTIC SOURDOUGH LOAF

YIELD: 1 BIG LOAF / **ACTIVE TIME:** 30 MINUTES / **TOTAL TIME:** 48 HOURS

Who said that bread can be baked only on weekends or vacations? Following the suggested time schedule, it is possible to fit a spectacular sourdough loaf in, even during a busy working week. Feel free to modify this basic recipe by playing with different flours.

**INGREDIENTS:**

5 oz (150 g) wheat sourdough starter (see page 59)

11⅘ oz (350 g) water

17½ oz (500 g) bread flour

1¾ tsp salt

## DAY 1, MORNING

Prepare the young sourdough starter and let it rise, covered.

## DAY 1, EVENING

1 Combine all the ingredients except for the salt. You can use your hands and scrape the dough off with a dough scraper or tablespoon. Let rest, covered, for 40 minutes.

2 Add the salt and combine well. Again, don't be afraid to use your hands!

3 Let rest, covered, for 3 hours, stretching and folding the dough on itself like a package every ½ hour. The dough will be sticky in the beginning and become smoother after each fold.

4 Place the dough in an airtight container or bowl sealed with plastic wrap and place in the fridge to rest until the next evening.

## DAY 2, EVENING

1 After about 24 hours in the fridge, the dough should have risen about 1 ½ of its volume and look smooth.

2 Take the dough out of the fridge and transfer it to a work surface. Fold the dough, stretching the 4 corners as if you were closing a package. Use a scraper to help you if you see that the dough is sticking to the surface.

3 Flip the "package" upside-down and let rest for 1 hour, covered.

4 After 1 hour, the dough will have spread and look soft.

5 Cut the dough in 2 parts, one larger (about ⅔) and one smaller (⅓). I use the large piece to shape the loaf and the rest to make a small *batard* (or *filone,* in Italian). This dough also makes excellent pizza and can be used up to 1 day after if kept in the fridge.

6   Sprinkle the working surface with a little rice flour and shape the larger piece of dough into a round by folding the corners all around and pinching to seal them on the top of the round.

7   Flip the dough upside-down and gently round it out by letting it slide on the clean surface and creating tension with the palms of your hands.

## DAY 3, EVENING

1   Take the loaf out of the fridge. If it does not look like it has risen about ½ of its initial volume, let it rest outside the fridge for a few hours before baking. Meanwhile, turn on the oven to its maximum temperature.

2   As soon as your loaf looks like it has risen by about 1½ compared to the night before, transfer it onto a peel or a baking tray covered with parchment paper and put it in the hot oven, reducing the temperature right away

8   Place the round seam side–down on a proofing basket that has been heavily floured with rice flour.

9   Place the basket in a large plastic bag (food-approved) and close the bag. Let rest in the fridge until the evening of the following day.

to 480°F. Create initial steam by throwing a few ice cubes in a hot baking dish placed on the bottom of the oven.

3   Bake for 20 minutes and then lower the temperature to 430°F and bake for 20 more minutes. Lower the temperature further to 390°F and bake for an additional 20 minutes (1 hour overall). Let cool on a rack for at least 1 hour before cutting.

# BLUEBERRY SOURDOUGH

YIELDS: 1 LOAF / **ACTIVE TIME:** 30 MINUTES / **TOTAL TIME:** 5 HOURS

Blueberries give a tangy bite to a rustic sourdough, which can match incredibly well with good cheese and honey or jam. The addition of condensed milk makes the crust softer and complements the tanginess of the blueberries.

**INGREDIENTS:**

- **14** oz (400 g) bread flour
- **3½** oz (100 g) whole-wheat flour
- **5.3** oz (150 g) sourdough starter (see page 59)
- **12.3** oz (350 g) water
- **2½** oz (70 g) sweetened condensed milk
- **1½** tsp (8½ g) salt
- **6.3** oz (180 g) fresh blueberries

1 In a large bowl, combine all the ingredients, except the salt and the blueberries. Make a series of folds and let rest for 20 minutes.

2 Add the salt and combine until fully incorporated. Transfer the dough to a clean surface, spread with your hands, and delicately fold the blueberries in without breaking them.

3 Make into a ball and transfer back to the bowl. Make another two series of folds after 20 and 40 minutes. Let the dough rest, covered, for 1½ hours.

4 Transfer the dough to a clean surface and shape into a round. Place the round in a proofing basket lined with a floured kitchen towel.

5 Preheat oven to maximum temperature, with the stone in if you own one.

6 Let rest, covered (for instance by placing the loaf into a clean, plastic bag), for 2 to 2½ hours.

7 Invert the loaf on a baker's peel or flat tray dusted with coarse semolina or corn flour. Transfer to the hot oven, producing steam (for instance, by throwing some ice cubes on the bottom part of the oven). Immediately reduce heat to 480°F and bake for 25 minutes.

8 Let the steam out, reduce heat to 430°F and bake for 20 to 25 minutes or until deep golden brown.

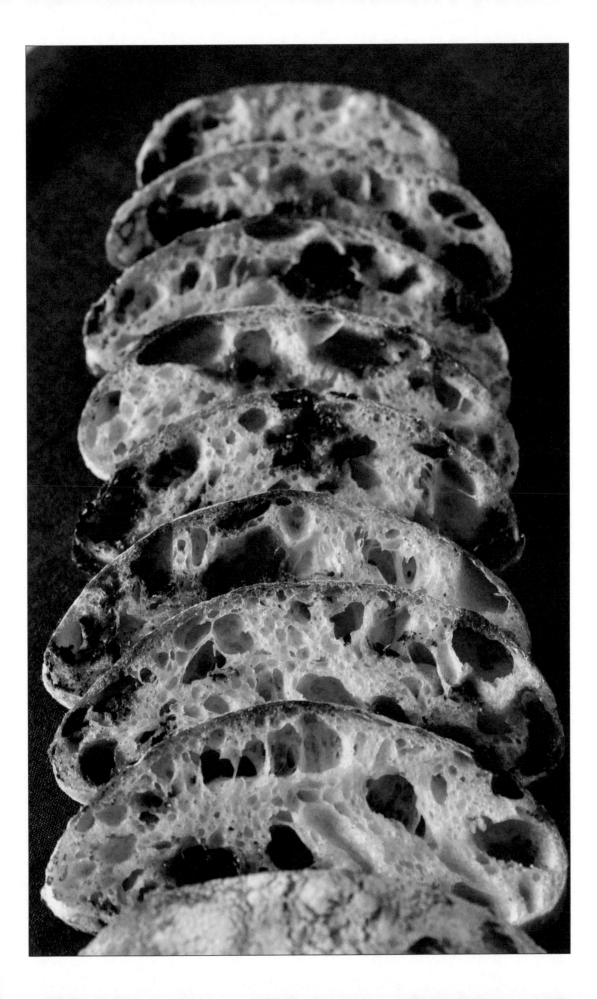

# COFFEE SOURDOUGH

YIELD: 1 LOAF / *ACTIVE TIME:* 30 MINUTES / *TOTAL TIME:* 5 HOURS

The addition of espresso coffee to sourdough gives a lovely dark crust, a *macchiato* crumb, and a hint of coffee in the taste. Coffee can affect dough development, so make sure you begin with a healthy starter.

**INGREDIENTS:**

- 1 lb (450 g) bread flour
- 1.8 oz (50 g) whole-wheat flour
- 5.3 oz (150 g) sourdough starter (see page 59)
- 8.8 oz (250 g) water
- 1 tbsp honey
- 1¾ tsp (10 g) salt
- 3½ oz (100 g) strong espresso

1 In a large bowl, combine all the ingredients, except the salt and the coffee. Make a series of folds and let rest for 20 minutes.

2 Add the salt and the coffee and combine until fully incorporated. Make another two series of folds after 20 and 40 minutes. Let the dough rest, covered, for 1½ hours.

3 Transfer the dough to a clean surface and shape into a round. Place the round in a proofing basket lined with a floured kitchen towel.

4 Preheat oven to maximum temperature, with the stone in if you own one.

5 Let rest, covered (for instance by placing the loaf into a clean, plastic bag), for 2 hours.

6 Invert the loaf on a baker's peel or flat tray dusted with coarse semolina or corn flour.

7 Transfer to the hot oven, producing steam (for instance, by throwing some ice cubes on the bottom part of the oven).

8 Immediately reduce heat to 480°F and bake for 25 minutes.

9 Let the steam out, reduce heat to 430°F, and bake for 20 to 25 minutes, or until deep golden brown.

# OLIVE SOURDOUGH

YIELDS: 1 BIG LOAF OR 2 SMALLER ONES / ACTIVE TIME: 50 MINUTES / TOTAL TIME: ABOUT 5 HOURS + STARTER

Olives are a wonderful addition to a basic sourdough, enhancing its rustic character and enriching the bread with precious nutrients and Mediterranean flavors. Feel free to try different types of olives as well as play with different types of flour.

**INGREDIENTS:**

- 12 oz (about 350 g) water
- 5 oz (150 g) wheat sourdough starter (see page 59)
- 14½ oz (410 g) bread flour
- 3 oz (90 g) whole-wheat flour
- 5.3 oz (150 g) olives, pitted and drained
- 1½ tsp salt

1 Combine the water (at room temperature) with the sourdough starter.

2 Add the flour, combine well, and let rest for 20 minutes, covered.

3 Add the salt and the olives and knead by hand for a couple of minutes.

4 Make a series of folds in short intervals for the first 1½ hours (see page 63 for tips about folding techniques).

5 Let the dough rest, covered, for 1 to 1½ hours, or until it is nearly doubled.

6 Preheat oven to maximum temperature, with the stone in if you own one.

7 Transfer the dough to a clean and floured surface and shape into 1 large round or 2 smaller ones without deflating the dough.

8 Place the round/rounds into proofing baskets lined with a kitchen towel and dusted with flour.

9 Cover and let rest for 1½ to 2 hours.

10 Invert the loaf/loaves on a baker's peel or flat tray dusted with coarse semolina or corn flour and transfer into the oven, creating steam (see page 49) and lowering the temperature to 460°F.

11 Bake for 20 minutes, then open the oven and release the steam, lowering the temperature to 410°F and baking for 25 to 30 minutes, or until pleasantly browned.

# CHICKPEA SOURDOUGH LOAF

YIELD: 1 LOAF / *ACTIVE TIME:* 30 MINUTES / *TOTAL TIME:* 5 HOURS

If you want to lower the gluten content of your bread and increase the protein content, chickpeas are a great option. This loaf is also incredibly tasty and it is goes well with earthy spreads, like liver or olive pâté.

1 In a large bowl, combine all the ingredients, except the salt. Knead by hand or with a stand-mixer for a few minutes. Let rest for 30 minutes. Add the salt and work the dough more, until it appears elastic when pulled.

2 Let the dough rest, covered, until it has increased 1.5 times its original volume. This should take about 2–2½ hours.

3 Transfer the dough on a clean surface and shape into 1 big round. Place the loaf in a proofing basket lined with a floured kitchen towel.

4 Preheat oven to maximum temperature, with the stone in if you own one.

5 Let rest, covered (for instance by placing the loaf into a clean plastic bag), until the loaf appear to have risen 1½ compared to its initial volume. This could take 2–2½ hours.

6 Invert the loaf on a baker's peel of flat tray dusted with coarse semolina or corn flour. Transfer to the hot oven producing steam (for instance, by throwing some ice cubes on the bottom part of the oven). Reduce immediately heat to 480° and bake for 25 minutes.

7 Let the steam out, reduce heat to 430° and bake for 25–30 minutes or until deep golden brown.

INGREDIENTS:

12.3 oz (350 g) bread flour

5.3 oz (150 g) chickpea flour

5.3 oz (150 g) sourdough starter (see page 59)

12 oz (340 g) water

1¾ tsp (10 g) salt

# DURUM WHEAT SOURDOUGH

**YIELD:** 2 LOAVES / **ACTIVE TIME:** 30 MINUTES / **TOTAL TIME:** 5½ HOURS

Whole wheat semolina flour (or durum flour) gives a golden touch to your crumb and an extra crunch to your crust. It is also a healthy choice, because it is rich in fiber and highly digestible.

**INGREDIENTS:**

- 14 oz (375 g) bread flour
- 3½ oz (125 g) whole-wheat semolina flour
- 5 oz (150 g) sourdough starter (see page 59)
- 12 oz (350 g) water
- 1¾ tsp (10 g) salt

1 In a large bowl, combine all the ingredients, except the salt. Knead by hand or with a stand-mixer for a few minutes. Let rest for 30 minutes. Add the salt and work the dough more, until it appears elastic when pulled. Let the dough rest, covered, until it has increased 1½ times its original volume. This should take about 2–2½ hours.

2 Transfer the dough on a clean surface and shape into two batards (see page 63). Place the loaves in two proofing baskets lined with floured kitchen towels. Preheat oven to maximum temperature, with the stone in if you own one.

3 Let rest, covered (for instance by placing the loaf into a clean plastic bag) until the loaves appear to have risen 1½ compared to their initial volume. This could take 1½ to 2½ hours, depending on several factors, like room temperature and power of the starter, for instance.

4 Invert the loaves on a baker's peel of flat tray dusted with coarse semolina or corn flour. Transfer to the hot oven producing steam (for instance, by throwing some ice cubes on the bottom part of the oven). Reduce immediately heat to 480°F and bake for 25 minutes.

5 Let the steam out, reduce heat to 425°F and bake for 15–20 minutes or until golden brown.

# Zingerman's Bakehouse

3711 Plaza Drive
Ann Arbor, MI 48108
(734) 761-2095
www.zingermansbakehouse.com

For bread enthusiasts, it's impossible to hear the words "rye bread" without immediately thinking of Zingerman's. Michiganders know the Deli for its overflowing, Jewish Deli–style sandwiches, made with corned beef, pastrami, and several other traditional favorites. But the real magic happens at the Bakehouse nearby, where head baker Amy Emberling and Frank Carollo and their crack team whip up loaves and pastries from all over the world. Everything at Zingerman's is delicious, but even among their many standouts, the rye has received special attention. *Saveur* named it "America's best deli rye…no contest." *The Atlantic* champions their rye as well, calling it "one of the best" in the country. And the list of accolades only continues from there.

Of course, the bread from Zingerman's Bakehouse is not *literally* magic. Like all breads, it must be built, cared after, and baked to perfection—and that's where Emberling and partner Frank Carollo come in. Making delicious loaves since 1992, the Bakehouse has a singular goal: make the best bread possible. Carollo, who started the bakery with the support of Zingerman's founders Ari Weinzweig and Paul Saginaw, was lucky enough to hire Emberling as one of the shop's original eight bakers, and the rest was history.

Emberling is not a perfectionist by nature, but one would be forgiven for thinking otherwise. When asked for her golden rule of baking, she can't help but list five. Her younger brother nicknamed her "Baker Woman" when she was only 10. And then there's the bread itself. Rustic Italian, German spelt, challah, even bagels—Zingerman's Bakehouse offers dozens of different loaves every week, each requiring its own specific precision and understanding. On top of it all, the Bakehouse manages BAKE!, a baking school that teaches the craft to hundreds every year. It adds up to a lot more hours in the kitchen than anyone would have time for, but Emberling and Carollo juggle their obligations with stunning composure.

At Zingerman's, growing fame led to an increased sense of community; the bakery has only become more entrenched in Ann Arbor as its notoriety spreads. As Emberling says, "What's most interesting about us is the continuing choice of all of Zingerman's partners (there are about 20 of us) to keep our businesses in the Ann Arbor area. We are deeply committed to our community and understand the reciprocal relationship between a business and its local community. We've been local in a very rooted physical way long before 'local' entered the food world's conversation." And the partners have done more than just stay put. "We also share with our community, giving 10% of our profits back to non-profit organizations. We realize that we're nothing without our greater community."

# IN HER OWN WORDS:

## AMY EMBERLING

*How and when did you get your start baking?*

I started baking at about age 10. I loved dessert. My mother hated to bake and we didn't have a traditional bakery in my hometown, so I decided to try it out myself. Even at 10 I loved looking through recipe books and daydreaming about what this list of ingredients and set of instructions would create. It all seemed mysterious and intriguing. I used recipes from *The Joy of Cooking* and from *McCall's Magazine*. They had a section at the back of the magazine every month, and sometimes I was lucky and it was something baked. That was the beginning.

*Who inspired you to bake?*

I had many inspirations before I turned 20, somewhat because I was very drawn to anyone who engaged with food and baking, and would let me participate. My Nanny, my father's mother, was a very good cook and baker. She was a typical self-taught baker who didn't measure anything—so challenging to learn from but inspiring nonetheless. My other grandmother, my New York Grandma, only bought cakes and cookies. They were inspiring though because they introduced me to my first experience of professional baking. I was fascinated by checkerboard cakes. I remember wondering, "How did they do that?" And I loved the names—"Charlotte Russe," so fancy! And then

there was our Italian babysitter/housekeeper Elva Pezzarello who made special cookies for us, and pizzas on Friday. She introduced me to yeast for the first time. The list goes on, but I have to come back to my mother. Although she was a reluctant baker, she did it from time to time. I now realize that some of her reluctance may have come from her perfectionism. If you're a perfectionist, baking can either make you very happy, or very crazy. Well, it made her crazy. But she inspired me to be more of a perfectionist (I'm not one by nature) because it's a valuable trait when you're trying to make truly great baked items, every time. Thanks Mom!

*Who inspires you now?*

I am super appreciative of the many bakers and baking instructors in America (famous and little known) who do what looks like the same thing everyday but continue to learn about the process and make their bread better and better. Examples of famous people are Jeffrey Hammelman, Frank Carollo (my partner at Zingerman's Bakehouse), Peter Reinhart, and Chad Robertson. They go deep in their study of bread making and bring progress to the field in important ways. I'm more drawn to world cuisines, and educating the public on breads that are not well known, or on the verge of being forgotten. The work these other bakers do educates me and enables me to make better versions of these breads. It's a great relationship for me. I'm not so drawn to exploring the intricacies, but am happy to learn them from those who are and then spread the word.

*What is your golden rule(s) for baking?*

These are some of my rules:

• Bake in a neat and clean environment. I'm addicted to order and need it in my work environment. For me it allows for the possibility of a well executed recipe. Disorder clutters my mind, distracts me, and leads to mistakes.

• Weigh ingredients. A scale is a must in my baking. Volume measures introduce too much variation.

• Measure everything prior to starting the process. This sets the stage for success. No missed items. No unexpected ingredients and order because all of the bags and boxes can be put away where they belong prior to starting the work.

• Do a double check. Everything measured? Measured correctly?

• Always do a recipe as written the first time through and then start to change it.

*What does a bakery represent to you?*

At Zingerman's Bakehouse we're very clear about what a bakery means. It's a community of people working toward an agreed upon and documented mission and vision. Our Mission, created in 1994, is, "At Zingerman's Bakehouse, we are passionately committed to the relentless pursuit of being the best bakery we can imagine." As part of this "best" we are deeply engaged in our greater community. We are in daily conversations with our customers about what's going well and not so well, receiving at least 100 points of feedback every week.

*Favorite thing to bake? Why? Least favorite thing to bake? Why?*

I love baking things that have very few ingredients, but an involved process. That's where the skill of a baker comes into play for me. I find it super rewarding when the seemingly simple, nondescript ingredients are transformed into a tasty and multi-textured treat. Examples of this are French baguettes and palmiers. They both use five ingredients or fewer, and are amazing in their complex end result.

On the other side, I like to stay clean when I bake and there are some steps that can make that difficult, like using cocoa powder or cinnamon in large quantities. I'm a small person and am usually quite close to the mixing bowls when I work, so it's easy to get enveloped by the clouds of items like this as they enter the bowl. So, if they're in the recipe I won't love that particular mix.

*Why Ann Arbor? How did Zingerman's come to be?*

Zingerman's Bakehouse is one of 10 food-related business that work together under the umbrella name "Zingerman's Community of Businesses." The bakery was opened in 1992, the second business after Zingerman's Delicatessen, which started in 1982. The founders of the Deli and the Zingerman's Community of Businesses are Ari Weinzweig and Paul Saginaw. They both went to university in Ann Arbor, love great food and the food business, and met working in an Ann Arbor restaurant.

*Where do you get your tools/materials?*

Oh, they come from all over our state, the country, and the world. We are most interested in great flavor and choose our ingredients based on that. We are fortunate to live in a state with a large agricultural community so we are able to get great tasting and fresh dairy, eggs, fruit, and vegetables. Grains are obviously critical to our bakery. We can get local rye and oats, and we're working on developing wheat with some local farmers. We then travel farther away when we want to use items not created here, like Parmigiano Reggiano cheese or vanilla.

# RYE SOUR

The foundation of some of the great rye breads, including Jewish rye, is an acidic "sour," or starter. The sour may be kept alive and well in the refrigerator forever if it is fed regularly. The chopped onion and whole caraway seeds should be removed and discarded after the first day and not used in future feedings. Once the mixture has fermented all night, the helpful organisms and flavor boosters will have moved off the onions and seeds and into the mixture you have created. If you are going to make this recipe infrequently, just make fresh sour each time. There's no need to keep your sour alive for weeks or months in between uses. If you are going to bake weekly, feed your sour at least once between baking sessions.
—*Amy Emberling, Zingerman's Bakehouse*

INGREDIENTS:

**TO MAKE YOUR SOUR:**

1 cup medium rye flour

¾ cup water, room temperature

⅛ teaspoon instant yeast

½ cup onion, coarsely chopped

1½ teaspoon caraway seeds

**TO FEED YOUR SOUR:**

¾ cup water, room temperature

1 cup medium rye flour

**TO MAINTAIN YOUR SOUR:**

1 cup rye sour

¾ cup water, room temperature

1 cup medium rye flour

## DAY 1: MAKE THE RYE SOUR

1 In a medium bowl, mix the rye flour, water, and yeast. Stir until the mixture is completely smooth.

2 Tie the onion and caraway seeds together tightly in cheesecloth (like a homemade tea bag), then sink the whole package completely into the flour mixture.

3 Cover the bowl tightly with plastic wrap and put it in a nice warm spot (70° to 75°F) overnight.

## DAY 2: FEED THE RYE SOUR

1 Remove the onion/caraway bag and scrape the sour off the bag and back into the bowl. To your sour, add the water and rye flour, and mix until smooth. Cover with plastic. Let it ferment for 3 to 4 additional hours—until it is visibly fermented and frothy.

2 The rye sour can now be used in your rye bread recipe, with plenty left over to put in the fridge until the next feeding. Store it in a tightly sealed container. Any subsequent feedings need to ferment at room temperature for only 3 to 4 hours.

## ONCE A WEEK:

To maintain your sour, add the water and rye flour to your sour and mix until smooth. Cover with plastic wrap and let ferment at room temperature for 3 to 4 hours, until it is nice and frothy and full of fermentation bubbles. Use the sour to make more rye bread, or put it back in the refrigerator, where it will be okay for another week. Feed the sour at least once per week and you will be able to keep it indefinitely.

# JEWISH RYE BREAD

YIELD: 2 LOAVES / ACTIVE TIME: 1 HOUR / TOTAL TIME: 3 HOURS 40 MINUTES

In order to open Zingerman's Bakehouse, we had to be able to bake great Jewish rye bread for Zingerman's Delicatessen, which was our first (and, at the beginning, our only) customer. It's not possible to have a superb Reuben sandwich without authentic Jewish rye bread! We wanted our Jewish rye to be an essential part of the sandwich, not just a structural element that didn't really add to the flavor. So right from the beginning, we used and further evolved the excellent recipe and techniques we learned from our first teacher, Michael London.

So, what makes this a great Jewish rye?

First, we use a sour starter (see page 198), which is unusual these days. It adds a little bit of leavening to the recipe, but mainly it provides depth and complexity of flavor. We created the starter in the fall of 1992, and we've been feeding it every day since to keep it healthy, with just the right amount of tang. This version of rye bread was the one made most often by the Polish Jewish bakers in New York and was called sour rye. It later became known as Jewish rye.

Second, we use "Old"—rye bread from the previous day's bake that we slice and soak in water and then add to the dough. It adds a layer of texture, flavor, moisture, and color to the bread. It's also a tradition for Jewish bakers to take something from yesterday and put it in today's recipes, representing the continuity and interconnectedness of life.

Third, there's actually some rye in the recipe. Many rye breads are made from white-wheat flour with a touch of rye added. We use lots of medium rye (rye flour that has some of its bran) in our sour starter.

Finally, we create a real crackly crust. We brush each loaf with water before it goes into the oven and then again when it comes out. The contrast of the cool water on the hot loaf causes the crust to crack in a distinctive way that is characteristic of Jewish rye.

This recipe takes some planning because you need to prepare the sour a day in advance. Nothing is too hard—but it isn't instantaneous, either. The most inconvenient steps of any recipe are the ones that bring the food from good to great. Our rye sour is an example of this.

—*Amy Emberling, Zingerman's Bakehouse*

## INGREDIENTS:

- ¼ cup day-old bread, preferably rye, torn into pieces
- 2¼ cups rye sour (see page 200)
- ¾ cup water, room temperature
- 1½ teaspoons instant yeast
- ½ teaspoon ground caraway
- 3½ cups + 1 tablespoon all-purpose flour
- 1 tablespoon sea salt
- Cornmeal, for dusting

## MIX THE DOUGH

1 Prepare the "Old." Take some bread—really of any age, preferably rye, though an unflavored white bread will work—break it into pieces, and moisten it with ½ cup minus 1 tablespoon of water. Let sit for 15 minutes. Measure out ¼ cup.

2 In a large, wide mixing bowl, combine the rye sour, water, Old, instant yeast, and ground caraway. Stir with a wooden spoon until well blended. Add half of the flour and stir until the mixture looks like thick pancake batter. Add the salt and remaining flour and stir until it starts to form a shaggy mass.

3 Scrape the dough out of the bowl onto a clean, unfloured work surface and knead for 6 to 8 minutes, until it forms a smooth ball. If the dough begins to stick, use a plastic scraper to clean the surface. Rye has a different chemical makeup than wheat flour and tends to be sticky. Don't be alarmed if that's the case, and resist the temptation to add flour. Keep gently kneading and the dough will come together.

4 Lightly oil the mixing bowl, place the dough in the bowl, and cover with plastic. Allow it to ferment for 1 hour. It will increase in size by about 50%.

## SHAPE AND BAKE THE DOUGH

1 After 1 hour, uncover the dough and turn it out onto a lightly floured work surface. Divide the dough into two equal pieces. Pre-shape both pieces into rounds and cover with plastic. Let rest for 30 minutes.

2 Shape the rounds into loaf shapes. Place on a cornmeal-coated board and cover with plastic.

3 Preheat the oven along with a baking stone and cast iron skillet (for creating steam) to 450°F for 45 minutes before baking. Ferment the loaves for 40 minutes to an hour. Use the touch test to see if the dough is ready for the oven.

4 Uncover the loaves and spray heavily with water. Place the loaves on a corn-meal-dusted wooden peel. With a razor blade or sharp knife, score the tops of the loaves with 5 uniform slices perpendicular to the length of the loaf.

5 Slide the loaves onto the hot baking stone. Bake for 8 minutes with steam, uncover, then bake for an additional 32 to 35 minutes, or until the desired color has been achieved. Baking times will vary depending on the size of your loaves.

6 Remove from the oven, place on a cooling rack, and spray heavily with water. Let cool completely before cutting.

---

### IMPORTANT NOTES

If you are not baking weekly, only feeding, you will end up throwing away or composting some rye sour.

If you use most of the rye sour to make bread and you are left with less than 1 cup, you can still use the steps in "Maintain the Rye Sour" to feed whatever amount you have left. Even if all you have left is a tablespoon, that is enough. Just feed it as directed, and in a matter of hours you'll have a cup of rye sour bubbling away!

# AMY'S RYE *with* CARAWAY *and* MUSTARD SEEDS

YIELD: 3 14-OUNCE LOAVES / ACTIVE TIME: 1 HOUR / TOTAL TIME: 5 HOURS

*Made with a Levain Sourdough Starter*

This is a wonderfully chewy, tangy, and very flavorful loaf that goes well with cured or smoked meats, poultry, or fish. This bread has a tight crumb because it is made with a high proportion of rye flour, which is low in gluten, and so doesn't rise high in the oven.
—*Amy Scherber, Amy's Bread*

**INGREDIENTS:**

- 1½ teaspoons active dry yeast
- ¼ cup very warm water (105–115°F)
- 2½ cups organic rye flour
- 1 cup unbleached bread flour
- 2 tablespoons mustard seeds
- 1 tablespoon + 2 teaspoons caraway seeds
- ½ cup cooked rye berries
- 1 tablespoon + 1 teaspoon kosher salt
- 1¾ cups water (75°F)
- 1¼ cups firm levain, room temperature
- Cornmeal for sprinkling, as needed

1. Combine the yeast and warm water in a small bowl and stir with a fork to dissolve the yeast. Let stand for 3 minutes.

2. Combine both flours, the caraway and mustard seeds, rye berries, and salt in a large mixing bowl. Pour in the cool water and the yeast mixture and stir with your fingers to combine. Bring the dough together into a rough mass and knead and fold it over onto itself for 3 minutes. If the dough seems too stiff, knead in up to 3 tablespoons of water, 1 tablespoon at a time. (The dough should be very sticky and gloppy, almost like clay, through most of the kneading process.)

3. Place the dough on a floured work surface and flatten it into a rough rectangle. Place the firm levain on top of the rye dough, stretching it to cover the rye dough. Fold the whole mass up like a business letter, folding the top third of the rectangle down and the bottom third up over it, then gently knead to blend both doughs together. Continue to knead until the dough becomes smooth and supple, about 4 minutes total. Cover the dough with a cloth or plastic wrap and let it rest for 20 minutes.

4. Loosen the dough from the work surface with a bench scraper, lift it up, and lightly flour the work surface. Knead the dough for 2 to 3 minutes, until it feels gluey, airy, and supple. It should still feel slightly firm, almost like aerated modeling clay.

5. Shape the dough into a loose ball and place it in a lightly oiled bowl. Turn the dough to coat with oil. Cover the bowl tightly with oiled plastic wrap and let the dough rise at room temperature (75 to 77°F) for 1 ½ to 2 hours, or until doubled in bulk. (This dough will not develop and rise as well at cooler temperatures.)

6. Generously sprinkle a peel or the back of a baking sheet with cornmeal or line it with parchment paper. Place the dough on a lightly floured surface and divide it into 3 equal pieces (about

16 ounces each). Shape each piece of dough into a boule. Place the loaves seam side–down on the peel or pan, leaving 2 to 3 inches between them for rising. These loaves are small, so they should all fit on one baking stone. Cover them with oiled plastic wrap and allow to rise at room temperature for 1 ½ to 2 hours, or until doubled in bulk. (Rye bread lacks gluten and the dough has the tendency to crack. If the loaves start to split or tear, they have become too acidic and have over-risen, and they should be baked right away. Don't worry: They'll still taste good, just with a tangier flavor.)

7 Thirty minutes before baking, preheat the oven to 425°F. Place a baking stone in the oven to preheat and place an empty water pan directly below the stone.

8 Sprinkle a little rye flour on top of each loaf, then cut the top of each loaf with a razor blade, making 3 lines that connect at one end like the prongs of a fork. Gently slide the loaves onto the stone. Quickly pour 1 cup of very hot water into the water pan and immediately shut the oven door. After about 1 minute, using a plant sprayer, mist the loaves 6 to 8 times and then quickly shut the oven door. Mist again after 2 more minutes.

9 Bake for 20 minutes, then reduce the oven temperature to 400°F and bake for 15 to 20 minutes longer, until the loaves are a rich reddish brown and sound hollow when tapped on the bottom. Transfer the bread to a rack to cool completely. (Make sure the loaves are completely cool before slicing, or they will be gummy inside.) This bread is great on the second day.

# HEIRLOOM RYE COUNTRY BREAD

YIELD: 2 2-POUND LOAVES / ACTIVE TIME: 2½ HOURS / TOTAL TIME: 16 HOURS

From Graison Gill and Bellegarde (see page 156) comes an absolutely gorgeous loaf with just the right amount of tang. Gill uses Seashore Black Rye, an heirloom rye variety from South Carolina grown by farmer Greg Johnsman. Johnsman, who has been growing the variety in the Carolina Lowcountry, said in an interview with Slow Food USA (www.slowfoodusa.org), "Rye is grown to protect and stop the sand from blasting a vegetable crop. After years of wind breaks, I asked my father-in-law if I could mill some. We were blown away with the flavor of this rye. No other rye compares with its texture and non-tacky quality." On its inclusion to the Ark of Taste, Johnsman add, "Our goal is to preserve and continue to keep the strain. I am excited to link his beginning as a farmer with the future."

—*recipe courtesy of Graison Gill, Bellegarde Bakery*

## INGREDIENTS:

- 797 millilitres water, 78°F (hold back some water)
- 24 grams salt
- 300 grams levain (see page 160)
- 440 grams freshly milled whole wheat flour, 78°F
- 337 grams rye flour, freshly milled, 78° F
- 194 grams bread flour, 78° F
- 2 grams malt powder (for flavor and color, if desired)

1 Add flour, levain, and about 90% of the water into a shaggy mass. Sprinkle the salt and remaining water on top. Mix by hand in a bus tub or large bowl. Once combined, the ingredients should have a mutual temperature of 78°F. If this temperature is not achieved, place the covered dough in a drafty or warmer area of the kitchen in order to reduce or increase its overall temperature. Then cover with a lid or towel and let rest for 90 minutes. This is your autolyse period.

2 After 90 minutes, fold the dough 5 to 7 times, depending on its strength and elasticity (see pages 62-63 for instruction on folding). Do this every 12 minutes.

3 Divide dough into 2 equal portions, shape tightly and place into bread pans. Store covered in fridge overnight.

4 Preheat oven to 550°F. When the oven is ready, gently score the loaves, transfer them into the oven, and immediately drop the temperature to 450°F. Bake to desired doneness, about 35 minutes or until golden brown.

# SWEDISH LIGHT RYE

**YIELDS:** 2 SMALL LOAVES / **ACTIVE TIME:** 30 MINUTES / **TOTAL TIME:** ABOUT 3 HOURS

The most common and traditional Swedish loaf is soft, slightly sweet, and based on light rye and wheat flour. It is generally made with commercial yeast, and it makes a good and versatile sandwich bread.

**INGREDIENTS:**

2½ tsp (7 g) active dry yeast

½ lb (250 g) all-purpose flour

½ lb (250 g) light rye flour

5.2 oz (160 g) water

5.2 oz (160 g) milk, lukewarm

2 tbsp light syrup or barley malt

1 tbsp butter

1¼ tsp (10 g) salt

1 In a large bowl, activate the yeast in the water warmed to 100–105°F maximum for 10 minutes.

2 Add all other ingredients except the butter and the salt and knead by hand or with a stand mixer for 15 minutes, adding the butter and the salt towards the end of the kneading (see page 142 for tips on kneading).

3 Let the dough rest, covered, in a warm spot, such as in the oven with the light on and the oven door open, until it doubles (about 1½ hours).

4 Preheat the oven to 400°F.

5 De-gas the dough and divide in 2 pieces.

6 Shape each piece of dough into a log and transfer to two oval or rectangular floured proofing baskets.

7 Let rest, covered, until the dough has risen 1½ times (about 1 hour).

8 Invert the loaves on a baker peel or flat tray covered with parchment paper and transfer into the oven.

9 Bake for 30 to 35 minutes or until golden brown.

# POLISH LIGHT RYE

YIELDS: 2 SMALL LOAVES / ACTIVE TIME: 30 MINUTES / TOTAL TIME: ABOUT 3 HOURS

Poland has a rich bread-baking tradition and its light rye breads are particularly delicious. This is a quite typical version, flavored by caraway seeds and perfect for sandwiches with deli meats.

**INGREDIENTS:**

| | |
|---|---|
| 11 | oz (325 g) water |
| 1 | tbsp caraway seeds |
| 1 | tsp sugar |
| 2½ | tsp (7 g) active dry yeast |
| 5.3 | oz (150 g) medium rye flour |
| 12.4 | oz (350 g) all-purpose flour |
| 1 | tbsp butter |
| 1¾ | tsp (10 g) salt |

1 In a large bowl, combine the water with the caraway seeds, the sugar, and the rye flour and warm to 100–105°F. Activate the yeast in the water for 25 minutes.

2 Add the wheat flour and knead for 10 minutes by hand or with a stand mixer, adding the butter and the salt towards the end of the kneading (see page 207 for tips on kneading).

3 Let the dough rest, covered, in a warm spot, such as in the oven with the light on and the oven door open a crack, until it doubles (about 1 hour).

4 Preheat the oven to 360°F.

5 De-gas the dough and divide in 2 pieces.

6 Shape each piece of dough into two rounds and transfer to two floured proofing baskets.

7 Let rest, covered, until the dough has risen 1½ times (about 1 hour).

8 Invert the loaves on a baker peel or flat tray covered with parchment paper and slash as desired.

9 Spray with some water and transfer into the oven.

10 Bake for about 40 minutes or until golden brown.

# OLIVE OIL LOAF

**YIELDS: 1 SMALL ROUND / ACTIVE TIME: 25 MINUTES / TOTAL TIME: 3 HOURS**

Make this bread when you are going tailgating or you have a crowd of people coming for lunch. When it's cooled, cut it in half like a cake, then make a giant sandwich with mayo, cold cuts, cheeses, tomatoes, onions, peppers—think of it as a round submarine sandwich loaf, but it'll taste so good! Serve in wedges with other picnic foods.

—*Dominique DeVito*

**INGREDIENTS:**

- ¼ teaspoon instant yeast
- ¼ teaspoon sugar
- 1½ cups water (110 to 115°F)
- 1 teaspoon kosher salt
- 3 cups all-purpose flour plus more for kneading and dusting
- 1 tablespoon freshly ground black pepper
- 1 tablespoon extra virgin olive oil

1 Put the yeast and sugar in a measuring cup and add about ½ cup warm water in a drizzle. Hot water will kill the yeast, so it's important that the water be warm without being hot. Cover the measuring cup with plastic wrap and set it aside for about 15 minutes. If the yeast doesn't foam, it is not alive and you'll need to start over.

2 When the yeast is proofed, pour it into a large bowl and add the additional cup of warm water. Stir gently to combine. Add the salt and pepper to the flour, and add the flour to the yeast mixture. Add the olive oil. Stir with a wooden spoon until combined. The dough will be sticky.

3 Put a dusting of flour on a flat surface and lift out the dough. With flour on your hands and more at the ready, begin kneading the dough so that it loses its stickiness. Don't overdo it, and don't use too much flour; just enough that it is more cohesive.

4 Place the dough in a large bowl, cover the bowl with plastic wrap, and allow to rise untouched for at least 1 hour, and up to several hours. On a piece of parchment paper, remove from the bowl and gently punch it down, shaping it into a round that will fit inside the Dutch oven (approximately 8 inches in diameter). Cover with the plastic and allow to rise again for another 30 minutes or so. Brush with the olive oil.

5 While the dough is on its final rise, preheat the oven to 450°F. Put a piece of parchment paper on the bottom of the Dutch oven and put it in with the lid on so it gets hot. When the oven is ready and dough has risen, carefully remove the lid and gently scoop the flattened dough from the bowl into the pot. Cover and bake for 15 minutes. Remove the lid and continue to bake for another 15 to 20 minutes until the top is golden and it sounds hollow when tapped.

6 Remove the pot from the oven and use tea towels to carefully remove the bread. Allow to cool completely.

# LIMPPU

YIELDS: 1 LOAF / ACTIVE TIME: 30 MINUTES / TOTAL TIME: ABOUT 15 HOURS

Traditional Finnish dark rye bread is made lighter by a proportion of wheat flour. As other similar dark rye breads, its preparation needs to start the night before the baking day.

**INGREDIENTS:**

- 14 oz (350 g) dark rye flour
- 7 oz (250 g) all-purpose flour
- ¼ cup (60 g) rye sourdough starter OR 1 tsp active dry yeast
- 15.2 oz (about 450 g) water
- 2 tbsp molasses
- 1 tsp (about 6 g) salt

1 Combine the water with ½ of the flours and the sourdough starter OR the yeast.

2 Let rest at room temperature for about 12 hours. Before adding the sourdough starter or the yeast to the dough, allow it to cool down to 85°F if using a sourdough starter, OR to 100–105°F if using active dry yeast.

3 Let rest, covered, overnight (about 12 hours), at room temperature.

4 Add the remaining flours and the molasses and knead for 10 minutes, by hand or with a stand-mixer, adding the salt towards the end.

5 Transfer the dough to a greased, medium-sized (8½ x 4½ x 2½) loaf pan, and let rest until nearly doubled (about 3 hours).

6 Preheat the oven to 350°F and bake for about 80 minutes.

7 Let cool for several hours before slicing.

# RUGBRØD

YIELDS: 2 LOAVES / ACTIVE TIME: 30 MINUTES / TOTAL TIME: 4½ HOURS

This quintessential Danish bread used to be used to make the traditional Danish sandwich, *smørrebrød*, an open sandwich spread with butter and topped in various ways, from liver pâté and pickles, to eggs and caviar, or cold cuts and spreads, among others.

1 Combine all ingredients but the salt and let rest for 15 minutes, covered.

2 Add the salt and combine well.

3 Place in two small (8 x 4 x 2½ inches) loaf pans and place in two food-approved plastic bags.

4 Let rest at room temperature until the dough has nearly doubled, about 4 hours.

5 Preheat the oven to 320°F and bake for about 2½ hours.

6 Let cool for a whole day before slicing.

**INGREDIENTS:**

| | |
|---|---|
| 14 | oz (600 g) dark rye flour |
| 5.3 | oz (150 g) rye chops, soaked in water overnight, boiled for 15 minutes and drained |
| 10½ | oz (300 g) rye sourdough starter |
| 13½ | oz (400 g) lukewarm water |
| 7 | oz (about 200 g) dark beer |
| 2 | tbsp molasses |
| 1½ | tsp (about 8½ g) salt |

# BAGUETTE

The baguette was initially called "Viennese bread" because it was inspired by the bread made in Vienna at the beginning of the 19th century. In Vienna, bakers had started to use steam ovens to cook bread faster and to get a crunchy crust and a light crumb. However, the bread baked this way had, and still has, a short shelf life, just like a regular baguette. From 1830 onwards, many Parisian bakers adopted the use of steam ovens, and began to produce this type of bread originally called pain de fantasie, which soon became pain baguette (that means "stick" or "wand"). With white wheat finally accessible to most, the baguette became the bread of the city workers, because it could be baked faster and it cost less than other loaves.

The baguette then gave birth to other types of bread made with the same method, but smaller in size, like pain batard, which is shorter and larger, and the pain flute, which is slimmer.

In 1920, after WWI, the French government issued an edict prohibiting bakeries from starting work before 4 a.m. This further increased baguette sales, because bakers had to give up producing other breads with slower rising times. The baguette was the fastest solution because it was yeast-based, and the long and narrow shape allowed for a faster baking time.

More recently, in the 1980s, large companies began using frozen baguette dough in the industrial scale, contributing to the spread of poor quality baguettes around the world. Since the 1990s, however, a long wave of artisan bread revival has grown in France and Paris. The government released a law to restore quality in French bread. According to this law, the only ingredients allowed in bread were water, flour, salt, and yeast (including sourdough), with the possibility of adding a minimal amount of wheat malt. Different versions of the baguette have since been developed to meet the re-acquired taste for long fermented bread. Now it is not uncommon to taste baguettes that have slowly risen with a preferment, rather than made in 4 hours from start to finish.

# BOULANGERIE'S BAGUETTE

YIELD: 4 LOAVES / ACTIVE TIME: 30 MINUTES / TOTAL TIME: 24 HOURS

There are many ways to make a baguette—Pâte Fermentée, poolish, straight method. Boulangerie uses Pâte Fermentée, or old dough, in our baguette. This creates a chewy texture while maintaining a crispy crust.

—*Amy and Zachary Tyson, Boulangerie*

## DAY 1

1 Begin by making your Pâte Fermentée a day in advance. Mix all ingredients by hand until incorporated. Cover and rest overnight. If you bake regularly, reserve this amount from your previous bread and use the old dough in the next mix. It can be held up to 48 hours.

## DAY 2

1 The next day, make your dough. Combine all ingredients and mix for 6 minutes on low speed. Increase speed to medium and mix for 5 additional minutes. Place dough in an oiled bin and refrigerate overnight. If baking the same day, let proof for 45 minutes in a warm spot.

2 When you're ready to bake, turn out the dough onto a floured surface and divide into 4 pieces (each a loaf). Save about half a loaf's worth of dough to ensure the correct size, and to use in future recipes if you bake regularly.

3 Pre-shape each piece into a rectangle. Flatten out each piece, fold top side–down, and bottom side–up. Pull both sides together and seal the seam.

4 Set your pre-shaped baguettes aside on a floured surface and cover with linen. Let rest 20 minutes.

5 While the dough rests, prepare your linen canvas, or "couche." Dust with flour and place on tray or board.

6 After 20 minutes, shape the baguettes. Again, flatten out, fold top-down, fold bottom-up, fold together, seal seam and roll from the center out until you've reached your length—approximately 2 feet. Place baguette on the couche, seam side–down. Pleat a nice fold of linen between and repeat for the others. If you do not have a couche, place baguettes on a parchment-lined tray. But beware: these baguettes tend to flatten. Let proof for 1 hour.

## INGREDIENTS:

### PÂTE FERMENTÉE

| | |
|---|---|
| 1 | cup + 2 tablespoons water |
| 2¼ | teaspoons fresh yeast |
| 3⅓ | cups Sir Galahad all-purpose flour |
| 1½ | teaspoons salt |

### DOUGH

| | |
|---|---|
| 2½ | cups water |
| 1⅔ | tablespoons fresh yeast |
| 7½ | cups Sir Galahad all-purpose flour |
| 1 | tablespoon salt |
| 1⅓ | cups Pâte Fermentée (see page 257) |

7 Preheat the oven to 470°F. Using a baguette board, turn the baguettes out from the couche and place on tray, or on a peel to slide onto a baking stone.

8 Bake at 470°F for 25 minutes, until golden brown. When first placing baguettes in oven, be sure to introduce steam by squirting a water bottle around the oven or putting some ice cubes on a hot tray that is already in the oven.

# BOULTED BREAD'S FRENCH BAGUETTE

YIELD: 5 BAGUETTES / ACTIVE TIME: 45 MINUTES / TOTAL TIME: 24 HOURS

Baguettes are my favorite thing to bake and the ultimate challenge for me: the purest expression of a baker's proficiency, focus, and ethos. A perfect baguette requires so many distinct skills and such precise execution. If you're even fractionally off your game, the whole thing can fall apart. For the same reason, baguettes are also my least favorite thing to bake. Nothing has caused me more stress, grief, and sleepless nights!
—*Joshua Bellamy, Boulted Bread*

## DAY 1

1 Eight hours prior to your mix, make your levain. Mix the whole wheat flour with ¼ cup cold water. Let sit at room temperature in a cool kitchen.

2 In a mixer with a dough hook attachment, mix bread flour, warm water, yeast, malt, and levain until all ingredients are evenly incorporated, then allow the dough to rest for 30 minutes at room temperature.

3 Add the salt and a small splash of water to the dough and mix on low speed for an additional 5 minutes.

4 Cover the mixing bowl with plastic wrap and place dough in a warm location. Allow to bulk ferment for 1 hour.

5 Wet your hand and fold all of the sides into the center of the bowl. Cover the bowl tightly in plastic wrap and place in refrigerator overnight.

## DAY 2

1 Dump cold dough onto a floured surface and divide the dough into 1-pound pieces. Loosely round each piece and let rest seam side–down on your work surface.

2 Dust the tops of the dough pieces lightly with flour. Turn the piece of dough upside-down and fold the bottom up to the center of the piece. Fold the top down to the center of the piece. Fold the new "top" down to the new bottom so that you now have a cigar-shaped loaf. Applying gentle pressure with both hands, gently roll out the cigar into a tube. [NOTE: This takes immense amounts of practice—it's best to embrace the imperfections. And if you want extra help, there are thousands of tutorial videos online!]

### INGREDIENTS:

**FOR LEVAIN:**

¼ cup cold water

½ cup whole wheat flour

**FOR DOUGH:**

8⅔ cups bread flour

⅓ cup cornmeal

4⅛ cups warm water

1½ tablespoons salt

1 gram malt

2 grams yeast

3 Place tubes onto a floured linen with a crease between each loaf.

4 Let proof in a warm location for 2 hours or until the dough slowly springs back when firmly poked.

5 Place a small baking sheet on the bottom rack of your oven and fill with water. Place your pizza stone on the rack above this and preheat the oven to 500°F. This will help to steam the top of the loaf.

6 Gently and carefully place each tube on the pizza stone. Using a sharp, serrated knife or razor blade, cut longways down the center of each tube

7 Bake at 500°F for approximately 20 minutes or until desired doneness is achieved. Live a little and let them get some color!

# METROPOLITAN'S FRENCH BAGUETTES

YIELD: 3 BAGUETTES / ACTIVE TIME: 1 HOUR / TOTAL TIME: 17–18 HOURS

Our baguette uses a preferment, which helps to create a crisper, crunchy crust with a moist interior and an irregular crumb. The small amount of yeast and the longer fermentation impart a decisively nutty flavor.

— *Wendy Smith Born and James Barrett, Metropolitan Bakery*

1 In a large bowl, dissolve the yeast in warm water. Stir in the flour and salt until a soft dough is formed. Cover and refrigerate for 12 hours.

2 Remove the preferment from the refrigerator. Let stand until at room temperature for 1 hour.

3 In the bowl of a heavy-duty mixer, combine the preferment, flour, and water. With a dough hook attachment at low speed, mix until the dough forms a shaggy mass, about 4 minutes. Sprinkle the salt over the dough. Let the dough rest 15 minutes.

4 At low speed, mix the salt into the dough. Increase the speed to medium. Knead the dough for 8 to 10 minutes. Test for proper gluten development—the dough should be smooth and elastic and pull away from the sides of the mixing bowl.

5 Lightly oil a large mixing bowl and transfer the dough to the prepared bowl. Cover the bowl with plastic wrap and let it rise in a cool, draft-free place for 1 hour. Fold the dough down to deflate. Cover the bowl and let the dough rise until doubled in size, about 1 hour.

6 Turn the dough out onto a lightly floured surface and divide into 3 equal parts. Flatten 1 piece of dough into a rectangle, with 1 long side facing you. Fold the bottom third of the dough, letter-style, up to the center of the rectangle. Fold the remaining dough over the top to meet the opposite edge. Starting from the left, use the palm of your hand to seal the seam. Gently roll the baguette back and forth into an 18-inch-long log, tapering the ends. Repeat with the remaining 2 pieces of dough.

7 Line a large baking tray with clean tea towels. Sprinkle the towels lightly with flour. Arrange the baguettes, seam side–up and about 1-inch apart, on the prepared towels. Gently pull up the towel between each baguette to form a pleat 1 ½ to 2 inches higher than the tops of the baguettes. Cover the baguettes with damp tea towels and let rise in a cool place until doubled in size, about 2 hours.

## INGREDIENTS:

### FOR PREFERMENT:

1    teaspoon active dry yeast

¾    cup lukewarm water (80°F)

1 ½  cups all-purpose flour

### FOR THE DOUGH:

     Preferment

¼    teaspoon fine sea salt

2½   cups all-purpose flour, plus extra flour for preparation

1¼   cups water

1¼   teaspoons fine sea salt

     Yellow cornmeal, for preparation

8 Meanwhile, at least 20 minutes before baking, place a large baking stone on the center oven rack. Preheat the oven to 450°F.

9 Sprinkle a baker's peel with cornmeal. Carefully transfer 1 baguette, seam side–down, to the prepared peel. With a lame or a sharp serrated knife, cut 3 shallow diagonal slashes, slightly overlapping, lengthwise down the center of the baguette. Working quickly, open the oven door and generously spray the entire oven cavity with water (taking care not to spray the oven lightbulb) in order to create steam. (If you don't have a spray bottle, place a baking pan at least 2 inches deep on the floor of your oven. Preheat the pan along with the baking stone at least 20 minutes before baking. Just before placing the loaf in the oven, very carefully pour lukewarm water into the pan.)

10 Slide the baguette onto the baking stone and close the oven door. Bake for 3 minutes. Open the oven door and spray all around the baguette. Close the oven door and bake for 3 minutes. Repeat spraying the oven walls. Close the oven door and bake for about 25 minutes, until the baguette is a dark golden brown. Transfer the baguette to a wire rack and let cool completely. Repeat with the remaining baguettes.

A "lame" is a 3-inch-long stainless steel rod to which a double-edge razor is attached. It is used to score the surface of breads.

## Swiss Bakery

143 East 3rd Avenue
Vancouver, BC V5T 1C7
Canada
(604) 736-8785
www.swissbakery.ca

For a man of so few words, Michael Siu is a tenacious baker. But he couldn't be any other way. "You need to be [tenacious]," he says. "And organized and attentive to detail. Don't be sloppy." Easier said than done, yes, but Siu makes it look simple. Having earned his status as a Certified Master Baker from Retail Bakers of America, he is not simply a good cook but also a smart manager, understanding the nuances of keeping the bakery clean and running smoothly.

Swiss Bakery is perhaps most famous for its frissant. Or, as many Americans refer to it, a cronut. And it's easy to see why. Fried, buttery and flaky, it is every bit the delicious treat that once took New York by storm. Siu refers to this recipe as his most memorable collaboration. "My daughter Annette and I worked tirelessly for at least a month in improving the dough, and she has created all the monthly flavors and presentations to this day." Michael

and Annette's hard work paid off, helping the bakery join *HuffPo*'s "Best Bakeries in Canada" list in 2016.

For Siu, the sort of creativity and self-confidence required to execute his complex recipes results directly from the time he spent abroad. Sourdough in San Francisco, pretzels in Germany, donuts in New York, and croissants in France—Siu has gone to great lengths to leave no stone unturned. His refusal to shy away from the hard tasks is what makes Swiss Bakery so special. Ask him his least favorite thing to bake, and he'll say, "muffins." Why? "Too simple."

Everything at Swiss Bakery is of the highest quality and is made with unwavering technical brilliance. Whether sampling one of their must-try pretzels, delicious baguettes, or the famous frissant, customers can always trust in Siu's consistency. For most bakers, that's half the battle.

# IN HIS OWN WORDS:

## MICHAEL SIU

*How and when did you get your start baking?*

About 35 years ago, my friend called me to join a small Greek bakery. At that time, I was an engineer working in an office and was not happy. I decided to take the risk and change my career and took on this new challenge. I fell in love with it right away because it gave me an opportunity to run around and work with my hands.

*Who inspired you to bake? Who inspires you now?*

My desire to learn, experiment, and to try new things always inspires me to bake. Nowadays, it's the young talented bakers that inspire me with their new ideas or products.

*What is your golden rule for bakers?*

My golden rule for bakers is to be passionate. If you don't have passion, baking is not for you, because the routine is tedious and tough. It's also good to upgrade by reading books.

*What does Swiss Bakery represent to you?*

Swiss Bakery represents high-quality products and the merging of European and North American baked goods. We are proud to only use scratch baking techniques and slow fermentation times to produce our pastries and breads.

*What is your favorite thing to bake?*

My favorite thing to make is artisan bread. Most of our breads require over 48 hours to make. I enjoy culturing the ideal starter because it needs the right balance of time and temperature to help bring out the natural flavors within a loaf of bread.

*How and when did Swiss Bakery get its start?*

Swiss Bakery started in 1992 when I purchased the business from the owner who wanted to retire. It started out as an 800-square-foot location to now a combined space of 10,000 square feet in the Vancouver area.

*What are your most popular items?*

The most popular items at Swiss Bakery are the butter croissants, "frissant"—fried croissant donut hybrid, hand-made soft pretzels, and our sourdough bread.

*What non-essential items should every baker have?*

A non-essential item every baker should have is a good cup of coffee, and a substantial breakfast every morning.

*What food outlets/periodicals/newspapers do you read or consult regularly, if any?*

Items I read or consult regularly include: *Professional Bakers Manual* by G. Rudolph and K. Sohm, *Bread Lines from the Bakers Guild*, *Advanced Bread and Pastry* by Michel Suas, and *Baking: The Art and Science* by Claus Schunemann.

*What is your proudest moment as a chef?*

My proudest moment as a chef is achieving my Certified Master Baker certification. It signified my highest level of accomplishment. It does not mean I stopped learning, though—there is always more to explore in baking.

*Where did you learn to bake?*

I first attended the Professional Baking Program at Vancouver Community College.

# SWISS BAKERY'S FRENCH BAGUETTE

**YIELD:** 10–12 BAGUETTES / **ACTIVE TIME:** 90 MINUTES / **TOTAL TIME:** 12-16 HOURS

There are many benefits to being a Certified Master Baker, but knowing how to make a perfect baguette is perhaps the best of all. Michael Siu (see page 227) is living proof, and these crunchy delights are perfect whether paired with butter and jam or building a banh mi.

—*recipe courtesy of Michael Siu, Swiss Bakery*

## DAY 1

1. At least 18 hours prior to baking, prepare your sponge and poolish. Gather 2 buckets and scale water, flour, and yeast accordingly. Cover with lid and store in a room-temperature environment.

## DAY 2

2. Place flour, malt powder, poolish, sponge, and water into mixer with dough hook. Mix at slow speed for about 2 minutes. Rest in bowl for 30 minutes

3. Add yeast and mix at slow speed for 2 minutes to incorporate the yeast. Once incorporated, switch to fast speed and mix for another 2 minutes to develop gluten. Add salt and mix for another minute to incorporate and let the gluten fully develop. Remove bowl from mixer, cover it with a towel, and let rest for 2 hours.

4. Flour your work surface and place dough on top. Flour generously and cut into 480-gram pieces. Roll dough into baton shape and rest for 30 minutes.

5. Shape the dough by folding one side of the dough over to the middle. Rotate dough 180°F and repeat. Once finished, fold the dough over in half and gently seal the open side.

6. Roll dough, starting with both hands in the middle working slowly outwards. Taper the ends to seal the dough.

7. Preheat oven to 450°F. Proof your dough at room temperature for at least 45 minutes, until the baguettes have doubled in size.

8. Mist baguettes with water and place into oven. Bake for 15–20 minutes or until the baguettes are golden brown. Remove from oven and enjoy.

## INGREDIENTS:

**POOLISH:**

| | |
|---|---|
| 2½ | cups bread flour |
| | Pinch of salt |
| .55 | grams fresh yeast |
| 2⅓ | cups water |

**SPONGE:**

| | |
|---|---|
| 3⅔ | cups bread flour |
| | Pinch of salt |
| .37 | grams fresh yeast |
| 1 | cup water |

**FINAL DOUGH:**

| | |
|---|---|
| 9¼ | cups bread flour |
| ½ | tablespoons salt |
| 2½ | teaspoons (9 g) malt |
| 1 | tablespoon fresh yeast |
| 2⅕ | cups water |
| | Poolish |
| | Sponge |

# CLASSIC CHALLAH

YIELDS: 1 LOAF / ACTIVE TIME: 50 MINUTES / TOTAL TIME: ABOUT 3½ HOURS

Possibly the most popular of Jewish breads, it is supposed to be eaten during the Jewish Sabbath and other Jewish holydays. It has Eastern European origins and it has much in common with other European sweet breads.

**INGREDIENTS:**

6 oz (180 g) water

2¼ teaspoons (7 grams) active dry yeast

17.6 oz (500 grams) all-purpose flour

2 eggs

2.7 oz (80 g) honey

2.7 oz (80 g) vegetable oil

1¾ tsp (10 grams) salt

1 egg for the egg wash

Poppy seeds (optional)

1 Heat the water to 100–105°F.

2 Dissolve the yeast in the water and let rest for 5 minutes.

3 In a large bowl, combine the water-yeast mixture with ½ of the flour.

4 Add 1 egg at a time and incorporate well. Add the honey and the rest of the flour and start working the dough, either with a stand mixer or by hand (see page 62 for tips on kneading).

5 Gradually add the oil, continuing to work the dough, and incorporate the salt towards the end of the kneading.

6 Work the dough until it feels smooth. The mixing process will take about 25 minutes from start to finish.

7 Let the dough rest, covered, in a warm spot until it looks fully risen (doubled or even tripled). This should take about 1½ to 2 hours.

8 Transfer the dough to a clean surface. Depending on how skilled you are at making dough braids, divide the dough in 3, 4, OR 6 pieces. A four-strand challah is almost as pretty as a six-strand one, and is much easier to braid.

9 Roll each piece of dough into a log, making sure that the resulting logs are of the same length.

10 Prepare a baking dish with oiled parchment paper, and seal together the ends of the dough strands. Start braiding the strands, hiding the ends under the finished braid. You can also roll the braid into itself like a snail, creating a beautiful effect.

11 Preheat oven to 375°F.

12 Let the braid rest, covered, for 40 to 60 minutes, depending on room temperature.

13 Brush the braid with the egg lightly whisked with 1 tablespoon water, and, if preferred, sprinkle with poppy seeds (optional).

14 Bake for 30 to 40 minutes, covering with aluminum foil if the challah is browning too fast.

## Community Grains

Oakland, CA
510.547.3737
www.communitygrains.com

For 30 years, Bob Klein has owned and operated Oliveto, a renowned farm-to-table Italian Restaurant in Oakland, CA. About 10 years ago, he started thinking about the gap between how much local produce they used and how little their flour varied. As Community Grains writer Phoebe Plank says, "as if wheat wasn't an agricultural product as well." Plank continues, "thus Bob set out to source heirloom wheat seeds from friends in Italy, roped in a couple of the same local farmers that the restaurant had been buying vegetables from for years, and gave it a go! The resulting flavors were exciting and spurred the vision to build this alternative grain economy that would innovate towards flavor and nutrition rather than just efficiency and uniformity. What began as the Oliveto Wheat Project slowly developed into its own whole grain products company, Community Grains."

Community Grains doesn't grow itself, but its work with mills and farmers has reinvigorated the grain community in northern California. And for good reason. "The change from thousands of local stone mills to a few hundred, centralized, high-speed roller mills has had a significant effect on both the flour coming out of it and the industry behind it." And while Plank and Klein acknowledge the importance of modern roller mills, they also note that "[in light of the] renewed demand for whole grains, however, the roller mill is sub-par in that it inevitably separates the components of the kernel, which can arguably not be recombined in the same way."

Of course a focus on local, sustainable grains is essential to Community Grains' vision, but there is plenty of focus on quality as well. Their grains are grown in nutrient-rich soil on farms that have been organically building soil for 30 years—and it shows in the quality of the wheat. This allows farmers more flexibility in their planning and the option to profit off fields that would otherwise lie fallow and subject to erosion. Add Plank and Klein, "Everything we sell is 100% whole grain, so you get the whole thing. Wheat, when consumed whole, is actually a superfood in terms of the essential minerals and nutrients it contains. The problem is that the most nutritious parts of a wheat kernel—the bran and the germ—are completely sifted out to create white flour (leaving only the starchy gluten-protein rich endosperm). Furthermore, the bran and the germ are often grossly underrepresented in most "whole grain" flours on the market, so we offer grain that has been milled whole, and never sifted to improve the health of our community."

## IN THEIR OWN WORDS:

## BOB KLEIN AND PHOEBE PLANK OF COMMUNITY GRAINS

*Who—or what—first inspired you to begin work-*
*ing with locally grown whole grains? Who inspires*
*you now?*

Initially it was food historian William
Ruble and Glenn Roberts of Anson Mills who
opened our eyes to the possibilities of growing
grain here. Since then, it has been the farmers
we work with. They were harvesting such fantastic produce when we started out, and have
continued to do so, inspiring us with their
ingenuity, energy, and grit.

*What is your golden rule(s) for growing grains?*

Our golden rule really is to look at the
whole thing; in the same way that a good farm
is a whole system, a grain economy is a whole
system. Good organic, sustainable farming is
incredibly complex. We certainly agree with
the farmers that believe you need to focus on
building nutrient-rich soil, and then the crops
will grow themselves. As a company that buys

grain, we don't require farmers we work with to
be doing anything in particular, just that they
are completely transparent and excited to share
with us all that they're trying out.

*What does Community Grains represent to you?*

A community of people excited about the
potential for grains, executing on an alternative
to commodity wheat, and creating exceptional
whole wheat products.

*Tell me a little bit about the different grains you*
*grow. What's the importance of growing the grains*
*sustainably?*

Our farmers grow an array of different
wheat varieties, some old heirloom varieties
bred and cultivated in Europe, some pre-industrial northern American varieties, and even
some newer varieties adapted for our growing
conditions here in northern California. Besides
needing to able to be grown organically, they

have to be healthy, flavorful, and have pretty good yield. Right now we use a mix of hard red, hard white, soft white, and hard amber durum varieties.

Growing grains sustainably is of the utmost importance because it is a virtuous circle that produces healthier better tasting food, a healthier environment, and healthier farm communities!

*What is your favorite type of grain? Why? Least favorite grain? Why?*

Dwarf modern varieties that can't survive without pesticides and herbicides and are essentially a product of all the wrong turns that the grain industry has made in regards to flavor and nutrition of grain. We like all the other ones.

*What are your most popular items?*

It's hard to say what our most popular items are—we have a lot of different types of customers, from grocery and online shoppers to restaurants and cafeterias. Perhaps our pastas and Red Flint polenta are the most beloved.

*Where do you get your tools/materials? What mill(s) do you work with and why?*

We work with a mill in Woodland, CA that has an air classifier mill, an innovative mill from Japan. We really like it because unlike a roller mill, which is what the vast majority of flour is milled with, it allows you to mill grains whole into very uniform flour particles. In addition, even though the whole kernel is together the entire time, the flour that comes out is shelf-stable. Initially the kernel is cracked and we presume the endosperm coats the germ (which is the part that contains the nutritious oils that cause rancidity) and keeps it from going off.

*What outlets/periodicals/newspapers do you read or consult regularly, if any?*

Most often we're up on *Civil Eats, The Atlantic,* and *The New York Times.*

*Tell me about your most memorable collaboration with another mill/farmer/etc.*

Our friends at Full Belly Farm have experimented with a bunch of our odd wheat ideas over the years. When we were first starting out, the harvest analysis came back with a very low protein reading, and everyone (the farmer and the miller) simply thought the wheat was going to have to end up as pig feed. Bob disagreed, bought a bag of it and convinced the miller to mill it, convinced a few bakers to play with it, and it turned out to be a crowd favorite! It made delicious bread despite the fact that by "industry standards" it was of a quality below human consumption.

*Please tell me about the type of mill you use.*

The mill we use is an Air Classifier Mill (ACM), which gives us true whole grain by milling it whole like a stone mill. Unlike a stone mill however, the ACM consistently puts out very uniform granulation and is more efficient for the scale that we operate at. The ACM operates by blowing the kernels around at high speeds so they smash into themselves and metal pegs in the mill until they are the desired size and are blown up and out.

*Brag about yourselves a bit. What are your highest achievements and/or proudest moments in this industry?*

We've put on two major conferences over the years, bringing together some brilliant minds in farming, nutrition science, plant science, history, journalism, and baking to discuss the future of wheat. Starting these conversations and executing on the vision they put forth is what it's all about.

*Please tell me about your education and experience.*

We don't grow grains ourselves, but have learned a ton about it from our farmer partners over the years. When Bob first got excited about growing grains, he learned from farmers and millers in Italy as well as in California.

*Please tell me about the growing and milling processes.*

The grain is planted in the spring or winter, grows green and heads-out as the kernels swell, and then is dried on the stalk (hopefully without getting too top-heavy and falling over). Once the wheat is thoroughly dried out in the hot summer, the wheat is harvested using harvesting machines that drive through the fields thrashing the stalks and separating and cleaning the grain in rotating cylinders. Once the farmer has harvested and cleaned the wheat, he'll have it analyzed by the California Wheat Commission for protein percentage amongst other metrics. Our process is then to mill a small batch of it up in Woodland and distribute samples to the bakers we're closest with to get a good read on it. The grain is stored at the farm or chilled at our warehouse in 2,000-pound super totes and ultimately milled fresh to fill orders and stock inventory.

# WHOLE WHEAT CHALLAH

YIELDS: 1 LARGE OR 2 SMALL LOAVES / ACTIVE TIME: 1½ HOURS / TOTAL TIME: 4 HOURS

Simple, pillowy, and delicious, this whole wheat loaf gives challah a whole new dimension.
—*recipe and image courtesy of Lena Miller of Community Grains*

**INGREDIENTS:**

- 2¼ teaspoons active dry yeast (1 packet)
- ¾ cup warm water
- 1 teaspoon sugar
- 1¼ cups Community Grains Hard Red Winter Wheat Flour
- 2 cups Community Grains Hard White Wheat Flour
- 1 teaspoon kosher salt
- 2 large eggs
- ¼ cup canola oil
- ¼ cup honey

**Egg wash:** 1 egg, beaten, a pinch of salt

**Optional:** raisins, sesame seeds, or poppy seeds

1 In a medium bowl, combine the yeast, warm water, and sugar and stir with a rubber spatula. Let sit until foamy.

2 In large bowl combine the flour, salt, and raisins (if using).

3 Whisk the eggs, oil, and honey in with the yeast and water.

4 Pour the wet ingredients into the flour. Using a rubber spatula, stir until the mixture becomes too thick. Using one hand, begin forming into a ball and then begin kneading. Dust with a small handful of flour when the dough begins to stick. You may need to do this 2 or 3 times. Knead until the dough becomes smooth and shiny, about 10 minutes.

5 Cover the dough with a thin layer of olive oil and cover with a towel. Let the dough rise in a warm spot for 2 to 3 hours, until it has doubled in size.

6 After the 2 to 3 hours, preheat your oven to 375°F. Line a baking sheet (or two if you're making two small loaves) with parchment paper. Turn your dough out onto a lightly floured work surface. There are many different challah braiding techniques—I suggest searching for your favorite online and following a photo or video tutorial. The one pictured here is a 4-stranded, round challah.

7 Brush your loaf or loaves with the egg wash and sprinkle with optional toppings. Cover with plastic wrap until the oven is ready. Bake challah for 25 minutes or until dark golden brown. Place on cooling rack for 15 to 20 minutes and serve. Store in an airtight bag or wrap in foil for up to 5 days.

# RAISIN CHALLAH

YIELDS: 1 LOAF / ACTIVE TIME: 50 MINUTES TOTAL TIME: ABOUT 4 HOURS

Raisins are the most common addition to challah, and they make this bread into a real treat. Don't be worried about having to make complicated braids with multiple strands. A three-strand braid works great with this type of challah.

1  Heat the water to 100–110°F.

2  Dissolve the yeast in the water and let rest for 5 minutes.

3  In a large bowl, combine the water-yeast mixture with ½ of the flour and the sugar.

4  Add one egg at a time and incorporate well. Add the honey and the rest of the flour and start working the dough, either with a stand mixer or by hand (see page 63 for tips on kneading).

5  Gradually add the oil, continuing to work the dough, and incorporate the salt and the raisins towards the end of the kneading.

6  Work the dough until it feels smooth. The mixing process takes about 25 minutes from start to finish.

7  Let the dough rest, covered, in a warm spot until it looks fully risen (doubled or even tripled). This should take about 1 to 1½ hours.

8  Transfer the dough to a clean surface. Depending on how skilled you are at making dough braids, divide the dough in 6, 4, or 3 pieces. A 3-strand challah still looks beautiful, but is much easier to make than a 6-strand braid.

9  Roll each piece of dough into a log, making sure that the resulting logs are the same length.

10  Prepare a baking dish covered with oiled parchment paper, place the strands over it, and seal the dough strands together at one end. Start braiding the strands, tucking the ends under the finished braid. You can also roll the braid into itself like a snail, creating a beautiful effect.

11  Preheat oven to 375°F.

12  Let the braid rest, covered, about 1 to 1½ hours, depending on the room temperature.

13  Brush the braid with the white egg wash.

14  Bake for 30 to 40 minutes, covering with aluminum foil if the challah is browning too fast.

## INGREDIENTS:

| | |
|---|---|
| 2½ | teaspoons (7 grams) active dry yeast |
| 7.8 | oz (220 g) water |
| 17.6 | oz (500 grams) all-purpose flour |
| 2.3 | oz (65 g) sugar |
| 2 | eggs |
| 2 | tbsp (40 g) honey |
| 2.7 | oz (80 g) vegetable oil |
| 1¾ | tsp (10 grams) salt |
| 4½ | oz (120 g) raisins |

## WHITE EGG WASH

| | |
|---|---|
| 1 | egg white |
| 1 | tsp water |

# IRISH SODA BREAD

It is impossible to think of Ireland or Irish people without thinking of soda bread. This bread, however, is not originally from Ireland. The first mention of a bread resembling soda bread appeared in 1817 in an English magazine, *The Gentleman's Magazine.* It contained sodium bicarbonate acidified with muriatic acid, something we would not think to put in food nowadays. A more wholesome version of soda bread was finally found in an Irish source from Northern Ireland in 1836. The recipe was similar to the classic soda bread recipe, and contained the typical four ingredients (plus a bit of water): wheat flour, baking soda, salt, and buttermilk. In this version, the naturally occurring acid in buttermilk replaced chemical acid. In order for sodium bicarbonate to make the bread leaven, an acidic ingredient is needed. Irish people found it in buttermilk, with delicious results.

This bread became extremely common in Ireland during the Great Famine, between 1845 and 1852. A plant disease destroyed potato harvests, starving Irish people who heavily depended on potatoes, both as sustenance and for exports. Extreme poverty also made it difficult to find yeast. However, sodium bicarbonate was cheap. When combined with buttermilk, it worked well with weak, local wheat, which was very low in protein, and did not rise well with yeast, anyway.

A couple of decades later, baking powder was invented in North America. In baking powder, baking soda is combined with an acidic compound, with a resulting rising power similar to that obtained in soda bread. Although, the many Irish immigrants, now residing in the United States, did not give up their traditional soda bread and kept using baking soda and buttermilk.

With time, soda bread had spread out of the Irish community, large and wide. This has also caused the original recipe to undergo an infinite number of variations. It is not uncommon to find recipes for soda bread that use baking powder, or that are enriched with sugar and other ingredients.

Recently, a private organization was funded to promote and protect authentic soda bread. The Society for The Preservation of Irish Soda Bread has set clear standards regarding what is considered soda bread. There is no space for fancy versions with chocolate or raisins. No, the authentic soda bread, according to the aforementioned association, is composed of only four ingredients: flour, baking soda, salt, and buttermilk. Any other interpretation, it specified, does not make soda bread, but rather a tea cake.

# ZINGERMAN'S IRISH BROWN SODA BREAD

YIELD: 2 LOAVES / **ACTIVE TIME:** 45 MINUTES / **TOTAL TIME:** 1 HOUR 30 MINUTES

Sometimes a bread just doesn't make sense to me; I don't "get it" until I eat it in its original context, baked by folks who understand it and serve it to me properly. I knew how beloved Irish soda bread was in Ireland, but to me it seemed a bit dry and crumbly. Then I went to the Slow Food Convivium in Turin, Italy. Artisan food producers from all over the world came to Turin to celebrate Slow Food. There was an Irish Pavilion where they were serving very traditional brown soda bread, baked on a hearth using wholemeal flour from Ireland. They offered us thinly sliced pieces with either smoked salmon or raspberry preserves. Finally, I got it! Full flavored and properly paired, it was delightful.

There's a wonderful bit of Irish storytelling that adds a whimsical element to this bread. After you form it into a round you make four long slashes into it dividing the loaf equally from the center into quarters. These represent the four counties of Ireland. Then you make four short slashes in each quarter to let the fairies out! This ritual adds an extra element of fun to the baking process.

—*Amy Emberling, Zingerman's Bakehouse*

**INGREDIENTS:**

- **4** cups wholemeal flour
- **1** cup all-purpose flour
- **⅓** cup oatmeal, rolled oats
- **1** teaspoon baking soda
- **1 ½** teaspoons sea salt
- **2** tablespoons brown sugar
- **¼** cup butter, room temperature
- **1** each egg, extra-large, room temperature
- **2¾** cups buttermilk, room temperature

1 For conventional ovens, preheat the oven to 425°F 20 minutes prior to baking. For convection ovens, preheat the oven to 400°F 20 minutes prior to baking.

2 In a mixing bowl, combine the whole wheat flour, all purpose flour, oatmeal, baking soda, salt, and brown sugar and stir together with a fork.

3 Add the butter to the dry ingredients. Using your hands, rub the butter together with the dry ingredients until well blended. Create a well in the center of the dry ingredients and set aside.

4 In a separate container, combine the egg and buttermilk and mix with a fork until well blended.

5 Pour the buttermilk/egg mixture into the well of dry ingredients and blend with a fork until the mixture is moistened.

6 In the bowl, fold and knead the dough 8 times. Mix until there is no dry flour remaining in the bowl. The dough should be evenly moistened.

7 Lightly flour the work surface and scrape the dough out of the bowl and onto the floured surface. Sprinkle the top of the dough with flour. Divide into 2 equal-sized pieces. Working quickly, shape each piece into a round shape. Sprinkle flour on top as needed to make sure the dough isn't sticking, but do not knead or fold the flour into the dough. Place the rounds on to parchment-lined sheet tray and cut a deep "X" into the tops of each loaf using a bench knife. Then make a small slash in each of the quarters to let the fairies out.

8 Bake the loaves at 425°F for 35 to 45 minutes or until the loaf has taken on a deep golden brown color. The loaf should sound hollow when thumped on the bottom. You can also use a digital thermometer to check the internal temperature. Once the loaf registers 190°F, it is baked through.

9 Remove from the oven and cool before cutting and eating.

# CLASSIC SODA BREAD

YIELDS: 1 BIG LOAF / ACTIVE TIME: 10 MINUTES / TOTAL TIME: 10 MINUTES

There are infinite variations of soda bread. The one that follows is a close approximation of the original Irish soda bread, which used buttermilk to activate baking soda.

**INGREDIENTS:**

- 1 lb (500 g) all-purpose flour
- 15 oz (about 450 g) buttermilk
- 1 tsp (about 4½ g) baking soda
- 1 tsp (about 6 g) salt

1 Preheat oven to 430°F.

2 Combine all ingredients in a bowl.

3 Transfer to a clean surface and knead for 3 to 5 minutes.

4 Make into a ball and transfer to a baking dish coated with some coarse flour or with parchment paper.

5 Flatten the ball with your palms to make a thick disk, and slash a deep cross on the top of the cake.

6 Bake for 20 minutes, then reduce heat to 340°F and bake another 20 to 25 minutes.

# SIMPLY SENSATIONAL IRISH SODA BREAD

**YIELDS** 1 LOAF / **ACTIVE TIME:** 30 MINUTES / **TOTAL TIME:** 90 MINUTES

Make this on a weekend morning when you have some extra time, then have slices of it later in the day with a cup of coffee or tea.
—*Dominique DeVito*

**1** Preheat the oven to 450°F.

**2** Combine the flour, sugar, salt, baking powder, baking soda, and caraway seeds. Add the beaten eggs and stir to combine. Gradually add the buttermilk until the dough is sticky and messy. Stir in the raisins.

**3** Generously butter the skillet, and scoop and spread the dough in it.

**4** Bake for about 1 hour, until the top is crusty and brown and the bread sounds hollow when tapped. Insert a toothpick in the center, too, to be sure the dough is cooked through. It should come out clean.

**5** Serve with fresh butter and orange marmalade.

**INGREDIENTS:**

| | |
|---|---|
| 4 | cups flour |
| ½ | cup sugar |
| ⅛ | teaspoon salt |
| 3¼ | teaspoons baking powder |
| ½ | teaspoon baking soda |
| 2 | tablespoons caraway seeds |
| 2 | large eggs, lightly beaten |
| 1½ | cups buttermilk |
| 8 | ounces golden raisins |

It wouldn't be St. Patrick's Day without Irish Soda bread. According to the Culinary Institute of America, "With a history spanning more than two centuries, soda bread is a traditional Irish specialty. The first loaf, consisting of little more than flour, baking soda, salt, and sour milk, made its debut in the mid-1800s when baking soda found its way into Irish kitchens." They don't mention the raisins or caraway seeds, but I consider these essential!

# CHEESY CHIVE SODA BREAD

**YIELDS** 1 LOAF/ **ACTIVE TIME:** 40 MINUTES / **TOTAL TIME:** 90 MINUTES

If you're looking for a savory version of a simple soda bread to serve with something like soup or stew, this is a great recipe.
—*Dominique DeVito*

**INGREDIENTS:**

- 3 cups white flour
- 2 cups spelt flour
- ¾ cup rolled oats (not instant)
- 2 tablespoons sugar
- 1 tablespoon baking powder
- 1 teaspoon salt
- 1 teaspoon baking soda
- 8 tablespoons (1 stick) butter, melted, and cooled
- 2½ cups buttermilk
- 1 large egg, lightly beaten
- ¼ cup chopped chives
- 1¼ cups grated sharp white cheddar cheese
- Freshly ground pepper

1 Preheat the oven to 350°F.

2 In a large bowl, combine the flours, oats, sugar, baking powder, salt, and baking soda. Whisk to combine thoroughly. In another bowl, combine the butter, buttermilk, and egg.

3 Add the milk mixture to the flour mixture and stir vigorously to blend. Dough will be sticky. Stir in the chives and 1 cup of the grated cheese.

4 Liberally grease the skillet with butter. Scoop and spread the dough into the skillet. Grate pepper over the top, then sprinkle the remaining cheese over it. Using a sharp knife, make an "x" in the center, about ½-inch deep, to settle the cheese further into the dough as it cooks.

5 Bake in the oven for about 1 hour and 15 minutes until golden on top and a toothpick inserted in the center comes out clean. Allow to sit in the skillet for a few minutes before serving.

> Soda bread doesn't keep so well, so if you happen to have any left over, be sure to wrap it tightly in plastic wrap. Store it in the refrigerator. It will last for about 3 days this way. The bread makes great toast!

# CHOCOLATE SODA BREAD

YIELDS: 1 BIG LOAF / ACTIVE TIME: 10 MINUTES / TOTAL TIME: 60 MINUTES

The addition of chocolate chips and a little sugar to a classic soda bread makes for a quick and delicious treat, which keeps some of the rustic charm of traditional version of this bread.

**INGREDIENTS:**

1   lb (500 g) all-purpose flour

15   oz (about 450 g) buttermilk

1   tsp (about 4½ g) baking soda

3   tbsp sugar

1   tsp (about 6 g) salt

⅔   cup chocolate chips

1   Preheat oven to 430°F.

2   Combine all ingredients except the chocolate chips.

3   Transfer to a clean surface and knead for 2 minutes, then quickly incorporate the chocolate chips, trying not to melt them with your hands.

4   Make into a ball and transfer to a baking dish coated with some coarse flour or with parchment paper.

5   Flatten the ball with your palms to make a thick disk, and slash a deep cross on the top of the cake.

6   Bake for 20 minutes, then reduce heat to 340°F and bake another 20 to 25 minutes.

# BARLEY SOURDOUGH

YIELDS: 2 LOAVES / ACTIVE TIME: 30 MINUTES / TOTAL TIME: 4½ HOURS

Barley is a fantastic cereal, rich in nutrients and enzymes that will give a beautiful, deep brown color to your crust. The gluten contained in barley is not ideal for bread baking, but when combined with wheat, it can give you gorgeous bread.

**INGREDIENTS:**

- 3 cups + 2½ tablespoons (14.1 oz) bread flour
- 1 cup (3.5 oz) barley flour
- 5.3 oz sourdough starter (see page 59)
- 1⅓ cups (11.3 oz) water
- 1¾ teaspoons salt

1 In a large bowl, combine all the ingredients, except the salt.

2 Knead by hand or with a stand-mixer for a few minutes.

3 Let rest for 30 minutes.

4 Add the salt and work the dough more, until it appears elastic when pulled.

5 Let the dough rest, covered, until it has risen to 1 ½ times its original volume. This should take about 2 hours.

6 Transfer the dough on a clean surface and shape into two batards (see page 63).

7 Place the loaves in two proofing baskets lined with floured kitchen towels.

8 Preheat oven to maximum temperature, with a pizza stone in if you own one.

9 Let rest, covered (for instance by placing the loaf into a clean plastic bag), until the loaves appear to have risen 1 ½ times their previous volume. This could take 1 ½ to 2 hours, depending on several factors, like room temperature and power of the starter, for instance.

10 Invert the loaves on a baker's peel or a flat tray dusted with coarse semolina or corn flour.

11 Throw a few ice cubes on a hot baking dish at the bottom of the oven to create steam, then transfer loaves to the oven.

12 Immediately reduce the temperature to 480°F and bake for 25 minutes.

13 Let the steam out, reduce heat to 425° and bake for 15–20 minutes or until golden brown.

# DEUX

## BAKERY

## Deux Bakery

824 Reddick Street
Santa Barbara, CA 93103
(805) 770-3109
www.deuxbakery.com

Tucked away in beautiful Santa Barbara, Deux is a beloved local spot. And for owner Wendy Fleming, "local" is not a word she uses lightly. The staff, always charming and helpful, is more family than company. When asked to brag a bit about herself, Fleming can't help but bring it back to her employees: "I do feel that most everything I have done is with someone else— whether it be my husband, daughter, Leo (my right-hand man), or Jesse (my breadbaker), it is always a group effort. The fact that I have these people with me is something to brag about, and I am very lucky in that respect."

Deux has grown from the most modest beginnings; at first, Fleming was just trying to help her daughter open a restaurant. "My daughter Crista has always loved to cook, but not bake. Her father is a wonderful cook and she loved standing by his side and cooking and talking about different foods. When she decided to open her restaurant, Scarlett Bego-nia, she asked me to help design a pastry menu, but there was no money for a pastry chef. And so I was called on to launch the pastry depart-ment of her new venture. It became a labor of love, and during this time at her restaurant, I

began to accumulate customers of my own. Eventually it got to be too big an endeavor to continue in her small kitchen!"

Fleming is mostly self-taught, though she attributes much of her ability to her mother's lessons growing up. "She was very patient and I always got to do my own pie or cake—a small portion of whatever she was doing." Despite her relatively informal training, the bread-and-pastry bakery is incredibly popular in the com-munity. Items often sell out before noon, so it can be a bit of a race to beat out other custom-ers. More than once, customers have let slip to Fleming that they keep mum on her little shop in order to prevent it from being overrun.

Still, Fleming doesn't mind. "I went into this endeavor with no idea what to expect. Certainly, I did not expect the endless hours of hard work, sometimes working more than 24 hours straight. All my husband and I wanted to achieve was a quality product for our daugh-ter's restaurant that reflected the best ingredi-ents and emphasized what bread and pastries used to be, before the main concern was shelf life and shipping."

# IN HER OWN WORDS:

## WENDY FLEMING OF DEUX BAKERY

*Who inspired you to bake? Who inspires you now?*

My mother, of course, but as I began to think professionally I found inspiration in Nancy Silverton of La Brea Bakery. In the old days, when Deux was a very small bakery, three or four customers made a crowd.

*What is your golden rule(s) of baking?*

Bring back the taste of something without the preservatives and colors—just the true flavor of the product.

*What does Deux represent to you?*

Deux is me. I have created and overseen every pastry recipe we use, plus most of the breads. I also have a very talented baker, Jesse, who has created breads that far surpass my expertise in the field. And now I have Mauricio, who is a supremely talented pastry chef!

*What is your favorite thing to bake? Why? Least favorite thing to bake? Why?*

I love trying out new things. I get an idea in my head, think about the right way to approach it, and then I bake it off and taste. Leo, my right-hand man since the beginning, has a great palate and tells me if it is good or bad. If bad, I'll try again until I get the thumbs up from Leo. The sense of accomplishment this provides is very satisfying for me! My least favorite thing to bake is dinner rolls—I get rave reviews from everyone about my dinner rolls, so you'd think I'd love making them, but it's like factory work. I'd say I could probably do them in my sleep, except that yesterday I forgot the yeast. Oops!

*What are your most popular items?*

We sell out of most everything in the pastry section every day, but Mauricio's Danish pastries always sell first. For the breads, our sourdough is the most popular, but our multigrain whole wheat sourdough is beginning to rival the plain sourdough.

*Where do you get your tools/materials? What non-essential items should every baker have?*

A non-essential tool for me, not necessarily as a baker, but as an employer and business owner is an understanding of each person's personality. I respect everyone who works for me very much, from the dishwasher to the head baker, but boy are they different personalities. It is essential to treat each person in a way they relate to you so that they feel special and instrumental in making our business successful.

*What book(s) go on your required reading list for bakers?*

We have so many books here at the bakery and we read them all to get ideas, and bakers percentages when doing new products. When I first started, my "bible" was a collection of Ciril Hitz books, as I took several weeks of classes with him before opening the bakery.

Also, Peter Reinhart's books, Nancy Silverton's books, and Sherry Yard, with whom I was lucky enough to take a seminar in Los Angeles.

*What outlets/periodicals/newspapers do you read or consult regularly, if any?*

We love to read *Bread Lines,* the *Bread Bakers Guild Magazine,* in order to learn about trends and the classes and clinics going on. We try to go to the ones in LA, but unfortunately there are not too many in this part of the world.

*Do you follow any chefs or cooking shows? If so, which is your favorite?*

My whole family loves Top Chef—it is very innovative and fun. We can't wait for each episode!

*Where did you learn to cook?*

I am always embarrassed to say that I am basically self-taught. My mother taught me about pies, cakes, and candy, and my husband, Morry, has always been there to help with whatever I try. He also often has suggestions about doing new things. He reads constantly about the interesting things going on in the pastry world and keeps me up to date. I have taken several classes with Ciril Hitz, who is a wonderful bread baker, and I've learned so much from him.

# SOURDOUGH MULTI-GRAIN

YIELD: 4 34-OUNCE LOAVES / ACTIVE TIME: 30 MINUTES / TOTAL TIME: 5 HOURS

This is fast becoming the bestselling loaf at Deux Bakery, and for good reason. The grains give extra flavor to an already delicious, tart sourdough.

*—courtesy of Wendy Fleming of Deux Bakery*

1 First, combine all soaker ingredients and soak for 1 hour.

2 Mix all the dough ingredients except the soaker on 1st speed for 4 minutes, then on 2nd speed for 2 minutes.

3 Mix in the soaker for 1 to 2 minutes on 1st speed.

4 Put the dough mix in a greased container and stretch and fold after 1 hour.

5 Cover and let rise for 1 to 2 hours in a warm—but not hot—environment. Form and let rise 2 to 4 hours.

6 Preheat oven to 450°F. Bake for 40 minutes and serve.

## INGREDIENTS:

**DOUGH:**

10⅙ cups flour

5 ⅛ cups water

5 ⅔ cups whole wheat flour

17⅛ ounces starter

Soaker (see below)

6⅓ tablespoons honey

2⅓ tablespoons salt

⅛ ounce dry yeast

**SOAKER:**

5¼ ounces oats

3½ ounces sunflower seeds

2⅛ ounces flax seeds

2⅛ ounces sesame seeds

2⅛ ounces poppy seeds

2⅛ ounces cornmeal

1½ cups water

# MULTIGRAIN SOURDOUGH

YIELDS: 1 LOAF / ACTIVE TIME: 30 MINUTES / TOTAL TIME: 4½ HOURS

This is a typical Scandinavian-style, whole-grain sourdough. The process needs to start the night before, as the starter needs to be fed and the grains soaked overnight.

1 Combine all the ingredients in a large bowl.

2 Work the dough by making a series of folds at regular intervals, for instance, 3 folds every 20 minutes during the first hour (see page 63 for tips on kneading and folding techniques).

3 Let rest, covered, for another hour at room temperature.

4 Grease a ⅗ gallon loaf pan and line with parchment paper.

5 Transfer the dough into the loaf pan.

6 Cover and let rest until it does not rise further (about 2½ hours).

7 Preheat oven to 360°F.

8 Bake for about 70 minutes and let cool completely before cutting the loaf.

## INGREDIENTS:

- 1.8 (50 g) buckwheat groats + 2½ (70 g) rye berries soaked overnight and boiled for 20 minutes, then drained well and let to cool down (soaker)

- 14 oz (200 g) sourdough starter (see page 59)

- 7.9 oz (225 g) water

- 2½ oz (70 g) coarse rye flour

- 2½ oz (70 g) whole-wheat flour

- 3½ oz (100 g) all-purpose flour

- 3½ oz (100 g) bread flour

- 2 tbsp mixed seeds

- 1 tbsp honey

- 1 tsp salt

- 2 small loaf pans (1.5 liter/0.4 gallons) or one big loaf pan

# BOULANGERIE'S FOUGASSE

YIELD: 6 LOAVES / ACTIVE TIME: 1 HOUR / TOTAL TIME: 3 HOURS IF USING PREPARED PÂTE FERMENTÉE, 15-27 HOURS IF MAKING IT ON THE SAME DAY

We love our Fougasse recipe because it is quite easy to translate to a home oven. There is no need to shape the dough to a perfect form, as long as it is thoroughly mixed and given time to get bubbly and grow. To have a flexible, stretchy dough we use a premixed portion called Pâte Fermentée, which you'll need to make 16 to 24 hours in advance.
—*Amy and Zachary Tyson, Boulangerie*

## FOUGASSE DOUGH

1 Add all of the ingredients to the mixing bowl except the Pâte Fermentée. In a mixer, or by hand, mix together to incorporate the ingredients. As the dough begins to come together, add the Pâte Fermentée in chunks. If necessary, correct the hydration of the dough by adding water (if too dry) or flour (if too wet) in small amounts.

2 Once all the Pâte Fermentée is added, continue to mix until the dough is smooth and supple. The dough should be moderately loose but still fight when you pull on it.

3 Let the dough sit in the bowl covered with plastic for approximately 2 hours. After the first hour, fold the dough over itself from different directions 8 times.

4 After the second hour, turn the dough out on a floured surface, sprinkle with flour and divide it into 6 8-ounce pieces, roughly 4 inches by 4 inches.

5 Once all the pieces are cut out, begin shaping by stretching the dough and cutting holes in it with a small plastic scraper or knife. Pull to the shape or design you desire, cover with toppings, then place on a greased sheet pan and put in a preheated oven at 420°F.

6 Bake for approximately 13 minutes or until the dough is golden with a brown bottom. Let cool and devour.

## INGREDIENTS:

### FOUGASSE DOUGH
5 ½    cups bread flour

2    cups water

2    teaspoons salt

1¼    teaspoons instant dry yeast

13 ½    ounces Pâte Fermentée (mixed the day before, recipe below)

### PÂTE FERMENTÉE
1¾    cups bread flour

⅝    cup water

1    teaspoon salt

⅛    teaspoon instant dry yeast

## PÂTE FERMENTÉE

1 Prepare the Pâte Fermentée 24 hours ahead of the final mix. Disperse the yeast in the water, add the flour and salt, and mix until just smooth.

2 Cover the bowl with plastic and let stand for 12 to 16 hours at room temperature. Alternatively, you can refrigerate up to 24 hours.

Fougasse can be topped with anything you like, like pizza without sauce. We like jalapeño and Asiago cheese, but you could go plain with sea salt and olive oil or savory with sun-dried tomatoes and goat cheese. Even cinnamon sugar is nice on a cold morning.

# LEMON CHOCOLATE FOUGASSE

YIELD: 2 LOAVES / ACTIVE TIME: 50 MINUTES / TOTAL TIME: 3 HOURS

Fougasse is the French word for the Italian "focaccia." It is from southern France and it has a very typical shape, given by a special scoring of the dough. This is a sweet version of it.

**INGREDIENTS:**

- 2½ teaspoons (7 g) active dry yeast
- 1 cup warm (105-110° F) water
- 1⅙ lbs (500 grams) bread flour
- 1 egg
- 1½ tablespoons olive oil
- 1½ teaspoons sea salt
- 2½ ounces caster sugar
- Peels of 2 organic lemons
- Juice of 1½ organic lemons
- 8⅘ ounces dark chocolate (70–75% cocoa), chopped
- Confectioner's sugar + a little water for final brushing

1 Dissolve the yeast in the warm water then add the flour and start kneading. Add the sugar, the egg, and finally the salt and olive oil. Keep kneading until the dough looks smooth—about 20 minutes by machine.

2 Incorporate the chocolate and the lemon peel and juice, and knead quickly until the dough appears reasonably smooth again.

3 Place the dough in a tall, airtight container and let rest for 1 hour, covered.

4 Shape 2 balls out of the dough and place on a floured surface to rest for 30 minutes. You can use salad bowls to create a vacuum over the balls.

5 Shape each ball into an oval (*batard*, in French) then flatten the oval well with the palms of your hands.

6 With a sharp knife, make 1 central cut and 6 lateral cuts, 3 on each side, to give the typical fougasse look to your dough.

7 Let rest, covered, for 20 to 30 minutes. Preheat your oven to 445°F.

8 Bake until the fougasse appears golden brown.

9 Brush with a mixture of confectioner's sugar and water while still hot.

# COUNTRY LOAF

YIELD: 3 LOAVES, OR 2 LARGE LOAVES / **ACTIVE TIME:** 1 HOUR / TOTAL TIME: 24 HOURS

Inspired by old versions of French country breads, this is a favorite of our customers—and especially our bakers.
—*Jim Williams, Seven Stars Bakery*

## DAY 1

1 For both sourdough cultures, mix until incorporated and leave to ferment for 12–16 hours at room temperature (ideally 70°F). They can be doubled or tripled for ease of use—just discard whatever you don't need.

## DAY 2

2 Mix all ingredients except rye starter, levain, and salt in a bowl to incorporation, either by hand or using a mixer. Let rest for 30 minutes.

3 Add rye starter, levain, and salt and mix the dough until it has lightly developed.

4 Bulk fermentation should take 3 hours at 77–80°F. During this time, give the dough 3 folds. Simply take the dough and fold it upon itself several times. Each time, the dough will feel stronger and more resilient.

5 After bulk fermentation, divide the dough into loaves. Give the dough a light pre-shape and let rest for 30 minutes.

6 Shape into final shapes and proof. The proof should last 3–5 hours, depending on the temperature and humidity in your kitchen.

7 Preheat a cast iron Dutch oven, with the lid, in your oven. Turn heat up as hot as it will go.

8 Once proofed, lightly insert the proofed dough into the Dutch oven and score it. Put the lid on and into the oven. After 30 minutes of baking, remove the lid and finish to desired color. Let cool and enjoy!

INGREDIENTS:

RYE STARTER

2¾ ounces whole rye

¼ cup water

¼ ounce sourdough culture

LEVAIN

¼ cup stone ground, fresh-milled wheat flour

¼ cup white all-purpose flour

⅛ cup water

¼ ounce sourdough culture

DOUGH

4⅛ white all-purpose flour

3½ cups fresh-milled, stone-ground whole wheat flour

3 cups water

5¼ ounces rye starter

7¼ ounces levain

1⅓ tablespoons salt

# FRESH FLOUR COUNTRY BREAD

YIELD: 2 2-POUND LOAVES / ACTIVE TIME: 2 HOURS / TOTAL TIME: 16 HOURS

This crunchy, hole-ridden loaf uses freshly milled whole wheat flour to set itself apart from other country breads. A two-day process, it's worth the wait; serve it fresh out of the oven before dinner and prepare for plenty of leftovers as guests go for slice after slice. —*recipe courtesy of Graison Gill, Bellegarde Bakery*

**INGREDIENTS:**

869 millilitres water, 78° F (hold back some water)

25 grams salt

195 grams levain

993 grams fresh-milled whole wheat flour, 78° F

1 Add flour, levain and 90% of the water into a shaggy mass. Sprinkle the salt and remaining water on top, then mix by hand in a bus tub or large bowl. Once combined, the ingredients should have a mutual temperature of 78°F. If this temperature is not achieved, place the covered dough in a drafty or warmer area of the kitchen in order to reduce or increase its overall temperature. Then cover with a lid or towel and let rest for 90 minutes. This is your autolyse period.

2 After 90 minutes has elapsed, fold the dough 5 to 7 times, depending on its strength and elasticity (see pages 62-63 for instruction on folding). Wait 12 minutes between every fold.

3 Divide dough into 2 equal portions, shape tightly, and store in proofing baskets overnight.

4 Preheat a Lodge cooker in your oven to 550°F. When the oven is ready, gently score the loaves, transfer them into the cooker in your oven, and immediately drop the temperature to 450°F. Bake to desired doneness, about 35-45 minutes.

# EXTREME COUNTRY SOURDOUGH

YIELD: 2 SMALL LOAVES OR 1 LARGE LOAF / ACTIVE TIME: 40 MINUTES / TOTAL TIME: 5½ HOURS

This is a very easy way to approach for the first time a highly hydrated country loaf. Make sure you work your dough until you see that it becomes very elastic and do not add more water if the dough does not absorb it. Every flour is different, so add as much water as yours can take.

1 Mix all the ingredients except the salt and the extra water. Knead for a few minutes. Let stand, covered, for 50 minutes.

2 Add the salt dissolved in 1⅘ ounces water and knead until the dough becomes very elastic when stretched.

3 Let rise at room temperature in a capable container, tightly closed, and make 2 folds at intervals of 40 minutes. Add more water if the dough needs and accepts it.

4 From the moment you mix the ingredients, a total of 3½ hours should pass before you form the loaves. Once formed, let the loaves rise for another 2 hours, covered.

5 Preheat the oven to 480°F with baking stone or baking dish inside. Add the dough to the oven and create initial steam by throwing a few ice cubes in the bottom of the oven.

6 Bake at high heat for the first 10 to 15 minutes, then gradually lower the temperature and bake until the loaf feel lighter when lifted.

## INGREDIENTS:

**YOUNG STARTER:**

- 1 ounce 100% hydration sourdough starter
- 7 ounces water
- 7 ounces bread flour

**FINAL DOUGH:**

- 15 ounces active young sourdough starter
- 1½ pounds bread flour
- 8⅘ ounces all-purpose flour
- 1⅖ pounds water
- 1⅘ ounces water, to be added with salt
- 3½ ounces water, to add when you make the folds (check your dough before adding)
- 3½ teaspoons sea salt

CAST-IRON RECIPE

# WHEAT BREAD

When you discover how easy it is to make such a tasty loaf of bread with all-purpose flour, you'll want to start experimenting with other flavors and textures, found in flours, nuts, and so on. Here's a wheat bread recipe that uses enough all-purpose flour to ensure adequate rising and fluffiness upon baking.
—*Dominique DeVito*

**INGREDIENTS:**

¼ teaspoon instant yeast

¼ teaspoon sugar

1½ cups water (110 to 115°F)

1 teaspoon kosher salt

2 cups whole wheat flour

1 cup all-purpose flour plus more for kneading and dusting

1 Put the yeast and sugar in a measuring cup and add about ½ cup warm water in a drizzle. Hot water will kill the yeast, so it's important that the water be warm without being hot. Cover the measuring cup with plastic wrap and set it aside for about 15 minutes. If the yeast doesn't foam, it is not alive and you'll need to start over.

2 When the yeast is proofed, pour it into a large bowl and add the additional cup of warm water. Stir gently to combine. Add the salt to the flour, and add the flour to the yeast mixture. Stir with a wooden spoon until combined. The dough will be wet and sticky.

3 Put a dusting of flour on a flat surface and lift out the dough. With flour on your hands and more at the ready, begin kneading the dough so that it loses its stickiness. Don't overdo it, and don't use too much flour; just enough that it is more cohesive.

4 Place the dough in a large bowl, cover the bowl with plastic wrap, and allow to rise untouched for at least 1 hour, and up to several hours. Gently punch it down, recover with the plastic, and allow to rise again for another 30 minutes or so.

5 While the dough is on its final rise, preheat the oven to 450°F. Put a piece of parchment paper on the bottom of the Dutch oven and put it in with the lid on so it gets hot. When the oven is ready and dough has risen, carefully remove the lid and gently scoop the dough from the bowl into the pot. Cover and bake for 15 minutes. Remove the lid and continue to bake for another 15 to 20 minutes until the top is golden and it sounds hollow when tapped.

6 Remove the pot from the oven and use tea towels to carefully remove the bread. Allow to cool before slicing.

# GLUTEN-FREE BREAD

**YIELDS** 1 SMALL ROUND / **ACTIVE TIME:** 25 MINUTES / **TOTAL TIME:** 3 HOURS

We are fortunate to live in a time when gluten-free options are numerous. If you love bread and can't or don't want to eat gluten, make this recipe and dig in! You'll be amazed at the result—an equally crusty yet fluffy loaf that tastes great!
—*Dominique DeVito*

**INGREDIENTS:**

| | |
|---|---|
| ½ | teaspoon instant yeast |
| ¼ | teaspoon sugar |
| 1½ to 2½ | cups water (110 to 115°F) |
| 1 | teaspoon kosher salt |
| 1½ | teaspoons xanthan gum |
| 3 | cups Bob's Red Mill gluten-free flour plus more for kneading and dusting |
| ⅓ | cup Bob's Red Mill sweet rice flour (glutinous rice flour) |

1 Put the yeast and sugar in a measuring cup and add about ½ cup warm water in a drizzle. Hot water will kill the yeast, so it's important that the water be warm without being hot. Cover the measuring cup with plastic wrap and set it aside for about 15 minutes. If the yeast doesn't foam, it is not alive and you'll need to start over.

2 When the yeast is proofed, pour it into a large bowl and add an additional cup of warm water. Stir gently to combine. Add the salt and xanthan gum to the flour, and add the flour to the yeast mixture. Stir with a wooden spoon until combined. Add up to an additional cup of warm water to accommodate the rice flour, which is tackier than regular flour. The dough should be wet and sticky.

3 Put a dusting of flour on a flat surface and lift out the dough. With flour on your hands and more at the ready, begin kneading the dough so that it loses its stickiness. Don't overdo it, and don't use too much flour; just enough that it is more cohesive.

4 Place the dough in a large bowl, cover the bowl with plastic wrap, and allow to rise untouched for at least 1 hour, and up to several hours. Gently punch it down, recover with the plastic, and allow to rise again for another 30 minutes or so.

5 While the dough is on its final rise, preheat the oven to 450°F. Put a piece of parchment paper on the bottom of the Dutch oven and put it in with the lid on so it gets hot. When the oven is ready and dough has risen, carefully remove the lid and gently scoop the dough from the bowl into the pot. Cover and bake for 15 minutes. Remove the lid and continue to bake for another 15 to 20 minutes until the top is golden and it sounds hollow when tapped.

6 Remove the pot from the oven and use tea towels to carefully remove the bread. Allow to cool before slicing.

# NO-KNEAD BREAD

**YIELDS** 1 SMALL ROUND / **ACTIVE TIME:** 20 MINUTES / **TOTAL TIME:** UP TO 2 DAYS

There is really nothing easier than this recipe for making a delicious loaf of fresh bread. The only thing is you need to give it up to two days, so plan ahead!
—*Dominique DeVito*

**INGREDIENTS:**

   **Dry yeast**

¼ **teaspoon sugar**

1½ **cups water (110 to 115°F)**

1½ **teaspoons kosher salt**

3 **cups all-purpose flour, plus more for dusting**

1 In a large bowl, add the yeast and sugar and top with the warm water. Stir to dissolve the yeast. Cover the bowl with plastic wrap and allow to proof for about 15 minutes. Add the flour and salt. Stir until just blended with the yeast and water. The dough will be sticky.

2 Cover the bowl with plastic wrap and set aside for at least 15 hours and up to 18 hours, preferably in a place that's 65 to 70°F.

3 The dough will be bubbled when you go to work with it. Lightly dust a work surface and scoop the dough out onto it. Dust your fingers with flour so they don't stick to the dough. Fold it gently once or twice.

4 Transfer the dough to a clean bowl that is room temperature and cover with a dish towel. Let rise another 1 to 2 hours until doubled in size.

5 While the dough is on its final rise, preheat the oven to 450°F, placing the Dutch oven inside with the lid on so it gets hot. When the oven is ready and dough has risen, carefully remove the lid and gently scoop the dough from the bowl into the pot. Cover and bake for 20 minutes. Remove the lid and continue to bake for another 25 minutes until the top is golden and it sounds hollow when tapped.

6 Remove pot from oven and use tea towels to carefully transfer bread to a rack or cutting board, and allow to cool at least 20 minutes before serving.

# WHOLE WHEAT CRANBERRY PECAN

YIELDS: 1 SMALL ROUND / ACTIVE TIME: 25 MINUTES / TOTAL TIME: 3 HOURS

This is a delicious and dense bread that is especially good toasted and served with fresh butter or cream cheese. It also makes a great complement to soft cheeses when cut into small pieces and served instead of crackers.

—*Dominique DeVito*

**INGREDIENTS:**

- ¼ teaspoon instant yeast
- ¼ teaspoon sugar
- 1½ cups water (110 to 115°F)
- 1 teaspoon kosher salt
- 2 cups whole wheat flour
- 1 cup all-purpose flour plus more for kneading and dusting
- 1 cup dried cranberries
- 1 cup chopped pecans

1 Put the yeast and sugar in a measuring cup and add about ½ cup warm water in a drizzle. Hot water will kill the yeast, so it's important that the water be warm without being hot. Cover the measuring cup with plastic wrap and set it aside for about 15 minutes. If the yeast doesn't foam, it is not alive and you'll need to start over.

2 When the yeast is proofed, pour it into a large bowl and add the additional cup of warm water. Stir gently to combine. Add the salt to the flour, and add the flour to the yeast mixture. Stir with a wooden spoon until combined. The dough will be wet and sticky.

3 Put a dusting of flour on a flat surface and lift out the dough. With flour on your hands and more at the ready, begin kneading the dough so that it loses its stickiness. As you're kneading, add in the cranberries and pecans so that they're distributed evenly in the dough. Don't overdo it, and don't use too much flour; just enough to make it more cohesive.

4 Place the dough in a large bowl, cover the bowl with plastic wrap, and allow to rise untouched for at least 1 hour, and up to several hours. Gently punch it down, recover with the plastic, and allow to rise again for another 30 minutes or so.

5 While the dough is on its final rise, preheat the oven to 450°F. Put a piece of parchment paper on the bottom of the Dutch oven and put it in with the lid on so it gets hot. When the oven is ready and dough has risen, carefully remove the lid and gently scoop the dough from the bowl into the pot. Cover and bake for 15 minutes. Remove the lid and continue to bake for another 15 to 20 minutes until the top is golden and it sounds hollow when tapped.

6 Remove the pot from the oven and use tea towels to carefully remove the bread. Allow to cool before slicing.

# ROMAN COUNTRY BREAD

**YIELDS:** 1 BIG LOAF / **ACTIVE TIME:** 50 MINUTES / **TOTAL TIME:** 5–6 HOURS

Rome is surrounded by lovely countryside with beautiful hills and volcanic lakes, an area that locals call *Castelli Romani*. The traditional country sourdoughs of this region have a chewy and pitted interior, and a thick and dark crust.

**INGREDIENTS:**

- ⅔ cup (ca. 150 grams) 100% hydration sourdough starter (page 59)
- 1½ cups (350 grams) water
- 12⅕ ounces (350 grams) bread flour
- 3½ ounces (100 grams) all-purpose flour
- 1⅕ ounces (50 grams) whole wheat flour
- 1¾ teaspoons (10 grams) salt

1   Combine the sourdough starter with the water. Add the flours to the water and the starter and mix well. Knead by hand or with a stand-mixer, alternating a few minutes of kneading/folding (page 63) to a few minutes rest (always covered).

2   After 20–30 minutes, incorporate the salt and work the dough more intensively, either by hand (page 63) or by increasing the speed on the stand-mixer. The dough should appear sticky but elastic, when pulled. Let the dough rest, covered, for 2 hours.

3   Preheat the oven to maximum temperature—with the baking stone in, if you have one.

4   Transfer the dough to a clean surface dusted with some semolina flour and fold the 4 corners of the dough to form a rectangular "package." Flip the "package" over a semolina flour covered kitchen towel, making sure that the top of the folds is on the bottom. Delicately close the kitchen towel, leaving enough space for the loaf to rise, and heavily sprinkle with semolina flour.

5   Let the dough rest at room temperature until it has almost doubled (this could take 2 to 3 hours). When your fingerprint on the dough springs back slowly, the dough is ready.

6   Prepare a baking peel or flat tray sprinkled with coarse semolina or corn flour and invert the loaf on it. Do not slash.

7   Add very little steam (you could throw 2–3 ice cubes in the lower rack) and bake for 15 minutes at maximum temperature.

8   Lower the temperature to 460°F and let the steam out.

9   Bake for 20 more minutes, then lower to 390°F and bake for a further 20–25 minutes, or until brown. The crust is supposed to look dark.

# COTTAGE LOAF

YIELDS: 1 BIG LOAF / ACTIVE TIME: 30 MINUTES / TOTAL TIME: ABOUT 3 HOURS

Possibly the most traditional British loaf, it is now rarely found in bakeries. Relatively easy to make, it is a lovely bread to serve thanks to its mild taste and its interesting shape.

**INGREDIENTS:**

| | |
|---|---|
| 2½ | tsp (7 g) active dry yeast |
| 10.2 | to 11.8 oz (350 g) water |
| 1 | lb (500 g) all-purpose flour |
| 1 | tbsp honey |
| 2 | tbsp butter |
| 1 | tsp (about 6 g) salt |

1 Activate the yeast in the water warmed to 100–105°F for 10 minutes. In a large bowl, combine the water-yeast mixture with the flour and the honey, and knead by hand or with a stand mixer for 10 minutes. Add the butter in small pieces and continue kneading for 5 minutes, adding salt towards the end (see page 63 for tips on kneading).

2 Let the dough rest, covered, in a warm spot, such as in the oven with the light on and open a crack, until it doubles (about 1½ hours).

3 Preheat the oven to 445°F. If you have a baking stone, place it in the oven to preheat.

4 Transfer the dough to a clean and floured surface and de-gas the dough by folding it on itself like a letter a couple of times. Divide the dough in 2 pieces, one bigger (about ⅔ of the dough) and 1 smaller (about ⅓ of the dough), and shape into two rounds.

5 Place the bigger round over a tray covered with parchment paper, and place the smaller round over the bigger one. Seal them together by placing a finger in the middle of the smaller round and pressing it against the bigger round. Let rest, covered, for an hour.

6 Transfer the proofed loaf with the parchment paper to a flat tray, or peel and load into the oven to the preheated stone.

7 Let rest, covered, until the dough has risen 1½ times.

8 Invert the loaves on a baker peel or flat tray dusted with coarse semolina or corn flour, slash as desired, and transfer into the oven. Bake with steam (see page 49) for 15 minutes.

9 Let the steam out by opening the oven door, lower the temperature to 375°F, and bake for 25 to 30 minutes or until golden brown.

# PUGLIESE BREAD

YIELDS: 1 BIG LOAF / ACTIVE TIME: 30 MINUTES/ TOTAL TIME: 5-5 ½ HOURS

This is a traditional bread from Apulia, in Southeast Italy. It tends to have a regular and tight crumb, because it is based on durum wheat, the same type of wheat used to make pasta.

**INGREDIENTS:**

- 3⅗ ounces (100 grams) 100% hydration sourdough starter (page 59) or old dough (page 65)
- 1½ cups (325 grams) water
- 14⁷⁄₁₀ ounces (400 grams) super fine semolina flour, also called *semola rimacinata*
- 3½ ounces (100 grams) bread flour
- 1¾ teaspoons (10 grams) salt

1 In a large bowl, combine the sourdough starter with the water. Add the flours and mix well. Then, knead for 15 minutes by hand or with a stand-mixer, incorporating the salt towards the end of the kneading. Let the dough rest, covered, until it is 1½ of the initial volume (around 2 ½ hours).

2 Transfer the dough on a clean surface and shape it into a tight round and let proof in a round proofing basket lined with a heavily floured kitchen towel. Cover and let rest for further 2½ hours (or more) at room temperature. Check the dough: if it rose 1½ its original volume, then it is proofed (do not wait until it doubles).

3 Preheat the oven to 480°F—with a baking stone in, if you have one. Prepare a baking peel or flat tray sprinkled with coarse semolina or corn flour, invert the dough, score a cross on top, and transfer to the oven (without steam).

4 After 20 minutes, lower the temperature gradually to 360°F and bake for further 30–40 minutes.

# OATMEAL LOAF

YIELD: 3 LOAVES / ACTIVE TIME: 45 MINUTES / TOTAL TIME: 2 HOURS 35 MINUTES

Our head baker, Bre, created this dough so we could offer a soft, moist, vegan sandwich bread. Our other sandwich loaves (white, wheat, multigrain) are all made with eggs, milk, and butter.
—*Amy and Zachary Tyson, Boulangerie*

**INGREDIENTS:**

- **3** cups water (scantly filled)
- **1** tablespoon + 1 teaspoon gold yeast
- **½** cup wheat flour
- **7** cups King Arthur Special Patent Flour
- **3¾** cups oats, soaked in ½ cup of water
- **⅔** cup honey
- **1½** tablespoon salt

1 Soak the oats for a minimum of 10 minutes and maximum of 1 hour.

2 Mix all the ingredients except for the oats on low speed for 5 minutes.

3 Mix on 2nd speed for 3–4 minutes. Check dough for window (see sidebar).

4 Let sit, covered, for 30 minutes prior to proof—preferably in a warm spot.

5 Divide dough into 3 equal portions. Pre-shape into an oval or rough loaf shape. Cover with a linen or cloth and let rest for 20 minutes.

6 Do a final shape and place seam side–down in a 1-pound loaf pan (approximately 9 inches x 4½ inches) that has been sprayed with Pam nonstick spray.

7 Proof until the dough comes above the edges of the pan. This should take about an hour, depending on the temperature.

8 Bake in a preheated oven at 350°F for 30–35 minutes.

A "window" exists when you can stretch the dough until a thin, transparent membrane forms. If the dough is developed enough—elastic enough—it will be able to form a "window" without tearing. If the dough does tear, it isn't developed enough. This is also a good test if mixing by hand.

# PRETZEL DOUGH

YIELD: 20 PRETZELS / ACTIVE TIME: 90 MINUTES / TOTAL TIME: 2 HOURS 10 MINUTES

Dependably chewy, warm, and salty, the pretzels at Swiss Bakery (see page 226) are worth traveling for. This recipe works whether you're making hot pretzels or pretzel buns—simply adjust the mold to your preferred shape!

—*recipe courtesy of Michael Siu, Swiss Bakery*

**INGREDIENTS:**

- 12¾ cups all-purpose flour
- 1⅔ tablespoons salt
- ¼ cup butter
- 1⅔ ounces malt liquid
- 1⅛ ounces fresh yeast
- 3⅔ cups water
- Lye or baking soda solution

1 Lye or baking soda solution: Swiss Bakery makes their own lye solution using 1¼ cups of water and 1⅓ ounces of sodium hydroxide. If you don't have sodium hydroxide, just mix 1 part baking soda to 9 parts warm water.

2 Add all ingredients into mixer bowl with a dough hook. Mix for about 5 minutes—2 minutes on slow and 3 minutes on fast, until gluten looks well developed.

3 Remove bowl from mixer and cover with a towel. Let rest for 20 minutes.

4 Flour table and remove dough from bowl. Flatten and cut into 20 or so equal pieces and roll out each piece until it's elongated. Place onto a baking sheet lined with parchment paper.

5 Take the first piece you've cut and slowly roll it out until it is about arm's length long. Taper the ends to your liking to have either a bigger or smaller knot. Try to use less flour, and if the dough is too floury, wet your hands a little bit.

6 Twist the middle and then place the ends back onto the round pretzel so that the sides stay. Place all finished pretzels onto a baking sheet.

7 Preheat the oven to 350°F. Take each pretzel and dip into the lye solution. If not available, baking soda solution can be used. Use slotted spoon to dip and remove.

8 Place back onto parchment and use a sharp paring knife to score the thick part of the pretzel. Sprinkle salt all over the pretzel, as much or as little as you desire.

9 Bake at 350°F for 15 minutes or until shiny and brown.

# FOCACCIA

YIELDS 4 TO 6 SERVINGS / **ACTIVE TIME:** 90 MINUTES / TOTAL TIME: 3 HOURS

This is essentially a raised flatbread—like a crustier pizza—to which all kinds of yummy things can be added. It's become synonymous with Italian cuisine, and it's certainly popular in Italy, but it's also made throughout the Mediterranean countries, from Istria through southern France. You can find it in grocery stores, but there's nothing like a fresh piece right out of the skillet, still warm, with toppings just the way you want them. This one is a simple salt/parmesan focaccia.
—*Dominique DeVito*

**INGREDIENTS:**

| 1 | packet active dry yeast (2 teaspoons) |
| 2 | teaspoons salt |
| 2 | cups water (110 to 115°F) |
| 4 to 4½ | cups flour |
| 3 | tablespoons olive oil, plus more for drizzling over bread before baking |

Sea salt (coarse grained) and freshly ground black pepper

Grated parmesan for topping

1 Proof the yeast by mixing it with the warm water. Let sit for 10 minutes until foamy.

2 In a bowl, combine the flour, salt, and yeast mix. Stir to combine well. Transfer to a lightly floured surface and knead the dough until it loses its stickiness, adding more flour as needed, about 10 minutes.

3 Coat the bottom and sides of a large mixing bowl (ceramic is best) with olive oil. Place the ball of dough in the bowl, cover loosely with plastic wrap, put it in a naturally warm, draft-free location, and let it rise until doubled in size, about 45 minutes to 1 hour.

4 Preheat the oven to 450°F.

5 When risen, turn the dough out onto a lightly floured surface and divide it in half. Put a tablespoon of olive oil in the skillet, and press one of the pieces of dough into it. Drizzle some olive oil over it and sprinkle with salt and pepper, then with parmesan cheese. Cover loosely with plastic wrap and let rise for about 20 minutes. With the other piece, press it out onto a piece of parchment paper and follow the same procedure to top it and let it rise.

6 Put in the middle of the oven and bake for 25 to 30 minutes until golden and hot. Remove from oven and let rest for 5 minutes before removing from skillet to cool further. Wipe any crumbs off the skillet, coat with some more olive oil, and transfer the other round to the skillet. Bake for about 25 minutes.

7 If desired, you can put the extra dough in a plastic bag and store it in the refrigerator for up to 3 days to use later.

# APPLE *and* RAISINS SOURDOUGH FOCACCIA

YIELD: 1 FOCACCIA / ACTIVE TIME: 50 MINUTES / TOTAL TIME: 4 HOURS

This is a delicious sweet version of focaccia. It is very easy to make by simply preparing a double batch of your basic white sourdough dough and using half of it for the focaccia.

**INGREDIENTS:**

1¹⁄₁₀ pounds (500 grams) basic white sourdough bread dough, to use right after baking

3½ ounces (100 grams) apples

3½ ounces (100 grams) raisins

1½ tablespoons olive oil

3 tablespoons sugar

2 tablespoons butter

1 Peel, core, and slice the apple and dry it on paper or a kitchen towel. Soak the raisins in water for 30 minutes.

2 Rinse the raisins and let them dry on paper or a kitchen towel.

3 Oil a bowl with 1 tablespoon of olive oil and place the bread dough in it.

4 Add the apple, the raisins, and 1 teaspoon of sugar and knead by hand for 2 minutes.

5 Let rest, covered, for ½ hour. Fold 1 or 2 times during the interval.

6 Repeat the fold for another ½ hour and then let rest for 2 hours.

7 Place the dough in an oiled baking dish and slightly flatten it with your hands. Cover and let rest for 2 hours. Preheat the oven to 480°F.

8 Place tiny pieces of butter on the focaccia and sprinkle with half of the sugar.

9 Bake for 30 minutes. Create initial steam by throwing a few ice cubes in the bottom rack when putting the focaccia in the oven.

10 Lower the temperature to 445°F and then lower further to 390°F after 10 minutes. Toward the end of baking, sprinkle the remaining sugar and the remaining butter pieces over the focaccia.

CAST-IRON SKILLET RECIPE

# ITALIAN HERB FOCACCIA

YIELDS: 4 TO 6 SERVINGS / ACTIVE TIME: 90 MINUTES / TOTAL TIME: 3 HOURS

Infused with oregano, thyme, and basil—and with garlic, too—this herbed focaccia is sensational dipped into olive oil infused with red peppers, or topped with an olive tapenade.
—*Dominique DeVito*

**INGREDIENTS:**

| | |
|---|---|
| 1 | teaspoon active dry yeast |
| 1 | cup water (110 to 115°F) |
| 2 to 2½ | cups flour |
| 1 | teaspoon salt |
| ½ | teaspoon dried oregano |
| ½ | teaspoon dried thyme |
| ¼ | teaspoon dried basil |
| 1 | clove garlic, minced |
| 3 | tablespoons olive oil, plus more for drizzling over bread before baking |
| | Sea salt (coarse grained) and freshly ground black pepper |
| | Grated Parmesan for topping |

1 Proof the yeast by mixing it with the warm water. Let sit for 10 minutes until foamy.

2 In a bowl, combine the flour, salt, oregano, thyme, and basil, and stir into yeast mix. Stir to combine well. Stir in the garlic. Transfer to a lightly floured surface and knead the dough until it loses its stickiness, adding more flour as needed, about 10 minutes.

3 Coat the bottom and sides of a large mixing bowl (ceramic is best) with olive oil. Place the ball of dough in the bowl, cover loosely with plastic wrap, put it in a naturally warm, draft-free location, and let it rise until doubled in size, about 45 minutes to 1 hour.

4 Preheat the oven to 450°F.

5 Put a tablespoon of olive oil in the skillet, and press the dough into it. Drizzle some olive oil over it and sprinkle with salt and pepper, then with Parmesan cheese. Cover loosely with plastic wrap and let rise for about 20 minutes.

6 Put in the middle of the oven and bake for 25 to 30 minutes until golden and hot. Remove from oven and let rest for 5 minutes before removing from skillet to cool further.

# ROSEMARY OLIVE FOCACCIA

**YIELDS:** 4 TO 6 SERVINGS / **ACTIVE TIME:** 90 MINUTES / **TOTAL TIME:** 3 HOURS

This is another traditional flavor combination for focaccia. Be sure to use fresh rosemary, a combination of olives from an olive bar in a grocery or specialty store, and the red pepper flakes for a nice spicy heat. This is a great focaccia to serve with a large green salad for a summer lunch.

—*Dominique DeVito*

**INGREDIENTS:**

1   teaspoon active dry yeast

1   cup water (110 to 115°F)

2   to 2½ cups flour

1   teaspoon salt

1   tablespoon fresh rosemary leaves

1   teaspoon red pepper flakes

1   clove garlic, minced

½   cup olives, pitted and cut in half

3   tablespoons olive oil, plus more for drizzling over bread before baking

Sea salt (coarse grained) and freshly ground black pepper

1   Proof the yeast by mixing it with the warm water. Let sit for 10 minutes until foamy.

2   In a bowl, combine the flour, salt, rosemary, and red pepper flakes, and stir into yeast mix. Stir to combine well. Stir in the garlic and olives. Transfer to a lightly floured surface and knead the dough until it loses its stickiness, adding more flour as needed, about 10 minutes.

3   Coat the bottom and sides of a large mixing bowl (ceramic is best) with olive oil. Place the ball of dough in the bowl, cover loosely with plastic wrap, put it in a naturally warm, draft-free location, and let it rise until doubled in size, about 45 minutes to 1 hour.

4   Preheat the oven to 450°F.

5   Put a tablespoon of olive oil in the skillet, and press the dough into it. Drizzle some olive oil over it and sprinkle with salt and pepper. Cover loosely with plastic wrap and let rise for about 20 minutes.

6   Put in the middle of the oven and bake for 25 to 30 minutes until golden and hot. Remove from oven and let rest for 5 minutes before removing from skillet to cool further.

# CARAMELIZED ONION *and* LEEK FOCACCIA

YIELDS: 4 TO 6 SERVINGS / ACTIVE TIME: 2 HOURS / TOTAL TIME: 3 HOURS

I'm a sucker for caramelized onions, which are onions that have been sautéed in butter and oil until soft and browned. They lose their bite, transformed instead into something almost sweet. The combination of leeks with the onions makes for a more subtle and even slightly sweeter topping.
—*Dominique DeVito*

1 In a skillet (cast-iron or otherwise), melt butter and 2 table-spoons of oil over medium-low heat. When melted, add the onion and leek slices. Increase the heat to medium-high and cook, stirring, until onions and leeks start to soften, about 5 minutes. Reduce heat to low and allow to cook, stirring occasionally, until cooked down and browned, about 10 to 15 minutes. Set aside.

2 Proof the yeast by mixing it with the warm water. Let sit for 10 minutes until foamy.

3 Combine the flour, salt, and pepper, and stir into yeast mix. Stir to combine well. Dough will be sticky. Transfer to a floured surface and knead the dough until it loses its stickiness, adding more flour as needed, about 10 minutes.

4 Coat the bottom and sides of a large mixing bowl (ceramic is best) with olive oil. Place the ball of dough in the bowl, cover loosely with plastic wrap, put it in a naturally warm, draft-free location, and let it rise until doubled in size, about 45 minutes to 1 hour.

5 Preheat the oven to 450°F.

6 Put a tablespoon of olive oil in the skillet, and press the dough into it. Top with the caramelized onion/leek mix. Season generously with sea salt and pepper, then with Parmesan cheese. Cover loosely with plastic wrap and let rise for about 20 minutes.

7 Put in the middle of the oven and bake for 25 to 30 minutes until golden and hot. Remove from oven and let rest for 5 minutes before removing from skillet to cool further.

## INGREDIENTS:

- 8 tablespoons (1 stick) butter
- 3 tablespoons olive oil
- 1 medium yellow onion, peeled and sliced into thin slices
- 1 large leek, white and light green part only, sliced thin and rinsed of any sand
- 1 teaspoon active dry yeast
- 1 cup water (110 to 115°F)
- 2 to 2½ cups flour
- 1 teaspoon salt
- 1 teaspoon freshly ground black pepper

  Sea salt (coarse grained)

  Grated Parmesan for topping

# BRIOCHE

YIELDS: 12 BUNS OR 2 SMALL LOAVES / ACTIVE TIME: 50 MINUTES / TOTAL TIME: ABOUT 4 HOURS

The quintessential French sweet dough, brioche is the base for many other French sweet breads. It originated during the Middle Age and became increasingly common as centuries passed, so common that it became the subject of the famous quote "let them eat brioche [if they do not have bread."

1 Heat the milk to 100–110°F. Dissolve the yeast in water and let rest for 5 minutes. In a large bowl, combine the water-yeast mixture with the warmed milk, ½ of the flour and the sugar.

2 Add 1 egg at a time and incorporate well. Add the rest of the flour and start working the dough, either with a stand-mixer or by hand (see page 63 for tips on kneading).

3 Add the butter in pieces, continuing to work the dough, and incorporate the salt towards the end of the kneading. Work the dough until it feels smooth. The mixing process takes about 20 minutes from start to finish.

4 Let the dough rest, covered, in a warm spot until it looks fully risen. This should take about 1 to 2 hours.

5 Divide the dough in 12 pieces if you like to make the dough in individual brioche buns, or cut in 6 pieces if you prefer the pan loaves version.

6 For the buns option: roll the dough pieces into rounds and place in greased individual brioche tins.

7 For the loaves: make 2 braids out of the 6 pieces by rolling each piece into a log, connecting the top ends of 3 pieces, and braiding them together, then repeating with the last 3 pieces of dough. Place into 2 small, greased loaf pans.

8 Cover with an oiled plastic film or place into big, clean plastic bags and let rest for about 1 to 1½ hours.

9 Preheat oven to 355°F.

10 Brush with the egg slightly whisked with the water. Bake for 20 to 30 minutes depending on the size of your brioches.

## INGREDIENTS:

- 1 tbsp (8.50 g) active dry yeast
- 3½ oz (100 g) water, warmed
- 7 oz (200 g) milk
- 17.6 oz (500 g) all-purpose flour
- 3½ oz (100 g) sugar
- 2 eggs
- 3½ oz (100 g) butter
- 1 tsp (6 g) salt

### EGG WASH
- 1 egg
- 1 tbsp water

# COPPIA FERRARESE

YIELD: 3 BREADS / **ACTIVE TIME:** 50 MINUTES / **TOTAL TIME:** 3½ HOURS

This is a traditional bread from Ferrara, in Northern-Central Italy. Because of its x-like shape, the bread has a crunchy exterior and a soft interior at the junction of the two arms.

**INGREDIENTS:**

- ⅔ cup (175 grams) water
- 1⅔ teaspoons (5 grams) active dry yeast
- 1 pound (500 grams) all-purpose flour
- ¼ cup (50 grams) extra virgin olive oil
- 1¾ teaspoons (10 grams) salt

1 Heat the water to 110°F maximum. Combine the yeast with the water and let rest for 10 minutes.

2 If mixing dough by hand: place the flour in a large bowl and create a well in the center. Pour the water-yeast mixture in the flour well and gently incorporate the water to the flour. Add the oil and the salt and incorporate gently. Knead for a few minutes and then let rest for a few minutes and knead again. Continue like this for about 20 minutes.

3 Or, if mixing with a stand-mixer: mix water with flour at low speed for a few minutes. Add the oil and gradually increase speed, to reach medium speed after 10–15 minutes. Add the salt and mix for further 5 minutes.

4 Let the dough rest, covered, until it doubles. Preheat the oven to 430°F—with the baking stone in, if you own one.

5 Take a little piece of dough (smaller than a golf ball) and put aside, covered. Make the dough into a ball and roll it out to a large disk, to a thickness between ⅒ and ⅕ inches. With a pizza cutter or other sharp instrument, cut the disk in 6 triangular slices.

6 Roll-up each slice into itself starting from the base of the triangle, to form a log. Take 2 rolled-up logs and place them near to each other, lengthwise, on a baking tray covered with parchment paper.

7 Use a small piece out of the piece of dough that you put aside to seal the 2 rolled-up logs to each other on their central part, leaving most of each log free.

8 Turn the free ends of the logs so that they form an arch facing the outside of the couple. Repeat for the remaining rolled-up logs. Let rest, covered, for 30–40 minutes.

9 Bake for 20 minutes.

# MAROCCA DI CASOLA

YIELD: 2 LOAVES/ ACTIVE TIME: 30 MINUTES / TOTAL TIME: 7 HOURS

Marocca di Casola is an ancient bread from one small rural area (Casola, Lunigiana) in Northern Italy. It is made almost entirely of chestnut flour, which is what the locals had in the past, when wheat flour was too expensive. It makes a very interesting bread with unusual aromas.

**INGREDIENTS:**

- 1 medium-small potato (2½ ounces)
- 12 ounces chestnut flour
- 5½ ounces all-purpose flour
- 5 ounces stiff sourdough starter
- 9 ounces water
- 2 teaspoons salt
- 1½ tablespoons olive oil

1 Boil 1 medium-small potato and set it aside to cool.

2 Combine the flours with the sourdough starter and water.

3 Make a ball, cover, and let rest for 2 to 3 hours.

4 Add the salt, the potato, and the olive oil. Knead until all ingredients are incorporated.

5 Divide the dough into 2 rounds and place in small baskets dusted with chestnut and wheat flours to rest, covered.

6 Let rest for several hours, until the loaves look risen. They do not grow much, but you can see cracks on the surface. Preheat oven to 390°F.

7 When ready, invert onto a baking dish, make 1 slash in the center (or none at all), and bake 35 to 40 minutes.

# MUFFOLETTE

YIELD: 8–10 SMALL LOAVES / ACTIVE TIME: 30 MINUTES / TOTAL TIME: 3½ HOURS

Traditional Sicilian semolina buns take on different names in different areas of Sicily. In Palermo, they are called *vastedda* and are filled with meat. This version is usually filled with olive oil and pecorino cheese, or tomatoes and anchovies.

1 Heat the water to 105°F maximum. Add the yeast to the water and let rest for 10 minutes.

2 In a large bowl, combine the water-yeast mix with remaining ingredients, except salt. Knead by hand or with a stand-mixer for 10 minutes, add the salt toward the end of the kneading. Let the dough rest, covered, until it doubles (about 2 hours).

3 Preheat the oven to 430°F—with the baking stone in, if you own one.

4 Transfer the dough to a clean and floured surface and divide into 8–10 pieces, depending on desired size. Form each piece into a tight round and place on 2 baking dishes covered with parchment paper, making sure to leave plenty of space in between the rounds.

5 Let rest, covered for an hour.

6 Flatten each round with the palm of your hand (floured) and place 1 tray at the time in the middle rack of your oven. Bake for 10 minutes.

## INGREDIENTS:

- 1 cup plus 1 tablespoon (265 grams) water

- 2½ teaspoons (ca. 7 grams) active dry yeast

- 1 pound (500 grams) super fine semolina flour, also called *semola rimacinata*

- 3 tablespoons extra virgin olive oil

- 2 tablespoons honey

- 1¾ teaspoons (10 grams) salt

# SICILIAN BREAD

YIELD: 2 LOAVES / ACTIVE TIME: 30 MINUTES / TOTAL TIME: 4 HOURS

Sicilian bread comes in many shapes, but it has one main characteristic: it is based on semolina flour. Traditionally made with old dough from a previous bake, it can also be made with yeast (or sourdough). This is a typical example of Sicilian daily bread.

**INGREDIENTS:**

- 1½ cups (325 grams) water
- 2½ teaspoons (7 grams) active dry yeast
- 1 teaspoon honey
- 2⅖ ounces (350 grams) super fine semolina flour, also called *semola rimacinata*
- 5⅓ ounces (150 grams) bread flour
- 2 teaspoons extra virgin olive oil
- 1¾ teaspoons (10 grams) salt
- Sesame seeds for coating

1 Heat the water to 105°F maximum. Add the yeast and honey to the water and let rest for 10 minutes.

2 In a large bowl combine the water-yeast mix with remaining ingredients, except salt. Knead by hand or with a stand-mixer for 10 minutes, add the salt towards the end of the kneading. Let the dough rest, covered, until it doubles (around 1 ½ hours).

3 Preheat the oven to 360°F—with the baking stone in, if you own one. Transfer the dough on a clean and floured surface and divide into 2 pieces. Flatten each piece into a rectangle and roll it up, from its shorter side and place on a tray coated with sesame seeds.

4 Preheat the oven to 430°F—with the baking stone in, if you have one. Let the dough rest, covered, for another 1 ½ hours.

5 Prepare a baking peel or flat tray sprinkled with coarse semolina or corn flour, invert the loaves on the peel, with the sesame seeds side on top, and make 3 light transversal cuts on top of each loaf.

6 Transfer the loaves in the oven and bake, without steam, for 15 minutes, then lower the temperature to 375°F and bake for further 30–40 minutes or until golden brown.

# BORODINSKY BREAD

**YIELDS:** 2 SMALL LOAVES / **ACTIVE TIME:** 30 MINUTES **TOTAL TIME:** 14½ HOURS

This popular Russian dark rye bread is flavored with coriander seeds. Its origin is mysterious, but its charm is certain. It needs to be started the night before the baking day, and it is easy in this recipe to substitute the traditional rye sourdough starter with commercial yeast.

**INGREDIENTS:**

- 10 oz (about 300 g) + 3.4–5 oz (100–150 g) water
- 1.3 lb (600 g) dark rye flour
- 2 tsp ground coriander seeds
- ¼ cup (60 g) rye sourdough starter **OR** 1 tsp active dry yeast
- 3 oz (85 g) whole-wheat flour
- 2 tbsp molasses
- 1 tsp (about 6 g) salt

1 Combine 10 oz of the water, brought to a temperature close to boiling, with ⅓ of the rye flour and the coriander seeds.

2 Before adding the sourdough starter or the yeast to the dough, allow it to cool down to 85°F if using a sourdough starter, OR to 100–105°F if using active dry yeast.

3 Let rest, covered, overnight (about 12 hours), at room temperature.

4 Add the remaining rye flour, the whole wheat flour and the molasses.

5 Add remaining water 1 tablespoon at a time, and stop when the dough reaches a consistency easy to knead and not too sticky.

6 Knead for 10 minutes, by hand or with a stand-mixer.

7 Transfer to a heavily floured surface, roll, fold like a letter a couple of times, and shape into 2 tight rounds.

8 Transfer the rounds into 2 proofing baskets heavily dusted with rye flour.

9 Preheat the oven to 320°F.

10 Let rest, covered, for about 2 hours.

11 Bake for about 1½ hours.

12 Let cool for several hours before slicing.

# PAIN DE CAMPAGNE

This is the traditional French country bread that many modern bakers took inspiration from. There is no right recipe for it, as it comes in infinite variations. What is quite constant is the use of natural fermentation and a percentage of whole wheat or whole rye.

**INGREDIENTS:**

- ⅔ cup (ca. 150 grams) 100% hydration sourdough starter (page 59)
- 1⅖ cups (350 grams) water
- 7 ounces (200 grams) bread flour
- 7 ounces (200 grams) all-purpose flour
- 3½ ounces (100 grams) rye flour
- 1¾ teaspoons (10 grams) salt

1 Combine the sourdough starter with the water.

2 Add the flours to the water and the starter and mix well. Knead for a few minutes by hand or with a stand-mixer. Let the dough rest, covered, for 40 minutes.

3 Incorporate the salt. Knead more, by hand or with a stand-mixer, until the dough appears elastic when pulled. Let the dough rest, covered, for 2 hours.

4 Transfer the dough to a clean surface. Divide in two, shape into 2 rounds, and transfer in a flour bread basket, or banneton.

5 Preheat the oven to maximum temperature—with the baking stone in, if you have one.

6 After 2 hours (or more depending on how fast your dough is fermenting), prepare a baking peel or flat tray sprinkled with coarse semolina or corn flour, slash the top of the rounds with 2 cuts crossing each other, and transfer the round—or boule—into the hot oven.

7 Immediately lower the temperature to 480°F and bake with steam for 25 minutes (see page 49).

8 Let the steam out by opening the oven door and bake for 20–30 minutes at 440°F, or until golden brown.

# PAIN DE MIE

YIELD: 1 BIG LOAF / ACTIVE TIME: 50 MINUTES / TOTAL TIME: 4 HOURS

Pain de Mie is the progenitor of our common sliced and packaged bread, so it is a real treat to be able to taste and offer the real thing. This bread uses a special tin with a lid, which gives it a more regular shape and crumb, but can also be baked in a regular loaf pan.

**INGREDIENTS:**

- 2½ teaspoons (7 grams) active dry yeast
- 3½ ounces (100 grams) water
- 1 tablespoon and 1 teaspoon (20 grams) sugar
- 7 ounces (200 grams) warm milk
- 1 pound (500 grams) all-purpose flour
- 2 ounces (57 grams) butter
- 1½ teaspoons (10 grams) salt

1 Activate the yeast in the water combined with the sugar and warmed to 105°F maximum, for 10 minutes.

2 Add the milk and the flour to the water and knead for 10 minutes, by hand or with a stand-mixer.

3 Add the butter and the salt and knead for another 10 minutes.

4 Let the dough rest, covered, in a warm spot (the oven with the light on and a crack open will do) until it doubles.

5 Preheat the oven to 430°F. Grease a loaf tin of approximately 10 x 4 x 2.8 inches. The proper Pain de Mie tin comes with a lid.

6 De-gas the dough, shape it into a long log and transfer into the tin. Cover with plastic wrap and let rest until the dough has reached ¾ of the loaf tin.

7 If the tin has a lid, close it. If the tin does not have a lid, brush the dough with milk and water and place in the oven. Immediately reduce the temperature to 360°F and bake for 40–45 minutes.

8 Take the tin out and let it cool (remove the lid if there is one). Invert the loaf on a grid and let cool completely before slicing.

# PAIN DE PROVENCE

YIELD: 2 SMALL LOAVES / ACTIVE TIME: 30 MINUTES / TOTAL TIME: 3½ HOURS

This is a simple white rustic bread, flavored with plenty of herbs from Provence, which is the French region from which this bread originates. Needless to say, it goes well with cheese.

**INGREDIENTS:**

- 2½ teaspoons (7 grams) active dry yeast
- 1½ cups (340 grams) water
- 1 tablespoon and 1 teaspoon (20 grams) sugar
- 1 pound (500 grams) all-purpose flour
- 3 tablespoons dry herbs de Provence
- 1¼ teaspoons (10 grams) salt
- 2 tablespoons olive oil

1 Activate the yeast in the water and warmed to 105°F maximum, for 10 minutes.

2 In a separate bowl, combine flour, herbs, and salt.

3 Add the flour-herbs mix to the water-yeast mix and knead, by hand or with a stand-mixer, for 10 minutes.

4 Add the olive oil and the salt and knead for further 10 minutes.

5 Let the dough rest, covered, in a warm spot (the oven with the light on and a crack open will do) until it doubles.

6 Preheat the oven to maximum temperature—with a baking stone in if you own one.

7 De-gas the dough and divide in 2 pieces. Shape each piece of dough into a round and transfer to a floured proofing basket (banneton). Let rest, covered, until the dough has risen 1 ½ times.

8 Invert the loaves on a baker peel or flat tray dusted with coarse semolina or corn flour and transfer into the oven. Immediately reduce the temperature to 480°F and bake with steam for 20 minutes (page 49).

9 Let the steam out by opening the oven door and bake for 20–25 minutes at 440°F, or until golden brown.

# CAFONE BREAD

YIELD: 1 BIG LOAF OR 2 SMALL ONES / ACTIVE TIME: 20 MINUTES / TOTAL TIME: 7 HOURS

This is a traditional bread from Campania, in South-West Italy. In Neapolitan, the term "*ca' fun*" (cafone) means peasants, and, in fact, this bread was brought to Naples and its coast by the inhabitants of the inner part of the region, which was less urbanized.

1 Combine the sourdough starter with the water. Add the flours to the water and the starter and mix well. Knead for no more than 10 minutes by hand or with a stand-mixer, incorporating the salt towards the end of the kneading.

2 Let the dough rest, covered, until it doubles (around 4 hours).

3 Transfer the dough on a clean surface. Divide the dough in two equal parts, flatten each piece and roll it up, lengthwise. Pull the two ends gently to elongate it and place on a heavily flour tray. Let rest, covered, until your fingerprint leaves a mark in the loaves. It is okay to slightly over proof this type of bread.

4 Preheat the oven to the maximum temperature—with the baking stone in, if you have one.

5 Prepare a baking peel or flat tray sprinkled with coarse semolina or corn flour, slash the loaves on the sides to prevent them from opening on the top, and transfer them into the hot oven without steam or with just a minimal amount of it.

6 Immediately lower the temperature to 480°F and bake for 25 minutes.

7 Lower temperature to 440°F and bake for 20–30 minutes, or until golden brown.

## INGREDIENTS:

- 3⅗ ounces (100 grams) 100% hydration sourdough starter (page 59) or old dough (page 65).

- 1½ cups (335 grams) water

- 10 ⅗ ounces (300 grams) bread flour

- 7 ounces (200 grams) all-purpose flour

- 1¼ teaspoons (10 grams) salt

# ROASTED GARLIC BREAD

YIELDS 1 SMALL ROUND / **ACTIVE TIME:** 25 MINUTES / **TOTAL TIME:** 3 HOURS

Be forewarned: If you love garlic (as I suspect you do if you want to make this recipe), the smell of this bread baking will make you drool. Once you can slice into it, eat it as-is, toast it and top with a thin smear of pesto, or serve it as a wonderful substitute for traditional garlic bread.
—*Dominique DeVito*

**INGREDIENTS:**

| | |
|---|---|
| 1 | head garlic |
| ¼ | cup olive oil |
| ¼ | teaspoon instant yeast |
| ¼ | teaspoon sugar |
| 1½ | cups water (110 to 115°F) |
| 1 | teaspoon kosher salt |
| 3 | cups all-purpose flour plus more for kneading and dusting |

1 Preheat the oven to 375°F.

2 Take as much of the paper skin off the head of garlic as possible without separating the cloves. With a sharp knife, cut off only as much of the top of the head as necessary to expose the cloves in their sleeves. Put the garlic cut side up on a piece of heavy-duty aluminum foil or in a garlic roaster. Pour the olive oil over the top of the head of garlic. Fold the aluminum foil up and over the garlic to cover it, crimping any edges together, or put the lid on the garlic roaster. Roast in the oven for 50 to 60 minutes.

3 Open the foil or roaster and allow the garlic to cool slightly. Extract the roasted cloves from their sleeves by squeezing the bottom so the cloves pop out. Put them on a plate or in a shallow bowl. Keep the cooking oil.

4 Put the yeast and sugar in a measuring cup and add about ½ cup warm water in a drizzle. Hot water will kill the yeast, so it's important that the water be warm without being hot. Cover the measuring cup with plastic wrap and set it aside for about 15 minutes. If the yeast doesn't foam, it is not alive and you'll need to start over.

5 When the yeast is proofed, pour it into a large bowl and add the additional cup of warm water. Stir gently to combine. Add the salt to the flour, and add the flour to the yeast mixture. Stir with a wooden spoon until combined. The dough will be wet and sticky.

6 Put a dusting of flour on a flat surface and lift out the dough. With flour on your hands and more at the ready, begin kneading the dough so that it loses its stickiness. Don't overdo it, and don't use too much flour; just enough that it is more cohesive. Add the roasted garlic cloves while you're gently kneading the dough.

7 Lightly grease a large bowl with some of the garlic-infused olive oil and place the dough in it. Cover the bowl with plastic wrap, and allow to rise untouched for at least one hour, and up to several hours. Gently punch it down, recover with the plastic, and allow to rise again for another 30 minutes or so. Brush the surface with the garlic-infused oil.

8 While the dough is on its final rise, pre-heat the oven to 450°F. Put a piece of parchment paper on the bottom of the Dutch oven and put it in with the lid on so it gets hot. When the oven is ready and dough has risen, carefully remove the lid and gently scoop the dough from the bowl into the pot. Cover and bake for 15 minutes. Remove the lid and continue to bake for another 15 to 20 minutes until the top is golden and it sounds hollow when tapped.

9 Remove the pot from the oven and use tea towels to carefully remove the bread. Allow to cool before slicing.

# HONEY BREAD

**YIELDS** 1 SMALL ROUND / **ACTIVE TIME:** 30 MINUTES / **TOTAL TIME:** 3 HOURS

The combination of honey and egg yolks in this bread creates something like a challah—with a beautiful yellow color on the inside and toasty brown crust on the outside. The dense, buttery bread is slightly sweet, too. It's a lovely loaf for eating, toasting, and making French toast.

—*Dominique DeVito*

**INGREDIENTS:**

| | |
|---|---|
| 1 | tablespoon active dry yeast |
| 1 | tablespoon sugar |
| 3 | tablespoons water |
| 4 | tablespoons butter |
| 1 | cup milk |
| ¼ | cup honey |
| 1 | tablespoon salt |
| 2 | egg yolks |
| 3 | cups flour |
| 1 | egg yolk beaten with 1 tablespoon milk |

1 Put the yeast and sugar in bowl and add about ½ cup warm water in a drizzle. Hot water will kill the yeast, so it's important that the water be warm without being hot. Cover the bowl with plastic wrap and set it aside for about 15 minutes. If the yeast doesn't foam, it is not alive and you'll need to start over.

2 In a saucepan, melt the butter over low heat. Stir in the milk, honey, and salt. Remove from the heat and allow to cool slightly. Pour this over the yeast/sugar combination and stir.

3 Add the egg yolks and flour and stir with a wooden spoon until the flour is blended in well.

4 Put a dusting of flour on a flat surface and lift out the dough. With flour on your hands and more at the ready, begin kneading the dough so that it loses its stickiness. The kneading process will take about 10 minutes, forming an elastic, smooth dough.

5 Place the dough in a large bowl, cover the bowl with plastic wrap, and allow to rise in a warm spot, untouched for at least one hour, and up to several hours. Gently punch it down, recover with the plastic, and allow to rise again for another 30 minutes or so.

6 While the dough is on its final rise, preheat the oven to 450°F. Put a piece of parchment paper on the bottom of the Dutch oven and put it in with the lid on so it gets hot. When the oven is ready and dough has risen, carefully remove the lid and gently scoop the dough from the bowl into the pot. Cover and bake for 15 minutes. Remove the lid and brush the surface of the loaf with the egg/milk mixture. Continue to bake for another 15 to 20 minutes until the top is golden and it sounds hollow when tapped.

7 Remove the pot from the oven and use tea towels to carefully remove the bread. Allow to cool on a dish for 15 minutes or so before slicing.

# CHOCOLATE-CINNAMON BREAD

**YIELD** 1 SMALL ROUND/ **DUTCH OVEN:** 4.5 QUART / **ACTIVE TIME:** 25 MINUTES / **TOTAL TIME:** 3 HOURS

This is like an exotic *pain au chocolat*—crunchy and crispy on the outside, fluffy yet chocolately and spicy on the inside. Be patient when it comes out of the oven and allow the bread to cool for 15 to 20 minutes so that it slices more easily and cleanly.
—*Dominique DeVito*

**INGREDIENTS:**

- ¼ teaspoon active dry yeast
- ¼ teaspoon sugar
- 1½ cups lukewarm water
- 2 tablespoons unsalted butter
- 1 cup semi-sweet chocolate morsels
- 1 teaspoon ground cinnamon
- 3 cups all-purpose flour plus more for kneading and dusting
- 1 teaspoon salt

1 Put the yeast and sugar in a measuring cup and add about ½ cup lukewarm water in a drizzle. Hot water will kill the yeast, so it's important that the water be warm without being hot. Cover the measuring cup with plastic wrap and set it aside for about 15 minutes. If the yeast doesn't foam, it is not alive and you'll need to start over.

2 Cut the butter into thin slices and put it with the chocolate morsels in a medium-sized, microwave-safe bowl. Melt the chocolate and butter in the microwave, working in 20-second increments. After each 20 seconds, stir the butter and chocolate. Microwave just until melted, about 40 to 60 seconds. Stir in the cinnamon and set aside to cool. It must be cool when added to the dough.

3 When the yeast is proofed, pour it into a large bowl and add the additional cup of lukewarm water. Stir gently to combine. Add the salt to the flour, and add the flour to the yeast mixture. Stir with a wooden spoon until combined. The dough will be wet and sticky.

4 Put a dusting of flour on a flat surface and lift out the dough. With flour on your hands and more at the ready, begin kneading the dough so that it loses its stickiness. Don't overdo it, and don't use too much flour—just enough that it is more cohesive. While kneading, add the chocolate/cinnamon in increments, using as much as you want. You may not choose to use it all. Work it into the dough gently.

5 Place the dough in a large bowl, cover the bowl with plastic wrap, and allow to rise untouched for at least 1 hour, and up to several hours. Gently punch it down, recover with the plastic, and allow to rise again for another 30 minutes or so.

6 While the dough is on its final rise, preheat the oven to 450°F. Put a piece of parchment paper on the bottom of the Dutch oven and put it in with the lid on while the oven reaches 450°F. When the oven is ready, use pot holders to remove the lid of

the Dutch oven, scoop the dough from the bowl to the pot, put the lid back on and close the oven door.

7 Bake with the lid on for 15 minutes, then remove the lid. Allow to bake for another 15 to 20 minutes until the top is golden and the bread sounds hollow when tapped.

8 Remove the pot from the oven and use tea towels to carefully remove the bread. Allow to cool before slicing.

## VARIATION:

Add a subtle yet delightful heat to the bread by adding 1 teaspoon cayenne pepper along with the cinnamon.

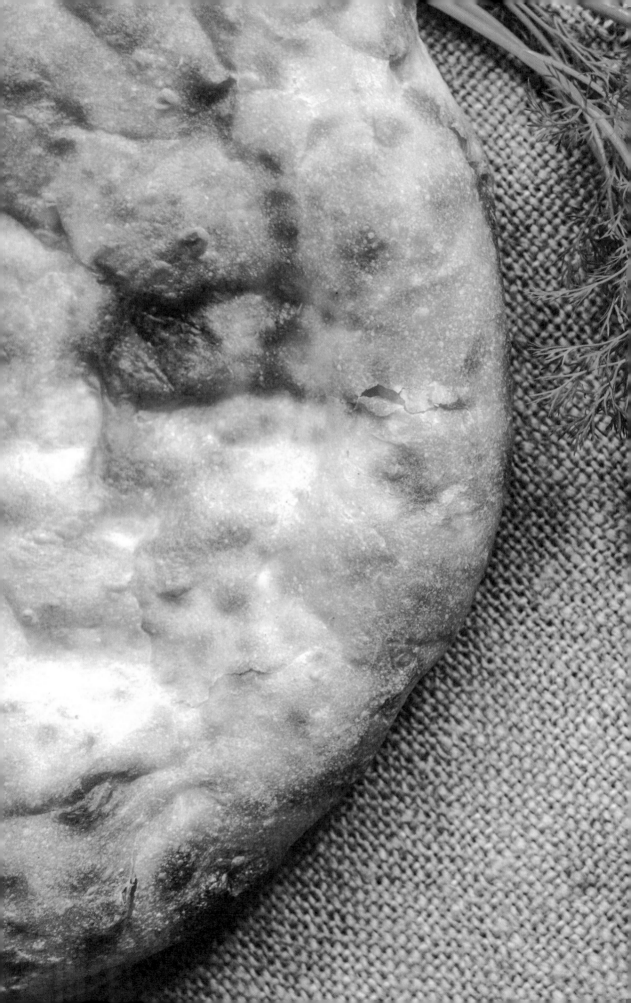

# FLATBREADS & UNLEAVENED BREADS

The simplest type of bread is an unleavened flatbread. This type of bread does not require a long fermentation process, and it does not even require an oven. It can be cooked on a griddle, or even on a camping stove or open fire.

Leavened flatbreads are more demanding. They require fermentation and traditionally are baked in special ovens (see page 106) but your own oven or pan with a lid can do the trick very well.

Flatbreads were the first type of bread ever baked, historically, but in many cultures, they were later replaced by loaves and buns when baking techniques evolved. In particular, flatbreads were abandoned in areas where wheat was widely available, since wheat is the only grain that can make well risen loaves.

If we look at today's map of flatbreads, we can easily see that they are still very popular in geographical areas that are either too cold, too humid, or to hot and arid for the proper growth of wheat.

From up North and in the high mountains, we have Scandinavian *knäckebröd* (or knækbrød, or knekkebrød) and Alpine *schüttelbrot*, which tend to be on the crunchy side and go wonderfully with butter. Far South, we have a nearly endless variety of different flatbreads: from Mexican *tortillas*, to Indian *roti* and all the different types of Arabic *pita*-like breads. Not to mention Ethiopian *injera* or Italian *piadina*. While Nordic flatbreads call for butter, Southern flatbreads call for sauces and stews and every sort of savory filling.

Making your own flatbreads at home will make your meals a real feast and surprise your family and friends with a world of new flavors and textures.

# TORTILLA

**YIELDS:** 6–12 (ABOUT 12 LARGE TORTILLAS) / **ACTIVE TIME:** 30 MINUTES / **TOTAL TIME:** 50 TO 60 MINUTES

We are covering flatbreads from around the world, so now, on to Mexico! These are even simpler to make than the ones that involved yeast. There's no need to let the dough rise for tortillas—simply mix, knead, and shape—all with your hands, which is really fun. Then cook. Oh, and eat!
—*Dominique DeVito*

**INGREDIENTS:**

3   **cups flour**

1   **teaspoon salt**

2   **teaspoons baking powder**

3   **tablespoons Crisco shortening (or 4 tablespoons chilled butter)**

1½   **cups water at room temperature**

1   Put the flour in a large bowl. Mix in the salt and baking powder.

2   Add the shortening (or butter), and using your fingers, blend it into the flour mix until you have a crumbly dough. Add 1 cup of the water and work it in, then portions of the additional ½ cup, working it in with your hands, so that you create a dough that's not too sticky.

3   Lightly flour a work surface and turn out the dough. Knead it for about 10 minutes until it's soft and elastic. Divide it into 12 equal pieces.

4   Using a lightly floured rolling pin, roll each piece out to almost the size of the bottom of the skillet.

5   Heat the skillet over high heat. Add a tortilla. Cook for just 15 seconds a side, flipping to cook both sides. Keep the cooked tortillas warm by putting them on a plate covered with a damp tea towel. Serve warm.

A homemade tortilla begs for a filling of sliced, grilled meat with shredded cheese, chopped tomatoes, chopped red onions, chopped lettuce, and sliced jalapeños.

# CORN TORTILLA

YIELDS: 15 TORTILLAS / ACTIVE TIME: 30 MINUTES / TOTAL TIME: ABOUT 30 MINUTES

Nowadays tortillas are made mainly with wheat flour, but the authentic Mexican version is based on corn flour. It may take some time to get the right consistency for the perfect corn tortilla.

**INGREDIENTS:**

**10.6** oz (300 g) masa harina, white corn flour

**¾** tsp (4.3 g) salt

**14.8** oz (420 g) water

1 In a large bowl, combine the flour with the salt.

2 Cover with boiling water and combine with a spoon.

3 As soon as the temperature allows, work the dough enough to make it come together, and shape it into a large ball. If the consistency is too dry, add more water, if too sticky, add more harina.

4 Heat a cast-iron pan or frying pan on medium-high.

5 Take one small ball of dough at a time and flatten it into a thin disk between two layers of parchment paper, using something heavy and flat to press the dough, or a tortilla press if you own one.

6 Cook from both sides, about 30 seconds on each side, or until some brown spots are visible on the surface.

7 Place the cooked tortilla between kitchen towels, to keep them soft.

# AREPAS

YIELDS: 6–7 AREPAS / ACTIVE TIME: 20 MINUTES / TOTAL TIME: ABOUT 50 MINUTES

This traditional corn bread is commonly eaten in Venezuela and Columbia, as well as other Central and South American areas. It can be eaten with a dip or split and filled like a sandwich.

**INGREDIENTS:**

1 lb (450 g) harina, white corn flour

7 oz (400 g) water

1 tsp (ca. 6 g) salt

Vegetable oil

1 In a large bowl, combine all the ingredients.

2 Let the dough rest, covered, for half an hour.

3 Roll the dough to ⅘ inch thickness and cut 6 to 7 disks out of it.

4 Fry in little vegetable oil on pan over medium-high heat for 2 minutes on each side.

5 Transfer to the oven, preheated to 400°F, and bake for 10 minutes.

6 Make each disk even by cutting any irregular side, making it as close as possible to a circle.

7 Heat a cast-iron skillet to medium-high.

8 Cook one disk at a time, a couple of minutes on each side.

# PÃO DE QUEIJO

**YIELDS:** 30–50 LITTLE BUNS / **ACTIVE TIME:** 30 MINUTES / **TOTAL TIME:** 30 MINUTES

This is a Brazilian cheese roll eaten as a snack or for breakfast. This bread was developed by enslaved miners in the 18th century. It used tapioca instead of wheat flour, which was scarcely available in Brazil at that time.

**INGREDIENTS:**

8.8 oz (250 g) milk

3½ oz (100 g) vegetable oil

8.8 oz (250 g) tapioca flour

1 tsp (about 6 g) salt

2 eggs

3½ oz (100 g) grated cheese

1 Preheat oven to 430°F and prepare two oven trays covered with parchment paper.

2 Bring the milk, emulsified with the oil, to a boil. Turn off and remove from the heat as soon as the liquids start to boil.

3 Add the tapioca and the salt, and beat with energy.

4 Continue to beat the batter and incorporate one egg at the time.

5 Finish by beating in the cheese.

6 Scoop teaspoon-sized dollops of batter over the baking trays, making sure to leave some space for them to puff.

7 Transfer to the hot oven, immediately reducing the temperature to 350°F.

8 Bake for 10–15 minutes (depending on size), or until golden-brown.

# PITA

**YIELDS:** 9 PITA / **ACTIVE TIME:** 30 MINUTES / **TOTAL TIME:** 3 HOURS

Pita is a soft, Middle Eastern flatbread that is common to most Arabic and Mediterranean countries, as well as in Northern Africa. It is a very ancient form of leavened bread, and it constitutes a staple in many cuisines. It goes well with dips, such as *hummus* and *baba ganoush*.

**INGREDIENTS:**

| | |
|---|---|
| 2 | tsp (6 g) active dry yeast |
| 1 | tsp (4.3 g) sugar |
| 8.8 | oz (250 g) water |
| 14.1 | oz (400 g) all-purpose flour |
| 2½ | tbsp (34 g) olive oil |
| 1⅖ | tsp (8 g) salt |

1 Heat the water to 100–105°F.

2 Dissolve the yeast with the sugar in the water and let rest for 5 minutes.

3 In a large bowl, combine the water-yeast mixture with the rest of the ingredients.

4 Start working the dough, either with a stand-mixer or by hand (see page 63 for tips on kneading).

5 Work the dough until it feels smooth. This should take about 10 minutes.

6 Let the dough rest, covered, in a warm spot until it looks fully risen. This should take about 1 to 1½ hours.

7 Preheat the oven to maximum temperature, with the baking stone in if you own one.

8 Transfer the dough to a clean and floured surface, divide in 9 pieces, and shape into rounds.

9 Place the rounds on a tray covered with parchment paper and let rest, covered, for 30 to 45 minutes.

10 On a clean and floured surface, flatten one round at a time into a ⅛-inch thick disk.

11 Bake for about 3 minutes on each side.

# PITA

YIELDS: 16 SERVINGS / ACTIVE TIME: 60 MINUTES / TOTAL TIME: 2 HOURS

And here's an easy recipe for another flatbread that originated in the Mediterranean region, purportedly ancient Greece, as the word itself is Greek—*pektos*—meaning solid or clotted. It is popular around the world, but especially in Middle Eastern countries.
—*Dominique DeVito*

**INGREDIENTS:**

- **1** packet active dry yeast (2¼ teaspoons)
- **2½** cups water (110–115°F)
- **3** cups flour
- **1** tablespoon olive oil
- **1** tablespoon salt
- **3** cups whole wheat flour

**1** Proof the yeast by mixing with the warm water. Let sit for about 10 minutes until foamy.

**2** In a large bowl, add the yeast mix into the regular flour and stir until it forms a stiff dough. Cover and let the dough rise for about 1 hour.

**3** Add the oil and salt to the dough and stir in the whole wheat flour in half-cup increments. When finished, the dough should be soft. Turn onto a lightly floured surface and knead it until it is smooth and elastic, about 10 minutes.

**4** Coat the bottom and sides of a large mixing bowl (ceramic is best) with butter. Place the ball of dough in the bowl, cover loosely with plastic wrap, put it in a naturally warm, draft-free location, and let it rise until doubled in size, about 45 minutes to 1 hour.

**5** On a lightly floured surface, punch down the dough and cut into 16 pieces. Put the pieces on a baking sheet and cover with a dish towel while working with individual pieces.

**6** Roll out the pieces with a rolling pin until they are approximately 7 inches across. Stack them between sheets of plastic wrap.

**7** Heat the skillet over high heat and lightly oil the bottom. Cook the individual pitas about 20 seconds on one side, then flip and cook for about a minute on the other side, until bubbles form. Turn again and continue to cook until the pita puffs up, another minute or so. Keep the skillet lightly oiled while processing, and store the pitas on a plate under a clean dish towel until ready to serve.

# SOURDOUGH PITA

YIELDS: 10 PITA / **ACTIVE TIME:** 30 MINUTES / **TOTAL TIME:** 4 HOURS

Since pita is a very ancient bread, it was originally leavened with a natural starter. Although the preparation of the starter needs to be done ahead, this recipe is not much more time or energy consuming than the more common yeast-based recipe.

**INGREDIENTS:**

- 14.1 oz (400 g) all-purpose flour
- 7.8 oz (220 g) water
- 4.9 oz (140 g) sourdough starter (see page 59)
- 2½ tbsp (34 g) olive oil
- 1 ⅖ tsp (8 g) salt
- 1 tsp (4.3 g) sugar

1 In a large bowl, combine all the ingredients.

2 Start working the dough, either with a stand-mixer or by hand (see page 63 for tips on kneading).

3 Work the dough until it feels smooth. This should take about 10 minutes.

4 Let the dough rest, covered, in a warm spot until it looks fully risen. This should take about 2 hours.

5 Preheat the oven to maximum temperature, with the baking stone in if you own one.

6 Transfer the dough to a clean and floured surface, divide in 10 pieces, and shape into rounds.

7 Place the rounds on a tray covered with parchment paper and let rest, covered, for 1½ hours.

8 On a clean and floured surface, flatten one round at a time into a ⅛-inch thick disk.

9 Bake for about 3 minutes on each side.

# NAAN

**YIELDS:** 8 NAAN / **ACTIVE TIME:** 30 MINUTES / **TOTAL TIME:** 3 HOURS

Naan is the most common type of leavened bread in both Central and Southern Asia. It is generally baked in a tandoor-like oven—although this type of oven takes on many different names. It can also be cooked in a frying pan, like in the version below.

**INGREDIENTS:**

1    tsp (3 g) active dry yeast

4.4   oz (125 g) water

10.6   oz (300 g) all-purpose flour

4.4   oz (125 g) plain yoghurt

1.4   (40 g) vegetable oil

     Melted, salted butter for topping

1   Heat the water to 100–105°F. Dissolve the yeast in the water and let rest for 5 minutes. In a large bowl, combine the water-yeast mixture with the rest of the ingredients.

2   Start working the dough, either with a stand-mixer or by hand (see page 63 for tips on kneading). Work the dough until it feels smooth. This should take about 10 minutes.

3   Let the dough rest, covered, in a warm spot until it looks fully risen. This should take about 1 to 1½ hours.

4   Transfer the dough to a clean and floured surface, divide in 8 pieces, and shape into rounds. Place the rounds on a tray covered with parchment paper and let rest, covered, for 30 to 45 minutes.

5   Preheat a cast-iron pan or frying pan on medium-high.

6   Take one round at a time and flatten it thin.

7   Cook on both sides on the slightly greased frying pan, until some browned bubbles form on both surfaces. Brush with melted, hot butter when still hot.

# NAAN

YIELDS: 4-8 SERVINGS (8 PIECES) / ACTIVE TIME: 60 MINUTES / TOTAL TIME: 3-4 HOURS

This is the bread that is traditionally served with Indian cuisine, from spicy to saucy. It's cooked in a tandoor (clay oven) in India, but the cast-iron skillet turns out a very good replication!
—*Dominique DeVito*

**INGREDIENTS:**

- 1½ teaspoons active dry yeast
- ½ tablespoon sugar
- 1 cup water (110–115°F)
- 3 cups all-purpose flour or 1½ cups all-purpose and 1½ cups whole wheat pastry flour
- ¼ teaspoon salt
- 1 teaspoon baking powder
- ½ cup plain yogurt
- 4 tablespoons unsalted butter
- ¼ cup olive oil

1 Proof the yeast by mixing it with the sugar and ½ cup of the warm water. Let sit for 10 minutes until foamy.

2 In a bowl, combine the flour, salt, baking powder, remaining water, and yeast mix. Stir to combine well. Add the yogurt and 2 tablespoons of the butter, melted, and stir to form a soft dough.

3 Transfer to a lightly floured surface and knead the dough until it is springy and elastic, about 10 minutes.

4 Coat the bottom and sides of a large mixing bowl (ceramic is best) with butter. Place the ball of dough in the bowl, cover loosely with plastic wrap, put it in a naturally warm, draft-free location, and let it rise until doubled in size, about 1 to 2 hours.

5 Punch down the dough. Lightly flour a work surface again, take out the dough and, using a rolling pin, make a circle with the dough and cut it into 8 slices (like a pie).

6 Heat the skillet over high heat until it is very hot (about 5 minutes). Working with individual pieces of dough, roll them out to soften the sharp edges and make the pieces look more like teardrops. Brush both sides with olive oil and, working one at a time, place the pieces in the skillet.

7 Cook for 1 minute, turn the dough with tongs, cover the skillet, and cook the other side for about a minute (no longer). Transfer cooked naan to a plate and cover with foil to keep warm while making the additional pieces. Serve warm.

## VARIATIONS

- You can add herbs or spices to the dough or the pan to make naan with different flavors.
- Add ¼ cup chopped fresh parsley to the dough.
- Sprinkle the skillet lightly with cumin or coriander or turmeric (or a combination) before cooking the pieces of naan.
- Use a seasoned olive oil to brush the pieces before cooking—one with hot pepper flakes or roasted garlic.

# LEFSE

YIELDS: 12 LEFSE / ACTIVE TIME: 1 HOUR / TOTAL TIME: ABOUT 40 MINUTES

Making good Norwegian *lefse* is a craft that takes time to refine. This potato-based flatbread has been made popular in the United States thanks to Norwegian immigrants in the Midwest, and it is now easy to find all the specific tools to make it like a real Norwegian grandma. The recipe below is adapted to require no specific tools.

**INGREDIENTS:**

1 lb    (450 grams) starchy potatoes

⅓      cup (75 g) butter

5.3–7  oz (150-200 g) flour

½      tsp (3 g) salt

1  Peel, cut in chunks, and boil the potatoes.

2  Mash the potatoes with a fork.

3  In a large bowl, combine the mashed potatoes with the butter.

4  Add half of the flour and start kneading.

5  Transfer the dough to a clean surface and add remaining flour little by little, stopping if you reach a consistency that allows you to roll the dough.

6  Make the dough into a ball and divide into 12 pieces.

7  Roll each piece into a round and flatten into a thin disk. Use flour to prevent the dough from sticking.

8  Heat a cast-iron skillet to medium-high.

9  Roll one disk at a time around a floured rolling pin and transfer the lefse to the pan.

10  Cook a couple of minutes on each side.

11  Transfer to a kitchen or paper towel and proceed with the other disks.

# ROTI

YIELDS: 15 ROTI / ACTIVE TIME: 30 MINUTES / TOTAL TIME: 1½ HOURS

This is one of the most traditional breads of the whole Indian subcontinent, a staple food eaten with classic local dishes. It is also known as *chapati*. It is important to find the right whole-wheat flour for this recipe.

**INGREDIENTS:**

10.6 oz (300 g) finely ground all-wheat flour

1 tbsp + 1 tsp vegetable oil

1 tsp (5.7 g) salt

7.3 oz (207 g) water

1 In a large bowl, combine all ingredients with ¾ of the water.

2 Start working the dough by hand or with a stand-mixer, checking for consistency. The dough needs to be soft, but not sticky. Add the rest of the water, if needed, and a little at a time.

3 Keep kneading the dough, 10 minutes overall (check page 63 for tips about kneading).

4 Let rest, covered, for 1 hour.

5 Transfer to a clean surface and divide the dough into 15 pieces.

6 Heat a cast-iron pan or frying pan on medium-high.

7 Flatten one ball at a time into a thin disk and transfer to the frying pan.

8 Cook 30 seconds on each side, then repeat on the other side, pressing the surface of the bread to cause it to puff.

9 Place in aluminum foil to keep warm.

# MANTOU

YIELDS: 14 SMALL BUNS / ACTIVE TIME: 30 MINUTES / TOTAL TIME: 2.5–3 HOURS

Steamed wheat buns have been a staple food in China since antiquity. In their unfilled form, they are rather bland, but just because they are supposed to be eaten with food rather than on their own.

**INGREDIENTS:**

8.1 oz (230 g) all-purpose flour

5.6 oz (160 g) water

1.5 tsp (4.3 g) active dry yeast

1 Dissolve the yeast in water heated to 100–105°F and let sit for 5 minutes.

2 Add the flour and knead until the dough is elastic and smooth (check page 63 for tips).

3 Let rest covered until the dough has risen about one and a half times its original volume, 1 to 1½ hours.

4 Transfer on a lightly floured surface and divide the dough in 2 parts.

5 Make one log out of each piece of dough. Divide each log into 7 pieces and shape each piece into a round.

6 Let rest, covered, for 1 hour or until they have risen one and a half times their initial volume.

7 Place the buns over little squares of baking paper and put the pieces of paper and the buns over a steamer grid placed over a pot with water. Do make sure that the water does not overflow out of the grid and over the buns.

8 Cover tightly with a lid and cook on the stove on moderate-high heat for 20 minutes.

9 Remove from the stove and wait for further 5 minutes before removing the lid.

# TUNNBRÖD

There are several versions of these Swedish flatbreads. This one is supposed to be soft and it can be eaten with a soft cheese spread paired with smoked salmon or cold cuts. In Sweden this bread is sold on the streets filled with steamy hot mashed potatoes, sausage and mustard, perfect for a snowy day.

INGREDIENTS:

| | |
|---|---|
| 2½ | tsp (7 grams) active dry yeast |
| 12.3 | oz (350 g) milk |
| 8.8 | oz (250 g) all-purpose flour |
| 5.3 | oz(150 g) graham flour |
| 3.5 | oz (100 g) rye flour |
| 1.8 | oz (50 g) light molasses |
| 1 | tsp (6 g) fennel or anise seeds, crushed |
| 1.8 | oz (50 g) butter |
| 1 | tsp (6 g) salt |

1 Heat the milk to 100–105°F. Dissolve the yeast in the milk and let rest 5 minutes. In a large bowl, combine the milk-yeast mixture with the flours, the molasses and the crushed seeds.

2 Knead the dough either with a stand-mixer or by hand (see page 63 for tips on kneading).

3 Add the butter in pieces, continuing to work the dough, and incorporate the salt towards the end of the kneading (about 10 minutes).

4 Let the dough rest, covered, in a warm spot until it looks fully risen. This should take about 1 to 1½ hours.

5 Divide the dough in 12 pieces and roll each piece into a round. Let the rounds rest on parchment paper for 1 hour, covered.

6 On a floured surface, roll one round at a time with a rolling pin, to ⅕-inch thick disks. Make some shallow holes with a fork on top of each disk.

7 Heat a cast-iron skillet to medium-high. Cook one disk at a time, a couple of minutes on each side.

# AUTHENTIC INJERA

YIELDS: 10–12 INJERA / ACTIVE TIME: 30 MINUTES / TOTAL TIME: 2–3 DAYS

To make authentic *injera,* all you need is time. By leaving the dough to ferment for days, the flavor improves along with the nutritional properties of this traditional Ethiopian bread.

**INGREDIENTS:**

- 12.7 oz (360 g) teff flour
- ¼ gallon (1 liter) water + 10½ oz (300 g)
- 1 tsp (6 g) salt

1 In a large bowl, combine the flour with ¼ gallon water.

2 Cover with plastic wrap and let rest at room temperature for 2 to 3 days.

3 The batter is ready when bubbles have formed and the mixture has a sour smell.

4 Do not stir yet, but instead pour out as much of the water as possible, being careful not to pour out the wet flour that should be in the bottom.

5 In a small saucepan, bring the water to a boil.

6 Take 1½ cup of the fermented batter and add it to the boiling water, stirring vigorously, until it thickens.

7 Incorporate the thickened batter into the original batter and stir well.

8 Add the salt and more water, if needed. You need to reach the consistency of a pancake batter.

9 Heat a medium a cast-iron skillet or shallow frying pan.

10 Grease the pan with a little oil and pour enough batter to cover the whole surface of the skillet, as you would do for a French crepe, but aim for a slightly thicker "crepe."

11 After the first 2 minutes of cooking, cover with a lid and cook until bubbles have formed and the bottom side of the injera detaches easily from the pan.

12 Place parchment paper between cooked injera so they will not stick together.

# INJERA *with* YEAST

YIELDS: 15 INJERA / ACTIVE TIME: 30 MINUTES / TOTAL TIME: 4½ HOURS

This is a quicker version of the delicious Ethiopian bread that is generally fermented for several days. This recipe gives you a good approximation of the "real thing" in a much shorter time. Do try the original version, too!

**INGREDIENTS:**

3    tsp (8½ g) active dry yeast

21.2   oz (600 g) water

17.6   oz (500 g) teff flour

1    tsp (6 g) tsp salt

1   Heat the water to 100–105°F. Dissolve the yeast in the water and let rest for 5 minutes. In a large bowl, combine the water-yeast mixture with the flour.

2   Let rest, covered with plastic wrap, for 3 to 4 hours.

3   Whisk in the salt.

4   Heat a cast-iron skillet or shallow frying pan to medium heat.

5   Grease the pan with a little oil and pour enough batter to cover the whole surface of the skillet, as you would do for a French crepe, but aim for a slightly thicker "crepe."

6   After the first 2 minutes of cooking, cover with a lid and cook until bubbles have formed and the bottom side of the injera detaches easily from the pan.

7   Place parchment paper between cooked injera so they will not stick together.

# ETHIOPIAN INJERA

**YIELDS:** 1 INJERA / **ACTIVE TIME:** 60 MINUTES / **TOTAL TIME:** 3 DAYS

If you've ever eaten at an Ethiopian restaurant, you'll remember that the centerpiece of the meal is the thick, spongy bread that's placed in the middle of the table. The dishes go around it, and you eat by ripping apart the bread and scooping up the other foods. I like to use it as almost a polenta or spongy pizza crust, topping with whatever leftovers I can combine to taste good. While the ingredients are minimal, you have to plan ahead for the day you want to serve the injera, as the "flour" needs to sit for several days to break down the grain.

*—Dominique DeVito*

**INGREDIENTS:**

½ teaspoon active dry yeast

2 cups water (110–115°F)

1½ cups ground teff (put the seeds in a food processor or blender to reduce to "flour")

Salt

Vegetable oil

1 Proof the yeast by mixing with the warm water. Let sit for about 10 minutes until foamy.

2 Put the ground teff in a bowl and add the water/yeast. Mix thoroughly until a stiff dough forms. Put a dish towel over the bowl and stick it in a draft-free, fairly warm place in your kitchen. It will bubble and turn brown and smell sour. Let it sit for 2 to 3 days.

3 When ready to make the injera, add salt to the mix until some of the sour "bite" has dissipated. The mix at this time should resemble pancake batter.

4 Heat the skillet over medium heat and brush with vegetable oil. Pour enough batter on the pan to coat the bottom less than a pancake but more than a crepe. Tilt to spread the batter over the bottom of the skillet. Cook until holes form in the bread and the edges crisp up and lift away from the pan. The bread should not be flipped so be sure to let it cook thoroughly.

5 When cooked, lift it out with a spatula and put it on a plate or platter to cool. Place plastic wrap between injeras as you cook a batch of them. Serve warm with bowls of things like sautéed vegetables, grilled meat pieces, creamed spinach, sautéed mushrooms, or authentic Ethiopian dishes you can make—or Indian dishes you can find in grocery stores.

# KNÄCKEBRÖD

YIELDS: 12 LARGE CRACKERS / ACTIVE TIME: 50 MINUTES / TOTAL TIME: ABOUT 2½ HOURS

Knäckebröd means crispy bread, or crackers, in Swedish. These crunchy and flavorful flatbreads stay fresh for a long time and can accompany a variety of foods. They are a traditional part of the Swedish smörgåsbord.

**INGREDIENTS:**

- 1¾ tsp (about 5 g) active dry yeast
- 12.3 oz (300 g) water
- 1 tbsp whole caraway seeds
- 1.8 oz (50 g) light rye flour
- 9 oz (300 g) bread flour
- 1.8 oz (50 g) whole-purpose flour
- 1 cup mixed seeds (sesame, sunflower, etc.)
- 1½ tsp salt

1 Dissolve the yeast in the water and add the caraway seeds. Let rest for 15 minutes.

2 Add all the other ingredients, salt last, and knead for 6 to 7 minutes at low speed or for about 10 minutes by hand.

3 Let rest covered for about 1½ hours.

4 Roll into a long log and cut in 12 pieces. Form each piece into a round and let rest on parchment paper for 40 minutes, covered.

5 On a floured surface, flatten one round at a time with a rolling pin, making it as thin as possible without tearing the dough.

6 Make some shallow holes with a fork on top of each round.

7 Start baking a couple of rounds at a time at maximum heat. They are ready when they are slightly browned and look crunchy. It takes about 10 minutes. Remember to keep the other rounds covered while you cook each batch.

# SCHÜTTELBROT

YIELDS: 8 FLATBREADS / **ACTIVE TIME:** 40 MINUTES / **TOTAL TIME:** ABOUT 2½ HOURS

This is a crunchy flatbread common in South Tyrol (Trentino Alto Adige). It is eaten with earthy cheeses or smoked cured ham (speck). Originated during the Middle Age, it was a bread of the common people, supposed to last through the long winters when food was scarce.

1 Heat the water to 100–105°F. Dissolve the yeast in the water and let rest 5 minutes. In a large bowl, combine the water-yeast mixture with remaining ingredients.

2 Knead the dough either with a stand-mixer or by hand (see page 63 for tips on kneading), for about 15 minutes.

3 Let rest covered for about ½ hour.

4 Roll into a long log and cut in 8 pieces. Form each piece into a round and let rest on parchment paper for 1 hour, covered.

5 On a floured surface, flatten one round at a time with your hands, in a circular manner, as if you were flattening a pizza disk. You need to reach a thickness of ⅕ inch. Use a rolling pin if the hand rolling feels too difficult.

6 Preheat oven to 410°F, with the stone in if you own one.

7 After rolling the disks, let rest covered for 15 to 20 minutes. Bake for 20 minutes, or until lightly browned.

**INGREDIENTS:**

- 2½ tsp (7 grams) active dry yeast
- 1½ cups (350 g) water
- 3⅘ cups (350 g) medium rye flour
- 1½ cups (150 g) all-purpose flour
- 2 tsp mixed seeds (fennel, caraway, coriander, anise)
- 1½ tsp salt
- 1 tsp sugar
- 3¼ tablespoons (50 g) buttermilk

# PIADINA

YIELDS: 7 PIADINE / ACTIVE TIME: 30 MINUTES / TOTAL TIME: ABOUT 1 HOUR

Piadina is a flatbread traditional of the Central-Eastern area of Italy. Generally filled with cold cuts and cheese, it is delicious if grilled after being filled to allow the cheese to melt.

**INGREDIENTS:**

- 17½ oz (500 g) all-purpose flour
- 7 oz (200 g) water
- 2.2 oz (60 g) lard
- 1 tsp (about 6 g) baking soda
- 1 tsp (about 6 g) salt

1 In a large bowl, combine all the ingredients.

2 Knead the dough either with a stand-mixer or by hand (see page 63 for tips on kneading) for 10 minutes.

3 Let the dough rest, covered, for ½ hour.

4 Divide the dough in 7 pieces, shape into rounds, and roll into thin disks.

5 Make each disk even by cutting any irregular side, making it as close as possible to a circle.

6 Heat a cast-iron skillet to medium-high.

7 Cook one disk at a time, a couple of minutes on each side.

# SPECIALTY BREADS
## & SIDES

When we use the term specialty breads, we generally mean something that is different from our daily bread. A special bread will always have extra ingredients compared to regular bread, or be made in a special way, either because of the technique used or the shape it is given.

Croissants, bagels and scones satisfy all of these "special" conditions: their ingredient list exceeds the usual flour, water, and yeast found in ordinary bread. They are made following specific techniques that give each of them a very special consistency, and they are all shaped in a characteristic way.

All of these breads have become internationally popular, but originate from very specific regional contexts.

# CROISSANT DOUGH

YIELD: 18 CROISSANTS / ACTIVE TIME: 3½ HOURS / TOTAL TIME: 4 HOURS

Croissants are the true test for any good bakery. Before trying anything else, I always eat a croissant at a new place. If I can't taste the butter or if the layers are too heavy, I turn on my heels and leave! However, if the croissant is a dark brown color, flaky, crispy, moist, and buttery, I may spend my entire paycheck in one sitting. In other words: the stakes are high.

This recipe will be buttery and light if you take your time with it.

—*Stephany Buswell*

---

1 In a stand mixing bowl, pour in the milk and the yeast and mix until the yeast dissolves. Add the flour, sugar, salt and, on top, the soft butter.

2 Mix with a dough hook on low speed for one minute and then on medium speed for 3 minutes. Careful not to over-mix this dough!

3 Make a rectangle shape about 6 inches by 10 inches. Wrap in plastic to keep from drying out and put in the refrigerator for 1 hour.

4 Make your butter block while the dough rests: First cut your butter into 1-inch-thick pieces. Place them next to one another like puzzle pieces. Sprinkle 1 tablespoon of flour on your counter and line the butter pieces up in a square. Sprinkle another tablespoon of flour over the top. Take your rolling pin and pound the butter until it is soft and pliable but not lumpy. Pick up the block turn it over and pound some more. You should have a block of butter that is now 4 inches by 6 inches. Keep this wrapped up and stored at room temperature, unless your room is warmer than 70°F, in which case store in the refrigerator until your dough is ready to roll. Ideally, the dough and the butter should be the same consistency.

5 Take your dough out and on a lightly floured surface and roll the dough out to about 8 inches by 12 inches. Place your butter block on one side of the dough. Fold the other side over the butter. There should only be a small piece of dough around the outside that you can pinch to seal the butter inside. This is called the butter lock in.

## INGREDIENTS:

### DOUGH (DÉTREMPE):

- 3 cups cold milk
- 1 package active dry yeast
- 4 cups bread flour
- 3 tablespoons sugar
- 4 tablespoons soft butter, unsalted
- 1 teaspoon salt

### BUTTER BLOCK (BEURRAGE):

- 14 ounces cold butter, unsalted
- 3 tablespoons bread flour

6 Immediately, roll the dough out to the 8 by 16-inch rectangle and fold the dough as you would fold a letter: one side into the middle and an equal-sized side over the top of that. This is called a letter turn, or a single fold.

7 Cover the dough with plastic wrap and put in the refrigerator for 30 minutes.

8 Repeat the turns 2 more times. As you do your next turn, make sure you turn the dough 90 degrees so that when the dough is rolled, the layers of the previous fold now become the short end of the new rectangle. Do this each time you turn the dough. When you have completed the last turn, you can either freeze the dough for later use or, after 30 minutes of rest, roll it out and make your croissants.

## HOW TO FORM THE CLASSIC CROISSANT

1 On a floured surface, roll the dough to ¼ inch thick. You should have a long rectangle that is 9 inches wide by about 20 inches long.

2 Make sure you relax the dough a bit before you begin to cut in order to prevent shrinkage.

3 Cut triangles 9 inches long and 4 inches wide at the bottom. Cut a 1-inch slit at the bottom of each triangle.

4 Start by stretching the corners of the slit out toward the outside edges of the triangle. Grab the point and begin stretching with one hand while rolling up the croissant with the other.

5 You should have a nicely rolled croissant with 3 steps in the top of the roll.

6 Tuck the tail under the bottom and curl the ends in to form the famous shape.

7 Egg wash and place on parchment paper lined sheet pan, let rise in a warm spot until they jiggle when you shake the edge of the pan.

8 Egg wash again carefully not deflating the dough. Bake at 375°F for 15 to 18 minutes or until a nice caramelized brown color.

## CHOCOLATE CROISSANTS

1 Roll the dough out to a 12-inch by 16-inch rectangle and cut 4-inch squares.

2 Egg-wash the ends of each square.

3 Place a chocolate baton (long pieces of chocolate made exclusively for chocolate croissants) on the top and fold the dough into the center of the square. Press the edge down firmly and place another baton on the folded edge. Now fold the top over so there are 2 pieces of chocolate wrapped into the dough.

4 Place on parchment and egg wash.

5 Let rise as you did the classic. Bake at 375°F for 15 to 18 minutes or until a nice caramelized brown color.

# ALMOND CROISSANT FILLING

YIELD: 1¼ CUPS WORTH OF FILLING

Make the classic croissants and fill each one before rolling up with this almond filling. After egg-washing, sprinkle sliced almonds on top and finish with powdered sugar.

Put into a food processor and chop until a smooth fine paste.

INGREDIENTS:

ALMOND FILLING:

1    cup sliced almonds

½    cup melted unsalted butter

5    tablespoons powdered sugar

1    egg yolk

½    teaspoon vanilla

## A BRIEF HISTORY OF CROISSANTS

The word "croissant" derives from its crescent moon shape. Surprising to some, its origin is not French, but rather Austrian, deriving from the German word "kipferl", or crescent.

There is a legend that links the Viennese croissant to the Ottoman siege of Vienna. The story says that the croissant was created by local bakers at the end of the Siege (in 1683 or during the earlier siege in 1529) to celebrate the victory of the Christian coalition. Supposedly, it was inspired by the Turkish flag, which displays the effigy of a crescent.

The crescent moon pastry arrived in France around 1839, when Austrian artillery officer August Zang founded the Boulangerie Viennoise in Rue de Richelieu, in Paris. This bakery, serving Viennese specialties, quickly became extremely popular, and inspired numerous French imitations. Thus, the croissant was born.

# BOULTED BREAD'S CROISSANTS

YIELD: 14 CROISSANTS / ACTIVE TIME: 45-60 MINUTES / TOTAL TIME: 14-18 HOURS

Our plain croissants are built around extracting as much flavor as possible from traditional ingredients. A large percentage of the flour is pre-fermented for 8 to 12 hours. This, combined with cultured butter in the laminations, helps to create a croissant that hits every part of the mouth.

—*courtesy of Joshua Bellamy, Fulton Forde, and Sam Kirkpatrick of Boulted Bread*

## DAY 1

1 The night before you plan on croissant production, mix poolish flour with warm poolish water and 1 gram of instant yeast. Place immediately into refrigerator for 8 to 12 hours.

2 Mix levain flour with lukewarm levain water and 10 grams of sourdough starter. Leave at room temperature for approximately 1 hour, then place into refrigerator for 8 to 12 hours.

## DAY 2

1 Mix all dry ingredients, butter, poolish, levain, and cold milk on low speed with dough hook attachment until ingredients are just evenly incorporated, approximately 2 minutes.

2 Let dough rest in bowl for 20 minutes. Continue mixing for another 2 minutes on low speed.

3 Transfer dough to a separate bowl, cover with plastic wrap, and allow dough to bulk ferment for approximately 1 hour at room temperature.

4 While dough is fermenting, soften lamination butter in mixing bowl for approximately 2 minutes or until the butter is smooth, free of lumps, but still cool.

5 Remove butter and smash into a rectangle on a piece of parchment paper. It should be 6½ inches by 9 inches and evenly thick throughout. Allow the butter rectangle to cool in refrigerator for the final 20 minutes of dough's bulk fermentation.

6 Thoroughly flour your work surface and roll out dough into a rectangle, approximately 13 inches by 9 inches, using a rolling pin.

**INGREDIENTS:**

**POOLISH:**

1 ¾ cups all-purpose flour

1 g instant yeast

Just under 1 cup water

**LEVAIN:**

¾ cup whole wheat flour

Just over ⅓ cup water

5 g sourdough starter

**DOUGH:**

5 ⅔ cups all-purpose flour

½ cup cane sugar

1 tablespoon salt

4 g instant yeast

1 cup whole milk

1¼ ounces butter

17⅔ ounces cured and unsalted butter, for lamination

1 egg and splash of heavy cream, for egg wash

7 Place the butter on the right half of the dough rectangle and fold the left side over, being sure to completely cover the butter and essentially making a butter sandwich.

8 Using the rolling pin and a light touch, roll the butter sandwich to 12 inches by 27 inches. Fold the length in half so the rectangle is now 12 inches by 13½ inches. Fold in half again so the rectangle is 12 inches by 6 ¼ inches.

9 Let dough rest for 1 hour in refrigerator wrapped in plastic wrap.

10 Gently roll out dough to 12 inches by 31½ inches.

11 Using a ruler and a sharp knife, cut alternating triangles out of the rectangle with 4 ½-inch bases.

12 Roll the bottom edge of each triangle base until the tip of the triangle tucks neatly under the bottom of the croissant. Place each croissant on a baking tray with parchment paper, being sure not to overcrowd the tray.

13 Cover the croissants with a towel and allow to sit at room temperature for approximately 4 hours. After this, croissant can be baked or placed in refrigerator until the following day.

14 Preheat your oven to 420°F. Prepare egg wash by thoroughly mixing egg yolk and a splash of heavy cream.

15 Using a brush, coat the top of the croissants with egg wash and bake for 20 to 25 minutes or until croissants are golden brown.

# BOULANGERIE'S CROISSANTS

**YIELD:** 30 CROISSANTS / **ACTIVE TIME:** 3 HOURS / **TOTAL TIME:** 3 DAYS

Boulangerie (see page 130) is famous for its incredible croissant, and with recipes this involved, that's no surprise. Though not for the faint of heart, these flaky, buttery pastries might just be the best you've ever had.

*—courtesy of Amy and Zachary Tyson of Boulangerie*

### INGREDIENTS:

- **3** cups water
- **1⅔** cups milk
- **2** tablespoons gold yeast
- **16** cups Sir Galahad all-purpose flour
- **1** cup + 1 tablespoon sugar
- **1** tablespoon + 1 teaspoon malt (optional)
- **2½** tablespoons salt
- **⅓** cup pliable butter

## DAY 1

**1** Mix all ingredients except the butter for 5 minutes on low speed.

**2** Increase speed to medium for 2 minutes. While mixing, gradually add pliable butter. Mix for an additional 2 minutes until dough comes together and butter is incorporated.

**3** Remove dough from bowl and tuck under sides so it forms a nice, taut ball. Place in oiled bowl or container. Refrigerate overnight.

## DAY 2

**1** Pull butter block and dough out of the refrigerator 1 hour before use. The ideal dough temperature for lamination is 48–50°F.

**2** Make butter block: beat butter with a rolling pin until pliable, then place between sheets of parchment 9 inches by 13 inches.

**3** If butter block is too soft, place in refrigerator for a few minutes. It should be pliable but cool.

---

If you want to bake some of your croissants the next day, place 6 on a tray (using as many trays as necessary) and refrigerate. The next day, pull and proof. Then egg wash and bake at 375°F for 25 minutes.

You can make monkey bread with the dough scraps!

4 Roll dough into a rectangle of 1-inch thickness, approximately a 21-inch width by 13-inch length.

5 Place butter block in middle and fold sides over to meet in middle. Press seams together but do not stretch.

6 Roll out to 1-inch thickness and give a book fold. The dough should measure roughly 55 inches wide by 15 inches long. Trim ends.

7 Repeat your book fold: Fold long edges in to meet in the middle, then fold over to close the "book." Let rest at room temperature for 30 minutes.

8 Place the book in front of you as before, turn sideways, and roll until it is again 1-inch thick.

9 Trim the ends and fold in thirds. Wrap in plastic and freeze.

## DAY 3

1 Pull out the dough 1 ½ hours before working with it. Roll to a 32-inch width and 20-inch length.

2 Cut into croissant shapes—4 inches by 10 inches for a traditional croissant, 4 inches by 5 inches for filled croissants.

3 If you're making filled croissants, fill the dough with dark chocolate batons, almond cream or cream cheese flavored with everything spices, or any other ingredient of choice.

4 Place 6 on a tray and either pull or proof until doubled in size. Egg wash and bake at 375°F for 25 minutes, until golden brown. Repeat the process for the remaining dough.

# KOUIGN-AMANN

**YIELDS:** 12 SMALL CAKES / **ACTIVE TIME:** 2 HOURS / **TOTAL TIME:** 5 HOURS 30 MINUTES

A specialty of Brittany, the small, rich kouign-amann, literally "butter cake," is possibly the most extraordinary pastry of all time. Imagine a flaky croissant–type pastry filled with layers of butter and sugar, and then more butter and sugar, and baked until the sugar caramelizes into a marvelously sticky, crispy coating. The first time I had one—in Paris, of course—I knew I had to make it at Flour. It remains for me the most delicious pastry I've ever eaten.

Nicole, our executive pastry chef, spent hours perfecting the recipe to make sure it has the right balance of sugar to butter to dough, and then tweaked it so that it could be baked in a muffin tin rather than ring molds. Read through the recipe a few times to make sure you understand the directions. If you've made laminated doughs of any kind before (puff pastry, croissant), you'll have no problem with this one. If you haven't, it is not difficult to make, but you'll need to familiarize yourself with the simple technique of folding and turning the dough, explained in the recipe. These small cakes are more of an after-party treat or decadent breakfast than an opulent plated dessert, although if you were to serve them with some ice cream and berries, I guarantee that you would be showered with compliments.

—*recipe and photo courtesy of Joanne Chang, Flour Bakery*

**INGREDIENTS:**

- 1⅛ tsp active dry yeast, or 0.35 oz (10 grams) fresh cake yeast

- 2¾ cups (385 grams) all-purpose flour

- 1¼ tsp kosher salt

- 1 cup (225 grams) unsalted butter, at warm room temperature, plus 1 tbsp melted

- 1½ cups (300 grams) granulated sugar, plus more for rolling and coating

  Special equipment: stand-mixer with dough hook (optional), baking sheet, rolling pin, bench scraper (optional), 12-cup standard muffin tin

1 In the stand-mixer, mix together the yeast and 1 cup/240 ml tepid water until the yeast dissolves. Add the flour, salt, and 1 tbsp melted butter and mix on low speed for 3 to 4 minutes, or until the dough comes together and is smooth. (If the dough is too wet, add 2 to 3 tbsp flour; if it is too dry, add 2 to 3 tsp of water.) The dough should be soft and supple and should come away from the sides of the bowl when the mixer is on. To make the dough by hand, in a medium bowl, dissolve the yeast in 1 cup/240 ml water as directed and stir in the flour, salt, and melted butter with a wooden spoon until incorporated. Then turn the dough out onto a floured work surface and knead by hand for 8 to 10 minutes, or until the dough is soft, smooth, and supple.

2 Transfer the dough to the baking sheet and cover with plastic wrap. Leave in a warm place for 1 hour to allow the dough to proof. Then transfer the dough to the fridge and leave it for another hour.

3 Transfer the dough from the fridge to a generously floured work surface. Roll it into a rectangle about 16 in/40.5 cm wide and 10 in/25 cm from top to bottom. With your fingers, press or smear the room-temperature butter directly over the right half of the dough, spreading it in a thin, even layer to cover the entire right half. Fold the left half of the dough over the butter, and press down to seal the butter between the dough layers. Turn the dough 90 degrees clockwise so that the rectangle is about 10 in/25 cm wide and 8 in/20 cm top to bottom, and generously flour the underside and top of the dough.

4 Press the dough down evenly with the palms of your hands, flattening it out before you start to roll it out. Slowly begin rolling the dough from side to side into a rectangle about 24 in/61 cm wide and 12 in/30.5 cm from top to bottom. The dough might be a little sticky, so, again, be sure to flour the dough and the work surface as needed to prevent the rolling pin from sticking. Using the bench scraper or a knife, lightly score the rectangle vertically into thirds. Each third will be about 8 in/20 cm wide and 12 in/30.5 cm from top to bottom. Brush any loose flour off the dough. Lift the right third of the dough and flip it over onto the middle third. Then lift the left third of the dough and flip it on top of the middle and right thirds (like folding a business letter). Your dough should now be about 8 in/20 cm wide, 12 in/30.5 cm from top to bottom, and about 1½ in/4 cm thick. Rotate the dough clockwise 90 degrees; it will now be 12 in/30.5 cm wide and 8 in/20 cm from top to bottom, with the folded seam on top. The process of folding in thirds and rotating is called turning the dough.

5 Repeat the process once more, patiently and slowly roll the dough into a long rectangle, flipping it upside down as needed as you roll it back and forth, and then fold the dough into thirds. The dough will be a bit tougher to roll out and a bit more elastic.

6 Return the dough to the baking sheet and cover it completely with plastic wrap, tucking the plastic wrap under the dough as if you are tucking it into bed. Refrigerate the dough for about 30 minutes. This will relax the dough so that you'll be able to roll it out again and give it more turns. Don't leave the dough in the fridge much longer than 30 minutes, or the butter will harden too much and it won't roll out properly.

7 Remove the dough from the refrigerator and place it on a well-floured work surface with a long side of the rectangle facing you and the seam on top. Again, roll the dough into a rectangle about 24 in/61 cm wide and 12 in/30.5 cm from top to bottom. Sprinkle ½ cup/150 g of the sugar over the dough and use the rolling pin to gently press it in. Give the dough another fold into thirds and turn as directed previously. The sugar may spill out a bit. That's okay, just scoop it back in.

8 Once again roll the dough into a rectangle 24 in/61 cm wide and 12 in/30.5 cm from top to bottom. Sprinkle the remaining ½ cup/150 g sugar over the dough and use the rolling pin to press the sugar gently into the dough. Give the dough one last fold into thirds and turn. Return the dough to the baking sheet, cover again with plastic wrap, and refrigerate for another 30 minutes.

9 Meanwhile, liberally butter the cups of the muffin tin and set aside.

10 Remove the dough from the refrigerator. Sprinkle your work surface generously with sugar, place the dough on the sugar, and sprinkle the top with more sugar. Roll the dough into a long rectangle 24 in/61 cm wide and 8 in/20 cm from top to bottom. The sugar will make the dough gritty and sticky, but it will also make the dough easier to roll out. Using a chef's knife, cut the dough in half lengthwise. You should have two strips of dough, each 24 in/61 cm wide and 4 in/10 cm from top

to bottom. Cut each strip into six 4-in/10-cm squares.

11 Working with one square at a time, fold the corners of the square into the center and press down so they stick in place. Shape and cup the dough into a little circle, and press the bottom and the top into more sugar so that the entire pastry is evenly coated with sugar. Place the dough circle, folded-side up, into a cup of the prepared muffin tin. It will just barely fit. Repeat with the remaining squares. Cover the tin with plastic wrap and let the cakes proof in a warm place (78° to 82°F/25° to 27°C is ideal) for 1 hour to 1 hour and 20 minutes, or until the dough has pouffed up.

12 About 20 minutes before you are ready to bake, preheat the oven to 400°F/200°C, and place a rack in the center of the oven.

13 When the dough is ready, place the muffin tin in the oven, reduce the heat to 325°F/165°C, and bake for 30 to 40 minutes, or until the cakes are golden brown. Remove the cakes from the oven and let them cool just until you can handle them, then gently pry them out of the muffin tin onto a wire rack and leave them to cool upside down. They are extremely sticky and will stick to the muffin tin if you don't pop them out while they are still warm. Let cool completely before serving.

# PAIN AU CHOCOLAT

YIELD: 18 PAIN AU CHOCOLAT / **ACTIVE TIME:** 45 MINUTES / **TOTAL TIME:** 14-18 HOURS

All else being equal, pain au chocolat are distinguished by the quality of chocolate used to fill the croissant. At the bakery, we are lucky enough to have access to world-class Escazu chocolate. But these are your croissants so use whatever chocolate brings a shameful grin to your face.
—*courtesy of Joshua Bellamy, Fulton Forde, and Sam Kirkpatrick of Boulted Bread*

## DAY 1

1 The night before your making the pain au chocolat, mix poolish flour with warm poolish water and 1g of instant yeast. Place immediately into refrigerator for 8 to 12 hours.

2 Mix levain flour with lukewarm levain water and 10 grams of sourdough starter. Leave at room temperature for approximately 1 hour, then place into refrigerator for 8 to 12 hours.

## DAY 2

1 In a mixer with a dough hook attachment, mix all dry ingredients, butter, poolish, levain, and cold milk on low speed until ingredients are just evenly incorporated. This should take approximately 2 minutes.

2 Let dough rest in bowl for 20 minutes. Continue mixing for another 2 minutes on low speed.

3 Transfer dough to a separate bowl and cover with plastic wrap. Allow dough to bulk ferment for approximately 1 hour at room temperature.

4 While dough is fermenting, soften lamination butter in mixing bowl for approximately 2 minutes or until the butter is smooth, free of lumps, but still cool.

5 Remove butter and smash into a rectangle on a piece of parchment paper. It should be 6½ inches by 9 inches and evenly thick throughout. Allow the butter rectangle to cool in refrigerator for the final 20 minutes of dough's bulk fermentation.

6 Thoroughly flour your work surface and roll out dough into a rectangle, approximately 13 inches by 9 inches, using a rolling pin.

### INGREDIENTS:

**POOLISH:**

| | |
|---|---|
| 1¾ | cups all-purpose flour |
| 1 | g instant yeast |
| | Just under 1 cup water |

**LEVAIN:**

| | |
|---|---|
| ¾ | cup whole wheat flour |
| | Just over ⅓ cup water |
| 5 | g sourdough starter |

**DOUGH:**

| | |
|---|---|
| 5⅔ | cups all-purpose flour |
| ½ | cup cane sugar |
| 1 | tablespoon salt |
| 4 | g instant yeast |
| 1 | cup whole milk |
| 1¼ | ounces butter |
| 17⅔ | ounces cured and unsalted butter, for lamination |
| 1 | egg and splash of heavy cream, for egg wash |
| | Individual squares of your favorite chocolate |

7 Place the butter on the right half of the dough rectangle and fold the left side over, being sure to completely cover the butter and essentially making a butter sandwich.

8 Using the rolling pin and a light touch, roll the butter sandwich to 12 inches by 27 inches. Fold the length in half so the rectangle is now 12 inches by 13½ inches. Fold in half again so the rectangle is 12 inches by 6¼ inches.

9 Let dough rest for 1 hour in refrigerator wrapped in plastic wrap.

10 Gently roll out dough to 12 inches by 31 ½ inches.

11 Using a ruler and a sharp knife, cut dough block in half lengthwise, so you have two 6-inch by 31½-inch pieces. Cut these pieces at 3½-inch increments so you have rectangles that are 6 inches by 3½ inches. Place a piece of your favorite chocolate in the center of each rectangle.

12 Fold the top of the rectangle down, and then the bottom of the rectangle up over the top of the chocolate. The chocolate should be completely hidden. Place each croissant (folded side–down) on a baking tray with parchment paper, making sure not to overcrowd the tray.

13 Cover the croissants with a towel and allow to sit at room temperature for approximately 4 hours. After this, croissants can be baked or placed in refrigerator until the following day.

14 Preheat your oven to 420°F. Prepare egg wash by thoroughly mixing egg yolk and a splash of heavy cream. Using a brush, coat the top of the croissants with egg wash.

15 Bake at 420°F for 20 to 25 minutes or until croissants are golden brown.

# FRISSANT

YIELD: 8 FRISSANTS / ACTIVE TIME: 2 HOURS / TOTAL TIME: 5½ HOURS

Skip the cronut line in your city and just make them yourself with Michael Siu's "frissant," a pastry that is as visually stunning as it is delicious. Experiment with fillings and toppings to determine your favorite flavor!

—*recipe courtesy of Michael Siu, Swiss Bakery*

**INGREDIENTS:**

- 3 cups bread flour
- 3 ¼ tablespoons sugar
- ¾ teaspoon salt
- ¾ ounce fresh yeast
- ⅔ tablespoon egg
- 1⅓ tablespoons butter
- ¾ cup water
- Grapeseed oil, for frying
- ½ cup roll-in butter, set aside

1 Combine all ingredients aside from your roll-in butter in a mixer with a dough hook. Mix on slow speed for about 5 minutes. The dough should look underdeveloped.

2 Remove the dough from mixer and flatten onto sheet tray. Cover with plastic wrap and place in the freezer for 1 hour.

3 Place your roll-in butter into a large ziplock bag and use your rolling pin to flatten the butter, filling the edges of the bag as much as possible. Make sure the butter is pliable and you can easily poke a finger into it. The butter should not be melted.

4 Remove the dough from the freezer and place onto a sparingly floured surface. Roll the dough out with a rolling pin so that it can envelope the pliable butter.

5 Remove the butter from the ziplock bag and place onto one side of the dough.

6 Fold the dough over so that the butter is fully blanketed and enclosed by the dough.

7 Roll out dough and give it one single fold, then let it rest in the fridge for 30 minutes.

8 Remove the dough from the fridge and roll it out. Give it 1 double-fold, then let rest it in the fridge for 30 minutes. When the 30 minutes is up, repeat this step one more time.

9 Remove dough from fridge and flour surface sparingly. Roll the dough out so that it is about 5 millimeters thick.

10 Cut out frissants and place onto a greased parchment paper. Proof in a warm area until the frissant has at least doubled in size. That will take at least an hour at around 84°F.

11 Pour grapeseed oil int a large pot to prepare to fry the frissants. Use a deep fry thermometer to figure out when oil is heated to 360°F.

12 Place up to 4 frissants into the hot oil. Try not to overcrowd the pan as it will lower the oil temperature. Flip when one of the sides is golden brown.

13 Prepare a tray with paper towels to drain the frissants after frying. Using a slotted spoon, remove from oil and place onto the prepared tray to drain the oil. Cool for at least 15 minutes, then roll each side in cinnamon sugar to coat.

14 Inject cream or jam into the frissants by poking 4 holes from the top.

15 Glaze the top with fondant, ganache or powdered sugar to finish.

# MORNING BUNS

YIELD: 12 BUNS / ACTIVE TIME: 30 MINUTES / TOTAL TIME: 90 MINUTES

These buns are so good that you may want to make sure you have a crowd to feed lest you eat them all yourself. If not, don't worry: The smell of cinnamon and sugar coming from your oven will draw a crowd! These must be eaten fresh, and are perfect on a holiday morning.

—*Stephany Buswell*

1 Preheat the oven to 350°F. In a medium bowl, mix together the sugars, cinnamon, and chopped walnuts.

2 Roll the dough out to a 6-inch by 20-inch rectangle. Paint the dough with the melted butter.

3 Sprinkle ⅔ of the sugar mixture over the dough, leaving a 1-inch strip at the top uncovered by the sugar.

4 Starting at the end closest to you, roll the dough up into a spiral.

5 Butter a muffin tin well and line with granulated sugar. Cut 1 ½-inch slices and place them in the prepared muffin tins.

6 Keep the pan in a warm place until the buns have risen 1½ times their size.

7 Place the muffin tin in a sheet pan and bake for 40–50 minutes. They should be well browned on top and when you poke the top it should feel firm.

8 When they are done, cool for 5 minutes and then turn them out onto a cooling rack. Immediately roll each bun in the leftover sugar/nut mixture.

**INGREDIENTS:**

1    **batch Stephany's croissant dough (see page 341)**

½    **cup white sugar**

½    **cup light brown sugar**

2    **tablespoons cinnamon**

½    **cup finely chopped walnuts (best to chop in a food processor for extra fine chop)**

4    **tablespoons melted butter**

# CUSTARD RAISIN ROLLS

YIELD: 18 ROLLS / ACTIVE TIME: 45 MINUTES / TOTAL TIME: 1 HOUR 45 MINUTES

If I may generalize a bit, the French are not the biggest fans of cinnamon in pastries. So they created this tasty alternative to our cinnamon rolls. Still, I'm sure these are much older than the cinnamon roll—the French pretty much invented all these pastries anyway.
—*Stephany Buswell*

**INGREDIENTS:**

1   batch of Stephany's croissant dough (see page 341)

1   batch of pastry cream (see page 364)

3   cups raisins soaked in dark rum for at least 2 hours, but preferably overnight

**Egg wash**

1   Preheat the oven to 375°F. Drain the raisins in a strainer and set aside.

2   Roll the dough out to a 8-inch by 16-inch rectangle about ¼-inch-thick.

3   Spread the custard on the dough about ¼-inch-thick. Sprinkle the raisins over the dough.

4   Starting at the edge closest to you, roll the dough into a spiral.

5   Cut 1½-inch-thick slices and place them on a parchment-lined sheet pan. Tuck in the loose end so it doesn't burn.

6   Let rise in a warm place for about 45 minutes, depending on how warm the spot is.

7   Egg-wash and bake for 20 minutes or until golden brown.

# CLASSIC PUFF PASTRY

YIELD: 2½ LB. / **ACTIVE TIME:** 1 HOUR / **TOTAL TIME:** 4 HOURS

Who doesn't love puff pastry? Here is my tried-and-true recipe for the delicious dough and a few of my favorite puffy recipes (plus a faster alternative for cooks on a deadline).

Whether you use this classic recipe or its quicker sibling, you must keep the dough cold to get the best results. After each step, put the dough back in the refrigerator to keep the butter firm and cold. This way, the butter will melt while it bakes, creating steam and ensuring proper puffing.
—*Stephany Buswell*

1   Begin by mixing your dough. Place the flour, salt, and softened butter in the mixing bowl of a stand mixer. Using the paddle, gently mix the ingredients together.

2   Put ice into a large container and fill with water. Measure the water from this container to get the coldest possible water. Add the lemon juice.

3   Pour all of the liquid into the dry mix. Mix slowly with the paddle until a shaggy dough forms. Now switch to the paddle with the dough hook and mix the dough until it is hydrated and no dry spots show. Do not over-mix!

4   Take the dough out of the bowl and round it into a ball. Wrap with plastic and refrigerate for 1 hour.

5   Now make your butter block: Place the cold butter cubes on a clean work surface and sprinkle with half of the flour.

6   Begin pounding the butter with your rolling pin until it is a smooth flat piece. Use the flour as needed in order to keep it from sticking to the pin and surface.

7   Fold it into a block and pound it until it is pliable. Shape it into a 5-inch by 5-inch square.

8   After your dough has chilled for 1 hour, take it out and use a sharp knife to cut a cross 1-inch deep into the top of the dough ball.

9   Gently pull each corner of the dough one at a time until you have a square piece. Place the butter block in the center.

10  Take each corner and pull it up and over the butter until you have completely covered the block of butter with the dough.

11  Roll the dough with butter into a rectangle approximately 10 inches long and 5 inches wide.

12  Give the dough a book turn (fold one end into the center and then the other end, meeting in the middle, and then fold the entire piece in half). Let rest for 20 minutes in the refrigerator.

13  Give the dough 3 more of these turns and rest for at least 1 hour. Freeze or refrigerate the dough until you are ready to form your pastries.

**INGREDIENTS:**

**DOUGH (DÉREMPE):**

3   cups bread flour

½   cup cake flour

1½  teaspoons salt

2   tablespoons softened butter

1   teaspoon lemon juice

¾   cup + 2 tablespoons ice water (7 fluid ounces)

**BUTTER BLOCK (BEURRAGE):**

1   pound unsalted butter, cut into 1-inch cubes

5   tablespoons bread or all-purpose flour

# QUICK PUFF PASTRY

YIELD: 1½ POUNDS / ACTIVE TIME: 30 MINUTES / TOTAL TIME: 2 HOURS

I often get asked, "When should I use quick and when should I use classic puff pastry?" Personally, I will use the quick for most items simply because...it's quick! However, you won't get the even layers you see in the classic recipe. The layers are plentiful, light, and flaky—just not as even. So if you want vol au vents then you want to make the classic. Most all other puff pastry items are fine using the quick method. Especially if you want the layers and flakiness but not the height, like gallettes or Napoleons. —*Stephany Buswell*

**INGREDIENTS:**

- **3** cups all-purpose flour
- **1** cup cold unsalted butter
- **½** cup ice water
- **1½** teaspoons salt

1 Cut the butter into 1-inch cubes. Dissolve the salt into the ice water.

2 Put the flour in the mixing bowl of a stand mixer with paddle attachment. On slow speed, cut the butter pieces into the flour, leaving large pieces of butter intact. You should only mix for about 1 minute.

3 Pour in the water-salt mix and again on slow speed mix the dough until it forms a shaggy mass. You should still be able to see chunks of butter and dry flour—don't worry, the dough will work itself together as you do the folds. Pour the dry shaggy dough onto a well-floured surface.

4 Using your hands, push the dough together into a rectangle block. It should be dry and barely hold together. If you're thinking, "How in the world is this ever going to work," you are doing this right! Chill for 1 hour.

5 Using a floured rolling pin, roll your rectangle out to form a large rectangle about 16 inches by 8 inches.

6 Use a bowl scraper or spatula of some sort to pick up ⅓ of this crumbly mess and fold it onto the dough. Then take the other side and fold it over the first. You now have a single or letter fold. Immediately turn the dough 90 degrees and roll out again to a rectangle.

7 Continue rolling and folding the dough 3 more times. Chill for 1 hour or overnight. This dough freezes well for future use.

8 When you are ready to form your pastries, do one last fold and let rest for 15 minutes in the refrigerator. You are now ready to use your dough!

To make the classic puff pastry you need time and attention. This dough requires four book folds, with appropriate resting time between each fold. And pay special attention to the way to form your layers—making your corners meet perfectly and rolling the dough into even layers. You want the dough and the butter at the same firm consistency.

# SPINACH-RICOTTA PASTRY

**YIELD:** 4 PASTRIES / **ACTIVE TIME:** 15 MINUTES / **TOTAL TIME:** 1 HOUR 45 MINUTES

This is one of my favorite fillings to use with my puff pastry dough. You can use this with either the fast or classic recipe—no matter what, it's sure to taste delicious.
—*Stephany Buswell*

1 Sauté the onion and garlic in olive oil until translucent. Add the spinach and put a top on the pot for a few minutes to wilt. Stir, adding salt and pepper to taste. While still warm, stir in the cheese to create a creamy spinach filling. Let cool.

2 Prepare the dough: Roll your puff pastry out to ⅛-inch-thick rectangle. Cut the dough into 4-inch by 4-inch squares. It will reduce waste if you can roll the dough out to 16 inches by 8 inches so you get maximum amount of pastries. You will need 2 squares for each pastry.

3 Using egg wash, paint the edges of half the squares. Then fold each unpainted square in half. With a sharp knife, make 1-inch cuts on the folded side of the pastry. When you open it you should have slats cut into the center of the dough.

4 Take a heaping spoonful of your spinach filling and place it in the center of the uncut pieces. Now place the cut pieces on top of each one. Using a fork, seal the edges gently so not to compress the dough's layers.

5 Chill for 1 hour. Bake at 400°F for 30 to 35 minutes or until golden all around. Serve at room temperature.

**INGREDIENTS:**

- ½ **pound spinach**
- ½ **yellow onion, finely chopped**
- 1 **batch puff pastry (see pages 358-359)**
- 1 **clove garlic, chopped**
- ½ **cup ricotta cheese**
- 3 **tablespoons olive oil**
- **Salt and pepper**

# VOL-AU-VENT

**YIELD:** 6 2½-INCH ROUNDS / **ACTIVE TIME:** 40 MINUTES / **TOTAL TIME:** 2 HOURS 40 MINUTES, OR UP TO 8 HOURS IF MAKING PASTRY ON SAME DAY

These are small flaky cups formed and baked from puff pastry. They are great for filling with creamy rich fillings like creamed mushroom or creamed salmon. And of course you can make small fruit tarts too, filling them with pastry cream and fresh berries. These light, flaky delights are hard to rest!
—*Stephany Buswell*

**INGREDIENTS:**

1½ **lb. puff pastry (see pages 358-359)**

1 **egg**

1 **teaspoon water**

**Pinch of salt**

**Sweet or savory filling of your choice**

1 Roll out the puff dough to ¼ inch thick. Chill.

2 After about 30 minutes, bring the dough out to a clean work surface dusted with flour. Using a 2½-inch biscuit cutter, cut as many rounds as you can. Make sure you cut closely in order to minimize waste.

3 With a 1½-inch cutter, cut the center out of half your pieces. Place on a half sheet pan lined with parchment. Place the solid pieces on the pan as well.

4 Preheat your oven to 400°F. Make an egg wash with 1 egg, 1 teaspoon of water and a pinch of salt. Using a small pastry brush, carefully brush the egg onto the solid pieces, making sure not to let the egg drip down the sides. This will stop the layers from puffing evenly. Now place the rings you have on top of the rounds. Egg wash the small rounds and refrigerate for 30 minutes.

5 Bake for 20 to 25 minutes or until golden brown all around. Leave no white or pale spots.

6 Fill with desired filling or store at room temperature in an airtight container.

# PÂTE À CHOUX (CHOUX PASTRY)

**YIELD:** 16 LARGE PUFFS OR ECLAIR SHELLS / **ACTIVE TIME:** 1 HOUR / **TOTAL TIME:** 1 HOUR 45 MINUTES

**INGREDIENTS:**

| | |
|---|---|
| 1 | cup water |
| 1 | cube unsalted butter |
| ½ | teaspoon salt |
| 1¼ | cups all-purpose flour |
| 4–5 | large eggs |

I absolutely love this dough! You can use it for so many different pastries, both sweet and savory! Here I will share two base recipes that you can fill with pastry cream, whipped cream, flavored buttercream, herbed cream cheese, smoked salmon, fried shrimp... really, the sky's the limit.

The beautiful thing about the baked puffs it that they are all crusts! You bake them in a hot oven and then turn it down to dry them out. When you cut them open they are hollow inside just waiting for you to fill them with a creamy filling.

Pipe them in either the traditional eclair shape which is 4 inches long and 1 ½ inches wide or a 2-inch-diameter ball.

With the savory dough, I pipe very small 1-inch balls and fill them with the herbed or plain cream cheese, sour cream and smoked salmon for hor d' oeuvres.

—*Stephany Buswell*

1 Preheat your oven to 450°F. In a medium saucepan, bring the water, butter, and salt to a rapid boil.

2 Stir in the flour all at once. Stir rapidly until you achieve a thick paste. Continue stirring over low heat until the paste pulls away from the sides and a skin forms on the bottom of the pan. Then transfer the hot dough to a mixing bowl on a stand-mixer. Mix on low speed with a paddle, releasing the steam from the dough.

3 When all the steam disappears, begin adding the eggs one by one. Allow each egg to totally absorb into the dough before adding another egg.

4 You need to only add the eggs until the dough forms a V shape when you pull the paddle straight up out of the dough. If the dough looks dry or drops off in blobs, it needs another egg. The dough should be shiny and smooth but not liquidy at all. When you pipe them they should hold their shape.

5 Line sheet pans with parchment, using little dabs of the dough in the corners under the paper to glue it down.

6 Use a ½-inch round tip to pipe the cream puffs and a large star tip to pipe the eclairs. Pipe 2-inch rounds for cream puffs and 1-inch rounds for smaller pastries. For eclairs, pipe 4-inch-long tubes, using a wet finger to press down the pointed ends.

7  Whip up an egg and a pinch of salt to use as egg wash for your pastries. Paint each pastry before putting them in the oven.

8  Place the pans in the hot oven for 10 minutes, and then turn it down to 350°F for another 30 to 40 minutes.

9  Break one open to make sure the dough inside has shrunk back to the crust and they have dried a bit. They should be hollow. For an extra crispy crust you can turn off the oven and prop it open a little, leaving the puffs in there to dry out some more.

10  When cool, fill with your favorite fillings and top with chocolate icing or liquid fondant glaze. For savory fillings just served filled.

## TOMATO HERB VARIATION

Use the Pate a Choux recipe but replace half the water with tomato juice and add dried herbs (oregano, basil, thyme, garlic granules) to the water/juice mix. They will come out the prettiest pink-peach color and taste great with savory fillings!

# PASTRY CREAM FOR CREAM PUFFS

YIELD: 16 CREAM PUFFS / ACTIVE TIME: 15 MINUTES / TOTAL TIME: 1 HOUR

To make cream puffs, simply incorporate this cream recipe into my Pâte à Choux dough (see page 362)!
—*Stephany Buswell*

1 In a small bowl, whisk together the sugar and cornstarch. Add the eggs and immediately whisk until smooth and creamy.

2 Meanwhile, have the milk in a small saucepan on medium heat on the stove bring to a simmer. Pour half of the hot milk over the egg mixture and stir until all incorporated. Pour this back into the rest of the hot milk and cook on medium heat, stirring constantly until the mixture is very thick and boiling.

3 Take off heat and pour into a bowl. Place plastic wrap directly on top of the custard to prevent a crust from forming. Put into the refrigerator until cool, then pipe into your finished puff pastries (see page 362)!

**INGREDIENTS:**

2 large eggs

3 tablespoons cornstarch

2 cups milk

½ cup sugar

Pinch of salt

1 tablespoons butter

½ teaspoon vanilla extract

1 batch of finished Pâte à Choux pastry puffs (see page 362)

# GOUGERES

**YIELD:** 36 PUFFS / **ACTIVE TIME:** 1 HOUR 15 MINUTES / **TOTAL TIME:** 1 HOUR 45 MINUTES

For a cheesy snack you will not be able to stop eating try this savory spin on Pâte à Choux.

—*Stephany Buswell*

1 Preheat your oven to 450°F. In a medium saucepan, bring the water, butter, and salt to a rapid boil.

2 Stir in the flour all at once. Stir rapidly until you achieve a thick paste. Continue stirring over low heat until the paste pulls away from the sides and a skin forms on the bottom of the pan. Then transfer the hot dough to a mixing bowl on a stand-mixer. Mix on low speed with a paddle, releasing the steam from the dough.

3 When all the steam disappears, begin adding the eggs one by one. Allow each egg to totally absorb into the dough before adding another egg.

4 You need to only add the eggs until the dough forms a V shape when you pull the paddle straight up out of the dough. If the dough looks dry or drops off in blobs, it needs another egg. The dough should be shiny and smooth but not liquidy at all. When you pipe them they should hold their shape.

5 After you have added your eggs to the batter, pour in a cup of grated Parmesan cheese and the cayenne pepper or smoked paprika. Pipe the dough out as 1-inch rounds and sprinkle more cheese on top with a few grains of salt. Not table salt—use Fleur de Sel (French sea salt) or some fancy salt you have been dying to use.

6 Whip up an egg and a pinch of salt to use as egg wash for your pastries. Paint each pastry before putting them in the oven.

7 Place the pans in the hot oven for 10 minutes, and then turn it down to 350°F for another 30 to 40 minutes.

8 Break one open to make sure the dough inside has shrunk back to the crust and they have dried a bit. They should be hollow. For an extra crispy crust you can turn off the oven and prop it open a little, leaving the puffs in there to dry out some more.

9 When cool, fill with your favorite fillings.

**INGREDIENTS:**

1 cup water

1 cube unsalted butter

½ teaspoon salt

1¼ cups all-purpose flour

4–5 large eggs

1 cup Parmesan cheese, grated

⅛ teaspoon cayenne pepper or smoked paprika

Pinch of Fleur de Sel or any sea salt

# BIALYS

YIELD: 8 BIALYS / ACTIVE TIME: 1 HOUR / TOTAL TIME: 3 HOURS 30 MINUTES

Created in Bialystock, Poland, I refer to these tasty bread treats (with an onion–poppy seed center) as the bagel's first cousin. The ones you'll usually find in America are soft and chewy all over, but the original versions had crisp centers that cracked when torn and chewy, soft edges. They were eaten with butter in Poland, while in the United States they're often used as a bread to eat with smoked fish. This recipe will give the desired Old World crispy effect if you make the centers thin and then bake them long enough.
—*Amy Emberling, Zingerman's Bakehouse*

## INGREDIENTS:

4   cups + 1 tablespoon bread flour

1½   cups + 1 tablespoon water, room temperature

1   teaspoon instant yeast

2   teaspoons sea salt

¼   cup + 2 tablespoons onion filling

## FOR THE ONION FILLING:

1¾   cup + 3 tablespoons onion (medium size, chopped)

2   tablespoons vegetable oil

2   teaspoons sea salt

2   tablespoons + 1½ teaspoons poppy seeds

1   In a large bowl, add the water, yeast and half of the flour. Mix with a wooden spoon until the mixture looks like a thick pancake batter.

2   Add the salt and remaining flour, then stir the mixture to incorporate the dry and wet ingredients.

3   Continue mixing the dough until the dough becomes shaggy. Scrape the side of the bowl with the dough and spoon to pick up any dry bits.

4   Remove the dough from the bowl and knead for 5 minutes.

5   Spray your mixing bowl with non-stick spray or brush with oil. Put the dough into the mixing bowl and cover with plastic. Ferment for 30 minutes.

6   Turn dough onto the bench. With a bench knife, divide the dough into 8 pieces. Round each piece. Dust with flour and cover with plastic. Let rest for 30 minutes.

7   Prepare your onion mix: For conventional ovens, preheat the oven to 400°F 20 minutes prior to baking; for convection ovens, preheat to 375°F 20 minutes prior to baking.

8   Mix the onions, salt, oil and poppy seeds in a small bowl, then spread the mixture out on a rimmed baking sheet. Bake for 30 minutes or until the onions pass through the translucent stage and are just starting to brown. Cool the mixture completely before adding to your dough.

9   Take each piece and create a thin center and raised sides. Place on a lightly floured surface. Place 1 tablespoon of onion mix in the center of each bialy. Proof for 1 hour.

10 Press the center down again before baking. Bake for 12 to 14 minutes, until just golden with some darker spots.

11 Remove from the oven, and enjoy while slightly warm, or cooled to room temperature.

# BAGELS:
# THE EAST COAST OBSESSION

The origin of the bagel is quite mysterious. There is a story that connects them to the Austrian croissant, but the most credited origin is that they were given to puerperal women as a gift in the Polish Jewish community. There is no agreement on how long bagels have been around, but we know that they were already popular in the 16th and 17th century.

Bagels build on the same baking tradition of pretzels, as they both required a pre-boiling before baking. This process gives bagels their shiny appearance and chewy texture.

When Polish Jewish immigrants reached Northern America, they brought their bagel tradition with them. The impact of the Jewish baking tradition was particularly strong on the East Coast, starting in New York, the now-recognized capital of bagels. Up until the first half of the 20th century, New York bagels were made with the traditional method, and the skill of the bagel bakers was guaranteed by a local trade union Bagel Bakers Local 338. Later on, automation of the process came into the scene and bagels became available to masses through supermarket distribution. Industrial bagels are often baked in steam ovens, skipping the boiling step.

The best bakeries still make bagels following the old method, and the East Coast passion for bagels is constantly on the rise.

**Montreal vs New York** Arguably, New York is not the only capital of bagels. Montreal has long disputed New York's lead in the bagel-mania. In the Canadian metropolis, bagels have a different character compared to those made in the Big Apple. Montreal's bagels are sweeter, crunchier, and darker, mostly coated with sesame seeds. This Canadian variety tends to be smaller than their New-York opponent, with a larger hole in the middle. New York-style bagels, on the other hand, are paler, moist and less sweet, and generally coated with poppy seeds.

Differences are of course due to differences in baking methods. Unlike New York-style bagels, Montreal Bagels are boiled in honey-sweetened water and contain malt, then baked in a wood-fired oven.

A Montreal-style bagel is often eaten alone, or with a spread placed on top, unlike the filled New York-style bagel. The crumb is denser, and New York-style fans complain that Montreal-style bagels get stale too easily. On the other hand, fans of Montreal bagels are not attracted by the pale look and the softer crust of the East Coast version.

In the end, it is all about individual preferences and acquired taste. Both types of bagels are authentic. It is generally acknowledged that the two bagel styles are simply due to influences from Polish-Jewish immigrants coming from different parts of Poland.

# St-Viateur Bagel

MONTRÉAL
Depuis 1957

www.stviateurbagel.com

263 Rue Saint Viateur O
Montréal, QC H2V 1Y1
Canada
(514) 276-8044

158 St-Viateur O
Montreal, QC, H2T 2L4
(514) 270-2972

1585 Dagenais O.
Laval, QC. H7L 5A3
(450) 625-5552

821 Tecumseh
DDO, QC. H9R 4X8
(514) 542-3344

5629 Monkland Avenue
Montréal, QC. H4A 1E2
(514) 487-8051

1127 Mont-Royal E.
Montréal, QC. H2J 1X9
(514) 528-6361

Quite simply, St-Viateur Bagel is one of the most popular bagel shops in the entire world. Vince Morena's shop—first located in Montreal's trendy Mile End neighborhood but now found across Montreal—is known as the standard-bearer of the Montreal bagel scene. A scene, of course, that is unrivaled anywhere outside of New York—and even there it's hotly contested.

"We're the best because we still do it the old fashion way," says Morena (after a bit of prompting). "We really love what we do, and care about it, and the bagels are just different. Meaning that they're not as big and doughy and salty as the New York style bagels. And there will be New Yorkers who argue the opposite. They'll call our bagels small and sweet. So, there is a division. But Montreal bagels are the best, definitely because the way we do it."

"We've grown to 8 locations, we have an online store, we have three restaurants, a food truck, and we're at about 600 grocery stores, so we're still growing." A trip to St-Viateur and it's not hard to understand the magic bakery's growth. In fact, there's a specific answer: the sesame bagel. Morena estimates that about 95 percent of their bagels sold are sesames—and if that's hyperbole, it's not as much as one might think. One bite of this iconic recipe justifies everything—the press, the longevity, and, yes, even the lines.

"When it comes to bagels, I have a master's degree, everything else I'm just a dummy. I always tell people I got two educations; I got one education in school, and I got another education in the bagel shop. Experience is everything. I've been making bagels for so long that when it comes to bagels I really know what I'm doing."

"When it comes to bagels, I have a master's degree, everything else I'm just a dummy..."

# IN HIS OWN WORDS:

## VINCE MORENA OF ST-VIATEUR BAGEL

*How and when did you get your start baking?*

My first shift in the bagel shop was in 1984 when I was 13 years old. I learned to roll bagels and make bagels the following year in 1985. My brothers all did the same thing. When we all finished our schooling, however, we all ended up back in the bagel business and we bought the whole thing in 1994.

*Who—or what—first inspired you to bake?*

My father, because he was in the business. You always look up to your dad, so when he started working in the bagel shop, it was just a natural progression. Coming out of the early '90s there was a bagel boom, so I felt that because I already knew the business and had a business background from my school-ing, that I could expand the business that we already owned. At that time, all we had was two spots, and then in '94 we opened a third, in '96 a fourth, and then we kept on growing and growing.

*Who inspires you now?*

Well when it's your own business, you always care for it more than if you worked somewhere else. And there's always been, and there always continues to be, so much potential for us, because we do things differently. We're not any run of the mill bagel company. We're trying to see how far we can take it.

*What is your golden rule(s) for baking?*

The golden rule is to get golden nuggets. When the bagels are perfectly cooked, we call them golden nuggets. That means that they're perfectly golden and symmetrical in their cook-ing. That's not as easy as it sounds, because we

are dealing with a wood fired oven. Our goal is to always get those perfectly golden-brown bagels.

We're only as good as our last bagel. So, our main goal is to keep the bagel consistent. There's people from all around the world who have heard about us, and we want them to have that great experience every time.

*What does St-Viateur Bagel represent to you?*

Well right now it represents my life. I've been here since I was a kid, and it's more than a bagel shop. It's part of the fabric of Montreal. Especially in the last ten years, we've really become a local landmark, and a tourist site. And, for me it really is my life. A lot of the other parts of my life revolve around the bagel shop.

*What is your favorite thing to bake? Why?*

Well, bagels are all similar to bake. The question would be what is my favorite bagel to *eat*. And, I would say the sesame is the golden standard. It's a different mentality from America. A lot of people come here from the States and say, "our bagel shop has 32 flavors," whereas up until about 10 years ago we only had three flavors. Now, we have some of the other flavors, and we're up to about nine. But my favorite is still the sesame seed.

*How did St-Viateur Bagel come to be? Why Mon-tréal?*

St-Viateur is a family business. It was started by a Holocaust survivor named Myer Lewkow-icz. My father started working for Myer as a boy in 1962, and then in 1974 he became a full partner. They kept growing the business.

There was just one shop back in the old days, and we didn't grow to two shops until 1984. In fact, there were only two bagel shops in all of Montreal at that time making bagels the way we do. So, we were the only game in town for a long time.

Montreal is the birthplace for Montreal-style bagels. So, now you'll see some Montreal-style bagels popping up all around the world, but I think the way it happened here was with the immigration patterns. Montreal had a similar immigration pattern to New York City, where at the turn of the century there were a lot of Eastern European Jewish people that came over, and they brought their bagels. We get compared to New York all the time, because we're both bagel meccas so to speak. And so, the main difference we tell people is that we never evolved.

At a certain point of time, bagels were made the same way everywhere, because it got brought over from Europe a long time ago. However, with people, technology, and machinery, got in the way. The American bagel is machine-made, and is made in gas or electric ovens, and with time it got bigger and bigger. Whereas our bagel, it fits in the size of your hand. We never changed. We make a lot smaller by batches, but they're tastier.

*What tools/materials do you use?*

Well the tools are easy. We build the brick ovens in house. We make every bagel by hand, so you need your hands. Then, we have a boiler, a knife, and a shibba. A shibba is used to shift the bagels in the oven. That's about it. And a mixer, obviously. It's very simple!

*Tell me about your most memorable collaboration with another chef.*

One of the most memorable collaborations would probably have to be with Bob Blumer. He had this TV show called Glutton for Punishment. In that show, we had to teach him how to make bagels in five days. So, that was his challenge, and it was probably one of the more memorable TV shows we have ever done. He did it, and we're still friends today.

*Brag about yourselves a bit. What are your highest achievements and/or proudest moments as chefs?*

We just celebrated our 60th anniversary with a big block party. So, we're just proud of the fact that we've been around for so long. We're the furthest thing from an overnight success. My dad's been here for 50 years, and my brothers and I have been here for 30 years, so it's the long process that I'm proud of.

*Where did you learn to cook? Please tell me about your education and apprenticeships.*

I started as a boy. It's a simple process, but it takes some time to master. Once you learn to bake bagels, you can't unlearn—it's like learning to ride a bicycle.

*Tell me about your bagel baking process.*

We put the ingredients together in a mixer, and we make batches of about 100 pounds at a time. We take the large dough, put it on the table, and cut it in strips. Then we roll the strips by hand into bagels. The bagels all weigh about two and a half or three ounces each.

It's a five-minute cycle. So, every five minutes we put four dozen bagels into a large pot of boiling water, and in the boiling water there is some honey that gives the bagels a little bit of sweetness, a little glow, that helps the sesame seeds stick. Then, we take the bagels out of the water, and cover them in sesame seeds, and put them on these wooden boards and into the oven to dry. There's always 20 dozen bagels in the oven, because it takes them about 18-20 minutes to cook. Then, we pull the ones that are cooked out of the oven, and through a chute, and then we start the whole process over again five minutes later. 24 hours a day, 365 days a year.

# ST-VIATEUR'S SESAME BAGEL

YIELD: 30 BAGELS / ACTIVE TIME: 50 MINUTES / TOTAL TIME: 1 ½ HOURS

The most popular bagel from one of the world's most revered bagel shops, St-Viateur's sesame bagel is the ultimate when it comes to Montreal-style bagels.

**INGREDIENTS:**

16 cups enriched white flour

3¾ cups water

1½ ounces malted barley flour

⅛ cup canola oil

2 ounces fresh yeast,

3 ounces sugar

1 pound sesame seeds

2 ounces honey

1 Mix all the ingredients besides seeds and honey together in a spiral mixer for 8 minutes. The dough should be a little sticky to the touch, but not too much. Let rest in the mixer or on the table for another 20 minutes.

2 Cut the dough into 1½-inch strips and roll them out into 9-inch cylinders. Attach both ends to form a bagel. (This is on Youtube, if you want to check out the visual!)

3 Bring a large pot of water to boil and dissolve honey into the water.

4 Boil the bagels in the pot, about 6 at a time, for 4 minutes. They should rise to the top when finished.

5 Remove bagels from hot water with a strainer and let cool for 1 minute.

6 Preheat oven to 325°F.

7 Put the sesame seeds in a bowl and generously cover the bagels in seeds.

8 Put the bagels in a tray and put in oven for 16 to 18 minutes. Remove when golden brown. Make sure to flip the bagels halfway through baking.

For added authenticity, you can cook the bagels for the first 9 minutes on wood planks. Just be sure to wet the planks beforehand!

# IN HIS OWN WORDS:

## JOSH POTOCKI OF 158 PICKETT STREET CAFÉ

*How and when did you get your start baking?*

I began baking at a small vegetarian restaurant in Asheville, North Carolina circa 1996. The job I was hired for was doing prep for dinner service and working the juice bar. There was a small bread program and I was very hungry to learn. The baker at the time there was Alison Reid a mentor and future business partner. I went in on my own time about 2-3 times to learn from her at which point she asked me to cover her shift. I was nowhere near ready for this but I agreed and baked the shift. She left me some detailed notes on paper and I went from there…twenty one years later, here I am, still in the baking business!

*Who—or what—first inspired you to bake? Who inspires you now?*

My love for bread came from my Dad's fresh baked rye bread. Currently, I'm inspired by our team who is constantly creating, producing and evolving.

*What are your golden rules for baking?*

Don't forget the salt and trust your gut.

*What does 158 Pickett Street Café represent to you?*

158 and Southside, our production bakery, prove to that if you really love what you do it's not work, it's a way of life. These are not just places of work, they are communities.

*What is your favorite thing to bake? Why? Least favorite thing to bake? Why?*

My favorite thing to bake is the baguette. It is unforgiving but when you get it just right there is nothing more beautiful.

*How did 158 Pickett Street come to be? Why Portland? What are your most popular items?*

158 started with a conversation with a friend who was visiting town. He went to get bagels and came back with a big bag. He looked at us and said can you guys make bagels? We didn't say no. Several weeks later I was riding my bike past the current location of the shop and saw a "for rent" sign in the window and next thing you know, we're incorporating in a lawyer's office. Sixteen years later, 158 still sits in that location! We have since moved the baking production across town to a large warehouse-turned-commercial kitchen and bakery. There, we have expanded our operation to include baking for wholesale clients as well as our full-service catering company, The Bread + Butter Catering Company.

Our most popular items are the Bacon + Egg + Cheese and our Salmon Bagel.

# 158 Pickett Street Café

158 Benjamin W Pickett St
South Portland, ME 04106
(207) 799-8998

Southside Bakery
73 Main St
South Portland, ME 04106
(207) 619-7031

*Where do you get your tools/materials? What non-essential items should every baker have?*

We get the tools necessary at restaurant and bakery supply companies, we have a lot of large equipment these days. We source many of our grains locally. All other items come from general food purveyors.

The nonessential needs for a baker would be a passion for bread and openness to trial and error.

*What books go on your required reading list for bakers?*

*Flour, Water, Salt, Yeast, Artisan Baking*, and *Tartine Bread*.

*What outlets/periodicals/newspapers do you read or consult regularly, if any?*

*Lucky Peach*.

*Tell me about your most memorable collaboration with another chef or baker, if any.*

My wife, myself and a friend created a pop-up brunch series called "Pocket Brunch" as we began building our catering company. Each brunch was in a different location and was based on a theme, collaborating with a guest chef. Through this I was able to work with the best old and new chefs in the area. The constant change in theme and location really forced us to push boundaries and get creative as chefs.

*Do you follow any cooking shows or chefs? If so, which is your favorite?*

I am constantly watching what's happening in the food world. I really like the work both Enrique Olvera and Alex Atala are doing these days.

*Brag about yourselves a bit. What are your highest achievements and/or proudest moments as chefs/bakers?*

Many years ago, we were mentioned in a New York Times article and I remember how proud I was that our little pirate shack in Maine was on the map. These days I am most proud to have workplaces that promotes free thinking and self-expression.

*Where did you learn to cook? Please tell me about your education and apprenticeships.*

I started learning to cook from my beautiful grandmother Julia Kovach. She was from Austria-Hungary and showed me the way of the old world. After that, I learned and continue to learn through observation, travel, and experimentation.

*Tell me about your bagel baking process.*

We use our 16-year-old wild ferment starter, flour, water, yeast, and salt. We mix, then proof in bulk. Then we cut, weigh and round. We let the dough proof more at this point. Then we form the hole, proof again, boil, add toppings, then it's oven time!

*What makes your bagels the best?*

The salty bakers who bake them.

# SEAWEED BAGEL

YIELD: 18 4 OZ. BAGELS/ **ACTIVE TIME:** 2 HOURS / **TOTAL TIME:** 5-6 HOURS

We began topping our bagels with Maine seaweed 5 years ago after participating in the Maine Seaweed Festival. We fell in love with salty sea flavor immediately. We brought the flavor back to the shop and it has been a customer fave ever since! It's wonderful to be able to utilize an element of the ocean we are so lucky to be so very close to.

—*158 Pickett Street Café*

## INGREDIENTS:

9   cups all-purpose flour

2⅔  cups lukewarm water

10  ounces sourdough starter

2   teaspoons instant yeast

1   tablespoon + ½ teaspoon salt

   **Cornmeal**

   **Dulse (seaweed) flakes**

## MIXING

1 Water should be room temperature or slightly warmer. Weigh out and pour into mixing bowl.

2 Add sour culture. It should be active and bubbly when you mix. When added to water it should float on the top. If it sinks it needs more time to ripen before it can be used.

3 Add flour and instant yeast. Mix on speed one for 2 minutes. The dough should come together in a rough mass, but not be entirely combined. Let rest 20 minutes in mixer.

4 Add salt. Mix on speed one for 2 minutes, then speed two for 3 minutes. The dough should feel strong, but not stiff or dry. If it does you may need to add a small amount of water. You should be able to grab a handful and pull it a few inches away.

5 Transfer dough to a large bowl or bin and cover. Keep in a warm, but not hot area. After 1 hour pull out edges and gently stretch, folding it back in on itself. Let rest another hour.

## SHAPING

1 Place pizza stone in oven and preheat to 500°.

2 Dump dough onto a lightly floured table. Use bench knife to cut into 16 or so evenly-sized pieces. Roll into balls, leaving the seam side down. The surface of the rounds should be taut, but not so tight it tears. Cover them and let rest until rounds have relaxed and flattened slightly, 30–60 minutes.

3 Poke a hole in the center of the ball and stretch gently to widen. If they are difficult to stretch and the dough resists, they need more time to rest. If they are slack and loose they have sat for too long. Let shaped bagels rest another 30–60 minutes.

4 Fill roasting pan with water and boil.

## BAKING

1 Gently lift bagel from underneath with bench knife and drop into boiling water, flipping top side down. Multiple bagels can be baked at once depending on the size of the pan, but make sure they are not overcrowded. Bagels should float (if not, more rest time is needed). After edges begin to darken, flip (about 30 seconds). After second side is boiled scoop out with spatula and place on cooling rack to drain.

2 Dust the back of a sheet pan with cornmeal and use spatula to place bagel on it. Make sure to space them out so they don't stick together. Sprinkle with dulse flakes. Gently slide bagels into oven onto pizza stone. Check after 10 minutes and rotate individually with tongs. Bake another 10–15 minutes, or until golden brown. Pull from oven with tongs and place on a rack to cool.

# GRAIN CRAFT

## Grain Craft

201 West Main St, Suite 203
Chattanooga, TN 37408
(423) 265-2313
www.graincraft.com

It should come as no surprise that a major independent miller like Grain Craft is so efficient, but it's still incredible to learn about how its mills (15 facilities in total from coast to coast) operate. According to Milling Superintendent Ian Tillinghast, "our mill in Rosedale, Kansas is what we call a swing mill—we can mill soft wheat or we can 'swing' the mill in order to mill hard wheat. Both present their challenges because we do not shut the process down to change the variety of wheat. We have a very good crew that can operate the mill and handle most problems that might occur."

It's amazing, but it makes more sense if you learn more about Tillinghast's bona fides. "I got my formal education in milling from Kansas State University with a Bachelor of Science in Milling Science and Management. I have worked full-time in three flour mills with over 10 years of experience. I learned how to become a miller on top of my education by working in the mill and learning something new every day. Numerous people have helped me along the way, whether supervisors or subordinates. They have all helped!"

That experience has led to a simple but effective company philosophy: "Learn from your mistakes." Says Tillinghast, "Milling is all about experience. Most experienced millers have made mistakes and they learn from those mistakes, which is why they are experienced." Milling flour requires patience, which is why the Rosedale mill's deliberate approach is so reliably successful.

# IN HIS OWN WORDS:

## IAN TILLINGHAST OF GRAIN CRAFT

*Who—or what—first inspired you to begin milling? Who inspires you now?*

My family has always played a big influence in any success that I have had. My parents always pushed me in school and work at a young age. They instilled that when you work hard and you try, you will have success. My family still inspires me to keep doing what I love to do.

*What does Grain Craft represent to you?*

Grain Craft is a very close-knit company that values their employees. They trust us to do our jobs. They appreciate and trust their employees, which allows employees to be successful within the company.

*What is your favorite type of grain? Why? Least favorite grain? Why?*

I enjoy milling hard red winter or hard red spring wheat. It presents challenges with all the different varieties that can be grown. We can utilize most of our equipment by making fine adjustments that allow us to get the most amount of flour out of a kernel of wheat. I'm a wheat miller and don't normally get to mill any other types of grains, so I'd say low quality wheat is my least favorite grain. It presents a whole new set of challenges that are not always easy to deal with.

*How did Grain Craft come to be? Why Rosedale? What are your most popular items?*

Grain Craft is the product of the merging of Milner Milling, Pendleton Flour Mills, and Cereal Food Processors in 2014. The Rosedale mill originally belonged to Cereal Food Processors. We make a variety of flours but the most popular one here at the Rosedale mill is Sunny Kansas Pastry, which is used in crackers.

*Where do you get your tools/materials? What non-essential items should every home baker have?*

We have a wide range of milling equipment that is used in our process. Most comes from milling equipment companies. Our material, which is soft wheat or hard wheat, comes from grain elevators around the Kansas City Metro area. My wife, who loves to bake, says a cookie scoop is a non-essential item a home baker should have.

*What outlets/periodicals/newspapers do you read or consult regularly, if any?*

I normally read *Milling and Baking News* and *Milling Journal*.

*Brag about yourself a bit. What have been your proudest moments as a miller?*

I don't have any outstanding achievements as an individual, but I have worked with some great people in my career, and have helped the mills that I worked at make a great finished product while doing it in a safe manner.

# JEWISH BAGELS

YIELD: 16 BAGELS / ACTIVE TIME: 45 MINUTES / TOTAL TIME: 2 HOURS

I consider a good bagel to be hard and chewy on the outside and firm but soft in the center. Not a fluffy bready number that squishes flat when you try to bite into it. I have a friend who grew up in New York City and her Jewish heritage has made her a bagel snob. When she offered a recipe that she used to make bagels I jumped all over it. This one is an adaptation to her original recipe and I think it is the closest thing to a good New York style bagel. Of course you can top them with whatever toppings you like but my favorite will always be the everything bagel. You just mix together all your seeds, dehydrated onion and garlic and a touch of coarse kosher salt. Perfect!

—*Stephany Buswell*

1 Put the hot water, sugar and yeast in a large bowl and whisk to dissolve.

2 Add about three cups of the flour and the salt to the water/yeast mixture.

3 Using a dough hook or paddle mix until the dough is thick but very wet.

4 Add more flour, one cup at a time but as the dough begins to thicken add it in smaller quantities. When the dough pulls away from the sides and forms a ball on the hook, take it off the mixer and begin to knead by hand. Dust the table with flour to prevent sticking. Soon you should have a nice stiff dough, stiffer than a regular bread dough but not dry! It should still give easily and stretch easily without tearing, forming a nice window.

5 Put the dough in a lightly oiled bowl turn it over to cover the dough in oil and cover with plastic wrap and put in the proof box or a warm moist place to rise.

6 While the dough is rising, fill a stockpot with about a gallon of water and set it on the fire to boil. When it reaches a boil, add the sugar and reduce the heat so that the water just barely simmer, the surface of the water should barely move.

7 Once the dough has doubled in size, turn it onto your work surface, punch it down to expel the gas that has formed and divide into 16 pieces.

## INGREDIENTS:

**FOR THE BAGELS:**

3 cups water heated to 105–110°F

¾ cup sugar

3 tablespoons Saf instant yeast

6–8 cups of bread (high gluten) flour

2 teaspoons salt

**FOR COOKING THE BAGELS:**

Vegetable oil or spray

16 cups (1 gallon) of water

4 tablespoons sugar

A few handfuls of cornmeal

8 To form the bagels there are two ways to do this; one is to form the dough into a sphere and then poke a hole in the middle with a finger and turn the dough around the hole to make the bagel shape. Then there is the hole-centric method. This involves rolling each piece into a long cylindrical snake of dough and wrapping it around your hand into a loop and then rolling the ends together on the table with your hand in the middle. Either way will work fine. Don't get discouraged if your bagels are misshapen and funny looking. Each one will be its own bagel—this is ok, enjoy the diversity.

9 Preheat your oven to 400°F.

10 Once all the bagels are formed let them rest for 10–15 minutes so they can begin to rise slightly, they should rise about ¼ in volume which is called half proofing.

11 When the bagels are ready drop them one by one into the simmering water. Do not crowd them boil only 3–4 at a time. The bagels should first sink and then begin to float. Let the bagel simmer for about another 3 minutes and then lift them out of the water and place them on a clean towel. Sprinkle cornmeal on parchment that has been placed on your full sheet pan. Arrange the bagels on the prepared sheet pan and bake them for about 25 minutes. Then remove them from the oven and turn them over and bake them for another 10 minutes or so. This will prevent flat bottomed bagels.

12 When done cool on a wire rack. Do *not* cut them while they are hot. They will be a wadded gummy mess—it isn't worth it!

---

**VARIATIONS:**

If you want flavored bagels, after boiling them you can wash them with a mixture of egg white and water and sprinkle toppings of your choice; poppy seeds, sesame seeds, caraway, toasted onion, raw garlic bits, or salt.

If you want more grains, replace ¼ of the bread flour with whole wheat flour.

# IN HER OWN WORDS:

## BETTE DWORKIN OF
## KAUFMAN'S BAGEL & DELICATESSEN

*How did Kaufman's Bagel & Delicatessen come to be? What are your specialties?*

Established in Skokie in 1963, Kaufman's Bagel & Delicatessen was built and operated by the late Maury Kaufman. Today Kaufman's continues to be a family owned and operated business, run by me and my Mom (Judy). We specialize in Eastern European breads and pastries—all manufactured on site—and a deli counter which has become a landmark in the Chicago-land area. We were chosen as one of the top 10 bakeries in the country by USA Today and the best bagel in the country by AOL's Kitchen's Best. Kaufman's has received awards from North Shore Magazine, Restaurant News; made the pages of Saveur Magazine, Chicago Magazine, Time-Out Chicago, Make It Better and The Chicago Tribune to name a few, along with a recently earned Zagat rating.

Our specialties include the artisan breads of Eastern Europe—those heavy, dense ryes and pumpernickels with a wonderfully fermented flavor; bagels made the traditional way—boiled and hearth baked for a great crust and chewy interior. And our sweet shop is a constantly changing selection of cakes, cookies, pies and strudels.

*How and when did you get your start in the bakery business?*

I am a bakery baby… what does that mean? Well, to some it means I have flour running through my veins, (after 4 generations I'm beginning to think there's some truth to that). It means I am used to the phone ringing at all hours of the day and night—along with very early mornings. It means dealing with the pressure of manufacturing and delivering a perishable product; coping with the whims of nature during the growing season—not to mention those commodity traders who wreak their own havoc on the flour market. It's the frustration of being part of an industry that has become a job rather than what it once was—a craft, a trade, a métier. I consider bread and pastry chefs to be artisans—people who studied years to learn their craft.

*Who—or what—first inspired you? Who inspires you now?*

To me bakery is a passion and an art—an environment full of creativity. While unfortunately a few years ago I had to give up flour and white sugar myself for health reasons, I believe bread and sweets are part of everyone's

# *Kaufman's Bagel & Delicatessen*

4905 W. Dempster St.
Skokie, IL 60077
(847) 677-6190
www.kaufmansdeli.com

world. As a child in this business I found magic in every corner of the bakery. I mean seriously-imagine a machine that just keeps pumping out butter cream frosting or hot donuts; walking the 80-foot length of an oven with windows watching the bread grow and become golden brown, or watching 800 pounds of dough smelling wonderfully fermented flipped out of a mixer…I am not a baker—but luckily, I still find my industry magical to this day.

*What does Kaufman's Deli represent to you?*

We had a major fire in 2011, and since then I think of Maury Kaufman and my late father, Arnold Dworkin, more often than ever—especially when I have difficult decisions to make. The past few years have been full of those. I have come to a better understanding that Kaufman's is about far more than the food, although that's a very big piece. But it's also about a sense of community, a place to meet, see old friends, and comfort; it was the outpouring of support from the community that kept us moving forward while we were closed. Kaufman's, through the visions of both Maury Kaufman and Arnold Dworkin, is about tradition.

*What are your proudest moments?*

I pride myself on having the best; all of the salads, dinners and soups are made in house. The fish counter boasts 4 types of lox, house-smoked sable, trout, sturgeon and gefilte fish like Grandma made. Corned beef comes in 4 different cuts depending on your cholesterol level, and the turkey and veal pastrami are cured and smoked in-house. There are seasonal items on both the deli counter and in the bakery, like Cranberry Applesauce and Pumpkin Blintzes. We love to experiment. Our staff hails from all over the world; at any given time you can hear English, Spanish, Hebrew, Yiddish, Assyrian, Arabic, Russian, French or German spoken in the store. Our goal is to make our customers feel at home.

I take tremendous pride in making some of the finest product available. We use no preservatives, chemicals or additives in our bakery—only the finest ingredients; whole eggs, chocolate, real vanilla, sour cream, cream cheese, whole grains and, of course, butter. I was really concerned about the trans-fat issue—we haven't had margarine or shortening in the bakery for years.

We're simply bakers who find joy in what we do and who make outstanding products—there's a little bit of our heart in every piece. We are a quality house. Always have been. Always will be…After all, I have over 100 years of family history to protect.

# PLAIN BAGELS

YIELD: 12 BAGELS / ACTIVE TIME: 45 MINUTES / TOTAL TIME: 11 HOURS

Delicious with sweet or savory fillings (or simply on its own), these chewy bagels are as versatile as they come.
— *courtesy of Kaufman's Bagel & Delicatessen*

**INGREDIENTS:**

- 7 cups high gluten flour
- ¼ cup granulated sugar
- 1 tablespoon + 1 teaspoon alt
- 1 egg
- ¼ cup vegetable or soybean oil
- 1½ cups cold water
- 2 teaspoons fresh yeast

1 Combine all ingredients in a mixer fitted with a dough hook. Mix on low until it forms a cohesive ball. Divide into 12 evenly-sized pieces. Roll into hot dog shape and form into bagels. Transfer to a pan or board with a light coating of cornmeal and place in the refrigerator to hold overnight. Dough can be frozen raw up to a week.

2 When ready to bake, remove bagels from the refrigerator and place in a warm, moist (if possible) environment to proof for approximately 2 hours (or until puffy).

3 Preheat your oven to 450°F and line your baking sheet with parchment paper.

4 Boil a pot of water and drop a few bagels at a time into the boiling water; as soon as the bagels pop up to the top of the water (30–60 seconds) remove them with a strainer and place them on your parchment paper lined pan. Bake for approximately 18–20 minutes.

# CINNAMON RAISIN BAGELS

YIELD: 12 BAGELS / **ACTIVE TIME:** 45 MINUTES / **TOTAL TIME:** 11 HOURS

Warm cinnamon and juicy raisins make these the perfect breakfast bagels, especially when they've come straight out of the oven.
— *courtesy of Kaufman's Bagel & Delicatessen*

**INGREDIENTS:**

- 7 cups high gluten flour
- ¼ cup granulated sugar
- 1 tablespoon plus 1 teaspoon salt
- 1 egg
- ¼ cup vegetable or soybean oil
- 1½ cups cold water
- 2¼ teaspoons fresh yeast
- 1 tablespoon cinnamon
- 1 cup dark midget raisins

1 Combine all ingredients in a mixer fitted with a dough hook. Mix on low until it forms a cohesive ball. Divide into 12 evenly-sized pieces. Roll into hot dog shape and form into bagels. Transfer to a pan or board with a light coating of cornmeal and place in the refrigerator to hold overnight. Dough can be frozen raw up to a week.

2 When ready to bake, remove bagels from the refrigerator and place in a warm, moist (if possible) environment to proof for approximately 2 hours (or until puffy).

3 Preheat your oven to 450°F and line your baking sheet with parchment paper.

4 Boil a pot of water and drop a few bagels at a time into the boiling water; as soon as the bagels pop up to the top of the water (30–60 seconds) remove them with a strainer and place them on your parchment paper lined pan. Bake for approximately 18–20 minutes.

Always bake a plain bagel with the cinnamon raisin and pumpernickel as a color guide.

# PUMPERNICKEL BAGELS

YIELD: 12 BAGELS / ACTIVE TIME: 45 MINUTES / TOTAL TIME: 11 HOURS

Caraway seeds and rye meal pack these hearty bagels with flavor.
— *courtesy of Kaufman's Bagel & Delicatessen*

**INGREDIENTS:**

7 cups high gluten flour

¼ cup granulated sugar

1 tablespoon plus 1 teaspoon salt

¼ cup vegetable or soybean oil

1 ¾ cups cold water

2 teaspoons fresh yeast

¼ cup whole caraway seeds

½ cup rye meal or chops

⅓ cup caramel color (burnt sugar)

1 Combine all ingredients in a mixer fitted with a dough hook. Mix on low until it forms a cohesive ball. Divide into 12 evenly-sized pieces. Roll into hot dog shape and form into bagels. Transfer to a pan or board with a light coating of corn meal and place in the refrigerator to hold overnight. Dough can be frozen raw up to a week.

2 When ready to bake, remove bagels from the refrigerator and place in a warm, moist (if possible) environment to proof for approximately 2 hours (or until puffy).

3 Preheat your oven to 450°F and line your baking sheet with parchment paper.

4 Boil a pot of water and drop in a few bagels at a time; as soon as the bagels pop up to the top of the water (30–60 seconds) remove them with a strainer and place them on your parchment paper lined pan. Bake for approximately 18–20 minutes.

Always bake a plain bagel with the cinnamon raisin and pumpernickel as a color guide.

# SCONES

The history of scones is quite mysterious. It is generally acknowledged that they were initially popular in Scotland, and from there they imposed themselves to the whole of Great Britain.

Traditionally, scones are slices of a simple unleavened round bread cooked on a griddle and called bannock. Bannock, however, is a rather common rudimental way to make bread, and different versions of bannocks are found among the Inuit and Native Americans. In Britain, the earliest bannocks (and scones) were made with oats and were rather dense. Bannocks were already mentioned back in the 8th century.

It is not clear how the word scone developed. While the word bannock seems to derive from the Latin panicium (baked bread), the word scone is probably derived from the Dutch word schoonbrood (fine white bread) or even from the Gaelic term sgonn (large mouthful).

With time scones developed into their own being, and the sliced bannock began being baked in pieces, or scones. Scones can also be shaped like rounds, rather than triangles, and are often flavored with a variety of additions. Initially, scones were unleavened and quite heavy, but after baking soda and baking powder became available, scones became the light and delicious tea accompaniment we know today.

The use of serving scones with tea and butter started in the 19th century England, where they became a real institution. While, in the beginning, wheat was not available and oats or barley were the grains mostly used, nowadays scones are made with wheat flour. This, plus rising agents, contributes to make them much lighter and more appealing than their original versions.

Different regional contexts contributed to different scone traditions. In England scones are sweet, rich, and buttery, often savored with raisins or black currants. In Scotland, potato scones, known as tattie scones, are a savory version; it is still common to cook them on a griddle, or in a pan on the stove instead of baking the scones in an oven. There is also a dropped scone which is similar to a pancake, and even a scone that uses lemonade instead of milk.

## BRITISH VS AMERICAN SCONES

In the United States, scones often resemble the consistency of American biscuits, which is something uniquely American.

Early settlers developed biscuits as a type of bread to accompany food, and, therefore, they tend to be less sweet and less cakey than scones, which are meant to accompany tea. American biscuits have a different consistency compared to scones, even if they look alike. British scones are indeed quite easily distinguished from typical American biscuits. While scones are sweet and crumbly, biscuits are less sweet and are flaky.

The difference in texture is due to a higher shortening-to-flour ratio in typical biscuits, and also to the absence of eggs in biscuit dough.

When scones are made in North America, they are basically biscuits with the addition of sugar, more than what would be typically present in an authentic British scone. Moreover, British scones rarely come with additions other than raisins and currants, while American scones are present with any possible addition, like chocolate, blueberries, cinnamon, and nuts (to mentions just a few). They are also often glazed, while British scones never are.

## SCONE DEBATE

In the scone's homeland, Great Britain, the last few years have seen a heated debate over one fundamental issue: should jam or cream butter go first on a scone?

It sounds like a laughable topic for a debate but, apparently, different English regions take the issue very seriously. Specifically, Cornwall supports the "jam first, cream on top" option, while Devonshire is a strong supporter of the "cream first, jam on top".

The rivalry between Devonshire and Cornwall over scones is livelier than ever after Devon dairy applied for Protected Designation of Origin (PDO) for "Devon cream tea", which are tea scones with clotted cream. Apparently, Cornwall already has PDO for clotted cream, but not for clotted cream scones. New evidence coming from a book fragment found in Devonshire supports the hypothesis that the use of topping scones with cream and jam originated there, some 1,000 years ago. Therefore, the "cream first" is gaining further support.

# CLASSIC SCONES

**YIELD:** 10-16 SCONES (DEPENDING ON CUTTER SIZE) / **ACTIVE TIME:** 20 MINUTES / **TOTAL TIME:** 20 MINUTES

Scones are the most typical accompaniment of the unmissable English tea break. They are eaten in different ways, depending on personal taste but also on regional variations. One popular version is smothered with a generous layer of clotted cream, preceded or followed by a layer of jam.

1 Preheat oven to 450°F.

2 Combine dry ingredients in a bowl.

3 Add the butter in pieces and incorporate well.

4 Add the buttermilk and work the dough until it comes together, then make it into a ball.

5 Transfer to a clean surface and roll 1½ inches square.

6 Cut disks with a floured cutter—fluted ones make lovely scones.

7 Transfer to a baking dish lined with parchment paper.

8 Brush with buttermilk.

9 Bake for 15 minutes.

**INGREDIENTS:**

- 17.6 oz (500 g) all-purpose flour
- 1½ tsp (7 g) baking soda
- 1 tsp (4.6 g) cream of tartar
- 1 tbsp sugar
- 2.8 oz (80 g) butter
- 10.6 oz (300 g) buttermilk, plus extra for the finish

# CLASSIC CREAM SCONES

YIELD: 18 LARGE OR 24 MEDIUM-SIZED SCONES / ACTIVE TIME: 40 MINUTES / TOTAL TIME: 55 MINUTES

These are my all-time favorite scones. They come from Chef Bo Friberg, my mentor and former pastry director at a school where I also taught. Chef Bo was the kind of pastry chef who loved flavors, textures, and the classics. He wrote two books, *The Professional Pastry Chef* and *The Advanced Professional Pastry Chef*. Unfortunately, he passed away before he could write the 5th edition of his popular book, but I will never forget Chef Bo or everything he taught me. This recipe has been adjusted for the home baker.
—*Stephany Buswell*

**INGREDIENTS:**

- 4½ cups all-purpose flour
- ⅓ cup sugar
- 3 tablespoons baking powder
- 1 teaspoon salt
- ½ cup currants or raisins
- ½ cup candied orange peel or 6 tablespoons lemon zest
- 3¼ cups heavy cream
- ¼ cup light clover honey
- ¼ cup cream
- Granulated sugar

1 In the bowl of a stand-mixer, mix together the flour, sugar, baking powder, salt, raisins or currants, and orange or lemon. If mixing by hand, a large bowl will do fine.

2 Mix together the cream and honey. Be sure to mix well so the honey is dissolved into the cream.

3 Pour all the wet ingredients into the dry and mix only until the dough is slightly wet and shaggy.

4 Pour out the shaggy dough onto a board and knead it by hand a few times until it comes together.

5 Divide the dough into 3 pieces. Pat the pieces into 8-inch rounds.

6 Cut each round into 6 or 8 triangle-shaped pieces. Paint each scone with cream and sprinkle with sugar.

7 Bake at 425°F for about 15 minutes or until golden brown and springy to the touch.

# GRANOLA SCONE

**YIELD:** 10 SCONES / **ACTIVE TIME:** 30 MINUTES / **TOTAL TIME:** 1 HOUR

Loaded with whole grains, dried fruits and nuts, this granola scone is unlike any you've ever had.
—*Jim Williams, Seven Stars Bakery*

1 Preheat your oven to 375°F. Combine dries and mix well. Add butter.

2 Add dried fruit and nuts and mix just until combined.

3 Add cream and mix lightly until combined.

4 Roll your dough out on table about 1-inch thick and then cut into individual shapes.

5 On a sheet pan, bake for 25–30 minutes.

**INGREDIENTS:**

- 1⅔ cups fresh-milled, stone-ground whole wheat flour
- 1⅛ teaspoons baking powder
- 1⅛ teaspoons baking soda
- ⅓ teaspoon salt
- 1⅛ teaspoons cinnamon
- ⅓ cup sugar
- ½ cup butter, cubed and chilled
- ½ cup heavy cream
- 2 cups rolled oats
- ½ cup raisins
- 1 cup tart dried cherries
- ½ cup pumpkin seeds
- ¾ cup whole, roasted almonds

# BACON CHIVE SCONES

YIELD: 24 2½-INCH SCONES / **ACTIVE TIME:** 1 HOUR / **TOTAL TIME:** 1 HOUR 15 MINUTES

Few snacks are as criminally underrated as the savory scone, and few savory snacks that aren't improved by bacon. This is a classic combination that allows for tons of variation. Try adding cheese and really making a meal out of it!
—*Stephany Buswell*

**INGREDIENTS:**

- ½ cup crispy bacon, cut into small pieces
- ¼ cup chives or green onions, chopped
- 6¾ cups all-purpose flour
- 1 tablespoon baking powder
- ¾ teaspoon baking soda
- 2 tablspoons sugar
- 1¼ teaspoons salt
- 2 sticks unsalted butter, cubed into ½-inch pieces
- 1½ cups buttermilk

**FOR THE TOPPING:**

- Cream or melted butter
- Sea salt

1 Combine the first 7 ingredients in a bowl mixer with a paddle attachment.

2 Add the cold cubed butter and mix until butter pieces are the size of hazelnuts. Add the buttermilk and mix just until it comes together.

3 Press the dough down and roll flat with a rolling pin.

4 Preheat the oven to 375°F. Using a 2½-inch round cutter, cut dough into desired shapes. Brush the tops with cream or butter and sprinkle with sea salt.

5 Bake at 375°F for about 12 to 15 minutes or until golden brown and springy in the center.

# CREAMY LEMON CURRANT SCONES

YIELD: 18 SCONES / ACTIVE TIME: 30 MINUTES / TOTAL TIME: 50 MINUTES

I developed these scones in the 1980s when I had my own bakery in Santa Cruz. My favorite breakfast place serves scones that have chunks of cream cheese inside—this is my version!
—*Stephany Buswell*

**INGREDIENTS:**

| | |
|---|---|
| 3½ | cups all-purpose flour |
| 1 | tablespoon baking powder |
| ½ | teaspoon baking soda |
| ¼ | cup sugar |
| ½ | teaspoon salt |
| 4 | ounces cold unsalted butter |
| 4 | ounces cold cream cheese |
| 3 | each eggs |
| ¼ | cup buttermilk |
| 3 | ounces dried currants |
| | Zest of 1 small lemon |

1 In a large bowl, mix together all the dry ingredients.

2 Using a pastry cutter or a stand-mixer with a paddle attachment, cut the butter and cream cheese into the flour until it looks like peas and walnuts. Be careful not to overmix at this point.

3 In a measuring cup, crack your eggs and add the buttermilk. Because egg sizes vary so much, make sure your total liquid is at least ½ cup. Add the lemon zest.

4 Pour all of the liquid ingredients into the dry bowl and mix on low—just until it barely comes together. Turn it out onto the table and, by hand, finish kneading the dough until it is a nice ball. Pat it into a rectangle and divide it into 3 sections.

5 With the ball of your hand pat each piece into a nice round circle, about ½ inch thick. Cut each patty into 6 pieces.

6 Preheat the oven to 375°F. Place the pieces on a sheet pan with parchment paper and egg-wash the top before baking.

7 Bake at 375°F for about 20 minutes or until golden brown and springy when touched.

# OAT SCONES *with* RAISINS *and* WALNUTS

YIELD: 12 LARGE SCONES / ACTIVE TIME: 20 MINUTES / TOTAL TIME: 50 MINUTES

These crunchy, freeform scones are fun to make, and with the endless possible combinations of fruits (bananas and pecans, figs and hazelnuts, golden raisins and walnuts, and pears and almonds, to name a few that we use at the bakery) it's easy to create a new taste sensation with every batch. In this recipe we use raisins and toasted walnuts.

—*Amy Scherber, Amy's Bread*

1 Position one rack in the top third of the oven, one rack in the bottom third of the oven, and preheat the oven to 400°F. Line the sheet pans with baking parchment.

2 In a food processor fitted with the metal blade, combine the 2 flours, sugar, baking powder, salt, cinnamon, and baking soda and process them for 5 seconds until they are just combined. Add the butter and process again for 10 to 15 seconds, until the mixture looks like coarse meal. The largest pieces of butter should be about the size of tiny peas. (If you don't have a food processor, mix the dry ingredients in a large bowl with a wire whisk and cut in the cold butter with a pastry blender or 2 knives.) The butter should be suspended in tiny granules throughout the flour, not rubbed into it to make a doughy mass.

3 Transfer this mixture to a large bowl and stir in the oats, raisins, and walnuts until they are evenly distributed.

4 In a small bowl, whisk together the buttermilk and egg. Remove ⅓ cup of this mixture and set it aside. Pour the remaining liquid over the dry ingredients and lightly and briefly stir them together, just until everything is barely moistened. It's fine if there is still a little bit of unmoistened flour in the bottom of the bowl. Don't overmix or your scones will be heavy and doughy. This dough won't be a single cohesive mass—it should look more like moistened clumps of flour and fruit.

5 Using your hands, drop free-form portions of dough about 3 ½ inches in diameter (4 ¼ ounces each) onto the prepared baking sheets. Evenly space 6 scones on each sheet. Don't try to press them down or squeeze them together—they should look like irregular mounds or clumps. Using a pastry brush, dab the reserved buttermilk/egg mixture all over the tops of the scones and sprinkle them lightly with turbinado sugar.

## INGREDIENTS:

- 1¾ cups + 1 tablespoon unbleached all-purpose flour
- ⅔ cup whole wheat pastry flour
- ½ cup sugar
- 1 tablespoon baking powder
- 1¼ teaspoons kosher salt
- 1 teaspoon cinnamon
- ¾ teaspoon baking soda
- 1¼ cups cold butter, unsalted and diced into ½-inch cubes
- 2⅓ cups old-fashioned rolled oats
- ⅞ cup raisins
- ¾ cup toasted walnuts, coarsely chopped
- 1½ cups buttermilk
- 1 large egg
- Turbinado sugar, for sprinkling

6 Place a pan on each oven rack and bake for 15 minutes. Reduce the oven temperature to 375°F and rotate the pans from top to bottom. Bake for 10 to 15 minutes longer, until the scones are a deep golden brown on both the top and bottom. A toothpick inserted in the center of a scone should come out clean.

7 Remove the scones from the pans to cool on a wire rack. Serve slightly warm or at room temperature. Store any leftovers in an airtight container. They're best if eaten within 2 days.

# BLUEBERRY SCONES

YIELD: 10 SCONES / **ACTIVE TIME:** 20 MINUTES / **TOTAL TIME:** 2½ HOURS

A classic breakfast pastry, every home baker should have a reliable blueberry scone recipe. Perfect for sit-down brunch or on-the-go eaters, this one should keep you stocked with scones for some time! (Read more on Winslow's Home on page 630.)
—*courtesy of Ann Lipton and Anna Long of Winslow's Home*

**INGREDIENTS:**

4½ cups all-purpose flour

¾ cup sugar

2 tablespoons baking powder

1 teaspoon salt

3 sticks butter

1½ cups cold heavy whipping cream, plus more for brushing

1 cup frozen blueberries

1 Cut butter in ½-inch cubes and put in the freezer for at least 45 minutes and up to overnight.

2 Mix flour, sugar, baking powder, and salt in a large bowl.

3 Toss butter in the dry ingredients, rubbing the butter between your fingers until it is the size of pea.

4 Add blueberries and toss in the flour/butter mixture until evenly distributed.

5 Drizzle in cream and work dough together until it forms one homogeneous mixture. Mixture may seem dry, but don't overmix!

6 Pat mixture into ¾-inch mound. Using a 3-inch ring cutter, cut scones out of dough. Gently work leftover dough back together and continue to cut scones until the dough runs out. Scones can be baked right away or frozen for up to 1 month. For best results, freeze for at least 1 hour before baking.

7 Preheat the oven to 375°F. Before baking, brush the tops with heavy cream and sprinkle with sugar.

8 Bake at 375 for 18 to 25 minutes, until golden brown. Scones should be served same day.

# WHOLE WHEAT CHERRY SCONE

YIELD: 18 SCONES / ACTIVE TIME: 20 MINUTES / TOTAL TIME: 2 HOURS 45 MINUTES, MORE IF CHILLING OVERNIGHT

This recipe is easy, fast, and—best of all—delicious; whole wheat lovers will find themselves coming back to it time and time again! — *Wendy Smith Born and James Barrett, Metropolitan Bakery*

1 In the bowl of a heavy-duty mixer, combine all-purpose and whole wheat flours, 1¼ cups of the granulated sugar, baking powder, baking soda, salt, oats, and orange zest. Add the butter to the flour mixture and toss.

2 With a paddle attachment at low speed, mix the butter into the flour mixture until the mixture resembles a coarse meal. Stir in the dried cherries. Add the buttermilk and mix until the dough is evenly moistened and beginning to come together.

3 Scoop the dough onto a lightly floured surface. With lightly floured hands, press the dough together into a ball. Divide the dough into 3 equal pieces. Gently round and flatten each piece into a ¾-inch-thick disk. Wrap each disk in plastic wrap and refrigerate for at least 2 hours, or overnight if possible.

4 When ready to bake, preheat the oven to 375°F. Line 2 large baking sheets with parchment paper or use nonstick baking sheets.

5 Unwrap the disks and place on a cutting board. Cut each disk into 6 equal wedges. Brush the tops lightly with the cream and sprinkle with the remaining 2 tablespoons granulated sugar. Separate the wedges, then transfer, 2 inches apart, to the preparing baking sheets.

6 Bake for 25 minutes or until golden, rotating the baking sheets between the upper and lower oven racks halfway through baking. Cool on wire racks and serve lightly warm.

## INGREDIENTS:

- 3 cups all-purpose flour
- 1½ cups whole wheat flour
- 1¼ cups + 2 tablespoons granulated sugar
- 1 tablespoon plus 1 ¼ teaspoons baking powder
- 1½ teaspoons baking soda
- 1½ teaspoons kosher salt
- 3¾ cups old-fashioned oats
- Grated zest of 2 oranges
- 2 cups (4 sticks) cold unsalted butter, cut into small cubes
- 1½ cups dried tart cherries
- 1¼ cups buttermilk
- 2 tablespoons heavy or whipping cream

# BLUEBERRY SCONES

**YIELDS:** 4 TO 6 SERVINGS / **ACTIVE TIME:** 30 MINUTES / **TOTAL TIME:** 50 MINUTES

These are delicious whenever you eat them, but they're especially good about 15 minutes after you take them out of the oven, slathered with butter!
—*Dominique DeVito*

**INGREDIENTS:**

- 3 cups flour
- ⅓ cup sugar
- 2½ teaspoons baking powder
- ½ teaspoon baking soda
- 1 teaspoon salt
- ¾ cup (1½ sticks) unsalted butter, chilled and cut into pieces
- 1 tablespoon orange zest
- 1 cup milk or half-and-half
- 1 cup fresh blueberries

1 Preheat the oven to 400°F. Position a rack in the middle of the oven.

2 In a large bowl, whisk together the flour, sugar, baking powder, baking soda, and salt. Add the butter pieces and mix with an electric mixer until just blended, or mix with a fork so that the dough is somewhat crumbly.

3 Stir in the orange zest and milk, and gently fold in the blueberries, being careful not to overmix.

4 With flour on your hands, transfer the dough to a lightly floured surface. Form the dough into a circle about ½-inch thick. With a long knife, cut the dough into 12 wedges.

5 Butter the skillet, and put the scone wedges in a circle in it, leaving some space between the pieces. Bake for 20 to 25 minutes, or until golden.

6 If desired, sprinkle with some additional sugar when just out of the oven.

## VARIATIONS:

Substitute fresh cranberries for the blueberries, or use a blend of ½ cup blueberries and ½ cup cranberries.

Substitute dried fruit for the blueberries: ½ cup dried cherries or dried sweetened cranberries.

CAST-IRON SKILLET RECIPE

# SAVORY SCONES

**YIELDS:** 4 TO 6 SERVINGS / **ACTIVE TIME:** 30 MINUTES / **TOTAL TIME:** 50 MINUTES

These cheesy scones with extra black pepper are a nice complement to scrambled eggs. You can also split them and use them as the bread for a nice ham-and-egg breakfast sandwich. Or enjoy them in the afternoon with a cup of tea.
—*Dominique DeVito*

**INGREDIENTS:**

- **2** cups flour
- **1** teaspoon baking powder
- **½** teaspoon salt
- **1** teaspoon freshly ground black pepper
- **½** teaspoon dry mustard
- **4** tablespoons butter, chilled, cut into pieces
- **½** cup grated sharp cheddar cheese
- **½** cup milk
- **1** egg beaten with a little milk

**1** Preheat the oven to 400°F. Position a rack in the middle of the oven.

**2** In a large bowl, whisk together the flour, baking powder, salt, pepper, and dry mustard. Add the butter pieces and mix with an electric mixer until just blended, or mix with a fork so that the dough is somewhat crumbly.

**3** Stir in the cheese and milk, being careful not to over-mix.

**4** With flour on your hands, transfer the dough to a lightly floured surface. Form the dough into a circle about ½-inch thick. With a long knife, cut the dough into 6 to 8 wedges.

**5** Butter the skillet, and put the scone wedges in a circle in it, leaving some space between the pieces.

**6** Brush with the beaten egg. Bake for 20 to 25 minutes, or until golden.

## VARIATIONS:

Substitute ½ cup freshly grated aged cheese like Pecorino-Romano or a nutty-flavored cheese like Havarti for some different flavor profiles.

For an added breakfast treat, include bacon bits in the dough. Add about ⅓ cup crumbled bacon or bacon bits to the dough when adding the cheese and milk.

# CHEDDAR JALAPEÑO SCONES

**YIELDS:** 4 TO 6 SERVINGS / **ACTIVE TIME:** 30 MINUTES / **TOTAL TIME:** 50 MINUTES

The spiciness of the jalapeño livens up any breakfast. I like to split the cooked scones in half and top with a spoonful of sour cream and some sliced avocado.

—*Dominique DeVito*

1 Preheat the oven to 400 degrees. Position a rack in the middle of the oven.

2 In a large bowl, whisk together the flour, baking powder, salt, and pepper. Add the butter pieces and mix with an electric mixer until just blended, or mix with a fork so that the dough is somewhat crumbly.

3 Stir in the cheese, peppers, and milk, being careful not to overmix.

4 With flour on your hands, transfer the dough to a lightly floured surface. Form the dough into a circle about ½-inch thick. With a long knife, cut the dough into 6 to 8 wedges.

5. Butter the skillet, and put the scone wedges in a circle in it, leaving some space between the pieces.

6 Brush with the beaten egg. Bake for 20 to 25 minutes, or until golden.

**INGREDIENTS:**

- 2 cups flour
- 1 teaspoon baking powder
- ½ teaspoon salt
- 1 teaspoon freshly ground black pepper
- 4 tablespoons butter, chilled, cut into pieces
- ¾ cup grated sharp cheddar cheese
- ½ cup sliced or chopped jalapeño peppers
- ½ cup milk
- 1 egg beaten with a little milk

Wear gloves when working with hot peppers so you don't get the oils in your eyes or other thin-skinned areas, as they irritate and burn.

CAST-IRON SKILLET RECIPE

# SOUR CREAM *and* DILL SCONES

YIELDS: 4 TO 6 SERVINGS / ACTIVE TIME: 30 MINUTES / TOTAL TIME: 50 MINUTES

Dill is so fragrant and distinctive—you either like it or you don't. If you do, these scones will have you coming back for seconds or thirds. Try serving them with smoked salmon.
—*Dominique DeVito*

**INGREDIENTS:**

- 2 cups flour
- 1 teaspoon baking powder
- ½ teaspoon salt
- 1 teaspoon freshly ground black pepper
- 4 tablespoons butter, chilled, cut into pieces
- ¾ cup sour cream
- 1 tablespoon finely chopped fresh dill
- 1 egg beaten with a little milk

1 Preheat the oven to 400°F. Position a rack in the middle of the oven.

2 In a large bowl, whisk together the flour, baking powder, salt, and pepper. Add the butter pieces and mix with an electric mixer until just blended, or mix with a fork so that the dough is somewhat crumbly.

3 Stir in the sour cream and dill, being careful not to overmix.

4 With flour on your hands, transfer the dough to a lightly floured surface. Form the dough into a circle about ½-inch thick. With a long knife, cut the dough into 6 to 8 wedges.

5 Butter the skillet, and put the scone wedges in a circle in it, leaving some space between the pieces.

6 Brush with the beaten egg. Bake for 20 to 25 minutes, or until golden.

# ROSEMARY BLACK PEPPER SCONES

**YIELDS:** 4 TO 6 SERVINGS / **ACTIVE TIME:** 30 MINUTES / **TOTAL TIME:** 50 MINUTES

While these are a bit savory for an early breakfast, they are a hit for brunch, when they can very nicely complement a simple omelet and a mimosa with fresh orange juice.
—*Dominique DeVito*

1 Preheat the oven to 400°F. Position a rack in the middle of the oven.

2 In a large bowl, whisk together the flour, baking powder, baking soda, and salt. Add the butter pieces and mix with an electric mixer until just blended, or mix with a fork so that the dough is somewhat crumbly.

3 Stir in the rosemary, black pepper, and milk, being careful not to overmix.

4 With flour on your hands, transfer the dough to a lightly floured surface. Form the dough into a circle about ½-inch thick. With a long knife, cut the dough into 12 wedges.

5 Butter the skillet, and put the scone wedges in a circle in it, leaving some space between the pieces. Bake for 20 to 25 minutes, or until golden.

**INGREDIENTS:**

3 cups flour

2½ teaspoons baking powder

½ teaspoon baking soda

1 teaspoon salt

¾ cup (1½ sticks) unsalted butter, chilled and cut into pieces

1 tablespoon crumbled dried rosemary

1 tablespoon freshly ground black pepper

1 cup milk or half-and-half

# OLIVE-FETA SCONES

CAST-IRON SKILLET RECIPE

YIELDS: 4 TO 6 SERVINGS / ACTIVE TIME: 30 MINUTES / TOTAL TIME: 50 MINUTES

Here's a recipe that shines with the flavors of Greece and the Mediterranean. Another great accompaniment to eggs at breakfast, or salad at lunch, or eggplant parmigiana at dinner. Who's hungry?
—*Dominique DeVito*

**INGREDIENTS:**

- 1¾ cups all-purpose flour
- 2 teaspoons baking powder
- ¼ teaspoon salt
- 6 tablespoons unsalted butter, chilled, cut into pieces
- ½ cup crumbled feta cheese
- ½ cup pitted Kalamata olives, chopped, drained on paper towels
- 1 teaspoon ground black pepper
- ½ cup plain yogurt
- 5 tablespoons milk, divided

1 Preheat the oven to 400°F.

2 In a large bowl, whisk together the flour, baking powder, and salt. Add 4 tablespoons of the butter pieces and mix with an electric mixer until just blended, or mix with a fork so that the dough is somewhat crumbly. Stir in the feta, olives, and pepper.

3 In small bowl, combine yogurt with 3 tablespoons of the milk. Add this to the flour mixture and stir until the dough comes together. It will be moist.

4 With flour on your hands, transfer the dough to a lightly floured surface. Form the dough into a circle about ½-inch thick. With a long knife, cut the dough into 6 to 8 wedges.

5 Melt the additional 2 tablespoons butter in the skillet, and put the scone wedges in a circle in it, leaving some space between the pieces. Brush with the remaining milk, and bake for 20 to 25 minutes, or until golden.

# LEMON POPPY SEED MUFFINS

YIELD: 12–15 MUFFINS / ACTIVE TIME: 45 MINUTES / TOTAL TIME: 1 HOUR 10 MINUTES

Lemon is such a bright and refreshing flavor—it brightens all it comes in contact with. This recipe uses lemon juice, but if you'd like to bump up the lemon flavor you can add the zest of the lemons you are juicing.
—*Stephany Buswell*

1 Preheat the oven to 350°F. Line muffin tins with paper liners.

2 In the bowl of a stand-mixer, cream the butter and sugar until smooth. Add the eggs one at a time. Scrape the sides of the bowl down well and mix the batter until smooth.

3 Add the sour cream and lemon juice. Mix until combined.

4 Add the dry ingredients and the poppy seeds. Do not overmix at this point—mix just until the dry ingredients are incorporated.

5 Scoop the batter into the muffin cups and bake for 18–20 minutes.

**INGREDIENTS:**

1 cube (4 ounces) butter, unsalted

¾ cup sugar

2 eggs

1 cup sour cream

3 tablespoons lemon juice

1⅔ cups all-purpose flour

1 teaspoon baking soda

1 teaspoon salt

2 tablespoons poppy seeds

You can also make a simple glaze from powdered sugar (1 cup) and lemon juice (3 tablespoons). Pour this over the muffins while they are still hot—it will keep them moist and lemony!

# PUMPKIN WALNUT MUFFINS

YIELD: 12 MUFFINS / ACTIVE TIME: 30 MINUTES / TOTAL TIME: 55 MINUTES

Nothing could be better on a crisp autumn day than Metro's pumpkin walnut muffins and a cup of coffee. Try making the puree yourself or substitute canned pumpkin.
— *Wendy Smith Born and James Barrett, Metropolitan Bakery*

1 Preheat the oven to 375°F. Butter 12 2½-inch (½ cup) muffin-pan cups.

2 In the bowl of a heavy-duty mixer, sift together the flour, cinnamon, baking powder, baking soda, salt, ginger, nutmeg, and cloves. Stir in the granulated and brown sugars. Add the butter with the flour mixture and toss. With a paddle attachment at low speed, mix the butter into the flour mixture until the mixture resembles a coarse meal.

3 In a medium bowl, whisk the eggs; stir into the flour mixture. Stir in the pumpkin puree, milk, and vanilla, just until blended. With a rubber spatula, fold in the walnuts.

4 Spoon the batter evenly into prepared muffin pan cups. Bake 15 to 20 minutes, rotating the muffin pans between upper and lower oven racks halfway through baking until a wooden skewer inserted in the center of a muffin comes out clean. Cool the muffins in the pan 5 minutes. Remove the muffins from the pans and cool completely on wire racks.

## PREPARING PUMPKIN PUREE

1 To prepare pumpkin puree, preheat the oven to 375°F. Cut 1 sugar pumpkin in half and scoop out the seeds.

2 Place the pumpkin halves, cut side–down, in a roasting pan. Add 1 cup water to the pan and bake for 45 minutes or until the skin wrinkles.

3 Remove the pumpkin from the pan. When cool enough to handle, scoop out the flesh.

**INGREDIENTS:**

- 2 cups all-purpose flour
- 1 ½ teaspoons ground cinnamon
- 1 ⅛ teaspoons baking powder
- 1 ⅛ teaspoons baking soda
- ½ teaspoon salt
- ¼ teaspoon ground ginger
- ¼ teaspoon ground nutmeg
- ⅛ teaspoon ground cloves
- 1 cup granulated sugar
- 1 cup dark brown sugar, firmly packed
- 5 tablespoons cold butter, unsalted and cut into small cubes
- 3 large eggs
- 1 cup + 2 tablespoons pumpkin puree, fresh or canned (see "Preparing Pumpkin Puree")
- ⅓ cup of milk
- 1 teaspoon vanilla extract
- 1⅓ cups chopped walnuts, toasted (see "Toasting Nuts")

4 Press the flesh through affine sieve set over a bowl. Clean the sieve, then line it with a double layer of cheesecloth and set over another bowl.

5 Spoon the puree into the sieve and drain in the refrigerator overnight.

## TOASTING NUTS

Toasting nuts releases their natural oils. If toasted too long, nuts become bitter, so it's best to toast lightly to bring out a robust nutty flavor. To toast, preheat oven to 325°F. Spread nuts evenly on a baking sheet. Bake on the center oven rack for 10 to 12 minutes, or until fragrant and toasted. Let cool.

# METROPOLITAN MILLET MUFFIN

YIELD: 24 MUFFINS / ACTIVE TIME: 30 MINUTES / TOTAL TIME: 55 MINUTES

Millet, a grain that has been around for generations, is prized for its high protein content. Toasting it lightly will give this otherwise bland grain a crunchy texture and nutty flavor that really shines through in these tasty muffins.

— *Wendy Smith Born and James Barrett, Metropolitan Bakery*

**INGREDIENTS:**

- 4 cups all-purpose flour
- 2½ teaspoons baking powder
- 1½ teaspoons kosher salt
- 1 teaspoon baking soda
- 2 cups millet, lightly toasted and cooled (see "Toasting Millet")
- 6 large eggs
- ½ cup milk
- 2 teaspoons vanilla extract
- ¾ cups (1½ sticks) unsalted butter, softened
- 2 cups dark brown sugar, firmly packed

1 Preheat oven to 375°F. Butter 2 regular-sized muffin tins (24 cups total).

2 In a large bowl, sift together the flour, baking powder, salt, and baking soda. Stir in the millet. In a small bowl, whisk together the eggs, milk, and vanilla.

3 In the bowl of a heavy-duty mixer with a paddle attachment, beat the butter and brown sugar until light and fluffy. At low speed, add the flour mixture alternately with the egg mixture, beginning and ending with the flour mixture, just until blended. Careful not to overmix!

4 Spoon the batter evenly into the prepared muffin cups. Bake for 15 to 20 minutes, rotating the muffin pans between the upper and lower oven racks halfway through the baking, until a wooden skewer comes out clean from the center of a muffin.

5 Cool the muffins in the pans for 5 minutes. Remove the muffins from the pans and cool completely on a wire rack.

## TOASTING MILLET

To toast your millet properly, preheat the oven to 350°F. Spread the millet in an even layer on a baking sheet. Bake on the center oven rack for 12 to 15 minutes, or until golden brown.

# (LIGHTER THAN A) CLOUD BISCUITS

YIELD: 16 BISCUITS / ACTIVE TIME: 45 MINUTES / TOTAL TIME: 1 HOUR 45 MINUTES

These are amazing with butter and honey or with gravy…really, they're amazing with anything. I can't stop eating them! Remember: You will need a 2½-inch round biscuit cutter for this recipe.
—*Stephany Buswell*

1 Adjust oven racks to upper-middle and lower-middle positions and heat oven to 150°F. Maintain temperature for 10 to 15 minutes, then turn off oven. Line two baking sheets with parchment paper.

2 Stir buttermilk and yeast together until dissolved. In standing mixer bowl fitted with paddle attachment, mix flour, baking powder, baking soda, sugar, and salt on low speed until combined.

3 Add the chilled butter and mix until just incorporated, about 1 minute. Slowly mix in buttermilk mixture until dough comes together, about 1 minute. Fit mixer with dough hook and mix on low speed until dough is shiny and smooth, about 3 minutes.

4 On lightly floured surface, knead dough briefly to form smooth ball. Roll dough into 10-inch circle, about ½ inch–thick. Using a 2½-inch biscuit cutter dipped in flour, cut out rounds and transfer to prepared baking sheets. Gather remaining dough and pat into ½-inch-thick circle. Cut remaining biscuits and transfer to baking sheets. Cover dough with kitchen towels and place in warm oven. Let rise until doubled in size, about 30 minutes.

5 Remove baking sheets from oven and heat oven to 350°F. Once the oven is fully heated, remove kitchen towels and bake until biscuits are golden brown, about 12 to 14 minutes, switching and rotating sheets halfway through baking. Remove from oven and brush tops with melted butter. Serve while warm.

## INGREDIENTS:

- **1** cup buttermilk, heated to 110°F
- **1** envelope (2 ¼ teaspoons) instant or rapid-rise yeast
- **2½** cups bleached all-purpose flour, plus extra for work surface
- **2** teaspoons baking powder
- **½** teaspoon baking soda
- **½** tablespoon sugar
- **1** teaspoon salt
- **8** tablespoons chilled butter, unsalted and cut into ½-inch pieces
- **2** tablespoons melted butter, unsalted

# BUTTERMILK BISCUITS

YIELD: 6-8 SERVINGS / *ACTIVE TIME:* 15 MINUTES / TOTAL TIME: 1 HOUR

In my experience, the best way to make the perfect flaky, melt-in-your-mouth biscuit is by turning the dough a few times like would with croissants, being careful not to overdevelop the dough and make them tough. Be sure to flour your cutter after each cut so the layers do not stick together, ensuring the highest and most even rise.

—*Stephany Buswell*

**INGREDIENTS:**

2    cups all-purpose flour

1    cup cake flour

1    tablespoon baking powder

½    teaspoon baking soda

¾    teaspoon salt

1½   cubes cold butter, unsalted

1¼   cups cold buttermilk

1  Mix all the dry ingredients together in a medium bowl.

2  Using either a pastry blender or a box grater, cut in the butter until hazelnut- or macadamia-nut-sized pieces are formed. Using a fork, toss the dry ingredients while pouring in the buttermilk. Only use enough to create a shaggy dough—it should still have dry parts. Reserve any remaining buttermilk.

3  Form a ball in your hands. If it is not holding together, add a bit more buttermilk.

4  Place the dough on a floured surface and pat the dough into a ½-inch-thick rectangle. Fold the dough in half and pat it out again. Do this 3 times total, then roll the dough out to a 1-inch-thick rectangle.

5  Using a 2-inch round cutter dipped in flour, cut out biscuits and place on a parchment lined sheet pan. Reroll the scraps and refrigerate the dough for 30 minutes.

6  Brush the tops with the remaining buttermilk.

7  Bake at 425°F in the oven for 14 to 16 minutes or until golden.

# MAINE GRAINS.

## Maine Grains

42 Court Street
Skowhegan, Maine 04976
(207) 474-8001
www.mainegrains.com

Not every local grain movement can be traced to a specific event—but then again, Skowhegan's wasn't exactly a normal graine renaissance. "Having lost jobs in the paper, shoemaking, agricultural, and woolen industries, Skowhegan was focused on its assets. Then grassroots organizers co-founded The Kneading Conference, a gathering of bakers, grain growers, millers, and wood-fired oven builders who planned to rebuild a lost grain economy. We took local expertise and convened with people from around the world to form a conference that would focus on "local bread." So says Amber Lambke of Maine Grains and the Maine Grain Alliance. Situated in the Somerset Grist Mill, a repurposed historic jailhouse, Maine Grains is helping to restore downtown Skowhegan's vibrant economic center.

Since the first Kneading Conference in 2007, the movement has grown significantly. Today, places like Maine Grains seek to both inspire and learn from independent mills all across the world. As Lambke puts it, "Our mill has created opportunity and hope, for farmers, bakers, brewers, and our employees. The mill connects people around a basic thing—grain, a staple food that sustains us. Maine Grains restores a sense of self-reliance and instills shared purpose in our foodshed."

It's a testament to Lambke's passion that "a small scrappy mill town in central Maine has taken center stage in the revival of regional grain farming, village bakeries, and real bread." How do they do it? Easy: "focusing on the grains!" The mill at Maine Grains turns slowly, keeping the flour cool and preserving its inherent flavor. Moreover, it preserves many of the nutrients found in the grains prior to the milling process. Their high quality products have made for some very happy—and very successful—bakers.

# IN HER OWN WORDS:

## AMBER LAMBKE OF MAINE GRAINS

*Who—or what—first inspired you to begin milling and baking? Who inspires you now?*

At that first Kneading Conference in 2007, I was inspired to learn that in 1837, our county produced 239,000 bushels of wheat—enough to feed 100,000 people in a county that only has half that number now. This helped me see that it was not a question of if we could grow wheat in Maine, but how we would regain that capacity. I traveled around the northeast, visited Kansas State University, and later went to Denmark. The millers I met there inspired me to focus on organic grain production and stone milling as a pathway to restoring good bread in my community.

*What are your golden rules for milling? What about for baking?*

Start with high quality grain, mill slowly, keep the stones cool, and the flour will feel alive. As a home baker using our freshly milled grains, I approach baking as though there is no such thing as mistakes! Experimentation leads to discovery. The future of bread lies in age-old techniques that we are only just beginning to re-learn.

*What is your favorite thing to bake? Why? Least favorite thing to bake? Why?*

I love to make pie crust with our stone-milled flour. It is the perfect vehicle to deliver the fresh fruit of the season, as well as our local eggs and garden vegetables. That said, I also love making biscuits, which are an important part of our local heritage; our gristmill (page 434) is housed in an old jail building that was once home to Alley Perry, a famed inmate baker who made biscuits for the community.

*What is your favorite type of grain? Why? Least favorite grain? Why?*

I love heritage red fife wheat. It makes the most aromatic flour and flavorful, sweet loaves. My least favorite grain is quinoa because it has an awkward texture and a peculiar cult status.

*How did Maine Grains come to be? Why Skowhegan, ME? What are your most popular items?*

Before this, I was a community organizer and speech pathologist. Maine Grains came to be when I partnered with friend and baker Michael Scholz to restore the infrastructure for processing organic locally grown grain in Maine. We launched the mill in 2012, and our most popular products are now the stone-ground whole wheat and sifted flours, and rolled oats.

*Where do you get your tools/materials? What non-essential items should every home baker have?*

I like to shop antique stores for old baking tools. Every home baker should have a cast iron griddle for making English muffins, baskets for proofing loaves, and a Dutch oven or cloche for baking loaves with a shiny crisp crust.

*What book goes on your required reading list for bakers?*

Being a homemaker, I particularly enjoy the very approachable message in Andy and Jackie King's *Baking By Hand*.

*What outlets/periodicals/newspapers do you read or consult regularly?*

I read *BREAD Magazine*, the *New York Times* Food Section, the *FeedFeed*, and the Bread Bakers Guild of America newsletter.

*Tell me about your most memorable collaboration with another chef.*

I am always inspired to watch Amy Halloran, "Flour Ambassador" and author of *The New Breadbasket*, teach workshops on baking and making pancakes. Amy boils baking down to a simple and intuitive process that can be easily accessed by all. She follows grain from the field to the griddle and uses pancakes as a means to teach about history and agriculture.

*Do you follow any cooking shows or chefs? If so, which is your favorite?*

I have lived without a television for the last 20 years and so have missed some of the pop culture around cooking shows and chef personalities. That said, I do enjoy the TED Talks and writings of Dan Barber, Michael Pollan, Mark Bittman, Alice Waters, and others who understand food in the context of agriculture.

*Where did you learn to bake? Please tell me about your education and apprenticeships.*

From my Mom! I am not formally trained at all. I benefitted from baking in the home growing up, and now from the world-class talent that convenes here in my hometown each July for The Kneading Conference, two full days of baking, oven building, and grain workshops.

# PERRY'S JAILHOUSE BISCUITS

YIELD: ABOUT 12 BISCUITS / ACTIVE TIME: 45 MINUTES / TOTAL TIME: 1 HOUR

I love making biscuits, and I make these to acknowledge Alley Perry, the famed inmate baker who made biscuits for the community out of our old jail building where the gristmill is housed.
—*Amber Lambke of Maine Grains*

**INGREDIENTS:**

- 1¾ cups Maine Grains sifted flour
- 2½ teaspoons baking powder
- 1 teaspoon coarse salt
- 6 tablespoons chilled butter, unsalted
- ¾ cup buttermilk

1 Whisk together flour, baking powder, and salt in a bowl. We like to use a cheese grater to grate the cold butter stick into the flour bowl. Toss the flour and grated butter together. Add buttermilk slowly, stirring with a fork to moisten all of the dry ingredients evenly.

2 Turn the dough out onto a clean, lightly floured surface and gently knead just to bring the dough together. Gently roll out the dough about ¾ inch–thick.

3 Using a biscuit cutter or bench scraper (depending on whether you want round or square biscuits), cut about 12 biscuits, rerolling any scraps.

4 Place on a baking sheet lined with parchment paper. Bake the biscuits at 400°F for 13 to 15 minutes until golden brown. Cool slightly and serve warm with butter, homemade preserves, or as Alley Perry did, with molasses.

# WHOLE WHEAT YOGURT BISCUITS

**YIELD:** 18 MEDIUM-SIZED BISCUITS / **ACTIVE TIME:** 30 MINUTES / **TOTAL TIME:** 45 MINUTES

Biscuits are the best. All that butter, and you can put on the same delicious toppings you would on a piece of toast. Half-and-half and Greek yogurt make these rich and fluffy, and you can make them even fluffier by refrigerating the dough between steps. Consider adding finely chopped herbs, grated cheese, or black pepper. —*courtesy of Bob Klein and Phoebe Plank of Community Grains and adapted from www.thekitchn.com*

1 Preheat the oven to 450°F. Line a sheet pan with parchment paper.

2 In a medium mixing bowl, combine flour, baking powder, salt, baking soda, and salt, plus any additions, and stir to incorporate. Cut the butter into razor-thin slices, then add to the dry ingredients and toss to coat with flour. (Optional: place the bowl in the freezer for 5 to 10 minutes before continuing.)

3 Gently fold the Greek yogurt into the dry ingredients, stirring until most of the flour is mixed in. Stir in the half-and-half a splash or two at a time, until the dough begins to come together. Then, turn the dough out onto a floured work surface and knead just until it forms a smooth ball, about 10 to 15 seconds. (Optional: chill the dough in the fridge for 15 to 30 minutes before rolling.)

4 Pat the dough into a ½ inch–thick round. Flour a sharp biscuit or circular cutter and cut out biscuits as close together as possible. Do not twist the cutter—press straight down and pull straight up. Use a bench scraper or spatula to transfer biscuits to the prepared baking sheet, spacing them about ½ inch apart. Reroll the scraps and cut to make more biscuits.

5 Bake the biscuits for 12 to 14 minutes, rotating halfway through cooking time, until tall and golden brown. Remove from the oven and allow to cool for 5 minutes before serving, then get out the butter and jam!

**INGREDIENTS:**

- 2 cups Community Grains Hard Red Winter Wheat, plus more for rolling
- 1 tablespoon baking powder
- 1¼ teaspoons kosher salt
- 1 teaspoon baking soda
- 4 tablespoons (2 ounces) cold butter, unsalted
- ½ cup + 2 tablespoons nonfat Greek yogurt, plain
- ½–1 cup (or more!) of cold half-and-half

CAST-IRON SKILLET RECIPE

# BISCUITS

YIELDS: 4 TO 6 SERVINGS / ACTIVE TIME: 20 MINUTES / TOTAL TIME: 40 MINUTES

For fluffy biscuits, you need to work with a very hot skillet. The golden brown crust on the bottom is as much of a delight as the airy, warm dough.
—*Dominique DeVito*

**INGREDIENTS:**

| | |
|---|---|
| 2 | cups flour |
| 1 | teaspoon sugar |
| 1 | teaspoon salt |
| 1 | tablespoon baking powder |
| 6 to 8 | tablespoons butter, cut into pieces |
| ½ | cup + 2 tablespoons buttermilk |

**1** Preheat oven to 450°F.

**2** In a large bowl, combine the flour, sugar, salt, and baking powder.

**3** Using a fork or pastry knife, blend in 6 tablespoons of the butter to form crumbly dough. Form a well in the middle and add ½ cup buttermilk. Stir to combine and form a stiff dough. Using your fingers works best! If it seems too dry, add 1 tablespoon more of the buttermilk, going to 2 tablespoons if necessary.

**4** Put 2 tablespoons butter in the skillet and put it in the oven to melt while the skillet heats.

**5** Put the dough on a lightly floured surface and press out to a thickness of about 1 inch. Press out biscuits using an inverted water glass. Place the biscuits in the skillet and bake for about 10 minutes, until golden on the bottom.

Biscuits are another buttery bread that can be served with savory or sweet additions. You can make mini ham sandwiches by splitting the biscuits, putting some mayonnaise and grainy mustard on them, and putting in a slice of fresh-baked ham. You can fill them with scrambled eggs and bacon bits. Or you can slather them with butter and your favorite jam or honey. Or just eat them as-is.

# GLUTEN-FREE BISCUITS

**YIELD:** 4 TO 6 SERVINGS / **ACTIVE TIME:** 20 MINUTES / **TOTAL TIME:** 40 MINUTES

It is possible to make delicious gluten-free biscuits, though they'll be a bit more crumbly than those made with regular flour.
—*Dominique DeVito*

**1** Preheat oven to 450°F.

**2** In a large bowl, combine the flours, baking powder, sugar, cream of tartar, salt, and xanthan gum. Using a fork or pastry knife, blend in 5 tablespoons of the butter to form crumbly dough.

**3** Form a well in the middle and add ½ cup buttermilk. Stir to combine and form a stiff dough. Using your fingers works best! If it seems too dry, add 1 tablespoon more of the buttermilk, going to 2 tablespoons if necessary.

**4** Put 2 tablespoons butter in the skillet and put it in the oven to melt while the skillet heats.

**5** Put the dough on a lightly floured surface and press out to a thickness of about 1 inch. Press out biscuits using an inverted water glass. Place the biscuits in the skillet and bake for about 10 minutes, until golden on the bottom.

**INGREDIENTS:**

| | |
|---|---|
| 1½ | **cups rice flour** |
| ⅓ | **cup potato starch** |
| 3 | **tablespoons tapioca flour** |
| 1 | **tablespoon baking powder** |
| 3 | **teaspoons maple sugar, or 1 tablespoon maple syrup** |
| 2 | **teaspoons cream of tartar** |
| ¼ | **teaspoon salt** |
| 1 | **teaspoon xanthan gum** |
| 5 to 7 | **tablespoons butter** |
| ½ | **cup + 2 tablespoons buttermilk** |

# POPOVERS

YIELD: 12 PASTRIES / ACTIVE TIME: 15 MINUTES / TOTAL TIME: 35 MINUTES

Popovers and Yorkshire pudding are very similar pastries. The main difference is that Yorkshire pudding is baked in very hot meat fat rendered from your beef roast, while popovers are baked in a hot pan without any fat at all. The best pan to use is a popover pan; it typically has six vessels for the batter and they are much deeper than muffin tins, providing you with a very tall and hollow type of biscuit.

Popovers must be eaten immediately from the oven since they will collapse. Personally, I have no problem breaking one open, slathering it with fresh butter, and eating it piping hot!

One last note: Have all your ingredients at room temperature. If they are not but you are ready to bake, put the eggs in a bowl of hot water for a few minutes and heat the milk to lukewarm in the microwave.

—*Stephany Buswell*

### INGREDIENTS:

3  eggs

1½  cups milk

1½  cups all-purpose flour

½  teaspoon salt

2  tablespoons melted butter

1 Preheat your oven to 450°F. Whisk together the milk and eggs until you cannot see any sign of the egg yolk. Whisk briskly, making a nice foamy liquid. This will help the dough to rise.

2 Now whisk in the flour and salt. Make sure all the large lumps are worked out and creating bubbles is a good thing. Stir in the melted butter.

3 Put the popover pan in the oven for 2 minutes right before you are to pan the batter. After 2 minutes, fill the cups up ¾ of the way.

4 Place in hot oven for 20 minutes. Reduce heat to 350°F and bake for another 20 minutes, checking to make sure they don't get too brown on top. If they begin to get too dark, place your pan on a sheet pan and move it lower in the oven. If you want them to be crispier, you can keep them in the oven a bit longer. Just be careful that they don't get too dark!

5 Remove from heat, immediately turn them out of the pan, and serve.

# GIANT YORKSHIRE PUDDING

**YIELDS:** 4 TO 6 SERVINGS / **ACTIVE TIME:** 30 MINUTES / **TOTAL TIME:** 60 MINUTES

This incredible treat is like a savory Dutch baby—a large (and so delicious!) popover. It's traditionally served with roast beef and is, in fact, made with the juices from the meat. Begin your preparation about an hour before the meat will be ready, as the batter needs to sit for a while. My mouth waters just thinking about this classic combination.

—*Dominique DeVito*

**INGREDIENTS:**

- 1½ cups flour
- ¾ teaspoon salt
- ¾ cup milk, room temperature
- 3 large eggs, room temperature
- ¾ cup water, room temperature
- ½ cup beef drippings

1 Preheat the oven to 400°F or increase the temperature when you take your roast beef out of the oven.

2 In a large bowl, mix the flour and salt together with a whisk. Make a well in the center of the flour, add the milk and whisk until blended. Next beat the eggs into the batter until thoroughly combined. Add the water, stir this in thoroughly, and set aside for about an hour.

3 When your roast comes out of the oven, pour off ½ cup of drippings and put them in the skillet. Put the skillet in the oven and let the drippings get very hot so that they sizzle. Stir the batter while you're waiting so it's blended. Remove the skillet from the oven, pour the batter in, and return it immediately.

4 Bake for about 30 minutes or until the sides have risen and are gently browned.

5 Bring to the table where the roast beef awaits, and serve with extra juices on the side.

If you want to make this delicious side dish but you're not having roast beef, you can substitute ½ cup melted butter for the drippings. Their smoking point is lower than the drippings, so keep an eye on the skillet as it heats up in the oven. The butter will be sizzling before long.

# YORKSHIRE PUDDINGS

These lovely light breads are a modern invention. It seems like they were unknown before the end of the 18th century, and were created to use the wheat flour that was suddenly available in Great Britain, thanks to the industrialization of wheat farming. Yorkshire puddings are designed to use up fat drippings from the roasting of meat, and were traditionally served before the meat, together with the roasted meat gravy. The wonderful chemical reaction that happens in this preparation is due to the combination of flour with eggs in the presence of hot fat in a hot oven. Yorkshire puddings are supposed to expand notably in the oven, and, according to the Royal Society of Chemistry, they need to be at least four inches tall. In North America, Yorkshire puddings are called popovers.

# MARY JENNIFER RUSSELL'S DOUBLE CORNBREAD

YIELD: 6 SERVINGS / ACTIVE TIME: 20 MINUTES / TOTAL TIME: 55 MINUTES

Buttery and sweet, this cornbread is sure to appease even the biggest corn-lovers!
—*Sugaree's*

1  Preheat oven to 425°F. Put lard in 12-inch cast-iron skillet and place in oven to heat.

2  When the skillet is hot and all of the lard has melted, remove from oven and swirl fat around the sides of pan to coat.

3  In a mixing bowl, stir together the yellow cornmeal, white cornmeal, brown sugar, baking powder, and salt.

4  In a separate bowl, stir together eggs, buttermilk and thawed (but still cold) corn. Pour wet ingredients into the dry ingredients and mix quickly, then pour the hot lard into the batter and stir to incorporate.

5  Sprinkle coarse cornmeal in bottom of hot skillet to prevent sticking, then pour the batter in. Bake for 30–35 minutes or until done.

**INGREDIENTS:**

½  cup rendered leaf lard (any butter or oil will work as a substitution)

1  cup yellow cornmeal, plus 2–3 tablespoons for the skillet

1  cup self-rising white cornmeal

2  tablespoons dark brown sugar

1  tablespoon baking powder

½  teaspoon salt

4  large fresh farm eggs

1  cup buttermilk

20  ounces frozen creamed corn, thawed

CAST-IRON SKILLET RECIPE

# BACON CHEDDAR CORNBREAD

**YIELDS:** 6 TO 8 SERVINGS / **ACTIVE TIME:** 20 MINUTES / **TOTAL TIME:** 1 HOUR

The smoky-salty combination of bacon and cheddar are a perfect complement to so many foods—burgers, grilled cheese sandwiches, fried eggs—and now, cornbread. If you have a houseful of guys on a Sunday morning (especially if they're teenagers), whip this up and watch it disappear.

—*Dominique DeVito*

1 Preheat the oven to 400°F.

2 In a large bowl, combine the cornmeal, flour, sugar, baking powder, baking soda, and salt. Put ½ cup milk in a measuring cup. Add the 2 tablespoons butter, cut into pieces. Put in the microwave and heat on high for 1 minute so that butter is melted into the milk. Pour this over the dry ingredients and begin stirring. Gradually add the additional cup of milk and stir until thoroughly combined. When batter is mixed, fold in most of the bacon pieces and grated cheese, saving some to sprinkle on top.

3 Heat the skillet over medium heat and melt the 2 remaining tablespoons of butter in it. Add the batter and shake the pan gently to evenly distribute. Sprinkle the top with the extra bacon and cheese.

4 Transfer the skillet to the oven and cook for 25 to 30 minutes, until light golden brown and a toothpick inserted in the middle comes out clean.

5 Using pot holders or oven mitts, remove the skillet from the oven and let the bread cool for 10 to 15 minutes before slicing and serving.

**INGREDIENTS:**

- 2 cups finely ground yellow cornmeal
- 1 cup flour
- ¼ cup sugar
- 2 teaspoons baking powder
- 1 teaspoon baking soda
- 1 teaspoon salt
- 4 tablespoons unsalted butter, divided
- 1½ cups milk
- 2 eggs
- 1 cup crunchy bacon bits
- 4 oz. (½ to ¾ cup) sharp cheddar cheese, grated

# CORNBREAD

CAST-IRON SKILLET RECIPE

**YIELDS:** 6 TO 8 SERVINGS / **ACTIVE TIME:** 20 MINUTES / **TOTAL TIME:** 1 HOUR

If you're going to make bread in a cast-iron skillet, you have to make cornbread! Many restaurants serve cornbread in a cast-iron skillet, which adds something to the flavor, if you ask me. No matter how you serve it, it tastes great.

—*Dominique DeVito*

**INGREDIENTS:**

- 2 **cups finely ground yellow cornmeal**
- 1 **cup flour**
- ¼ **cup sugar**
- 2 **teaspoons baking powder**
- 1 **teaspoon baking soda**
- 1 **teaspoon salt**
- 5 **tablespoons unsalted butter, divided**
- 1½ **cups milk**
- 2 **eggs**

1 Preheat the oven to 400°F.

2 In a large bowl, combine cornmeal, flour, sugar, baking powder, baking soda, and salt. Put ½ cup milk in a measuring cup. Add 2 tablespoons butter, cut into pieces. Put in the microwave and heat on high for 1 minute so that butter is melted into the milk. Pour this over the dry ingredients and begin stirring. Gradually add the additional cup of milk and stir, then add the eggs and continue stirring until thoroughly combined.

3 Heat the skillet over medium heat and melt the 3 remaining tablespoons of butter in it. Add the batter and shake the pan gently to evenly distribute.

4 Transfer the skillet to the oven and cook for 25 to 30 minutes, until light golden brown and a toothpick inserted in the middle comes out clean.

5 Using pot holders or oven mitts, remove the skillet from the oven and let the bread cool for 10 to 15 minutes before slicing and serving.

Cornbread recipes are as varied and plentiful as those for chili. A great way to discover different ones that you like without having to go through multiple cookbooks and lots of time in the kitchen yourself is to invite friends and family to a Cast-Iron Cornbread Cook-Off. Make the chili the way you like it (and plenty of it), then have people bring over their cornbreads with recipes.

# CORNY-SPICY CORNBREAD

YIELDS: 6 TO 8 SERVINGS / ACTIVE TIME: 25 MINUTES / TOTAL TIME: 1 HOUR

Now that I've suggested the family or neighborhood cornbread challenge, I have to offer my own contender for first prize, since I love a cornbread that actually has kernels of corn in it. If you like spicy, toss in the jalapeños, too.
—*Dominique DeVito*

1 Preheat the oven to 400°F.

2 In a large bowl, combine the cornmeal, flour, sugar, baking powder, baking soda, and salt. Put ½ cup milk in a measuring cup. Add the 2 tablespoons butter, cut into pieces. Put in the microwave and heat on high for 1 minute so that butter is melted into the milk. Pour this over the dry ingredients and begin stirring. Gradually add the additional cup of milk and stir, then add the eggs and continue stirring until thoroughly combined. When batter is mixed, fold in the corn kernels and jalapeños.

3 Heat the skillet over medium heat and melt the 2 remaining tablespoons of butter in it. Add the batter and shake the pan gently to evenly distribute.

4 Transfer the skillet to the oven and cook for 25 to 30 minutes, until light golden brown and a toothpick inserted in the middle comes out clean.

5 Using pot holders or oven mitts, remove the skillet from the oven and let the bread cool for 10 to 15 minutes before slicing and serving.

**INGREDIENTS:**

| | |
|---|---|
| 2 | cups finely ground yellow cornmeal |
| 1 | cup flour |
| ¼ | cup sugar |
| 2 | teaspoons baking powder |
| 1 | teaspoon baking soda |
| 1 | teaspoon salt |
| 4 | tablespoons unsalted butter, divided |
| 1½ | cups milk |
| 2 | eggs |
| 1 | cup corn kernels (can be from fresh-cooked corn on the cob, or use canned being sure to drain the liquid) |
| ¼ to ½ | cup diced jalapeño peppers |

# PERFECT CRUST

YIELDS: 2 CRUSTS / **ACTIVE TIME:** 15 MINUTES / **TOTAL TIME:** 75 MINUTES

Made in a cast-iron skillet, pie crust finishes to a lovely crispness. We'll use this recipe for a whole bunch of pies and quiches, though you always have the option of using store-bought crusts, if you're in a hurry.
—*Dominique DeVito*

1 To make the crust, combine flour, sugar, and salt in a large bowl.

2 Using a pastry knife or a large fork, work the butter cubes into the flour mixture until the butter pieces are no larger than a pebble and the dough is crumbly.

3 Add the very cold water 2 tablespoons at a time and work the dough with your hands until it holds together. Form it into two pieces, wrap them in plastic wrap, and refrigerate for 1 hour before rolling out.

**INGREDIENTS:**

| 2½ | cups flour |
| 1 | teaspoon sugar |
| 1 | teaspoon salt |
| 1 | cup (2 sticks) unsalted butter, cut into small cubes |
| 4 to 6 | tablespoons very cold water |

# CLASSIC QUICHE

**YIELDS:** 2 QUICHES / **ACTIVE TIME:** 1 HOUR / **TOTAL TIME:** 4 HOURS

This tried and true recipe from the folks at Boulangerie (see page 130) will give your brunches a catered feel without any of the extra time or work.

—*courtesy of Amy and Zachary Tyson of Boulangerie*

1 Cut your cold butter into cubes. On low speed, mix flour, salt, and cold butter briefly—just until the butter is distributed but still in chunks larger than a pea. Pour in water while mixing and stop mixing as soon as it comes together.

2 Form dough into a fat loaf or tube shape and wrap in plastic. Let rest in the refrigerator for an hour.

3 Divide the dough in half and roll out to line a 9-inch pie pan or a 10-inch tart pan with a removable base. We prefer the tart pan. Freeze or refrigerate shells for an hour.

4 Preheat the oven to 350°F. Blind bake with parchment and weights in the shell for 20 minutes.

5 Mix your filling ingredients together, adding fillings of your choice—ham, asparagus and cheese, spinach and cheese, and tomato and cheese are some of our favorites. Remove the shell from the oven and pour in the quiche filling.

6 Bake the quiche for 30 minutes at 350°F. Cover with foil and bake an additional 30 minutes.

**INGREDIENTS:**

**QUICHE SHELLS:**

¾ cup + 1 tablespoon water

½ cup + 1 tablespoon butter

3 cups all-purpose flour

2 tablespoons salt

**FILLING:**

9 eggs

2½ cups heavy cream

½ cup Greek yogurt

½ teaspoon salt

¼ teaspoon pepper

# SMOKED SALMON *and* DILL QUICHE

**YIELDS:** 6 TO 8 SERVINGS / **ACTIVE TIME:** 30 MINUTES / **TOTAL TIME:** 60 MINUTES

Any good deli in New York City will serve smoked salmon for breakfast—typically on a bagel with a schmear of cream cheese, a few capers, and a sprig of dill. What a treat! Putting smoked salmon and dill in a quiche makes for a dish that is still fantastic for fans of the fish, but is mellower and therefore more palatable for those who might not be…though no one can resist.
—*Dominique DeVito*

1 Preheat the oven to 350°F.

2 Allow the refrigerated pie dough to come to room temperature. On a lightly floured surface, unroll and smooth it. Gently fold it and place in the skillet, pressing gently into place. Crimp the edges at the top of the skillet for a decorative touch.

3 Brush the mustard over the bottom of the dough. Place the salmon pieces in the pie.

4 In a large bowl, whisk the eggs, half-and-half, salt, and pepper together until combined. Add the dill and mix well.

5 Pour the egg mixture over the salmon pieces, giving the skillet a gentle shake to distribute the liquid. Sprinkle the cubes of cream cheese evenly on top.

6 Put the skillet in the oven and bake for 35 to 40 minutes or until the quiche is puffy and golden brown and the eggs are set. Use pot holders or oven mitts to take the skillet out of the oven. Allow to sit for 10 minutes before slicing and serving.

**INGREDIENTS:**

1 homemade pie dough (page 444) or pre-made refrigerator pie dough (14.1 oz) or

1 teaspoon Dijon mustard

1 pound smoked salmon, cut or torn into nickel-sized pieces

4 eggs

1 cup half-and-half

1 teaspoon salt

½ teaspoon ground black pepper

1 tablespoon dill, finely minced

1 (3-oz.) package cream cheese, cut into small cubes

# QUICHE LORRAINE

**YIELD:** 1 9-INCH TART / **ACTIVE TIME:** 30 MINUTES / **TOTAL TIME:** 1 HOUR

Some may remember that in the 1970s there was this saying that "Real men don't eat quiche." Well, I say balderdash! I already gave my age up when I starting talking about the '70s so that old expression works, right?

In any case, quiche is a wonderful, quick way to fancy up a luncheon or picnic, and quiche Lorraine is the most classic quiche. Of course, you can make variations with broccoli and cheddar, or spinach and mushroom, but you can't go wrong serving bacon to a bunch of meat-eaters.

—*Stephany Buswell*

**INGREDIENTS:**

- 1 flaky pie crust (see page 603)
- ½ cup crispy bacon, cut into ¼-inch pieces
- ½ cup milk
- ½ cup cream
- 2 large eggs
- ⅛ teaspoon salt
- Pinch of nutmeg
- ½ cup Gruyère cheese, grated

1 Roll out and line the tart pan with the pie crust. Be careful not to leave any holes in the crust or the liquid custard filling will leak out and cause the tart to cook into the pan. Chill dough.

2 Cook your bacon until crispy and drain on paper towel.

3 Blind bake the pie shell by lining it with parchment paper and pouring in pie weights or dry beans. Place in the oven for 15 to 20 minutes at 375°F, making sure it is light brown and done through.

4 In a medium bowl, mix together the milk, cream, eggs, and spices.

5 When the crust is out of the oven. and cooled, place the bacon pieces on the bottom of the crust evenly.

6 Pour the custard filling over the bacon and then sprinkle your grated cheese over the top.

7 Bake in a cool oven—250°F—for 20 to 30 minutes or until the custard is set. There should be no color on top and the center shouldn't wiggle when shaken. Serve at room temperature.

# HAM N' CHEESE QUICHE

**YIELD:** 2 QUICHES (6 SERVINGS EACH) / **ACTIVE TIME:** 20 MINUTES / **TOTAL TIME:** 55 MINUTES

Sometimes I mix in ½ cup of Parmigiano-Reggiano cheese with spinach or broccoli. Fresh chives are good as well as substituting crisp bacon for ham.

—*Jane Jaharian, The Sweetery*

1 Preheat oven to 400°F. Unroll pastry sheets into two 9-inch pie plates and flute the edges.

2 Line the unpricked pastry shells with a double thickness of heavy-duty foil. Fill with pie weights—dried beans or uncooked rice works.

3 Bake for 10 to 12 minutes or until light golden brown. Remove the foil and weights and bake 3 to 5 minutes longer, or until bottom is golden brown. Cool on wire racks.

4 Divide ham, cheese and onion between shells. In a large bowl, whisk eggs, half-and-half, salt, and pepper until blended. Pour into shells.

5 Cover edges loosely with foil. Bake 35 to 40 minutes or until a knife inserted near the center comes out clean. Let stand 5 to 10 minutes before cutting.

6 Freeze option: Cover and freeze unbaked quiche. To use, remove from freezer 30 minutes before baking (do not thaw). Preheat oven to 350°F and place quiche on a baking sheet, covering the edge loosely with foil. Bake as directed, increasing time as necessary for a knife inserted near the center to come out clean.

**INGREDIENTS:**

- 1 homemade pie dough or 1 pre-made refrigerator pie dough (14.01 oz)

- 2 cups fully cooked ham, diced

- 2 cups (8 ounces) shredded sharp cheddar cheese

- 2 teaspoons dried minced onion

- 4 large eggs

- 2 cups half-and-half

- ½ teaspoon salt

- ¼ teaspoon pepper

# SUGAREE'S BAKERY COLLARD *and* HAM QUICHE

YIELD: 6–8 SERVINGS / ACTIVE TIME: 30-45 MINUTES / TOTAL TIME: 5 HOURS 30 MINUTES

Everyone loves a spinach quiche, but not enough attention gets paid to the beautiful leafy collard green as an egg complement. Mix it with ham and bacon and you get southern comfort with a crust.

—*Mary Jennifer Russell, Sugaree's*

1 Preheat your oven to 375°F. Using a pastry cutter, cut together flour, salt, butter and lard until the bits are the size of sunflower seeds.

2 Use a pastry fork to cut in ice water two tablespoons at a time, slowly decreasing the amount until the mixture sticks together when you form a ball. Work quickly to avoid overworking dough.

3 Roll out your dough between two pieces of plastic wrap. Add to pie pan and shape.

4 Freeze crust completely, then lightly brush cream/yolk glaze on crust while frozen.

5 Blind bake for 30 minutes until light golden brown.

6 While the crust bakes, make your filling: Put collards, bacon, vinegar, and sugar in crock pot with enough water to just cover for 4 hours. Drain and chop 2 cups of greens.

7 Preheat your oven to 375°F. Mix collards with all other ingredients and pour into partially baked pie crust. Bake for 50–60 minutes or until it is set in the center (a knife inserted in center comes out clean).

## INGREDIENTS:

### CRUST

| | |
|---|---|
| ⅗ | pound cake flour |
| ½ | teaspoon salt |
| 2 | ounces butter, frozen and grated |
| 2 | ounces lard |
| 2½ | ounces ice water |
| 1 | tablespoon heavy cream |
| 1 | egg yolk |

### FILLING:

| | |
|---|---|
| 1 | bunch collard greens |
| 3 | slices bacon |
| 2 | tablespoons vinegar |
| 1 | tablespoon sugar |
| 4 | large eggs |
| 1¼ | cups heavy cream |
| 1½ | cups gruyere, grated |
| 1½ | cups ham steak, cubed |
| ½ | teaspoon salt |
| ½ | teaspoon pepper |
| ¼ | teaspoon nutmeg, freshly grated |

# BROCCOLI-SWISS QUICHE

YIELDS: 6 TO 8 SERVINGS / ACTIVE TIME: 30 MINUTES / TOTAL TIME: 70 MINUTES

A quiche is essentially a savory pie, and like any good pie, it can be so satisfying. There's something simple yet elegant about pie, and a quiche is no exception. This is a recipe that features broccoli paired with Swiss cheese and artichoke hearts, accented with Italian seasoning. It's delicious heated or at room temperature, and, served with a salad, makes a great meal.
—*Dominique DeVito*

**INGREDIENTS:**

- **1** homemade pie dough (see page 444) or 1 pre-made refrigerator pie dough (14.01 oz)
- **1** teaspoon Dijon mustard
- **1¼** cup grated/shredded Swiss cheese
- **3** cups broccoli florets and stems, cooked but not too soft
- **6** eggs
- **¾** cup half-and-half
- **1** teaspoon salt
- **1** teaspoon Italian seasoning
- **½** teaspoon ground black pepper
- **1** (6-oz.) jar quartered, marinated artichoke hearts, drained
- **½** cup grated Parmesan cheese

**1** Preheat the oven to 350°F.

**2** Make homemade pie crust (page 444) or get out your store-bought refrigerated pie dough and roll it out if needed.

**3** Brush the mustard over the bottom of the dough. Next, use about ¼ cup of the cheese and sprinkle it over the dough. Place the broccoli pieces in the pie.

**4** In a large bowl, whisk the eggs, half-and-half, salt, Italian seasoning, and pepper together until combined. Add the remaining Swiss cheese and mix well.

**5** Pour the egg mixture over the broccoli pieces, giving the skillet a gentle shake to distribute the liquid. Arrange artichoke hearts on top. Sprinkle the Parmesan over everything.

**6** Put the skillet in the oven and bake for 35 to 40 minutes or until the quiche is puffy and golden brown and the eggs are set. Use pot holders or oven mitts to take the skillet out of the oven. Allow to sit for 10 minutes before slicing and serving.

CAST-IRON SKILLET RECIPE

# QUICHE *with* SAUTÉED LEEKS

YIELDS: 6 TO 8 SERVINGS / ACTIVE TIME: 30 MINUTES / TOTAL TIME: 60 MINUTES

The leeks in this recipe are sautéed until soft and golden, which brings out their delectable mild onion flavor. Swiss or gruyére cheese is the perfect complement. This is an easy-to-make quiche that is nonetheless quite elegant.

—*Dominique DeVito*

**INGREDIENTS:**

| | |
|---|---|
| 1 | pre-made refrigerator pie dough (14.1 oz) or homemade pie dough (page 444) |
| 3 | large leeks, white and light green parts only |
| 2 | tablespoons olive oil |
| 3 | eggs |
| 1 | cup whole milk or half-and-half |
| ½ to ¾ | cup shredded Swiss or gruyére cheese |
| | Salt and pepper to taste |

1 Preheat the oven to 400°F.

2 Allow the refrigerated pie dough to come to room temperature. On a lightly floured surface, unroll and smooth it. Gently fold it and place in the skillet, pressing gently into place. Crimp the edges at the top of the skillet for a decorative touch.

3 Prepare the leeks by cutting the white and light green parts only into thin slices. Separate the rings in a colander, and rinse thoroughly to remove any sand or grit. Pat dry.

4 In another skillet, heat the olive oil over medium-high heat. Add the leeks and cook, stirring, for a minute or two. Lower the heat and continue to cook so that the leeks become tender and golden, not overly browned, about 10 to 15 minutes. Stir frequently.

5 In a large bowl, whisk the eggs and milk or half-and-half until thoroughly combined. Add the shredded cheese and season with salt and pepper. Stir.

6 Spread the sautéed leeks over the crust in the skillet. Pour the egg/cheese mixture over them.

7 Put the skillet in the oven and bake for about 30 minutes or until the quiche is puffy and golden brown and the eggs are set. Use pot holders or oven mitts to take the skillet out of the oven. Allow to sit for 10 minutes before slicing and serving.

# CORN CHOWDER CORNBREAD

**YIELDS:** 6 TO 8 SERVINGS / **ACTIVE TIME:** 20 MINUTES / **TOTAL TIME:** 1 HOUR

I was going through my cans of soup one day and thought, "Why not use chicken corn chowder soup instead of milk in a cornbread recipe?" So I tried it. Super easy. Nice, moist result. And this leads, of course, to thoughts of other soups as flavor additives for cornbread. I'm sure you can think of some, too.

—*Dominique DeVito*

**INGREDIENTS:**

- 2 cups finely ground yellow cornmeal
- 1 cup flour
- ¼ cup sugar
- 2 teaspoons baking powder
- 1 teaspoon baking soda
- 1 teaspoon salt
- 1 teaspoon cayenne pepper (optional)
- ¼ cup milk
- 4 tablespoons unsalted butter, divided
- 1 (18.5-oz.) can of chicken corn chowder soup
- 2 eggs

1 Preheat the oven to 400°F..

2 In a large bowl, combine the cornmeal, flour, sugar, baking powder, baking soda, salt, and cayenne pepper. Put the ¼ cup milk in a measuring cup. Add the 2 tablespoons butter, cut into pieces. Put in the microwave and heat on high for 1 minute so that butter is melted into the milk. Pour this over the dry ingredients and begin stirring. Add the can of soup and stir, then add the eggs and continue stirring until thoroughly combined.

3 Heat the skillet over medium heat and melt the 2 remaining tablespoons of butter in it. Add the batter and shake the pan gently to evenly distribute.

4 Transfer the skillet to the oven and cook for 25 to 30 minutes, until light golden brown and a toothpick inserted in the middle comes out clean.

5 Using pot holders or oven mitts, remove the skillet from the oven and let the bread cool for 10 to 15 minutes before slicing and serving.

# FOOLPROOF SOURDOUGH ROLLS

YIELD: 2 BATCHES OF ROLLS / ACTIVE TIME:30 MINUTES/ TOTAL TIME: 2 HOURS

This is a great recipe to use sourdough starter leftovers, and it's also a fantastic way to have freshly baked bread on in the morning without having to plan ahead. These rolls are also a great way to break the ice with a new sourdough starter, as they do not require any special skill.

## DAY 1

1 In the evening, combine the starter with the water and add all the flours. Let rest covered for 45 minutes, add the salt, and combine well.

2 Let rest, covered, for 30 minutes, then fold the dough 3 times. Let rest, covered, for another 30 minutes, then perform 3 more folds.

3 Cover and let rest at room temperature until the following morning.

## DAY 2

1 In the morning, preheat the oven to 475°F. Transfer the dough onto a floured surface and fold like a package. Let rest 10 minutes and fold again.

2 Delicately flip the dough upside-down and let rest another 40 to 60 minutes.

3 Cut the dough into small pieces with the help of a dough scraper and bake for 15 minutes. Use parchment paper to easily transfer the rolls to the hot oven.

INGREDIENTS:

- 2½ ounces (70 grams) 100% sourdough starter
- 19 ounces (540 grams) water
- 12⅓ ounces (350 grams) bread flour
- 7 ounces (200 grams) all-purpose flour
- 5⅓ ounces (150 grams) whole-wheat flour
- 2½ teaspoons salt

# SAVORY KALE-FILLED BUNS

YIELD: 10-12 BUNS / ACTIVE TIME: 30 MINUTES/ TOTAL TIME: 2½ HOURS

These buns build on the same concept of cinnamon buns, but instead use a savory filling. Here is one possible filling, but feel free to try different combinations.

1 Clean and sauté the kale with salt, pepper, cheese, olive oil, and minced garlic.

2 To make your dough, dissolve the yeast in the water and milk, both lukewarm.

3 Add the other liquid ingredients and then the flours and the salt.

4 Knead for 8 minutes and let rest, covered, for 45 minutes.

5 Transfer the dough on a floured surface and shape it into a rectangular log.

6 Spread the filling on the dough and roll it lengthwise.

7 Cut dough into small pieces and place them in muffin molds. Let rest, covered, for 45 minutes.

8 Bake at 430°F for 8 to 10 minutes or more, depending on the size of your rolls.

INGREDIENTS:

DOUGH:

| | |
|---|---|
| 2½ | teaspoons instant yeast |
| 3½ | ounces milk |
| 5⅓ | ounces water |
| 2 | tablespoons olive oil |
| 1 | tablespoon honey |
| 1 | teaspoon salt |
| 7 | ounces all-purpose flour |
| 7 | ounces white spelt flour |

KALE FILLING:

| | |
|---|---|
| 7 | ounces kale |
| 4 | ounces grated cheese |
| 1 | clove garlic, minced |
| | Olive oil |
| | Salt, to taste |
| | Pepper, to taste |

# DINNER ROLLS

**YIELDS:** 8 TO 10 SERVINGS (12 ROLLS) / **ACTIVE TIME:** 60 MINUTES / **TOTAL TIME:** 3 HOURS

These classic dinner rolls are light, flaky, and buttery perfection. Once found on the tables at fine restaurants everywhere, they're now commonly replaced by sliced loaf breads. See if these will even make it to your table when they come out of the oven.

—*Dominique DeVito*

1 In a small bowl, combine ½ cup warm milk and the sugar. Sprinkle the yeast over it, stir, and set aside so the yeast can proof (about 10 minutes).

2 While the yeast is proofing, melt the butter in the skillet over low to medium heat, and remove from heat when melted.

3 When the yeast mix is frothy, stir in 3 tablespoons of the melted butter, the remaining milk, the salt, and the eggs. Then stir in the flour, mixing until all ingredients are incorporated. Transfer to a lightly floured surface and knead the dough for 5 to 10 minutes until it is soft and springy and elastic.

4 Coat the bottom and sides of a large mixing bowl (ceramic is best) with butter. Place the ball of dough in the bowl, cover loosely with plastic wrap, put it in a naturally warm, draft-free location, and let it rise until doubled in size, about 45 minutes to 1 hour.

5 Prepare a lightly floured surface to work on. Punch down the dough in the bowl and transfer it to the floured surface. Warm the skillet with the butter so that it is melted again.

6 Break off pieces of the dough to form into rolls, shaping them into 2-inch balls with your hands. Roll the balls in the butter in the skillet, and leave them in the skillet as they're made and buttered.

7 Cover the skillet loosely with a clean dish towel, put it in the warm, draft-free spot, and let the rolls rise until doubled in size, about 30 minutes. While they're rising, preheat the oven to 350°F.

8 When the rolls have risen and the oven is ready, cover the skillet with aluminum foil and bake in the oven for 20 minutes. Remove the foil and finish cooking, another 15 minutes or so, until the rolls are golden on top and light and springy. Serve warm.

**INGREDIENTS:**

- 1¼ cups whole milk, heated to 110°F
- 3 tablespoons sugar
- 1 tablespoon active dry yeast
- 8 tablespoons (1 stick) unsalted butter
- ¾ teaspoon salt
- 2 eggs at room temperature, lightly beaten
- 3½ cups cake or bread flour (not all-purpose flour)

# DATE-AND-FIG WINTER ROLLS *with* SPELT

**YIELD:** 10–12 ROLLS / **ACTIVE TIME:** 40 MINUTES/ **TOTAL TIME:** 3½ HOURS

These rolls are wonderful for a winter breakfast or brunch ,and they are a great way to use sourdough starter leftovers. The overnight fermentation allows you to save some time and it gives a more complex flavor.

1 Combine all the ingredients with a spoon and then by hand, without kneading.

2 Let rest, covered, at room temperature for 1 hour, making folds every 30 minutes. Transfer in the fridge and let rest overnight.

3 In the morning, take the dough out of the fridge and let rest at room temperature for 1½ hours.

4 Preheat the oven to 480°F and shape the rolls into assorted shapes—rounds, ovals, and so on. Let the buns rest, covered, for 1 hour.

5 Brush the buns with water and sprinkle with spelt bran or chia seeds, depending on your preference.

6 Bake for 12 to 15 minutes, then lower the temperature and bake for an additional 12 to 15 minutes.

**INGREDIENTS:**

- 6 ½ ounces 100% hydration sourdough starter
- 10⅗ ounces organic bread flour
- 3½ ounces organic whole spelt flour
- 10⅗ ounces water
- 1 teaspoon sea salt
- ½ teaspoon malt syrup
- 2⅗ ounces dried figs, chopped
- 2⅗ ounces dried dates, chopped
- Water, spelt bran, and chia seeds for finishing

# GARLIC ROSEMARY ROLLS

**YIELDS:** 6 TO 8 SERVINGS (8 ROLLS) / **ACTIVE TIME:** 90 MINUTES / **TOTAL TIME:** 3 HOURS

If you're a fan of garlic as my family is, you will be swooned by the scent these rolls give off as they're baking. Better yet is the taste. Mangia!

—*Dominique DeVito*

**1** In a large bowl, mix the yeast, warm water, and sugar and let the yeast proof for about 10 minutes, until foamy.

**2** Next add the melted butter, salt, garlic, and half the flour. Mix until the dough forms a sticky dough. Continue to add flour, mixing to form a soft dough. Add the rosemary with the last addition of flour.

**3** Coat the bottom and sides of a large mixing bowl (ceramic is best) with butter. Place the ball of dough in the bowl, cover loosely with plastic wrap, put it in a naturally warm, draft-free location, and let it rise until doubled in size, about 45 minutes to 1 hour.

**4** Put the skillet in the oven and preheat the oven to 400°F.

**5** Transfer the dough to a lightly floured surface. Divide into 8 pieces and form into balls.

**6** Remove the skillet from the oven and melt the butter in it. Place the rolls in the skillet, turning to cover them with butter. Wash the rolls with the beaten egg and sprinkle with sea salt.

**7** Bake in the oven until golden and set, about 40 minutes.

**INGREDIENTS:**

- 1 **packet active dry yeast (2¼ teaspoons)**
- 1 **cup water (110–115°F)**
- 1 **tablespoon sugar**
- 1 **tablespoon butter, melted**
- 1 **teaspoon salt**
- 2 **cloves garlic, minced**
- 4 **cups flour**
- 1 **teaspoon fresh rosemary leaves, chopped, or 2 teaspoons dried, crushed rosemary**
- 1 **tablespoon butter**
- 1 **egg, lightly beaten**
- **Sea salt**

Make cheesy garlic-rosemary rolls by sprinkling Parmesan or pecorino romano cheese on the tops after washing with the beaten egg. Skip the sea salt.

# SWEET POTATO ROLLS

**YIELDS:** 8 TO 10 SERVINGS (18 SMALL ROLLS) / **ACTIVE TIME:** 60 MINUTES / **TOTAL TIME:** 3 HOURS

There's something about the color and flavor of sweet potatoes that says "goodness." These rolls won't disappoint. They're delicious served with savory dishes like roast pork or chicken, but also great for breakfast with homemade jam.
—*Dominique DeVito*

1 Cook the sweet potatoes by putting the cubes in a saucepan, covering them with water, bringing the water to a boil, and simmering them in the boiling water until they're soft, about 20 minutes. When they can be easily pierced with the tip of a knife, drain them in a colander. While they're warm, put them in a large bowl and mash them with a potato masher or fork.

2 In a large bowl, combine the yeast and the warm water. Add the brown sugar and ¼ cup of the flour, stirring well. Set aside so the yeast can proof (about 10 minutes).

3 Melt 5 tablespoons of the butter and add it to the large bowl with the sweet potatoes. Stir in the honey, egg, salt, ginger, and nutmeg. Stir well until smooth.

4 Add the sweet potato mixture to the yeast and stir to combine. Add the remaining all-purpose flour and the whole wheat flour. Stir to form a soft dough, adding additional whole wheat flour a tablespoon at a time until it holds together. Transfer to a lightly floured surface and knead the dough for 5 to 10 minutes until it is soft and springy and elastic.

5 Coat the bottom and sides of a large mixing bowl (ceramic is best) with 2 tablespoons of melted butter. Place the ball of dough in the bowl, cover loosely with plastic wrap, put it in a naturally warm, draft-free location, and let it rise until doubled in size, about 1 to 2 hours.

6 Prepare a lightly floured surface to work on. Punch down the dough in the bowl and transfer it to the floured surface. Warm the skillet with the butter so that it is melted again.

7 Break off 18 pieces of the dough to form into rolls, shaping them into balls with your hands. Roll the balls in the butter in the skillet, and leave them in the skillet as they're made and buttered.

## INGREDIENTS:

| | |
|---|---|
| 1 | large or 2 small sweet potatoes, peeled and cut into cubes |
| ½ | cup water (110–115°F) |
| 1 | packet active dry yeast (2¼ teaspoons) |
| 2 | tablespoons light brown sugar |
| 2 | cups all-purpose flour |
| ¾ | cup (1½ sticks) unsalted butter |
| ⅓ | cup honey |
| 1 | egg, lightly beaten |
| ½ | teaspoon salt |
| ½ | teaspoon ground ginger |
| ¼ | teaspoon ground nutmeg |
| 1½ | cups whole wheat flour |

8 Cover the skillet loosely with a clean dish towel, put it in the warm, draft-free spot, and let the rolls rise until doubled in size, about 30 minutes. While they're rising, preheat the oven to 375°F.

9 When the rolls have risen and the oven is ready, bake for 30 to 35 minutes until golden on the top. Serve warm.

# SOURDOUGH CROUTONS

YIELD: 2 LARGE BOULES, PRE-SLICED / ACTIVE TIME: 45 MINUTES / TOTAL TIME: 5 HOURS, 45 MINUTES

Whipping up some homemade croutons is fairly simply no matter how you do it, but if you're going to make them from scratch, it's worth using the Boulangerie sourdough recipe (see page 179). They use their old loaves to make delicious croutons in-house!
—*courtesy of Amy and Zachary Tyson, Boulangerie*

**INGREDIENTS:**

- 5⅙ cups water
- 1½ cups culture
- 5⅙ cups Sir Galahad all-purpose flour
- 1¾ cups King Arthur Special Patent flour
- 1½ tablespoons salt

1 Mix water, culture, and flours in a large bowl. Let sit for 30 minutes. This is your autolyse period.

2 In a mixer with a dough hook attachment, mix in the salt on 1st speed for 5 minutes. Then mix on 2nd speed for 3 minutes.

3 Allow to bulk ferment for 3 hours, or overnight if possible. If baking the same day, fold the dough every hour as you wait.

4 Divide the dough in half and preshape into a rough ball. Let rest for 30 minutes.

5 Do your final shaping and place dough bottom side–up in a basket or bowl lined with a floured cloth.

6 Proof for 45 minutes and preheat the oven to 450°F.

7 Invert dough onto a peel dusted with semolina or flour. Score the dough.

8 Spray oven with water bottle and bake for 30–45 minutes, until the bread sounds hollow.

## MAKING YOUR CROUTONS

1 Cut day-old sourdough into small cubes.

2 Preheat oven to 350°F. Toss cubes with olive oil and Maldon sea salt.

3 Bake for 30 minutes at 350°F until firm and golden brown.

# PIZZA & CALZONES

The first written record of the word "pizza" dates back to 997 in a document from Gaeta, an Island near Naples. Later on, the term was found in records from other Italian cities. The word pizza, however, meant different things depending on the place, and this ambiguity is still present in contemporary Italian language. In some regions, for instance, pizza is a round, leavened, cake. The type of pizza that became worldwide popular, however, is a very specific incarnation of Italian pizza. What we commonly refer to when we speak of pizza outside of Italy is mostly Neapolitan pizza. We also call many focaccias related to Neapolitan pizza with the same name, both in Italy and abroad, though they are not quite the same thing and do not have the same history.

The history of Neapolitan pizza starts before the 18th century, in Naples. At that time, it was common to use flattened rounds of dough to test the oven's temperature before baking bread. The discarded baked dough became a plate for the poor, because it was quick to bake, and, therefore, less valuable. It was sold in the streets, topped with a white sauce. The white sauce topping was later replaced with bacon, lard, cheese, tomatoes or fish, as described in 1843 by the writer Alexandre Dumas, visiting Naples. As Dumas recounted, pizza was the food of the lazzaroni, the people who inhabited the streets of Naples, doing small jobs or not working at all. Pizza was the food eaten in the streets during the winter and the topping depended on what was most abundant at every moment. If fishing had been good, then plenty of fish-topped pizza was sold, if there was a lot of leftover lard from butchers' shops, then there was plenty of pizza with lard, and so on.

It is quite certain that by the early 1820's there were already pizzerias in Naples, since we know that Naples' King, Ferdinand I of Bourbon (who died in 1825), visited one of them. The story says that Ferdinand, always very close to his people and to the lazzaroni in particular, wanted to taste some freshly baked pizza and so he violated court etiquette and visited a pizzeria in a poor district of Naples—and we are sure he did not regret it.

In a few decades, pizza became popular also among the middle and privileged classes, and after Piedmont's Kingdom took over Italy, a special pizza was dedicated to the new visiting queen, Margherita di Savoia. That version of pizza had a simple topping of tomato sauce, mozzarella cheese, and basil, to honor the three colors of the national flag set by the Savoia.

From there pizza spread to the whole Italian Kingdom, and it travelled with the early Italian migratory wave to Northern America, where it soon became an extremely popular food. From the United States, and other countries that experienced the smaller waves of Italian migration, Neapolitan pizza has spread to every corner of the world.

## MAKING PIZZA AT HOME

As you have read in the above section, the humble origins of pizza should reassure you about your capability of making it at home. Pizza, in fact, became popular just because it was easy and quick to make. So, do not be frightened by the fuss for the "perfect" pizza. There is no perfect pizza. There is instead the pizza that you can make the best or that you like the best, and with a few tips it is very possible that the two will soon coincide.

### Basic Pizza Dough

If you have never made pizza, it is best to start with an easy dough, and then move from there. See pages 45-51 for tips on basic baking equipment.

### Mixing the dough

*Flour to water ratio.* You want your pizza dough to be quite firm, so consider using 65% of water over the total amount of flour used. For example, for 2 pounds (1 kg) of flour, you will use 23 ounces (650 g) of water. If you are using 1 pound (500 g) flour, you will instead need 11½ ounces (325 g) of water, and so on.

*Yeast.* Pizza is usually made as a direct dough, which means, a dough made by adding the yeast directly to the flour and water, without using a preferment. Feel free to make your first dough with a good amount of baker's yeast, so that you aren't turned away by the long rising time. If using instant or dry yeast, 1½% would make your dough rise in just a few hours. This means 5⅓ teaspoons (15 g) of yeast for 2 pounds (1 kg) of flour. Remember to activate your yeast in warm water, with a good pinch of sugar if using active dry yeast.

*Salt.* You want the pizza crust to be tasty, so why not use 2½% of salt? This means adding 4 ½ teaspoons (25 g) to a dough made with 2 pounds (1 kg) of flour. If you do not want the crust to be very savory, or if you are expecting to use salty toppings, stick to the usual 2% salt used for bread dough, which for 2 pounds (1 kg) of flour means using 3½ teaspoons of salt (20 g).

### Kneading the dough

*If you own a stand-mixer.* Put the dough hook on and knead at a slow speed for 5 minutes. Then, increase to the medium speed and work the dough further for 5 more minutes. Check the dough: If you pick a piece, does it crumble away from the rest of the dough? Or, does the dough stick together? In these first two scenarios (crumbling or too tight dough), keep kneading at a low speed. Increase the dough mixer speed to medium high in the last few minutes of the kneading process. If the piece of dough in your fingers elongates elastically without detaching completely from the dough, while forming a long filament as you pull it away, then your dough is ready.

*By hand.* Make sure to have a solid kneading surface and start working the dough, letting it rest every few minutes. This will help the gluten form on its own and have time to relax. Keep working the dough at regular intervals, always covering it in between intervals, until it feels smooth and elastic when you pull it away from one corner. Do not worry too much about your technique. Hand kneading is a very intuitive process: let your hands do the job and learn to feel the dough. It is also a wonderful way to relieve stress, so enjoy the process and technique will follow.

### First fermentation (or bulk)
When the dough feels smooth and elastic, make a ball out of it and place it in an airtight container or in a bowl sealed with plastic wrap, making sure that the dough has enough space to triple (but it does not need to). Depending on room temperature, the dough will take between 1½ to 2 hours to double in volume if the % of yeast is 1½ over the total flour amount.

### Shaping the rounds
This is where having a scale comes in handy. It is now time to transfer your dough on a clean working surface, divide it into pieces of equal weight and make them into rounds. A good weight for a regular home oven with a firm yeasted dough is 9 ounces (250 g). See section 63 for tips on shaping rounds.

### Second fermentation (or final proof)
Once the rounds are shaped, they can be placed in a heavily floured oven pan, leaving enough space between one another so that they can rise in volume. After placing the dough rounds in the pan, they need to be sprinkled with flour and the whole pan can be placed in a food-approved plastic bag, making sure that the bag is big enough to leave plenty of space on top of the buns to prevent them from sticking to the bag. It is also possible to cover them with a kitchen towel, but make sure they do not dry, or it will be difficult to flatten them later on. The second fermentation should allow the rounds to increase to 1½ their volume. Do not let them ferment too long, because the dough will soften excessively and it will become difficult to shape them.

### Shaping the pizzas
This may be the hardest part of all. However, you will become better and better as time goes by. As a rule of thumb, you may want to avoid using a rolling pin on your pizza. The dough should be spread out with your hands, with movements that will become more and more accurate as you keep repeating the process. Make sure to always leave a border where the dough is higher, while spreading the pizza and flattening if from inside out. The border, *cornicione* in Italian, is very important as it will become a barrier that prevents the toppings from spilling out in the oven. Try not to spread the round all at once, but let it open up little by little, allowing the tension in the dough to naturally decrease.

### Dressing the pizza
Once you spread your pizza, it is now time to proceed with the toppings. Turn to pages 477-489 for some suggestions.

### Baking in a hot oven
A hot oven is essential for good pizza. See page 48 for tips on what oven to use and read page 49 for tips on how to make your home oven hotter. Baking time depends on how hot your oven manages to get. Of course, a shorter baking time is best for pizza, but it is essential that the pizza is properly cooked in the center and is not doughy. Practice will make you extremely good at judging how cooked your pizza is by just looking at it.

## Long-fermented Pizza
Now that you have practiced with a fast dough, you can approach a long-fermented pizza. In the classic method, pizza dough is fermented with a minimal

amount of yeast, which will make the dough rise slowly over many hours. At home, you can make your life easier by using cold bulk, with the help of nothing more than your household fridge.

### Mixing the dough

One can use the same type of dough used in basic pizza dough (page 469), but start the process one day ahead. The only difference, when mixing the dough, will be to reduce the amount of yeast to 1% on the total amount of flour. This means, 3½ teaspoons (10 g) of active dry or instant yeast for 2 pounds (1 kg) flour.

### Kneading the dough

Proceed as you would for basic pizza dough (page 469).

### First fermentation (bulk)

This will be different than when making a basic pizza, and will extend over several hours, using the aid of your household fridge. After letting the dough rest, covered, for 1 hour at room temperature, you can proceed with a cold bulk. This simply means putting the dough in an airtight container or a bowl sealed with plastic wrap, and placing it in the fridge, possibly not in the coldest part of it, 0 for a minimum of 16 hours.

### Shaping the rounds

Bring the pizza dough to room temperature again and shape it as described previously (page 63). After shaping into rounds, the pizza dough can also be placed back into the fridge, and used the day after. The flavor will further improve with prolonged fermentation.

### Second fermentation, pizza shaping, toppings, and baking

Proceed as you would with the basic pizza dough (page 470).

## Pan Pizza (Pizza in Teglia)

Before pizza became popular in Naples, and later on in the world, focaccias were extremely common. A very common way to make focaccia is in a baking tray, and so when we talk about pizza in teglia, pizza in a baking pan, we are talking about a focaccia with pizza toppings.

This pizza is possibly the easiest version of pizza you can make. You will not need to shape the pizza dough into rounds, nor to shape them into individual pizzas. You will instead need a very soft dough with a high hydration, which simply means a dough with a high water to flour ratio.

### Mixing the dough

*Flour to water ratio.* You may want to start with an 80% hydration, which means, a dough with 80% the amount of water compared to flour. For 2 pounds (1 kg) of flour, this means adding 12 ounces (800 g) of water. When you are more comfortable with soft doughs, you can add more water. 14 ounces (850 g) of water to 2 pounds (ca. 1 kg) flour will give you a hydration of 85%.

*Yeast.* This type of pizza benefits even more than Neapolitan pizza from a long fermentation. So, use the same percentage of yeast (1%) as the long fermented pizza dough (page 472).

*Salt.* Pan pizza cooks more slowly than free-form pizza, so it has more time to absorb the liquids of the savory condiments. You may want to use less salt than in the basic pizza dough. Use about 2% on the total flour amount, meaning 3½ teaspoons (20 g) per 2 pounds (1 kg) of flour.

### Kneading the dough

This is possibly the best part of pan pizza—you do not need to knead it. Just combine all ingredients for 3–4 minutes.

### First fermentation (or bulk)

After letting the dough rest, covered, for 1 hour at room temperature, put the dough in an airtight container or a bowl sealed with plastic wrap, and place in the fridge for a minimum of 16 hours. Avoid placing the dough in the coldest part of the refrigerator.

### Second fermentation (or final proof)

Bring the dough to room temperature again and let it rest for 1 hour. Then pour an abundant amount of olive oil in a baking tray that will fit the amount of dough you intend on baking. Consider 1½ pounds (750 g) of dough for a tray that fits a regular home oven. You will want a shallow and rectangular baking tray, which is the type traditionally used for this type of pizza in Italy. Transfer your dough directly onto the oiled tray, and spread it with the tip of your fingers, but do not do it all at once. Allow the dough to slowly relax on its own and accompany this process with your hands. The best way to spread a pan pizza dough is to alternate your hand movements in intervals, in which one interval lets the dough rest. When the pizza is covering the whole baking pan, drizzle it with olive oil and let it rest for an hour, while your oven is warming-up.

### Toppings

See pages 477-489 for some suggestions.

### Baking the pizza

Preheat your oven to 446°F (230°C), and when transferring the pizza in the oven, lower immediately to 410°F (210°C). Bake for 30 minutes.

## Sourdough Pizza

It seems strange to think that a traditional bread is not based on sourdough, but this is the case with pizza. When pizza became popular in Naples in the 19th century, baker's yeast was already used by bakers. Pizza was made by these bakers, in the city, and not by women at home in the countryside, where sourdough was used for bread. Nowadays, we know of all the added bonuses given by sourdough fermentation, and, therefore, many now prefer to use sourdough to make pizza crust.

### Preparing the pre-ferment

This type of pizza needs your sourdough starter to be fed, so that it will have enough power to make the pizza rise properly without giving it a sour taste (see page 60 on how to maintain your sourdough starter). Make sure to have enough active starter to use for the amount of pizza dough you are going to make. Consider using a 25% starter to your total flour amount, which means ½ pound (250 g) starter per 2 pounds (1 kg) of flour.

### Mixing the dough

Follow the same method used for basic pizza dough (page 469) and start it one day ahead like for long-fermented pizza dough (page 472). The only difference is that you are using a sourdough pre-ferment. Your dough will be slightly more hydrated than in the basic pizza dough, even if using the same amount of water, because there is some extra water in the starter. This is good, because sourdough pizza benefits from a higher water to flour ratio.

### Kneading the dough

Proceed like for basic pizza dough (page 469).

### First fermentation (bulk)

Proceed like for long-fermented pizza dough (page 472).

### Shaping the rounds

Bring the pizza dough to room temperature again and shape it as shown previously (page 63). When forming the pizza rounds using a sourdough dough, it is recommended to make bigger rounds, of 10.5-12.3 ounces (300-350 g) each. This is because sourdough dough does not bounce back as much as a yeast-based dough, and, therefore, the pizza rounds should not be flattened as much as those made with a yeast-based dough. Delicate handling will ensure you a soft pizza, otherwise you may end up with a tough crust.

### Second fermentation, pizza shaping, toppings, baking

Proceed as for basic pizza dough (page 470).

## CALZONE AND POCKETS

Calzone is a traditional variation of Neapolitan pizza, and its name is, in fact, derived from Neapolitan dialect "*o cazone 'mbuttunat*," which means sock, a long sock full of delicious food.

The calzone was probably born at the same time as pizza, in the late 18th century, out of the creativity of some Neapolitan pizzaiolo who decided to use the classic pizza dough in a different way. Instead of baking it open, the pizza was sealed in a crescent shape and stuffed with leftovers, including the poorest parts of pork, cheese, and tomatoes.

The calzone is generally baked in an oven, but it can also be fried, and then it becomes Neapolitan fried pizza. Pockets are an American delicacy that remind us of calzones, but are instead mostly inspired by Latin America's empanadas. Empanadas are made with a pastry-like dough, traditionally not leavened, filled with meat or vegetables and fried rather than baked. Pizza pockets are empanadas made with pizza dough and baked instead of being fried.

## BAKING APPARATUSES

The way you bake your pizza will strongly impact the quality of your pizza. This does not mean that you have to buy an expensive pizza oven. Your home oven, if you know a few tricks, can give you amazing pizza, too. It is good, though, to know all the possible options you may have to bake awe-inspiring pizzas. Only you know where you want to set the limit.

### Wood-fired Oven

Wood-burning ovens have been used since ancient Roman times. A classic wood-burning oven is entirely made of refractory material, which means, a material that retains its strength at high temperatures. In a wood-fired oven, the baking chamber has a base made of stone, summoned by a vault also made of refractory material. A chimney is connected to the vault to allow the discharge of fumes from the wood burning. The hearth is almost always started in the center and then moved to the side before baking.

The refractory stones on the base and on the vault are heated by the hearth and maintain a constant temperature, thanks to the thermal accumulation guaranteed by the building materials.

In a wood-fire oven, the pizzas bake in direct contact with the stone receiving heat from it and also baking for irradiation and convection thanks to the heat of the flames present in the baking chamber.

Cooking times of a wood-burning oven are reduced compared to an electric oven. A few minutes, or even just 60 seconds, for a Neapolitan pizza, which ensures the characteristic soft texture of this pizza. A pizza baked in a wood-fired oven has a different flavor compared to a pizza baked in an electric oven. The flames burning in the cooking chamber transfer the aromatic components developed by the various types of wood to the pizza.

A wood-fired pizza has a different aroma and taste, but with regard to the actual baking process there will be no difference. Handling a wood-fired oven is more difficult than an electric oven: the flame should be followed carefully and the pizza turned a couple of times to ensure homogeneous heat exposure. An experienced baker will pay careful attention, as it is common to have pizzas cooked in an inconsistent way or even get burned due to poor oven management. If you own a garden, it may not be complicated to build your own wood-fired oven, with some help. Your pizza will surely become unbeatable this way, with practice.

### Grill

The closest cooking apparatus to a wood-fire oven is your barbeque grill. With the right accessories, a regular barbeque grill can make a fantastic pizza with a wood-fire oven "touch."

What you need to make a pizza on a grill is two things: 1) a grill lid and 2) a baking stone. The lid will keep the steam from the pizza dough in, allowing the pizza to properly cook, and will also help keep the temperature high. The stone will allow the temperature of the grill to be max-

imized, and not be dispersed. Of course, you should seek out baking stones that are suitable for grills. They are generally lighter than the ones used for home ovens, and they are round while oven models are generally rectangular.

There are also special mini baking chambers made for the grill, which make very good pizza, as well. Choose based on your budget and also on the frequency with which you will be baking pizza. If that is no more than a few times a year, maybe you could instead look at the following section and use your regular kitchen oven. If you are instead motivated to bake on your grill and have bought the appropriate baking stone, this can be an extremely fun endeavor.

### Standard Kitchen Oven

It may surprise you, but a common kitchen oven can make great pizza. If you aim to make a Neapolitan-style pizza, you will want to invest in a baking stone, which will also be the best investment if planning to bake bread at home (see page 49 on using baking stones).

As for bread, heat is fundamental for making a good pizza crust. You will want to have your oven set to its maximum temperature, with the stone in, and allow the stone to get really hot, which could take up to a couple of hours, depending on the oven and on the thickness of the stone.

Generally, the stone is placed in the middle rack, just like for bread baking. However, for pizza, you can also place the stone on a higher rack. With this method, after keeping the oven on maximum temperature for one to two hours, it is necessary to switch to the grill function and allow the stone to become extremely hot (but check if this works with your oven, it would not be worth it to damage it or start a fire). At this point the oven needs to go back to regular heating, still on max, and the pizza can be transferred onto the hot stone. Using this method, baking time should be shortened, and the pizza crust should remain softer compared to when baking it over the middle rack.

## SAUCES AND TOPPINGS

The original Neapolitan pizza toppings were very different from what we can nowadays find in Neapolitan-style pizzerias. It was only toward the middle of the 19th century that tomato sauce started to become a favorite pizza (and pasta) topping. Even if the history of tomato sauce is not a very long one, its relevance skyrocketed soon after it was introduced. According to the association for the preservation of authentic Neapolitan pizza (Associazione Verace Pizza Napoletana, AVPN), tomato sauce is the only real, acceptable, Neapolitan pizza topping. In particular, there are only two orthodox pizzas, which both include tomato sauce as the base: Pizza Marinara and Pizza Margherita.

However, even if the toppings that made pizza popular in Naples were only two, things changed when pizza spread to other Italian regions and to the world. Over time, any possible edible combination has been used to top Neapolitan-style pizza crust. Sweet toppings have also made their appearance, and it is now not uncommon to be served a Nutella pizza in a Roman or in a NY pizzeria–and why not?

### The Perfect Neapolitan-style Pizza Sauce

The perfect pizza sauce is of course tomato-based. However, one should be aware that the sauce to go over a Neapolitan-style pizza crust is not supposed to be cooked, otherwise it will overcook in the hot oven. Instead, what should be used is raw canned, or fresh peeled, tomatoes, roughly squeezed into a sauce with a fork or a food processor. This is the best pizza sauce; and, the better quality of the tomatoes, the better sauce, and the better pizza. It is okay to season the raw tomato sauce with salt and olive oil. In this case you do not need to add much salt as a finishing when assembling the pizza toppings.

## Toppings

The beauty of pizza is that, with the same exact pizza dough recipe, one can make a nearly infinite variety of pizzas, just by changing the toppings. Sometimes, even daring combinations end up being winners. You have to be willing to try, and time and experience will tell what you and your family or friends like best. Of course, being inspired by local and seasonal ingredients is best. Here some suggestions to start.

These ingredients are meant for one Neapolitan pizza round, and, if multiplied by three, they all make perfect toppings for pan pizzas, too. See page 469 for details on how to make pizza dough and page 470 on how to bake the pizzas.

# TRADITIONAL

There are only two traditional pizza toppings, so if you really want to make Neapolitan pizza, try serving one of these two variations.

## MARINARA

This is the most traditional type of Neapolitan pizza topping, as it was already popular before the Margherita topping became a hit. It consists of tomato sauce, olive oil, oregano, and garlic.

According to the AVPN (Associazione Verace Pizza Napoletana), the crushed tomato sauce is placed at the center of the pizza disc and then spread. The garlic clove is then cut into thin slices and distributed over the tomato sauce base. The oregano is distributed on the tomato and the garlic. Salt (if not added to the tomato sauce before) is evenly sprinkled over the pizza. Olive oil is poured with a spiral motion, starting from the center towards the periphery, using an olive oil dispenser.

**INGREDIENTS:**

- 2½ ounces (70 g) crushed peeled tomatoes (canned or fresh)
- 1 garlic clove
- 1 pinch of oregano
- Salt
- 1 teaspoon olive oil

# MARGHERITA

Developed by a Neapolitan pizzaiolo when Queen Margherita of Savoy visited Naples. It included three colors to represent the flag of the newly united Italy: green, white, and red.

According to the AVPN, the crushed tomato sauce is placed at the center of the pizza disc and then spread. The mozzarella is sliced in strips and distributed over the tomato sauce base. The grated cheese is sprinkled over the tomato and the mozzarella. The basil leaves are placed over the other toppings. Salt (if not added to the tomato sauce before) is evenly sprinkled over the pizza and, to finish, olive oil is poured with spiral motion, starting from the center towards the periphery, using an olive oil dispenser.

INGREDIENTS:

- 2½ ounces (70 g) crushed peeled tomatoes (canned or fresh)
- 3 ounces (85 g) fresh mozzarella (with liquid well drained)
- 1 tablespoon grated hard cheese
- Basil, a few leaves
- Salt
- 1 teaspoon olive oil

# VEGETARIAN

The original pizza is vegetarian, and the most traditional one is even vegan. This happened, because in 19th century Naples, tomatoes, herbs, and fresh cheese were more abundant and cheaper than meat and fish. Pizza was born as a *piatto povero*, a poor dish. Nowadays, even the vegetarian versions of pizza can be sultry and include luxury ingredients, but the simplicity of the original recipes is not to be overlooked.

## WILD MUSHROOMS, BUFALA, *and* PECORINO

If the mushrooms are fresh, wash them and dry them. Chop the mushrooms in big chunks and sauté in 1 tablespoon olive oil and the garlic clove, seasoning with salt and pepper. Pour and distribute 1 tablespoon of olive oil over the pizza disk. Slice the mozzarella in strips or simply pull it apart in big chunks and distribute it over the oiled pizza. Distribute evenly the sautéed mushrooms over the mozzarella. Distribute the pecorino over the mozzarella and top with the parsley. Season with salt and drizzle the remaining olive oil over the other ingredients.

INGREDIENTS:

3 ounces (85 g) wild mushrooms (fresh or frozen)

3 tablespoons olive oil

1 garlic clove

Salt

Black pepper

3 ounces (85 g) fresh mozzarella (with liquid well drained)

1 tablespoon pecorino flakes

Parsley, a handful, chopped

## GRILLED VEGGIES *and* TOFU CREAM CHEESE (VEGAN)

Wash the vegetables and cut in strips or big chunks and grill in a grilling pan. Place in a bowl and season with salt and 2 tablespoons of the olive oil. You can do this just before making the pizza, or the day before, leaving the grilled vegetables to marinate in the fridge, covered, overnight. Spread the crushed tomatoes sauce over the pizza starting from the center of the disk. Evenly distribute the grilled vegetables over the raw tomato sauce. Top with small dollops of tofu cream cheese. Sprinkle the chopped parsley over the other ingredients. Season with salt and drizzle with the remaining olive oil.

INGREDIENTS:

6 ounces (170 g) mixed vegetables to grill (zucchini and bell peppers are a good choice, among others)

Salt

3 tablespoons olive oil

2½ ounces (70 g) crushed peeled tomatoes (canned or fresh)

1½ tablespoons tofu cream cheese

Parsley, one handful fresh

# CHERRY TOMATOES, PESTO, *and* SMOKED CHEESE

Spread the pesto over the pizza disk. Slice the cheese in strips and distribute it over the pesto. Evenly distribute the cherry tomatoes cut in half. Distribute the Parmesan flakes over the other ingredients and finish with a drizzle of olive oil.

INGREDIENTS:

- 2½ ounces (70 g) basil pesto
- 3 ounces (85 g) smoked cheese, like provola
- 4–5 cherry tomatoes, halved
- 1 tablespoon Parmesan cheese flakes
- 1 tablespoon olive oil

# BOK CHOY, PINE NUTS, *and* RAISINS (VEGAN)

Wash the bok choy and cut in strips or big chunks, and sauté in 2 teaspoons of the olive oil with the garlic clove, seasoning with salt. Put the raisins in warm water for 10 minutes and then squeeze the liquid out. Spread the crushed tomatoes sauce over the pizza starting from the center of the disk. Evenly distribute the sautéed bok choy over the tomato sauce. Sprinkle the raisins and the pine nuts over the bok choy. Season with salt and drizzle the remaining olive oil over the other ingredients.

INGREDIENTS:

- 6 ounces (170 g) bok choy
- 3 teaspoons olive oil
- 1 garlic clove
  Salt
- 1 tablespoon raisins
- 2½ ounces (70 g) crushed peeled tomatoes (canned or fresh)
- 1 tablespoon pine nuts

# MEAT-BASED

Although Neapolitan pizza reached the apex of popularity in its vegetarian version, before that it was common to use leftover bacon and lard as toppings. Meat condiments are always best if paired with a vegetable, in honor of the true Southern Italian style.

## BROCCOLI *and* ITALIAN SAUSAGE

Wash the broccoli and boil in salted water for three minutes. Drain and cut in big chunks and let them sauté with 1 tablespoon olive oil and the garlic for another three minutes. Pour and distribute 1 tablespoon of olive oil over the pizza disk. Slice the mozzarella in strips or simply pull it apart in big chunks and distribute it over the oiled pizza. Evenly distribute the sautéed broccoli over the mozzarella. Distribute the Italian sausage, in pieces, over the broccoli. Season with salt and pepper, top with the pecorino flakes, and finish by drizzling the remaining olive oil.

INGREDIENTS:

3½ ounces (100 g) broccoli (fresh or frozen)

3 tablespoons olive oil

1 garlic clove

3 ounces (85 g) fresh mozzarella (with liquid well drained)

3 ounces (85 g) Italian sausage

Black pepper

Salt

1 tablespoon Pecorino cheese flakes

## PARMA HAM *and* SMOKED CHEESE

Pour and distribute 1 tablespoon of olive oil over the pizza disk. Slice the mozzarella in strips or simply pull it apart in big chunks and distribute it over the oiled pizza. Slice the smoked cheese in strips and distribute it over the mozzarella. Season with salt and pepper. Top with the Parma ham and Parmesan flakes, and finish with a drizzle of olive oil.

INGREDIENTS:

2 tablespoons olive oil

3 ounces (85 g) fresh mozzarella (with liquid well drained)

3 ounces (85 g) smoked cheese, like provola

Salt

Black pepper

3 slices of Parma ham

1 tablespoon Parmesan cheese flakes

## GRILLED BELL PEPPERS *and* CHORIZO

Wash the bell pepper, cut in strips or big chunks and grill in a grilling pan. Place in a bowl and season with salt and 1 tablespoon olive oil. You can do this just before making the pizza or the day before, leaving the grilled bell pepper to marinate in the fridge, covered, overnight. Spread the crushed tomato sauce over the pizza starting from the center of the disk. Slice the mozzarella in strips or simply pull it apart in big chunks and distribute it over the tomato sauce. Evenly distribute the grilled pepper over the mozzarella. Top the mozzarella with the chorizo slices and finish with the Parmesan flakes. Season with salt and pepper, and drizzle with the remaining olive oil.

**INGREDIENTS:**

| | |
|---|---|
| 1 | bell pepper |
| | Salt |
| 2 | tablespoons olive oil |
| 2½ | ounces (70 g) crushed peeled tomatoes (canned or fresh) |
| 3 | ounces (85 g) fresh mozzarella (with liquid well drained) |
| 2½ | ounces (70 g) sliced chorizo |
| 1 | tablespoon Parmesan cheese flakes |
| | Black pepper |

## ROAST BEEF *and* SPINACH

Wash the spinach and toss in a bowl with 1 tablespoon olive oil. Pour and distribute 1 tablespoon of olive oil over the pizza disk. Slice the mozzarella in strips or simply pull it apart in big chunks and distribute it over the oiled pizza. Distribute the spinach over the mozzarella and then the roast beef over the spinach. Top with little dollops of béarnaise sauce. Season with salt and pepper and finish by drizzling the remaining olive oil.

**INGREDIENTS:**

| | |
|---|---|
| | Spinach, fresh, one big handful (or baby spinach) |
| 3 | tablespoons olive oil |
| 3 | ounces (85 g) fresh mozzarella (with liquid well drained) |
| 3½ | ounces (100 g) thinly sliced roast beef (cut in strips) |
| 2 | tablespoons béarnaise sauce |
| | Salt |
| | Black pepper |

# FISH-BASED

Fish can perfectly complement a pizza, particularly small and savory fishes like anchovies or fish that have been processed in a way to make it savory, like canned tuna fish or smoked salmon.

## ANCHOVIES *and* MOZZARELLA

Spread the crushed tomato sauce over the pizza starting from the center of the disk. Slice the mozzarella in strips or simply pull it apart in big chunks and distribute it over the tomato sauce. Cut the anchovies in half and distribute them evenly over the mozzarella. Season with salt and oregano, finish with the Parmesan flakes and drizzle with the olive oil.

INGREDIENTS:

- 2½ ounces (70 g) crushed peeled tomatoes (canned or fresh)
- 3 ounces (85 g) fresh mozzarella (with liquid well drained)
- 5–6 canned anchovies

  Salt

  Oregano
- 1 tablespoon Parmesan cheese flakes
- 1 teaspoon olive oil

## SHRIMP, PINK MAYONNAISE, *and* LETTUCE

Spread the crushed tomato sauce over the pizza starting from the center of the disk. Drizzle with olive oil, season with salt, and bake as usual. Once the pizza is fully baked, let it cool and spread the mayonnaise over the tomato sauce. Top with the shrimp and the lettuce and season with salt and pepper. Finish with an abundant drizzle of olive oil.

INGREDIENTS:

- 2½ ounces (70 g) crushed peeled tomatoes (canned or fresh)
- 2 tablespoons olive oil

  Salt
- 2 tablespoons pink mayonnaise
- 3½ ounces (100 g) cooked and peeled shrimp (canned or fresh)

  Lettuce, a handful, washed and chopped

  Black pepper

# TUNA FISH, RED ONIONS, BLACK OLIVES

Spread the crushed tomato sauce over the pizza starting from the center of the disk. Slice the mozzarella in strips or simply pull it apart in big chunks and distribute it over the tomato sauce. Evenly distribute the tuna fish over the mozzarella, and then finish with the red onion slices and olives. Season with salt and pepper and drizzle with the olive oil.

**INGREDIENTS:**

- 2½ ounces (70 g) crushed peeled tomatoes (canned or fresh)
- 3 ounces (85 g) fresh mozzarella (with liquid well drained)
- 3 ounces (85 g) canned tuna fish in olive oil (well drained)
- Red onion, a few thin slices
- Black olives, a handful
- Salt
- Black pepper
- 1 tablespoon olive oil

# SMOKED SALMON, SPINACH, *and* RICOTTA

Wash the spinach and toss in a bowl with 1 tablespoon olive oil. Pour and distribute 1 tablespoon of olive oil over the pizza disk. Slice the mozzarella in strips or simply pull it apart in big chunks and distribute it over the oiled pizza. Distribute the spinach over the mozzarella, and the salmon over the spinach. Top with little dollops of ricotta cheese. Season with salt and pepper and finish by drizzling the remaining olive oil.

**INGREDIENTS:**

- Spinach, fresh, a big handful (or baby spinach)
- 3 tablespoons olive oil
- 3 ounces (85 g) fresh mozzarella (with liquid well drained)
- 2½ ounces (70 g) smoked salmon, cut in thin slices
- 2 tablespoons ricotta cheese
- Salt
- Black pepper

# PIZZA *in* TEGLIA

**YIELD** 2 PAN PIZZAS (10 SERVINGS)/ **ACTIVE TIME:** 40 MINUTES / **TOTAL TIME:** 2 HOURS
PLUS 12–16 HOURS IN THE FRIDGE

This is a lovely and simple vegetarian pan pizza that is easy to make and can feed many with just one bake. It's best to top it with wild mushrooms like chanterelle, which are lovely on pizza, but any mushroom will do. Check pages 472-473 for more in-depth directions on pan pizza making.

## DAY 1

1  The night before, activate the yeast in 5 tablespoons of the water, heated to 105°F and let rest for 10 minutes.

2  In a large bowl, combine the activated yeast to the rest of the water, then add the flour and combine well. Let rest for a half hour, then add the salt. Place the dough in an airtight container and let rest in the fridge until the day after.

3  It's also better to make the mushrooms ahead: Sauté the mushrooms with the garlic cloves (whole) in a little olive oil. Toward the end, add the chopped parsley and remove the garlic. Refrigerate until needed.

## DAY 2

1  The afternoon or night of the next day, preheat the oven to maximum temperature.

2  Oil 2 baking dishes. Pour the dough in one of them and divide it in half (the other half goes in the second baking dish).

3  Preheat the oven to maximum temperature, with the baking stone (if available) in the middle rack.

4  This is the most important step: Very gently, without pressing out the air pockets, try to spread the dough in the pan. It's best to do this incrementally, allowing the dough to spread (relax) by itself with time.

5  Do the same with the second piece of dough and let both pieces rest, covered, in the pans for 30 minutes to 1 hour. Do not use a kitchen towel to cover, as it will stick to the dough.

6  Sprinkle with olive oil and place the first pan directly on the bottom of the oven. Bake for 10 minutes.

**INGREDIENTS:**

- 2⅕ pounds (1 kg) all-purpose flour

- 3½ cups (840g) lukewarm water

- 3⅕ teaspoons active dry yeast

- 3½ teaspoons sea salt

- 1 pound fresh mushrooms, washed and roughly chopped (I recommend chanterelle)

- 2 cloves garlic

- 1 handful of fresh parsley, chopped

- 5 ounces olive oil–marinated artichokes, sliced lengthwise

- 1 medium-sized mozzarella (firm flesh), diced

- 1 medium-sized buffalo mozzarella, torn apart with your hands

- Olive oil and marine salt, to season

7 Lower the oven temperature to 430°F and take the pizza out and cover with the firm mozzarella, mushrooms, and half of the artichokes. Place back in the oven, this time on the middle rack.

8 Bake until it looks golden (but not burned) and looks cooked through (but not dry)—about 10-15 minutes, depending on your oven. It may take longer if your oven does not get very hot.

9 Once out, finish with the buffalo mozzarella and remaining artichokes.

**LA SVOLTA**

*La Svolta*

450 Hampton Street
Hampton Victoria 3188
Australia
+61 3 9521 8990
www.lasvolta.com.au

It's often said that the truest test of any pizzeria is their Margherita pizza. If that's true, then La Svolta has nothing to worry about. Known for their simplicity and passion, owners Valerio Calabro and Giueseppe "Pino" Russo consistently make one of the best Margherita pizzas in Australia.

"We always dreamed of having our own place, the space in Hampton came up and the feeling was right, so we made it our home," says Calabro. But Calabro and Russo's pizza-baking roots go back much further than that. When asked where they learned to cook, both cite their mothers and grandmothers in Italy. Whether the owners of La Svolta had any previous jobs or apprenticeships almost becomes irrelevant—at La Svolta, the only way to make authentic pizza is to have lived that authenticity. Considering the final product, it's hard to argue.

"'La Svolta' literally translates to 'the turning point.' It was a huge turning point in our lives to be able to open our own restaurant and showcase our style of Italian food and pizza," says Russo. But it isn't just the food on display—it's the entire culture. La Svolta's open, friendly space ensures that guests can experience the feel of a local Naples pizzeria as well. For Russo and Calabro, though, it all comes back to simplicity. What non-essential item should every pizza-maker have? That's easy— "a great set of hands!"

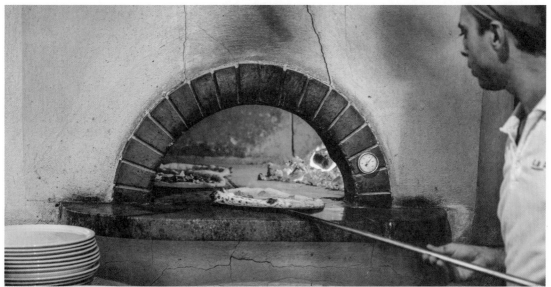

"But it isn't just the food display—it's the entire culture."

# IN THEIR OWN WORDS:

## VALERIO CALABRO AND GIUSEPPE "PINO" RUSSO OF LA SVOLTA

*How and when did you get your start baking? Why pizza over other breads or pastries?*

Our passion has always been for making pizza—not baking! We began making pizza together in 2006 and opened La Svolta in 2010.

*Who—or what—first inspired you to make pizza? Who inspires you now?*

We were inspired by the art of cooking good, traditional Italian food and pizza is a part of that tradition. And always our mothers in the kitchen, of course.

*What is your golden rule(s) for baking?*

Cook the pizza for 60 to 90 seconds in a wood oven set at 400°Celsius.

*What is your favorite pizza to bake? Why? Least favorite pizza to bake? Why?*

The classic Margherita—it's a classic, and delicious! We don't have a least favorite.

*How did La Svolta come to be? Why Hampton? What are your most popular items?*

Our most popular pizzas are the Signor George (San Marzano tomato, fior di latte mozzarella, salami, olives, and chili), the Linda (San Marzano tomato, bocconcini, cherry tomatoes, rocket, prosciutto di Parma, shaved Parmigiano), and the classic Margherita.

*What book(s) go on your required reading list for bakers?*

While we don't really use guidebooks, La Svolta is part of the Associazione Verace Pizza Napoletana (www.pizzanapoletana.org). We prepare our pizzas based on the guidelines of the association, which has given us a global accreditation.

*What outlets/periodicals/newspapers do you read or consult regularly, if any?*

We read *The Age*, *Herald Sun*, and *Broadsheet.com.au*—these are the strongest supporters of Melbourne's restaurant industry.

*Tell me about your most memorable collaboration with another chef.*

We work together every day…its always memorable!

*Do you follow any cooking shows or chefs? If so, which is your favorite?*

Salvatore Santucci is a master pizza maker from AVPN who we follow online.

*Brag about yourselves a bit. What are your highest achievements and/or proudest moments as chefs?*

Opening La Svolta and winning Melbourne's Best Pizzeria Award in 2012. Seven years later, we were recently listed in the top-20 pizzerias in Victoria—a huge honor.

*Tell me about your baking process.*

Proof the dough twice over 36 hours, and cook the pizza in a wood fire oven for 60 to 90 seconds at 400°Celsius.

*What's your favorite kind of pizza crust, and why? Favorite toppings?*

Naples-style pizza is the best for us; that's what we make, and why we belong to the prestigious AVPN.

# LA SVOLTA PIZZA DOUGH

YIELD: 4-6 PIZZA BASES / ACTIVE TIME: 20 MINUTES / TOTAL TIME: 6 HOURS 15 MINUTES

This is the traditional method for making pizza dough in Italy's iconic pizza mecca, Naples.
—*courtesy of Valerio Calabro and Pino Russo, La Svolta*

**INGREDIENTS:**

- 4¼ cups water
- 3½ pounds 00 flour, plus extra for dusting
- ⅛ ounce fresh yeast
- 2¼ tablespoons salt

1 Put 3⅓ cups of water into a bowl add salt and dissolve the water.

2 In a separate bowl use the remaining water to melt the yeast.

3 Add 7 ounces of the flour to the water and salt, then add the dissolved yeast.

4 Add the rest of the flour gradually until the dough achieves achieve a smooth and elastic consistency. Leave dough in the bowl, cover with a damp cloth and set aside to proof for about 2 hours.

5 When it has doubled in size, roll the dough into individual-sized balls (approximately 7 ½ to 8 ounces each) and proof for another 4 hours. When the balls have doubled in size, your dough is ready!

# PIZZA MARGHERITA

YIELD: 1 LARGE PIZZA / ACTIVE TIME: 20 MINUTES / TOTAL TIME: 30 MINUTES

A firm favorite of most Italians, Pizza Margherita is a classic for good reason - these simple ingredients come together to make something really special.
—*courtesy of Valerio Calabro and Pino Russo, La Svolta*

1 Preheat oven to 425°F. Put your pizza stone or tray into the oven to preheat.

2 Hand stretch or roll the pizza dough to form a 10-inch disc and place onto your hot pizza stone or tray.

3 To make the Napoli Sauce: put tomatoes in a bowl and add all the remaining ingredients.

4 Using a stick mixer, combine the ingredients together until the sauce has a chunky texture.

5 Spread napoli sauce over the base and top with quality mozzarella cheese (we use either Fior di Latte or Buffalo). Place 3 to 4 basil leaves on top and drizzle with extra virgin olive oil.

6 Cook for 10 minutes, or until cooked to your liking. When the base is crisp and brown, it's ready.

7 Drizzle with extra virgin olive oil and serve immediately.

## INGREDIENTS:

- 8 ounces pizza dough (see page 495)
- 2½ ounces napoli sauce (see recipe below)
- 2 ounces quality mozzarella cheese, sliced
- 3–4 fresh basil leaves

  Drizzle of extra virgin olive oil

## NAPOLI SAUCE

- 2 14-ounce tins of whole peeled Italian tomatoes
- 6 basil leaves, finely chopped
- 2 tablespoons extra virgin olive oil
- 1 teaspoon salt

# 400 GRADI

## 400 Gradi

99 Lygon Street
East Brunswick, Victoria 3057
Australia
+61 3 9380 2320
www.400gradi.com.au

"There's only one type of pizza crust," says Johnny Di Francesco. "The one on a Napoletana pizza." The 400 Gradi owner is a purist in every sense of the word, and it shows in his pizza. His Margherita is one of the best in the world—literally. In 2014, Di Francesco took home top honors in the Pizza World Championship (Campionato Mondiale Della Pizza) in Parma, Italy, where he faced off against 600 competitors from 35 countries.

It's a great honor, but for the Naples-descended *pizzaiolo*, success is nothing without family. "I'm inspired by a lot of chefs from around the world, the ones who are fusing tradition with trends, but I'm mostly inspired by my Dad—his love of good food and family, and making sure the two came together often, is something I think about every time I cook."

Di Francesco's hard work has helped put Australia's pizza scene on the map, and rightfully so. The tangy, crispy crust is as true a taste of Italy as one can find outside of the old country. No wonder, then, that he serves as the Australasian Principal of the AVPN—personally testing other pizzaiolos before inducting them into the association. For Di Francesco, it's just a labor of love. "I never thought about cooking anything else; pizza became my absolute passion."

## IN HIS OWN WORDS:

## JOHNNY DI FRANCESCO OF 400 GRADI

*How and when did you get your start baking? Why pizza over other breads or pastries?*

As a true *pizzaiolo*, I'm not sure I'd call it baking—but I started making pizza when I was 12 years old, and I did it to buy myself a pair of sneakers. My family couldn't afford designer shoes, so I realized that if I wanted them, I had to buy them myself. I started working in a pizza shop washing dishes and literally worked my way up from there—it just found its way into my blood.

*What is your golden rule(s) for baking?*

Hero your ingredients. The end result of any dish is only ever going to be as good as the

ingredients in it. Traditional Napoletana pizza uses very few, but very good, ingredients and they each need to shine.

*What does 400 Gradi represent to you?*

It represents so much. The name itself represents the temperature that a traditional pizza needs to be cooked at.

*Flavor-wise, why do you love Napoletana crust so much?*

It's full of air, chewy, light, and a delight to eat!

# 400 GRADI'S NAPOLETANA MARGHERITA PIZZA

**YIELD:** 1 PIZZA / **ACTIVE TIME:** 30 MINUTES / **TOTAL TIME:** 40 MINUTES, PLUS 10-12 HOURS FOR RISING

A traditional Napoletana Pizza Margherita is the ultimate crowd pleaser. Made with love, the dough is fluffy and just the right amount of chewy, and this is the same recipe that won me the title of the best in the world at The World Pizza Championships in Parma.

*—courtesy of Johnny Di Francesco, 400 Gradi*

## NAPOLETANA PIZZA DOUGH (MAKES 4-5 DOUGH BALLS)

1 In a bowl, combine water and salt and allow to dissolve.

2 Add about 10 percent of the flour and mix. Mix well, then add more flour and the yeast. Continue to add the remaining flour and mix well until combined.

3 Turn dough onto a lightly floured surface and knead until smooth and elastic. This can take up to 10 minutes. Place the dough into a lightly floured bowl, cover with a damp cloth and set aside.

4 Let the dough rest for 30 minutes, then divide into 4 to 5 round balls. Cover with a damp tea towel and allow the dough balls to rise. This can take up to 10 to 12 hours.

5 Once the dough has doubled in size place on a lightly floured bench, and stretch the dough by hand into pizza bases. Alternatively, dough balls can be wrapped in plastic and stored in the freezer or refrigerator for later use.

## MARGHERITA PIZZA

1 Roll out one ball of dough to desired size.

2 Spread the San Marzano tomato and top with buffalo mozzarella.

3 Place 4 basil leaves on top and drizzle some extra virgin olive oil.

4 Bake at 500–535°F for 10 minutes (domestic oven) or 750°F for 90 seconds (woodfire oven).

### INGREDIENTS:

**NAPOLETANA PIZZA DOUGH**

2½ pounds 00 flour, sieved (roughly 8 cups)

2 tablespoons fine sea salt

¼ teaspoon fresh yeast

2½ cups water

**MARGHERITA PIZZA**

1 ball pizza dough (see above)

San Marzano tomatoes, crushed by hand

Buffalo mozzarella

Fresh basil

Extra virgin olive oil

## Dante's Pizzeria

www.dantespizzeria.co.nz

136 Ponsonby Road
Ponsonby, Auckland 1011
New Zealand
+64 9-378 4443

2/40 Hurstmere Road
Takapuna, Auckland 0622
New Zealand
+64 9-486 3668

How does *pizzaiolo* Kevin Morris (he of the Michelin-starred Dante's Pizzeria; host to prime ministers, advisor to celebrity chefs, television *pizzaiolo*) make such a brilliant Margherita? According to him, love. "The most important rule for me, before I start any recipe or idea, is that it has to come from the heart. Most bakers will tell you baking requires some luck. I choose to replace luck with love. When you put love and care into your baking, your finished dish will smile back at you with much more love when taken out from the oven."

Ah, if only it was so simple. But there's no denying Morris' passion, which has been cultivated over years of experience in Italy and elsewhere. What began with him watching his Italian mother bake focaccia in London, and continued during frequent visits to his grandparents' home in Italy, has led him to become one of the Southern Hemisphere's most respected authorities on pizza Napoletana. And that's not just a platitude.

His was only the second pizza in the Southern Hemisphere to receive "La Vera Pizza Napoletana," a title that indicates his pizza (specifically, the Margherita) counts as true pizza Napoletana and is a legitimate member of the Naples pizza scene—protected by European law!

It is easy to lose track of the the many achievements Morris has reached in his career. Dante's has been awarded "Best Pizza in Auckland" by *Metro Magazine* four years in a row. In 2014, they also won "The Best Pizza in NZ" by Campionato Mondiale Della Pizza. He has appeared on New Zealand television to spread his gospel, and received countless write-ups in local and national publications.

For Kevin Morris, though, it all comes back to his mother's focaccia bread in the kitchen all those years ago. Without it, he would have never fallen in love with dough—and the world would never get to enjoy his true pizza Napoletana.

"When it comes to food, I like simple dishes done well,
with the best ingredients you can get."

# IN HIS OWN WORDS:

## KEVIN MORRIS OF DANTE'S PIZZERIA

*How did Dante's come to be? What are your most popular items?*

One afternoon at a friend's barbecue, I was talking about pizza Margherita and how I wished I could find one to eat. As a result, a friend suggested I open a pizzeria myself. So I did. At this time, Auckland's restaurant scene was growing, so I started my first pizzeria in Kumeu, and Dante's Pizzeria Napoletana was born. Later on, we moved to Ponsonby, Auckland. We are most famous for our Margherita, along with the sourdough Panouzzi (A Napoli Street sub sandwich), and our fried sourdough dressed in tomato sauce and mozzarella.

*Who—or what—first inspired you to make pizza? Who inspires you now?*

In 2008, I was invited by Associazione Verace Pizza Napoletana in Naples to experience their culture and advance my knowledge of pizza Napoletana. During this time, I was honored to meet and work at Pizzeria Gaetano along with Gaetano himself in Ischia. Even now, he is still the man who inspires me to uphold the art of the perfect "cornicione"—the perfect crust of the true pizza Napoletana.

*What does Dante's mean to you?*

Dante was my Italian grandfather. Every Christmas as kids, we would fly to Italy to visit my grandparents. All my memories of that time were always about food. As a result, I wanted to use my grandfather's name to tie in my Italian side when opening my pizzeria.

*What is your favorite pizza to make? Can you talk a bit about your process?*

When it comes to food, I like simple dishes done well, with the best ingredients you can get. Therefore, the pizza Margherita. It begins with the two-day sourdough base, after which the dough is stretched by hand. I then spread on hand-crushed San Marzano tomatoes imported from Italy, sprinkle with freshly picked basil, hand-broken buffalo mozzarella, and finish with a drizzle of extra virgin olive oil. It's important to remember that less is more. Finally, the pizza is cooked in a very hot wood-fired oven for just over a minute. During this time, I use the turning peel to turn the pizza in order to achieve an even cook. As the pizza arrives on the table, the aroma of the wood fire blended with the sourdough base and basil is what makes the Margherita a Michelin star winning dish.

*Where do you get your tools/materials? What non-essential items should every pizza baker have?*

The oven is the most important item. We imported our ovens from Naples and pizza tools from different parts of Italy. Every Naples oven has a dome shape, which allows a swirling effect of intense heat to create the pizza Napoletana's signature blisters around the crust. In addition, a marble work bench is necessary to open (stretch) the pizza dough. Marble has a cool and even temperature all year, so the dough is always easy to work with. Last but not least, a good pizza peel and a turning peel are essential to place the pizza into the oven and help with even cooking. I also recommend a pizza stone for even cooking and to improve your crust.

*What book(s) go on your required reading list for bakers?*

One of my favorite books to read is *Bread* by Dean Brettschneider. Dean explains how simple baking can be as long as you prioritise the basic products. As we all say, practice makes perfect; once you have mastered the basics and understood the taste, texture and feel of the dough, other baking will come easily.

*Brag about yourself a bit. What are your proudest moments as a chef?*

When I decided to open my own pizzeria, I started looking for the best pizza recipe. After days and days of trying different recipes, I made my mind up on pizza Napoletana. However, I kept practising and changing the recipe until I was able to achieve the light, fluffy and chewy crust of the traditional Pizza Napoletana. That was when Dante's Pizzeria was born. As I learned more about pizza Napoletana, I found AVPN (see page 477), which is an organization that protects the art and craft of the true Naples Pizza. After contacting them and discussing what I do with them, they invited me to Naples to advance my knowledge of "opening the dough."

In early 2008, New Zealand Prime Minister and National Party leader John Key visited Dante's. He was not just happy enjoying his pizza, he also rolled up his sleeves and joined me in my kitchen for a one-on-one pizza making lesson. Key also made a joke that the chance to swap politics for pizza could also be tempting. I told him with a smile that if he ever wanted a part-time job, I'd happily employ him.

*Favorite crust?*

Napolitana crust is always the best. It's light, fluffy, crispy, and chewy, all at once. Since the dough is a two-day fermentation, the pizza base and crust can be digested easily and are light on your stomach, leaving room for your favorite dessert. Besides Margherita, my other favorite pizza topping is hot calabrese salami, another must-have in my pantry.

# DANTE'S MUM'S KICKBUTT PIZZA

**YIELD:** 6 5-INCH PERSONAL PIZZAS / **ACTIVE TIME:** 1 HOUR / **TOTAL TIME:** 12-30 HOURS + 5 MINUTES

These personal pizzas are packed with flavor and perfect for sharing with family and friends.

— *courtesy of Kevin Morris of Dante's Pizzeria*

1 In a large saucepan, heat the olive oil over medium heat. Add the onion and garlic and season with the flaky sea salt. Cook until soft, light and golden 8–10 minutes. Add the thyme and carrot and cook until the carrot is quite soft, about 5 minutes.

2 Add the tomatoes with their juice and bring to a boil, stirring often. Lower the heat, crush the chicken or veggie stock cube. Now simmer until it thickens, about 30 minutes. When finished, cover and set aside for later use.

3 Now for the fun part: pour the water into a bowl and mix the salt and yeast together (yes, this is the correct way).

4 Gradually add the flour to the water, kneading until the dough starts pulling away from the sides and becomes ball.

5 Remove to a lightly floured work top and start to knead the ball of dough with light "crisscross" punches, folding the dough back on to itself. Keep working in the dry flour, and continue until the dough has absorbed all of the flour from the work bench.

6 Now divide the dough into 3 evenly sized portions and work each into a small ball. Place them in a large tray, with plenty of space between each of the balls, and cover with a wet cloth. Allow them to rest for 6 to 8 hours before use (preferably maintaining a temperature of around 70°F if possible).

7 After 6 to 8 hours, your dough is ready to be used. Using your hands, flatten each ball until they are about 5 or 6 inches in diameter.

8 Once they are shaped, preheat your oven on 480°F and turn on the broiler. Bake them on the on the top rack, watching them closely. Once they start to fill with steam and brown a little on top, flip them to brown the other side.

9 Remove them from the oven and let cool a little. Cut each crust in half horizontally (like you are making a sandwich), making two pizza bases each. Now it's ready for Mum's pizza sauce.

## INGREDIENTS:

### FOR MUM'S PIZZA SAUCE:

¼ cup extra-virgin olive oil

1 large white onion, cut into quarters then cut into chunks to the thickness of your little finger (do not dice)

4 cloves of garlic, thinly sliced

1 medium carrot, finely grated

3 tablespoons chopped fresh thyme

2 400g cans of Italian whole peeled tomatoes, crushed by hand

1 chicken stock cube, or vegetable stock cube if preferred

Good quality flaky sea salt, to taste

### FOR THE DOUGH:

1 cup cool water (50°F-60°F)

2½ tablespoons fine sea salt

½ teaspoon fresh yeast

3½ cups Italian 00 flour (available in most specialty stores)

### FOR THE TOPPING:

Pizza sauce (see above)

Buffalo mozzarella

Fresh basil

10 Cover the pizza bases with the warm sauce, fresh basil, and buffalo mozzarella cheese.

11 Place the finished bases on aluminum foil or a baking sheet and gently return to oven, placing them under the broiler as before. Keep your eyes on them as you only need to melt the cheese and char the exposed pizza base. This should only take 3 to 5 minutes. Remove and enjoy.

Tip: If you don't feel like kneading the dough by hand, you can use a mixer. Set it to speed 1 and leave it for 20 minutes.

# PIZZA PILGRIMS

## Pizza Pilgrims

www.pizzapilgrims.co.uk

| | | |
|---|---|---|
| 11 Kingly Street<br>W1B 5PW<br>+44 20-7287-2200 | 136 Shoreditch High Street<br>E1 6JE<br>England<br>+44 20-3019-7620 | 12 Hertsmere Road<br>London, E14 4AE<br>England<br>+44 20-3019-8020 |
| Covent Garden<br>23 Garrick St<br>WC2E 9BN<br>England<br>+44 20-7240-4145 | 11 Dean Street<br>W1D 3RP<br>England<br>+44 20-7287-8964 | Westgate Roof Terrace<br>OX1 1PG<br>England<br>+44 18-6580-8030 |
| 15 Exmouth Market<br>EC1R 4QD<br>England<br>+44 20-8069-6969 | 8 Browns Buildings<br>EC3A 8AL<br>England<br>+44 20-3846-3222 | |

If the name "Pizza Pilgrims" just strikes you as a fun, lighthearted title, you're not thinking literally enough. Thom and James Elliott's pizzeria was not named flippantly—the brothers had to live it before they could create it.

Let's backtrack. The Elliott Brothers sat in the London pub where they worked, thinking about the future. "We were in the pub and drew a picture of a three-wheeled van with a pizza oven in the back. It has been a pretty mad ride since then." This kernel of an idea brought them to Sicily, where they purchased a three-wheeled tuk-tuk and began what can only be called a "pizza pilgrimage." "We knew nothing when we set out," says James. "It took six weeks driving at 18 mph, but we got to spend time working in the best pizzerias across the country."

The long, delicious journey was more than a spiritual awakening—it was the beginning of a major pizza enterprise. Today, there are eight Pizza Pilgrims locations, all known for their reliably delicious pizza Napoletana. "[Neapolitan crust] immediately jumped at us while we were travelling through Italy. The only other style that came close was Roman, where the crust is thinner and a little more 'sophisticated.' I really love how hearty Neapolitan pizza is without being heavy and doughy."

Customers seem to agree. Says James, "Opening our first restaurant was very stressful and took long hours, but the sense of achievement in seeing a happy, busy restaurant on a Friday night is hard to beat!" It helps that, despite their relative inexperience with cooking, the two men spent years working in and around in kitchens and knew how they wanted customers to feel. "We sell pizza, and that is very important to us, but it has also become about creating spaces and food that we really love."

# IN HIS OWN WORDS:

## JAMES ELLIOTT OF PIZZA PILGRIMS

*Who—or what—first inspired you to make pizza? Who inspires you now?*

My brother and I had much more normal jobs and hated them! The first pizzaiolo I worked with was Antonino Esposito from a pizzeria in Sorrento. He taught me the basics of pizza and we still use the dough recipe he taught us! We are inspired from everywhere now, not just pizza places. The London food scene is really exciting, with a lot of independent companies trying new things. London is the place to be at the moment.

*What is your golden rule(s) for baking?*

The wetter the better! We try to keep our dough at as high a hydration level as possible to ensure a gloriously soft crust.

*What is your favorite pizza to bake? Why? Least favorite pizza to bake? Why?*

My favorite pizza to bake is that with a Nduja topping. It is a smoked and cured pork sausage with chili we found in Calabria. You bake it on the pizza and it melts, dressing the pizza in amazing smoky oils. Otherwise, I'd say chicken on pizza is my absolute no-no.

*Where do you get your tools/materials? What non-essential items should every pizza baker have?*

Our ovens are actually produced in Dorset, UK. We work with this amazing company called Gozney Ovens who produce fantastic Naples-style ovens.

*What book(s) go on your required reading list for bakers?*

Chris Bianco has a fantastic book on pizza, *Bianco: Pizza, Pasta, and Other Food I Like,* which was great bedtime reading while we were setting up. We have also written a cookbook on pizza—*Pizza Pilgrims: Recipes from the Backstreets of Italy.* It was a really fun process and brings together everything we learned about pizza and Italian cooking during our travels.

*What outlets/periodicals/newspapers do you read or consult regularly, if any?*

I have to say we find ourselves looking at what others do less and less. If you are constantly checking out what the rest of the world is doing you stop concentrating on what you're doing.

*Tell me about your most memorable collaboration with another chef.*

We are currently collaborating with British cured meat specialist Cannon and Cannon. We thought it would be fun to re-invent the Meat Feast pizza using great British ingredients. It is on our menu for the month and people are loving it!

*Do you follow any cooking shows or chefs? If so, which is your favorite?*

I grew up watching cooking shows. It was basically how I learned to cook. I used to watch a lot of Jamie Oliver when he was doing the Naked Chef stuff. These days I love watching people like Nigel Slater and Simon Hopkinson.

Basically, great home cooking—not *Boiling Point* or *Kitchen Nightmares!*

*Where did you learn to cook? Please tell me about your education and apprenticeships.*

We both grew up in a pub, so we always had summer jobs in the kitchen. Apart from that we were very much self-taught. As I said, we were not chefs before we started Pizza Pilgrims, so it has been a steep learning curve.

*Tell me about your baking process.*

Our process is exactly the same as they do in Naples pizzerias. We make very simple dough from tipo 00 Caputo blue flour, cold water, sea salt, and fresh baker's yeast. We mix it for a short time to not overdevelop the glutens, then roll it into individual balls. It proofs at room temperature for approximately 12 hours and then is blocked in the fridge for an additional 24 hours to slow proof. We then bring the dough out and bring it back to room temperature, and it ready to use.

# PIZZA PILGRIMS' NEAPOLITAN PIZZA DOUGH

**YIELD:** 10 BALLS OF PIZZA DOUGH / **ACTIVE TIME:** 25 MINUTES / **TOTAL TIME:** 8½ - 24 HOURS

There are three stages to this recipe – making and proving the dough, making the pizza base and then making the pizza itself in a frying pan. This recipe is for a traditional Margherita, but you can of course add other toppings once it is in the frying pan – just remember that less is more! So here goes…

—*Pizza Pilgrims*

**INGREDIENTS:**

- **8** cups flour with a high gluten content
- **⅔** teaspoon fresh baker's yeast
- **2½** cups cold water
- **3½** teaspoons table salt

1 Tip the flour onto your work service and make a well in the center. Dissolve your yeast in the water and pour into the middle of the well a little at a time whilst using your hands to bring the walls of the flour in so that the water begins to thicken. Once you've reached the consistency of custard, add the salt and bring in the rest of the flour until it comes together as a dough. Knead for 10–15 minutes.

2 Cover and leave to rest for 10 minutes before kneading again quickly for 10 seconds (this helps to develop the flavor and the gluten).

3 Divide the dough into 10 or so evenly sized balls and leave to rest overnight or for at least 8 hours (24 hours is optimal, 48 hours maximum) in a sealed container or a deep baking dish sprinkled with flour and covered in cling film. Remember to leave space for each of your dough balls because, as the gluten relaxes, they will spread out to take up twice the diameter that they do initially.

4 After proving, the dough balls are ready to use straight away. We would recommend always making this amount of dough, even if you are only making pizza for a few people. There is a good chance you might want a second (or third, or fourth, etc.) and pizza dough is actually fine to freeze once it has proved. Just defrost it in the fridge next time you want pizza—it's easier and quicker than ordering a takeaway!

5 Scrape a dough ball out of its container using a spatula and as much flour as you need to ensure it doesn't stick. The rounder the dough ball comes out, the rounder the final pizza base.

6 Put the dough ball onto a well-floured surface (honestly, if you are going to get serious about pizza making, get used to having flour play a large part in your life).

7 Using your fingertips, press out the dough ball firmly, starting at the center and working out to the edge. Ensure you leave a half an inch around the rim of the pizza untouched.

8 Turn the dough ball over and repeat the pressing out process on the other side.

9 Using the palm of your hand, do one firm push in the center of the dough ball to ensure the thickness of the base is consistent (not counting the raised edges).

10 Take the newly flattened dough ball on the back of your hands, ensuring the weight is on your knuckles and that your fingertips and nails are not going to poke a hole in the dough.

11 Using the back of your hands, stretch the dough out as far as you can without tearing it (now there's a challenge). Turn the dough through 90 degrees and repeat this stretching. Do this a few times.

12 You should now have a disc of dough around 10 inches in diameter, consistently thin but with a slightly thicker rim. We are ready to cook.

# FRYING PAN MARGHERITA PIZZA

YIELD: 4 10-INCH PIZZAS / ACTIVE TIME: 20 MINUTES / TOTAL TIME: ABOUT 22-25 MINUTES

This method is the best way to make Neapolitan pizza at home, unless of course, you happen to have a Neapolitan stone oven in your kitchen. The frying pan and grill combo replicates the intense heat you need to cook the pizza quickly – and ensure that the dough does not dry out and become biscuit-y.
—*Pizza Pilgrims*

**INGREDIENTS:**

4   balls of Neapolitan Pizza Dough (see page 514)

1   can San Marzano (or any good-quality Italian) tomatoes

A good pinch of sea salt

Grated Parmesan

A handful of basil leaves

1   cup fior di latte cheese (cow's milk mozzarella), torn into pieces no bigger than a quarter

Extra virgin olive oil

1   Take the dough balls and press them out flat to make four 10 inch pizza bases using the tips of your fingers.

2   To make the tomato sauce, first crush the tomatoes by hand. This stops the seeds being whizzed up by the blender, which makes the sauce bitter. Add a pinch of salt, then blitz with a hand blender until you have a tomato sauce with a slightly rough texture.

3   Preheat the grill to its absolute highest setting.

4   Lay a pizza base flat in a dry frying pan (preferably non-stick) that has been on a high heat and is screaming hot.

5   Spread a thin layer of sauce with a ladle across the base, leaving a couple of centimetres round the edge for the crust. Add a pinch of Parmesan, basil leaves, and a quarter of the mozzarella, in that order. Drizzle with olive oil.

6   Once the base of the pizza has browned (about 1–2 minutes), take the frying pan and place it on the highest shelf, under the grill.

7   Once the crust has taken on some color (again about 1–2 minutes), the pizza is ready to go. Eat it fast (contrary to popular belief, pizza is not better cold the morning after!).

# Pizzaly

**Authentic Italian Pizza**
**Eat In & Take away**

## Pizzaly

561-565 Plenty Road
Preston Victoria 3072
Australia
+61 3-9470-2002
www.pizzaly.com.au

You love pizza. Everybody loves pizza. But do you love it more than Silvio Serpa and Anna Di Perna? Let's try a thought experiment—

You're in your 70's and you've reached retirement. A lifetime of work in the hospitality industry has brought you to this moment. You and your partner move away from your home of 20 years to a new country. You overcome the cultural and language barriers and become citizens—again, all after retirement. But something nags at you: Wherever you go, the pizza just isn't up to par. Do you A) keep trying new places, traveling the country to find one that satisfies your tastes, B) give up, and make do with what you have, or C) start your own pizza restaurant from scratch?

Unless you chose C, you probably don't love pizza as much as Silvio Serpa and Anna Di Perna, the married owners of Pizzaly in Preston, Victoria. "Silvio began his pizza making in 1982, transforming an existing restaurant in a beachside town in Tuscany into a pizzeria," says Di Perna. But Pizzaly wasn't born until much later, after the couple moved to Australia in 2008. "It was born out of Silvio's frustration in not being able to find a pizza in Melbourne that could satisfy his taste buds. He literally came out of retirement to start a pizza restaurant."

The returns have been promising, to say the least. Serpa won first place for Australia at the World Pizza Championship in Parma in 2016. That incredible honor aside, the couple have also received plenty of local attention as well. "At a local level, he was asked to participate in the "Local Legends Series" within the Darebin Food & Wine Festival in May 2017, where he gave a master class pizza demonstration to 50 participants." For the "local legend," though, there is no great mystery when it comes to good pizza. "Precise measurements, fresh ingredients, and a clean oven" are the rules to live by at Pizzaly—perhaps none more so than the last one, as Serpa bakes pizza directly on the oven floor.

Australia's pizza scene has blossomed in the last decade, and Serpa's discerning palate has much to do with that growth. Who knows where things would stand without his pizza particulars!

# IN HER OWN WORDS:

# ANNA DI PERNA OF PIZZALY

*What does Pizzaly represent to you?*

Pizzaly is the culmination of a lifelong career working in hospitality, and a wonderful opportunity to work as husband and wife again.

*What is your favorite pizza to bake? Why? Least favorite pizza to bake? Why?*

Silvio's favorite pizza to make is the Napoletana pizza with tomato, mozzarella, anchovies, and capers—because it's tasty! He dislikes making any pizza with too many ingredients because he does not believe you can distinguish the flavors as well. Toppings are there for a reason, and they should be balanced—not overbearing or overloaded.

*What book(s) go on your required reading list for bakers?*

There is no one "go-to book" for us, but a collection of recipe books and notes taken over the years of tried and tested recipes, quite a few of which have been handed down from both our families.

*What outlets/periodicals/newspapers do you read or consult regularly, if any?*

I like to get my hands on anything food-related. Silvio doesn't have time to read!

*Tell me about your most memorable collaboration with another chef.*

The input Silvio received from the man who showed him how to make an excellent pizza.

I have worked in hospitality for many years alongside my husband, but have also collaborated with highly acclaimed Italian chefs in both Italy and Australia.

*Do you follow any cooking shows or chefs? If so, which is your favorite?*

Neither of us are into the cooking shows—in our opinion, they don't depict real life kitchen or cooking experiences!

*Where did you learn to cook? Please tell me about your education and apprenticeships.*

Silvio began his cooking experience by taking over the restaurant by the sea all those years ago in 1982. He watched and learned, adding his own creative flare in the kitchen and then expanding to include pizza.

I have worked in numerous restaurants in Italy, from trattoria-style to high-end fine dining restaurants. I have collaborated with Silvio in this, our fourth restaurant together. My passion for cooking and baking stretches everywhere, from appetizers to handmade pastas to desserts. I prepare all the sweets served at Pizzaly, including short crust tarts, tiramisu, chocolate mousse, crème brûlée, and homemade ice cream.

*What's your favorite kind of pizza crust, and why? Favorite toppings?*

Silvio and I agree that our favorite pizza is a thin-based pizza cooked directly on the stone in a wood-fired oven. Toppings should be minimal, but of the highest quality available including, fior di latte mozzarella, crushed tomatoes, and extra virgin olive oil.

# PIZZALY'S WOOD-FIRED PIZZA

**YIELD:** 4 TO 5 200-GRAM-PIZZAS / **ACTIVE TIME:** 20 MINUTES / **TOTAL TIME:** 1½ - 2½ HOURS

There is nothing like the smell and warmth of a wood-fire oven, or the magic of watching raw ingredients transform into to a crisp, perfectly charred pizza in a matter of minutes.

— *courtesy of Silvio Serpa and Anna Di Perna, Pizzaly*

1 Preheat wood-fired oven to approximately 570°. For conventional home ovens, best results will be obtained with a ventilated oven at maximum heat.

2 Dissolve yeast in approx. ½ cup of the water. orm a small "volcano" of flour on a wooden board or clean kitchen work bench. If making the oven version, add the mashed potato to the flour before making your volcano.

3 Combine remaining water and oil and slowly add to the center of the flour well. Add dissolved yeast mixture and begin to slowly incorporate the wet and dry ingredients.

4 When the dough is almost fully combined, add the salt, which must not make contact with the yeast. Continue to knead vigorously for at least 5 minutes to obtain a smooth and lump free firm dough mixture. Divide into about 10 evenly sized balls and allow them to prove in a warm environment until they double in volume.

5 Once they have risen, these dough bases will need to be flattened out by use of a rolling pin or by hand, and can then be topped with your favorite ingredients before going into the oven (alternatively, these portions of dough can be refrigerated or frozen for later use and prepared at your leisure). These pizzas will bake in just a few minutes, so keep an eye on them. Once the crust is crisp and golden, remove from oven and serve.

**INGREDIENTS:**

**ORIGINAL WOOD-FIRED PIZZA DOUGH:**

8 cups all-purpose flour

2½ cups lukewarm water

⅔ cup extra virgin olive oil

4½ teaspoons fresh yeast

3½ teaspoons salt

**OVEN VERSION:**

8 cups all-purpose flour

2½ cups lukewarm water

½ cup extra virgin olive oil

4 teaspoons fresh yeast

1 small potato (boiled, peeled, and mashed)

3½ teaspoons salt

Pizza toppings of your choice (we recommend fior di latte mozzarella and crushed tomatoes)

## Tano's Pizzeria

www.tanoschicago.com
3038 W. Irving Park Road
Chicago, IL 60618
(773) 478-3070

When you think of Chicago pizza, your mind probably jumps to deep dish. And for good reason—cheesy, thick, and gooey, the Chicago deep dish has long been an icon of the area. Which is why it's a surprise to find out that Tano's, which has been named on several best-of lists for its deep dish, makes more thin-crust pizza on a daily basis than any other kind.

"Our most popular item is a thin-crust pizza, which is not what you might expect in a deep dish pizza town," says owner Tom Guagliardo. "But we cater to locals and neighborhood people and, truth be told, locals don't eat a lot of deep dish pizza. Buffalo wings are our second-bestselling item, and those two go hand-in-hand." Both styles of pizza have had a lot of local recognition, so it's a good idea to go with a big group and empty stomach to try some of each.

Tano's is a true neighborhood pizzeria, a descendent of the popular Manzo's down the street, which had been operated by Guagliardo's father for decades. "Tano's pizza is part of the community—we help find lost dogs, serve as a meeting place for friends and families, and have a voice in the neighborhood's future. But my proudest moments come from the customers. We had a chef come from Africa to try our deep dish pizza—that blows me away. More than anything, I am proud to have regulars; I've watched children grow up and I have mourned the loss of family members. I hear about bad first dates and I watch couples fall in love."

If pizza is family, then Tano's is the truest pizzeria. Recipes passed down over half a century have remained largely unchanged, and Guagliardo still uses tools passed down from his father and grandfather. While Guagliardo's pizza speaks for itself, you would be crazy not to visit and experience a meal at Tano's in person. By the end, West Irving Park Road might even start to feel like home.

# IN HIS OWN WORDS:

## TOM GUAGLIARDO OF TANO'S PIZZERIA

*How and when did you get your start in this industry?*

I grew up in restaurants. My father started in this industry when he was 16. He learned the business, and eventually opened up his own restaurant with the help of his brother and father. As I grew up, I helped out in the kitchen, first making bread baskets and then salads. Soon I was taking orders for delivery and routing delivery drivers. The real fun began when I learned the pizza station and then how to cook on the line.

*Who—or what—first inspired you to begin baking pizza? Who inspires you now?*

A restaurant kitchen is a magical place. It can be a hot, stress-laden environment or it can be a beautiful dance of flying dough and sauté pans. It's hard not to fall in love with it. When you're young in the kitchen, you get stuck doing boring tasks like slicing bread or making side salads, but it helps move the show along, and can be a lifesaver when a server has five or six tables. Plus, you get to see what's going on in other stations. You get to watch flames fly from the sauté station and pizza sauce spiral out of the center of a pizza skin. It gives you a drive to "level up" in the kitchen. Nowadays

I get a lot of inspiration from the Internet; viral videos of bakers giddy over yeasty, bubbly dough bins and before-and-after shots of pizzas keep me excited about what I'm doing next.

*What are your golden rules for baking pizza?*

My golden rules are:

1. Never use water over 100°F. "You don't want to kill the baby!" Yeast is a living organism—you need to keep it alive so it can transform your dough into a beautiful product. If the water is too hot it will kill the yeast.

2. Consistency is key. You have to do everything the same way each and every time. Baking is a science. Every batch of dough is an experiment; if you change one variable you will get a different outcome.

3. Time cooks the dough, temperature browns the cheese. This is great to remember when trying out new recipes or working on a new oven. You have to find the right temperature and time for a recipe. That little sentence will help zero in on the perfect bake.

*What does Tano's Pizzeria represent to you?*

Tano's Pizzeria is my family legacy. My father and his lessons are the foundation of this place. Many recipes have remained the same for over 50 years. But we are also looking to the future, and always trying new things and updating others.

*What is your favorite pizza to bake? Why?*

Least favorite pizza to bake? Why? Research and development for pizza is so much fun. Talk about a dream job! Who wouldn't want to make and eat pizza every day? When we have time, we test out new things. I'll hear about a new ingredient from a distributor or see something cool online. We jump on it and play around in the kitchen. It is a lot of fun.

*What is your favorite type of pizza crust? Why? Least favorite crust? Why?*

I have been into Neapolitan-style pizza for some time. I love the crispy exterior and the chewy interior of the crust. And, of course, the beautiful wood-fire ovens. I think it's great that they cook at such high temperatures—just 90 seconds and pizza is cooked! The blisters from the high heat give the pizza a great smokiness. I think it also has something to do with not being able to make it myself. My restaurant just doesn't have the right equipment for the job. My least favorite crust is something that's underdeveloped or overworked. Pizza dough needs time to ferment. The yeast does its thing, developing flavors and lightening the dough. Some places take shortcuts with fast rises or frozen dough, but nature cannot be rushed.

*How did Tano's Pizzeria come to be? Why Chicago?*

Tano's is a culmination of everything I have learned over the years. My father's last restaurant Manzo's was located only 3 blocks away from our location. That place raised my brother and me for 20 years. We celebrated and mourned inside those walls. The neighborhood was very good to my family and when my father decided to retire I knew I wanted to stay in the same neighborhood when I opened up Tano's.

Chicago is a world-class city, and the food here rivals that of anywhere else. We are lucky enough to have everything that makes a great pizza at our doorstep. Flour from the Great Plains. Lake Michigan gives us the best water. Wisconsin brings in the best cheese. Plus, Chicago is known as the sausage capital of the U.S., so it's no surprise we use a lot of it on our pizza. Our tomatoes take the longest trip—they come from California.

*Where do you get your tools/materials? What non-essential items should every home baker have?*

Most of the tools of the trade can be found online or at our distributors. Luckily I have some tools that are older than I am. I have a pizza peel that was made by my grandfather. And our oven, a beautiful stainless steel carousel oven, is from the 1950s. The great thing about pizza is that you don't need many tools to create it. For the home cook, there are a few basic tools that can help but nothing mandatory: Pizza stones are great for keeping a constant temperature in the oven and on the crust. A rolling pin is useful if you're making Chicago-style thin crust pizza. Dark metal pans work the best for deep dish pizza. The dark finish brings more heat to the pizza.

*What book(s) go on your required reading list for bakers?*

*The Pizza Bible* by Tony Gemignani. It has just about everything you need to know about pizza, from different types of flour, to the right kind of knife to use for pizza-cutting.

*What outlets/periodicals/newspapers do you read or consult regularly, if any?*

There are a lot of great industry magazines. I like *PMQ Pizza Magazine* and *Pizza Today*.

*Tell me about your most memorable collaboration with another chef.*

I love to cook with my dad. Even at 65 years old he is still one of the fastest pizza makers I know.

*Do you follow any cooking shows or chefs? If so, which is your favorite?*

I love *Chef's Table* on Netflix. It lets me nerd out on all things restaurant, from kitchen design to modern plating. I also love that it features chefs from all over the word and all different cuisines—from a farm-to-table chef in Colorado to a Jewish chef making ramen in the heart of Japan.

My favorite chef right now is Stefanie Izard. She's a Chicago girl who has three restaurants in the West Loop. I recently got to see her at the National Restaurant Association show, and her energy and excitement for food and cooking is infectious.

*Where did you learn to bake pizza? Please tell me about your education and apprenticeships.*

The restaurant business is in my blood. My father met my mother when she was waitress-ing at a restaurant; he used to close up shop and go out for breakfast, and that's where he met my mother. I learned everything from my father and, as his friends would say, you got the best education from the school of West Irving Park Road.

*Tell me about your pizza baking processes.*

It all starts with the dough. Our dough is mixed and rests for 24 to 48 hours. It is sheeted out to a thickness of about ¼ inch and placed in a dark round baking pan that has been buttered. Any ingredients are placed directly on the dough and that is topped with our mozzarella blend. A thin layer of dough is placed on top of the cheese and our thick pizza sauce is ladled on over that. It is then baked in our oven at 450°F for 35 minutes.

# CHICAGO DEEP DISH STUFFED PIZZA

**YIELD:** 1 PIZZA + 1 ADDITIONAL PIZZA CRUST / **ACTIVE TIME:** 3 HOURS 30 MINUTES
**TOTAL TIME:** ABOUT 33 HOURS

Almost more pie than pizza, this impressive stuffed deep dish is the ultimate version of the Chicago classic.
— *courtesy of Tom Guagliardo, Tano's Pizzeria*

1 Add the water to the mixing bowl, then add the salt and sugar. Add the flour, pour bloomed yeast on top of flour. Begin mixing at low speed and gradually pour in the oil over about 60 seconds. Continue mixing for a total of about 4 to 5 minutes at low speed.

2 Transfer the dough mix to a bowl and cover to prevent drying. Allow the dough to ferment/rise in the tub for 4 to 5 hours.

3 Bring the dough to the bench and divide into 3 evenly sized pieces, then form into balls. Place dough balls into dough boxes, lightly oil the top of the dough balls to prevent drying. Cover with plastic wrap. Dough will be ready to use after 24-hours in the cooler, and will last up to 48-hours.

4 To use the dough, remove from the cooler and allow to temper at room temperature for 2.5 to 3 hours, then begin opening the dough into pizza skins by your preferred method, I suggest using a rolling pin to a thickness of about ¼ inch.

5 Place dough in a buttered 10" cake pan. If there is extra hanging out of the pan us a paring knife to cut off the extra. Place desired ingredients on top of dough. Top with mozzarella.

6 Take another dough ball and roll that out to a thickness of about ⅛ inch. Cut the dough in a 9" circle. Use a paring knife to cut small slits for venting steam. Place the dough on top of the cheese and tuck it up against the dough rising up the side of the pan.

7 Top the second layer of dough with your favorite pizza sauce. Bake at 450°F for about 35 minutes or until the crust is a golden brown. Serve and enjoy!

### INGREDIENTS:

**FOR THE PIZZA DOUGH:**

7   cups + ¼ cup all-purpose flour

2   cups water heated to 70°F-75°F

6   tablespoons oil

2 ½ teaspoons salt

¼ + ⅛ teaspoons active dry yeast

1   tablespoon + ½ teaspoon sugar

**FOR THE FILLING AND TOPPING:**

1¼  cups mozzarella

Pizza toppings of your choice

Tomato sauce

# Scoozi

*"just like nonna made"*

## Scoozi

136 Union Road
Ascot Vale, Victoria 3032
Australia
+61 3-9370-0100
www.scoozi.net

Phillip Bruno is not your average pizza-maker. Bruno is the president of the Associazione Pizzaiuoli Napoletani Australasia (or, as he calls it, the "Pizza Police"), where he oversees the accreditation of countless pizza chefs and pizzerias all over the continent. As a pizza judge, he's travelled the globe, visiting places like New York, Taipei, and Naples, where he helps crown the world's best pizza chef every year. And then there's Scoozi itself, awarded Best Pizza in Melbourne 2014 and inducted into the Pizza Hall of Fame in 2017 by Melbourne's largest newspaper, *The Herald Sun.* The man lives and breathes pizza.

When Bruno is cooking, he says he likes to keep it simple. "I only have one golden rule: Follow the traditional pizza Napoletana recipe and have fun." His dough uses only four ingredients—flour, water, salt, and yeast—and cooks for 90 seconds, at most. But if you look a little closer you get a sense of the meticulous process he's managed to perfect over 35 years of making pizza. His oven is hand-built—by Bruno himself. His dough's leavening process takes about 30 hours, in a controlled lab, where the dough builds flavor while using very little yeast. Talk to Bruno a little about making pizza, and it becomes clear that "simple" does not really mean "simple." Of course, 35 years of practice will do that to you.

Bruno only began making pizza in order to pitch in at home—as the oldest child, he wanted to have dinner on the table for his parents, who both worked late hours. He never dreamed it would take him all around the country, visiting the most delicious restaurants and discussing the craft with their owners. Says Bruno, "I find true inspiration visiting local wood-fired pizzerias." And while he may not say it himself, his fantastic work at Scoozi ensures that this is a two-way street.

# IN HIS OWN WORDS:

## PHILLIP BRUNO OF SCOOZI

*How and when did you get your start in this industry?*

I started baking pizza in 1982, in my first pizza store.

*Who—or what—first inspired you to begin baking pizza? Who inspires you now?*

I have always enjoyed cooking, and who doesn't like pizza? My inspirations now come from some of the top pizza chefs in the world, who I get to visit and follow from afar.

*What does Scoozi represent to you?*

Scoozi represents all of my 35 years experience and true pizza Napoletana, as it was made 300 years ago.

*What is your favorite pizza to bake? Why? Least favorite pizza to bake? Why?*

My favorite pizza to bake is the Marinara: well-rested dough baked to a Napoletano crust, quality San Marzano tomatoes, fragrant dried oregano, strong extra virgin olive oil, and some fresh, thinly sliced garlic. I always say pizza is a celebration of dough, and simplicity is always the best. We call this Marinara, which translates to "sailor." Sailors were always in a rush before heading off to sea, so their pizza order would be, "Margherita, no cheese, just add a little garlic." I should add that this is also my favorite pizza to eat. I can't say I have a least favorite pizza to bake. I love them all!

*How did Scoozi come to be? Why Melbourne? What are your most popular items?*

It was always my dream to bring a true Napoletana pizza to Melbourne. Melbourne is my home!

*Where do you get your tools/materials? What non-essential items should every home baker have?*

The beauty of making pizza at home is you just need an oven—everything else is what you have at home. For a non-essential item, I recommend a terra cotta tile pizza stone.

*What book(s) go on your required reading list for bakers?*

*The Bread Baker's Apprentice*, by Peter Reinhart, is a good read. To really know your pizza, try *The Pizza Bible* by Tony Gemignani, a 12-time world champion. Both are amazing guys.

*Tell me about your most memorable collaboration with another chef.*

Working alongside some of world's finest chefs is a highlight for any chef, but the most memorable was at Napoli Pizza Village 2015 with American celebrity chef Lidia Bastianich and fellow pizza chefs Davide Civitiello and Teresa Iorio, both world champions.

*Where did you learn to bake pizza? Please tell me about your education and apprenticeships.*

I first started cooking at home. Both of my parents worked late and I was the oldest, so many times I had to prepare the evening meal.

I finished high school and returned to college a few years later to pursue Civil Engineering, but I always wanted a business of my own. So my (now) wife and I brought our first pizzeria and that's how it all started.

# MELANZANE PIZZA

YIELD: 2 PIZZAS / ACTIVE TIME: 50 MINUTES / TOTAL TIME: 11-13 HOURS

Melanzane Pizza is a simple way to enjoy two of Italy's favorites things; the Neapolitan pizza and *melanzane* - also known as eggplant.

— *courtesy of Philip Bruno, Scoozi Traditional Pizza & Pasta*

1 Combine water, sea salt, sugar and olive oil in a large bowl, stirring continually till the salt and sugar have dissolved.

2 Add half of the flour, stirring it until the mixture becomes soupy. Then put some of the flour in the palm of your hand and rub the yeast to it, allowing it to fall into your container. Add the rest of the flour gradually, kneading for approximately 20 to 25 minutes, until it reaches the desired consistency. You are looking for soft, smooth, elastic dough. Once this is achieved, cover bowl with a loosely fitting lid or a damp cloth. Allow the dough to rest at room temperature for 10 to 12 hours.

3 After the dough has rested, divide into 2 evenly sized portions. Roll each portion into a tight ball. Place each ball in a bowl and cover once more with a loosely fitting lid or damp cloth. Let rest for a further 5 hours.

4 Once the dough is ready, place each ball on a pizza tray or pan. Stretch the dough by using your fingertips to press the air from the center of each ball to the edges, until each ball becomes a 10"-12" circle. Leave a 1" border for the crust, and allow a further 15 minutes rest.

5 Cut eggplants into very thin slices and layer in a colander, lightly salting each layer. Leave for 15 minutes (this allows the eggplant to release some of its moisture and bitterness). Heat a slightly oiled griddle or frying pan then cook the eggplant for 2 to 3 minutes on each side, until each piece is light brown with grill marks. Allow to cool in refrigerator.

6 Squash the whole peeled tomatoes by hand (do not use a blender, it will break the seeds and cause the tomatoes to become bitter).

7 Preheat oven to 460°F- 480°F.

## INGREDIENTS:

### FOR THE PIZZA DOUGH:

| | |
|---|---|
| ½ + ⅓ | cup room-temperature water |
| 2 | teaspoons sea salt |
| ¼ | teaspoon yeast |
| ½ –¾ | teaspoon olive oil |
| ¼ | teaspoon sugar |
| 2⅓ + 2⅔ | cups flour |

### FOR THE TOPPING:

| | |
|---|---|
| 1 | eggplant |
| | Olive oil, for frying |
| | Salt & pepper to taste |
| 1 | can whole peeled tomatoes (We recommend San Marzano or other good quality tomatoes) |
| | Fresh basil |
| 1 | cup fior di latte or fresh mozzarella cheese, chopped into matchstick-sized pieces |
| | Grated parmesan cheese, to taste |

8 Prepare both pizzas to be baked at once or bake each at your leisure. Spread 2 to 3 table spoons of tomatoes on the base, then add fresh basil (a good 6 to 8 leaves) and half of the cheese. Top with 5 to 6 pieces of eggplant.

9 Bake each pizza for approximately 15 minutes, until the crust is crisp and the cheese is melted and bubbly. Top with grated parmesan cheese and serve.

Note: If baking in a wood-fire oven, omit the oil and sugar from the dough recipe and be aware that each pizza will cook much quicker.

Recommended drink: A strong full body Shiraz as it will cut through the taste of the pizza but retain the sweetness, if you prefer beer try a full strength crisp beer.

# Theo & Co

838 Albany Highway
East Victoria Park, WA 6101
Australia
+61 9361 6776

147 Oxford Street
Leederville, WA 6007
Australia
+61 9201 9638

When Theo Kalogeracos set out to become a pizza maker, it wasn't for fame. He just wanted to make fun pizzas. But that penchant for creative baking has made him famous all the same, as his big personality and out-of-the-box thinking have helped him become one of Australia's most well known pizzaiolos.

Walk into one of Theo & Co.'s two locations and the first thing you'll notice is the sheer number of pizzas. Starters, entrees, desserts—if you were so incli ned, you could have a full course meal comprised entirely of pizza. And the options are tempting. Stone-baked pizzas, skillet pizzas, and grandma-style pizzas on fluffy focaccia are just three of the varieties Kalogeracos has mastered.

What's amazing about Theo & Co. is how close it came to never existing. Kalogeracos was already a star pizza maker in his own right when he worked at Little Caesars Pizzeria in Perth (unrelated to the popular pizza chain). A dispute with management, however, led Kalogeracos to leave the restaurant and open his own pizzeria mere feet from his old employer.

"It came down to quality… I wasn't happy with what we were producing but the owners wanted to maximize their returns and I don't blame them for that," he said in an interview with WAtoday. Neither do Theo & Co. customers, who have enjoyed his reliably fun and delicious pizzas ever since.

# THEO & CO.'S BASIC PIZZA DOUGH

YIELD: 8 200-GRAM PIZZA DOUGH BALLS / ACTIVE TIME: 30 MINUTES / TOTAL TIME: 40-45 MINUTES

This method tells you how to make my basic pizza dough by hand. This is a great way to develop a 'feel' for making dough. This dough is used for our Salt-N-Pepa Prawn, Farmer's Market & Custom Royal Pizzas.

—*courtesy of Theo Kalogeracos, Theo & Co. Pizzeria*

**INGREDIENTS:**

- 7½  cups strong bakers flour
- 2  tablespoons + 1 teaspoon dry yeast
- 1¾  teaspoons salt
- 2  teaspoons caster sugar
- 2½  cups + ¼ cup cold (not chilled) water

1 Start by mixing all the dry ingredients together and creating a well in the center. Carefully pour 600 ml of water into the well and gradually incorporate the water into the flour mixture. It will take three to four minutes for the dough to come together. The remaining ¼ cup of water is only added if necessary, depending on the gluten content of the flour.

2 Knead the dough for about 10 minutes, but avoid watching the clock and try instead to develop a feel for what is right. A well-kneaded ball of dough should be smooth and springy, yet soft. At this stage it should be possible to stretch the dough quite thinly, so it is translucent when held up to the light.

3 Divide the dough into eight even-sized balls and leave them to rest under a tea towel for 10 to 15 minutes.

4 Then roll, throw, or stretch the dough with the palm of your hand to the desired size. A 200 g dough ball will make a 10 inch (25 cm) pizza. Make up all eight pizza bases as quickly as you can. If you don't have enough pizza trays, you can place them on non-stick paper sprinkled with semolina – these can be stacked in threes and kept in the fridge until you are ready to cook. I always do this when I make wood-fired pizzas which are cooked directly on the hot bricks without a tray.

# THEO & CO.'S SKILLET PIZZA DOUGH

**YIELD:** 6 TO 8 200-GRAM PIZZA DOUGH BALLS / **ACTIVE TIME:** 25 MINUTES
**TOTAL TIME:** ABOUT 2½ HOURS

This recipe makes almost 3 pounds of pizza dough, which is enough for one big and one small deep-dish skillet pizza.

I know it might seem like a long process (and it is), but skillet pizza is like no other, and you need to go through these stages to get that rich, flaky crust. It is kind of a combination of a quiche base and a pizza base, so you really need to follow these guidelines to make it.

*—courtesy of Theo Kalogeracos, Theo & Co. Pizzeria*

1 Using a mixer with a dough hook, place water, butter, and olive oil into the mixing bowl. Then place half flour, half the semolina, all the yeast, salt, and sugar and mix for 3 to 4 minutes until all the ingredients make a nice smooth batter. Remove and cover the bowl with a tea towel or cling wrap and leave to rest for 20 minutes.

2 Return bowl to mixer, add remaining flour and semolina, and mix on low speed for 7 minutes.

3 Take the slightly yellow dough and divide into for a big pan and for a small pan, if you have an extra-large pan use it all. It will be a soft and tacky dough, looking more like a batter. Mold the dough into a smooth ball and rub evenly with the extra olive oil. Place it in a large bowl and cover with a tea towel and let it rest for 1 hour.

4 Put about a teaspoon of olive oil in your deep-dish pan and use a brush to coat the surface entirely. Grab your dough ball and place it in the middle of the pan, and using your fingers and palm, push and spread the dough evenly around the pan, getting it to about 1 inch from the top as you push it up the edge of the tray. Once you have done that, cover the pan with a tea towel and let it rest for 30 minutes. Now it is ready to use.

**INGREDIENTS:**

1¾ cups water

3 tablespoons butter

¾ cup olive oil + 1 tablespoon for rubbing the dough just before proofing

4¾ cups all-purpose flour (8% protein)

½ cup fine semolina

2 tablespoons + 1 teaspoon dry yeast

1 teaspoon salt

1 teaspoon sugar

# NOTORIOUS P.I.G SKILLET PIZZA

YIELD: 1 PIZZA/ ACTIVE TIME: 45 MINUTES / TOTAL TIME: 1 HOUR

Chicago and Detroit are both famous for their respective styles of Deep Dish Pizza cooked in a heavy cast-iron skillet. We've combined the deep pie of The Chi and the charred crust of The D to bring you our own unique flavor.
—*courtesy of Theo Kalogeracos, Theo & Co. Pizzeria*

1 The first thing you do is start by sprinkling half of the mozzarella around the edge of the pizza base. This will help toast the cheese and give a beautiful crunchy cheese crust.

2 Place the first cup of eye bacon on top of cheese, then place the rest of the cheese evenly over the bacon touching the skillet's edge again.

3 Then place the rest of the bacon, sprinkle the parmesan cheese all over the pizza, then place small dollops of the bacon jam evenly around the pizza now it is ready to go in the oven.

4 Bake in the center of the oven (fan off), without opening the door for about 10 minutes, then have a look: it may need another 5 minutes. You are after a really golden crust and a bubbling bacon jam with golden brown melted cheese.

5 Once you have taken the pizza out of the oven let it sit in the skillet for 5 minutes before you serve it. Like lasagna, the skillet pizza needs this time to sit so it stops cooking and it all comes together. After 5 minutes make sure that all the crust has come away from the edges of the skillet serve in the skillet with maple syrup on the side so you can pour as much or as little as you want.

## BACON JAM

1 Combine oil, bacon, tomatoes, and onions, and cook on medium-high for 10 minutes, stirring occasionally.

2 Add stock, water, sugar, molasses, cayenne pepper, and cook for another 30 minutes, stirring occasionally.

3 Remove from the stove and leave to cool. The jam can be stored in the refrigerator for 2 to 3 weeks.

### INGREDIENTS:

- 1 roughly 11-inch skillet dough base, in skillet, rested and ready to go (see page 537)
- 1½ cups grated mozzarella
- ½ cup roughly cut eye bacon
- 1 tablespoon parmesan cheese, grated
- 2 tablespoons bacon jam (see below)
- Maple syrup

### BACON JAM

- 1 tablespoon oil
- 1 cup eye bacon roughly chopped up
- 1 cup cherry tomatoes, thinly sliced
- 1 cup red onion chopped fine
- 1 cup chicken stock
- 1 cup sugar
- 4 tablespoons molasses
- 1 cup water
- ½ teaspoon fine cayenne pepper

# FARMER'S MARKET

**YIELD:** 1 PIZZA / **ACTIVE TIME:** 40 - 50 MINUTES / **TOTAL TIME:** 1 HOUR

You can buy pretty much everything you need for this pizza from your local farmer's market, and if the ingredients are not in season, you can find great marinated vegetables at any good deli. This pizza has no sauce on it, it only has the juices of the vegetables and their marinades, and the yogurt on top. You will notice as you are eating the pizza that all the flavors of the vegetables stand out and the yogurt on top gives it a really light fresh zing.

I've assumed that the veggies you are going to use are in season, so I've given you a step-by-step run-down on how to grill and marinate each one separately. If you want to try just one of the veggies at a time on a pizza you can, or you can try them all - it's up to you.

—*courtesy of Theo Kalogeracos, Theo & Co. Pizzeria*

1 Preheat oven to 480°F.

2 In a small bowl, combine Greek yoghurt, chives, and a squeeze of lemon juice. Set aside.

3 Sprinkle the mozzarella evenly across the pizza base. Top evenly with squash, peppers, zucchini, and beetroot. This ensures that each slice will have a bit of everything.

4 Bake for 7 to 10 minutes until the base is crisp and the cheese is melted and bubbling. Drizzle with Greek yoghurt sauce just before serving.

## ROASTED RED PEPPERS

1 On a grill or gas range, flame grill each of the peppers one at a time. Place the peppers directly over the flame (trust me on this, it is easy and really tasty) and burn one side at a time. Keep turning until the pepper is fully burnt. Remove from the flame and wrap loosely in plastic wrap. Repeat for each pepper.

2 Leave the peppers to sweat for 10 to 15 minutes, then remove the plastic wrap and rub off the burnt skin with your hands. Don't worry too much about removing every bit of skin - it will give the pepper a great charcoal flavor.

3 Cut the top of each pepper off and slice lengthways. Scrape out the seeds, and slice into strips. Combine peppers with

### INGREDIENTS:

- 2 tablespoons Greek yoghurt

  Fresh chopped chives

  Squeeze of lemon juice

- 1 basic pizza dough ball – rolled, rested & ready (see page 536)

- 1 teaspoon chia seeds, sprinkle on bench then roll dough so the seeds stick on the bottom

- ¾–1 cup grated mozzarella

- ½ cup roasted red peppers squash (see subrecipe)

- ½ cup roasted butternut squash (see subrecipe)

- ½ cup roasted marinated zucchini (see subrecipe)

- ½ cup roasted beetroot (see subrecipe)

### ROASTED RED PEPPERS

Red bell peppers, as many as desired (green and yellow also work well)

Garlic, minced

Salt

Parsley, finely chopped

Extra virgin olive oil

### ROASTED BUTTERNUT SQUASH

- 1 butternut squash

- 1 tablespoon basil pesto

  Extra virgin olive oil

- 2 cloves garlic, minced

  Pinch of rock salt

garlic, parsley, salt, and a drizzle of extra virgin olive oil in a small bowl. Leave to marinate for at least 10 minutes before using. Make sure to marinate the peppers while they are still warm, as they will absorb more flavor.

## ROASTED BUTTERNUT SQUASH

1 Preheat oven to 440°F.

2 Skin and deseed your squash, cut into 1-inch strips, place on a baking tray, top with garlic, a pinch of salt, and drizzle with olive oil.

3 Place in the oven for 10 to 15 minutes. You only want the squash to be semi-cooked as it's going on the pizza where it will cook some more.

### ROASTED MARINATED ZUCCHINI

3 zucchinis

Extra virgin olive oil

Pinch of salt

Pinch of pepper

2 cloves garlic, minced

### ROASTED BEETROOT

Beetroot (as many as desired)

Pinch of salt

Pinch of pepper

Balsamic glaze

4 Once cooked, take the squash out of the oven and cut into cubes. Combine in a bowl with pesto and mix until squash is fully coated. Allow to squash to cool before using on the pizza.

## ROASTED MARINATED ZUCCHINI

1 Preheat oven to 440°F.

2 Wash the zucchini and slice the lengthways into half-inch strips. Make sure to leave the skin on as this will lend texture and color. Place on a baking tray and top with a drizzle of olive oil and a pinch of salt.

3 Roast in the oven for 5 to 10 minutes.

4 Remove zucchini from oven and cut into chunks. Combine in a bowl with garlic, as well as a little more extra virgin olive oil and salt. Stir and allow zucchini to cool before using.

## ROASTED BEETROOT

1 Preheat oven to 440°F.

2 Wrap each beetroot in foil and place them in the oven for 20 to 30 minutes, depending on their size (the bigger they are, the longer it will take to cook). When the beetroot is easily pierced with a skewer or fork, it is done.

3 Remove the beetroot from the oven and discard the foil. Peel off the skin and cut into wedges. Place wedges in a bowl and top with salt, pepper, and a light drizzle of balsamic glaze.

# SALT-N-PEPA PRAWN PIZZA

YIELD: 1 PIZZA / ACTIVE TIME: 10 MINUTES / TOTAL TIME: 20 MINUTES

Let's talk about prawns coated in garlic & sesame seeds, lime salt & pepper, then push it real good by finishing it off with avocado, rocket & mayo.

—*courtesy of Theo Kalogeracos, Theo & Co. Pizzeria*

1 Preheat oven to 430°F.

2 Combine all ingredients for the Sriracha mayonnaise in a small bowl and whisk until incorporated. Cover and set aside.

3 Combine all ingredients for the avocado mousse in a small bowl and whisk until incorporated. Cover and set aside.

4 Sprinkle the garlic over the pizza base and top with mozzarella. Mix the sesame seeds with the salt and pepper. Toss the prawns in the salt and pepper mixture, making sure they are each evenly coated.

5 Distribute the prawns evenly across the pizza and bake for 7 to 10 minutes.

6 Once the pizza is out of the oven, top it with arugula and drizzle with the Srirachanaise sauce (see step 2). Dollop avocado mousse (see step 3) evenly around pizza and sprinkle with sesame seeds before serving.

## INGREDIENTS:

### "SRIRACHANAISE" SAUCE:

1 cup Sriracha sauce

1 cup whole egg mayonnaise

Juice of 1 lemon

Pinch salt

### AVOCADO MOUSSE:

2 avocados soft and ready

Pinch salt

Juice of 1 lemon

### PIZZA:

1 basic pizza dough ball – rolled, rested & ready (see page 536)

1 teaspoon garlic, finely chopped

¾–1 cup grated mozzarella

1 teaspoon sesame seeds

¼ teaspoon of salt & pepper, mixed

10 large raw prawns, shelled & de-veined

1 cup arugula leaves, dressed with olive oil & a pinch of salt

# CUSTOM ROYAL DESSERT PIZZA

YIELD: 1 PIZZA / **ACTIVE TIME:** 1 HOUR / **TOTAL TIME:** 1 HOUR 10 MINUTES

The only reason I ever wanted to go to the Perth Royal Show (imagine a *giant* state fair) was for a toffee apple. This pizza is my interpretation!

—*courtesy of Theo Kalogeracos, Theo & Co. Pizzeria*

1 Preheat oven to 430°F.

2 Place the butter and sugar into your mixing bowl and, using the flat paddle attachment, cream together on a medium speed for one minute, scrape down. Add the egg and mix for one minute, scrape down.

3 Add flour and vanilla paste and mix on a low speed for one minute, scrape down, then mix on a medium speed for another minute.

4 Remove bowl from mixer and spread over the pizza base.

5 Spread the custard over the batter mix gently.

6 Distribute sliced apples evenly across pizza, and sprinkle with brown sugar.

7 Bake for 7 to 10 minutes.

8 When cooked, cut into eight pieces, decorate with a dusting of powdered sugar and sprinkles of toffee pieces. Place cotton candy in the middle and drizzle with caramel sauce.

## CUSTARD

1 Whisk the custard powder and sugar with milk in a small bowl and then transfer to a small heavy-based saucepan.

2 Place on low heat and stir until the custard starts to boil and thicken. Remove from the heat and add the vanilla bean paste.

3 Pour into a bowl and allow to cool completely before spreading on a pizza base. The custard can be made in advance, placed in a sealed container and stored in the fridge for up to seven days.

## INGREDIENTS:

- 1 basic pizza dough ball – rolled, rested & ready (see page 536)
- 5 tablespoons unsalted butter, softened
- ½ cup caster sugar
- ½ teaspoon vanilla bean paste
- 1 egg
- 1 cup self-raising flour
- 2 tablespoons custard (see subrecipe)
- 1 Royal Gala apple cored & sliced into thin half-moons.
- 1 tablespoon brown sugar
- 2 tablespoons crushed up toffee (see subrecipe)
- 1 handful cotton candy
- 2 tablespoons caramel sauce (see subrecipe)

## CUSTARD

- 1 tablespoon custard powder (look for it in the International Foods aisle or in specialty stores)
- 1 tablespoon caster sugar
- ½ cup milk
- ½ teaspoon vanilla bean paste

## TOFFEE

- 2 ½ cups sugar
- 1 cup water
- 2 drops red food coloring

## TOFFEE

1 Line a tray with baking paper.

2 In a pot or nonstick pan, dissolve the sugar in the water. Stir over a low heat until the syrup starts to boil. Keep stirring until the syrup turns a light brown.

3 Drizzle the hot toffee over the tray and leave for 20 minutes to cool and set before breaking into small pieces.

## CARAMEL SAUCE

1 Combine butter, brown sugar, golden syrup and pinch of salt in a non-stick pot and cook over medium heat. Stir until the sugar dissolves – this will take about 3 minutes.

2 Add the cream and continue to stir and cook for another 3 minutes. The sauce will be ready when its smooth and slightly thicker than honey.

3 Remove from heat and allow to cool somewhat before serving.

## CARAMEL SAUCE

5 tablespoons unsalted butter

1 cup soft brown sugar

2 tablespoons golden syrup pinch salt

1 cup fresh cream

# Otto Pizza

www.ottoportland.com

| | | |
|---|---|---|
| 250 Read Street<br>Portland, ME 04103<br>(207) 358-7551 | 159 Cottage Road<br>S. Portland, ME 04106<br>(207) 517-3051 | 1432 Massachusetts Ave<br>Cambridge, MA 02138<br>(617) 873-0888 |
| 225 Congress Street<br>Portland, ME 04101<br>(207) 358-7870 | 367 Main Street<br>Yarmouth, ME 04096<br>(207) 846-1325 | 289 Harvard St<br>Brookline, MA 02446<br>(617) 232-0014 |
| 576 Congress Street<br>Portland, ME 04101<br>(207) 358-7090 | 202 Massachusetts Ave<br>Arlington, MA 02474<br>(781) 859-5378 | 1210 Market St<br>Lynnfield, MA 01940<br>(781) 872-6991 |
| 125 John Roberts Road<br>S. Portland, ME 04106<br>(207) 772-0900 | 888 Commonwealth Ave<br>Boston, MA 02446<br>(617) 232-0447 | 202 Merrimac St<br>Newburyport, MA 01950<br>(978) 225-6161 |

Even if OTTO pizza was just so-so, owners Mike Keon and Anthony Allen would still deserve a spotlight for their desire to give back. Allen started Nantucket's first-ever pizza joint at age 17—before his senior year of high school—because he knew how badly his fellow islanders were clamoring for it. In 2012, Keon and Allen traveled to New York City in the wake of Hurricane Sandy, armed only with 600 pizzas and a grill. After hours of travel and coordinating, they spent five days handing out free pizza and rations to storm victims, leaving only once everything was gone. They've worked closely with local organizations to aid fundraising efforts in Maine and Massachusetts as well, and Keon once tried to cook a full Thanksgiving dinner on a fishing boat…during a storm. In other words: They're men of the people.

Of course, the pizza *is* good—good enough, actually, to be included in Food Network's "50 Pizzas, 50 States," where it was named one of the best pizzas in America. Good enough to have grown from one little shop in Portland in 2009 to 12 locations today. They have also been featured on the Cooking Channel and numerous local "best-of" lists.

"We had talked for many years about working together and made steps toward larger scale restaurants in Boston. For many different reasons in many different locations we never opened in Boston," says Allen. "Mike moved to Portland in '07 and was taken by the vibrant food culture. When a tiny space on Congress Street became available in '09, Mike called me and asked to come up and take a look. We agreed that rather than open a big restaurant in a big city, maybe starting a very small slice shop that focused on one thing had its upsides. Having never worked together, it made sense to start small and see how it went as a team. It went remarkably well from the very start."

And it continues to go well, as Allen and Keon feed the hungry masses from Boston to Maine.

## IN THEIR OWN WORDS:

## MIKE AND ANTHONY OF OTTO PIZZA

*How and when did you get your start baking? Why pizza over other breads or pastries?*

Anthony opened Anthony's Pizza, the first pizza shop on Nantucket, where he grew up. He was 17, and opened the shop at the start of the summer leading into his senior year in high school. Pizza was a much-needed commodity on the island. Anthony and his wife D.D. would later open a café in Gloucester, MA, where they would bake a daily array of fresh breads and pastries.

*Who—or what—first inspired you to make pizza? Who inspires you now?*

We continue to inspire each other with the passion from which we began in 2009, searching for the perfect pie; a combination of the best ingredients we can source (or produce ourselves), the art of making a balanced pie, and focusing on the quality of the ingredients rather than the quantity. It's prepping the dough so it's just the right temperature and elasticity before being topped and baked. And it's about using the right equipment—the Marsal oven, a brick-lined cavity with consistently high, intense heat that bakes an unusually even pie with a golden crown and crispy bottom. As a company, we're more inward-looking, constantly asking how we can improve our consistency, our process, and delivery of our product. We make sure to remain current with all things pizza, but it's our commitment to ourselves, to constantly challenging what we do and how we do it, that enables us to produce our pie with consistency.

*What is your golden rule(s) for baking?*

"Golden" is the key word—it marks that the dough is perfectly proofed (62°F), ready for the oven, resulting in an airy, open cell–structured, crispy bake. The optimal point of doneness for our product is golden with slight blistering or char. If it's pulled too early, it can be bland, flaccid, and unremarkable. Left in too long, it can take on bitter and unwanted flavors.

*What does Otto's represent to you?*

An interest in re-engineering a ubiquitous food. Our studied approach to pie was one which we transformed what is often blandly accepted into an exceptionally envisioned pie—one that ignites curiosity and a slow nod of approval as one begins to enjoy the often unusual combination of flavors, created and executed by a devoted and caring team.

*What is your favorite pizza to bake? Why? Least favorite pizza to bake? Why?*

Anthony: Plain cheese is the go-to for anyone in the business. It's the 'vanilla' of pizza. If I can belt out a killer cheese slice, chances are we know what we're doing. If I've got company over, it's the sausage, Vidalia, and Fontina pie, with a little scallion and fresh herb.

Mike: Plain cheese with a little basil because it is simple and perfect. My least favorite is any half-and-half—they're messy, busy, and slow down production.

*What are your most popular items?*

Our most popular pie is "The Masher"— mashed potato, bacon, and scallion.

*Where do you get your tools/materials? What non-essential items should every pizza baker have?*

Mike: Cornmeal to create a gap between the dough and the stone.

Anthony: Cornmeal is *absolutely* essential. Essential equipment for the home pizza chef: a pizza stone and hopefully a gas-fired oven that

cranks to 550°F. We use Marcel Ovens in all our shops; their brick-lined cavities allow for even heat distribution and recover exceptionally well.

*What book(s) go on your required reading list for bakers?*

*My Pizza* by Jim Lahey, *Flour, Water, Salt, Yeast* by Ken Forkish, and *American Pie* by Peter Reinhart. We're also big fans of Zingerman's Training Seminars in Ann Arbor, MI (www.zingtrain.com, see page 196).

*What outlets/periodicals/newspapers do you read or consult regularly, if any?*

Mark Bittman, *NYT*, *Food and Wine*, *Saveur*, and Anthony Bourdain's *Parts Unknown*.

*Tell me about your most memorable collaboration with another chef.*

OTTO's Master Baker, Alex Castiello, knows more about the history of dough, the science behind the dough, and industrial dough production than anyone we've ever met. We're lucky he sought us out and we're lucky we listened to 'the dough whisperer.'

*Where did you learn to cook? Please tell me about your education and apprenticeships.*

Ant learned how to make pie on his own when he opened his first shop at the young age of seventeen. He was also inspired after a trip to Naples. Mike first started cooking on a fishing vessel in Alaska and then at a very busy restaurant in Boston. He opened his own bistro north of Boston in 2000.

# THE MASHER: MASHED POTATO, BACON, & SCALLION PIZZA

YIELD: 1 PIZZA / ACTIVE TIME: 25 MINUTES / TOTAL TIME: 45 MINUTES

When we opened OTTO, we began with thinking about Maine. Kinda tough to put a lobster on a pie, so Maine potatoes it was; rich, creamy mashed potatoes, complemented with smoked bacon and scallion. We had to give these slices away at first, but once we started offering a money back guarantee, we got 'em hooked, and the rest is history.

—*courtesy of Mike Keon and Anthony Allen, OTTO Pizza*

1 Preheat oven to 500°F-550°F (or as hot as you can).

2 Bring dough to room temperature (about 65°F) and flatten to about an 8" disc. Allow to rest for 10-15 minutes, then stretch to 16" circle and place on a cornmeal-dusted wooden pizza peel.

3 Brush the dough with olive oil. Season with the black pepper and Asiago. Smooth mashed potatoes around the pizza, spreading all the way to the crust and top with the mozzarella. Drizzle generously with cream. Top with the bacon, scallions, parsley, and salt.

4 Slide pizza off wooden peel onto preheated (hot) pizza stone. Bake until golden brown. Rotate the pizza halfway through cooking for even browning. Cut and serve.

**INGREDIENTS:**

- 1 16-ounce proofed pizza dough
- 2 tablespoons olive oil
- Black pepper, to taste
- 2 tablespoons Asiago cheese, grated
- 1 cup mashed potatoes (your recipe – we recommend making it with lots of cream and butter)
- 7 ounces grated Whole Milk low moisture mozzarella
- Heavy cream, to taste (about an ounce)
- ½ cup chopped cooked bacon
- ½ cup bias-cut green onion (⅛-inch thick)
- 1 tablespoon of parsley, rosemary, and thyme, mixed
- Salt, to taste

# Settebello Pizzeria Italiana

3/1 Rata Street
New Lynn, Auckland 0600
New Zealand
+64 9-826-0777
www.settebello.co.nz

For Francesco Acri, pizza is great—but the process is better. "Settebello is my way to communicate to people, telling them everything about pizza, but without using words—just baking." When asked what his favorite pizza to bake is, he says "all kinds, simply because I love the baking process itself." It is clear after only the briefest interaction that Acri makes pizza as a labor of love. And while there are other factors—his Naples heritage, his genuine love of pizza, his desire to see his culture represented in new areas—it always comes back to his golden rule: "Take your time."

Acri may take his time when making pizzas, but that's nothing compared to his professional career. Acri moved to New Zealand in 2011 after spending 11 years in the Italian navy. He always loved and appreciated the pizza he grew up eating, but never found his professional calling until settling down in a new country. After gaining experience for a year, he was able to open Settebello in 2012.

Still, his pizza career has been anything but slow-and-steady. Though he began baking professionally in 2011, he has already been declared the best pizza-maker in New Zealand after winning the pizza Neapoletana category in 2015's New Zealand Pizza Championship. From there, he was off to Parma, Italy for the World Final Pizza Championship, where he placed in the top 30. Acri is pleased with the result, but insists that "the most memorable part of that experience was competing with many of the greatest pizza-makers in the world."

Settebello is a small pizzeria, tucked away in New Lynn, but in its kitchen Acri is able to make magic. His approach—deliberate, passionate, and local—has made ripples reaching Italy itself. For the kid from Naples, that's a dream come true.

# IN HIS OWN WORDS:

## FRANCESCO ACRI OF SETTEBELLO

*How and when did you get your start baking? Why pizza over other breads or pastries?*

Baking has always been part of my life, but my professional baking career started when I moved to New Zealand in 2011. Why Pizza? A few different reasons, but the most important is that pizza Napoletana is part of my culture. I was inspired by Napoli, my native city and the birthplace of pizza.

*How did Settebello come to be? Why Auckland?*

When I moved to Auckland with my family I wanted to start my own pizzeria and bring a touch of Napoli to the area.

*What are your most popular items?*

Our most popular pizzas on the menu are: Margherita DOC with buffalo mozzarella, Rossa Settebello, Capricciosa, Calzone Napoli, and Scugnizzielli Napoletani, which is a fried dessert dough with Nutella, hazelnut, and few more ingredients.

*Where do you get your tools? What non-essential tool should every pizza-maker have?*

It's very important to handle professional tools when you operate a pizzeria. It just makes life easier. It's been always hard to get good tools here in New Zealand, so I get most of my tools from a company in Italy called Gi Metal.

*What book(s) go on your required reading list for bakers?*

If you are passionate about pizza Napoletana, I suggest a book called *Farina, Acqua, Lievito, Sale, Passione* from the Associazione Pizza Verace Napoletana (APVN, see page 477). Another great book is *The Neapolitan Pizza,* by Paolo Masi, Annalisa Romano, and Enzo Coccia, a scientific guide about the artisanal process.

*Do you follow any cooking shows or chefs? If so, which is your favorite?*

I don't really have time to follow cooking or chefs shows, my pizzeria takes most of my time, but when I can I keep an eye on social media for some cooking shows.

*Where did you learn to cook? Please tell me about your education and apprenticeships.*

I've been making pizza since I came to New Zealand. During my time living here, I've also spent time in Napoli, where I trained with the master pizza-makers of Associazione Verace Pizza Napoletana. From the association, I have to say: I learned a lot.

I think when it comes to baking it's very important to maintain the right process for whatever you're baking. To make a Pizza Napoletana, you must have the wood-fired oven at right temperature, around 840°F, and the pizza should take only 60 to 90 seconds. You can also make a pizza Napoletana at home, but most domestic ovens don't get hot enough so you'll have to change your dough recipe and get a nice pizza stone. It will take 5 or 6 minutes, but still taste beautiful.

*What's your favorite kind of pizza crust, and why? Favorite toppings?*

Clearly my favorite is pizza Napoletana, but the best part is the outer edge called cornicione—the frame of your topping. I love it because it's puffy and thick, crunchy on the outside, soft and chewy on the inside, and covered with leopard spots. I love to dip it into the tomato sauce and mozzarella. I really love Margherita, which is just peeled tomatoes, mozzarella, basil, extra virgin olive oil, and a little bit of Parmigiano. And of course, you need to cook this pizza the right way! Otherwise don't call it Margherita—just tomato and cheese! Plus, if you don't cook properly you will never appreciate the flavors of all these ingredients together.

# SETTEBELLO'S WOOD-FIRED NEAPOLITAN PIZZA DOUGH

**YIELD:** 10 TO 11 250-GRAM PIZZA BASES / **ACTIVE TIME:** 25 MINUTES
**TOTAL TIME:** 10½ - 12½ HOURS

You can really smell the wheat of the flour in this award-winning dough, and if you don't have enough mouths to feed, use whatever is left over to make bread for the table!
—*recipe courtesy of Francesco Acri, Settebello*

**INGREDIENTS:**

4      cups lukewarm water

12–13  cups 00 flour

3      tablespoons sea salt

1      teaspoon fresh yeast

1 In a bowl, combine water and sea salt, stirring until the salt dissolves. Incorporate some of the flour and then the fresh yeast.

2 Start kneading and gradually add the rest of the flour. If using a domestic oven, add the sugar and olive oil. Continue to knead the dough for about 20 minutes until it reaches the desired consistency. is achieved. The dough should be sticky, soft, and elastic to the touch.

3 Cover your dough with a bowl or damp cloth and let it rest for 2 hours. During this time the dough will double the volume.

4 Using a spatula, divide the dough into 10 to 11 evenly sized pieces, and form each piece into a ball. These will be your pizza bases. Place these dough balls into any plastic container and cover, allowing them to rise to close for 8 to 10 hours at room temperature (between 70° and 75°). After 8 to 10 hours your pizza bases will be ready to bake and make pizza.

If using a domestic oven instead wood-fired oven, add the following: 3 tablespoons + 2 teaspoons olive oil, and 2 tablespoons sugar.
    Note: If you want to make this recipe using a domestic oven, we strongly recommend using a pizza stone.

# BIANCA CON SALSICCIA DI FINOCCHIETTO (WHITE PIZZA WITH FENNEL SAUSAGE)

YIELD: 1 PIZZA / ACTIVE TIME: 25 MINUTES / TOTAL TIME: 25 MINUTES AND 60-90 SECONDS IN A WOOD-FIRED OVEN, 31-32 MINUTES IN A DOMESTIC OVEN

This savory pizza is so tasty that it's worth the extra heaviness. Be sure to go easy on the truffle oil until you've tasted the pizza, as it can be very overpowering!
—*recipe courtesy of Francesco Acri, Settebello*

1 Preheat wood-fired oven to 840°F (if using a conventional oven, preheat it to its highest possible temperature).

2 Take one ball of pizza dough and place it lightly on a floured surface. Using your fingertips, press into your pizza base, making sure to leave the edges a little thicker. Keep pressing with the fingertips of your right hand and use the left hand to rotate the pizza base till it reaches 10 to 12 inches in diameter. Remove excess flour.

3 Top with smoked Mozzarella, potato, sausage pieces, baked potatoes, red onion, a pinch of salt, and a few sprigs of rosemary.

4 Lightly dust a pizza peel or stone with flour and carefully transfer your pizza onto it, using both hands, and put in the oven. If using a wood-fired oven your pizza will be ready in 60 to 90 seconds, however if you are using a domestic oven this will take 6 or 7 minutes.

5 Once the pizza is cooked, drizzle with truffle oil and garnish with more rosemary before serving.

**INGREDIENTS:**

- 1     ball of pizza dough (see page 558)
- ¾–1     cup smoked mozzarella, cut into thin rectangles
- 1     pork fennel sausage, cut into pieces and fried until fully cooked

     Half of a potato, boiled for 2 minutes and then baked with some rosemary at 390°F for 7 minutes

- ¼     of a red onion, finely sliced

     A few sprigs of rosemary

     Pinch of salt

     Drizzle of truffle oil

# ROSSA CON FILETTI DI ACCIUGHE (TOMATOES, ANCHOVIES, AND OLIVES PIZZA)

**YIELD:** 1 PIZZA / **ACTIVE TIME:** 25 MINUTES / **TOTAL TIME:** 25 MINUTES + 60–90 SECONDS IN A WOOD-FIRED OVEN, 31–32 MINUTES IN A DOMESTIC OVEN

These classic Mediterranean flavors pair beautifully with Francesco's tangy crust, creating a finished product that brings you straight to Naples.

—*courtesy of Francesco Acri, Settebello*

1 Preheat wood-fired oven to 840°F (if using a conventional oven, preheat it to its highest possible temperature).

2 Take one ball of pizza dough and place it lightly on a floured surface. Using your fingertips, press into your pizza base, making sure to leave the edges a little thicker. Keep pressing with the fingertips of your right hand and use the left hand to rotate the pizza base till it reaches 10 to 12 inches in diameter. Remove excess flour.

3 Top with crushed tomatoes, then buffalo mozzarella, anchovy fillets, capers, olives, salt, oregano, and a drizzle of extra virgin olive oil.

4 Lightly dust a pizza peel or stone with flour and carefully transfer your pizza onto it, using both hands, and put in the oven. If using a wood-fired oven your pizza will be ready in 60 to 90 seconds, however if you are using a domestic oven this will take 6 or 7 minutes. Serve and enjoy!

**INGREDIENTS:**

- 1 ball of pizza dough (see page 558)
- ½ cup whole peeled San Marzano tomatoes, crushed by hand
- ¾–1 cup buffalo mozzarella, cut into thin rectangles and allowed for drain for at least 1 day
- 8–10 anchovy fillets
- 7–8 pitted Kalamata olives
- 9–10 capers
- Pinch of oregano
- Drizzle of olive oil
- Pinch of salt

# CALZONE VULCANO

YIELD: 1 CALZONE / **ACTIVE TIME:** 25 MINUTES **TOTAL TIME:** 25 MINUTES + 90-100 SECONDS IN A WOOD-FIRED OVEN, 33-34 MINUTES IN A DOMESTIC OVEN

If you like strong flavors, this beautiful (and beautifully simple) calzone is perfect for you. And if spice isn't your thing, no problem—just go easy on the chili oil.
—*courtesy of Francesco Acri, Settebello*

1 Preheat wood-fired oven to 840°F (if using a conventional oven, preheat it to its highest possible temperature).

2 Take one ball of pizza dough and place it lightly on a floured surface. Using your fingertips, press into your pizza base, making sure to leave the edges a little thicker. Keep pressing with the fingertips of your right hand and use the left hand to rotate the pizza base till it reaches 10 to 12 inches in diameter. Remove excess flour.

3 Top one side of your base with most of the mozzarella and tomatoes, Salame Napoli, and Kalamata olives, along with some of the bell peppers and red onion. Drizzle with a little chili oil and season with a pinch of salt.

4 Pick up the edges of the empty side of your pizza base and fold it over the other half, joining the edges. It should look like a half-moon. Cut a few holes in the top of the calzone, and then top with remaining mozzarella, tomatoes, peppers, and red onion.

5 Lightly dust a pizza peel or stone with flour and carefully transfer your calzone onto it, using both hands, and put in the oven. If using a wood-fired oven your calzone will be ready in 90 to 100 seconds, however if you are using a domestic oven this will take 8 or 9 minutes. Serve and enjoy!

### INGREDIENTS:

- 1 ball of pizza dough (see page 558)
- ⅓ cup whole peeled San Marzano tomatoes, crushed by hand
- ¾ cup buffalo mozzarella, cut into thin rectangles and allowed for drain for at least 1 day
- ¼ cup sliced Salame Napoli
- 9 pitted Kalamata olives
- Handful of roasted bell peppers, mixed colors
- ¼ of a red onion, finely sliced
- Drizzle of chili oil, mixed with dried chili flakes
- Pinch of salt

# PIZZA DOUGH

**YIELDS:** 2 SERVINGS (4 LARGE PIECES) / **ACTIVE TIME:** 30 MINUTES / **TOTAL TIME:** UP TO 3 DAYS

This is breadmaking at its simplest: flour, water, salt, and yeast. There's actually a cookbook with that title! With this super-easy recipe, you can create amazing pizzas that can be completely individualized with almost anything you have in the fridge or pantry, from traditional cheese to "gourmet." And while the flavor will become more complex and the crust crispier if you allow the dough to rise for a couple of hours (or up to 3 days in the refrigerator), you can also roll it out and bake it within 15 minutes of making it.
—*Dominique DeVito*

**INGREDIENTS:**

- ¾ **cup water (110 to 115 degrees)**
- 1 **teaspoon active dry yeast**
- 2 **cups all-purpose flour**
- 1½ **teaspoons salt**
- 1 **tablespoon olive oil**

  **Toppings (see pages 477–489)**

1 Traditional pizza toppings include the base of marinara topped with mozzarella cheese, as well as ricotta cheese, Italian seasonings, garlic, fresh tomatoes, pepperoni, sausage, meatballs, spinach, olives, mushrooms, peppers, onions— almost anything!

2 If you'll be making pizza within the hour, preheat the oven to 450 degrees.

3 In a large bowl, add the warm water and yeast, stirring to dissolve the yeast. Stir in the flour and salt and mix until the dough is just combined. It will be sticky.

4 Turn out on a floured surface and start kneading until the flour is incorporated, adding more if necessary until the dough is malleable and smooth, but not overdone.

5 Allow the dough to rest for 15 minutes. While it's doing so, put the skillet in the oven to get hot. Prepare the toppings for the pizza.

6 After 15 minutes or when ready, put a piece of parchment paper under the dough. Start rolling and pushing it out to form a 9-inch disk that will fit in the skillet. If it bounces back, let it rest before pushing or rolling it out again.

7 When the disk is formed, use pot holders or oven mitts to remove the skillet from the oven. Add the olive oil and brush to distribute over the bottom. Transfer the dough to the skillet and add the toppings.

8 Bake for 12 to 15 minutes until the crust starts to brown and the toppings are hot and bubbling. Use caution taking the hot skillet from the oven. Allow to cool for 5 minutes before lifting or sliding the pizza out and serving.

# WHOLE WHEAT PIZZA DOUGH

**YIELDS:** 2 SERVINGS (4 LARGE PIECES) / **ACTIVE TIME:** 30 MINUTES / **TOTAL TIME:** 30 MINUTES TO 3 DAYS

If you like an earthier-tasting crust with the added health benefits of whole wheat, this is another easy recipe to follow. Because pizza dough needs to be elastic, it's best to keep some of the regular flour in the blend. The honey helps activate the yeast, and mellows the whole wheat flavor just a bit.

—*Dominique DeVito*

**INGREDIENTS:**

- ¾ cup water (110 to 115 degrees)
- ½ teaspoon honey
- 1 teaspoon active dry yeast
- 1½ cups wheat flour
- ½ cup all-purpose flour
- 1½ teaspoons salt
- 1 tablespoon olive oil

1 If you'll be making pizza within the hour, preheat the oven to 450 degrees.

2 In a large bowl, add the warm water, honey, and yeast, stirring to dissolve the yeast. Stir in the flours and salt and mix until the dough is just combined. It will be sticky.

3 Turn out on a floured surface and start kneading until the flour is incorporated, adding more if necessary until the dough is malleable and smooth, but not overdone.

4 Allow the dough to rest for 15 minutes. While it's doing so, put the skillet in the oven to get hot. Prepare the toppings for the pizza.

5 After 15 minutes or when ready, put a piece of parchment paper under the dough. Start rolling and pushing it out to form a 9-inch disk that will fit in the skillet. If it bounces back, let it rest before pushing or rolling it out again.

6 When the disk is formed, use pot holders or oven mitts to remove the skillet from the oven. Add the olive oil and brush to distribute over the bottom. Transfer the dough to the skillet and add the toppings.

7 Bake for 12 to 15 minutes until the crust starts to brown and the toppings are hot and bubbling. Use caution taking the hot skillet from the oven. Allow to cool for 5 minutes before lifting or sliding the pizza out and serving.

# PALEO PIZZA DOUGH

**YIELDS:** 2 SERVINGS (4 LARGE PIECES) / **ACTIVE TIME:** 30 MINUTES / **TOTAL TIME:** 30 MINUTES TO 3 DAYS

Paleo Bonus: You can make a great paleo-friendly pizza crust with that most wonderful of vegetables, cauliflower!
—*Dominique DeVito*

**INGREDIENTS:**

- 1 head cauliflower
- 2 eggs, lightly beaten (or use just whites if you prefer)
- 1 tablespoon Italian seasoning

  Salt and pepper to taste

1 Preheat the oven to 450 degrees.

2 Use a food processor to render the cauliflower florets into a rice-like consistency.

3 Fill a large pot about ⅓ full of water, bring to a boil, and cook the cauliflower in it until soft, about 5 minutes. Allow to drain thoroughly, then transfer cooked cauliflower to a clean dish towel and squeeze out as much water as possible. Put the cooked, dried cauliflower in a bowl.

4 Add the eggs, Italian seasoning, and salt and pepper to taste and mix thoroughly.

5 Take enough of the "dough" and, on a piece of parchment paper, shape it into a circle that will fit in the skillet. Lightly grease the skillet with coconut oil. Use a spatula and carefully transfer the crust to the skillet. Bake for about 10 minutes, until golden. Remove from the oven, allow to cool slightly, add toppings and bake again for 10 to 12 minutes.

CAST-IRON SKILLET RECIPE

# PEPPERONI BREAD

YIELDS: 6 TO 8 SERVINGS/ ACTIVE TIME: 1 HOUR / TOTAL TIME: 3 HOURS

This is a favorite during football season, when the game hasn't actually started until this makes an appearance in front of the TV. Start in the morning for an afternoon game, as the dough needs to rise several times. But it's so delicious!
—*Dominique DeVito*

**INGREDIENTS:**

1¼ cups water (110 to 115 degrees)

1 tablespoon sugar

1 oz. active dry yeast

1 tablespoon melted butter

1½ teaspoons salt

3½ cups flour

Salt and pepper

½ pound pepperoni, slivered

2 cups grated mozzarella cheese

1 teaspoon hot pepper flakes

1 teaspoon dried oregano

1 teaspoon garlic powder

1 Proof the yeast by mixing it with the water and sugar in a large bowl and then adding the yeast, stirring. Let sit until foamy, about 10 minutes. Add the salt and about half the flour to form a sticky dough. Cover the bowl with plastic wrap or a clean dish towel and let rise in a warm, draft-free place until it is double in size, about 1 hour.

2 Punch down the dough and add more flour to make it less sticky. Transfer to a floured surface and work the dough until it's smooth and elastic. Transfer to a lightly greased bowl and let sit for about 15 minutes.

3 On the floured surface, roll the dough out into a rectangle about 14x16 inches. Sprinkle with salt and pepper, spread the dough with pieces of pepperoni, then cheese, and top with a sprinkling of hot pepper flakes, oregano, and garlic powder. Roll up like a jellyroll, pinching the ends to secure filling.

4 Grease the skillet with the butter and lay the roll in it in a circle, working from the edges toward the center. Cover with a clean dish towel and let it rise again for about 1 hour. Preheat the oven to 375 degrees.

5 Bake the pepperoni bread for about 30 minutes, until golden on top and bubbling in the center. Serve immediately.

## VARIATION

It's easy to make this into a full-blown Meat Lover's Bread. In addition to the pepperoni, add about ¼ to ½ cup of any or each of diced pancetta, diced smoked ham, crumbled cooked bacon, sautéed sausage, or diced cooked mini meatballs.

## Sugaree's Bakery

110 West Bankhead Street
New Albany, MS 38652
(662) 534-0031
www.sugarees.com

Every state in the south has its own baking tradition, each wonderful in its own right. That said, you could do a lot worse than Mississippi, where recipes are often passed down through generations of at-home bakers. And if you are in Mississippi, it's hard to do much better than Sugaree's, where owner Mary Jennifer Russell has been creating delicious goodies for the masses since 1997.

Of course, Mary began baking much earlier than 1997. Her education began at 7 years old, learning from her first and most important teacher: her mother. Mary says, "She was that mom who made thirty different candies and baked goods every year to give as Christmas gifts to all of our teachers, church friends, and family. I loved getting a free pass on our normally early bedtime to stay up late every night in December to help her!" This background led Mary to revisit baking after bouncing around pharmaceutical sales jobs after graduation. While the jobs may have bored her, the connections she made went a long way toward getting Sugaree's off the ground. "I borrowed a calligraphy book from the library, hand wrote a price list and took samples to all the downtown

merchants, teachers' lounges, and local business break rooms. Orders slowly started coming in. When I finally got another part-time contract pharmaceutical sales job, it was approved in the interview stage that I could use my entire $300 monthly expense account to purchase my own cakes and give them to the doctors' offices—and that's exactly what I did for the next three years, which helped spread my footprint to all of North Mississippi."

The enterprise grew from local to wholesale before Mary opened her first brick-and-mortar space in New Albany. And while she still does most of her business wholesale, Sugaree's remains a staple in the community, evoking the "childhood memories of growing up with a master baker in your life" and staying true to the traditional flavors of the Deep South. Her mastery of this difficult balance is what earned Mary the 2017 award for Mississippi SBA Small Business Person of the Year—and what's kept customers coming back for more over the last 2 years.

# IN HER OWN WORDS:

## MARY JENNIFER RUSSELL

*Who inspired you to bake? Who inspires you now?*

I have always been inspired by my mom's baking abilities and aware of the reactions her desserts generated when she walked into a church pot luck or a holiday dinner at my grandmother's house. My local farmers, my culinary graduate employees, and my customers also inspire me.

*What is your golden rule(s) of baking?*

Mo' butter, Mo' better!

What does Sugaree's represent to you?

I hope to distill the classic flavor profiles of the Deep South into nostalgic taste experiences for my customers with Southern roots…and for anyone else who just appreciates especially rich and moist homemade desserts!

*What is your favorite thing to bake? Why? Least favorite thing to bake? Why?*

My favorite thing to bake is the chocolate meringue pie. I prefer to do the finishing steps in all of my kitchen processes—pulling cake layers from the oven, icing cakes, shaping pie crusts, and peaking meringue are some of my favorite tasks. My least favorite thing to bake might be petit fours. I think I have sworn them off every time I have ever made them—I tire quickly of slow, tedious decorating details.

*What are your most popular items?*

Our most popular item is our three-layer caramel cake, which of course is also the most difficult to make! Caramel cake is a regional specialty that embodies our brand mission, which is to help preserve and celebrate heirloom recipes and baking techniques unique to this area. We cook the caramel icing for one cake at a time all day long, starting with ½ cup of granulated sugar in a cast iron skillet. It is a very particular process that is sensitive to the humidity, temperature, and pressure conditions, which aren't completely in our control, so the icers have to make adjustments throughout the day to keep the finished icing product consistent with our quality standards. It's definitely a labor of love!

*Where do you get your tools/materials? What non-essential items should every baker have?*

We don't need a lot of specialty tools to do what we do—our primary tools are just bigger versions of home kitchen basics, like bigger mixers. For small wares, my go-to mail order companies are Webstaurant.com and Hubert.com. One of my favorite tools is the Kitchen Aid mixer with all its glorious attachments! I think every baker should have scales, a pastry blender, a lazy Susan, high-temperature spatulas, portion scoops, and a bench scraper.

*What book(s) go on your required reading list for bakers?*

All of Rose Levy Berambaum's books, *Baking with Julia, Cook's Illustrated Baking Book, Pastries from La Brea Bakery* by Nancy Silverton, *A Passion for Bread* by Lionel Vatinet, *Professional Baking* by Wayne Glissen.

*What outlets/periodicals/newspapers do you read or consult regularly, if any?*

I like to keep an eye on: *Cook's Illustrated, Milk Street, NY Times Cooking, Southern Living* and all of the Hoffman Media publications, *Bon Appetit, Food and Wine, Saveur,* and *Local Palate.*

*Tell me about your most memorable collaboration(s) with another chef.*

Sugaree's has hosted a couple of farm-to-table dinners in my hometown with the seating on a footbridge over the Tallahatchie River in our public park. It was fantastic to bring such a high level of quality chefs and meals to New Albany—our second dinner sold out in 15 minutes!

*Do you follow any cooking shows or chefs? If so, which is your favorite?*

I just started watching the Netflix shows *Cooked* and *Chef's Table* and love them both.

*Where did you learn to cook? Please tell me about your education and/or apprenticeships.*

I learned to cook and bake primarily from my mom. The only baking job I ever had was during one semester in Oxford at the Harvest Café. I think I was working three jobs at the time and quit that one when I started having trouble getting enough sleep to keep up with my Biology course load.

*Mississippi has a long, rich history of wonderful southern baking. How has that influenced you and your approach at Sugaree's?*

Mississippi has a long, rich history of wonderful baking that, when examined closely, I believe has deep ties to rural poverty. The caramel cake and red velvet cakes are great examples of how poor home cooks could take very inexpensive and simple basic ingredients (sugar, salt, and flour) and add their own home produced farm products (butter, buttermilk, eggs), ending up with a very special treat that didn't cost much money to produce. Since we now have access to higher quality ingredients, such as European butter and premium chocolates and extracts, we can produce the old recipes using the traditional techniques and get results with even more depth of flavor.

# SUGAREE'S BAKERY MISSISSIPPI POT ROAST HAND PIE

YIELD: 13 HAND PIES / ACTIVE TIME: 1 HOUR / TOTAL TIME: 3 HOURS 35 MINUTES

These fun hand pies can be used as starters, sides, or the main course. Just be sure to hide a few for yourself!
—*Mary Jennifer Russell*

## FILLING

1 Preheat oven to 450°F. Rinse and pat the roast dry. Salt and pepper all sides, then coat in seasoned flour.

2 Heat oil over medium-high heat in a Dutch oven. Sear meat on all sides for 3–5 minutes or until golden. Remove roast from pan, add carrots to the bottom, and place the roast on top of the carrots. Add the shallots, bay leaves, thyme, Worcestershire, and water. Cover and cook for 1 hour.

3 Turn oven down to 350°F and cook for 1 hour. In a mason jar with a lid, shake together flour and beef stock and pour through a strainer over the roast. Cover and cook another hour or until tender.

## CRUST

1 As your roast cooks, begin making your crust. Mix flour and salt. Grate butter into the flour mix and toss to coat. Use a pastry blender or two butter knives to cut butter into flour in small, evenly sized pieces.

2 Add ice water a few tablespoons at a time and incorporate by tossing with a large fork, working quickly to avoid overworking the dough. Form dough into a ball quickly to avoid overheating the dough.

3 Cut and weigh 2 ½-ounce portions. Roll each portion into an 8-inch circle between two pieces of saran wrap. Chill.

## COMBINE

1 When your roast is finished, remove everything from the pan except the gravy and cook the gravy over medium-high heat until it thickens. Season with salt and pepper and let cool.

2 Chop meat, carrots, and shallots and add back to gravy with the frozen peas. Season to taste.

### INGREDIENTS:

**FILLING**

| | |
|---|---|
| 2 | pounds bottom round |
| | Salt |
| | Pepper |
| 1 | cup flour, mixed with 1 tablespoon each salt and pepper |
| 3 | tablespoons grape seed oil |
| 2 | pounds carrots, peeled and whole |
| 8 | shallots, peeled and whole |
| 2–3 | bay leaves |
| 8–10 | fresh thyme sprigs |
| ¼ | cup Worcestershire |
| 1 | cup water |
| ¼ | cup flour |
| 2 | cups beef stock |
| 1 | pack frozen green peas |
| 1 | egg yolk |
| 1 | tablespoon cream |

**CRUST**

| | |
|---|---|
| 4 | cups flour |
| 1 | teaspoon salt |
| ½ | pound unsalted butter, frozen and grated |
| 1 | cup ice water |

3 Set your oven to 375°F. Put ⅓ cup cooled filling in the center of each pastry. Fold into a half moon shape and pinch edges to seal. Poke a hole in the top of each hand pie.

4 Brush with egg yolk and cream glaze. Bake at 375°F on the bottom rack of oven for 30–35 minutes. Remove and let cool.

# SAUSAGE CALZONE

**YIELDS:** 4 TO 6 SERVINGS/ **ACTIVE TIME:** 1 HOUR / **TOTAL TIME:** 2 HOURS

If you're looking for a meal that's more filling than just pizza, go for a calzone. Typically it's pizza dough folded over a filling into a half-moon shape. When made in a cast-iron skillet it's a double-crusted pizza. This allows for more filling to be piled inside, and as always with the cast-iron experience, the resulting dish will have a lovely bottom crust.

—*Dominique DeVito*

1  Make the dough by combining the warm water and yeast in a large bowl, stirring to dissolve the yeast. Stir in the flour and salt and mix until the dough is just combined. It will be sticky.

2  Turn out on a floured surface and start kneading until the flour is incorporated, adding more if necessary until the dough is malleable and smooth, but not overdone.

3  Lightly grease a bowl and put the dough in it. Allow to rise while you prepare the filling and preheat the oven, about 30 minutes.

4  Preheat the oven to 400 degrees.

5  Make the filling. In a large skillet over medium-high heat, cook the sausage in the olive oil, breaking up the meat into smaller pieces as it cooks. Stir continuously as it cooks, keeping the meat from sticking to the pan and making sure it is cooked evenly. Cook until the meat is no longer pink, about 15 minutes. Drain any excess fat. Reduce the heat to low and stir in the garlic and herbs. Season with salt and pepper. Set aside but do not refrigerate.

6  On a lightly floured surface, turn out the dough and separate it into two equal pieces. Roll each piece into a 12-inch circle.

7  Place one circle in the skillet. The dough should extend about half way up the side. Spread the marinara sauce over it, then add the cooked sausage, and top with the grated cheese. Place the other dough circle over the filling and crimp to seal the edges together with your fingers. Cut 4 slits in the top.

8  Bake for 25 minutes until the crust is a lovely golden brown. Use pot holders or oven mitts to remove the skillet. Allow to cool for about 10 minutes before slicing and serving. Serve with additional marinara sauce if desired.

## INGREDIENTS:

### FOR THE DOUGH

- 1½ cups water (110 to 115 degrees)
- 2 teaspoons active dry yeast
- 4 cups all-purpose flour
- 2 teaspoons salt

### FOR THE FILLING

- 1 tablespoon olive oil
- 1 pound sweet or hot Italian sausage, casing removed
- 2 cloves garlic, pressed
- ½ teaspoon dried oregano
- ½ teaspoon dried thyme
- Salt and pepper to taste
- ½ cup marinara sauce
- 2 cups shredded mozzarella
- Other filling ingredients as desired

# SAUSAGE, PEPPER, *and* ONION CALZONE

**YIELDS:** 4 TO 6 SERVINGS / **ACTIVE TIME:** 1 HOUR / **TOTAL TIME:** 2 HOURS

Eating one of these is like being at an Italian street fair. Load it up so that the ingredients and juices overflow the crust when you eat it. Fabuloso!

*—Dominique DeVito*

1 Make the dough by combining the warm water and yeast in a large bowl, stirring to dissolve the yeast. Stir in the flour and salt and mix until the dough is just combined. It will be sticky.

2 Turn out on a floured surface and start kneading until the flour is incorporated, adding more if necessary until the dough is malleable and smooth, but not overdone.

3 Lightly grease a bowl and put the dough in it. Allow to rise while you prepare the filling and preheat the oven, about 30 minutes.

4 Preheat the oven to 400 degrees.

5 Make the filling. In a large skillet over medium-high heat, cook the onions and garlic in the oil for about 2 minutes. Add the sausage slices and continue cooking until browned, another 5 minutes. Reduce the heat to medium, add the pepper slices, and stir to combine. Reduce the heat to low and continue cooking, stirring occasionally, until the pepper slices have softened and caramelized slightly in the oil, 10 to 15 minutes. Season with oregano, salt and pepper. Set aside but do not refrigerate.

6 On a lightly floured surface, turn out the dough and separate it into two equal pieces. Roll each piece into a 12-inch circle.

7 Place one circle in the skillet. The dough should extend about half way up the side. Spread the sausage and peppers over it, then top with the grated cheese. Place the other dough circle over the filling and crimp to seal the edges together with your fingers. Cut 4 slits in the top.

8 Bake for 25 minutes until the crust is a lovely golden brown. Use pot holders or oven mitts to remove the skillet. Allow to cool for about 10 minutes before slicing and serving. Serve with marinara sauce if desired.

## INGREDIENTS:

### FOR THE DOUGH

1½ cups water (110 to 115 degrees)

2 teaspoons active dry yeast

4 cups all-purpose flour

2 teaspoons salt

### FOR THE FILLING

3 tablespoons olive oil

1 medium onion, sliced

3 cloves garlic, minced

1 pound hot Italian sausage, sliced into thin rounds

1 teaspoon red pepper flakes (optional)

1 green pepper, seeds removed, sliced into strips

1 red pepper, seeds removed, sliced into strips

½ teaspoon oregano

Salt and pepper to taste

2 cups shredded mozzarella

# PHILLY CHEESESTEAK CALZONE

**YIELDS:** 4 TO 6 SERVINGS/ **ACTIVE TIME:** 1 HOUR / **TOTAL TIME:** 2 HOURS

If you want to be a hero for the meat-loving men in your household, serve up one of these. With the hot, crispy crusts, the experience may even exceed a Philly cheesesteak sandwich. Super Bowl party at your house!

—*Dominique DeVito*

1 Make the dough by combining the warm water and yeast in a large bowl, stirring to dissolve the yeast. Stir in the flour and salt and mix until the dough is just combined. It will be sticky.

2 Turn out on a floured surface and start kneading until the flour is incorporated, adding more if necessary until the dough is malleable and smooth, but not overdone.

3 Lightly grease a bowl and put the dough in it. Allow to rise while you prepare the filling and preheat the oven, about 30 minutes.

4 Preheat the oven to 400 degrees.

5 Make the filling. Put the olive oil in a large skillet over medium-high heat and add the onion. Cook, stirring, so that the onions soften and caramelize, about 5 to 8 minutes. Transfer the onions to a bowl. Following the package instructions, cook the sliced steaks, transferring the cooked pieces to a plate until all are done.

6 On a lightly floured surface, turn out the dough and separate it into two equal pieces. Roll each piece into a 12-inch circle.

7 Place one circle in the skillet. The dough should extend about half way up the side. Spread the steaks over the dough, season with salt and pepper, then distribute the cheese over the meat and top with the cooked onions. Place the other dough circle over the filling and crimp to seal the edges together with your fingers. Cut 4 slits in the top.

8 Bake for 25 minutes until the crust is a lovely golden brown. Use pot holders or oven mitts to remove the skillet. Allow to cool for about 10 minutes before slicing and serving. Serve with warmed marinara sauce on the side.

## INGREDIENTS:

**FOR THE DOUGH**

1½ cups water (110 to 115 degrees)

2 teaspoons active dry yeast

4 cups all-purpose flour

2 teaspoons salt

**FOR THE FILLING**

2 tablespoons olive oil

1 medium onion, sliced

1 package frozen sliced steaks

2 cups shredded American cheese (do not substitute)

Salt and pepper to taste

1 jar marinara sauce, heated

# BARBECUED CHICKEN *and* PEPPERONI CALZONE

**YIELDS:** 4 TO 6 SERVINGS/ **ACTIVE TIME:** 1 HOUR / **TOTAL TIME:** 2 HOURS

Using leftover barbecued chicken gives this calzone recipe an added layer of tang, but you can use plain cooked chicken, too. Either will delight when brought out of the oven.
—*Dominique DeVito*

1 Make the dough by combining the warm water and yeast in a large bowl, stirring to dissolve the yeast. Stir in the flour and salt and mix until the dough is just combined. It will be sticky.

2 Turn out on a floured surface and start kneading until the flour is incorporated, adding more if necessary until the dough is malleable and smooth, but not overdone.

3 Lightly grease a bowl and put the dough in it. Allow to rise while you prepare the filling and preheat the oven, about 30 minutes.

4 Preheat the oven to 400 degrees.

5 Make the filling. In a large skillet over medium heat, warm the marinara sauce. Add the garlic and cook for a couple of minutes. Add the chicken pieces, stir, then add the pepperoni slices. Season with salt and pepper. Reduce the heat to low and simmer, uncovered, until ready to use.

6 On a lightly floured surface, turn out the dough and separate it into two equal pieces. Roll each piece into a 12-inch circle.

7 Place one circle in the skillet. The dough should extend about half way up the side. Spread the chicken/pepperoni mix evenly over the dough, then cover with the mozzarella and sprinkle with the Parmesan. Place the other dough circle over the filling and crimp to seal the edges together with your fingers. Cut 4 slits in the top.

8 Bake for 20 to 25 minutes until the crust is a lovely golden brown. Use pot holders or oven mitts to remove the skillet. Allow to cool for about 10 minutes before slicing and serving.

## INGREDIENTS:

### FOR THE DOUGH

1½ cups water (110 to 115 degrees)

2 teaspoons active dry yeast

4 cups all-purpose flour

2 teaspoons salt

### FOR THE FILLING

1 cup marinara sauce

2 cloves garlic, pressed

3 cups cooked barbequed chicken, cut into dice

1 cup pepperoni slices

Salt and pepper to taste

2 cups shredded mozzarella cheese

Grated Parmesan

# CHICKEN *and* PESTO CALZONE

**YIELDS:** 4 TO 6 SERVINGS / **ACTIVE TIME:** 1 HOUR / **TOTAL TIME:** 2 HOURS

Calzones are great pockets in which to stuff leftovers and create something yummy and different at the same time.
—*Dominique DeVito*

1   Make the dough by combining the warm water and yeast in a large bowl, stirring to dissolve the yeast. Stir in the flour and salt and mix until the dough is just combined. It will be sticky.

2   Turn out on a floured surface and start kneading until the flour is incorporated, adding more if necessary until the dough is malleable and smooth, but not overdone.

3   Lightly grease a bowl and put the dough in it. Allow to rise while you preheat the oven, about 30 minutes.

4   Preheat the oven to 400 degrees.

5   On a lightly floured surface, turn out the dough and separate it into two equal pieces. Roll each piece into a 12-inch circle.

6   Place one circle in the skillet. The dough should extend about half way up the side. Spread the cooked chicken evenly over the dough, then dollop with the pesto. Sprinkle the mozzarella over everything, and then sprinkle with the Parmesan. Place the other dough circle over the filling and crimp to seal the edges together with your fingers. Cut 4 slits in the top.

7   Bake for 20 to 25 minutes until the crust is a lovely golden brown. Use pot holders or oven mitts to remove the skillet. Allow to cool for about 10 minutes before slicing and serving.

**INGREDIENTS:**

**FOR THE DOUGH**

1½   cups water (110 to 115 degrees)

2   teaspoons active dry yeast

4   cups all-purpose flour

2   teaspoons salt

**FOR THE FILLING**

3   cups cooked chicken, diced

1   cup pesto

2   cups shredded mozzarella cheese

Grated Parmesan

## VARIATION

Make this a Buffalo Chicken and Pesto Calzone. When making the filling, put the cooked chicken pieces in a small bowl and add ¼ cup Frank's Hot Sauce. Stir to coat and drain any extra. Proceed to fill the calzone as directed above.

# EGGPLANT, OLIVES, ONIONS, *and* ANCHOVIES CALZONE

YIELDS: 4 TO 6 SERVINGS/ ACTIVE TIME: 1 HOUR / TOTAL TIME: 2 HOURS

Here's a calzone inspired by the flavors of Greece. For a clean, just-right taste, use anchovies marinated in oil, not anchovy paste, which is too salty and can be somewhat bitter.

—*Dominique DeVito*

1 Make the dough by combining the warm water and yeast in a large bowl, stirring to dissolve the yeast. Stir in the flour and salt and mix until the dough is just combined. It will be sticky.

2 Turn out on a floured surface and start kneading until the flour is incorporated, adding more if necessary until the dough is malleable and smooth, but not overdone.

3 Lightly grease a bowl and put the dough in it. Allow to rise while you prepare the filling and preheat the oven, about 30 minutes.

4 Preheat the oven to 400 degrees.

5 Make the filling. In a large skillet, heat 1 tablespoon of oil over medium-high heat. Add the eggplant cubes and cook, stirring, until softened and browned, about 6 to 8 minutes. Use a slotted spoon and transfer the pieces to a plate covered with a paper towel to absorb extra oil. Add 2 tablespoons of oil to the hot pan and add the garlic and red pepper flakes. Cook until the garlic bits dance in the oil, about 2 minutes. Add the anchovy fillets and the olives and stir to combine, cooking for an additional minute or two. Add the eggplant pieces and combine.

6 On a lightly floured surface, turn out the dough and separate it into two equal pieces. Roll each piece into a 12-inch circle.

7 Place one circle in the skillet. The dough should extend about half way up the side. Spread the eggplant/olive mixture evenly over the dough, then sprinkle the mozzarella over everything. Place the other dough circle over the filling and crimp to seal the edges together with your fingers. Cut 4 slits in the top.

8 Bake for 20 to 25 minutes until the crust is a lovely golden brown. Use pot holders or oven mitts to remove the skillet. Allow to cool for about 10 minutes before slicing and serving with grated Parmesan cheese.

## INGREDIENTS:

**FOR THE DOUGH**

1½ cups water (110 to 115 degrees)

2 teaspoons active dry yeast

4 cups all-purpose flour

2 teaspoons salt

**FOR THE FILLING**

3 tablespoons olive oil

1 small eggplant, cubed

3 garlic cloves, minced

½ teaspoon red pepper flakes

4 to 6 anchovy fillets in oil (not anchovy paste)

½ cup pitted black olives, cut in half

2 cups shredded mozzarella cheese

Grated Parmesan

# SPINACH *and* RICOTTA CALZONES

**YIELDS:** 4 TO 6 SERVINGS/ **ACTIVE TIME:** 1 HOUR / **TOTAL TIME:** 2 HOURS

Such a great combination! The resulting pizza "pie" is gooey with cheese and plenty of lovely green spinach. I like to spice this up with hot pepper flakes, but you can serve them on the side if you prefer.

—*Dominique DeVito*

1 Make the dough by combining the warm water and yeast in a large bowl, stirring to dissolve the yeast. Stir in the flour and salt and mix until the dough is just combined. It will be sticky.

2 Turn out on a floured surface and start kneading until the flour is incorporated, adding more if necessary until the dough is malleable and smooth, but not overdone.

3 Lightly grease a bowl and put the dough in it. Allow to rise while you prepare the filling and preheat the oven, about 30 minutes.

4 Preheat the oven to 400 degrees.

5 Make the filling. Put the olive oil, garlic, and red pepper flakes in a large skillet over medium-high heat and add the frozen spinach. Stir while cooking as the spinach thaws, coating the leaves with the oil and garlic, about 5 minutes. Reduce the heat to medium-low and cover, stirring occasionally, until the spinach is cooked through, another 15 minutes. Season with salt and pepper. Set aside but do not refrigerate. In a bowl, mix together the ricotta, egg, and Parmesan cheese.

6 On a lightly floured surface, turn out the dough and separate it into two equal pieces. Roll each piece into a 12-inch circle.

7 Place one circle in the skillet. The dough should extend about half way up the side. Spread the cooked spinach evenly over the dough, then dollop with the ricotta cheese mix. Use a spatula or the back of a large spoon to distribute the ricotta. Place the other dough circle over the filling and crimp to seal the edges together with your fingers. Cut 4 slits in the top.

8 Bake for 25 minutes until the crust is a lovely golden brown. Use pot holders or oven mitts to remove the skillet. Allow to cool for about 10 minutes before slicing and serving.

**INGREDIENTS:**

**FOR THE DOUGH**

1½  cups water (110 to 115 degrees)

2  teaspoons active dry yeast

4  cups all-purpose flour

2  teaspoons salt

**FOR THE FILLING**

2  tablespoons olive oil

3  cloves garlic, minced

1  teaspoon red pepper flakes (optional)

1  (16-oz.) package frozen chopped spinach leaves

Salt and pepper to taste

2  cups fresh ricotta cheese

1  egg, lightly beaten

½  cup grated Parmesan cheese

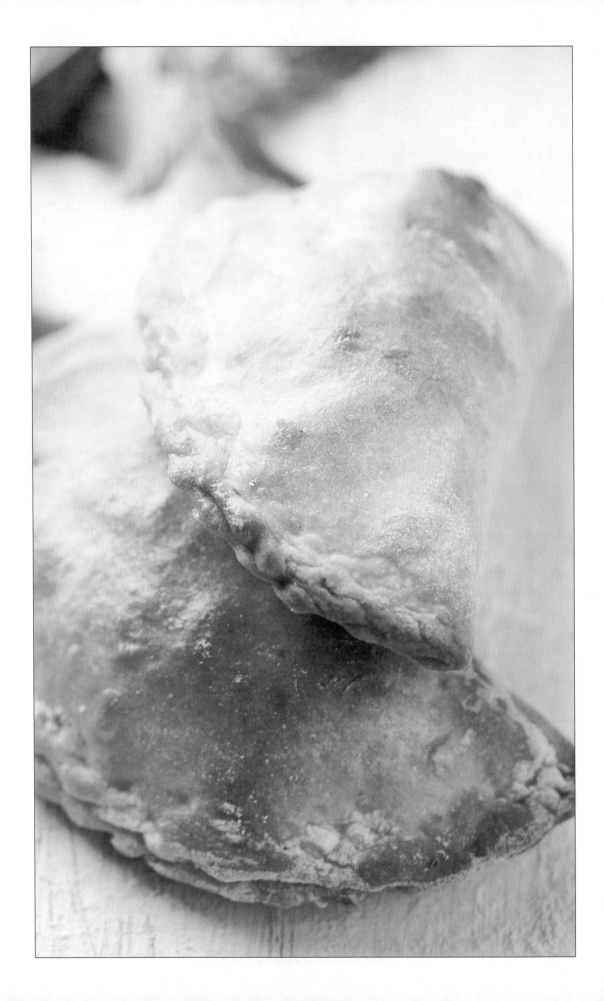

# KALE *and* MONTEREY JACK CALZONE

CAST-IRON SKILLET RECIPE

**YIELDS: 4 TO 6 SERVINGS/ ACTIVE TIME: 1 HOUR / TOTAL TIME: 2 HOURS**

Kale, like spinach, holds up well when sautéed. You can use all kale in this recipe, or you can substitute other substantial leafy greens, like spinach, Swiss chard, beet tops, or arugula. The Monterey Jack has a hint of heat, but if you want something milder, use mozzarella.

—*Dominique DeVito*

**INGREDIENTS:**

**FOR THE DOUGH**

1½ cups water (110 to 115 degrees)

2 teaspoons active dry yeast

4 cups all-purpose flour

2 teaspoons salt

**FOR THE FILLING**

2 tablespoons olive oil

3 cloves garlic, minced

1 pound fresh kale, woody stems removed and roughly chopped

Salt and pepper to taste

2 cups grated Monterey Jack cheese

1 egg, lightly beaten

½ cup grated Parmesan cheese

1 Make the dough by combining the warm water and yeast in a large bowl, stirring to dissolve the yeast. Stir in the flour and salt and mix until the dough is just combined. It will be sticky.

2 Turn out on a floured surface and start kneading until the flour is incorporated, adding more if necessary until the dough is malleable and smooth, but not overdone.

3 Lightly grease a bowl and put the dough in it. Allow to rise while you prepare the filling and preheat the oven, about 30 minutes.

4 Preheat the oven to 400 degrees.

5 Make the filling. Put the olive oil and garlic in a large skillet over medium-high heat. Add the kale and sauté, stirring, until the kale is wilted, about 5 minutes. Reduce the heat to low and cover, stirring occasionally, until the kale is soft, another 5 to 10 minutes. Season with salt and pepper. Set aside but do not refrigerate. In a bowl, mix together the Monterey Jack, egg, and Parmesan cheese. Add the kale and stir to combine.

6 On a lightly floured surface, turn out the dough and separate it into two equal pieces. Roll each piece into a 12-inch circle.

7 Place one circle in the skillet. The dough should extend about half way up the side. Spread the kale mix evenly over the dough. Sprinkle with additional Parmesan cheese if desired. Place the other dough circle over the filling and crimp to seal the edges together with your fingers. Cut 4 slits in the top.

8 Bake for 20 to 25 minutes until the crust is a lovely golden brown. Use pot holders or oven mitts to remove the skillet. Allow to cool for about 10 minutes before slicing and serving.

# GARLIC KNOTS

YIELDS: 3 DOZEN / **ACTIVE TIME:** 45 MINUTES / **TOTAL TIME:** 90 MINUTES

Use the pizza dough recipe to make the knots themselves. They'll get that great cast-iron crust when they bake, then they can be bathed with garlic-parsley butter and put on a plate. Don't expect them to hang around for long, which is why this is a double batch of dough.

*—Dominique DeVito*

1 In a large bowl, add the warm water and yeast, stirring to dissolve the yeast. Stir in the flour and salt and mix until the dough is just combined. It will be sticky.

2 Turn out on a floured surface and start kneading until the flour is incorporated, adding more if necessary until the dough is malleable and smooth, but not overdone.

3 Lightly grease a bowl and put the dough in it. Allow to rise for about an hour. Preheat the oven to 450 degrees.

4 Transfer to a lightly floured surface and push and stretch the dough into a large rectangle. If it resists, let it rest before stretching it further. Cut the rectangle into strips, and tie the strips into knots. Spread the tablespoon of olive oil over the bottom of the skillet. Tuck the knots into the skillet so there's just enough room separating them. Bake for about 15 minutes until golden brown.

5 While the knots are baking, prepare the garlic-dill sauce. In a saucepan on medium heat, melt the butter. Add the garlic and reduce the heat to medium-low. Allow to cook, stirring occasionally, for about 3 minutes. This takes some of the pungency out of the garlic and also infuses the butter with the flavor. Stir in the chopped dill and salt.

6 When the garlic knots come out of the oven, use a tea towel over your hand to pull them off the skillet and put them in a large mixing bowl. Scoop a large spoonful of the garlic-dill sauce over the knots and toss to coat, adding a bit more if necessary. Use another spoon to transfer the coated knots to a plate. Sprinkle with Parmesan if desired and serve.

7 Continue to work in batches in the skillet until the dough is used up, or save some of the dough in the refrigerator for up to 3 days. The sauce can also be refrigerated for several days and reheated.

## INGREDIENTS:

**FOR THE KNOTS**

1½ cups water (110 to 115 degrees)

2 teaspoons active dry yeast

4 cups all-purpose flour

2 teaspoons salt

1 tablespoon olive oil

**GARLIC-DILL SAUCE**

8 tablespoons (1 stick) unsalted butter

8 cloves garlic, minced

⅓ cup dill, finely chopped

2 teaspoons salt

Grated Parmesan if desired

# PIES

## WHAT A PIE IS AND WHAT A PIE IS NOT

There is no universal consensus on what a pie should look like. Should it have a crust? Should it have a bottom crust? Should it have a top crust? Should it be shallow or deep? Should the crust and the filling be savory or sweet?

There is quite the geographical variation in what a pie is supposed to be. In Northern America, pies are mostly sweet and deep. They can have a top crust but they always have a bottom crust. In Great Britain and Germany, pies are mostly savory and need to have a crust all around them: under, on the sides, and on top. In Sweden, pies are still savory but shallow and open-faced, and so are French and Italian pies, which are often sweet, and are called tarts. Thus, is pie a tart? Or is a tart a pie?

It is, however, internationally acknowledged that pies need to be baked and that a filling must be encased in, or placed over, a non-spongy *crust*, which must contain flour and a source of fat. A pie should not be something fried and should not be leavened. A pie is not a cake, nor a doughnut. Absolutely, not a pizza. Possibly, a pie is not even a tart. So, what is a pie?

The answer is that one cannot fully understand pies in their essence without deep-diving into pie history.

Just like what happened for leavened bread, pies started to be baked by the Egyptians and became known to Romans through the Greeks. Thereafter, the Romans made pies known to the rest of Europe.

Originally, pies developed together with wood-fired ovens. The crust was then both a pan and a lid, to allow food, mostly meat, to cook without drying or burning. It was tricky to make kitchenware that could resist the heat of a wood-fired oven without exploding or deforming. Thick dough was the ideal shell to protect the food from the fire and allow an even cooking. For a long time the crust was supposedly not eaten. Dried up and often burned, thick, unleavened and hardened, it must not have been the most appealing food to savor.

Pies were very popular in Northern Europe during the Middle Ages and were mostly savory, often meat-based. In Britain, the shell of pies was called *coffyn*, which by then did not evoke a burial, but simply referred to a container. Coffyns were made with wheat flour, water, and lard. Lard was considered much better than butter to make a crust, because it has less water content than butter and a much higher smoking point during baking at high temperatures. These pie shells were mostly not eaten, unless by servants or the very poor, waiting at the gates of the rich mansions.

Meat pies were also used as a mean to preserve the meat during winter. The shell, together with the cold, preserved cooked meat for months. This also allowed pies to travel long distances, brought on trips or sent to relatives.

Fruit pies made their appearance quite late in pie history, around the 14th or 15th century AD. Initially fruit pies were not sweetened, because sugar was expensive. There is one school of thought that ascribes the term "tart" to this reason: tarts were born as unsweetened fruit pies with a tart bite to them, meaning sour and acidic. Another school of thought

distinguishing fruit pies from tarts, stems from the Latin term *torta panis,* literally meaning "twisted bread [dough]", from tortus, "twisted" and "folded over". To make a tart, indeed, one needs to roll the dough with a rolling pin and fold the edges over the filling. Tarts, mostly linked to the French and Italian baking tradition, started to become popular around the same time as Northern European pies, but were different both in their context and in the quality of their crust.

British fruit pies, for instance, were unsweetened and were more a convenience type of cooking, like meat pies. Made to feed and use up ingredients, more than to delight. The crust was plain and was not supposed to be tasty. Tarts were instead developed around an enriched unleavened dough meant to be sweet and pleasant to the palate both in texture and in taste. These types of dishes were not everyday food and were instead linked to festive days, for ordinary people, and to fancy dining, for the few privileged. It is therefore likely that, although coming from a same common Roman ancestor, tarts and pies followed their own paths and developed within distinct traditions.

## THE RULES OF PIE BAKING

These rules mainly apply to American-style pies, but much of them can be used for pies from other local contexts.

### Ingredients

As it is often the case in the kitchen, to make a high quality baked good one needs high quality ingredients. This is particularly true for pies. While many other sweets kind of "cheat" altering the basic ingredients to a point where they are not distinguishable any longer, pies, especially American fruit pies, do not lie. They are meant to exalt the main ingredient rather than conceal it. Another important secret to pie success is that the crust needs heat only when in the oven. So here the first two rules of pies.

**1.** Use good quality ingredients and your pie will taste good.

**2.** Use cold ingredients and your crust will be impeccable.

### Dough

*Flour.* There are no specific requirements when it comes to flour. Pastry flour will work, but all-purpose wheat flour is fine as well. You can also use a proportion of whole wheat flour, as well as playing with different grains. Whatever grain you choose, make sure not to go 100% whole-grain, unless you don't care losing the flakiness. If there are no food sensitivities or allergies to wheat, it is also always good to use at least some wheat, even when using other types

of flour, to preserve some lightness in the crust. Always use fridge-cold flour.

*Shortening.* Butter is the usual way to go, but lard can also be used for a more old-fashioned effect. This may not please all palates, though. When butter is not viable because of specific dietary requirements, vegetable alternatives will do the job. Just make sure to adapt the recipe you are using, because every type of shortening impacts the dough. Give your choice of shortening a try, and thereafter try again. There are no specific requirements for the type of butter used. Unsalted is okay, but so is salted butter. In the latter case, just remember not to add salt to the dough. Always use refrigerated butter.

*Sweetener.* Caster sugar is a good option for the crust, unless you are aiming for a specific consistency or taste. Always use fridge-cold sugar.

*Salt.* If you are using salted butter, remember not to add salt to the dough. If you are using any unsalted shortening, a good way to add salt is using some slightly crushed fleur de sel (salt in flakes): the effect will be scrumptious.

*Water.* Most pie crust is water-based, and, therefore, it is fundamental to use the right amount of water, not more not less. However, there is no magical number. In other words, there is no rule regarding how many tablespoons of water are required by any specific amount of flour. Flour humidity and air humidity are subject to change. The butter, vegetable shortening, or lard you use will also have an impact on the dough humidity. Water is you best friend when it comes to perfect pie crust. It is the one ingredient that you can twist around to reach your desired dough consistency. It is also a great way to achieve the right dough temperature. Here some water-specific rules.

**1.** Keep a bowl of water with ice-cubes close to your kneading bowl.

**2.** Add one tablespoon of water at a time to your dough and keep adding only if your dough needs it. Stop when you reach desired consistency. Do not follow any fixed amount of water—your dough will "tell you".

**3.** You can also use cold water to make your hands colder. Just make sure to dry them before touching the dough or you will add more water without wanting to.

*Other Ingredients.* When using other ingredients, just remember to first refrigerate them.

### Filling

The wonderful thing about pies is that we can really use all of our creativity to vary the filling. Thousands and thousands of pie filling ideas are already out there, ready to be reinterpreted. You should, however, always feel free to re-invent an already popular filling or, why not, creating a completely new one. There are just a few rules to be followed.

**1.** Always wait for the ingredients of the filling to completely cool down before using them. Ideally, the filling should be fridge-cold before touching the uncooked pie shell.

**2.** Make sure to include a binding ingredient to your filling. This will give the cooked pie a creamy, rather than watery, consistency, and will help prevent a soggy crust.

### Mixing and Shaping

**1.** It is more than okay to use your hands to combine ingredients. You just have to be careful to quickly combine the ingredients and to not knead the dough, for two reasons:

**a.** your hands tend to be warm and your dough should be cold;

**b.** by working the dough, you help the gluten net to develop.

In the world of pies, gluten development is not something you should go after. There should only be enough gluten development to allow the dough to be rolled out, but not as much to make it tough and hard to bite into once baked.

**2.** It is OK also to use a stand-mixer to combine the ingredients, only make sure that you follow the same suggestion mentioned previously for hand mixing. Use quick and gentle mixing to avoid overheating and overworking the dough.

**3.** It is not necessary to make the dough rest, nor to refrigerate it (unless you are baking on a very hot day and you have no air conditioning at home). By making the dough rest, you help a process called autolysis (see page 134 that enables the gluten net to develop just by letting the dough rest. Make sure you instead followed the general suggestion of keeping all your ingredients cold. You could even use a cold bowl and cool your hands in cold water, as we mentioned earlier. Just be fast. The longer the dough rests, the more time the gluten net has to develop.

**4.** Rolling surface. Any surface will do, as long as it is abundantly coated with flour.

**5.** Pie dish. You absolutely do not need to go crazy finding a pie-approved ceramic dish. Anything reasonably deep will do. The rest is up to the skills of the baker.

### Finish

There are several options for the final finish of the pie and only one rule:

If you made a top crust, make sure there are holes in it. You can either make the holes with pastry cutters before covering the pie, or make little holes with a fork on once the top crust is already sitting in place.

Here some finish ideas to brush on the top of your pie crust before baking.

• Egg wash. There are different ways to do an egg wash. You can use only the egg yolk, the slightly whisked whole egg, or the slightly whisked whole egg combined with a couple of tablespoons of water, milk, or heavy cream. In all of these options, the egg yolk will cause the crust to be shiny and take up lots of color. If you are concerned that the edges of the pie will to look too browned, you don't have to use any finish on them, or maybe use a different finish on the edges.

• Egg white wash. This variation can be made either by slightly whisking the egg white alone or by combining it with 1 tablespoon water. It will make the crust slightly shiny and only slightly colored, which could work well for the edges of the crust.

• Milk wash. Simply brush the crust with some milk, or heavy cream. Results will be similar to those obtained with the egg white wash, but even less shiny.

Whatever type of finish wash you choose, a sprinkle of brown sugar on top will give a wonderful rustic look to the pie, and an extra sweet bite.

### Baking

It is good practice to begin baking at a high temperature, then decrease the temperature as the pie bakes. For example, pre-heat to 440°F and after 10–15 minutes lower the temperature to 350°F and cook for another 40–45 minutes; though exact times depend on the dimensions of the pie, on the filling, and also on your oven.

In order to prevent a soggy crust bottom, either cook the pie on the bottom rack of the oven for the first 10–15 minutes, or, even better, use a baking stone during the whole baking. The baking stone will help the heat reach the bottom of the pie in a more constant way (see pages 49 on baking stones).

If the edges of the pie are browning too fast, lower the temperature of your oven.

# SUGAR PIE BAKERY'S PIE CRUST

**YIELD:** 2 9-INCH PIE CRUSTS / **ACTIVE TIME:** 30 MINUTES / **TOTAL TIME:** 1½ -2 HOURS

This homemade pie crust will make all the difference in your pie! The buttery, flaky goodness will have your friends and family asking for more!

—*courtesy Gina Watts, Sugar Pie Bakery*

1 Measure and cut your butter into small pieces. Measure and add shortening and put both into the freezer.

2 Measure sugar, flour, and salt in a food processor. After butter and shortening have chilled for 30 minutes or more, slowly add them to the dry mixture in the food processor.

3 Begin adding the ice-cold water 1 teaspoon at a time while pulsing the food processor until dough starts to form. Be careful not to over-mix!

4 Wrap in plastic wrap and chill in refrigerator for 1 hour or more before rolling out.

**INGREDIENTS:**

| | |
|---|---|
| 2½ | cups flour |
| 1 | teaspoon salt |
| 1 | teaspoon sugar |
| 1 | cup cold butter, cut in small pieces |
| ¼ | cup shortening |
| 6–8 | teaspoons ice cold water |

# BAKED CRUST

YIELDS: 1 12-INCH CRUST / **ACTIVE TIME:** 20 MINUTES / **TOTAL TIME:** 2 HOURS

The pies in this cookbook may call for a simple, single baked crust. It's fast and easy to put together and the result is delicious. —*Dominique DeVito*

**INGREDIENTS:**

1¼  cups flour

¼    teaspoon salt

½    cup (1 stick) unsalted butter, chilled and cut into small pieces, plus

1    tablespoon butter for greasing the skillet

4    to 6 tablespoons cold water

1 In a large bowl, combine the flour and salt. Add the butter and work it into the flour mixture with a pastry blender or 2 knives until the dough resembles coarse meal. Add 3 tablespoons cold water to start, and using your hands or a fork, work the dough, adding additional tablespoons until it just holds together when you gather it in your hands.

2 Working on a lightly floured surface, gather the dough and place it on the work area, forming it into a solid ball or disk. Wrap tightly in plastic wrap and refrigerate for about an hour. Dough can be refrigerated for a couple of days or frozen for a couple of months.

3 Preheat the oven to 450°F. Take the dough out of the refrigerator to allow it to warm up a bit but work with it cold. Put the refrigerated dough on a lightly floured surface, and with a lightly dusted rolling pin, flatten the dough into a circle, working both sides to extend it to a 12-inch round.

4 Grease the cast-iron skillet with 1 tablespoon of butter.

5 Carefully position the crust in the skillet so it is evenly distributed, pressing it in lightly. Crimp the edges. Use a fork to prick the crust on the bottom and sides.

6 Bake for 10 to 12 minutes until lightly browned. Transfer to a wire rack to cool before filling.

# BUTTERY PIE DOUGH

**YIELD:** 1 9-INCH PIE CRUST / **ACTIVE TIME:** 30 MINUTES / **TOTAL TIME:** 1 HOUR

This buttery, satisfying crust is the perfect accompaniment to Sweet Life Patisserie's Sour Cherry, Pumpkin, and Strawberry Rhubarb Pies.

—*courtesy of Catherine and Cheryl Reinhart, Sweet Life Patisserie*

**INGREDIENTS:**

1½  cups all-purpose flour

1   tablespoons cane sugar

¼   teaspoon salt

6   tablespoons salted butter

6   tablespoons ice-cold water

1   teaspoon vinegar

1   tablespoon oil

1 Chop cold salted butter into pieces no larger than ½ inch in diameter. Use a bit of the flour to dust it as you cut; this prevents it from sticking together.

2 Combine flour, salt, and sugar in mixer bowl. Add cold butter to dry ingredients and mix with a paddle attachment for roughly 3 to 5 minutes. Butter should be incorporated into mix and be no larger than a pea.

3 Remove bowl from mixer. Pour in cold water and oil all at once and hand fold in with bowl scraper until the dough begins to come together. If dough is dry, add water carefully in small amounts so as not to over-wet dough. This is the tricky point, as it's easy to add too much water, making the dough unrecoverable. You're looking for dough that is light, flaky, and relatively dry. The dough should barely stick together when formed into ball.

4 Form dough into a flat disc. Wrap with plastic wrap and let rest for minimum of 20 minutes in the fridge.

5 Roll out to fit your pie tin. Depending on the size of the tin, you may have extra dough for lattice or a crust top. Chill until pie filling is ready.

# FLAKY PIE CRUST *with* CREAM CHEESE

**YIELD:** 1 9-INCH PIE CRUST / **ACTIVE TIME:** 30 MINUTES / **TOTAL TIME:** 1 HOUR 10 MINUTES

This very flaky, rich crust goes great with fruit pies. Be sure to hand-mix for best results.
—*Stephany Buswell*

**INGREDIENTS:**

- 1½ cubes unsalted butter
- 2 cups all-purpose flour
- ¼ teaspoon salt
- ¼ teaspoon baking powder
- 4 ounces (½ box) Philadelphia-style cream cheese
- 2 tablespoons ice water
- 1 tablespoon vinegar

1 Cut the butter into ¾-inch cubes and place in the freezer to chill.

2 Place the flour, salt, and baking powder in a medium bowl and whisk to combine.

3 Add the cream cheese and rub the mixture between your fingers, blending the cream cheese into the flour until it resembles coarse meal.

4 Spoon the mixture into a gallon sized freezer bag. Add the butter chunks and shake well. Expel any air from it and seal the bag.

5 Using a rolling pin, flatten the butter chunks into flat flakes. Place the bag back into the freezer for about 10 minutes.

6 Transfer the mixture into a large bowl and sprinkle the water and vinegar over, tossing lightly with a rubber spatula. Spoon back into the plastic bag.

7 Knead the mixture by alternately pressing the outside of the bag with the knuckles and heels of your hands until the mixture holds together in one single piece.

8 Divide into 2 pieces. Wrap with plastic wrap and refrigerate for 30 minutes.

# GLUTEN-FREE PIE CRUST

YIELD: 1 9-INCH PIE CRUST / **ACTIVE TIME:** 15 MINUTES / **TOTAL TIME:** 2 HOURS 15 MINUTES

I have to give my dear friend and mentor, Patricia "The Vanilla Queen" Rain, credit for this recipe; she is gluten-free and I am not. Though Patricia claims she is still working to create the perfect gluten-free crust, this is one of her favorites. Generously, she's allowed me to share it with you here.
—*Stephany Buswell*

**INGREDIENTS:**

1   8-ounce package cream cheese

1   cup butter

1¾ cups Bob's Red Mill gluten-free flour

¾   cup Pamela's gluten-free flour

½   teaspoon salt

Tapioca flour, for rolling out

1 Cream together the butter and cream cheese. Add the flours and salt and blend until smooth.

2 Wrap the dough in plastic wrap and refrigerate for 2 hours.

3 The dough will be very firm—take a rolling pin and pound the dough using a dusting of tapicoa flour until it is soft enough to roll out.

4 As it will be a little crumbly, roll the dough on wax paper or parchment paper.

5 Remove the paper and move your dough into the pie pan. Fill with your pie filling and bake as normal.

If you like vanilla—who doesn't?—then you might want to check out Patricia's web page at www.vanillaqueen.com. She is an advocate for tropical farmers worldwide. Her page has all kinds of information about vanilla and it's plight in the world today. She also sells all types of vanilla products.

# GRAHAM CRACKER CRUST

YIELD: 1 9-INCH CRUST / ACTIVE TIME: 10 MINUTES / TOTAL TIME: 15 MINUTES

This classic adds a little twist with cinnamon and walnuts. You can leave the nuts out if you like, but I love the texture they add.
*—Stephany Buswell*

**INGREDIENTS:**

1¾ cups graham cracker crumbs, finely ground

¼ cup walnuts, finely chopped

½ teaspoon cinnamon

½ cup melted butter

1 Combine the dry ingredients in a medium bowl.

2 Pour in the melted butter and rub the crumbs together using your hands.

3 Press into the desired 9-inch cake pan. Bake for 5 minutes at 350°F. Cool before filling.

# SUGAR PIE BAKERY'S GRAHAM CRACKER CRUST

**YIELD:** 2 9-INCH PIE CRUSTS / **ACTIVE TIME:** 10 MINUTES / **TOTAL TIME:** 20 MINUTES

Graham cracker crust is one of the easiest crusts to make but your guests will be able to taste the difference!
—*courtesy of Gina Watts, Sugar Pie Bakery*

**INGREDIENTS:**

2    cups graham cracker crumbs

6    tablespoons sugar

6    tablespoons butter, melted

1    Mix graham cracker crumbs and sugar until well incorporated. Melt butter then add to graham cracker and sugar mixture.

2    Pour mixture into pie pan and press until crumbs are packed tightly. Bake at 350°F for 7 minutes. Let cool.

# CHOCOLATE COOKIE CRUST

YIELD: 1 9-INCH PIE CRUST / **ACTIVE TIME:** 20 MINUTES/ **TOTAL TIME:** 1 HOUR

Chocolate crust for chocolate cream pie, or chocolate cheesecake, or any other chocolate goody that needs a crust. This one is very dark chocolate!

—*Stephany Buswell*

**INGREDIENTS:**

- 1½ sticks unsalted butter, room temperature
- ¾ cup light brown sugar
- ¾ cup granulated sugar
- 1 tablespoon vanilla extract
- 6 ounces semisweet chocolate, melted
- 8 tablespoons natural cocoa powder
- 1 teaspoon baking soda
- ½ teaspoon salt
- 1¾ cups all-purpose flour
- 4 tablespoons butter, melted
- ½ egg white

1 Cream the butter and sugars together until light. Add the vanilla. Add the melted chocolate and mix well, scraping between additions.

2 Sift together the cocoa powder, baking soda, salt, and flour. Add the dry ingredients and mix only until incorporated.

3 Roll dough out to fit a half sheet pan, ⅛-inch thick.

4 Bake at 300°F until firm, about 20 minutes. Check at minute 15 to make sure it doesn't get overdone. Because it's already dark, it'll be a bit hard to tell when it is done—as a rule, you shouldn't be able to leave fingerprints behind when you press gently in the middle.

5 Cool and then crumble using a rolling pin between paper or a food processor.

6 Place the crumbs in a bowl and pour the melted butter and egg white over them. Rub with your hands to properly mix in the butter. The crumbs should stick together when you squeeze them in your hand.

7 Press the crumb crust into the desired pan and bake at 300°F for 5 to 6 minutes, until the crust has set.

# CREAM CHEESE PIE CRUST

YIELDS: 1 9-INCH PIE CRUST / ACTIVE TIME: 20 MINUTES / TOTAL TIME: 45 MINUTES

This rich crust is a revelatory component of The Sweetery's Tomato Pie, and great way to amp up sweet pies, too.
—*The Sweetery*

**INGREDIENTS:**

- 3 teaspoons cold water
- 1 teaspoons cold apple cider vinegar
- 1½ cups all-purpose flour
- ½ teaspoon salt
- 4 ounces cold cream cheese, cut in small pieces
- 4 ounces cold butter, cut in small pieces

1 Mix the water and vinegar in a small bowl. In another bowl, mix flour and salt.

2 Cut the butter and cream cheese into the flour mixture until resembles coarse crumbs.

3 Add the water and vinegar to the dough, and mix until dough holds together.

4 Wrap in plastic wrap. Using a rolling pin, roll the wrapped dough into a disc and refrigerate until firm.

5 Roll dough into a 12-inch round circle on a lightly floured surface. Fit the dough over a greased 9-inch pie dish. Trim the edges, leaving a 1-inch overhang. Flute the edges. Refrigerate the dough for another 15 minutes.

6 Pour filling in crust and bake according to the pie's instructions.

# CORNMEAL CRUST

**YIELDS:** 1 12-INCH CRUST / **ACTIVE TIME:** 20 MINUTES / **TOTAL TIME:** 90 MINUTES

A crust that includes cornmeal will have more texture and flavor than a crust made from simple all-purpose flour. This distinctive texture and flavor is a perfect complement to savory fillings when prepared without sugar, and makes a great base for sweet pies as well. It's easy to make, too.

—*Dominique DeVito*

**INGREDIENTS:**

- ¾ cup all-purpose flour
- ¾ cup yellow cornmeal
- 3 tablespoons sugar, if making a sweet crust
- ½ teaspoon salt
- ½ cup (1 stick) unsalted butter, chilled and cut into small pieces, plus 1 tablespoon butter for greasing the skillet
- 1 egg, slightly beaten

1 In a large bowl, thoroughly combine the flour, cornmeal, salt, and sugar if making a sweet crust. Add the butter and work it into the flour mixture with a pastry blender or your fingers to form coarse meal. Add the egg and continue to blend until the dough comes together.

2 Shape into a disk, cover tightly with plastic wrap, and refrigerate for 30 minutes.

3 Preheat the oven to 375°F. Take the dough out of the refrigerator to allow it to warm up a bit but work with it cold. Put the refrigerated dough on a lightly floured surface, and with a lightly dusted rolling pin, flatten the dough into a circle, working both sides to extend it to a 10- to 12-inch round.

4 Grease the cast-iron skillet with 1 tablespoon of butter.

5 Carefully position the crust in the skillet so it is evenly distributed, pressing it in lightly. Crimp the edges. Use a fork to prick the crust on the bottom and sides.

6 Bake for 10 to 12 minutes until lightly browned. Transfer to a wire rack to cool before filling.

# BUTTER OAT CRUMBLE

YIELD: 1 TOPPING / ACTIVE TIME: 10 MINUTES / TOTAL TIME: 10 MINUTES

This crumble is a simple and delicious topping to any fruit pie.
—*courtesy of Catherine and Cheryl Reinhart, Sweet Life Patisserie*

**INGREDIENTS:**

½    **cup flour**

½    **cup brown sugar**

⅔    **cup regular oats**

6    **tablespoons cold butter**

1   Combine flour, oats and brown sugar in mixer.

2   Chop cold butter into 1-inch cubes and add to dry mix.

3   Mix until butter is mostly broken down and streusel begins to come together. Avoid a floury, dry–looking mixture, as that will create a dry non-crispy streusel. Streusel should be uniformly moist-looking and hold together when pressed lightly.

# PÂTÉ BRISÉE (FLAKY FRENCH PIE DOUGH)

YIELD: 2 9-INCH OR 10-INCH CRUSTS / ACTIVE TIME: 15 MINUTES / TOTAL TIME: 1 HOUR 15 MINUTES

I have been a pastry instructor for many years now and the number one thing I hear from potential students is, "I love to bake, but I can't make a decent pie crust!" Here I hope to dispel the notion that it is difficult to make a good crust.

This particular pie dough is crisp and flaky—not as tender at the traditional American pie dough with shortening (but then, I am a food snob who won't use shortening. Why would I when we have wonderful animal fats like butter and lard to use!). The French knew what they were doing when they began using butter in crusts; they first used olive oil, but the liquid oil produced a soft and crumbly crust. Butter gives more structure and flavor, not to mention a fabulous flakiness.

Last but not least, the use of cake flour will help keep the dough from becoming too tough. The golden rule: never over-mix your pie crust. In the end, it should have dry spots and chunks of butter showing. The rest in the refrigerator should finish the flour's hydration and rest it enough to roll out beautifully.

—*Stephany Buswell*

### INGREDIENTS:

- **3** cups cake flour
- **1** teaspoon salt
- **1** cup (2 cubes) very cold unsalted butter (I put it in the freezer 10 minutes before making the dough)
- **1** egg
- **2** tablespoons ice water

1 Using a mixer with a paddle attachment, mix the flour, salt, and butter cubes on medium-low speed until the pieces are the size of peas or hazelnuts. Be very careful not to over-mix. To guarantee a good crust, chop the butter in the flour, salt mixture using a pastry cutter or bench scraper.

2 Whisk the egg with the ice water. Drizzle enough of the egg mixture in the dry ingredients for the dough to start coming together, creating a shaggy dough that is not wet.

3 Divide the dough into 2 pieces, gathering all the loose bits wrap each piece in plastic and then push down with the palm of your hand to flatten them into round patties.

4 Refrigerate for at least one hour before rolling out.

# PÂTÉ SUCRÉE (SWEET TART CRUST)

**YIELD:** 3 8-INCH TARTS / **ACTIVE TIME:** 10 MINUTES / **TOTAL TIME:** 1 HOUR 10 MINUTES

This light, crisp crust is perfect for any sweet tart filling you want to use. In fact, I even use this recipe for sugar cookies during the holidays; the crispness just lends itself to decorating.

This dough also freezes very well, so if you only need one tart, divide the dough in three, wrap well, and freeze for future use!
—*Stephany Buswell*

**INGREDIENTS:**

½ cup sifted powdered sugar

1 cup unsalted butter, room temperature

3 eggs

2 cups all-purpose flour

½ teaspoon baking powder

½ teaspoon salt

¼ teaspoon vanilla

1 Put the room temperature butter into a mixing bowl of a stand-mixer. Mix with a paddle on low speed for about 1 minute until smooth.

2 Add the sugar and cream together on medium speed until smooth. Be careful not to whip air into the mixture or the dough will be very hard to handle.

3 Crack the eggs into a cup and begin adding them one by one. While you add the eggs, scrape the side of the bowl so the mixture becomes homogenous. Add the vanilla.

4 Add the flour, baking powder, and salt. Mix on low speed just until all the dry ingredients are incorporated.

5 Wrap the dough well and refrigerate for at least one hour before rolling out.

---

If you end up with scraps, you can roll the dough out one more time without it becoming tough. After that, though, you risk significant text changes. Just be mindful of how you use the dough and cut your pieces carefully to eliminate scrap.

## VARIATIONS

Since tarts allow for so much flavor variation, it can be fun to add a flavored crust to the recipe. Here are some of my favorite variations:

Chocolate Sucrée: Replace 3 tablespoons of flour with 2 tablespoons of cocoa powder

Lemon Sucrée: add the zest of 1 lemon

Almond Sucrée: replace ¼ cup of flour with ½ cup of almond flour. Since almonds do not contain gluten, we add more nuts to replace the flour. You can also add ⅛ teaspoon of almond extract to bring out the almond flavor.

# VEGAN PIE DOUGH

YIELD: 1 9-INCH PIE CRUST / ACTIVE TIME: 15 MINUTES / TOTAL TIME: 35 MINUTES

Sweet Life Patisserie started making egg- and dairy-free desserts long before it hit the mainstream, and this delicious vegan crust is one of their many tried-and-true favorites.

—*courtesy of Catherine and Cheryl Reinhart, Sweet Life Patisserie*

1 Finely chop your shortening. The average chunk should be about as small as a pea.

2 Combine flour, salt, and sugar in mixer. Add cold shortening to dry ingredients and mix for roughly 2 to 3 minutes. It should be incorporated into mix and no larger than a pea.

3 Remove bowl from mixer. Emulsify water, oil, and vinegar. Pour in all at once and hand-fold in with bowl scraper until the dough begins to come together. If dough is dry, add a very small amount water so as not to over-wet the dough.

4 Form dough into a flat disc. Wrap with plastic wrap and let rest for minimum of 20 minutes in fridge.

5 Roll out to fit your pie tin. Depending on the size of the tin, you may have extra dough for lattice or a crust top. Chill until pie filling is ready.

**INGREDIENTS:**

- 1⅔ cups all-purpose flour
- 1 tablespoons cane sugar
- ½ teaspoon salt
- 3 ounces cold shortening (we recommend organic palm shortening)
- 6 tablespoons cold water
- 1 teaspoon vinegar
- 1 teaspoon oil

# MERINGUE PIE SHELL

**YIELDS:** 1 12-INCH CRUST / **ACTIVE TIME:** 30 MINUTES / **TOTAL TIME:** 90 MINUTES

Making this crust is a great way to use up egg whites left over from another recipe, or just because! The baking time is long and slow, but the result is a light, delicious, gluten-free shell that's perfect for creamy or fruit fillings.
—*Dominique DeVito*

**INGREDIENTS:**

- **3** egg whites at room temperature
- **¼** teaspoon cream of tartar
- **¾** cup sugar
- **½** teaspoon vanilla
- **1** tablespoon butter for greasing the skillet

1 Preheat the oven to 225°F.

2 In a large bowl, beat egg whites and cream of tartar on high speed until foamy. Beating constantly, add sugar 2 tablespoons at a time, beating after each addition until sugar is thoroughly dissolved before adding the next. Beat until whites are glossy and stand in stiff peaks. Add and beat in vanilla.

3 Grease the skillet with the butter and spread the meringue over it, working it up the sides to form a rim.

4 Bake for 60 to 90 minutes until meringue is firm and a toothpick inserted in center comes out clean. Turn off the oven and allow to dry and crisp in the cooling oven for at least 1 hour. Remove from oven, cool completely on a wire rack, and fill as desired.

# AS AMERICAN AS APPLE PIE

Early British and Dutch settlers in North America imported pie to the new continent. They may not have brought actual pies on the long boat trips (although it could have come in handy), but they did bring pie's main ingredients: flour, molasses, lard, salt, and spices. Once settled in the new land, pies became a very easy and portable way to use local ingredients together with the few imported ones, like flour. Pumpkin and apple pies are among the first pies that we have record of, and it surely must have been due to the abundance of both apples and pumpkin in much of North America. We also have accounts of shoofly pie, from Pennsylvania, which uses all the basic ingredients and very little more.

Although Northern Americans did not invent pie, they did bring it to a whole new level. In fact, pie became so popular in the young United States of America that every state had its own version, to exalt and use up local ingredients. It is believed that in the early times of North American settlements pies became so popular, because fruit was so abundant. However, wheat was still not grown and had to be imported. Pie crust used so little wheat and it could also be made with ground corn, which was instead cheap and widely available. As a sweetener, instead of expensive sugar, settlers used the cheaper molasses and then maple syrup, after learning from native Americans how to extract it from trees.

The use of pumpkin for food is also something that settlers had to learn from the natives. Pies were possibly the first dish in which European settlers managed to use up these cheap extra calories from the orange fleshy vegetable, and pumpkin pie became a classic.

Apples were very abundant in many American states and so apple pie became an all-times favorite and is now the emblem of American pies, possibly, the pie of all pies. Besides these common American classics, different states developed different pies, based on local cultural influences on resulting cuisines and, even more, based on what grows best in each specific state. In Maine, the highly priced local blueberries make a fantastic blueberry pie, which is now the state's official sweet treat. In Louisiana, local strawberries are showcased in a celebrated Ponchatoula strawberry pie that has its own yearly fair. Florida is known worldwide for its Key lime pie, apparently born on a boat and without an oven. Many other states host yearly fairs with context to prize the best local pie, like peach pie in the annual contest "Oh My! It's Peach Pie!", at the Iowa State Fair. A sultry cherry pie was the winner of the last Ohio State Fair. The list is endless like the variation found in all the delicious American pies, a treasure to support and a tradition not to let go.

The British pie tradition brought to the United States happily coexists with French and Dutch tart tradition as well. Depending on the influence, North American pie can look like a tart, like pumpkin pie, or it can look like a proper pie, nowadays also called "deep-dish pie", like classic apple pie. To make matters even more complicated, French fruit galettes, which are similar to open-faced fruit pies, are also called pies in North America. Different words, one common love: a filled crust.

Pie's popularity decreased after the mid of the 19th century but became central again in the 1950s and '60s, thanks to the use of ready-made doughs for crust and instant custards for the fillings. After another period of decreased popularity in the '70s, pies are now back to their long-deserved glory and are recognized as a heritage of American history.

It has been observed that pies, particularly apple pie, belong to the American collective memory and this is why there is the saying "as American as apple pie", meaning that pies are so embedded with what is traditionally American that they define it. Most American pies conjure memories of the "good old times", home, and family. It is not coincidental that Disney's Snow White was singing while baking an apple pie, in her little and cozy cottage in the woods. Cakes are beautiful, but pies are bountiful. They transmit security, warmth, and hominess. They are always welcome gifts and... lets' face it: mastering the art of pies means mastering the hearts of many. Let's see how to achieve it—and remember: anyone can bake a pie!

# ALL-AMERICAN APPLE PIE

YIELD: 1 9-INCH PIE / ACTIVE TIME: 20 MINUTES / TOTAL TIME: 1 HOUR

This classic apple pie is wonderful, aside from one little problem: The apples shrink by half when you bake them, leaving a huge gap between the top crust and apple filling. What's the point of laboring over a tasty, impressive crust when the slices collapse upon being served? So to address that problem, we spend a little more time on our apples in this recipe, cooking them first before thickening the juices they yield.

For this recipe, choose two or three apple varieties that go well together. For instance, I like Fuji for the flavor and juiciness and Braeburn for their tartness and pulpiness. Put them together and you get one great apple pie!

—*Stephany Buswell*

**INGREDIENTS:**

- 2 **9-inch flaky pie dough (see page 603)**

  **About 3 pounds apples (6–8), peeled, cored, and sliced**
- 2 **tablespoons lemon juice**
- ½ **cup sugar**
- 2 **teaspoons cinnamon**
- ⅛ **teaspoon salt**
- ¼ **cup flour**

1 Place the apple slices, lemon juice, and sugar in a large saucepan. Cook on medium heat until all the juices have extracted and the apples are just beginning to soften. Do not overcook at this point or you will have applesauce pie.

2 Throw in the cinnamon and cook another minute or so.

3 Strain out the apples, leaving the juices. Whisk the flour into the juice making sure you whisk out all of the lumps. Put this back on the stove and cook until thickened.

4 Let cool while you roll out your crust. Never fill a crust with hot filling as it will become too soggy to bake properly.

5 Preheat your oven to 450°F. When all has cooled and the crust is chilled and ready to go, fill it up with all the apples and then pour the thickened juice over the top. Cover with the top crust and cut vents on top. Decorate as you like, egg-wash, and sprinkle with some sugar.

6 Bake in the lower half of the oven at 450°F for 15 minutes, then raise it up to the middle of the oven and turn the oven down to 350°F for another 30 to 40 minutes. You should see the juices oozing and bubbling out of the vents. If you feel the edges are getting too brown before the rest of the pie is done then cover the edges with foil and continue baking.

# SUGAR PIE BAKERY'S APPLE PIE

YIELD: 1 9-INCH PIE / ACTIVE TIME: 30-40 MINUTES / TOTAL TIME: 1½-2 HOURS

Our apple pie recipe is inspired by my grandmother and has been selected as West Virginia's Best Apple Pie two years in a row by DailyMeal.com.  The tart apples mixed with the sweet cinnamon pecan crumb is an award winning combination!
—*courtesy of Gina Watts, Sugar Pie Bakery*

1 Heat oven to 350°F. Peel and cut apples into thin slices.

2 Mix sugar, flour, nutmeg, cinnamon and salt with apples. Let sit and soak for 15 to 30 minutes.

3 Fill your pie crust. The apples will bake down, so overfill with whole recipe.

4 Cut the butter into pieces and add on top of apples.

5 Cover with Cinnamon Pecan Crumb or double crust. Bake for 40 to 50 minutes or until crust is brown and juice begins to bubble.

### INGREDIENTS:

1   cup sugar

⅓   cup flour

1   teaspoon nutmeg

1   teaspoon cinnamon

    Dash of salt

8   cups Granny Smith apples, peeled and thinly sliced

1   Sugar Pie Bakery's pie crust (see page 599)

2–3 tablespoons of butter, cut into pieces (optional)

1   Cinnamon Pecan Crumb (optional, see page 627)

# CINNAMON PECAN CRUMB

YIELD: 1 TOPPING / ACTIVE TIME: 15 MINUTES / TOTAL TIME: 15 MINUTES

Crumb topping is a great addition to any fruit pie! Whether it's cherry, apple, or mixed berry pie, this quick and easy crumb will top it off perfectly!
—*courtesy of Gina Watts, Sugar Pie Bakery*

Combine all dry ingredients in large bowl, adding the butter last. Use your hands to incorporate the butter by rubbing and working it together until it mixes into a crumb consistency.

**INGREDIENTS:**

- ⅔ cup pecans, shelled and chopped
- ¼ teaspoon cinnamon
- ½ cup flour
- 5 tablespoons unsalted butter, diced
- ¼ cup granulated sugar
- ¼ cup light brown sugar

CAST-IRON SKILLET RECIPE

# APPLE-CRANBERRY PIE WITH POMEGRANATE SAUCE

**YIELDS:** 6 TO 8 SERVINGS / **ACTIVE TIME:** 60 MINUTES / **TOTAL TIME:** 2 HOURS

This is the perfect pie for Thanksgiving, as it combines the fruits synonymous with late fall and the celebration of the harvest. The pomegranate sauce is the key to bringing it all together.
—*Dominique DeVito*

**1** Preheat the oven to 375°F.

**2** In a large pot, melt the butter. When melted, add the apples, flour, sugar, cinnamon, nutmeg, and salt. Stir to combine. Cook, stirring over medium heat until apples just start to soften, about 3 minutes. Stir in the cranberries and continue to cook, stirring, for another 2 minutes.

**3** Put the skillet over medium heat and melt the butter in it. Carefully remove pan from heat.

**4** Place the piecrust in the skillet. Fill with the apple/cranberry mix. Bake for 20 minutes.

**5** While the pie is baking, make the pomegranate sauce. In a saucepan over medium-high heat, cook the pomegranate juice until it's reduced slightly, stirring occasionally, about 5 minutes. Stir in the pomegranate seeds, sugar, and lemon juice. Continue to cook, stirring, until seeds are thawed, another 5 minutes or so.

**6** Remove pie from oven and pour sauce over the top. Return to the oven and finish baking, another 15 minutes or so, until bubbling.

**7** Allow to cool before serving. Serve with vanilla ice cream!

## INGREDIENTS:

- 1 flaky pastry crust recipe for a single crust (see page 603)
- 6 to 8 crisp-tart apples such as Macoun, Granny Smith, or Jonah Gold, peeled, cored, and cut into small pieces
- 3 tablespoons butter
- 2 tablespoons flour
- ½ cup light brown sugar
- 1 teaspoon cinnamon
- ¼ teaspoon nutmeg
- ¼ teaspoon salt
- 1 cup whole cranberries
- 1 tablespoon butter

### SAUCE

- ½ cup pomegranate juice (unsweetened)
- 1 cup frozen pomegranate seeds
- ¼ cup sugar
- 1 tablespoon fresh squeezed lemon juice

# BLACKBERRY-PEACH PIE

**YIELDS:** 6 TO 8 SERVINGS / **ACTIVE TIME:** 60 MINUTES / **TOTAL TIME:** 2 HOURS

Colorful and flavorful, and smacking of summer, this is the perfect pie for nights when the sun doesn't set until after 9. Ah, summertime!

—*Dominique DeVito*

**INGREDIENTS:**

- 2 **flaky pastry crust recipes for a double crust (see page 603)**
- 4 **cups fresh peaches, peeled, pitted, and cut into pieces**
- ¾ **cup sugar**
- 3 **tablespoons flour**
- ½ **teaspoon grated lemon peel**
- 1 **tablespoon fresh squeezed lemon juice**
- ¼ **teaspoon ground ginger**
- 1 **cup fresh blackberries**
- 1 **tablespoon butter**
- 1 **egg white**
- 2 **tablespoons sugar**

1 Preheat the oven to 375°F.

2 In a large bowl, toss peaches with sugar, flour, lemon peel, lemon juice, and ginger. Gently stir in blackberries.

3 Put the skillet over medium heat and melt the butter in it. Carefully remove pan from heat.

4 Place 1 of the piecrusts in the skillet. Fill with fruit mix. Roll out the top crust on a lightly floured surface, and cut 8 strips from the dough. Arrange them in an over-under lattice pattern, crimping the edges to connect them to the bottom crust, or use whole and cut 4–5 slits in the top.

5 Brush the top crust with the egg white, and sprinkle the sugar over it.

6 Put the skillet in the oven and bake for about 55 to 60 minutes, until golden brown and bubbly

7 Allow to cool before serving, and top with fresh whipped cream.

# WINSLOW'S HOME

## Winslow's Home

7213 Delmar Boulevard
St. Louis, MO 63130
(314) 725-7559
www.winslowshome.com

Though it is no worse for the journey, St. Louis' Winslow's Home had a particularly circuitous route toward bakery stardom. "My background is as a designer," says general manager Ann Lipton. "And I wanted to restore the inner suburb's century-old freestanding building. The first floor had always been a grocery store and I wanted it to remain a neighborhood establishment that sold essentials, but had doubts that it would remain so if I leased out the space post-renovation. So, I did it myself! We opened our doors in April of 2008." What began as a local store, though, grew rapidly more ambitious—today, Winslow's Home is equal parts restaurant, bakery, caterer, lounge, event space, and general store. Oh, and they own their own farm as well: Winslow's Farm has been part of the Lipton family since 1997, and provides most of the ingredients they use in the kitchen.

It sounds like a lot, but Winslow's Home is the exception that proves the saying, "jack of all trades, master of none." Everything they sell has been labored over by someone in the Winslow's family, and nowhere is that more apparent than in its renowned bakery, where head baker Anna Long works magic on a daily basis. Scones, cookies, fresh breads—if you can think of it, it's probably being sold at Winslow's. Everything Long bakes is worth trying, but there's no denying the bakery's chocolate chip cookie, which *Food & Wine* has named among

America's best, along with Zingerman's (page 196) and Sugar Bakeshop (page 744)

Still, Long prefers baking bread. "I love the science behind it," she says. "I love that you can collect yeast from the air in water and flour and continue to feed and care for it in order to make sourdoughs. When something is not right with bread, you can retrace your steps and figure out where you went wrong. And, most of all, I love eating it." Her customers do too—the bread Long makes in-house is used in several restaurant offerings, giving new meaning to the term "locally sourced." The resulting loaves are crunchy and chewy in all the right places, perfect for spreading jam and cheese or for a Cuban sandwich.

Whether in the market for a sit-down dinner or just looking for a cup of coffee and a scone, Winslow's Home is a wonderful option for anybody near St. Louis. Lipton puts it simply: "We strive for a warm and welcoming atmosphere, where simple food is prepared using time-honored cooking techniques and clean ingredients. It's a place where diverse members of the community gather to spend a quiet moment alone, share a meal, celebrate a special occasion in our private space, or grab something on the go." In this way, Winslow's will always have the spirit of a corner bakery, no matter what it's selling.

# IN THEIR OWN WORDS:

## ANN LIPTON AND ANNA LONG

*Who inspired you to bake? Who inspires you now?*

Ann Lipton: My little sister and I used to bake after school when I had to watch her. We'd always leave a plate of treats for everyone.

Anna Long: My family and friends have always inspired my baking. I love baking my dad's favorite cookies or bringing home a loaf of my brother's favorite bread. I think baking for someone is the best gift you can give them.

*Winslow's Home is not just a restaurant—what led you to include so many non-food items for sale? How has that decision impacted the customers' experience?*

Ann Lipton: Winslow's Home was originally a community-gathering place where you could pick up home essentials and food items, loosely based on a general store model. Since that time, it has evolved into more of a conventional restaurant.

*What is your golden rule for bakers?*

Anna Long: Make sure everything is at the correct temperature. Baking is a science—if things are at the incorrect temperature the emulsification you need to achieve the best end result can't happen.

*What are your most popular items?*

Anna Long: Our most popular items are our chocolate chip cookie and our lemon-ginger scone.

*What non-essential items should every baker have?*

Ann Lipton: Silpat, pastry cloth, NPR StoryCorps, mason jars, and a copy of *The Splendid Table* by Lynn Rosetta Casper.

Anna Long: A bench scraper and a scale.

*Where did you learn to bake?*

Ann Lipton: My home kitchen growing up in St. Louis.

Anna Long: I started baking in grade school with my Grandma and Aunt on the weekends. I went to baking and pastry school at Sullivan University in Louisville, KY.

*Can you talk a bit about Winslow's Farm? Was it founded with a specific goal in mind?*

Ann Lipton: I've focused on natural solutions to health and wellness since I was a teenager, and have cooked and gardened my entire life. What began as window boxes in my apartment turned into a small flower garden in my first house. Winter was a time to armchair garden, and I did so with a heavy dose of curiosity, planning for the season ahead, learning from my mistakes and expanding on small victories.

I tried to focus on organic farming principles, using plant-based solutions to the challenges of growing. This led me to volunteer for several community gardens, where I became a master gardener through the extension service. As a home cook, I began to scale up my passion for producing food herbs and fruits on five acres of a rich Missouri farmland located on a family farm in Augusta. When the plans for Winslow's Home started to take shape, it seemed logical that I would grow ingredients for the kitchen there.

Now in our 10th year of farming, we produce seasonal vegetables, flowers, fruits, herbs, eggs, and grass-fed Angus beef and goat for Winslow's Home, in addition to other restaurants, clubs, and florists in the St. Louis area.

# WINSLOW'S HOME'S APPLE PIE

YIELD: 1 9-INCH PIE / **ACTIVE TIME:** 1 HOUR / **TOTAL TIME:** 12 HOURS

This classic apple pie takes inspiration from time honored recipes and uses high quality ingredients to create an American classic.
—*courtesy of Ann Lipton and Anna Long, Winslow's Home*

1 Cut butter into ½-inch cubes and put in the freezer for at least 2 hours and up to overnight. Put flour, sugar, and salt in a large mixing bowl. Toss butter in dry and rub butter between your fingers until it is slightly larger than the size of a pea.

2 Add vinegar and ice water and work together. Divide into to round disks and refrigerate overnight or up to a week. Dough can be frozen for 1 month.

3 Pull dough out and let it set on counter for 30 to 45 minutes until dough is easily workable.

4 While dough is warming up, prepare your filling: Peel and cut apples into ¼-inch slices. Toss in lemon juice. Put the rest of the ingredients in the bowl and toss until apples are coated. Set aside.

5 Dust countertop with flour and, using a rolling pin, roll one piece of dough until it is 2 to 3 inches larger than the rim of your pie pan.

6 Carefully fit rolled-out pie dough into the bottom and up the sides of your pie pan. Shell should be ½ to ¾ inch larger than your pie pan on all sides. Brush egg on the rim on your pie shell. Pour filling into the bottom pie shell—your apples will have released some juices, which is okay.

7 Roll second pie shell into a circle that will cover your apples and overlap your base shell by about ½ inch on all sides.

8 Gently press together your shells to ensure the ends are sealed. Your shell should be hanging ½ inch off your pie pan. Cut any excess using a sharp paring knife or kitchen scissors. Using your index finger and thumb pin together dough to make a thick wall all the way around your pie. To create fluted edge, place index finger and thumb of right hand on outside of the "pie dough wall" and index finger of left hand on the inside of the "pie dough wall" and press together. Leaving visible indents, continue this around the pie until you get to where you started.

## INGREDIENTS:

### DOUGH:

| | |
|---|---|
| 8 | ounces butter |
| 3 | cups all-purpose flour |
| 2 | tablespoons sugar |
| 1 | teaspoon salt |
| 1 | cup ice water |
| 2 | teaspoons white vinegar |

### FILLING:

| | |
|---|---|
| 1 | egg, beaten |
| 6 | Granny Smith apples |
| ¼ | cup granulated sugar, plus extra for dusting |
| ½ | cup brown sugar |
| 2 | tablespoons lemon juice |
| 2½ | tablespoons cornstarch |
| 2 | teaspoons cinnamon |
| ¾ | teaspoon cardamom |
| | Flour for rolling |

9 Refrigerate for 45 minutes. Preheat oven to 375°F. Cut an "X" or any decorative design into the top of the pie. Brush with egg and top with sugar. Bake for 30 to 45 minutes, until juices are bubbling in the center of the pie.

# BLUEBERRY PIE

YIELDS: 6 TO 8 SERVINGS / ACTIVE TIME: 30 MINUTES / TOTAL TIME: 90 MINUTES

Blueberry pie is so easy to make and tastes so good with rich, creamy vanilla ice cream. Summer in a slice!

*—Dominique DeVito*

1 Preheat the oven to 350°F.

2 If using frozen blueberries, it's not necessary to thaw them completely. In a large bowl, toss blueberries with lemon juice, sugar, and flour, being sure to coat the pieces.

3 Put the skillet over medium heat and melt the butter in it. Add the brown sugar and cook, stirring constantly, until sugar is dissolved, 1 or 2 minutes. Carefully remove pan from heat.

4 Place 1 of the piecrusts over the sugar mixture. Fill with blueberries, and place the other crust over the blueberries, crimping the edges together. For a lattice crust: cut 1-inch strips across the round dough using a fluted rolling cutter (a knife will do if you don't have one).

5 Brush the top crust with the egg white, and sprinkle the sugar over it. Cut 4 or 5 slits in the middle.

6 Put the skillet in the oven and bake for 45 minutes until golden brown and bubbly. Cover the outermost edge with aluminum foil in the last 10 minutes of baking to prevent it from burning.

7 Allow to cool before serving.

**INGREDIENTS:**

2 flaky pastry crust recipes for a double crust (see page 603)

4 cups fresh or frozen blueberries

1 tablespoon fresh squeezed lemon juice

1 cup sugar

3 tablespoons flour

1 tablespoon butter

2 tablespoons brown sugar

1 egg white

2 tablespoons sugar

# PEACH PIE

YIELDS: 6 TO 8 SERVINGS  /  ACTIVE TIME: 60 MINUTES / TOTAL TIME: 2 HOURS

There's something otherworldly about a pie made with fresh peaches. It is just so good! With the way the cast-iron skillet yields a sugary, somewhat crunchy bottom crust, this will become your go-to recipe when peaches are in season.

—*Dominique DeVito*

**INGREDIENTS:**

| | |
|---|---|
| 2 | flaky pastry crust recipes for a double crust (see page 603) |
| 2–3 | pounds peaches to yield 4 cups, peeled (see step 2), cored, and sliced |
| 1 | teaspoon fresh squeezed lemon juice |
| ¾ | cup sugar |
| 4 | tablespoons flour |
| 1 | tablespoon butter |
| 2 | tablespoons light brown sugar |
| 1 | egg white |
| 2 | tablespoons sugar |

1 Preheat the oven to 350°F.

2 Bring a large pot of water to boil. Fill another large pot with cold water. When the water's boiling, submerge the peaches for a minute or two, then remove them with a slotted spoon and put them immediately into the cold water. This loosens the skin and makes them much easier to peel. Use enough peaches to yield 4 cups of peeled slices. In a large bowl, toss peaches with lemon juice, sugar, and flour, being sure to coat the pieces.

3 Put the skillet over medium heat and melt the butter in it. Add the brown sugar and cook, stirring constantly, until sugar is dissolved, 1 or 2 minutes. Carefully remove pan from heat.

4 Place 1 of the piecrusts over the sugar mixture. Fill with the peaches, and place the other crust over the peaches, crimping the edges together.

5 Brush the top crust with the egg white, and sprinkle the sugar over it. Cut 4 or 5 slits in the middle.

6 Put the skillet in the oven and bake for 60 to 70 minutes until golden brown and bubbly. Cover the outermost edge with aluminum foil in the last 10 minutes of baking to prevent it from burning.

7 Allow to cool before serving. Serve with bourbon whipped cream.

For this pie you have to try serving it with bourbon whipped cream. You'll understand why this is so popular in the south, from whence the best peaches—and bourbon—hail. Simply beat heavy or whipping cream until soft peaks form. Add about ¼ cup sugar and continue beating until stiff peaks form. Gently beat in ¼ cup bourbon. Serve immediately or cover with plastic wrap and refrigerate until ready to serve.

# GRAPE PIE

A refreshing twist on tarte tatin, though it's a similar concept: fruit embedded in pastry cream. Sliced grapes make a beautiful presentation, and the taste is just as nice. Serve with a white dessert wine, like an Ice Wine.

*—Dominique DeVito*

**INGREDIENTS:**

- **2** flaky pastry crust recipes for a single crust (see page 603)
- **1** (10-oz.) jar lemon curd
- **1** tablespoon fresh squeezed lemon juice
- **1** teaspoon lemon zest
- **1** tablespoon butter
- **1** tablespoon light brown sugar
- **2–3** cups seedless grapes, sliced in half (white, red or a combination)
- **2** tablespoons sugar

**1** Preheat the oven to 350°F.

**2** In a small bowl, combine the lemon curd, lemon juice, and lemon zest. Set aside.

**3** Put the skillet over medium heat and melt the butter in it. Add the brown sugar and cook, stirring constantly, until sugar is dissolved, 1 or 2 minutes. Carefully remove pan from heat.

**4** Place the piecrust over the sugar mixture. Spread the lemon curd mix over the piecrust. Place the grape halves in a decorative pattern on top of the lemon curd, skin side up. Sprinkle with sugar.

**5** Put the skillet in the oven and bake for 45 to 50 minutes until set.

**6** Allow to cool before serving.

# STRAWBERRY PIE

If you just can't get enough strawberries in early summer, this pie will surely satisfy. Topped with strawberry preserves, it's absolutely heavenly.

—*Dominique DeVito*

1 In a saucepan over medium heat, mix sugar, cornstarch, and water. Stir in 1 cup of strawberry pieces. Cook, stirring until mixture begins to boil and thicken. Continue to cook and stir for about 5 minutes. Remove from the heat and allow to cool, about 20 minutes

2 Spread the remaining strawberry pieces evenly in the pie crust. When cooked mixture is cool, pour it over the larger pieces of fruit.

3 In a microwave-proof bowl, melt the strawberry preserves until just melted, about 20 seconds. Stir and drizzle the melted jam over the pie to distribute evenly.

4 Cover with plastic wrap and refrigerate for at least 3 hours and up to 1 day. Serve with whipped cream or ice cream (strawberry, vanilla, or another fruit flavor).

INGREDIENTS:

- 1 baked crust (see page 600)
- 6 cups (about 3 pints) fresh strawberries, washed, tops trimmed, and sliced in half or quarters
- ¾ cup sugar
- 3 tablespoons cornstarch
- ½ cup water
- ½ cup unsweetened strawberry preserves

# SUGAR BAKESHOP'S LEMON MERINGUE PIE

YIELDS: 8 TO 10 SERVINGS / ACTIVE TIME: 1 HOUR / TOTAL TIME: 1 HOUR 25 MINUTES

A simple classic, you can't go wrong with lemon meringue. Just be careful—it's so well known that mistakes are easily noticed!
—*Sugar Bakeshop*

1 Begin by making your pie dough. Heat oven to 425°F and cut butter into small pieces. Keep the butter slices in the freezer.

2 Mix the flour and salt in food processor. Add shortening and pulse until small pieces. Add your sliced butter, mixing until small, pea-sized pieces form. Gradually add water and mix until combined. Finish mixing by hand, making sure not to over-mix.

3 Form the pie dough into a ball, wrap in plastic wrap and refrigerate for 1 hour.

4 After 1 hour, flatten the dough into a 6-inch disc. Roll it out over a large sheet to ¼-inch thick.

5 Line a 9-inch pie pan with the dough and pierce with fork. Brush pie dough with egg wash and bake until slightly brown. Remove from oven and set aside.

6 In a medium saucepan, combine cornstarch, flour, sugar and salt. Mix well. Gradually add water, stirring until smooth.

7 Over medium heat, bring the mixture to a boil, stirring occasionally for approximately 20 minutes or until thick and set-up. Remove from heat.

8 Quickly stir some of the hot mixture into the egg yolks. Then, add egg yolk mixture back to saucepan and return to heat. Stir in lemon juice, lemon zest and butter.

9 Remove filling from saucepan and allow to cool. Pour into your baked pie shell.

10 Heat your oven to 400°F.

11 Using a handheld mixer, beat the egg whites, cream of tartar and salt together until the mixture has stiffened. Gradually add sugar and continue to beat until well dissolved and very stiff.

12 Gently fold in fresh lemon juice. Spread the meringue over the lemon filling to top edge of pie crust, using a large spoon or spatula to create swirled peaks.

13 Bake for 6 to 8 minutes, until meringue is light brown at peaks. Let the pie cool completely before serving.

## INGREDIENTS:

### PIE DOUGH

| | |
|---|---|
| 6 | tablespoons unsalted butter |
| 1¼ | cups all-purpose flour |
| ¼ | teaspoon sea salt (local, if available) |
| 2 | tablespoons leaf lard (use shortening if leaf lard is not available) |
| 2½ | tablespoons cold water |
| 1 | egg, beaten for egg wash |

### LEMON FILLING

| | |
|---|---|
| ¼ | cup cornstarch |
| ¼ | cup all purpose flour |
| 1¾ | cup sugar |
| ¼ | teaspoon salt |
| 2 | cups water |
| 4 | egg yolks, slightly beaten |
| ½ | cup fresh squeezed lemon juice |
| 1½ | tablespoons zested lemon peel |
| 2 | tablespoons unsalted butter |

### MERINGUE

| | |
|---|---|
| 4 | egg whites |
| ¼ | teaspoon cream of tartar |
| | Salt, a pinch |
| ½ | cup sugar |
| 1 | teaspoon fresh lemon juice |

# CHERRY CRUMB PIE

YIELD: 1 9-INCH PIE / **ACTIVE TIME:** 15 MINUTES / **TOTAL TIME:** 1 HOUR 15 MINUTES

This is a slightly different from your traditional cherry pie, but almonds and cherries are a perfect marriage. I really love the crunch the nuts provide.

Of course, fresh cherries are the best, but the work it takes to pit each and every cherry leads me to use frozen or canned cherries. If you don't have time for pitting, I prefer frozen to canned!
—*Stephany Buswell*

1 To make your filling: Mix together all the ingredients and pour them into the prepared pie shell.

2 Preheat your oven to 350°F. To make the topping, mix flour, nuts, sugar, zest, and salt in a mixing bowl with a paddle. Slowly pour the melted butter into the ingredients and stop mixing when you have a nice, moist crumb.

3 Sprinkle the crumb topping over the cherries.

4 Bake for 50 to 60 minutes or until bubbling occurs around the pie's edges.

## INGREDIENTS:

### PIE FILLING:

- 6 cups fresh, frozen or canned cherries
- ⅔ cup sugar
- 2 tablespoons cornstarch
- ⅛ teaspoon salt
- 1 teaspoon almond extract
- 1 9-inch flaky pie shell (see page 603)

### ALMOND CRUMB TOPPING:

- 1 cup all-purpose flour
- ⅔ cup toasted chopped almonds
- ¾ cup light brown sugar packed
- Zest of 1 small lemon
- ¼ teaspoon salt
- 3 tablespoons melted butter

# CHERRY-APPLE PIE

YIELDS:6 TO 8 SERVINGS / ACTIVE TIME: 45 MINUTES / TOTAL TIME: 90 MINUTES

Cherries add a bit of tang and a refreshing texture to a more traditional apple pie. This one uses canned cherry pie filling and is really easy to make.

*—Dominique DeVito*

**INGREDIENTS:**

- **1** baked crust (see page 600)
- **3** large apples, peeled, cored, and sliced
- **1** tablespoon butter
- **1** tablespoon fresh squeezed lemon juice
- **¼** teaspoon ground ginger
- **1** (15-oz.) can cherry pie filling

**1** Preheat the oven to 350°F.

**2** In a skillet or sauté pan over medium heat, combine apple pieces with butter and cook, stirring, until apple pieces soften, about 10 minutes.

**3** Transfer apple pieces to a large bowl and add lemon juice, ground ginger, and cherry pie filling. Stir to combine well.

**4** Put apple/cherry filling into crust.

**5** Bake for 20 to 25 minutes until heated through and set. Allow to cool slightly and serve with vanilla ice cream.

# MIXED BERRY PIE

I especially like this pie in a cornmeal crust. It gives it extra texture since the berries soften as they cook. Try it with this or a regular crust and see which you prefer. Of course, it's best to use all fresh fruit, but if one of them isn't available, you can substitute frozen fruit (thaw it first).

—*Dominique DeVito*

**1** Preheat oven to 375°F.

**2** In a large bowl, toss berries with lemon juice, brown sugar, and cornstarch. Transfer fruit to a large saucepan and cook over medium heat for about 3 minutes, until the fruit just starts to warm and break down.

**3** Scrape fruit and resulting juices into pie crust.

**4** In a small bowl, stir the preserves until slightly liquefied. Drizzle over pie.

**5** Put the skillet in the oven and bake for about 30 to 40 minutes until bubbling.

**6** Allow to cool before serving. Serve with fresh whipped cream.

## INGREDIENTS:

- **1 cornmeal crust (see page 611)**
- **1½ cups fresh blueberries**
- **1 cup fresh blackberries**
- **1 cup fresh raspberries**
- **1½ cups fresh strawberries, washed and tops trimmed, and sliced in half**
- **1 tablespoon fresh lemon juice**
- **½ cup light brown sugar**
- **2 tablespoons cornstarch**
- **½ cup unsweetened raspberry preserves**

# SPICY PUMPKIN PIE

YIELD: 1 9-INCH PIE / ACTIVE TIME: 10 MINUTES / TOTAL TIME: 55 MINUTES - 1 HOUR

Warm spices on a cool fall evening—perfect for lifting spirits and taste buds. This pie base is covered in ginger snaps for some extra fun! Just pour the pie filling over and bake and you have an extra warm, spicy pie for your holiday.
—*Stephany Buswell*

1 Preheat your oven to 375°F. In a bowl, whisk together the sugar, eggs, and pumpkin until the sugar begins to dissolve. Add the spices and salt and then the cream.

2 Place the cookies over the bottom of the partially baked shell in a single layer and pour the filling over them.

3 Bake for 45 to 50 minutes or until the filling doesn't jiggle when you gently shake the pan.

**INGREDIENTS:**

| | |
|---|---|
| ⅔ | cup dark brown sugar, packed |
| 4 | eggs |
| 1 | 15-ounce can pumpkin puree |
| 1 | teaspoon cinnamon |
| 1 | teaspoon ginger |
| ½ | teaspoon nutmeg |
| ¼ | teaspoon clove |
| ¼ | teaspoon salt |
| 1½ | cups heavy cream or half-and-half |
| 12–14 | ginger snap cookies |
| 1 | 9-inch flaky pie shell, partially baked (see page 603) |

It's a good idea to partially bake your crust before filling so you don't end up with a soggy crust. Place paper and pie weights in the bottom and bake for about 10 to 12 minutes at 350°F.

# SOUR CHERRY PIE

YIELD: 1 PIE / **ACTIVE TIME:** 45 MINUTES / **TOTAL TIME:** 2 HOURS

This pairing of tart cherries with a rich, buttery crust is a match made in pie heaven.

—*courtesy of Catherine and Cheryl Reinhart, Sweet Life Patisserie*

**1** Preheat oven to 350°F.

**2** Combine cherries and sugar. Cook until hot and sugar is dissolved. Combined water, arrowroot starch and cornstarch. Add this mixture to cherries and cook until thick and clear.

**3** Let cool. Pour into your buttery pie crust (see page 601). Top with butter oat crumble (see page 613). Bake for 50 minutes to 1 hour.

**INGREDIENTS:**

- **2 pounds and 6 ounces sour cherries**
- **2 ¾ cups cane sugar**
- **2 ½ tablespoons water**
- **2 ½ tablespoons arrowroot starch**
- **2 ½ tablespoons cornstarch**
- **1 buttery pie dough (see page 601)**

  **Butter oat crumble (see page 613)**

## Sweet Life Patisserie

742 Monroe St.
Eugene, OR 97402
(541) 683-5676
www.sweetlifedesserts.com

Sisters Cheryl and Catherine Reinhart have always been bakers at heart—the issue has never been "what," but "where." Before they opened Sweet Life, Catherine had been working in local bakeries, practicing with wedding cake decoration, while Cheryl worked primarily in restaurants, baking whenever possible. Says Cheryl, "We wanted to work for ourselves and we owned a house together. We thought, why not convert our one-car garage into a certified kitchen and make wedding cakes? So that's what we did." Both women kept their other jobs for the first year, attending shows and marketing to restaurants in order to build a base. Before long, Sweet Life had earned a reputation as a go-to place for celebratory desserts.

The Reinharts have truly embraced this identity, even describing the bakery's essence as "a party every day, where everyone in the community can celebrate special occasions." And while the bakery has since moved out of the garage, this personal touch is what keeps Sweet Life so in touch with the community. That, and their eagerness to accept and promote different kinds of diets. "We were doing gluten-free and egg- and dairy-free desserts long before it caught on in the mainstream." Why? "Because the customers asked." This wasn't an easy transition—Cheryl and Sarah knew they wanted to keep their original recipes, but they wanted everyone to feel comfortable at Sweet Life. That

meant a lot of experimentation. "We didn't think it was possible until someone gave us a really good egg- and dairy-free chocolate cake recipe and we were sold on the idea. We kept at it until we felt our vegan and gluten-free dessert options were delicious for everyone."

Part of this can be attributed to Eugene, Oregon, where the bakery can be found. "Eugene is famous for its many alternative lifestyles, including dietary ones," says Cheryl. But different diets have only become more prominent since they expanded their menu, and the experimenting can be fun, if trying. Cheryl admits, "There are some desserts that just don't taste good when translated with certain dietary restrictions, and we just don't do them." In other words, quality is always the most important thing.

The treats at Sweet Life have resonated outside of the Eugene area, earning the bakery a place on *Buzzfeed*'s "23 Bakeries You Need to Visit Before You Die" list. Still, the Reinhart sisters take more pride in their partnership than anything else. "More than being a chef, I think running a successful business as sisters has been a journey that we're both proud of. We've learned a lot from each other and I feel like we have a huge community that supports us and we support them by giving a lot of people meaningful work in a supportive environment."

# IN THEIR OWN WORDS:

## CATHERINE AND CHERYL REINHART

*How and when did you get your start baking?*

We both started baking and cooking when we were young kids. Both of our grandmas and our mother were amazing cooks and made cakes, cookies and pies from scratch. We were immersed in a culture of home cooking and baking, so for us it was just natural to join in with the baking.

*Who inspired you to bake? Who inspires you now?*

When we started baking professionally, we were inspired by French pastry chefs and their beautiful creations. Our scratch baking roots provided inspiration as well. Today, we find inspiration from many sources, including the Locavore movement, our employees, and the wealth of food culture that has blossomed everywhere around us.

*What is your golden rule(s) of baking?*

We attempt to achieve the perfect balance of flavors and textures by combining complementary elements in our desserts.

*What is your favorite thing to bake? Why? Least favorite thing to bake? Why?*

My favorite is our passionfruit tart with fresh raspberries. We start with a shortbread shell, fill it with passionfruit curd, top with fresh organic local raspberries, glazed with apricot glaze. Why? Because, well, it's so delicious! Least favorite: Gluten-free cakes. Why? Because it's so tricky to get the texture just right.

*What are your most popular items?*

Our chocolate orgasm cake is one of our customers' all-time favorites. It's a chocolate cake, filled with vanilla custard and chocolate mousse and topped with blood orange buttercream. A few other favorites are: the Josephine (our version of a Napoleon, it's a crispy puff pastry shell filled with vanilla custard and

served with an organic raspberry puree); pumpkin cookies with brown sugar frosting; black bottom cupcakes (chocolate cake with a baked cheesecake top and milk chocolate chips) and cheesecake (we do all kinds of different cheesecakes and the customers love them all!).

*What non-essential items should every baker have?*

My favorite non-essential items are cool stencils for making fancy shaped designs on top of cakes.

*What book(s) go on your required reading list for bakers?*

There are so many options nowadays. I recommend experimenting with recipes that sound good to you and modifying them as needed whether it's adding darker chocolate or more salt to a recipe. As far as acquiring skills, libraries and the internet have a wealth of knowledge. Just Google what you want to know and you'll find hundreds of "how-to" resources.

*Tell us about your favorite part of collaborating on a recipe.*

What is really interesting to us is collaborating with our bakers. They all come with some experience and creativity so when we want to come up with a new dessert or an exciting flavor combination, we love to brainstorm together to make the perfect dessert.

*Where did you learn to cook? Please tell me about your education and/or apprenticeships.*

Mostly it was on the job experience. As mentioned before, we grew up in a family that loved food and cooking, so it's in our blood. We spent time in all sorts of kitchens from a galley on a crab processor in Alaska, to a homey bakery to a high-end restaurant in Eugene, Oregon. As for learning how to bake, we still continue to improve our recipes and refine our techniques. It's an ongoing education.

# PUMPKIN PIE

YIELD: 1 9-INCH PIE / ACTIVE TIME: 45 MINUTES / TOTAL TIME: 2 HOURS

This comforting seasonal classic gets an added touch of color and flavor from the addition of molasses.

—*courtesy of Catherine and Cheryl Reinhart, Sweet Life Patisserie*

1 Preheat oven to 350°F. Combine all ingredients and mix until evenly incorporated.

2 Pour approximately 5 cups of filling into unbaked pie shell.

3 Bake for 30 minutes at 350°F, then 30 to 40 minutes at 275°F. Pie should be firm and jiggle only slightly. The center should not be sticky, cracked, or dry looking.

**INGREDIENTS:**

| | |
|---|---|
| 2 | cups pumpkin purée |
| ¾ | cup sugar |
| ½ | tablespoon molasses |
| ½ | teaspoon salt |
| ¾ | cup cream |
| ¾ | cup milk |
| 2 | eggs |
| 2 | teaspoons vanilla |
| 2 | teaspoons cinnamon |
| ½ | teaspoon nutmeg |
| ½ | teaspoon ginger |
| ½ | teaspoon allspice |
| 1 | buttery pie dough (see page 601) |

# The Sweetery

1814 E Greenville St
Anderson, SC 29621
(864) 224-8394
www.thesweetery.net

When asked to describe what The Sweetery represents to her, owner Jane Jaharian has a specific answer in mind: "A child that never grows up." It is an apt description; the bakery has endured for over 30 years and barely aged a day. And though her son Ryan has indeed grown up, he hasn't strayed far—the mom-and-son duo work together in the bakery to bring sweetness to South Carolina.

A lifelong Anderson resident, Jane set out to help working mothers—baking homemade cakes for them to bring home after a long day so as not to "take precious time away from their families." Once people began tasting her cakes, though, word began to spread. Today, Jane is not only a master baker but also the president of the South Carolina Specialty Food Organization, where she helps local farmers and retailers expand their businesses.

As a bakery, The Sweetery doesn't overcomplicate things. In true southern fashion, simple ingredients and traditional flavors are the bakery's hallmarks. "I read a lot about cooking foods, techniques, ingredients and recipes from all generations—and also get a lot from the Food Network!" For Jane and the team, the proudest moments come from happy customers. And with The Sweetery's output, those moments occur every day.

# IN HER OWN WORDS:

## JANE JAHARIAN

*How and when did you get your start baking?*

I began baking pizza and pies—both sweet and savory—when I was 13 years old.

*Who inspired you to bake? Who inspires you now?*

From an early age, I think all southern women, or homemakers in general, are inspired by the satisfaction of seeing people enjoy food they've prepared. My Sweetery customers inspire me now!

*What is your golden rule(s) of baking?*

Use quality ingredients.

*What is your favorite thing to bake? Why? Least favorite thing to bake? Why?*

Favorite: A special holiday cake—it doesn't matter what kind. Least favorite—a recipe that leaves something out.

*What are your most popular items?*

Strawberry Cake, Brownies & Crème, and Tomato Pies are our best sellers.

*What book(s) go on your required reading list for bakers?*

I have several baking books I refer back to

from time to time, to list just some would be an injustice.

*What outlets/periodicals/newspapers do you read or consult regularly, if any?*

I like *Bake Magazine*, and the Retail Baker's Association also puts out good newsletters.

*Tell me about your most memorable collaboration with another chef.*

There have been many, but Paula Dean and I once had a conversation on Southern food that was like talking recipes with an old friend.

*Where did you learn to cook?*

I've always had a love of cooking and am self-taught through years of practice.

*What is your favorite thing about The Sweetery?*

The feeling of being a part of your community. When I was growing up in Anderson, we had our own town baker; when he retired, he began working part-time in The Sweetery, and was kind enough to pass some of his special recipes to us. This continuing of community traditions is very special to me.

# PECAN PIE

YIELDS: 8–10 SERVINGS / ACTIVE TIME: 20 MINUTES / TOTAL TIME: 1 HOUR 5 MINUTES

This 30-year-old recipe of a classic southern dish belongs in every bakery, southern or otherwise.

— *The Sweetery*

1 Begin by making your pecan filling. Preheat your oven to 350°F, and combine all ingredients in a large bowl.

2 Next, make your pie crust (page 610)

3 Roll dough into a 12-inch round circle on a lightly floured surface. Fit the dough over a greased 9-inch pie dish. Trim the edges, leaving a 1-inch overhang. Flute the edges. Refrigerate the dough for another 15 minutes.

4 Pour filling in crust and bake for 45 to 50 minutes.

**INGREDIENTS:**

1 cup light corn syrup

1 cup dark brown sugar, firmly packed

3 eggs, lightly beaten

⅓ cup butter, melted

½ teaspoon salt

1 cup pecans, halves or medium-sized pieces

**Cream Cheese Pie Crust (see page 610)**

# MAPLE PECAN PIE *with* BOURBON

YIELD: 1 9-INCH PIE/ ACTIVE TIME: 15 MINUTES/ TOTAL TIME: 1 HOUR 10 MINUTES

I always thought pecan pie was cloyingly sweet; although I loved the first bite, it was as far as I ever wanted to go. I began wondering if I could make this great pie using syrup that was less sweet but still flavorful. Well, maple syrup was the answer. Who doesn't love the earthy sweetness of a good maple syrup? Pair it with pecans and bourbon and you have a winner!
—*Stephany Buswell*

**INGREDIENTS:**

- 1½ cups pecans
- 1 cup brown sugar
- ⅔ cup maple syrup
- 1 tablespoon bourbon (optional)
- ¼ cup unsalted butter
- 3 large eggs (lightly beaten)
- ¼ cup heavy cream
- 1 teaspoon vanilla
- 1 teaspoon salt
- 1 pie crust (chilled in the fridge until time of use, see pages 603-607)

1 Bake the pecans in a preheated oven at 350°F until nicely toasted, about 8 to 10 minutes. Leave the oven heated at 350°F.

2 Heat the sugar, syrup, bourbon, and butter in a large saucepan until it boils, stirring constantly. Remove from heat and let cool.

3 Beat in the eggs, cream, vanilla and salt.

4 Spread the pecans over the bottom of the pie crust, then pour the liquid mixture into the pie crust.

5 Bake at 350°F until a toothpick inserted into the center comes out clean, about 40 to 50 minutes.

6 Remove from heat and serve with whipped cream.

# SALTED-CARAMEL PECAN PIE

YIELDS: 8 SERVINGS / ACTIVE TIME: 45 MINUTES / TOTAL TIME: 90 MINUTES

I'm a big fan of the salty-sweet confection craze, which features many kinds of salted-caramel foods. This recipe is a twist on traditional pecan pie, as the filling is cooked until it almost caramelizes. This gooey, almost smoky filling is topped with mixed-salted nuts in addition to pecans.

—*Dominique DeVito*

1 Preheat the oven to 350°F.

2 In a small bowl, combine the pecan pieces with the salted nuts and stir to combine. Set aside.

3 In a large, heavy-bottomed saucepan over medium heat, combine the sugar, corn syrup, and water. Cook, stirring constantly, until sugar is completely dissolved. Increase heat to medium-high and, while stirring, bring the mixture to a boil. Continue to stir as the mixture bubbles and begins to turn dark brown, about 10 minutes. Just before it starts to smoke, remove it from the heat.

4 Stand back from the saucepan and using a long-handled spoon, add the cream. The mixture will spatter. Stir until combined and settled. Return the saucepan to the heat. Add the rum and salt. Cook on medium-low until the mixture is smooth, another few minutes.

5 Ladle the mixture into a large bowl and allow to cool.

6 When cool, use a whisk and add the eggs. Pour the mixture into the pie crust. Sprinkle with the pecan/salted nut combination.

7 Put the skillet in the oven and bake for about 45 minutes or until a knife inserted toward the middle comes out clean.

8 Cool completely before serving. Serve with fresh whipped cream sprinkled with more salted nuts if desired.

## INGREDIENTS:

| | |
|---|---|
| 1 | flaky pastry crust recipe for a single crust (see page 603) |
| ½ | cup pecan pieces |
| 1½ | cups mixed salted nuts |
| 1¾ | cups granulated sugar |
| ⅓ | cup dark corn syrup |
| ¼ | cup water |
| ¾ | cup heavy cream |
| 2 | tablespoons dark rum |
| 1 | teaspoon salt |
| 3 | large eggs, beaten |

# CHOCOLATE MOUSSE PECAN PIE

**YIELDS:** 6 TO 8 SERVINGS / **ACTIVE TIME:** 40 MINUTES / **TOTAL TIME:** SEVERAL HOURS OR OVERNIGHT

Doesn't the name of this pie sound decadent? A combination of chocolate mousse and the buttery richness of pecans? Well, it is decadent in its flavor, but it is super-simple to make—it doesn't even need to be baked. Time to indulge!

*—Dominique DeVito*

**INGREDIENTS:**

1 **baked crust (see page 600)**

½ **cup coarsely chopped pecans, toasted**

12 **ounces semisweet chocolate morsels**

2½ **cups heavy cream, divided**

1 **tablespoon bourbon**

1 **teaspoon vanilla extract**

1 Preheat the oven to 350°F.

2 Spread the pecan pieces on a cookie sheet. Bake for about 8 minutes, checking on the nuts after 5 minutes to be sure they don't burn. Remove when just starting to brown. Allow to cool.

3 Put the chocolate morsels in a microwave-safe bowl. Add ½ cup of the cream and stir. Microwave on high in 30-second increments, stirring after each. When just melted, stir in the bourbon and vanilla. Let stand for about 5 minutes.

4 In a large bowl, beat the remaining 2 cups of cream at medium-high speed with an electric mixer for about 3 minutes or until medium peaks form. Fold the chocolate mixture into the whipped cream. Pour the chocolate into the pie crust, spreading with the back of a spoon to distribute evenly. Sprinkle the toasted pecans over the top.

5 Refrigerate for several hours before serving.

# GREEK-STYLE WALNUT PIE

YIELDS: 8 TO 10 SERVINGS / ACTIVE TIME: 90 MINUTES / TOTAL TIME: SEVERAL HOURS

If you like the Greek pastry Baklava, which is a nut-rich treat with honey and lemon, you'll love this pie. It's intense, and a little goes a long way…but you'll be back for more.

—*Dominique DeVito*

**INGREDIENTS:**

- 2 **flaky pie crust recipes for a double crust (see page 603)**
- 2½ **cups finely chopped walnuts**
- ¼ **cup packed brown sugar**
- 2 **tablespoons granulated sugar**
- 1½ **teaspoons ground cinnamon**
- ¾ **cup butter, split into 3 (¼ cup) rations, melted, plus 1 tablespoon for greasing the skillet**
- ¾ **cup honey**
- 1 **tablespoon fresh squeezed lemon juice**

1 Preheat the oven to 325°F.

2 In a medium bowl, mix walnuts, brown sugar, granulated sugar, and the cinnamon.

3 Put the skillet over medium heat and melt the butter in it. Carefully remove pan from heat.

4 Place 1 of the piecrusts in the skillet. Pour ¼ cup of melted butter over the bottom of the pie crust. Spread the walnut mixture evenly over butter. Melt and drizzle another ¼ cup butter over the nut mixture and place the other crust over it, crimping the edges together. Cut large slits in the middle of the top crust and drizzle the remaining ¼ cup melted butter over it, brushing to distribute evenly.

5 Put the skillet in the oven and bake for about 20 minutes. Cover the outermost edge with aluminum foil in the last 10 minutes of baking to prevent it from burning. Bake an additional 30 to 35 minutes or until golden brown.

6 When pie is nearly finished, put honey and lemon in a small saucepan. Heat over medium heat, stir, and cook, stirring constantly, until mixture is almost watery in consistency.

7 Remove pie from the oven and slowly and carefully pour the honey-lemon mixture over the top, allowing it to penetrate and drizzle into the crust.

8 Allow pie to cool for several hours before serving.

# STRAWBERRY-RHUBARB PIE *with* LATTICE CRUST

YIELD: 1 9-INCH PIE / ACTIVE TIME: 20 MINUTES / TOTAL TIME: 1 HOUR 20 MINUTES

I love rhubarb so much that I'm happy to enjoy it all by itself, but pairing rhubarb with strawberries makes for a classic combination nobody can pass up. This sweet, fragrant version adds only a little orange peel for an accent flavor.

The lattice crust will take a bit more time, but it looks so nice with the bright red peaking out between the dough. The crust's many holes operate as vents, allowing the fruit to bake and not steam under a solid crust. You may get some juices bubbling up and onto the crust, but in my opinion that just makes it look even tastier.

—*Stephany Buswell*

### INGREDIENTS:

- **4** cups (about 1¼ pounds) rhubarb, cubed
- **4** cups strawberries, halved
- **1** cup sugar
- **¼** cup cornstarch
- Zest of ½ orange
- **⅛** teaspoon salt
- **2** tablespoons unsalted butter
- **1** 9-inch unbaked pie shell
- **1** 10-inch-round rolled crust, chilled (see page 603)

1 In a large mixing bowl, combine all of the ingredients except the butter. Fill the unbaked shell with the fruit mix and dot with butter.

2 For the lattice crust: Take the rolled and chilled dough and, using a fluted rolling cutter (a knife will do if you don't have one), cut 1-inch strips across the round dough.

3 Trim the dough in the pie pan to the outside edge of the pan. Egg-wash the top edge.

4 Place one of the short strips on the top near the edge. Then continue placing strips across the pie using the strips that fit the space.

5 Preheat your oven to 400°F and begin making your lattice top. First, lift every other strip and fold it back enough so you can place a strip down over the pieces that remain lying down. Then fold the strips back over the cross strip. Repeat each time you place a new cross strip, folding back the strips that were not folded last time, placing a cross strip, and then folding back to create a woven lattice top.

6 When done, seal the edges with a fork and egg-wash the top strips, being careful not to get the egg on the fruit. Sprinkle with sugar.

7 Bake on a sheet pan at 400°F for 20 minutes, then turn down the oven to 350°F for another 40 minutes or until the center is bubbling.

# STRAWBERRY-RHUBARB PIE

YIELD: 1 9-INCH PIE / ACTIVE TIME: 45 MINUTES / TOTAL TIME: 2 HOURS

Sweet strawberries, sour rhubarb, and plenty of brown sugar combine to make a winning version of this classic dessert.
—*courtesy of Catherine and Cheryl Reinhart of Sweet Life Patisserie*

1  Preheat oven to 350°F.

2  Combine water, lemon juice, brown sugar, starches, and tapioca in a bowl. Pour over rhubarb and mix.

3  Heat over low until starches are clear and thick. Add strawberries. Cool.

4  Pour into pie shell and top with crust or butter oat crumble. Bake for 50 minutes to 1 hour.

**INGREDIENTS:**

- 2 pounds and 5 ounces strawberries (hulled and quartered)
- 1 pound and 2 ounces rhubarb (sliced in ½-inch slices)
- ⅓ cup water
- 2 tablespoon lemon juice
- 1 cup brown sugar
- 2½ tablespoons minute tapioca
- 2 tablespoons arrowroot powder
- 1½ tablespoons cornstarch
- 1 9-inch buttery pie shell (see page 601)

# Sugar Pie Bakery

3624 MacCorkle Ave SE
Charleston, WV 25304
(304) 205-7753
www.sugarpiebakerywv.com

Gina Watts' baking story is a testament to what happens when you know what you want. "I started working at the bakery one month after it opened. Before working there for a year, I was asked to buy in as an owner. At the age of 24, I was an owner in my own bakery. Working weekends, 12-hour days and constantly thinking (and dreaming) about the bakery had paid off. Five years after opening, I am the sole owner and operator of the bakery."

If it sounds straightforward, that's only because of Watt's persistence. She began her baking career with no guarantees—only a passion for sweets and a love of creative cooking. Having loved to cook since childhood, she took a ProStart cooking class during high school and captained its competition team to a second-place statewide finish. For Watts, the work was just beginning. Cooking school, internships and apprenticeships all awaited her before she found her home at Sugar Pie. Watts refers to these formative years as her "most memorable collaborations with other chefs." "It was fun being around so many people who shared my passion and who I could learn from."

Today, Sugar Pie is known for its many unique recipes and their endless variations—perhaps none more so than the New York cheesecake and its 20-plus flavors. Of course, this inventiveness comes at a cost: "My staff and I are always working on new ideas and flavors for the store. We come up with a new cupcake menu every month, as well as add new items in our cases daily. Most of our ideas come from flavors and combinations that we like. Depending on the recipe, it can take days to weeks to perfect a recipe and baking time for a product." Still, it's worth it; cheesecakes and cupcakes are Sugar Pie's two most popular options, often specifically because of their creativity. What could become an "old standby" transforms into a must-try item. Not every bakery has the time and staff to make this happen regularly, but Sugar Pie patrons are glad that this one does.

Ironically, for all of their ingenuity, Sugar Pie is perhaps best known for their mastery of an American classic: apple pie. A perennial bestseller at the bakery, it was named "Best Apple Pie in West Virginia" by *Mental Floss* in 2016. It is perhaps Watts' proudest moment as a baker, as apple pie is no small part of the state's food legacy. For fans of classics and concoctions alike, Sugar Pie is a southern bakery worth returning to—there's always another recipe to try!

# IN HER OWN WORDS:

## GINA WATTS

*How and when did you get your start baking?*

I started baking at a very young age. I'm fortunate to have wonderful and talented cooks throughout my family including my grandmothers and mother. I was always interested in what my mom was doing in the kitchen. She would let me watch and help cook often. We always had family meals at the dinner table every night. If my mom had to work late, she would have my sister and I finish dinner or add to the crock pot so we could eat when she got home.

*Who inspired you to bake? Who inspires you now?*

My mom inspired my love for food. She has always been an amazing cook and enjoys trying new recipes and using fresh ingredients that she grows in her garden.

I draw inspiration from everything I encounter. I have people suggest new flavors to me every day, or I see something that gives me an idea and I think of how I can incorporate it into a cupcake, cake, or pie. My staff does a great job of always thinking of new flavor ideas through their experiences as well.

*What is your golden rule(s) of baking?*

"Read the directions fully. If you mess up, try again."

*What is your favorite thing to bake? Why? Least favorite thing to bake? Why?*

I love baking cupcakes! They are so versatile and allow room for creativity. It is easy to bake a lot of them and different flavors quickly.

My least favorite thing to bake is bread. I

love to eat homemade bread, but I don't have the patience to make it.

*How and when did Sugar Pie come to exist? Tell us your origin story!*

Sugar Pie was originally opened with three owners, two friends who brought in a local cake decorator. As I mentioned before, I was hired exactly one month and one day after the doors first opened. I quickly became in charge of making many of the everyday sweets including buttercream for the cupcakes every morning. The friends who started the bakery together both left the next year one shortly after the other. The remaining owner asked if I would be interested in buying into the bakery, and taking over the managerial responsibilities along with being the main baker. Of course, I said, "Yes!" This past year, she had decided that it was time for her to spend more time with her children, leaving me as the sole owner and operator of the bakery. We have had many ups and downs owning a small business in Charleston, WV but I wouldn't change it for anything.

*What are your most popular items?*

Our best-selling items are cupcakes (especially our red velvet and chocolate peanut butter flavors), cheesecake, and French macarons. Our cupcakes are made in small batches and completely from scratch. Our red velvet cupcakes are mixed by hand, and is a traditional red velvet cake. Our New York cheesecake is smooth and not too sweet. We top them with strawberry sauce and homemade whipped cream. Our French macarons are made fresh, in house! We even make our own almond flour. We have spent hours perfecting the recipe and bake time. The vanilla, raspberry and chocolate peanut butter are the most popular.

*What non-essential items should every baker have?*

Every baker should have a sheeter. It is a lifesaver! It cuts down time while making pie crusts, sugar cookies and decorating cakes.

*What book(s) go on your required reading list for bakers?*

I love reading cookbooks in my spare time! When I get a new one, I'll sit down and look at every page. Some of my favorites are *Taste of Home* and *Better Homes and Garden* cookbooks.

*What outlets/periodicals/newspapers do you read or consult regularly, if any?*

Cooking magazines are also some of my favorite "books" to read in my spare time. I love *Southern Living*, *Taste of Home* and *Cooks Illustrated*.

*Where did you learn to cook? Please tell me about your education and/or apprenticeships.*

I learned a lot about cooking and baking from watching my family members as well as experimenting myself. However, I learned many of the basics, and that I had a real passion for cooking and baking, during my high school ProStart class. After taking general education classes at my state university, I moved away from home to attend Pierpont Community and Technical College in Fairmont, WV. They are the only ACF-certified baking school in the state of WV. On top of going to class, we had to complete three internships. The hands-on experience was irreplaceable.

*Do you follow any cooking shows or chefs? If so, which is your favorite?*

*Chopped* is my favorite cooking show to watch! I like to think about what I would make and compare it to what they come up with. It also reminds me of school because that is exactly how we did our finals. They were always timed, you had to incorporate certain elements, and you had to share equipment with the rest of the class.

# COCONUT DREAM PIE

YIELD: 1 9-INCH PIE / **ACTIVE TIME:** 30 MINUTES / **TOTAL TIME:** 1 HOUR

Real coconut milk and shredded coconut makes our coconut dream pie exactly that, a dream.
—*courtesy of Gina Watts, Sugar Pie Bakery*

**1** Stir together coconut milk, milk, shredded coconut, and ½ cup sugar in large saucepan.

**2** Bring to a bare simmer over medium heat.

**3** While milk mixture is heating, in large bowl, whisk together eggs, the remaining 2 tablespoons of sugar, and the cornstarch until smooth.

**4** Once milk mixture is at a simmer, slowly pour about ½ cup of hot milk mixture into the eggs while whisking constantly. Repeat until you have stirred in 2 cups of the mixture.

**5** Whisk the egg mixture back into the remaining milk mixture, stirring constantly.

**6** Bring to a boil. Once mixture is thick, remove from heat. Stir in butter, vanilla, and coconut extract. Scrape into Graham Cracker Crust pie shell (see page 608) or bowl, cover with plastic wrap and refrigerate until cool.

**7** Once cooled, top with whipped cream (see below).

## WHIPPED CREAM

Use a stand mixer and mix whipping cream and vanilla extract until fluffy. Add confectioner's sugar and mix on high, until medium-sized peaks form in the mixture.

### INGREDIENTS:

| | |
|---|---|
| 1 | **Graham Cracker Crust (see page 618)** |
| 1 | **14-ounce can coconut milk** |
| 3 | **tablespoons butter** |
| 1 | **cup whole milk** |
| 2 | **teaspoons pure vanilla** |
| ½–¾ | **cup shredded coconut** |
| 2 | **teaspoons coconut extract** |
| ½ | **cup + 2 tablespoons sugar** |
| 3 | **whole eggs** |
| 4½ | **tablespoons cornstarch** |

### WHIPPED CREAM

| | |
|---|---|
| 1 | **cup whipping cream** |
| 2 | **tablespoons confectioner's sugar** |
| | **Splash of pure vanilla extract** |

# ELVIS PIE (BANANA CREAM PIE)

YIELD: 1 9-INCH PIE / **ACTIVE TIME:** 30 MINUTES / **TOTAL TIME:** 1 HOUR

The King himself would approve this delicious treat! The pairing of banana, peanut butter and chocolate is unmatched in this creamy, delectable pie!
—*courtesy of Gina Watts, Sugar Pie Bakery*

## CHOCOLATE GRAHAM CRACKER CRUST

1 Mix graham cracker crumbs and sugar until well incorporated. Melt butter then add to graham cracker and sugar mixture.

2 Pour mixture into pie pan and press until crumbs are packed tightly. Bake at 350°F for 7 minutes. Let cool.

## BANANA CREAM PIE FILLING

1 In a saucepan, combine sugar, flour, and salt. Add milk gradually, stirring constantly. Cook over medium heat, stirring constantly, until mixture begins to simmer. Keep stirring and cook an additional 2 minutes. Remove from heat.

2 Stir a small amount of the hot milk mixture into the beaten egg yolks, then add egg yolk mixture to the hot milk mixture and return to heat. Cook for 2 more minutes while continuously stirring. Once mixture is thick and bubbling, remove from heat and add butter and vanilla. Stir until combined.

3 Add half of the sliced bananas and mix. Cover with plastic wrap to cool.

4 When you're ready to make your pie, melt peanut butter and pour into cooled chocolate graham cracker crust.

5 Take remaining bananas slices and lay on top of the peanut butter layer. Pour banana cream filling over top of banana slices.

6 Make whipped cream (see page 674). Use a piping bag and star tip to pipe and cover top of pie. Melt peanut butter and drizzle on top of the whipped cream. Garnish with dried banana chips.

## INGREDIENTS:

### CHOCOLATE GRAHAM CRACKER CRUST

2 cups chocolate graham cracker crumbs

¼ cup granulated sugar

8 tablespoons melted butter

### BANANA CREAM PIE FILLING

¾ cup granulated sugar

2 tablespoons butter

⅓ cup flour

1¼ teaspoons pure vanilla extract

¼ teaspoon salt

4 bananas, sliced

2 cups whole milk

3 egg yolks, beaten

Peanut butter, for drizzling

Dried banana chips, for garnish

# CHOCOLATE PUDDING PIE

YIELDS: 6 TO 8 SERVINGS / **ACTIVE TIME:** 20 MINUTES / **TOTAL TIME:** 90 MINUTES

Whatever you do, don't skip adding the whipped topping on this pie. It truly is the "secret ingredient" that brings it all together. Garnishing with fresh raspberries or strawberry pieces adds flavor and color.

—*Dominique DeVito*

1 In a large bowl, combine the pudding mix and milk. Whisk until all the lumps are broken up, the pudding is smooth, and it has started to thicken, about 5 minutes.

2 Put the pudding in the graham cracker crust and cover with plastic wrap. Refrigerate for an hour or longer.

3 Before serving, top with the whipped topping and garnish with the fruit, if desired.

**INGREDIENTS:**

1 graham cracker crust (see page 607)

2 (3.5-oz.) boxes instant chocolate pudding (dark chocolate is preferable)

3 cups whole milk

2 cups whipped topping (Cool Whip or fresh whipped cream)

Whole fresh raspberries or sliced strawberries for garnish (if desired)

# LEMON RICE PUDDING PIE

YIELDS: 6 TO 8 SERVINGS / ACTIVE TIME: 30 MINUTES / TOTAL TIME: 3 OR MORE HOURS

I had leftover rice one night and I thought that the rice would be a nice texture and flavor addition to a pudding pie. I chose lemon for the filling and enhanced the flavor with some fresh squeezed lemon juice and vanilla extract. This is now a family favorite.

—*Dominique DeVito*

1 In a large bowl, combine the lemon pudding mix and milk. Whisk until all the lumps are broken up, the pudding is smooth, and it has started to thicken, about 3 minutes. Stir in the lemon juice and vanilla, then stir in the rice.

2 Put the filling into the pie crust. Put a piece of plastic wrap over it, covering the filling, and refrigerate for 2 or more hours before serving.

3 Top with the whipped topping and sprinkle with cinnamon, if desired.

**INGREDIENTS:**

1   graham cracker crust (see page 607)

1   (3.4-oz.) box instant lemon pudding mix

2   cups whole milk

1   tablespoon fresh squeezed lemon juice

1   teaspoon vanilla extract

1½  to 2 cups cooked rice (brown rice is best)

1   cup whipped topping (Cool Whip or fresh whipped cream)

    Cinnamon (optional)

# PIÑA COLADA

**YIELDS:** 6 TO 8 SERVINGS / **ACTIVE TIME:** 45 MINUTES / **TOTAL TIME:** SEVERAL HOURS

Seriously, piña colada pie. If you think it sounds temptingly weird, you're right. If you love a good piña colada with its combo of fresh coconut and sweet pineapple, you're going to love this pie. It really is a cocktail in a crust.

—*Dominique DeVito*

1 Sprinkle the unsweetened coconut flakes in the bottom of the baked pie crust and set aside.

2 In a large bowl, combine the coconut pudding mix with the milk and piña colada mix. Whisk until all the lumps are broken up, the pudding is smooth, and it has started to thicken, about 3 minutes.

3 In a small saucepan, heat the rum over a low flame. When it's warm, add the cornstarch and stir with a fork or a small whisk until it is completely blended and warmed throughout. Remove from heat and continue to stir while allowing the mixture to cool slightly.

4 Add the rum mixture to the pudding and stir gently to combine.

5 Pour the filling into the baked pie crust. Cover with plastic wrap, press the plastic into the filling, and refrigerate for several hours before serving. Garnish as desired.

**INGREDIENTS:**

- 1 baked crust (see page 600)
- ½ cup unsweetened coconut flakes
- 1 (3.4-oz.) box instant coconut pudding mix
- 1 cup milk
- 1 cup piña colada mix (non-alcoholic)
- ¼ cup dark rum
- 2 tablespoons cornstarch

  Kiwi slices, pineapple slices, and coconut shavings for garnish (optional)

# PINEAPPLE CREAM PIE

**YIELDS:** 6 TO 8 SERVINGS / **ACTIVE TIME:** 40 MINUTES / **TOTAL TIME:** SEVERAL HOURS OR OVERNIGHT

This creamy pie has the great zing of pineapple, plus it's really fun to decorate with the pineapple rings and maraschino cherries. The result is a taste of the tropics with a modern take on pineapple upside down cake.

—*Dominique DeVito*

**INGREDIENTS:**

- **1** baked crust (see page 600)
- **½** cup sugar
- **3** tablespoons cornstarch
- **¼** teaspoon salt
- **1¾** cup milk
- **¾** cup pineapple juice from a can of sliced pineapple rings
- **3** egg yolks
- **1** tablespoon butter
- **1** (20-oz.) can pineapple rings or chunks

1 In a medium saucepan, combine sugar, cornstarch, and salt. Whisk to combine. Stir in the milk until smooth. Cook over medium-low heat, stirring constantly, until mixture begins to thicken and just begins to boil. Don't allow to boil. Add the pineapple juice and continue to stir until thoroughly combined. Remove from the heat.

2 In a small bowl, whisk egg yolks. Add a large spoonful of the pineapple cream and stir rapidly to prevent curdling or cooking. Repeat, being sure to stir rapidly. Next, stir the egg mixture into the saucepan with the pineapple cream, and stir that briskly to combine. Return saucepan to low heat, and stir in the butter. Continue to stir while cooking, until mixture thickens considerably, about 5 minutes.

3 Pour into pie crust and spread evenly. Cover with plastic wrap and refrigerate several hours or up to 1 day.

4 When ready to serve, remove plastic wrap and decorate with pineapple rings or chunks.

# SUGAREE'S BAKERY CHOCOLATE MERINGUE PIE

YIELDS: 8 SERVINGS / ACTIVE TIME: 45 MINUTES / TOTAL TIME: 1 HOUR 30 MINUTES

This southern classic proves that you don't need to love lemons to enjoy a nice meringue pie.

## CRUST

1. Preheat your oven to 375°F. Using a pastry cutter, cut together flour, salt, butter and lard until the bits are the size of sunflower seeds.

2. Use a pastry fork to cut in ice water two tablespoons at a time, slowly decreasing the amount until the mixture sticks together when you form a ball. Work quickly to avoid overworking dough.

3. Roll out your dough between two pieces of plastic wrap. Add to pie pan and shape.

4. Freeze crust completely. With a fork, mix together 1 tablespoon of heavy cream and 1 egg yolk. Using a pastry brush, lightly apply to frozen pastries. With a fork, poke holes all over the bottom and sides of pie crust.

5. Bake at 375°F for 10 minutes. Check on your dough—if it's puffing up, remove from heat and poke holes in the dough. Bake for another 20 minutes until light golden brown.

## FILLING

6. Whisk together dry ingredients until completely combined.

7. In a separate bowl, whisk egg yolks and water together, then pour into the milk through a strainer. Pour dry ingredients on top of liquid ingredients and whisk to combine.

8. Pour through strainer into 3-quart pot. Stir constantly over medium heat until the filling boils. Remove from heat. Add small butter chunks and vanilla and beat with a hand mixer until smooth. Cover to keep hot.

## MERINGUE

9. Preheat your oven to 325°F. Beat egg whites and cream of tartar at high speed until frothy.

## INGREDIENTS:

### CRUST

| | |
|---|---|
| ⅝ | pound cake flour |
| ½ | teaspoon salt |
| 2 | ounces butter, frozen and grated |
| 2 | ounces lard |
| 2½ | ounces ice water |
| 1 | tablespoon heavy cream |
| 1 | egg yolk |

### FILLING

| | |
|---|---|
| 5 | tablespoons cake flour |
| ½ | cup cocoa, sifted |
| ⅛ | teaspoon salt |
| 2¼ | cups granulated sugar |
| 1¾ | cups evaporated milk |
| ¾ | cups water |
| 5 | large egg yolks |
| 2½ | teaspoons vanilla extract |
| 2½ | tablespoons butter |

### MERINGUE

| | |
|---|---|
| 1½ | egg whites, room temperature |
| ½ + ⅛ | teaspoon cream of tartar |
| 1¼ | cups sugar |

10  Very slowly, add sugar while the mixer is running. Beat until meringue can hold a stiff peak.

11  Pour your filling into pie shell while it's still piping hot, then immediately top with meringue.

12  Seal edges of pie first, then fill in the center and pile up high on pie in the shape of a beehive. To form peaks, use a spoon and go around the pie starting as close as you can get to the bottom working around in circles up to the top.

13  Bake at 325°F for 45 minutes. A few cracks should start forming on the meringue when you're done. Remove from heat. With a knife, cut a slit between the crust and meringue and prop pie on lip of pan to drain any excess liquid. Use a damp cloth to clean pie pans.

# KEY LIME CHIFFON PIE

**YIELDS:** 6 TO 8 SERVINGS / **ACTIVE TIME:** 30 MINUTES / **TOTAL TIME:** 2 HOURS

This is a fluffier version of a classic key lime pie. What I love about this one is the cloud-like consistency of the filling, which is the perfect complement to the tangy taste of the lime. Don't omit the lime zest from this recipe.

—*Dominique DeVito*

**INGREDIENTS:**

- 1 **graham cracker crust (see page 607)**
- 2 **cups heavy cream**
- ¼ **cup sugar**
- ⅓ **cup fresh squeezed lime juice**
- **Zest from 2 limes**
- 1 **envelope (about 1 tablespoon) unflavored gelatin**
- ½ **cup sweetened condensed milk**
- **Whipped cream and lime zest or wheels for garnish**

1 In a large bowl, beat the cream on high until peaks just start to form. Add the sugar and continue to beat on high until stiff peaks form.

2 In a small saucepan, combine the lime juice, zest, and gelatin, and stir until gelatin is dissolved. Turn the heat on to medium and cook the mixture until it begins to thicken, stirring constantly, about 3 to 5 minutes. Do not let it boil or burn. Remove from heat and allow to cool slightly. Stir in the sweetened condensed milk.

3 Fold this mixture into the whipped cream until combined and smooth. Don't overwork it.

4 Pour the filling into the crust. Cover with plastic wrap and refrigerate until set, about 45 minutes (or refrigerate for up to a day).

# GLUTEN-FREE GRAPEFRUIT CUSTARD PIE

**YIELDS:** 6 TO 8 SERVINGS / **ACTIVE TIME:** 60 MINUTES / **TOTAL TIME:** SEVERAL HOURS OR OVERNIGHT

This came to a dinner party I attended by way of a native Texan. She claimed that the grapefruits that grew in her yard produced something far tastier than what she made for us in New York, and if so, I'm not sure why she ever moved. The pie became an instant favorite of mine. I like it with vanilla ice cream.

—*Dominique DeVito*

1 In a small bowl, stir 2 cups sugar and flour until combined. In another bowl, whisk the egg yolks until well combined. Set aside.

2 Place the grapefruit pieces in a saucepan and add the water. Cook over medium heat, stirring constantly, until the water comes to a boil. Add remaining ½ cup sugar and continue to stir while the mixture boils, another 10 or so minutes. The grapefruit sections will fall apart and yield a thick, pulpy mixture.

3 Remove from heat and stir in the sugar/flour mixture. Add the sweetened condensed milk and stir gently to combine.

4 Put a large spoonful of the hot grapefruit mix into the egg yolks and whisk or stir briskly to combine. Repeat, and then transfer the egg yolk mixture to the saucepan and stir to combine all. Return to the heat and bring to a boil, stirring constantly, and cook for about 10 minutes more. Remove from heat and stir in the vanilla.

5 Pour into the pie crust and distribute evenly. Cover with plastic wrap and refrigerate for several hours or up to a day. When ready to serve, remove the plastic wrap and garnish with fruit slices, if desired. Top slices with vanilla ice cream.

**INGREDIENTS:**

1 baked crust (see page 600) or gluten-free crust (see page 604)

2½ cups sugar, divided

½ cup all-purpose gluten-free flour

4 egg yolks

4 red grapefruits, peeled, pith removed, and sections cut in half

2 cups water

1 (16-oz.) can sweetened condensed milk

1 teaspoon vanilla extract

Vanilla ice cream

Grapefruit or kiwi slices for garnish

# TOMATO PIE

YIELD: 8 TO 10 SERVINGS / ACTIVE TIME: 40 MINUTES / TOTAL TIME: 1 HOUR 30 MINUTES

You can make this you own special recipe by switching out your favorite cheeses and add spices that you like dill or basil.
—*courtesy of Jane Jaharian of The Sweetery*

1 Begin by making your filling: Cut 2 pounds of the tomatoes into ¼-inch slices. Place tomatoes in a single layer on paper towels and sprinkle with 1 teaspoon of salt. Let stand 30 minutes.

2 Preheat oven to 425°F. In a large bowl, stir together both cheeses, mayonnaise, beaten egg, chives, parsley, vinegar, onion, sugar, pepper and the remaining salt until combined evenly.

3 Pat tomato slices dry with a paper towel. Sprinkle cornmeal over bottom of crust. Lightly spread ½ cup of your cheesy mixture onto the crust and layer with half of the tomato slices in slightly overlapping rows.

4 Spread tomatoes with ½ cup of the cheese mixture and repeat using the rest of the tomato slices.

5 Cut the remaining ¾ pound of tomatoes into ¼-inch slices and arrange on top of pie.

6 Bake at 425°F for 40 to 45 minutes, shielding edges with foil during last 20 minutes to prevent excessive browning. Let stand 1 to 2 hours before serving.

**INGREDIENTS:**

- 1 of your favorite pie crusts (see page 610 for Sweetery's cream cheese pie crust)
- 2¾ pounds large tomatoes, divided
- 2 teaspoons kosher salt, divided
- 1½ cups shredded sharp cheddar cheese
- ½ cup shredded Parmigiano-Reggiano cheese
- ½ cup mayonnaise
- 1 large egg, lightly beaten
- 1 tablespoon chopped chives
- 1 tablespoon chopped parsley (optional)
- 1 tablespoon apple cider vinegar
- 1 green onion, thinly sliced
- 2 teaspoons sugar
- ¼ teaspoon black pepper
- 1½ tablespoons plain yellow cornmeal

# PHYLLO DOUGH

Pies, including fruit pies, are sometimes made with a different type of crust than the one used in traditional Northern European and American pies. The Austrian strudel became popular in Western Europe in the 19th century. In this type of pie, apples, raisins and pine nuts are wrapped into a very thin pastry, crisp and soft at the time. It is likely that the pastry on which strudel is based came from the East, in particular from Turkey. In fact, strudel dough seems to be a simplified version of phyllo dough, which was developed in the Turkish Ottoman Empire, and from there spread to Eastern Europe, Greece, the Middle East, and Northern Africa. The name phyllo is actually derived from Greek language, and it means leaf, much like the layers of thin dough this pastry is made of. Phyllo is indeed very popular in Greece, as it is in all the countries that were under the influence of the Ottoman Empire. In Romania, for example, it is called plaçinta. On the outskirts of the Ottoman Empire, in Maghreb, the pastry has been somewhat modified to obtain a slightly less thin version called warka, also called brik or briwat. It is used in the all Middle East to make baklava.

In Turkey itself, phyllo is called yufka. Yufka is a name used to indicate three different preparations. There is baklava yufka, a pastry dough meant for a sweet filling; there is börek yufka, used in savory dishes; and there is a third type of yufka that is thicker.

We are lucky enough to have at least one type of phyllo (or yufka) available in grocery stores, because making it at home is not done effortlessly. Phyllo did not originate from the home kitchens of common people but from the professional kitchens of the Turkish royalty. It soon started to be made with the help of machines, and although it is not impossible to make it at home, it does require mastery of the technique.

Phyllo is a real work of pastry art: a mixture of just flour and water, sometimes with the addition of very little vinegar, that needs to be rolled in extremely thin layers using a precise technique. The rolling needs to be fast and simultaneous otherwise the layers will dry and then they will not stick to one another any longer. In between layers, just a minimal brush with oil at the very end of the process, and there you have phyllo pastry.

What is special about using this crust for a pie, is that the taste experience will be on the lighter side. Not only because of the crispy, airy, consistency of the baked phyllo dough, but because this pastry uses almost no fat. Something to consider when your filling is particularly rich.

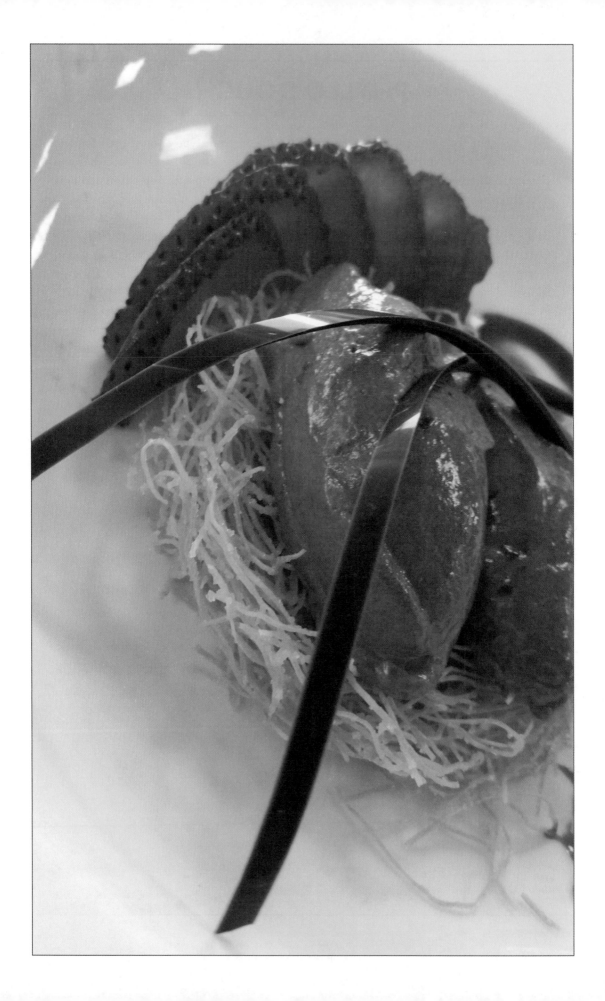

# KATAIFI *with* PISTACHIO AND HONEY

YIELD: 20 SMALL PASTRIES / ACTIVE TIME: 40 MINUTES / TOTAL TIME: 50-55 MINUTES

Kataifi, shredded phyllo dough that closely resembles noodles, needs to be treated just like regular phyllo dough in order to keep it from drying out. This is best done by covering it with a damp towel. Be generous with the butter to add as much flavor as you can.

—*Stephany Buswell*

1 Butter the sides and bottom of a 9-inch by 13-inch baking pan.

2 Make sure your kataifi is fully thawed. Take it out of the package and pull it apart very carefully. Place a slightly damp cloth over it so it doesn't dry out.

3 Make your syrup by combining sugar, honey, water, and lemon juice in a saucepan and bring to a boil. Stir until the sugar dissolves. Cook for another 4 minutes on medium heat. Turn off and let cool.

4 Preheat the oven to 350°F. Melt the butter in a saucepan. Pulse the nuts in a food processor until finely chopped.

5 Spread a portion of the kataifi out on a clean surface into a flat piece, about 6 inches by 4 inches. Paint it with the melted butter and place a spoonful of the nuts at the end of the piece of kataifi. Begin rolling it up, pulling the ends in as you roll it up to create small logs.

6 Continue this with the rest of the kataifi until the pan is filled with the little rolls.

7 Bake at 350°F for 10-12 minute or until golden brown. When you remove the pan, pour the syrup over it immediately.

INGREDIENTS:

1 package of thawed kataifi

1¼ cups (1½ sticks) unsalted butter

4 cups pistachios, finely chopped

2 tablespoons lemon juice

¾ cup water

1 cup sugar

½ cup honey (I prefer light honey, like clover honey)

# SPANIKOPITA TRIANGLES

**YIELD:** 24 TRIANGLES / **ACTIVE TIME:** 30 MINUTES / **TOTAL TIME:** 1 HOUR-1 HOUR 10 MINUTES

I love to travel to Greece and this is a classic pastry that you will find in almost every restaurant. It is often made like baklava, in a large pan cut into pieces; like little hand pies, these are easy and fun to eat with no utensils required. The filling varies but it always has spinach and feta cheese. I doctored this up with more flavor and you can adjust to your liking!

—*Stephany Buswell*

1 First, make your filling. Chop the onion and garlic and sauté in the oil until tender. Add the spinach and cook down. Add the dill and lemon juice and spread out on a plate to cool.

2 When cool add the cheese and the egg and stir until mixed.

3 Preheat oven 350°F. Place one sheet of the phyllo on a clean work surface. Paint it with melted butter and place another sheet on top.

4 With the longest end horizontal to the table, cut the sheet into 5 equal pieces. Each should be about 2 ½ inches wide.

5 Place a tablespoon of the filling at the end of each strip. Begin folding one into a triangle, like you would a flag. Continue folding until you reach the end. Place on a parchment-lined sheet pan. Continue this process until the filling is gone.

6 Paint the triangles with melted butter and bake in the oven for 25 to 30 minutes or until golden brown. Serve at room temperature.

## INGREDIENTS:

- 1 **package of thawed phyllo sheets**
- 4 **tablespoons melted butter**
- 2 **tablespoons olive oil**
- 1 **small onion, chopped**
- 2 **cloves garlic, chopped**
- 12 **ounces baby spinach**
- 8 **ounces feta cheese, crumbled**
- 1 **egg**
- 1 **tablespoon fresh dill, finely chopped**
- 1 **tablespoon lemon juice**

# TOP CRUST CHICKEN PIES

**YIELD:** 8 MINI PIES / **ACTIVE TIME:** 1 HOUR / **TOTAL TIME:** 3½ - 9½ HOURS

An instant favorite at our new Metropolitan Cafe, we fill this pie with chunks of roasted chicken thigh and breast. The addition of fresh thyme adds a surprise flavor. Few things compare to that first forkful, after piercing through the crust and watching the steam rise.

—*James Barrett and Wendy Smith Born, Metropolitan Bakery*

1 In the bowl of an electric mixer fitted with the paddle attachment, combine flour, sugar and salt. Add butter and mix on medium-low speed until mixture resembles coarse meal.

2 Cut the frozen shortening into small cubes and add to the flour. Mix only until evenly distributed. Large bits of shortening should remain visible as this will help create the flaky texture in the final pastry. Add the water and mix until combined.

3 Transfer the pastry to a work surface, and gather the pastry into a ball. Wrap in plastic and flatten to a disc. Refrigerate pastry for 2 hours or overnight.

4 Remove pastry from the refrigerator. Unwrap the pastry and on a lightly floured surface, roll the pastry to ¼-inch thickness. Cut 8 circles measuring 4 ¼ inches in diameter. Place them on a baking tray. Wrap the tray and refrigerate the pastry for 1 hour or overnight.

5 Preheat the oven to 375°F. Place chicken breast and thighs on a baking sheet and season with 1 teaspoon of salt and ¼ teaspoon of black pepper.

6 Place chicken in a preheated oven and roast for 30 to 35 minutes or until a thermometer plunged into the thickest part of the breast registers 160°F. Remove chicken from the oven and cool to room temperature. Remove the skin and pull the meat off the bones. Dice the chicken into medium-sized chunks and set aside.

7 Bring 1 quart of water to a boil and add potatoes and carrots. Return to boil and cook for 4 minutes. Strain the potatoes and carrots. Reserve the potatoes until needed.

8 Heat the olive oil in a large sauce pot. Add the onions, mushrooms, garlic, ½ teaspoon salt and ¼ teaspoon

**INGREDIENTS:**

**FOR THE FLAKY PIE CRUST:**

- 3 cups all-purpose flour
- ¼ cup granulated sugar
- 1½ teaspoons kosher salt
- 18 tablespoons cold, unsalted butter, cut into small cubes
- 4½ tablespoons vegetable shortening, frozen
- 10 tablespoons ice cold water

**FOR THE CHICKEN FILLING:**

- 1 chicken breast (2 halves), bone-in, skin-on
- 2 chicken thighs, bone-in, skin-on
- 1 tablespoon + 1 teaspoon kosher salt
- ¾ teaspoon ground black pepper
- 1 cup carrots, medium diced
- 1 cup yukon gold potatoes, medium diced
- 3 tablespoons extra virgin olive oil
- 1 medium onion, diced
- 2 cloves garlic, minced
- 1 cup cremini mushrooms, sliced
- ¼ cup dry vermouth or white wine
- 6 tablespoons unsalted butter
- ½ cup all-purpose flour
- 5 cups chicken stock, heated
- 1 cup frozen peas
- ½ cup flat leaf parsley, roughly chopped
- 2 tablespoons heavy cream
- 2 teaspoons fresh thyme leaves, roughly chopped
- 1 egg, beaten
- Coarse sea salt

black pepper. Sauté the vegetables on medium-low heat for 6 to 8 minutes until onions become translucent. Add vermouth or wine and cook 5 minutes longer. Add 5 tablespoon butter and stir until melted. Mix in the flour and cook for 3 minutes. Slowly pour in the warm chicken stock and stir until the stock thickens. Add the diced chicken, peas, potatoes, carrots, heavy cream, parsley, thyme, 2 teaspoons salt, and ¼ teaspoon black pepper. Continue to cook for 5 minutes. Remove from heat and cool. At this point, the filling may be refrigerated for 4 days.

9 To begin assembly, preheat oven to 350°F. Divide the chicken filling between eight 10-ounce ramekins on a baking tray. The ramekins we use measure 4 inches across the top and are 2 inches deep. Brush the rim and outside edge of each ramekin with the beaten egg. Place a ½ teaspoon of cold butter on the filling of in each ramekin. Remove pastry circles from the refrigerator and using the narrow end of a pastry tip, cut out the center of each circle. This is the vent that will allow steam to escape during baking.

10 Cover each ramekin with a pastry circle. Using your hands, gently smooth the edge of the pastry over the sides to adhere the pastry to the ramekins. Lightly brush the pastry with the beaten egg and sprinkle each with a pinch of sea salt. Bake for 40 to 50 minutes until the filling just begins to bubble and pastry is golden brown. Remove from the oven and cool for 3 to 5 minutes before serving.

# ASPARAGUS *and* GOAT CHEESE GALETTE

YIELD: 1 LARGE GALETTE, SERVES 4–6 / ACTIVE TIME: 10 MINUTES / TOTAL TIME: 1 HOUR

Because 100% whole wheat flour is highly absorptive, we added a touch of egg for additional moisture. We made this rustic tart to celebrate spring, dressing it with earthy, roasted asparagus and a tart layer of creamy goat cheese. Nutty whole wheat makes a perfect backdrop for these bold flavors. This would work beautifully with roasted mushrooms, carrots, or other spring vegetables—or, try sweetening the goat cheese with honey and sprinkling with dried lavender for a simple cheese galette.

—*recipe by Andrew Chaney of Oliveto and courtesy of Community Grains*

1 In a bowl, mix the flour with the salt. Using a pastry blender or your fingers, cut in half of the measurement of butter until the mixture resembles coarse meal. Cut in the remaining butter until the largest pieces are the size of peas. This can also be done in a food processor with a few short pulses. Stir in the egg and egg yolk until well combined, but be careful not to overwork.

2 Gather up the dough and knead it 2 or 3 times. Flatten the dough into a disk, wrap in plastic, and refrigerate for at least 30 minutes.

3 Preheat oven to 375°F. In a small bowl, combine the goat cheese, thyme leaves, and lemon juice. Mix until well combined.

4 Roll dough out on a floured work surface to a 14-inch-wide round, about ⅛ inch thick. Transfer to a baking sheet lined with parchment paper.

5 Spread the goat cheese mixture atop the dough, leaving about 2-inch border all the way around. Lay the asparagus atop the goat cheese mixture and fold up the edges of the dough over the asparagus and goat cheese. Leave the edges wild and rustic or use your thumb and index finger to form crimps around the edge.

6 Brush the crust with olive oil. Sprinkle the galette lightly with sea salt and freshly cracked pepper.

7 Bake for 20 to 25 minutes. Remove from oven and serve warm or at room temperature.

INGREDIENTS:

FOR CRUST:

1 cup Community Grains Hard White Whole Wheat Flour

⅓ cup Community Grains Hard Red Whole Wheat Flour

Pinch of salt

4 ounces (1 stick) cold unsalted butter, cut into ½-inch pieces

1 egg + 1 yolk, whisked

Zest of 1 lemon

FOR FILLING:

6 ounces goat cheese, room temperature

8 sprigs of thyme, stems removed

1½ teaspoons lemon juice

1 pound asparagus, washed and trimmed

# SUGAREE'S BAKERY HEIRLOOM TOMATO GALETTE

YIELDS: 14 GALETTES / ACTIVE TIME: 1 HOUR / TOTAL TIME: 1 HOUR 35 MINUTES

This crispy, buttery galette is simple in its execution but stunning in its finish, making it a hit at any party or bake sale.

1 Slice and lightly salt tomatoes, then put on cooling rack over sheet pan to drain for at least 30 minutes. Pat tomato slices dry with paper towels before using or put in a salad spinner to remove as much moisture as possible.

2 Mix pie crust and weigh out, wrap and chill 2½-ounce portions. Roll into 8-inch circles between two pieces of saran wrap.

3 Mix all non-tomato filling ingredients together and chill until ready to assemble.

4 Place 2–3 tablespoons filling in center of each crust. Top with tomato slices and sea salt. Fold and pinch crust around edges.

5 With a fork, mix together 1 tablespoon of heavy cream and 1 egg yolk. Using a pastry brush, lightly apply to crust and sprinkle with freshly grated Parmesan.

6 Cook on bottom rack of oven at 375°F for 30–35 minutes until golden and crispy. Top with fresh basil and serve.

## INGREDIENTS:

### CRUST

| | |
|---|---|
| 4 | cups flour |
| 8 | ounces butter |
| 1 | teaspoon salt |
| 1 | cup ice water |

### FILLING

| | |
|---|---|
| ¾ | cup freshly grated Parmigiano Reggiano |
| 2–3 | Purple Cherokee, or other red/purple tomatoes |
| 2–3 | Green Zebra, or other green tomatoes |
| 2–3 | Cream Sausage, or other yellow tomatoes |
| | Salt |
| 6 | ounces cream cheese |
| ¾ | cup mayo |
| ¾ | cup grated and squeezed onion |
| 2 | teaspoons fresh thyme |
| ¾ | teaspoons pepper |

### FINISHING INGREDIENTS

| | |
|---|---|
| 2 | tablespoons heavy cream |
| 2 | egg yolks |
| | Fresh basil |
| | Flake sea salt |
| ¾ | cup freshly grated Parmigiano Reggiano |

CAST-IRON SKILLET RECIPE

# PEANUT BUTTER PIE

YIELDS: 8 TO 10 SERVINGS / ACTIVE TIME: 30 MINUTES / TOTAL TIME: 90 MINUTES

Yes, peanut butter pie. And this pie tastes as amazing as it sounds. If you're looking for a peanut butter-cup kind of experience, you can also bathe the top in chocolate when cool. Try it, you'll love it.

—*Dominique DeVito*

1 Preheat the oven to 350°F.

2 In a large bowl, whisk the eggs until thoroughly combined. Add corn syrup and sugar, and whisk until sugar is completely dissolved. Whisk in the peanut butter and vanilla until smooth and combined. Don't over-whisk it.

3 Pour filling into the pie crust and sprinkle with the salted whole peanuts.

4 Put the skillet in the oven and bake for about 60 minutes or until a knife inserted toward the middle comes out clean. If the edge of the crust starts to overly brown, remove the skillet from the oven and put tin foil over the exposed crust until the filling is set. Allow to cool completely.

5 If you'd like to top with chocolate, put the morsels in a microwave bowl and heat in 15-second increments, stirring after each, until pieces are just melted. Drizzle over cooled pie and refrigerate until hard. Garnish with pecans, peanuts, or walnuts, if desired.

**INGREDIENTS:**

1 chocolate cookie crust (see page 609)

3 eggs

1 cup dark corn syrup

½ cup sugar

½ cup creamy all-natural peanut butter (with no added sugar)

½ teaspoon vanilla extract

1 cup salted peanuts (the higher the quality, the better)

6 ounces semi-sweet chocolate morsels (if desired)

Pecans, peanuts, or walnuts as garnish (if desired)

# TURKEY *and* SWEET POTATO POT PIE

YIELDS: 4 TO 6 SERVINGS / ACTIVE TIME: 45 MINUTES / TOTAL TIME: 90 MINUTES

This is a fun pot pie to make after Thanksgiving, when there tends to be leftover turkey and sweet potatoes. Feel free to add any other vegetable leftovers into the filling, such as green beans, creamed onions, or peas. If you're inspired, add the cumin. It adds an exotic flavor and gives a nice deep yellow color to the filling.

—*Dominique DeVito*

1 Preheat the oven to 350°F.

2 In a small skillet (not the cast-iron skillet), heat the olive oil. Add the onion and garlic and stir, cooking, for about 2 minutes. Add the sweet potato pieces and the thyme. Reduce the heat to low and cook, covered, stirring occasionally, until the sweet potatoes start to soften and the onions caramelize, about 5 minutes. Set aside.

3 Before starting to make the white sauce, be sure the milk is at room temperature. If it's not, microwave it so that it's just warm, about 15 to 20 seconds.

4 In the cast-iron skillet, over medium heat, melt the butter. Sprinkle the flour over it and stir quickly yet gently to blend the flour in with the butter. Reduce the heat slightly so the butter doesn't burn. Stir until the butter and flour are combined, a minute or so. They will form a soft paste.

5 Add just a little of the warm milk and stir constantly to blend it in. Add more milk in small increments, working after each addition to stir it into the flour and butter mixture smoothly. Work this way until all the milk has been incorporated. Continue to stir the sauce, cooking over low heat, until it thickens, about 5 minutes.

6 Add the turkey pieces, peas, and vegetable mixture from the other skillet, along with any other leftovers you think would taste good. If needed, add some additional milk so the filling isn't too thick. Season with salt, pepper, and cumin.

7 On a lightly floured surface, roll out the crust so it will fit over the filling. Lay it gently on top, push down slightly to secure, and cut 3 or 4 slits in the middle. Brush the crust with the half-and-half.

8 Put the skillet in the oven and bake for 30 to 40 minutes, until the crust is browned and the filling is bubbly.

9 Allow to cool slightly before serving.

## INGREDIENTS:

1 flaky pastry crust recipe for a single crust (see page 603)

2 tablespoons olive oil

½ yellow onion, diced

1 clove garlic, chopped

1 small sweet potato, peeled and cut into small cubes

½ teaspoon thyme

2 tablespoons butter, cut into smaller slices

2 tablespoons flour

1¼ cup milk at room temperature

1½ cups cooked turkey, cut into bite-sized pieces

1 cup frozen peas

Salt and pepper to taste

½ teaspoon cumin (optional)

1 tablespoon half-and-half

# BEEF *and* MUSHROOM POT PIE

**YIELDS:** 4 TO 6 SERVINGS / **ACTIVE TIME:** 45 MINUTES / **TOTAL TIME:** 90 MINUTES

When you're looking for something to pair with a big, dry red wine and it's a chilly fall day, remember this dish. Prepare the dish early in the day, then bake about an hour before you're ready for dinner, and this pot pie will be the perfect companion to that special bottle of wine.

—*Dominique DeVito*

**INGREDIENTS:**

| | |
|---|---|
| 1 | flaky pastry crust recipe for a single crust (see page 603) |
| 3 | tablespoons flour |
| 1 | teaspoon salt |
| 1 | teaspoon pepper |
| 1 | teaspoon paprika |
| ½ | cup beef pieces (stew meat) |
| 2 | tablespoons olive oil |
| ½ | yellow onion, diced |
| 2 | carrots, peeled and sliced |
| 1 | celery sticks, leaves removed, diced |
| 1 | cup mushrooms, sliced |
| ½ | cup beef broth |
| ¾ | cup stout beer |
| 2 | cloves garlic, crushed |
| ½ | teaspoon thyme |
| ½ | teaspoon rosemary |
| 1 | bay leaf |
| | Salt and pepper to taste |
| 1 | egg |
| 1 | tablespoon water |

**1** Preheat the oven to 400°F.

**2** In a large bowl, whisk together the flour, salt, pepper, and paprika. Add the beef pieces and toss to coat well. Set aside.

**3** In the cast-iron skillet, heat the oil over medium-high heat. Add the floured meat pieces and stir, cooking, until just browned on the outside. Add the garlic and stir, cooking together for a minute or so. Add the onion, carrots, celery, and mushrooms, and stir to brown the vegetables, about 2 minutes. Add the broth, beer, garlic, thyme, rosemary, and bay leaf. Stir and bring to a boil, stirring occasionally, then reduce the heat to low and simmer for 10 to 12 minutes, stirring occasionally, until meat and vegetables are tender. Remove from heat and allow to cool, about 30 to 40 minutes. Remove the bay leaf. Season with additional salt and pepper, if desired.

**4** On a lightly floured surface, roll out the crust so that it will just cover the meat mixture. Lay it gently on top, push down slightly to secure, and cut 4 or 5 slits in the middle. Beat egg with 1 tablespoon water and brush on the crust.

**5** Bake for about 30 to 40 minutes or until crust is browned and filling is bubbly.

**6** Allow to cool slightly before serving.

# BEET *and* RADICCHIO GALETTE

YIELDS: 4 TO 6 SERVINGS / ACTIVE TIME: 45 MINUTES / TOTAL TIME: 90 MINUTES

If you want to impress some lunch guests—or yourself, for that matter—make this beautiful galette. The flavors combine beautifully, and the deep red colors are as nice to look at as they are to eat.

—*Dominique DeVito*

**1** Preheat the oven to 400°F.

**2** Put the beet pieces in a large piece of aluminum foil. Drizzle with the olive oil. Bake for 30 to 40 minutes until the beets are soft. Carefully remove from the oven, open the foil packet so the beets cool, and reduce the temperature to 350°F.

**3** In a skillet other than the cast-iron, heat 1 tablespoon olive oil over medium heat, add the leeks, and cook , stirring, for about 5 minutes, until the leeks are soft and somewhat caramelized. Set half of the leeks aside, and add almost all the radicchio to the pan. Stir and cook over low heat, stirring occasionally, for about 8 minutes. Drizzle the balsamic over the mixture about half way through.

**4** In a bowl, combine the ricotta, parmesan, and egg, mixing well. Stir in the beets and the leek/radicchio mixture, and season with salt and pepper to taste.

**5** On a lightly floured surface, roll out the crust so that it is about 1 inch larger than the bottom of the pan. Melt 1 tablespoon of butter in the skillet, remove from heat, and lay the pastry crust in the pan.

**6** Place the ricotta/vegetable mixture in the center. Fold the edge up and so there is about an inch of crust along the outside. Brush with half-and-half.

**7** Put the skillet in the oven and bake for 25 to 30 minutes, until the crust is just golden.

**8** Top with the reserved radicchio, and continue to bake for another 10 to 15 minutes.

**INGREDIENTS:**

- **1** flaky pastry crust recipe for a single crust (see page 603)
- **1** large beet, peeled and cut into pieces
- **2** tablespoons olive oil, divided
- **2** leeks, white and light green parts only, cleaned and sliced very thin
- **1** head of red radicchio, sliced thin and separated so that some can be used on top
- **1** tablespoon balsamic vinegar
- **½** pound whole milk ricotta (don't substitute a lower-fat ricotta)
- **¼** cup grated parmesan cheese
- **1** egg
- Salt and pepper to taste
- **1** tablespoon butter
- **1** tablespoon half-and-half

# MUSHROOM, SPINACH, *and* LEEK GALETTE

YIELDS: 4 TO 6 SERVINGS / ACTIVE TIME: 30 MINUTES / TOTAL TIME: 90 MINUTES

Caramelized leeks are even sweeter than onions, and are a great, mellow complement to the earthy mushrooms and bright spinach that top this tart.

—*Dominique DeVito*

**INGREDIENTS:**

1   flaky pastry crust recipe for a single crust (see page 603)

4   tablespoons butter

2   leeks, white and light green parts only, washed and sliced thin

1½   cups sliced mushrooms (all white mushrooms or a combination of types)

4   cups baby spinach leaves

½   cup grated parmesan cheese

1   tablespoon half-and-half

1   Preheat the oven to 375°F.

2   In the cast-iron skillet, melt 2 tablespoons of the butter over medium heat and add the leeks. Cook, stirring, while leeks soften, about 2 minutes. Add the remaining 2 tablespoons of butter and mushrooms, and stir to combine. Allow to cook over low heat, stirring occasionally, until mushrooms are soft and leeks are caramelized, about 10 minutes.

3   Raise the heat to medium and add the baby spinach, stirring while the leaves wilt. When wilted, remove the skillet from the heat. Transfer the vegetables to a bowl but leave the melted butter on the skillet.

4   On a lightly floured surface, roll out the crust so that it is about 1 inch larger than the bottom of the pan and lay the pastry crust in the pan.

5   Place the vegetable mixture in the center. Fold the extra crust over to form a ring around the tart, and crimp the edges gently. Sprinkle with parmesan cheese and brush the crust with the half-and-half.

6   Put the skillet in the oven and bake for 20 to 30 minutes until the crust is golden and puffy.

# TOMATO, CHEVRE, *and* BASIL TART

**YIELDS:** 4 TO 6 SERVINGS / **ACTIVE TIME:** 30 MINUTES / **TOTAL TIME:** 90 MINUTES

If you want to throw together an elegant and easy-to-prepare tart that celebrates summer, this is it. Use a variety of tomatoes to add color and visual appeal, as the slice sizes will be different, too.

—*Dominique DeVito*

**1** Preheat the oven to 350°F.

**2** Put the tomato slices on a plate lined with paper towels, and sprinkle with the salt. Let the salt sit on the tomatoes for about 15 minutes, and turn the slices over.

**3** In the cast-iron skillet, heat the olive oil over medium heat and add the onions. Cook, stirring, until the onions are lightly browned, about 3 minutes. Season with salt and pepper. Transfer them to a bowl but keep the oil in the skillet.

**4** On a lightly floured surface, roll out the crust so that it is just larger than the bottom of the pan and lay the pastry crust in the pan.

**5** Spread the onions over bottom of the crust and dot with the goat cheese. Arrange the tomato slices so that they cover the bottom. Sprinkle with the crumbled feta or parmesan/romano blend. Drizzle lightly with olive oil.

**6** Put the skillet in the oven and bake at 350°F for 20 minutes then increase the heat to 400°F and bake an additional 10 minutes until top of tart is toasty.

**7** While tart is still warm, sprinkle with shredded basil leaves.

**INGREDIENTS:**

| | |
|---|---|
| 1 | flaky pastry crust recipe for a single crust (see page 603) |
| 1½ | pounds tomatoes, sliced about ¼-inch thick, seeds removed |
| 1 | tablespoon kosher salt |
| 2 | tablespoons olive oil, plus more for drizzling |
| 1 | Vidalia onion, thinly sliced |
| | Salt and freshly ground black pepper |
| 1 | cup (8 ounces) fresh chèvre (goat cheese) |
| ½ | cup crumbled feta or grated parmesan/romano |
| 8–10 | basil leaves, cut into threads |

CAST-IRON SKILLET RECIPE

# FIG, PROSCIUTTO, *and* CAMEMBERT TART

YIELDS: 4 TO 6 SERVINGS / ACTIVE TIME: 45 MINUTES / TOTAL TIME: 90 MINUTES

For this tart, it's important to use a baked crust, as this one doesn't need a lot of time in the oven. The figs are delicate and lose their flavor if overcooked.

—*Dominique DeVito*

1 Preheat the oven to 400°F.

2 In a skillet over medium heat, heat the olive oil and add the onions. Cook and stir until the onions are lightly browned, about 3 minutes. Add the prosciutto slices to the onions and cook, stirring, for an additional minute. Remove from heat.

3 Brush the Dijon mustard evenly over the bottom of the crust and top with the onion/prosciutto mix.

4 Cut the Camembert into ¼-inch thick wedges and place them decoratively over the onion mix. Next place the fig halves over the cheese. Don't overcrowd.

5 In a small bowl, whisk together the balsamic vinegar and honey. Drizzle the sauce over the tart.

6 Put the skillet in the oven and bake for 20 to 25 minutes until cheese is melted and figs are softened.

### INGREDIENTS:

| | |
|---|---|
| 1 | baked crust (see page 600) |
| 2 | tablespoons olive oil |
| ½ | onion, sliced thin |
| ½ | pound prosciutto, cut into 1-inch slices |
| 1 | tablespoon Dijon mustard |
| 1 | round Camembert, at room temperature |
| 6–8 | fresh figs, stems removed, cut in half |
| 3 | tablespoons aged balsamic vinegar |
| 1 | tablespoon honey |

# FRENCH POTATO TART

YIELDS: 4 TO 6 SERVINGS / **ACTIVE TIME:** 45 MINUTES / *TOTAL TIME:* 2 HOURS

I refer to this as a French potato tart because of the use of crème fraîche blanketing very thin potato slices, as in a traditional gratin. What takes it over the top is baking between two crusts. This is a fantastic side dish for roast meat or vegetables.

—*Dominique DeVito*

**INGREDIENTS:**

- **2** flaky pastry crust recipes for a double crust (see page 603)
- **2** pounds Yukon Gold potatoes, peeled
- **1¼** cups crème fraîche
- **1** tablespoon kosher salt
- **½** teaspoon black pepper

  **Pinch** of grated nutmeg
- **2** cloves garlic, crushed
- **2** teaspoons chopped fresh thyme
- **1** egg yolk
- **1** tablespoon half-and-half

**1** Preheat the oven to 400°F.

**2** Using a very sharp knife, a mandoline, or a spiralizer, slice the potatoes as thin as possible.

**3** In a bowl, combine the crème fraîche, salt, pepper, nutmeg, garlic, and thyme. Stir to combine.

**4** Add the potato slices and fold gently to cover with the crème, making sure slices are completely covered.

**5** On a lightly floured surface, roll out the crust so that it is just larger than the bottom of the pan and lay the pastry crust in the pan.

**6** Using your hands, start layering the potato slices in the crust, creating even, tight layers. When all the potatoes are in the crust, use a rubber spatula to scrape the cream mixture into the pie. Tap the edges of the skillet to distribute the mix evenly.

**7** On a lightly floured surface, roll out the top crust and crimp the edges with the bottom crust to seal. Blend the egg yolk with the half-and-half and brush the mixture over the top crust. Cut 4 to5 slits in the middle.

**8** Put the skillet in the oven and bake at 400°F for 15 minutes, then reduce oven temperature to 350°F and continue to bake for 1 hour until potatoes are tender.

**9** Serve hot or at room temperature.

## Lindley Mills

7763 Lindley Mill Road
Graham, NC 27253
(336) 376-6190
www.lindleymills.com

One would be hard-pressed to find a mill more historic than Lindley Mills, which has been around since 1755! The scene of the Revolutionary War's bloodiest battle in North Carolina—the Battle of Lindley's Mill—the mill has withstood the test of time to produce high-quality flour for centuries. Says President Joe Lindley, "Thomas Lindley, my six-times great-grandfather, built Lindley's Mill and passed it on to his children and grandchildren. While it hasn't always been in the family, the family milling heritage helped spark my interest. Today, I am inspired to make the best possible products for our customers and to continue to push the boundaries of flour milling to achieve the most flavorful and nutritious flours."

Today, Lindley Mills functions as a jack-of-all-trades, popular for everything from its Super Sprout™ Sprouted Whole Grain Wheat Flour to several specialty products like organic rye, spelt, whole wheat, and white flours and organic yellow cornmeal and grits. The mill is flexible, and that flexibility allows Joe Lindley to custom-mill whatever his client needs. The result is a North Carolina Mill that has earned—and maintained—respect over the course of three centuries.

# IN HIS OWN WORDS:

## JOE LINDLEY OF LINDLEY MILLS

*How and when did you get your start in this industry?*

My family purchased Lindley's Mill in 1975 after I graduated from college, and we worked together to begin restoration. As we looked into the area's rich milling history I learned a lot about water-powered flour mills. We refurbished the structure, built and installed the water wheel, moved and connected grinding stones, and began milling flour. I was hooked immediately. There is nothing quite like making flour. It's satisfying and challenging, taking skill, focus, science, and craftsmanship. Most flour today is milled by large, industrial flour mills which produce high volumes of three or four flours. Instead we custom-mill a wide variety of products using different types of grain.

*What is your golden rule for milling?*

One axiom the old-time millers shared when I was starting out was, "You can't make good flour out of bad wheat, but you can make bad flour from good wheat." So in order to provide the best possible flour you have to start with good wheat and treat the wheat, through the milling process, with care and respect. If you succeed, your reward will be the opportunity to mill more flour. Another rule we mill by is similar to the actual golden rule: "Make flour for others that you'd like to eat yourself." Not only do we frequently taste test our own products, but we buy most of our bread from local bakers and eat at local restaurants which use our flours. This is why we have always chosen to mill certified organic flours and why we have consistently pursued the most stringent Global Food Safety certifications. High quality and consistency is our standard and we want our customers to have the best.

*What does Lindley Mills represent to you?*

Lindley Mills represents a lifetime of work and accomplishment for both me and my wife, Teresa, who has been my partner in the mill. I couldn't have made it without all of her hard work and we are excited to be teaching the ropes to our daughter Caroline, who has just joined us full-time. The mill is a great teacher and we have enjoyed watching it grow. It has been a challenge and an opportunity to provide food for hundreds of millions of people over the years as well as innovate in a category with such a wide reach.

*What is your favorite type of grain? Why? Least favorite grain? Why?*

We mill a large variety of grains, but wheat is by far the most prevalent and provides one-fifth of the world's food calories. Its unique possession of gluten allows it to expand and be a vehicle for other nutritious inclusions such as other grains, fruits, and nuts. Wheat has significantly contributed to the development of human society as it has always provided a renewable and reliable source of food.

*How did Lindley Mills come to be? Why Graham, NC? What are your most popular items?*

My ancestor Thomas Lindley established Lindley Mills in 1755. He moved here from Pennsylvania in the 1750s and built his Mill on the Cane Creek. The location was likely chosen because of the unique shape of Cane Creek and the available water to provide power to the mill. It was also located at the intersection of the Western Trading Route and the Cape Fear Road to Wilmington, which were the major thoroughfares of the day.

Our Mill has had several brushes with Revolutionary War history, including at least one instance when flour was "requisitioned" from the Mill to feed the troops of British General, Lord Cornwallis when they were camped in the area.

In the foggy dawn of September 12, 1781, the Loyalist forces captured the Governor of North Carolina, Thomas Burke, in Hillsborough and were marching him to Wilmington. The next morning, on September 13th, Patriot forces laid an ambush on the ridge just yards from the Mill during a conflict that would later be called the Battle of Lindley's Mill. It was the bloodiest per-capita battle of the Revolutionary War in North Carolina. Ultimately, the Whig forces were not able to rescue the Governor and other prisoners who were being held in the Spring Friends Meeting House further up the road, but they did wound Colonel Fanning and slow the Tory forces down. Interestingly, the founder of the Mill, Thomas Lindley, died on the day of the battle, although it's unlikely that he was involved in the conflict.

Today we continue to honor the traditions of our ancestors by making the highest quality, certified organic flours we can and providing them to both large bakeries and our local neighbors. Some of our most popular items include our Super Sprout™ Sprouted Whole Grain Wheat Flour and several of our specialty products like organic rye, spelt, whole wheat, and white flours, as well as stoneground organic yellow cornmeal and grits.

*Where do you get your tools/materials? What non-essential items should every home baker have?*

We sample and test wheat from all across the United States in our state-of-the-art in-house lab. Then we buy the highest quality certified organic wheat to make our flours. We also make an effort to purchase certified organic North Carolina wheat from our neighbors whenever possible.

If you have an oven, water, salt, Lindley Mills flour, and yeast, you can make an excellent loaf of bread without fancy tools or gadgets.

*What outlets/periodicals/newspapers do you read or consult regularly, if any?*

I enjoy skimming *Milling & Baking Magazine, QA Magazine, Food Business News,* and *The Wall Street Journal* to see what's happening.

*Brag about yourselves a bit. What is your highest achievement and/or proudest moment as a miller?*

I'd have to say my highest achievement as a miller is the creation of Super Sprout™ Sprouted Whole Grain Wheat Flour. I always wanted to create a whole wheat flour that tasted better so that more people would be interested in eating whole grains. The sprouting of the wheat unlocks the live potential of the wheat seed, enhancing the digestibility, nutritional availability, and flavor. One day, I believe that 'all whole wheat, whole grain flour will be made this way since it's so much more nutritious and flavorful. Being able to develop something that encourages more people to eat whole grains is quite satisfying and has been a lifetime achievement.

*Where did you learn to become a miller? Please tell me about your education.*

My college degree was in science, but not milling science. My milling education was trial-and-error and fueled by my desire to meet bakers' directives. I tailored the entire process to make the specialty products requested by our customers in the historic space we had available. I have gradually made changes to update our equipment over time and keep up with changing tastes. Today we are certainly not a traditional industrial mill, but we use both modern equipment and old-world traditions to grind the best flour.

*Tell me about your milling process. What makes your mill special?*

Our mill is set up to do a variety of products and to custom-mill many different grains. This allows us to stay flexible and switch between different products to custom-mill our orders fresh for the customer. Furthermore, to be grinding grain into flour in the same space that our many times great-grandfathers did more than 260 years ago is really special. Knowing the Revolutionary Era history just adds another layer.

# SWEET BREADS *and* TARTS

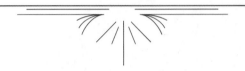

## BAKING TO CELEBRATE

Imagine that a festivity is approaching, or that you have a few days off to spend at home with family. What would your hands itch to knead and bake? Most likely something sweet. Probably a quick bread or a tart. This is not surprising because our taste for sweet breads comes from the traditional use of these types of breads for special occasions.

When looking at the rich display of treats at a downtown café, one might erroneously believe that sweet breads are a treat that people have always had the chance to enjoy daily. This is not the case and we know that, in the not so far away past, sweet treats were surely not an everyday pleasure. Typical ingredients of sweet breads are eggs, butter, honey, sugar, spices, dried fruit, and nuts. Anything that can make a dough sweet and rich. In professional baking jargon, sweet breads are in fact called *enriched doughs*. To use so many resources in just one bake was something the big majority of people could only afford in special occasions. Things were of course different for the privileged classes that could have cake all-year-round like we do today. *Noblesse oblige*–a surely sweet and delectable duty.

Every traditional sweet bread has its own history, but there is a common thread: the intention of baking something sultry, different from the daily bread. Something sweet, like what gods and goddesses ate, according to ancient populations' folklore. The tradition of sweet bread is in fact very ancient and often connected to religious celebrations.

From the German *Stollen* and the Italian *Panettone* for Christmas, to the English *Hot Cross Buns* and the Greek *Tsoureki* for Easter, and the *Kaffebröd* like *Kanelfläta* for the Swedish Sunday. From *Pan de Muerto* for the Mexican All Saints Day to the Muslim *Baklava* enjoyed during Ramadan and *Babka* for the Jewish Rosh Hashanah. Very different geographical areas, different religions, and festivities, but the common thread is that bread has to be sweet to make everyone acknowledge that the occasion is indeed a celebration.

Tarts are a special case of sweet breads linked to the European tradition and are made with unleavened enriched dough. The term tart defines an open-faced pie with a jam-based or creamy filling. This type of preparation has ancient origins, but became common in the 15th century. Many tarts developed on the tables of the rich, but others were instead linked to specific cultural traditions, like the Neapolitan *Pastiera*. This particular tart is filled with ricotta cheese and boiled wheat berries, and flavored with orange blossoms. It is still traditional in Naples, and surrounding areas, to bake several pastiera tarts before Easter and give them away to relatives and friends. It is believed that this tart may be a variation of an ancient Roman sweet bread containing cheese and wheat berries, which was part of a pagan ritual to celebrate spring and the goddess of grains, Ceres.

Nowadays, while some sweet breads and tarts continue being baked and eaten on their specific holidays, several of them have become available all-year-round. This is due to the increased availability of the main ingredients of sweet breads and tarts. Sugar, spices, dried fruit, eggs, and butter, once rare or expensive, now are considered basic food items. We can cheaply splurge on "enriching" ingredients and bake this incredible variety of sultry breads and pastries any day of the year. Surely one could be tempted to do so, having the time. Luckily, there is as a solution for everyone's baking needs. Quick breads only take a handful of minutes to mix, and some tarts can also be rather quick to make as well. For the more ambitious baker, yeasted sweet doughs are a stand-alone type of baking, which will completely thrill you once you put your hands at them. There are easy yeasted breads, like a Swedish *Saffransbröd* (bread with saffron), and more demanding ones, like *Panettone*. A sourdough-based panettone will keep you secluded in your own home for two whole days—but it may be all worth it.

Ultimately, it is entirely up to the baker to decide what can better satisfy the itch to do something special, happy, and celebrative. The fact that most sweet breads have origins connected to local folklore adds a certain ancient charm to these bakes. It is like baking a piece of culture and the best part of it is that the outcome will be time-tested delicious. It is also a wonderful way to share with your family and friends, and to have edible gifts to give away as presents. Sweet breads are in fact meant for sharing, enabling you to bake as many of them you want, without a hint of guilt.

# Flour Bakery

www.flourbakery.com

30 Dalton Street
Boston, MA 02115
(857) 233-2255

12 Farnsworth St.
Boston, MA 02210
(617) 338-4333

114 Mt. Auburn St.
Cambridge, MA 02138
(617) 714-3205

190 Massachusetts Ave.
Cambridge, MA 02139
(617) 225-2525

40 Erie St.
Cambridge, MA 02139
(617) 945-0322

131 Clarendon St.
Boston, MA 02116
(617) 437-7700

1595 Washington St.
Boston, MA 02118
(617) 267-4300

*Breadquarters*
9 Travis Street
Allston, MA 02134

It's nearly impossible to talk about the New England baking scene without going on a tangent about Flour Bakery + Café, Joanne Chang's highly acclaimed bakery chain. Chang, a true culinary star, has been featured or reviewed in too many publications to count—from *Zagat* to *Food & Wine* to dozens of Boston outlets. In 2007, she beat celebrity chef Bobby Flay on *Food Network's* "Throwdown with Bobby Flay," besting his sticky bun with her own now-famous recipe. And she won the James Beard Foundation's award for Outstanding Baker in 2016. In other words: Joanne Chang is a busy woman.

Incredibly, all of this could have never happened had Chang ignored her gut. After graduating from Harvard with a degree in Applied Math and Economics, she began her career as a management consultant at The Monitor Group in Cambridge. Thus began two years of spreadsheets and meetings that never quite suited Chang, despite the respect she held for her bosses. And so, she began applying for work at Boston's top restaurants. Chef Lydia Shire gave her a start at the bottom of the totem pole at Biba, where she worked for a year before leaving to work with Rick Katz at his bakery in Newton Center. Before long, Chang was working at Payard Patisserie with legendary pastry chef Francois Payard.

"He was the stereotypical French chef. He yelled a lot in French and English, threw things at times, was such a perfectionist." I spent a year with him working from 4 a.m. to

7 p.m., 6 days a week. I'm not exaggerating. We all worked this hard—it was sort of like boot camp. Of course, I learned so much! But I also realized that no one can work those hours and stay sharp and strong. It was while I was in NYC that I started thinking about opening a bakery of my own. I had loved working with Rick and all of the personal touches we were able to give our customers, and I dreamed of opening a place back in Boston in which we would make everything from scratch and we would give the best service ever. We would be like the bakery version of Cheers."

Chang realized her dream in 2000, opening the first Flour Bakery + Café in Boston's South End. She has skyrocketed since then, but the bakeries' collective mission statement has remained unchanged: "total unwavering com-mitment to excellence in every way." The afore-mentioned sticky buns are perhaps the best in the country, but everything baked at Flour is reliably delicious and fresh—so much, in fact, that you may have to prepare for a (well worth it) line!

Today, Chang owns seven Flour locations in addition to their "Breadquarters" (where Flour's offices and baking classes can be found) and Myers+Chang, a sit-down restaurant she operates with chef Karen Akunowicz and co-owns with her husband, Chris Myers. If this all sounds like too much, don't worry; Chang has been so successful at every level that it's fair to wonder if she's just getting started.

# IN HER OWN WORDS:

## JOANNE CHANG

*Who inspired you to bake? Who inspires you now?*

My first pastry chef, Rick Katz, was such a perfectionist. He taught me and inspired me to always make sure everything I made was so delicious you couldn't stop eating it. And that's the barometer I use today.

Today my husband Christopher is my biggest inspiration. Making something that knocks his socks off is the best feeling I know, and I'm always pursuing that elusive goal.

*How and when did Flour get its start?*

Once I had the idea to open my own bakery, I left New York and moved back to Boston, where I worked as the pastry chef at Mistral for two years while I planned. I found the location for the first Flour somewhat by chance. My best friend was getting married and I made her wedding cake. One of the guests told me I should do this professionally. I told him that I did and that I was looking for a space to open up my own place. He gave me his business card...and he is now our landlord at Flour.

We opened September 2000 in the South End, and my goal from the very beginning was to make the best pastry and food possible and provide super warm and genuine neighborhood service. I also wanted to give back to the neighborhood by giving a certain percentage of our sales to charity. Flour had to run efficiently as well in order for us to continue so I included "run profitably and efficiently" as another mission. Finally, my main mission at Flour was to make everyone's lives better—for our customers, through amazing food and service, and (more importantly) for the Flour employees by being an awesome, inspiring, and supportive place to work. Those were my missions in 2000 and they are my missions today.

*What is your golden rule for bakers?*

TASTE. Always. Everything. Constantly.

*What is your favorite thing to bake? Why? Least favorite thing to bake? Why?*

Anything laminated! I love the challenge and the beauty of laminated doughs.

I honestly can't think of anything I don't love to bake. Breads, tarts, cookies, brioche, danish, cakes… I love it all.

*What are your most popular items?*

Sticky buns, chocolate chip cookies, and banana bread. Oh, and egg sandwiches and BLTs.

*What food outlets/periodicals/newspapers do you read or consult regularly, if any?*

*Food & Wine*, *Boston Globe* and *NY Times* Food Section, *Eater*, Instagram.

**Tell me about your most memorable collaboration(s) with another chef.**

Chef Karen Akunowicz! She has made Myers+Chang so much stronger, and I love our collaboration.

**What is your proudest moment as a chef? Bragging is encouraged here.**

Honestly every time a guest comes up to me to tell me how great the staff is, what an incredible pastry they had, how M+C is their favorite restaurant, how Flour/M+C has made their trip memorable—that's when I'm super proud.

**What lessons did you learn during your first baking gig?**

Working for Rick Katz was like enrolling in the most rigorous baking school ever. He was fanatical about pastry and relentless in his pursuit of making the most delicious desserts I'd ever tasted. He only used the best ingredients. He preferred, for example, to make his own vanilla extract and to shred his own coconut. He was a stickler about perfect technique as well and the waste bins often overflowed after my shifts because he deemed one cake after another not tender enough or light enough.

# FLOUR'S FAMOUS BANANA BREAD

**YIELDS:** 1 9-INCH LOAF / **ACTIVE TIME:** 45 MINUTES / **TOTAL TIME:** 2 HOURS

I remember grocery shopping with my mom and toting home large bags of overripe bananas when we found them on special for ten cents a pound. My mom would encourage my brother, my dad, and me to "have a banana!" every time we were near the kitchen. My brother and I began to avoid the kitchen for fear of being accosted by Mom and her banana entreaties. In time, I developed this banana bread as a protection device for us. We loved it so much we sometimes found ourselves buying more bananas just to make it.

—*recipe and photos courtesy of Flour Bakery*

1 Position a rack in the center of the oven, and heat the oven to 325°F. Butter a 9-by-5-inch loaf pan.

2 In a bowl, sift together the flour, baking soda, cinnamon, and salt. Set aside.

3 Using a stand-mixer fitted with the whip attachment (or a handheld mixer), beat together the sugar and eggs on medium speed for about 5 minutes, or until light and fluffy. (If you use a handheld mixer, this same step will take about 8 minutes.)

4 On low speed, slowly drizzle in the oil. Don't pour the oil in all at once. Add it slowly so it has time to incorporate into the eggs and doesn't deflate the air you have just beaten into the batter. Adding it should take about 1 minute. Add the bananas, crème fraîche, and vanilla and continue to mix on low speed just until combined.

5 Using a rubber spatula, fold in the flour mixture and the nuts just until thoroughly combined. No flour streaks should be visible, and the nuts should be evenly distributed. Pour the batter into the prepared loaf pan and smooth the top.

6 Bake for 1 to 1¼ hours, or until golden brown on top and the center springs back when you press it. If your finger sinks when you poke the bread, it needs to bake a little longer. Let cool in the pan on a wire rack for at least 30 minutes, and then pop it out of the pan to finish cooling.

7 The banana bread can be stored tightly wrapped in plastic wrap at room temperature for up to 3 days. Or, it can be well wrapped in plastic wrap and frozen for up to 2 weeks; thaw overnight at room temperature for serving.

**INGREDIENTS:**

- 1½ cups (210 grams) unbleached all-purpose flour 1 teaspoon baking soda
- ¼ teaspoon ground cinnamon
- ½ teaspoon kosher salt
- 1 cup plus 2 tablespoons (230 grams) sugar
- 2 eggs
- ½ cup (100 grams) canola oil
- 3½ very ripe, medium bananas, peeled and mashed (1 cups mashed/ about 340 grams)
- 2 tablespoons crème fraîche or sour cream
- 1 teaspoon vanilla extract
- ¾ cup (75 grams) walnut halves, toasted and chopped

# LEMON ZUCCHINI BREAD *with* LEMON GLAZE

YIELD: 1 LOAF / ACTIVE TIME: 30 MINUTES / TOTAL TIME: 1 HOUR AND 15 MINUTES

This lemony, moist cake goes great with your morning coffee or afternoon tea!
—*Stephany Buswell*

1 Preheat the oven to 350°F. In a large mixing bowl, combine the flour, baking soda, baking powder, and salt. Mix with a spoon to combine.

2 In another bowl, mix together the oil, sugar, egg, lemon juice, zest, and zucchini to combine.

3 Pour the wet ingredients into the dry and stir to combine. When the dough is mixed about halfway, drop in the lemon pieces and mix very carefully—only until all the dry ingredients are wet.

4 Pour into a 9-inch by 5-inch buttered loaf pan. Bake at 350°F for 50–55 minutes or until a toothpick comes out clean.

5 While the bread bakes, make the glaze: Sift the powdered sugar into a bowl, add the lemon juice and zest, and stir until it is smooth and runs off a spoon in an even stream. Add more lemon if you need to.

6 When the cake is done, turn it out onto a cooling rack. Spoon the glaze over it after it has cooled.

## INGREDIENTS:

- 1 ½ cups all-purpose flour
- ½ teaspoon baking soda
- ¼ teaspoon baking powder
- ¼ teaspoon salt
- ¾ cup sugar
- 1 cup finely shredded, unpeeled zucchini
- ¼ cup sunflower oil
- 1 egg
- 2 tablespoon lemon juice + the meat of 1 lemon
- 2 tablespoons finely shredded lemon peel

## FOR THE GLAZE:

- ½ cup powdered sugar
- 1 tablespoon lemon juice
- Zest of 1 lemon

Peel the lemon with a paring knife, and use the blade to cut inside each membrane of the lemon, letting the "meat" of the lemon loose. Cut each piece in half.

# CHOCOLATE CHIP BANANA BREAD

**YIELD:** 1 9-INCH X 5-INCH LOAF / **ACTIVE TIME:** 15 MINUTES / **TOTAL TIME:** 1 HOUR

One of my favorite summertime treats growing up was a frozen banana dipped in chocolate. Chocolate and bananas are the best of friends. They go together like salt and pepper! This bread is a great breakfast loaf, but it works just as well with ice cream and chocolate sauce for a fast and delicious dessert. Make sure you use overripe bananas for this, as their sweetness is necessary to play off the dark chocolate.

—*Stephany Buswell*

1 Preheat the oven to 350°F and butter and flour your pan.

2 In the bowl of a stand-mixer, cream together the butter and brown sugar until light and fluffy.

3 Mix in the eggs one at a time, scraping the sides of the bowl between each addition. Add the bananas and sour cream.

4 Sift together the flour, salt, baking powder, and baking soda. Add it to the butter mixture. Stir gently until it is almost totally incorporated and then take the bowl off the mixer.

5 Pour in the chocolate and nuts. Mix by hand with a wooden spoon to ensure you do not over-mix.

6 Pour into the prepared pan and bake for 40 to 50 minutes or until a toothpick comes out clean.

**INGREDIENTS:**

- 1½ cubes unsalted butter, room temperature
- 1 cup light brown sugar, firmly packed
- 3 eggs
- 1 cup smashed overripe bananas
- 2 tablespoons sour cream
- 1¾ cup all-purpose flour
- 1 teaspoon baking soda
- ¼ teaspoon baking soda
- ¼ teaspoon salt
- 1 cup semisweet chocolate chips
- ½ cup chopped walnuts (optional)

# PUMPKIN GINGER LOAF

**YIELD:** 1 9-INCH X 4-INCH LOAF / **ACTIVE TIME:** 10 MINUTES / **TOTAL TIME:** 1 HOUR-1 HOUR 10 MINUTES

This spicy version is versatile and festive. Some folks enjoy putting chocolate chips in as well. Personally, I love to add toasted nuts—pecans in particular add a nice crunch to this velvety moist bread. It lasts a long time at room temperature and can be frozen for weeks. Try baking it as a holiday gift!
—*Stephany Buswell*

1 Preheat your oven to 350°F. Sift together the dry spices, flour, salt, baking powder, and baking soda.

2 In a large bowl, mix together the pumpkin, sugar, oil, and eggs. Pour the wet into the dry and gently stir together until incorporated.

3 Pour the batter into a greased and floured pan.

4 Bake 350°F for 50 to 60 minutes or until a toothpick comes out clean.

**INGREDIENTS:**

- 1½ cups all-purpose flour
- 1 teaspoon baking powder
- ½ teaspoon baking soda
- 1 tablespoon candied ginger, finely chopped
- 1 teaspoon ground cinnamon
- Pinch of cloves
- ¾ cup packed dark brown sugar
- 1 cup canned pumpkin puree
- ½ cup sunflower oil
- 2 eggs

# ORANGE CINNAMON-SCENTED YAM MUFFINS
## *with* HONEY CREAM CHEESE ICING

**YIELD:** 24 MUFFINS /**ACTIVE TIME:** 30 MINUTES /**TOTAL TIME:** 50 MINUTES

I was once hired by Toyota and the Monterey Farmers Markets to create recipes highlighting the local farmers and vendors. It was so much fun, and this recipe was one of my yummiest creations. Moist, sweet, and addictive, it uses the yams, honey, eggs, oranges, and cream cheese I found at the market.
—*Stephany Buswell*

1 Preheat your oven to 350°F. Sift all the dry ingredients together in a large bowl.

2 In another bowl, mix the oil, eggs, and zest. Pour the mixture into the dry ingredients.

3 Put the yams in last and stir only until mixed. A few lumps are okay.

4 Spoon into lined muffins tins and bake at 350°F for about 20 to 25 minutes or until springy when touched.

5 While your muffins bake, make your icing. First, cream the cream cheese and butter until there are no lumps left. Add the orange blossom honey, powdered sugar, and vanilla, and mix until smooth.

6 Remove your muffins and let cool briefly. While they're still warm, use a small butter knife or icing spatula to smear icing onto the muffins, then top with either chopped toasted walnuts or pecans.

**INGREDIENTS:**

- 2 cups all-purpose flour, sifted
- 1½ teaspoons baking soda
- ¼ teaspoon cloves
- 1½ teaspoons cinnamon
- 1 teaspoon salt
- 2 cups sugar
- 1½ cups vegetable oil
- 4 eggs
- 2 tablespoons orange zest
- 2 cups cooked yams

**FOR THE ICING:**

- 2 ounces unsalted butter, room temperature
- 3 ounces cream cheese, room temperature
- 3 ounces orange blossom honey
- 5 ounces powdered sugar
- 1 teaspoon vanilla

# KING CAKE (BRIOCHE DES ROIS)

YIELDS: 1 LOAF / ACTIVE TIME: 40 MINUTES / TOTAL TIME: 3½ HOURS

There are several versions of King Cake, which is a sweet bread traditional to several different countries. The original cake that probably inspired all the others is French and was eaten for the Epiphany, also called the Three King's Day.

**INGREDIENTS:**

| | |
|---|---|
| 1¾ | teaspoon (5 g) active dry yeast |
| 3 | ounces (85 g) milk |
| 12.3 | ounces (350 g) all-purpose flour |
| 1.8 | ounces (50 g) confectioner's sugar |
| 1 | egg plus 1 egg yolk |
| 1 | teaspoon orange blossoms water |
| 2.8 | ounces (80 g) butter |
| 1 | teaspoon (5.6 g) salt |

**FINISH**

| | |
|---|---|
| 1 | egg |
| | Sugar |
| | Candied fruit in big chunks |

1 Heat the milk to 100–110°F. Dissolve the yeast in the milk and let rest for 5 minutes. In a large bowl, combine the milk-yeast mixture with the flour, the sugar, the egg, and the orange blossoms water.

2 Start working the dough, either with a stand-mixer or by hand (see page 63 for tips on kneading). Gradually add the butter, continuing to work the dough, and incorporate the salt towards the end of the kneading. Work the dough until it feels smooth. The mixing process takes about 20 minutes from start to finish.

3 Let the dough rest, covered, in a warm spot until it looks fully risen. This should take about 1 to 1½ hours.

4 Transfer the dough to a clean and floured surface and shape into a ball.

5 Prepare a baking dish lined with parchment paper and dusted with flour. Place the dough ball in the center of the dish and slightly flatten it. Using your hands, make a hole in the center of the dough and gently enlarge the hole, creating a crown.

6 Preheat oven to 320°F.

7 Let the crown rest, covered, about 1 to 1½ hours, depending on room temperature.

8 Brush the crown with the egg, slightly whisked with 1 tablespoon of water.

9 Bake for 30 to 35 minutes, covering with aluminum foil if the crown is browning too fast.

10 Combine 3 tablespoon sugar with ⅓ cup water and heat until the sugar is dissolved. Brush the hot crown with the sugar bath and decorate with the candied fruit.

# HOT CROSS BUNS

**YIELDS:** 12-15 BUNS / **ACTIVE TIME:** 50 MINUTES / **TOTAL TIME:** ABOUT 4 HOURS

Traditional sweet buns originated in England, probably in St. Albans, during the Middle Age. They were supposed to be eaten only on the Friday preceding Easter or at burials. As delicious as they are, hot cross buns are now available all-year-round in several places.

1 Heat the water to 100–110°F. Dissolve the yeast in the water and let rest for 5 minutes. In a large bowl, combine the water-yeast mixture with the warmed milk, ½ of the flour, and the sugar.

2 Add one egg at a time and incorporate well. Add the rest of the flour and start working the dough, either with a stand-mixer or by hand (see page 63 for tips on kneading).

3 Add the butter in pieces, continuing to work the dough, and incorporate the salt towards the end of the kneading.

4 Work the dough until it feels smooth. The mixing process takes about 20 minutes from start to finish.

5 Let the dough rest, covered, in a warm spot until it looks fully risen. This should take about 1 to 2 hours.

6 Transfer the dough to a clean surface. Incorporate all other ingredients, folding them in until evenly distributed.

7 Divide the dough in 12 to 15 pieces of about 2½ to 2¾ oz (70-80 g) each. Roll into small rounds and place on one or two baking trays covered with parchment paper.

8 Cover with an oiled plastic film or place into a big, clean plastic bag and let rest for about 1 to 1½ hours.

9 Preheat oven to 425°F.

10 Prepare the finish for the cross by combining the flour with the water and filling a piping bag with it. Decorate the top of each bun by piping a cross over it. Bake for 20 to 25 minutes. Glaze while still warm with the warmed and sieved apricot jam.

## INGREDIENTS:

- 1 tablespoon (8.50 grams) active dry yeast
- 3½ ounces (100 g) water
- 4.9 ounces (140 g) milk
- 17.6 ounces (500 grams) all-purpose flour
- 2½ ounces (70 g) sugar
- 2 eggs
- 1.8 ounces (50 g) butter
- 1¾ teaspoons (10 g) salt
- 3½ ounces (100 g) raisins
- 2.8 ounces (80 g) chopped, candied orange/lemon peels
- 1 apple, peeled, cored, finely chopped
- Zest of 1 orange
- 1 teaspoon ground cinnamon

### FOR THE CROSS
- 2.8 ounces (80 g) all-purpose flour
- 2.8 ounces (80 g) water

### FOR THE GLAZE
- Apricot jam

# Sugar Bakeshop

59 ½ Cannon Street
Charleston, SC 29403
(843) 579-2891
www.sugarbake.com

Lost in all the talk of Charleston's rapidly growing foodie scene is its rich baking legacy, which has existed as long as the city itself. And few bakeries, in Charleston or otherwise, carry that legacy as elegantly as Sugar Bakeshop. Sugar is coziness incarnated—nuzzled in at 59 ½ Cannon Street, you would be forgiven for underestimating the bakery's prowess. But the bite-sized pastries in this small space have made waves well outside of Charleston, having merited the bakery's inclusion on *Travel + Leisure's* "Best Bakeries in America" list in 2013. "Our original goal was to be a neighborhood bakeshop," says co-owner Bill Bowick. "We're proud we have achieved that. What we didn't expect was attention on a more national level. But we're equally proud of both of those achievements."

Bill and David's path to baking was anything but direct. While originally from the South, both men began their careers as architects in New York City. Bill knew how to bake from his family of "from-scratch" bakers; David from his own sweet tooth and his grandmother's beloved apple pie. Says David, "It wasn't until I met Bill that I embraced the idea of baking as a creative and visual process. The idea of consuming this culinary item you've created is so satisfying. You can't eat a building!"

A spontaneous subway conversation made all the difference in their lives. Bill and David fell in love and immediately began planning the beginnings of Sugar Bakeshop. They moved to Charleston, spent some time in London and then returned home to South Carolina. All along, the plan was to open a bakery that would be woven into the fabric of the community. Bill and David accomplished that goal by embracing locally grown ingredients—in some cases, grown literally on the premises. Their rooftop garden is home to herbs like mint, lemongrass and rosemary, plus two beehives that produce honey used and sold in-store. "People may say buying an herb at the grocery store is easy, but I can tell you that growing mint is actually easier than a trip to the store. It's not harder. And tending your overgrown mint bed next to your neighbor's garden is a great way to build community. And it's a great way to live your life. Because of our efforts with these things, I think Charlestonians view us not as just a brand, or a purveyor of baked goods, but as friends and allies in building community."

In this way, Sugar is the embodiment of Charleston's baking scene—even if its founders did spend their formative years in the Big Apple!

# IN THEIR OWN WORDS:

## BILL BOWICK AND DAVID BOUFFARD

*Who inspired you to bake? Who inspires you now?*

Bill: My mom, grandmother, and aunts. They expressed their love through baking for others. That's what David and I do for others now. From that perspective, I guess you could say our customers inspire us now. We're baking for them, figuring out what baked treats bring them joy and taking pleasure in that.

I would also say Lee Bailey. He was a fellow southerner who approached the culinary arts as a lifestyle. He assembled delightful concoctions using his heritage, knowledge of French cooking, and his noggin. He's a bit forgotten now, but I reference his books often. A small note: when I first moved to New York, he happened to have a loft in the same building where I lived near Union Square. I had some happy interactions with him and he was gracious enough to sign one of his books for me.

David: I was inspired by my family bakers including my two sisters…and especially by Bill!

*What is your golden rule of baking?*

Use the best and the freshest ingredients available and never over-mix. In architecture school, we were taught to "keep a light hand" in sketching. We keep that phrase in mind when baking. Don't overwork it.

*What does Sugar Bakeshop represent to you?*

Sugar Bakeshop is the manifestation of an attitude and a philosophy. The design and brand of the shop reflect honesty, simplicity and purity of design, in both ingredients and method of baking. Our shop's name is actually a double entendre. Sugar is our primary ingredient. It is pure. Elemental. But it is also a term of endearment. What southerner (of a certain age) didn't grow up and hear an elder use the term "sugar" as a term of affection? It is the perfect embodiment of our shop: baked items, evocative of love and affection, translate to love and confection.

*What is your favorite thing to bake? Why? Least favorite thing to bake? Why?*

We love to bake tartlets—the yield of the simple dough recipe is plentiful, reliable, and easy to make. It complements available ingredients for fillings, which provide punchy bursts of flavor in your mouth when paired with the buttery crust.

Our least favorite is anything fussy and complicated. As any modernist architect would say—less is more.

*What are your most popular items?*

Our mini tartlets are always a crowd pleaser—especially the lemon tarts. We vary the tarts seasonally, so you may find heirloom pumpkin tarts in the fall, and strawberry-rhubarb in the spring. But everyone loves a pie. Our focus on freshness means we don't sell pie by the slice. Pies are made to order only—baked just for the customer.

*What non-essential items should every baker have?*

A fluted pastry wheel is a fine tool to have on hand. It helps make basket weave pie crusts even more beautiful. We also use a marble cutting board that we chill in the refrigerator before preparing pie dough. Pie crusts are best when worked cold, and a chilled pie board gives you a leg up there.

*What book(s) go on your required reading list for bakers?*

I find Nick Malgieri's *The Modern Baker* to be a thorough and handy reference for bakers.

Also, *The Fannie Farmer Cookbook*. Don't

laugh! Vintage cookbooks were written when many people didn't have ready access to ingredients or modern cooking. These books have practical knowledge, including substitutions, variations with available ingredients, and general wisdom passed from generation to generation on how to make your baking a success.

*What outlets/periodicals/newspapers do you read or consult regularly, if any?*

*The New York Times, Cooks Illustrated,Food & Wine, Bon Appetit, Lucky Peach, Kitchen52, Martha Stewart,* and *Kinfolk*

*Tell me about your most memorable collaboration with another chef.*

Well…we married each other!

*Who inspires you? Do you follow any cooking shows or chefs? If so, which is your favorite?*

Bill: I sometimes watch *The Great English Bake Off.* It's classy and full of smart feedback from the judges.

Otherwise, Ruth Reichl—her career is less about hype and more about authenticity and the relationship between food and our everyday lives. Oh, and I love old footage of Julia Child.

*Where did you learn to cook?*

Bill: I learned to cook over the phone from NYC to points south—conversations with my mom, grandmother, aunts. My first internship as an architect was with an old school fellow who imparted some sage advice. He said that some people expend a lot of time on marketing. He felt that if one does good, quality work, people respond to it. That advice has served me well in both my careers.

David: I've always enjoyed cooking, but didn't get into baking until I met Bill—so I would have to say I apprenticed with Bill. My love of numbers, formulas and chemistry has propelled me to the front line of our bakery. I have literally hijacked the oven and kicked my mentor out of the kitchen!

Bill: It's true! Over time our roles have shifted in our shop. Now, David and other bakers in our shop do most of the actually baking. Now I am more interested in the menu and what kinds of things we're actually baking as well as the presentation of our baked goods. Baking is such a visual pursuit.

# SUGAR BAKESHOP'S LEMON TARTS

**YIELDS:** 24 TARTS, 2-INCHES IN DIAMETER BY 1-INCH DEEP / **ACTIVE TIME:** 20 MINUTES
**TOTAL TIME:** 40–45 MINUTES

These bite-sized treats are one of our year-round favorites. The simple dough and tart lemon filling topped with powdered sugar work for both rustic outings and elegant events.

**INGREDIENTS:**

**TART DOUGH**

1½  sticks (¾ cup) unsalted butter

5  ounces cream cheese

1½  cups all-purpose flour

½ cup powdered sugar

**LEMON TART FILLING**

2  cups sugar

5  tablespoons flour

4  eggs

2  medium lemons, for zest

4  tablespoons fresh lemon juice (use zested lemon for juice)

1  Begin by making your dough. Warm butter and cream cheese to room temperature. Cream the butter and cream cheese in stand-mixer until just combined.

2  Combine flour and powdered sugar in a bowl, then add dry ingredients to butter and cream cheese and mix until just combined. Finish working the dough with your hands.

3  Spoon approximately 1 tablespoon of dough into each ungreased tart pan mold.

4  Press and spread dough in mold using fingers—it's okay if the dough extends slightly above top of mold. Note: dough can be made and pressed in advance and refrigerated until ready to fill and bake.

5  Now make your filling. First heat the oven to 350°F, then combine sugar and flour in a medium mixing bowl. Mix in eggs with a whisk or spatula until combined. Add lemon zest and juice and mix with whisk or spatula until combined.

6  Fill tart dough molds to top with filling. Bake for 20 to 22 minutes, or until tart dough is golden brown. Let cool for 15 minutes before removing from pan. To remove, run a knife around the edge of the tart and carefully pop out.

Add blueberries or raspberries to lemon filling for delicious fruit-filled variation!

# FRUIT TART

**YIELD:** 10-INCH TART OR 12 MINI TARTS / **ACTIVE TIME:** 1 HOUR / **TOTAL TIME:** 2 HOURS

This beautiful dessert is made to impress! It's unique, sweet and stunning appearance makes it great to take to parties, get-togethers or give as a gift. This addictive recipe can make one whole fruit tart or 12 mini fruit tarts, depending on your company!
—*recipe courtesy of Gina Watts of Sugar Pie Bakery*

1 Combine flour, sugar, and salt in a food processor. Slowly add pieces of butter, pulsing several times until mixture begins to crumble. Add egg yolk mixed with cream. Pulse until all ingredients are moistened. Mix until dough starts to stick together, being careful not to over-mix.

2 Add additional drops of cream if dough seems too dry. Press dough into a patty, wrap in plastic, and place in refrigerator to chill for 30 minutes.

3 Stir together milk, salt and sugar in large saucepan. Bring to a bare simmer over medium heat.

4 While milk mixture is heating, in large bowl, whisk together egg yolks and cornstarch until smooth.

5 Once milk mixture is at a simmer, slowly pour about ½ cup of hot milk mixture into the egg mixture while whisking constantly. Repeat until you have stirred in 2 cups of the mixture.

6 Whisk the egg mixture back into the remaining milk mixture while constantly stirring.

7 Bring to a boil and once mixture is thick, take off heat. Stir in butter and pure vanilla extract. Scrape into pie shell or bowl, cover with plastic wrap, and refrigerate until cool.

8 Once cooled, top with your favorite fruit, such as strawberries, blackberries, blueberries, raspberries, and kiwi.

## INGREDIENTS:

### CRUST:

| | | |
|---|---|---|
| 1½ | cups flour | |
| ⅓ | cup powdered sugar | |
| ¼ | teaspoon salt | |
| ½ | cup butter, chilled and cut into pieces | |
| 1 | egg yolk | |
| 1 | tablespoon heavy cream | |

### CREAM FILLING:

| | | |
|---|---|---|
| 2¾ | cups whole milk | |
| 4 | egg yolks | |
| ⅔ | cup granulated sugar | |
| 2 | tablespoons butter | |
| ¼ | cup cornstarch | |
| 1 | teaspoon pure vanilla | |
| ⅛ | teaspoon salt | |

# LEMON CURD TART *with* TORCHED MERINGUE TOPPING

**YIELD:** 1 TART / **ACTIVE TIME:** 35 MINUTES / **TOTAL TIME:** 45 MINUTES

Lemon curd is a versatile cream that be used for scones, angel food cake, pound cake, or cake fillings. What's more, it has a long shelf life and can sit in the refrigerator for a week or so.
—*Stephany Buswell*

**INGREDIENTS:**

- 1   9-inch sweet tart crust, pre-baked (see page 617)
- 6   eggs
- 1   cup sugar
- 1¼  cups lemon juice
-     Zest of 4 lemons
- 6   tablespoons unsalted butter

**MERINGUE TOPPING:**

- 1   cup sugar
- ½   cup egg whites
-     Pinch of salt

1   Place the eggs, sugar, juice, and zest in the top of a double boiler.

2   Cut the cold butter into 1-inch pieces and place on top of the lemon mixture.

3   Cook over medium heat, stirring occasionally, until the mixture reaches 180°F on a candy thermometer.

4   Cool lemon curd over an ice bath and then pour into your prepared shell.

5   In a large stainless-steel bowl, mix together the sugar, whites and salt with a whisk.

6   Place the bowl over a pot of boiling water and whisk until the mixture reaches 150°F. Immediately pour into a stand mixing bowl. Using the whip, mix on high speed until stiff peaks form. This will produce a fully cooked meringue that is strong and will hold up to cutting.

7   Pipe or spoon the meringue on top of the tart, making peaks with the back of the spoon or the piping bag.

8   Using either a brulée torch or the oven (400°F for 5 to 7 minutes), toast the top of the meringue to a golden-brown color.

# CLASSIC LINZER TART

YIELD: 1 9-INCH TART (SERVES 10) / *ACTIVE TIME:* 25 MINUTES / *TOTAL TIME:* 2 HOURS

There are many variations for this classic tart, but this one, with its cocoa powder and spices, is a personal favorite. Some will have ground almonds and hazelnuts, others cake crumbs, and still others will use hard-boiled egg yolks instead of whole eggs. They're all delicious, so start here and then find your favorite.
—*Stephany Buswell*

1 Cream the butter, sugar, and zest until smooth and creamy. Add the eggs one by one, scraping the bowl between each addition.

2 Mix all the dry ingredients together.

3 Add the dry ingredients to the butter mix and mix in slowly. Be careful not to over-mix.

4 Wrap the dough in 2 equal packages and chill until firm, about 1 hour.

5 Preheat your oven to 350°F. On a lightly floured surface, roll out half of the dough and line a 9-inch tart pan with it. You can use your fingers to press any dough that cracks or breaks off back into the pan. This is a very tender crust that will not toughen after being handled.

6 Roll the second piece out to a 10-inch round and use a knife to cut strips ¾-inch wide.

7 Fill the crust with the raspberry jam. Make a lattice top with the strips you cut (see Strawberry-Rhubarb Pie, page 666).

8 Bake 350°F for 35 to 40 minutes or until golden.

INGREDIENTS:

1 cup sugar

12 tablespoons unsalted butter, room temperature

1 teaspoon lemon zest

2 whole eggs

1¼ cups all-purpose flour

1 cup almond flour, toasted in the oven until golden

½ teaspoon cinnamon

¼ teaspoon cloves

1 tablespoon cocoa powder

¼ teaspoon salt

¾ cup quality raspberry jam, with or without seeds

# CARAMELIZED PEACH CUSTARD TART

YIELD: 1 9-INCH TART / ACTIVE TIME: 25 MINUTES / TOTAL TIME: 1 HOUR

This tart can be made with apples, pears, or any firm fruit able to withstand the flambé procedure. You will be creating a huge flame, so if fire frightens you I would skip the flambé step.
—*Stephany Buswell*

1 Melt the butter in a large fry or sauté pan. Place your fruit slices in and cook on medium-high heat until they are brown on all sides.

2 Sprinkle the sugar over and shake the pan vigorously until all pieces are coated in sugar. If you want to omit the flambé then continue to cook until caramelized.

3 For the flambé: When the pan is nice and hot and the fruit is caramelized, have ready a lighter and your brandy. Those long-handled lighters used for grills and fireplaces work best here.

4 Pour the brandy into the pan and light immediately. A huge flame may shoot up—shake the pan vigorously and the flame will die down. As soon as you lose the flame, pour the fruit onto a pan to cool.

5 Arrange the cooled fruit in an attractive circle in the baked tart crust.

6 Preheat your oven to 300°F and make your custard filling: Use a whisk to mix together all filling ingredients, being careful not to whip in too much air.

7 Strain the custard over the peaches in the tart shell.

8 Bake for about 20 to 30 minutes or until set. It's okay if the tart doesn't get much color on top.

## INGREDIENTS:

1 pre-baked 9-inch sweet tart crust (see page 617)

### FOR THE FRUIT:

2 large peaches, halved and then cut into 5 slices per half

2 tablespoons unsalted butter

3 tablespoons sugar

¼ teaspoon cinnamon

2 tablespoons brandy, kept covered until time of use

### FOR THE CUSTARD FILLING:

½ cup milk

½ cup heavy cream

2 eggs

1 yolk

¼ cup sugar

½ teaspoon vanilla

¼ teaspoon salt

# CHOCOLATE TRUFFLE TART

YIELD: 1 9-INCH TART / ACTIVE TIME: 20 MINUTES / TOTAL TIME: 2 HOURS 45 MINUTES

Great for that last minute dinner party you want to make a bit fancier, this is the most simple, beautiful tart you can whip up. A dark, rich chocolate ganache filling in a chocolate butter crust—what's not to love? Serve with whipped cream or fresh berries, or both.

—*Stephany Buswell*

**INGREDIENTS:**

1 Chocolate Sucrée recipe (see page 617)

1½ cups heavy cream

12 ounces bittersweet chocolate, chopped, 58-65% on the label

¼ cup unsalted butter, cubed

2 tablespoons of your favorite liqueur (optional)

1 Roll out and line one 9" fluted tart pan with the Chocolate Sucrée. Blind bake it by lining the dough with parchment paper and filling it with either pie weights, pinto bean, or dry rice.

2 Bake at 350°F for 15 minutes. Carefully lift out the paper filled with weights and check to make sure it is baked thoroughly. If not, place back in the oven (without the weights) for 5 more minutes to dry out. Let cool.

3 Bring the cream to a boil in a small sauce pan and add the chopped-up chocolate to a mixing bowl.

4 Pour the boiling cream over the chocolate and stir until smooth and no lumps show up on the back of your spatula or spoon. Stir in the butter pieces and then the flavoring.

5 Strain into the cooled tart shell and make sure it spreads evenly. Do not touch the top or you will ruin your glossy finish.

6 Chill for a couple hours until set.

# APPLE TART

**YIELDS:** 6 TO 8 SERVINGS / **ACTIVE TIME:** 60 MINUTES / **TOTAL TIME:** SEVERAL HOURS OR OVERNIGHT

Cast-iron skillets caramelize fruits to perfection. This recipe is the quintessential example. It's what the French call "tarte tatin," and for them it's a national treasure.

—*Dominique DeVito*

**INGREDIENTS:**

| | |
|---|---|
| 1 | cup flour |
| ½ | teaspoon salt |
| 1 | tablespoon sugar |
| 6 | tablespoons unsalted butter, cut into small pieces |
| 3 | tablespoons ice water |
| 1 | cup (2 sticks) unsalted butter, cut into small pieces |
| 1½ | cups sugar |
| 8 to 10 | apples, peeled, cored, and halved |

1 To make the pastry, whisk together the flour, salt, and sugar in a large bowl. Using your fingers, work the butter into the flour mixture until you have coarse clumps. Sprinkle the ice water over the mixture and continue to work it with your hands until it just holds together. Shape it into a ball, wrap it in plastic wrap, and refrigerate it for at least one hour, but even overnight.

2 Preparation for the tart starts in the skillet. Place the pieces of butter evenly over the bottom of the skillet, then sprinkle the sugar evenly over everything. Next, start placing the apple halves in a circular pattern, starting on the outside of the pan and working in. The halves should support each other and all face the same direction. Place either 1 or 2 halves in the center when finished working around the outside. As the cake bakes, the slices will slide down a bit.

3 Place the skillet on the oven and turn the heat to medium-high. Cook the apples in the pan, uncovered, until the sugar and butter start to caramelize, about 35 minutes. While they're cooking, spoon some of the melted juices over the apples (but don't overdo it).

4 Preheat the oven to 400°F, and position a rack in the center.

5 Take the chilled dough out of the refrigerator and working on a lightly floured surface, roll it out into a circle just big enough to cover the skillet (about 12 to 14 inches). Gently drape the pastry over the apples, tucking the pastry in around the sides.

6 Put the skillet in the oven and bake for about 25 minutes, until the pastry is golden brown.

7 Remove the skillet from the oven and allow to cool for about 5 minutes. Find a plate that is an inch or two larger than the top of the skillet and place it over the top. You will be inverting the tart onto the plate. Be sure to use oven mitts or secure pot holders, as the skillet will be hot.

8 Holding the plate tightly against the top of the skillet, turn the skillet over so the plate is now on the bottom. If some of the apples are stuck to the bottom, gently remove them and place them on the tart.

9 Allow to cool a few more minutes, or set aside until ready to serve (it's better if it's served warm).

CAST-IRON SKILLET RECIPE

# GLUTEN-FREE RASPBERRY ALMOND TART

YIELDS: 6 TO 8 SERVINGS / ACTIVE TIME: 30 MINUTES / TOTAL TIME: 90 MINUTES

What's amazing about this dessert is the sweetness of the raspberries with the nutty hints of almond. They are a great pair. And of course the custard is creamy, the colors are gorgeous, and the overall effect is of something irresistible.

—*Dominique DeVito*

**INGREDIENTS:**

1  gluten-free crust (see page 604)

5  tablespoons unsalted butter, softened

½  cup sugar, plus 1 tablespoon

Dash of salt

1  egg, plus 1 egg white

¾  cup almond flour

½  teaspoon almond extract

1½ cups fresh raspberries

1  Preheat the oven to 375°F.

2  In a large bowl, cream butter with sugar until mixture is light and fluffy. Add salt.

3  Stir in the egg and egg white until thoroughly combined, then the flour and almond extract. In a separate bowl, stir the raspberries with the extra tablespoon of sugar.

4  Sprinkle about ⅓ of the berries on the crust. Top with the almond/egg mixture, and add the remaining raspberries on top.

5  Put the skillet in the oven and bake for about 40 to 45 minutes, until a knife inserted near the center comes out clean.

6  Allow to cool completely.

# GINGER KEY LIME TART

**YIELDS:** 6 TO 8 SERVINGS / **ACTIVE TIME:** 40 MINUTES / **TOTAL TIME:** 60 MINUTES

To complement the zestiness of the key lime, the tart is baked in a gingersnap crust spiked with fresh ginger, which itself has a bright, zingy flavor. The result is an explosion in your mouth.

—*Dominique DeVito*

**1** Preheat the oven to 350°F.

**2** In a food processor, grind the cookie pieces until they form crumbs. If you don't have a food processor, you can also put the cookie halves in a resealable plastic bag and use a rolling pin to grind them into crumbs.

**3** Put the crumbs in a bowl and add the ginger. Stir in the 6 tablespoons of melted butter. Heat the remaining 2 tablespoons until just melted and put the butter in the cast-iron skillet to coat the bottom. Press the cookie crumb mixture into the skillet, extending the crust about half way up the sides of the skillet.

**4** Bake until the crust is firm, about 10 minutes. Allow to cool. Reduce oven temperature to 325°F.

**5** In a medium bowl, combine the condensed milk, key lime juice, egg yolks, and vanilla. Pour the filling into the crust.

**6** Put the skillet in the oven and bake for about 20 to 30 minutes, until the liquid has set into a soft custard.

**7** Allow to cool completely before serving.

**INGREDIENTS:**

8–10 gingersnap cookies

1 teaspoon fresh grated ginger

½ cup (8 tablespoons) unsalted butter, divided into portions of 6 tablespoons and 2 tablespoons

1 (14-oz.) can sweetened condensed milk

½ cup key lime juice

4 large egg yolks

1 tablespoon vanilla extract

# DOUBLE LEMON TART

**YIELDS:** 6 TO 8 SERVINGS / **ACTIVE TIME:** 30 MINUTES / **TOTAL TIME:** 60 MINUTES

Lemons are like sunshine—they brighten everything! Very thinly sliced lemons sit atop a lemon-drenched custard nestled in a graham cracker crust and make a dessert whose flavor shines through from the first to last bites.

—*Dominique DeVito*

1 Preheat the oven to 325°F.

2 In a medium bowl, combine the condensed milk, lemon juice, egg yolks, and vanilla. Pour the filling into the crust. Top with the very thin slices of lemon, arranged in a decorative pattern.

3 Put the skillet in the oven and bake for about 20 minutes, until the liquid has set into a soft custard.

4 Allow to cool completely before serving.

**INGREDIENTS:**

1 graham cracker crust (see page 607)

1 (14-oz.) can sweetened condensed milk

½ cup fresh squeezed lemon juice

4 large egg yolks

1 tablespoon vanilla extract

1 lemon, very thinly sliced, seeds removed

CAST-IRON SKILLET RECIPE

# STRAWBERRY KIWI TART

YIELDS: 6 TO 8 SERVINGS / ACTIVE TIME: 90 MINUTES / TOTAL TIME: SEVERAL HOURS

This is one of those desserts you marvel at in the display case of a high-end grocery store. It always looks perfect. When you make one yourself, you'll find that it's quite simple, and looks just as impressive.

—*Dominique DeVito*

1 In a large bowl, cream the softened cream cheese with the sugar, stirring until very smooth. Add the vanilla.

2 In a separate bowl, whip the cream with an electric mixer on high until it forms stiff peaks. Fold the cream into the cheese mixture until it's fully incorporated. Scrape into the crust and spread evenly.

3 Arrange the fruit in a pattern of circles, alternating the kiwis and the strawberries and working from the outside toward the center. Refrigerate until set, about 1 hour.

4 Melt the jelly and water in a small saucepan over low heat, cool slightly, then brush it over the entire surface of the tart.

5 Chill for several hours before serving.

6 Serve with fresh whipped cream, crème fraiche, or vanilla ice cream.

**INGREDIENTS:**

1 baked crust (see page 600)

½ cup (4 ounces) cream cheese, at room temperature

½ cup sugar

1 teaspoon vanilla extract

1 cup heavy cream

1½ cups fresh strawberries, stems removed and sliced in half

3 medium kiwis, peeled and sliced widthwise

3 tablespoons seedless strawberry jam

1 tablespoon water

# PECAN, CHOCOLATE *and* BOURBON TARTS

YIELD: 24 TARTS, 2-INCHES IN DIAMETER BY 1-INCH DEEP / ACTIVE TIME: 20 MINUTES
TOTAL TIME: 40–45 MINUTES

A favorite for holiday entertaining, the nutty flavor of pecans combined with chocolate and bourbon provides just the right amount of sweetness to complement a glass of milk or a cocktail!
*—Sugar Bakeshop*

1 Begin by making your dough. Warm butter and cream cheese to room temperature. Cream the butter and cream cheese in a stand-mixer until just combined.

2 Combine flour and powdered sugar in a bowl. Add the dry ingredients to the butter and cream cheese and mix until just combined. Finish working the dough with hands.

3 Spoon approximately 1 tablespoon of dough into each ungreased tart pan mold.

4 Press and spread dough in mold using fingers—it's okay if the dough extends slightly above top of mold. Note: dough can be made and pressed in advance and refrigerated until ready to fill and bake.

5 To make your filling, heat the oven to 350°F. In a small bowl or saucepan, melt the butter and set aside.

6 In a medium mixing bowl, mix together brown sugar and eggs with a spatula. Add the melted butter and mix well.

7 Fold in the chopped pecans, then add the chocolate morsels and bourbon. Mix with spatula until all ingredients are combined.

8 Fill tart dough molds with filling to just below the tops. Add pecan halves on top of each tart.

9 Bake for 20 to 22 minutes or until crust is a light golden brown. Let cool 15 minutes before removing from pan.

## INGREDIENTS:

### TART DOUGH

1½ sticks (¾ cup) unsalted butter

5 ounces cream cheese

1½ cups all purpose flour

½ cup powdered sugar

### TART FILLING

2 tablespoons unsalted butter

1½ cups brown sugar

2 eggs

1½ cups chopped pecans

½ cup semisweet chocolate morsels

1 tablespoon bourbon

24 pecan halves, for top of tart

# BREAD PUDDING

YIELDS: 8 TO 10 SERVINGS / ACTIVE TIME: 60 MINUTES / TOTAL TIME: 2 HOURS

Whoever invented bread pudding was on to something—use up some slightly stale bread, drench it in butter, sugar, and eggs, and bake. It's a bit trickier than that, but not much. Enjoy!
—*Dominique DeVito*

1 Prepare the skillet by coating it with 2 tablespoons of the butter. Make a layer of bread cubes using half the baguette. Sprinkle half of the raisins, nuts, and fruit over the cubes, and make another layer, starting with the bread cubes and topping with the raisins, nuts, and fruit.

2 In a large bowl, whisk the eggs until frothy and add the milk, cream, sugar, vanilla, and spices. Whisk briskly to blend thoroughly. Pour the mixture over the bread layers, shaking the pan slightly to be sure to distribute throughout and so that the top cubes are just moistened while the bottom layer gets most of the liquid.

3 Refrigerate for about an hour, pressing down on the bread occasionally.

4 Preheat the oven to 325°F and position a rack in the center. Before putting the skillet in the oven, cut up the remaining 4 tablespoons of butter into little pieces and place them over the top of the pudding. Bake in the oven for 1 hour.

5 Remove and allow to cool for about a half hour. Serve with fresh whipped cream, ice cream, or a Grand Marnier sauce (see below).

## GRAND MARNIER SAUCE

1 Melt the butter in a heavy-bottomed saucepan over medium heat. Add the sugar and stir constantly with a wooden spoon while it dissolves and begins to cook. Stir until dissolved, about 2 minutes, then stir in the Grand Marnier, continue to cook for a minute or two, and remove from the heat.

2 In a bowl, whisk the egg until frothy. Add a large spoonful of the warm Grand Marnier/sugar sauce to the egg and continue to whisk so that it combines. Transfer this to the saucepan and whisk it in with the rest of the sauce.

3 On low heat, cook the sauce, whisking constantly, until it starts to thicken (about 3 minutes). Remove from the heat and continue to whisk as it thickens. Drizzle it over bread pudding, or serve on the side.

### INGREDIENTS:

| | |
|---|---|
| 6 | tablespoons butter |
| 1 | large baguette, preferably a day old |
| ¼ | cup raisins (optional) |
| ⅔ | cup toasted almonds or walnuts (optional) |
| 1 | cup apples or pears, cored and diced |
| 3 | eggs |
| 1½ | cups milk |
| 1½ | cups heavy cream |
| 1 | cup sugar |
| 1 | tablespoon vanilla extract |
| ¼ | teaspoon cinnamon |
| ⅛ | teaspoon nutmeg |
| ⅛ | teaspoon ginger |

### GRAND MARNIER SAUCE

| | |
|---|---|
| 6 | tablespoons butter |
| ½ | cup sugar |
| ½ | cup Grand Marnier |
| 1 | egg |

# BUTTER PECAN BREAD PUDDING

**YIELDS:** 4 TO 6 SERVINGS / **ACTIVE TIME:** 45 MINUTES / **TOTAL TIME:** 2 HOURS

If you want a super-simple, irresistible recipe for no-fail bread pudding, look no further. The addition of toasted pecan pieces sets this dish apart. The better the quality of the ice cream, the tastier the bread pudding will be and the better it will set up.
—*Dominique DeVito*

**INGREDIENTS:**

- ½ cup chopped pecans
- 4 tablespoons butter
- 4 cups cubed bread from a day-old loaf of French or Italian bread
- 2 eggs
- ¼ cup rum
- 1 gallon vanilla ice cream, left out to soften (high-quality so that it is as rich as possible)

1 Place the skillet over medium-high heat. When hot, add the chopped pecans. Using pot holders or oven mitts, shake the pecans in the skillet while they cook. You want them to toast but not brown or burn. This should take just a few minutes.

2 When toasted, transfer the pecans to a plate and allow to cool.

3 Add the butter to the skillet and, over low heat, let it melt. Add the bread pieces to the skillet and distribute evenly. Sprinkle the pecan pieces over the bread cubes.

4 In a bowl, whisk the eggs with the rum. Add the softened or melted ice cream and stir just enough to combine. Pour the egg/ice cream mixture over the bread and nuts. Shake the skillet gently to distribute the liquid evenly.

5 Cover with plastic wrap, put in a cool place, and allow the mixture to rest for about 30 minutes so that the bread cubes are saturated with the ice cream.

6 Preheat the oven to 350°F.

7 Bake for 40 to 45 minutes until the cream mixture is set and it is slightly brown around the edges. Use pot holders or oven mitts to take the skillet out of the oven. Allow to cool for 5 to 10 minutes before inverting onto a serving dish. Serve immediately. No need for additional ice cream.

# KILLER VANILLA BREAD PUDDING

**YIELDS:** 4 TO 6 SERVINGS / **ACTIVE TIME:** 45 MINUTES / **TOTAL TIME:** 2 HOURS

Here's another variation on delicious and easy bread pudding that is sure to be loved by all members of the family. This is an easy, last-minute dessert you can throw together that will be gobbled up when it comes out of the oven—guaranteed! An important note, though: use high-quality ice cream so that it is as rich as possible.

—*Dominique DeVito*

1 Place the skillet over low heat. Melt the butter in the skillet. Add the bread pieces to the skillet and distribute evenly.

2 In a bowl, whisk the eggs and vanilla. Add the softened or melted ice cream and stir just enough to combine. Pour the egg/ice cream mixture over the bread. Shake the skillet gently to distribute the liquid evenly.

3 Cover with plastic wrap, put in a cool place, and allow the mixture to rest for about 30 minutes so that the bread cubes are saturated with the ice cream.

4 Preheat the oven to 350°F.

5 Bake for 40 to 45 minutes until the cream mixture is set and it is slightly brown around the edges. Use pot holders or oven mitts to take the skillet out of the oven. Allow to cool for 5 to 10 minutes before inverting onto a serving dish. Serve immediately. No need for additional ice cream.

**INGREDIENTS:**

4 **tablespoons butter**

4 **cups cubed pieces of croissants or a combination of baguette and croissant**

2 **eggs**

1 **teaspoon vanilla extract**

1 **gallon vanilla ice cream, left out to soften (high-quality so that it is as rich as possible)**

CAST-IRON SKILLET RECIPE

# RED, WHITE, *and* BLUE BREAD PUDDING

YIELDS: 4 TO 6 SERVINGS / ACTIVE TIME: 45 MINUTES / TOTAL TIME: 2 HOURS

This is one to make around 4th of July—or almost any time in the summer, as it just pops with the flavors of these fruits.
—*Dominique DeVito*

**INGREDIENTS:**

4   tablespoons butter

4   cups cubed bread from a day-old loaf of French or Italian bread

1   cup fresh or frozen blueberries

2   eggs

1   gallon strawberry ice cream, left out to soften (high-quality so that it is as rich as possible)

1   Place the skillet over low heat. Melt the butter in the skillet. Add the bread pieces to the skillet and distribute evenly. Sprinkle the blueberries over the bread pieces.

2   In a bowl, whisk the eggs. Add the softened or melted ice cream and stir just enough to combine. Pour the egg/ice cream mixture over the bread. Shake the skillet gently to distribute the liquid evenly.

3   Cover with plastic wrap, put in a cool place, and allow the mixture to rest for about 30 minutes so that the bread cubes are saturated with the ice cream.

4   Preheat the oven to 350°F.

5   Bake for 40 to 45 minutes until the cream mixture is set and it is slightly brown around the edges. Use pot holders or oven mitts to take the skillet out of the oven. Allow to cool for 5 to 10 minutes before inverting onto a serving dish. Serve immediately. No need for additional ice cream.

# BLOOD ORANGE CHEESECAKE

**YIELD:** 1 CHEESECAKE / **ACTIVE TIME:** 1 HOUR / **TOTAL TIME:** 2 HOURS

This decadent and rich cheesecake is sure to impress!
—*courtesy of Cheryl and Catherine Reinhart of Sweet Life Patisserie*

## DAY 1

1 First make your cheesecake crust: Mix crumbs and melted butter together and press mixture into bottom of a 10-inch springform pan.

2 Next, make your chocolate cookie crumbs. Begin by creaming the butter and sugar. Add in remaining ingredients and press into sheet pan.

3 Bake at 350°F for 30 minutes and let cool.

4 Once baked, break into pieces and chop in a food processor until cookies become fine crumbs.

5 Now make your cheesecake. Preheat the oven to 300°F, then blend the cream cheese and sugar together on medium speed.

6 Add the eggs, scraping down sides in after each egg. Mix to combine, then add the blood orange compound.

7 Bake for 1 hour at 300°F until the top jiggles evenly. Turn off oven and leave in for 1 additional hour.

8 Mix 2 cups of sour cream with ⅓ cup of sugar and spread on top of baked cheesecake. Bake for 20 minutes at 300°F.

9 Refrigerate overnight and remove from pan the following day.

## DAY 2

1 Before serving your cheesecake, make the chocolate ganache: Bring cream and sugar to a boil while stirring.

2 In a mixing bowl, pour the cream and sugar over the over chocolate and butter. Wait 5 minutes and stir until smooth.

3 Pour over cooled cheesecake and let sit for at least 5 minutes before serving. Serve and enjoy!

### INGREDIENTS:

**CHEESECAKE CRUST:**

- 2 ounces melted butter
- 2¼ cups chocolate cookie crumbs

**CHOCOLATE COOKIE CRUMBS:**

- 3 ounces butter or palm shortening
- 1½ tablespoons water
- 1 cup granulated sugar
- ⅓ cup cocoa powder
- 1½ cups flour

**CHEESECAKE:**

- 2¼ pounds cream cheese
- 1 cup + ⅓ cup sugar, separated
- 4 eggs
- 2 tablespoons blood orange compound
- 2 cups sour cream

**GANACHE:**

- 1⅓ cups heavy cream
- 3 tablespoons sugar
- ½ pound bittersweet chocolate
- 3 tablespoons butter

# CHOCOLATE FUDGE TART

**YIELDS:** 6 TO 8 SERVINGS / **ACTIVE TIME:** 45 MINUTES / **TOTAL TIME:** 90 MINUTES

When you know that nothing else will do for dessert except chocolate, you'll want to make this tart. The crust is crunchy chocolate, the filling is fudgy chocolate, and you can even drizzle white chocolate over it to hit a chocolate dessert home run.

– *Dominique DeVito*

**INGREDIENTS:**

**8–10** Oreo cookies, filling scraped off

**½** cup (8 tablespoons) unsalted butter, divided into portions of 6 tablespoons and 2 tablespoons

**10** ounces semisweet chocolate (morsels or a bar broken into pieces)

**½** cup (8 tablespoons) unsalted butter, cut into pieces

**2** eggs

**1** cups heavy cream

**½** cup sugar

**1** teaspoon vanilla extract

**1** pinch salt

**4** ounces white chocolate morsels or pieces

1 Preheat the oven to 350°F.

2 In a food processor, grind the cookie pieces until they form crumbs. If you don't have a food processor, you can also put the cookie halves in a resealable plastic bag and use a rolling pin to grind them into crumbs.

3 Put the crumbs in a bowl and add 6 tablespoons of melted butter. Heat the remaining 2 tablespoons until just melted and put the butter in the cast-iron skillet to coat the bottom. Press the cookie crumb mixture into the skillet, extending the crust about half way up the sides of the skillet.

4 Bake until the crust is firm, about 10 minutes. Allow to cool.

5 In a small saucepan, combine the chocolate and butter pieces. Heat over low until both are melted and combined, stirring frequently. Set aside.

6 In a bowl, whisk together the eggs, heavy cream, sugar, vanilla, and salt. Pouring gently and steadily, add the chocolate mixture to the egg mixture, whisking as the chocolate is added. Whisk or stir to combine thoroughly.

7 Pour the chocolate mixture into the crust and shake the skillet gently to evenly distribute the liquid.

8 Put the skillet in the oven and bake for 15 to 20 minutes until the filling is set around the edges but still soft in the center. It will continue to cook when it's removed from the oven.

9 Transfer to a wire rack and allow to cool completely. Before serving, put the white chocolate pieces in a microwave-safe bowl and microwave on high for 15-second intervals, stirring after each, until the chocolate is just melted. Drizzle in a decorative pattern over the tart.

# WHITE CHOCOLATE TART

YIELDS: 6 TO 8 SERVINGS / ACTIVE TIME: 45 MINUTES / TOTAL TIME: 60 MINUTES

This creamy, rich tart tastes really good in all kinds of cookie-based crusts. I made one with Pepperidge Farm Mint Milano cookies and loved the hint of mint. Almost any of the Milano flavors would work with this, so try different kinds.

— *Dominique DeVito*

## INGREDIENTS:

- 8–10 Mint Milano cookies
- ½ cup (8 tablespoons) unsalted butter, divided into portions of 6 tablespoons and 2 tablespoons
- 1 (12-oz.) package white chocolate morsels
- ½ cup (8 tablespoons) unsalted butter, cut into pieces
- 2 eggs
- 1 cups heavy cream
- ½ cup sugar
- 1 teaspoon vanilla extract
- 1 pinch salt

1 Preheat the oven to 350°F.

2 In a food processor, grind the cookie pieces until they form crumbs. If you don't have a food processor, you can also put the cookies in a resealable plastic bag and use a rolling pin to grind them into crumbs.

3 Put the crumbs in a bowl and add 6 tablespoons of melted butter. Heat the remaining 2 tablespoons until just melted and put the butter in the cast-iron skillet to coat the bottom. Press the cookie crumb mixture into the skillet, extending the crust about half way up the sides of the skillet.

4 Bake until the crust is firm, about 10 minutes. Allow to cool.

5 In a small saucepan, combine the white chocolate morsels and butter pieces. Heat over low until both are melted and combined, stirring frequently. Set aside.

6 In a bowl, whisk together the eggs, heavy cream, sugar, vanilla, and salt. Pouring gently and steadily, add the chocolate mixture to the egg mixture, whisking as the chocolate is added. Whisk or stir to combine thoroughly.

7 Pour the chocolate mixture into the crust and shake the skillet gently to evenly distribute the liquid.

8 Put the skillet in the oven and bake for 15 to 20 minutes until the filling is set around the edges but still soft in the center. It will continue to cook when it's removed from the oven.

9 Transfer to a wire rack and allow to cool completely. Serve with almost any flavor ice cream!

# CHOCOLATE CHEESECAKE TART

YIELDS: 6 TO 8 SERVINGS / **ACTIVE TIME:** 40 MINUTES / **TOTAL TIME:** 90 MINUTES

There's something so decadent about cheesecake! It's fantastic in a cookie crust, and this one is enhanced with cocoa powder and a dash of Kahlúa liqueur.

— *Dominique DeVito*

**1** Preheat the oven to 350°F.

**2** In a food processor, grind the cookie pieces until they form crumbs. If you don't have a food processor, you can also put the cookie halves in a resealable plastic bag and use a rolling pin to grind them into crumbs.

**3** Put the crumbs in a bowl and add the cocoa powder and Kahlúa. Stir in the 6 tablespoons of melted butter. Heat the remaining 2 tablespoons until just melted and put the butter in the cast-iron skillet to coat the bottom. Press the cookie crumb mixture into the skillet, extending the crust about half way up the sides of the skillet.

**4** Bake until the crust is firm, about 10 minutes. Allow to cool. Reduce oven temperature to 325°F.

**5** In a large bowl, mix the cream cheese with the sugar, unsweetened cocoa powder, vanilla and eggs, until thoroughly combined. Scrape the cream cheese mixture into the cooled crust.

**6** Put the skillet in the oven and bake for about 40 to 60 minutes, until set.

**7** Allow to cool, and refrigerate for up to 3 hours or overnight before serving.

**INGREDIENTS:**

8–10 **Oreo cookies, filling scraped off**

1 **tablespoon unsweetened cocoa powder**

2 **tablespoons Kahlúa or coffee liqueur**

½ **cup (8 tablespoons) unsalted butter, divided into portions of 6 tablespoons and 2 tablespoons**

2 **(8-oz.) packages cream cheese, softened**

1 **cup sugar**

1 **tablespoon cocoa powder**

½ **teaspoon vanilla extract**

2 **eggs**

# STICKY STICKY BUNS

YIELDS: 8 BUNS / ACTIVE TIME: 1 HOUR / TOTAL TIME: 4 HOURS

Flour's addictive sticky buns have been famous in Boston for years, but they received national attention in the summer of 2007, when they starred in an episode of the Food Network show *Throwdown with Bobby Flay.* I went head-to-head with chef Flay in a sticky bun bake-off—in front of television cameras and a live audience of about one hundred customers at Flour. After we both finished baking our buns, an agonizing hour passed during which customers were quizzed about which buns they preferred, mine or Chef Flay's, and the judges did their evaluations. Flour's sticky buns won! Many people wonder if television-show judging is fixed. But the visible sweat on my brow during that hour should assure them it definitely is not. These sticky buns are quite simply the stickiest, richest, gooiest, most decadent buns you'll ever eat. We start them with a brioche dough base, fill them with sugar, pecans, and cinnamon, and then top them with copious amounts of a sticky caramel concoction called, naturally, goo. When you eat them, be sure to have plenty of napkins nearby.

*—recipe and photos courtesy of Flour Bakery*

## INGREDIENTS:

### GOO

- ¾ cup (1½ sticks/170 grams) unsalted butter
- 1½ cups (330 grams) packed light brown sugar
- ⅓ cup (115 grams) honey
- ⅓ cup (80 grams) heavy cream
- ⅓ cup (80 grams) water
- ¼ teaspoon kosher salt

### STICKY BUNS

- Brioche dough (steps 1 to 4 on page 284)
- ¼ cup (55 grams) packed light brown sugar
- ¼ cup (50 grams) granulated sugar
- ⅛ teaspoon ground cinnamon
- 1 cup (100 grams) pecan halves, toasted and chopped

1 To make the goo: In a medium saucepan, melt the butter over medium heat. Whisk in the brown sugar until the sugar dissolves. Remove from the heat and whisk in the honey, cream, water, and salt. Let cool for about 30 minutes, or until cooled to room temperature. You should have about 2 cups. (The mixture can be made up to 2 weeks in advance and stored in an airtight container in the refrigerator.)

2 On a floured work surface, roll out the dough into a rectangle about 16 x 12 inches and ¼-inch inch thick. It will have the consistency of cold, damp Play-Doh and should be fairly easy to roll. Position the rectangle so a short side is facing you.

3 In a small bowl, stir together the brown sugar, granulated sugar, cinnamon, and half of the pecans. Sprinkle this mixture evenly over the entire surface of the dough. Starting from the short side farthest from you and working your way down, roll up the rectangle like a jelly roll. Try to roll tightly, so you have a nice round spiral. Even off the ends by trimming about ¼-inch from either side.

4 Use a bench scraper or a chef's knife to cut the roll into 8 equal pieces, each about 1½ inches wide. (At this point, the unbaked buns can be tightly wrapped in plastic wrap and frozen for up to 1 week. When ready to bake, thaw them, still wrapped, in the refrigerator overnight or at room temperature for 2 to 3 hours, then proceed as directed.)

5 Pour the goo into a 9 x 13-inch baking dish, covering the bottom evenly. Sprinkle the remaining pecans evenly over the surface. Place the buns, a cut side down and evenly spaced, 2-by-4 inches, in the baking dish. Cover with plastic wrap and place in a warm spot to proof for about 2 hours, or until the dough is puffy, pillowy, and soft and the buns are touching.

6 Position a rack in the center of the oven, and heat the oven to 350°F.

7 Bake for 35 to 45 minutes, or until golden brown. Let cool in the dish on a wire rack for 20 to 30 minutes. One at a time, invert the buns onto a serving platter, and spoon any extra goo and pecans from the bottom of the dish over the top.

8 The buns are best served warm or within 4 hours of baking. They can be stored in an airtight container at room temperature for up to 1 day, and then warmed in a 325°F oven for 6 to 8 minutes before serving.

# GREEN APPLE PECAN STICKY BUNS

YIELD: 12 STICKY BUNS / ACTIVE TIME: 2 HOURS / TOTAL TIME: 8-10 HOURS

Tart green apples perfectly balance the sweetness of these gooey, chewy buns.

*—courtesy of Cheryl and Catherine Reinhart of Sweet Life Patisserie*

## DAY 1

1 Combine flour, sugar, and salt in mixer. Add eggs, milk/yeast mixture and butter. Mix 3 minutes with dough hook. Refrigerate overnight!

## DAY 2

1 Roll dough out to a rectangle approximately ¼-inch thick. Spread dough with melted butter.

2 Sprinkle with brown sugar, chopped pecans and apples. Drizzle with heavy cream.

3 Roll up into a long cylinder. Cut dough into 2-inch rolls if you want large rolls, or 1-inch if you want smaller.

4 Preheat the oven to 300°F, then whip all the sticky bun goo ingredients in mixer for 5 minutes.

5 Grease 8 large muffin tins, or a 9 x 13–inch pan, with butter.

6 Divide sticky bun goo amongst pans. Sprinkle with untoasted pecans (enough to cover bottom). Place cut buns on top and let rise for 1 hour.

7 Bake for 30 to 40 minutes Buns should be golden brown on top. Flip out immediately after removing from oven. Be careful as there will be a lot of hot sugar at the bottom of the bun.

**INGREDIENTS:**

**DOUGH:**

| | |
|---|---|
| 1 | tablespoon yeast dissolved in 1 cup milk, warmed slightly |
| ½ | cup sugar |
| 7 | tablespoons salted butter, melted |
| 1 | teaspoon salt |
| 2 | eggs |
| 3¾–4 | cups flour |

**FILLING:**

| | |
|---|---|
| 2 | ounces butter |
| ¾ | cup brown sugar |
| ½ | cup toasted pecans, chopped |
| 1 | pound apples, peeled and chopped (approximately 2 apples) |
| ½ | cup cream |

**STICKY BUN GOO:**

| | |
|---|---|
| 1 | cup brown sugar |
| 2 | teaspoons cinnamon |
| 6 | ounces salted butter |
| 1 | tablespoon brown rice or corn syrup |
| 1 | tablespoon water |

# SWEET DOUGH

YIELD: ENOUGH FOR 16 SMALL ROLLS OR BUNS / ACTIVE TIME: 15 MINUTES
TOTAL TIME: 35 MINUTES-2 HOURS 35 MINUTES

This is an easy and delicious sweet dough for all types of breakfast pastries. Though it's less time consuming than the laminated doughs, you still get yummy, tender, sweet cinnamon rolls, sticky buns, or hot cross buns. The difference is what you mix in it.
—*Stephany Buswell*

**INGREDIENTS:**

- 3 cups all-purpose flour
- 2 packages dry yeast
- ½ cup sugar
- 1 ½ teaspoons salt
- 1 stick (4 ounces) unsalted butter
- 1 ½ cups warm water, around 110°F
- 2 eggs

1 Mix together 2 cups of the flour, yeast, sugar, and salt.

2 Cut in the butter using a paddle on a stand-mixer, or by hand using a pastry cutter, until it resembles coarse meal.

3 Mix together the water and eggs. Add this to the dry ingredients with 1 more cup of flour, continue to mix until a dough forms. If needed, you can add another ½ cup of flour. The dough should be tacky but not sticky to the touch, and definitely not dry!

4 Turn the dough into an oiled bowl and cover with a damp cloth. Rest for 20 minutes.

5 Deflate the dough and either form your pastries or refrigerate for up to 48 hours before forming into pastries. The dough will be much easier to use if you refrigerate for a couple hours before using.

For my sticky buns I replace half the water with orange juice and the zest of one orange. For hot cross buns I add to the orange, 1 tablespoon cinnamon, 1 teaspoon cloves, ½ teaspoon nutmeg and 2 cups of currants.

# STICKY BUNS / SWEET ROLLS

YIELD: 2 9-INCH CAKE PANS (APPROXIMATELY 16 PIECES) / ACTIVE TIME: 30 MINUTES / TOTAL TIME: 1½ HOURS

These spicy, nutty sticky buns are the ultimate sugar rush.
—*Stephany Buswell*

1 After you make your dough, divide it into 2 pieces.

2 Spread the toasted pecans on the bottom of the buttered cake pans

3 Make your sticky goo: Melt the butter in a saucepan, add the brown sugar, and cook until melted. Add the cream, honey and zest. Bring to boil and turn off to cool.

4 When cool, pour evenly over the nuts in the bottom of the two buttered cake pans.

5 Roll one piece of dough into a 6-inch-wide by 24-inch-long rectangle. Paint the melted butter over the entire surface of the sweet dough, then spread the cinnamon mix over the buttered dough. Roll up like a cinnamon roll.

6 Cut 1 ½-inch pieces and place on top of the sticky "goo" in a circle with one in the middle. 8 should work perfectly. Don't worry if they do not touch, this is good!

7 Repeat with the other piece of dough sitting in the fridge.

8 When both are formed, place the pans in a warm spot until they double in size.

9 Be sure and put the pans on a sheet pan with parchment paper—the goo cooks and bubbles over the side, making a sticky mess.

10 Bake at 350°F for about 25 to 30 minutes. They will be very dark brown on top, but that doesn't mean they are done underneath as the goo keeps the dough soft. To test it, push the center roll down. If it feels springy you are good. If the center stays down when you push on it, leave it in for 5 more minutes.

11 When they are done you need to have a dish or pan ready to turn them out while hot. Be very careful with the goo—you do not want it to burn your skin! Place the plate on top of the pan and with a glove or towel carefully turn the pan over onto the plate. Lift it off slowly and reveal the gooey goodness of the sticky bun.

## INGREDIENTS:

| | |
|---|---|
| 2 | cups toasted pecans, chopped |
| 1 | Sweet Dough Recipe, orange juice version (page 785) |

### STICKY GOO:

| | |
|---|---|
| ½ | cup unsalted butter |
| ½ | cup brown sugar |
| ½ | cream |
| ⅓ | cup honey |
| ¼ | teaspoon orange zest |

### CINNAMON MIXTURE:

| | |
|---|---|
| ½ | cup melted butter |
| ½ | cup brown sugar |
| ¾ | teaspoon cinnamon |
| ⅛ | teaspoon cloves |
| ¼ | teaspoon nutmeg |
| ⅛ | teaspoon salt |

# BANANA CREAM TART

YIELD: 1 9-INCH TART / ACTIVE TIME: 15 MINUTES / TOTAL TIME: 15 MINUTES

I love both banana cream and coconut cream pies, and this is a great combination of the two. If coconut isn't your thing and bananas are, just leave the coconut off the top and you have a perfect banana cream pie.

—*Stephany Buswell*

1 Cream you pastry cream in the mixer with a paddle until smooth and creamy.

2 Cut the bananas into ½-inch slices and stir them into the smooth pastry cream. Pour this mixture into the prepared tart shell and smooth the top.

3 Whip the cream with the sugar and vanilla until firm peaks appear.

4 Spread or pipe the cream on top of the banana filling for decoration. Sprinkle the toasted coconut on top. Keep refrigerated until ready to serve.

**INGREDIENTS:**

1    Pastry Cream recipe (page 364)

1    9-inch sweet tart shell, pre-baked (page 617)

2    large bananas, ripe

1    cup heavy whipping cream

1    tablespoon sugar

¼    teaspoon vanilla extract

½    cup toasted sweetened coconut flakes (shredded is fine)

# BEGGAR'S PURSE *with* APPLE COMPOTE

YIELD: 8 SERVINGS/ ACTIVE TIME: 30 MINUTES / TOTAL TIME: 1 HOUR

This a fun, non-traditional way of using phyllo dough. You can fill them with any fruit compote as long as it's not too juicy. We use pound cake or a similar type to soak up the juices from the fruit so the bottoms don't get too soggy.
—*Stephany Buswell*

## INGREDIENTS:

- 1 **package of thawed phyllo sheets**
- 4 **apples**
- ⅓ **cup sugar**
- ½ **vanilla bean or ½ teaspoon cinnamon (your choice)**
- 6 **tablespoons melted butter**
- **Small pound cake**
- 8 **pieces of foil, cut to 6 inches x 3 inches**

1 Make the apple compote: Peel, core, and dice the apples to about ½ inch. Place them in a sauce pan with 2 tablespoons of water, the sugar, and spice.

2 Cook apples on medium heat until they become soft and some become translucent. Do not overcook since they will get baked as well.

3 When finished, pour the apples into a strainer over a bowl to drain. Let cool.

4 Referring to the instructions on the baklava regarding its handling, begin to prepare your phyllo dough. First unroll the thawed phyllo and place a damp towel over the leaves of dough. You will use 4 sheets for each purse.

5 Remove 1 leaf from the pile and place it on your cutting board. Paint it will the melted butter and repeat with 3 more leaves.

6 Place a 2-inch by ½-inch round of cake in the middle. Spoon 1 large tablespoon of apple compote on top.

7 Fold your pieces of foil up so they become 6-inch by ½-inch strips.

8 Pick up the outside edges of the phyllo dough and gather them in the middle, forming your purse. Take the foil strip and wrap it around the middle so the top is opening like tissue paper.

9 Place them on a parchment-lined sheet pan and bake at 350°F for about 10 to 15 minutes or until golden and crisp. Serve warm with ice cream.

> If you want to fill your purse with a savory filling, be sure to use a piece of dry bread instead of cake.

# RUSTIC ONION TART

YIELD: 1 10-INCH TART / ACTIVE TIME: 25 MINUTES / TOTAL TIME: 45-55 MINUTES

This is a wonderful savory tart that goes well with a light lunch or to start off a light dinner. I cannot have enough caramelized onions, so if you want to be more generous with them go ahead! The cheese is also interchangeable—if Gorgonzola is too pungent for you, or if you just prefer something lighter, try goat cheese or fresh mozzarella with shaved Parmesan on top.
—*Stephany Buswell*

**INGREDIENTS:**

1    recipe flaky pie crust (see page 603)

3    medium onions, thinly sliced

1    small sprig of fresh thyme

½    cup Gorgonzola cheese, crumbled

⅓    cup walnuts, finely chopped

2    ripe tomatoes, thinly sliced

1    Roll the dough out to a 12-inch circle and place on parchment on a sheet pan. Chill in the refrigerator.

2    Sauté the sliced onions in 3 tablespoons of olive oil with thyme until golden brown, about 15 minutes. Stir often. When finished, spread onto a plate to cool.

3    Take the crust from the refrigerator and spread the cooled onions on top.

4    Preheat the oven to 350°F. Take the edge of the dough and fold it in about 1 inch toward the center, then take the edge next to it and pleat it over the first one continuing around the tart until the outside edge is pleated nicely. The tart should now be about 10 inches in diameter.

5    Place the sliced tomatoes on top, then the cheese. Sprinkle it with chopped nuts. Egg-wash the folded edges.

6    Bake at 350°F for about 20 minutes or until the crust is golden brown and the cheese is bubbly. Serve at room temperature.

# BLACK *and* BLUE GALETTE

**YIELDS:** 6 TO 8 SERVINGS / **ACTIVE TIME:** 30 MINUTES / **TOTAL TIME:** 60 MINUTES

This galette—open-faced "pie"—is made with blackberries and blueberries, a beautiful combination of colors and textures. Served warm with vanilla ice cream, it's lovely to see the white ice cream melting through the crevices of the dark fruit.

—*Dominique DeVito*

**1** Preheat the oven to 400°F.

**2** The crust in the skillet should be slightly larger than the bottom of the pan so that it can be folded over along the edges.

**3** In a large bowl, mix the fruit with the sugar, lemon juice, cornstarch, and pinch of salt. Stir well to be sure to coat all the fruit.

**4** Place the fruit in a mound in the center of the pie crust. Fold the edges of the crust over to form an edge of about 1 inch of crust. Brush the crust with the beaten egg and sprinkle it with sugar.

**5** Put the skillet in the oven and bake until the filling is bubbly, which is necessary for it to thicken sufficiently, about 35 to 40 minutes.

**6** Allow to cool before serving. Garnish with fresh berries.

**INGREDIENTS:**

1 **flaky pastry crust recipe for a single crust (see page 603)**

1½ **cups fresh blueberries**

1½ **cups fresh blackberries**

½ **cup light brown sugar**

**Juice of ½ lemon (seeds removed)**

3 **tablespoons cornstarch**

**Pinch of salt**

1 **egg, beaten**

1 **tablespoon granulated sugar**

**Fresh berries for garnish**

# TRIPLE BERRY GALETTE

**YIELDS:** 4 TO 6 SERVINGS / **ACTIVE TIME:** 30 MINUTES / **TOTAL TIME:** 60 MINUTES

You'll soon discover why this triple berry galette is a real home run. The fruits marry perfectly, with the raspberries sweetening everything just enough. If you want to kick it up some more, consider spreading some raspberry jam on the crust before adding the fruit and baking it.

—*Dominique DeVito*

1 Preheat the oven to 400°F.

2 The crust in the skillet should be slightly larger than the bottom of the pan so that it can be folded over along the edges.

3 In a large bowl, mix the fruit with the sugar, lemon juice, cornstarch, and pinch of salt. Stir well to be sure to coat all the fruit.

4 Place the fruit in a mound in the center of the pie crust. Fold the edges of the crust over to form an edge of about 1 inch of crust. Brush the crust with the beaten egg and sprinkle it with sugar.

5 Put the skillet in the oven and bake until the filling is bubbly, which is necessary for it to thicken sufficiently, about 35 to 40 minutes.

6 Allow to cool before serving.

**INGREDIENTS:**

1 flaky pastry crust recipe for a single crust (see page 603)

1 cup fresh blueberries

1 cup fresh blackberries

1 cup fresh raspberries

½ cup sugar

Juice of ½ lemon (seeds removed)

3 tablespoons cornstarch

Pinch of salt

1 egg, beaten

1 tablespoon granulated sugar

# SUMMER CHERRY GALETTE

YIELDS: 4 TO 6 SERVINGS / ACTIVE TIME: 30 MINUTES / TOTAL TIME: 60 MINUTES

You can use all of the same type of cherry for this galette, or you can mix varietals. It takes some work to remove the pits from the cherries, but it's so worth it!

—*Dominique DeVito*

**INGREDIENTS:**

1    flaky pastry crust recipe for a single crust (see page 603)

3    cups cherries, pitted and halved

½    cup light brown sugar

    Juice of ½ lemon (seeds removed)

3    tablespoons cornstarch

    Pinch of salt

1    egg, beaten

1    tablespoon granulated sugar

1    Preheat the oven to 400°F.

2    The crust in the skillet should be slightly larger than the bottom of the pan so that it can be folded over along the edges.

3    In a large bowl, mix the fruit with the sugar, lemon juice, cornstarch, and pinch of salt. Stir well to be sure to coat all the fruit.

4    Place the fruit in a mound in the center of the pie crust. Fold the edges of the crust over to form an edge of about 1 inch of crust. Brush the crust with the beaten egg and sprinkle it with sugar.

5    Put the skillet in the oven and bake until the filling is bubbly, which is necessary for it to thicken sufficiently, about 35 to 40 minutes.

6    Allow to cool before serving.

# PEACH GALETTE

**YIELDS:** 6 TO 8 SERVINGS / **ACTIVE TIME:** 45 MINUTES / **TOTAL TIME:** 90 MINUTES

When peaches are ripe in the mid-to-late summer, this is a super-simple way to turn them into a great dessert. Smearing some peach jam on the crust before adding the fruit will intensify the flavor of the peaches, and if you want something a little more "adult," consider adding some Amaretto liqueur to the jam instead of water.

—*Dominique DeVito*

**INGREDIENTS:**

1    **flaky pastry crust recipe for a single crust (see page 603)**

3    **cups fresh peaches, peeled, stones removed, and sliced**

½    **cup sugar**

     **Juice of ½ lemon (seeds removed)**

3    **tablespoons cornstarch**

     **Pinch of salt**

2    **tablespoons peach jam**

1    **teaspoon Amaretto liqueur (optional)**

1    **egg, beaten**

1    **tablespoon granulated sugar**

1   Preheat the oven to 400°F.

2   The crust in the skillet should be slightly larger than the bottom of the pan so that it can be folded over along the edges.

3   In a large bowl, mix the fruit with the sugar, lemon juice, cornstarch, and pinch of salt. Stir well to be sure to coat all the fruit.

4   If using the liqueur, mix it in with the jam in a small bowl before smearing the jam onto the center of the crust.

5   Place the fruit in a mound in the center of the pie crust. Fold the edges of the crust over to form an edge of about 1 inch of crust. Brush the crust with the beaten egg and sprinkle it with sugar.

6   Put the skillet in the oven and bake until the filling is bubbly, which is necessary for it to thicken sufficiently, about 35 to 40 minutes.

7   Allow to cool before serving.

CAST-IRON SKILLET RECIPE

# PLUM GALETTE

**YIELDS:** 4 TO 6 SERVINGS / **ACTIVE TIME:** 40 MINUTES / **TOTAL TIME:** 90 MINUTES

Here's another summer fruit-laden pie that is so easy to put together and tastes great! The flavor of the plums is definitely enhanced by the jam, and the whole thing is sublime when topped with ice cream and—try this—roasted and salted pumpkin seeds (just a sprinkle).

—*Dominique DeVito*

**INGREDIENTS:**

1 **flaky pastry crust recipe for a single crust (see page 603)**

3 **cups fresh plums, pits removed, and sliced**

½ **cup sugar**

**Juice of ½ lemon (seeds removed)**

3 **tablespoons cornstarch**

**Pinch of salt**

2 **tablespoons blackberry jam**

1 **egg, beaten**

1 **tablespoon granulated sugar**

1 Preheat the oven to 400°F.

2 The crust in the skillet should be slightly larger than the bottom of the pan so that it can be folded over along the edges.

3 In a large bowl, mix the fruit with the sugar, lemon juice, cornstarch and pinch of salt. Stir well to be sure to coat all the fruit.

4 Brush or smear the jam in the center of the pie crust. Place the fruit in a mound in the center, as well. Fold the edges of the crust over to form an edge of about 1 inch of crust. Brush the crust with the beaten egg and sprinkle it with sugar.

5 Put the skillet in the oven and bake until the filling is bubbly, which is necessary for it to thicken sufficiently, about 35 to 40 minutes.

6 Allow to cool before serving.

# BAKLAVA

YIELD: 48 PIECES / ACTIVE TIME: 1 HOUR / TOTAL TIME: 2 HOURS

Baklava is such a harmony of texture and flavor: layers of crisp pastry and buttery, crumbly nuts topped with sticky-sweet honey and spices. It's a bit of a process to make, but more than worth the effort.
—*Stephany Buswell*

**INGREDIENTS:**

- 1 package of phyllo dough, thawed
- 1¼ cups (1½ sticks) unsalted butter
- 4 cups walnuts, finely chopped
- 1 teaspoon cinnamon
- ¼ teaspoon cloves
- 2 tablespoons lemon juice
- ¾ cup water
- 1 cup sugar
- ½ cup honey (I like light honey, like clover honey)

1 Butter the sides and bottom of a 9-inch by 13-inch baking pan.

2 Make sure your phyllo is fully thawed. Take it out of the package and unroll very carefully. Place a slightly damp cloth over it so it doesn't dry out.

3 Make your syrup by combining sugar, honey, water, and lemon juice in a saucepan and bringing to a boil. Stir until the sugar dissolves. Cook for another 4 minutes on medium heat. Turn off and let cool.

4 Melt the butter in a saucepan. Pulse the walnuts in a food processor until finely chopped, then add 1 teaspoon of cinnamon and ¼ teaspoon of cloves.

5 Place 1 sheet of phyllo in your prepared pan and use a pastry brush to paint it with the melted butter. Stack another layer on top and paint with butter, continuing until you have 10 sheets of phyllo stacked on top of one another. Be sure and keep your phyllo covered with a cloth at all times.

6 Spread about ⅓ of the nuts over the dough.

7 Add 5 more layers of phyllo, buttering in between. Repeat 4 more times, alternating nuts to dough to nuts, and so on. Finish the top with 10 sheets of dough and butter.

8 Trim the edges of the dough to keep them even. Cut the pastry 6 by 4 to make 24 2 ¼-inch by 2-inch squares. Then cut each square into triangle halves.

9 Bake in the oven at 350°F for about 1 hour or until it is golden brown.

10 Remove from the oven and pour the syrup evenly over the entire pan immediately. You should hear it sizzle—this will keep the pastry from getting soggy. Let cool and enjoy!

# CINNAMON ROLLS *with* CREAM CHEESE ICING

YIELD: ABOUT 12 BUNS / ACTIVE TIME: 20 MINUTES / TOTAL TIME: 45 MINUTES

What better way to start a morning than with the aroma of freshly-baked cinnamon buns?
—*Stephany Buswell*

1 Roll the dough out to 12-inch by 24-inch rectangle. Paint with melted butter.

2 Combine the sugars and cinnamon, then cover the dough in the cinnamon mixture.

3 Starting at the bottom of the dough, begin a tight roll by folding the edge in little by little until you get to the end. With the palm of your hands, roll the dough up into a long log, keeping the roll tight by stretching back a little as you roll up.

4 Cut out rolls about 1 ½-inch thick and tuck the end under as you place it on a parchment-lined pan.

5 Cover loosely with plastic wrap and let rise in a warm place until soft and puffy. Do not over-proof them or they will fall.

6 Bake at 375°F for 12 to 15 minutes, until they are golden brown with no white stripes.

7 While they bake, make your glaze: Mix the sugar and cream cheese, add the vanilla, add the milk a little at a time until it is loose and easily spread over the hot cinnamon rolls.

## INGREDIENTS:

- 1   Sweet Dough Recipe (page 785)
- 1   cup white sugar
- 1   cup brown sugar
- 2   tablespoons cinnamon

### GLAZE:

- 1   cup powdered sugar, sifted
- 2   ounces cream cheese, room temperature and softened
- 2   tablespoons milk
- ½   teaspoon vanilla

# SURDEGS KANELBULLAR
## (SOURDOUGH CINNAMON BUNS)

YIELD: 20 BUNS / ACTIVE TIME: 40 MINUTES / TOTAL TIME: 9 HOURS

Cinnamon buns are a must in Sweden. They are generally eaten in the afternoon, with coffee and milk (called *latte* in Swedish, an abbreviation of the Italian *caffe-latte*) and they are usually yeast-based. This is a yummy sourdough version of these classic Scandinavian sweet buns.

1 Add all the ingredients except the butter and knead (by machine or by hand) until you have a smooth dough.

2 Add the butter little-by-little at room temperature, kneading consistently throughout. Keep kneading until the butter is fully incorporated and your dough does not break easily when stretched.

3 Transfer the dough to a plastic container or a large bowl and stretch and fold a few times. Let rest, covered, in a warm corner of your kitchen for about 4 hours.

4 Always check on the dough. When you see that volume has increased at least 1 ½ times since the start, roll the dough onto a heavily floured surface into a long rectangle about 1 centimeter thick. If you do not have much kneading space, divide the dough in half and make 2 shorter rectangles.

5 Prepare the filling by combining the ingredients in a little bowl.

6 Spread the filling on ⅔ of the dough, lengthwise, and then fold the dough on itself, making 3 lengthwise folds beginning from the part without filling.

7 Cut 1½-centimeter-wide strips from the folded dough.

8 Roll one end of each strip around your finger and roll the rest all around it, removing the knot from your finger at the end and closing the free edge underneath.

9 Place the buns on parchment paper–covered baking trays and let rest somewhere warm (in your oven with the light on, for instance) for about 4 hours.

10 Make a syrup with the brown sugar and the water in a small saucepan over medium heat. Let cool.

## INGREDIENTS:

5⅗ ounces active liquid starter

1⅕ pounds all-purpose flour

13⅘ ounces milk

1 ⅘ ounces water

3 ⅕ ounces caster sugar

½ teaspoon salt

1½ teaspoons ground cardamom

5⅓ ounces butter

## FILLING:

5⅓ ounces butter (room temperature)

3⅕ ounces sugar

2 tablespoons cinnamon

## COATING:

8⅓ ounces brown sugar

7 ounces water

Pearl sugar (optional)

11 Preheat your oven to 445°F. Brush the buns with some water or milk and eventually add pearled sugar if you can find it. Otherwise, leave them as they are.

12 Bake for 10 minutes, then lower the temperature to 375°F and bake until golden brown on both sides.

13 While the buns are cooling down, brush them with the syrup.

RESOURCES

# RESOURCES

Bjørnstad, Åsmund. *Wheat—Its Role in Social and Cultural Life. The World Wheat Book: A History of Wheat Breeding Volume 3*, by Alain Bonjean, William Angus, Maarten Van Ginkel, Collectif, Jean-Yves Foucault; Tec & Doc Lavoisier, 2016.

Bjørnstad, Åsmund. *Our Daily Bread—A History of the Cereals*. Vidarforlaget AS, 2012.

Buehler, Emily. *Bread Science: The Chemistry and Craft of Making Bread*. Two Blue Books, 2006.

De Cillis, Ugo. *I Frumenti Siciliani*. Editore Maimone; Catania, 2004.

Dickie, John. *Delizia! The Epic History of the Italians and Their Food*. Sceptre, 2008.

Gobbetti, Aldo e Corsetti, Marco. *Biotecnologia dei Prodotti Lievitati da Forno*. Casa Editrice Ambrosiana, 2010.

Halloran, Amy. *The New Bread Basket*. Chelsea Green Publishing, 2015.

Jacob, Heinrich Eduard. *Six Thousand Years of Bread: Its Holy and Unholy History*. Garden City NY: Double Day, Doran & Co., 1944.

Whitley, Andrew. *Bread Matters*. Fourth Estate, 2009.

For more resources that professional bakers consult, check out the In Their Own Words sections through the book to see which books, periodicals, and tools they recommend!

# METRIC EQUIVALENTS

## Weights

1 ounce = 28 grams
4 ounces (¼ pound) = 113 grams
8 ounces (½ pound) = 227 grams
16 ounces (1 pound) = 454 grams

## Volume Measures

¼ teaspoon = 1.25 ml
½ teaspoon = 2.5 ml
1 teaspoon = 5 ml
1 tablespoon (3 teaspoons) = ½ fluid ounce = 15 ml
2 tablespoons = 1 fluid ounce = 29.5 ml
¼ cup (4 tablespoons) = 2 fluid ounces = 59 ml
⅓ cup (5 1/3 tablespoons) = 2.6 fluid ounces = 79 ml
½ cup (8 tablespoons) = 4 fluid ounces = 118 ml
⅔ cup (10 2/3 tablespoons) = 5 ⅓ fluid ounces = 158 ml
¾ cup (12 tablespoons) = 6 fluid ounces = 177 ml
1 cup (16 tablespoons) = 8 ounces = 237 ml

## Length Measures

1/16 inch  =  1.5 mm
⅛ inch  =  3 mm
¼ inch  =  6.25 mm
½ inch  =  1.25 cm
¾ inch  =  2 cm
1 inch  =  2.5 cm

## Temperatures Equivalents

| °F | °C | Gas Mark |
|----|-----|----------|
| 250 | 120 | ½ |
| 275 | 135 | 1 |
| 300 | 150 | 2 |
| 325 | 165 | 3 |
| 350 | 175 | 4 |
| 375 | 190 | 5 |
| 400 | 205 | 6 |
| 425 | 220 | 7 |
| 450 | 230 | 8 |
| 475 | 245 | 9 |
| 500 | 260 | 10 |

IMAGE CREDITS

Barbara Elisi Caracciolo: pages 8, 34, 163, 171, 172, 183, 184, 189, 190, 195, 255, 269, 289, 296, 333, 491, and 809

Stephany Buswell: pages 363, 383, 622, 694, 735, 752, 755, 759, 787, and 791

158 Pickett Street Café & Southside Bakery: photo of café front courtesy of Kate Schier-Potocki, 158 Pickett Street Café, page 376; photo of seaweed bagel courtesy of Nate Butler, page 379

400 Gradi: pages 498, 499, 500, 501, 503

Amy's Bread: photos courtesy of Liz Clayman, page 115 (top, bottom left, and bottom right) and page 401; photos courtesy of Aimee Herring, pages 121 and 204

Barton Springs Mill: photos courtesy of Ian Van Alan, pages 74, 76-77

Bellegarde Bakery: photos courtesy of Morgan & Owens, pages 157, 158 and 161

Boulangerie, a Proper Bakery: photo courtesy of Troy R. Bennett (*Bangor Daily News*), page 131; photos courtesy of Regina Jenkins, pages 133 (all), 135, 164, 181, 219, 256, 465

Boulted Bread: photos courtesy of Jim Trice, pages 147, 148, 150, 221, 345 and 353

Community Grains: photo courtesy of LA Specialty and Community Grains, page 233; photos courtesy of Lena Miler and Community Grains, pages 235 (bottom left) and 236; photos courtesy of Jaclyn Coleman of Community Grains, pages 235 (top and bottom right), 430 and 701

Dante's Pizzeria: pages 505, 506, 509

Deux Bakery: photos courtesy of Emilio Millar, pages 251 and 252

Flour Bakery: Photos and recipes from *Flour* ©2010 by Joanna Chang. Used with permission of Chronicle Books LLC, San Francisco. Visit ChronicleBooks.com. Pages 348, 351, 727, 729, 730, and 781

Giuseppe Ninivaggi: page 99

Grain Craft: pages 380 and 381

Kaufman's Bagel & Delicatessen: photos courtesy of Michael Cookes, pages 384, 386, and 390

King Arthur Flour: pages 167 (all)

La Svolta: photo courtesy Kristyna Hess Photography, page 492; photos courtesy of Alison Mayfield Photography, pages 493 and 496

Lindley Mills: photos courtesy of Lindley Mills 2017, pages 719 and 721

INDEX

# D

## G

# M

## Q

## R

## S

## T

## U

## V

# Y

# Z

# ACKNOWLEDGMENTS

We would like to first thank Barbara Elisi Caracciolo for her incredible, in-depth, and passionate work on this book. Her diligence and attention to the finest detail has concluded in a true baker's book.

We'd also like to thank all of the amazing bakeries, bakers, and chefs who contributed their favorite recipes and most importantly, their time. Many thanks to:

Amber Lambke, Maine Grains
Amy and Zachary Tyson, Boulangerie
Amy Scherber, Amy's Bread
Amy Emberling and Sara Whipple, Zingerman's
Anna Di Perna and Silvio Serpa, Pizzaly
Ann Sheehan Lipton, Anna Long, and Angela Buckley-Martin, Winslow's Home
Jesse Merrill, Polestar Hearth Bread
Mary Jennifer Russell, Sugaree's Bakery
Joanne Chang, Flour Bakery
Bette Dworkin, Kaufman's
Caroline and Joe Lindley, Lindley Mills
Catherine and Cheryl Reinhart, The Sweet Life Patisserie
Courtney Jergins and Ian Tillinghast, Grain Craft
Mike Keon, Anthony Allen, and Eric Shepherd, OTTO Pizza
Francesco April, Settebello
Gina Watts, Sugar Pie Bakery
Graison Gill, Bellegarde
Jessie Morgan-Owens and James Owens, Morgan & Owens Photography
Gwen Adams, King Arthur Flour
James Brown, Barton Springs Mills
Jane Jaharian, The Sweetery
Jane Stabler, Evil Twin PR
Johnny Di Francesco, 400 Gradi
Joshua Bellamy, Fulton Forde, and Sam Kirkpatrick, Boulted Bread
Kate Schier-Potocki and Josh Potocki, 158 Pickett Street Cafe
Kevin Morris, Dante's Pizzeria
Jim and Lynn Williams, Seven Stars Bakery

Michael and Annette Siu, Swiss Bakery
Phillip Bruno, Scoozi
Phoebe Plank, Community Grains
Andrew Chaney, Oliveto
Rebecca Serra, James Elliot, and Thom Elliot, Pizza Pilgrims
Wendy Smith Born and James Barrett, Metropolitan Bakery
Stacey Himes, Stacey Himes PR
Theo Kalogeracos, Theo & Co.
Tom Guagliardo, Tano's
Valerio Calabro, Giuseppe "Pino" Russo, and Sally Calabro, La Svolta
Vince Morena, St-Viateur
Wendy Fleming, Deux Bakery

A special thank you to Stephany Buswell of the International Culinary Center for her many recipes!

Additionally, we wouldn't be anywhere without the talented Cider Mill Press team. Thanks to publisher John Whalen, editors Patrick Scafidi, Emma Kantola, Taylor Bentley, and Brittany Wason; designers Jaime Christopher, Cindy Butler, and Annalisa Sheldahl (who also illustrated the book!) and the rest of the team!

# ABOUT THE CONTRIBUTORS

### BARBARA ELISI CARACCIOLO

Barbara has a background in medical research and a long-standing interest in bread and grains. Originally from Italy, which remains her main bread baking inspiration, she is now living and working in Sweden. Barbara is the founder of Spigamadre, a small company focused on the promotion of artisan bread and quality grains. She has written extensively on bread in several languages and her work was published on magazines and books such as *Arte Bianca*, *BREAD Magazine*, and *Vårt Älskade Bröd*. Barbara's blog *Bread & Companatico* has been a reference for thousands of home bakers making their first steps into bread baking. She aims at further spreading her ever-growing passion for bread through her baking, milling, teaching and writing.

### DOMINIQUE DEVITO

Dominique has written more than a dozen books including *The Cast Iron Skillet Cookbook* and *The Cast Iron Baking Book*. She also edited *Country Living Kitchens* (Hearst). Dominique's work has been featured in *Martha Stewart Living*, *USA Today*, *Rural Intelligence*, and many other newspapers and magazines nationally. She writes for *Hudson Valley Wine Magazine*, *Main Street Magazine*, and a regular wine column for *The Register Star* newspaper. She is co-owner of the highly acclaimed Hudson-Chatham Winery.

* Her recipes are the cast-iron skillet (size 12.5") and Dutch oven (7-quarts) but you can adapt the recipe for your own pan!

### STEPHANY BUSWELL

Stephany, a Certified Master Baker, is a pastry chef-instructor at the International Culinary Center. In addition to teaching, she owns Chefany Cakes, a custom wedding cake business.

Stephany began teaching in 1989, but has been in the baking industry for over 40 years. Today, she enjoys sharing her wealth of bread baking, pastry, and cake decorating knowledge with students and others.

### PATRICK SCAFIDI (profile and interviewer writer)

Patrick Scafidi is an author and editor living in Brooklyn, New York. To see more of his work, go to www.patrickscafidi.com.

## ABOUT CIDER MILL PRESS BOOK PUBLISHERS

Good ideas ripen with time. From seed to harvest, Cider Mill Press brings fine reading, information, and entertainment together between the covers of its creatively crafted books. Our Cider Mill bears fruit twice a year, publishing a new crop of titles each spring and fall.

*"Where Good Books Are Ready for Press"*

Visit us online:
cidermillpress.com

or write to us at
PO Box 454
12 Spring St.
Kennebunkport, Maine 04046